Christendom Anno Domini
M D C C C C I

*Eleven hundred pages, Illustrated
In Two Octavo Volumes.*

VOL. II.

A Presentation of Christian Conditions and Activities in *Every Country of the World* at the Beginning of the Twentieth Century by more than sixty Competent Contributors

::::::::: EDITED BY :::::::::
REV. WILLIAM D. GRANT, Ph.D.
WITH INTRODUCTORY NOTE BY *President*
CHARLES CUTHBERT HALL, D.D.

NEW YORK
CHAUNCEY HOLT
1902

Copyright 1902
BY
WM. D. GRANT

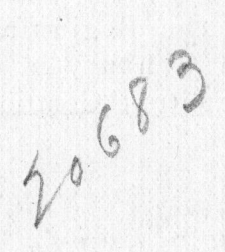

In
Sincere Loyalty
To Him
Whose I am
And
Whom I serve

To recognize as brethren those who differ from us in religion;

To accord to such the rights and privileges which belong to them;

To covet for them the best gifts and graces;

To give them full credit for the good that appears in them;

To speak well of their persons and to show interest in their work;

To rejoice in whatever success attends their labors;

To believe that their motives may be, at least, as pure as our own;

To bid them god-speed in life and action;

To follow after the things which make for peace and things wherewith one may edify another;

This is to manifest in no small degree the love of our Lord Jesus Christ; the spirit of tolerance and good will to men so fully exemplified in His life and enforced by His teachings.

CONTENTS.

VOLUME II.

NEW PROBLEMS OF CHRISTIANITY..............*Mancius H. Hutton, D.D.*
GAINS OF CHRISTIANITY................*President John H. Barrows, D.D.*
RELIGIOUS THOUGHT IN 19TH CENTURY.....*George T. Purves, D.D., LL.D.*
SOCIAL ASPECT OF CHRISTIANITY......*J. H. W. Stuckenberg, D.D., LL.D.*
REVIVALS IN 19TH CENTURY...................*J. Wilbur Chapman, D.D.*
CHRISTIANITY AND PHILANTHROPY...............*C. H. d'E. Leppington*
ART AND RELIGIOUS PROGRESS.................*Francis E. Marsten, D.D.*
RELIGIOUS LEADERS IN 19TH CENTURY
        "Simeon and Schleiermacher," by *Prof. Jackson;* "Bushnell," by *Dr. Munger;* "Martineau," by *Dr. Grant;* "Ritschl," by *Dr. Garvie;* "Brooks," by *Prof. Allen;* "Moody," by *Dr. Dixon.*
CRITICAL MOVEMENTS IN 19TH CENTURY....*Prof. Geo. H. Schodde, Ph.D.*
RELIGIOUS PRESS...........................*W. C. Gray, Ph.D., LL.D.*
ROMAN CATHOLIC CHRISTIANITY...........*Rev. Alex. P. Doyle (Paulist)*
ROMAN CATHOLIC MISSIONS...............*Rev. Alex. P. Doyle (Paulist)*
GREEK CHRISTIANITY...........................*Prof. A. C. Zenos, D.D.*
PROTESTANT CHRISTIANITY...................*Rev. Wm. D. Grant, Ph.D.*
PROTESTANT MISSIONS..............................*Judson Smith, D.D.*
ESSENTIAL CHRISTIANITY....................*Rev. Wm. D. Grant, Ph.D.*
RELIGIONS CONTRASTED......................*Prof. Allan Menzies, D.D.*
DISUNION OF CHRISTENDOM........................*A. S. Crapsey, D.D.*
CHURCH UNION.....................*Bishop John F. Hurst, D.D., LL.D.*
FEDERATION OF CHURCHES....................*Rev. Walter Laidlaw, Ph.D.*
THE SUNDAY-SCHOOL...............................*A. F. Schauffler, D.D.*
ORIGIN AND PROGRESS OF THE Y. M. C. A....*President L. L. Doggett, Ph.D.*
EVANGELICAL ALLIANCE......................*Rev. Wm. D. Grant, Ph.D.*
RESCUE WORK..................................*Kate W. Barrett, M.D.*
W. C. T. U. ORIGIN AND PROGRESS..............*Katharine L. Stevenson*
STUDENT FEDERATION...................................*John R. Mott*
THE SALVATION ARMY......................*Commander Booth Tucker*
SOCIAL SETTLEMENTS..............................*Robert A. Woods*
CHRISTIAN ENDEAVOR SOCIETY..................*Francis E. Clark, D.D.*
KING'S DAUGHTERS AND SONS................*Rev. Wm. D. Grant, Ph.D.*

CONTENTS.

VOLUME II.

                                                  PAGE

NEW PROBLEMS OF CHRISTIANITY, *Mancius H. Hutton, D.D.* 1
    Forenote: Getting people to attend church, p. 1.—Prediction perilous, p. 2.—The mission problem, p. 4.—Religious indifference, p. 5.—The resetting of the Bible, p. 6.—Sabbath observance, p. 7.—Family religion, p. 8.—Christian doctrine, p. 10.

GAINS OF CHRISTIANITY IN THE 19TH CENTURY, *President John Henry Barrows, D.D.* 12
    Christian progress—extensive and intensive, pp. 12-14.—The Bible better understood, p. 14.—Fellowship and tolerance, p. 14.—The century and the growth of toleration, p. 15.—Men and influences which have made for religious liberty, p. 18.—The true church better understood, p. 19.—The drawing together of Christian hearts, p. 20.—Change in religious form and method, p. 21.—The church beginning to take the view-point of Jesus Christ, p. 22.

RELIGIOUS THOUGHT IN THE 19TH CENTURY, *George T. Purves, D.D., LL.D.* 23
    Christianity claims the right to govern the whole man, p. 23.—Religious thought stirred by the thinking done in other lines, p. 24.—(1) Note emphasis laid on the soul's immediate relation to God, p. 24.—The Divine immanence, p. 26.—(2) The emphasis placed on the love of God, p. 27.—The Fatherhood of God, p. 28.—(3) Historical criticism, p. 29.—(4) Progress of physical sciences, p. 31.—(5) Christianity thought of as a social force, p. 33.—(6) Thought with regard to the comparative study of religions, p. 35.—Christianity the absolute religion, p. 36.

THE SOCIAL ASPECT OF CHRISTIANITY, *J. H. W. Stuckenberg, D.D., LL.D.* 37
    The new spirit in the Christian Church, p. 37.—The influences which begat the new order, p. 37.—The French revolution and the Socialist's aim, p. 38.—Religious life and metaphysical speculation, p. 41.—Attacks on Holy Scripture—Strauss, p. 41.—Recent social movements due to many causes, p. 42.—Clerical apathy in England, p. 42.—A great awakening in England, p. 45.—Social movement in Germany, p. 45.—Catholic and Protestant, p. 47.—Modern social movement in the United States, p. 48.—The pulpit and the social movement in the United States, p. 50.—Movement mainly begun by individuals in the U. S., p. 51.—Theories adopted not always uniform nor Biblical, p. 53.—The new social Gospel, p. 54.—The method

CONTENTS.

of Jesus, p. 55.—The study of Scripture and human relations, p. 56.—Social awakening of the church, p. 57.—Institutional church work, p. 58.—Religion brought out into daylight, p. 59.

NINETEENTH CENTURY REVIVALS, *J. Wilbur Chapman, D.D* 61
Forenote: Revivals still a need of the church, p. 61.—The closing years of the century not encouraging, p. 62.—Modern Christianity and revival movements, p. 62.—Revivals in colleges, p. 64.—The prince of evangelists, p. 65.—The revival of 1857, p. 66.—Mr. Dwight L. Moody, p. 68.—What has been accomplished by revivals? p. 70.

PHILANTHROPY IN THE 19TH CENTURY, *C. H. d'E. Leppington* 72
Forenote: Christianity and philanthropy, p. 72.—The altruistic spirit preceded Christianity, p. 72.—Liberality among the ancients, but no philanthropy, p. 73.—Christian benevolence embraces all men, p. 74.—No other religion has so insisted upon and inspired charity, p. 75.—Parish relief in the seventh century, p. 76.—Early and later provisions for the destitute in the United States, p. 77.—National provision for the poor in other countries—England, p. 79; Germany, p. 80; Scandinavia, Russia, France, p. 81; Belgium, Holland, p. 82; Italy, p. 83.—State and individual aid, p. 84.—Altered social conditions require new methods, p. 85.—Improved accommodation, p. 86.—Associations for philanthropic service, p. 86.—Kaiserswerth, the Salvation Army, p. 87.—Many fresh philanthropic shoots, p. 88.—Providing for defectives, p. 91.—The housing of the poor, p. 92.—Personal contact, p. 93.—"Friendly Visitor," p. 94.—Charity organization, p. 95.—Industrial co-operation, p. 96.—The evils of uninstructed philanthropy, p. 97.—Results of the survey, p. 98.

ART AND SOCIAL AND RELIGIOUS PROGRESS, *Francis E. Marsten, D.D.* .. 100
Forenote: Tendency of imagery in public worship, p. 100.—The relations of art to religious and social progress, p. 100.—Art and morals, p. 102.—Art and worship, p. 103.—Art and the reformation, p. 104.—Art and social well-being, p. 104.—Prof. Hamlin's observation, p. 107.—Robertson's picture and its effect, p. 108.—Art in kitchen stoves, p. 108.—Pullman's model town, p. 109.—Money valuation of things, p. 109.—Modern art an enrichment, p. 110.—Deformity and Divinity far apart, p. 112.—Much remains to be done, p. 112.

RELIGIOUS LEADERS 114
Forenote: The imperishable and the Carpenter's Son, p. 114.

CHARLES SIMEON, *Samuel Macauley Jackson, D.D., LL.D* 115
The evangelical movement in England, p. 115.—Early pastoral difficulties and ultimate success, p. 116.

FRIEDRICH SCHLEIERMACHER, *Samuel Macauley Jackson, D.D., LL.D*. 117
Early life and training, p. 117.—His "Speeches on Religion" and their effect, p. 118.—Becomes professor at Berlin, p. 119.

HORACE BUSHNELL, *Theodore T. Munger, D.D* 120

CONTENTS.

PAGE

His influence still growing, p. 120.—Early life and studies, p. 120.
—Mental powers and freedom, p. 121.—Pastoral labors and literary efforts, p. 122.—He is charged with heresy, p. 124.

JAMES MARTINEAU, *Rev. Wm. D. Grant, Ph.D* 127
Where and how his early years were spent, p. 127.—Pastoral charges—Dublin, Liverpool, London, pp. 128-9.—Professor at Manchester New College, p. 128.—Visits Germany, is chosen principal of New College, retires at the age of 85, p. 129.—The Metaphysical Society and Martineau's tolerance, p. 130.—Appearance and characteristics, p. 130.—As a preacher, p. 131.—The fruits of his literary activities, p. 132.—Theological bent—Unitarian, p. 134.—Academic honors and personal appreciation, p. 136.—The great address, p. 137. —His "unique personality" and pre-eminence among master minds, p. 138.

ALBRECHT RITSCHL, *Rev. Alfred E. Garvie, B.D* 139
By birth and breeding dedicated to theology, p. 139.—His mental history; professor at Bonn, then at Göttingen, p. 139.—Published works, p. 140.—The Ritschlian school of theologians and their distinctive doctrines, p. 141.—Merits and influence of the school, p. 142.

PHILLIPS BROOKS, *Alexander V. G. Allen, D.D* 144
The sphere and fruits of his activity, p. 144.—Conspicuous as a preacher, p. 144.—A mind capable of clear thinking, "The influence of Jesus," p. 147.—All sectarianism seemed to disappear in his presence, p. 148.

DWIGHT L. MOODY, *A. C. Dixon, D.D* 148
Forenote: By weight of personality born to command, p. 148.— He was honest and humble, p. 149.—He was practical, hopeful, brave, and tolerant, p. 150.—He made himself the servant of all; a preacher, rather than a teacher, p. 151.—He was a prophet of God and his message was "Salvation by Grace," p. 152.

MOVEMENTS CRITICAL AND ETHICAL, *George H. Schodde, Ph.D* 155
Forenote: The right and need of criticism, p. 155.—Criticism not regarding doctrine but the Scriptures themselves, p. 155.—Criticism has emphasized the human side of the Scriptures, p. 156.—Higher and lower criticism, p. 158.—Some distinguished names, p. 159.— Practical and theoretical aspects of the task, p. 160.—An attempt to restore the original readings of the O. T., p. 161.—Higher criticism has met with disfavor because unknown, p. 163.—A few great names and their work, p. 164.—In both the New and the Old Testament stress has been laid on the literary analysis of the various books, p. 166.—The movement originated by Ritschl, p. 168.—No ethical movement of a theoretical character outside that of Ritschl, p. 170.

THE RELIGIOUS PRESS, *Wm. C. Gray, Ph.D., LL.D* 171
Forenote: Possible union of the religious press, p. 171.—Origin of the religious paper, p. 172.—The quality and method of the religious journalism of the future, p. 174.—The aim of religious press, p. 175.

CONTENTS.

PAGE

ROMAN CATHOLIC CHRISTIANITY, *Rev. Alex. P. Doyle (Paulist)* 176
 Forenote: Confession made by non-Catholic when uniting with the church, p. 176.—Development of the church in doctrine and ritual, p. 177.—The church more an organism than an organization, p. 178.—The church's teaching authority, p. 179.—The doctrine of Papal Infallibility, p. 180.—The seven sacraments, p. 181.—The church's standards of holy living and saintly heroism, p. 183.—Her views regarding the social order, p. 183.—The church's sympathy with labor, p. 184.—The Catholic Church is the salt of the earth, p. 185.—Beliefs which all Christians have in common, p. 186.—Devotion to the Virgin Mary and the saints, p. 186.—Purgatory, p. 187.

ROMAN CATHOLIC MISSIONS, *Rev. Alex. P. Doyle (Paulist)* 188
 Forenote: Martineau's tribute to the Roman Catholic Church, p. 188.—At the beginning of last century, p. 189.—The external and internal growth of the church during the century, p. 191.—Large increase of orders and communities, p. 191.—Missionary enterprises, p. 192.—Rapid growth in Anam and China, p. 194.—Captain Younghusband's tribute, p. 195.—The origin of "Propaganda de Fide," p. 195.—Statistics, p. 197.

GREEK CHRISTIANITY, *Professor A. C. Zenos, D.D* 200
 Forenote: Reply of Greek Church to Pope's encyclical, p. 200.— What the Greek Church is and embraces, p. 201.—I. The influence of Greek thought on the church, p. 202.—Clement, p. 203.—The three Gregories, p. 205.—John of Damascus, p. 206.—The form of doctrine fixed, p. 207.—II. The polity of Greek Christianity, p. 207. —Holds to the oneness of church and state, p. 208.—III. Form of worship, p. 209.—The introduction of images, p. 210.

PROTESTANT CHRISTIANITY, *Rev. Wm. D. Grant, Ph.D* 212
 Forenote: Contemplating her conquests, the Church of Rome was led to believe that God was in her institutions and that she was necessary to God, p. 212.—The Church of Rome lays claim to man's confidence even when she has forfeited God's favor, p. 213.—Religious institutions can, no more than political or commercial, stand when they have proved recreant to trust, p. 214.—Luther's experience in Rome, p. 215.—Dr. Louis Pastor's "History of the Popes Since Close of the Middle Ages," p. 216.—Rome has lost her power, p. 217.—Rome is accountable to no one but herself, p. 217.—Gladstone, Manning, Rome's arrogant spirit, and the original protest, p. 218.—Attempts at reform, p. 219.—How shall Protestantism be defined? p. 219.—With the Roman Catholic the church is an end, with the Protestant it is but a means, p. 220.—The supremacy and sufficiency of Holy Scripture, p. 221.—The right of private judgment, p. 225.—Jesus Christ the only Mediator, p. 228.—Justification by faith alone, p. 231.—Why are Protestants disliked by Roman Catholics? p. 233.—Protestantism will deserve the Divine disfavor as Rome has, and meet with Divine condemnation, unless she serves His people with her best, p. 235.

CONTENTS.

PAGE

PROTESTANT FOREIGN MISSIONS, *Judson Smith, D.D*............... 236
Forenote : The spirit of union more manifest in the foreign field than at home, p. 236.—The achievements of missions during the century as great as in any other line of progress, p. 237.—Missionary organization, p. 237.—The state of world one hundred years ago, p. 238.—Missionary expansion, p. 238.—Statistics, p. 239.—Some great names, p. 240.—Difficulty in enlisting the church in the great work, p. 240.—The native agencies, p. 241.—Evidences of progress in Madagascar, Fiji, China, p. 241.—At the opening of the century the great religions of the East seemed formidable, p. 242.—The message of the missionary, p. 243.—In the main the world is now open, and in most countries substantial foundations have been laid and foregleams of final victory have been seen, p. 243.

ESSENTIAL CHRISTIANITY, *Rev. Wm. D. Grant, Ph.D*............... 245
Systems soon depart from original simplicity, p. 245.—Christianity no exception to the rule, but possesses the power of self-renewal, p. 246.—The Reformation an attempt to return to primitive Christianity, p. 246.—What are fundamentals, and what circumstantials? p. 247.—No formulated system in the Gospels, p. 247.—Need not go beyond the Gospels for essential Christianity, p. 249.—We are as capable now, as in any previous period, of determining what Christianity is, p. 249.—The essential and distinguishing feature of Christianity—life in and union with Jesus Christ, p. 250.—How much knowledge is needful? p. 250.—Opinions may be held tenaciously, while fellowship with Christ in life and service are unknown, p. 251. —Life in and union with Jesus Christ the secret of all spiritual greatness and power, p. 253.—Whittier's poem, p. 254.

RELIGIONS CONTRASTED, *Professor Allan Menzies, D.D*.............. 255
Forenote : The pre-Christian religions, p. 255.—How can comparison be made? p. 255.—If we send missionaries to heathen peoples we should know the reason why ; why are we ourselves Christians, rather than Mohammedans? p. 256.—Wrong ways of making a comparison, p. 257.—Christianity difficult to define, equally true of other religions, p. 258.—Neither history nor statistics will help us, p. 259.— Religions can be judged only by their comparative value for the human spirit and for human society, p. 260.—The morphological method, p. 260.—The various stages of a religious development, p. 263.—Christianity is higher in the scale of religions than any other, p. 264.—The Chinese, Greece, Assyria, Egypt, even Judaism, p. 264. —Two national religions—Chinese and Judaism, p. 265.—Three universal religions—Buddhism, Christianity, Islam, p. 266.—How shall we compare these three? p. 267.—Buddhism, p. 267.—Islam, p. 269.—Christianity, p. 270.

THE DISUNION OF CHRISTENDOM, *Algernon S. Crapsey, D.D*.......... 272
Lines of progress and unification, p. 272.—Our Lord disappointed, p. 272.—There was disunion everywhere in our Lord's day, p. 273.— Our Lord's plan of unification, p. 274.—Success of the plan, p. 275.

CONTENTS. 11

PAGE

—Failure of plan since fourth century, p. 276.—Cause of failure, p. 278.—Doctrinal unity, p. 282.—Reunion of the church in God and in humanity, p. 288.

CHURCH UNION MOVEMENTS, *Bishop John Fletcher Hurst, D.D., LL.D*. 290
Forenote: Defeat due to disunion, p. 290.—Division of Greek and Latin churches, p. 290.—First attempts at union, p. 292.—Irenic movements since the Reformation, p. 293.—The Formula of Concord, p. 294.—Efforts for the union of the Reformed and Lutheran bodies, p. 296.—Labors of Durie, Calixtus, Grotius, Owen, Baxter, pp. 297-301.—English Presbyterians and Congregationalists. p. 302.—The union of 1817, p. 305.—Protestantism and the Greek Church, p. 306. —Van Dyke, p. 310.—Recent unions and negotiations, p. 312.

CHURCH FEDERATION, *Rev. Walter Laidlaw, Ph.D* 321
Organic union is not in sight, p. 322.—Old World, church and state, p. 322.—England's early congresses, p. 323.—Contrasts with America, p. 324.—Sociological objects, p. 326.—Council membership, p. 327.—Catechism on church and state, p. 328.—South Africa, Jamaica, and Scotland, denominational inclusion, p. 332.—Intolerance, London's federation, p. 333.—Special services, p. 334.—Mission results, p. 335.—The co-operative parish idea, p. 336.—Federation extension, p. 337.—New World federation, p. 337.—A national church, p. 338.—Political federation, p. 339.—America's problem, p. 340.—Urban population, p. 340.—Alien population, p. 341.—Congestion, church extension, New York's federation, p. 342.—Creeds in New York, p. 343.—Sociological bureau, p. 344.—Co-operative district plan, p. 346.—Co-operative calendars, p. 347.—Inductive church extension, p. 347.—Chicago and other cities, p. 348.

THE SUNDAY-SCHOOL, *A. F. Schauffler, D.D* 353
Forenote: God's instrument for fashioning human lives, p. 353.— Origin and growth of the Sunday-school, p. 353.—Means and methods, p. 354.—No teaching nor accommodation too good for the Sunday-school, p. 355.—Though great progress has been made in equipment and conduct, much still remains to be done, p. 355.—Leadership is the first consideration, and the second is like unto it, the systematic preparation of the teacher for his work, p. 356.

THE Y. M. C. A., *President L. L. Doggett, Ph.D* 358
Forenote: The practical character and fruits of the association, p. 358.—Young men and the city, p. 359.—The origin of the association, p. 359.—International work, p. 360.—Revival of 1857 and the Y. M. C. A., p. 360.—Evangelistic work, p. 361.—Work for young men, p. 361.—The building movement, p. 362.—The meeting at Louisville in 1877, p. 363.—The work in non-Christian countries, p. 363.—Boys' work, p. 364.—American international committee, p. 364.—The growth of the association, p. 364.—The founder of the Y. M. C. A., p. 365.—The Boston Jubilee, p. 366.

EVANGELICAL ALLIANCE, *Rev. Wm. D. Grant, Ph.D* 368
Forenote: The unity is needful for the efficiency of the Christian

CONTENTS.

PAGE

Church, p. 368.—The origin and aim of the alliance, p. 369.—Some account of the life of Dr. Wm. Patton, p. 370.—The spread of the alliance, p. 372.—The work of the alliance, p. 372.—King of Portugal and the alliance, p. 374.

Rescue Work, *Kate Waller Barrett, M.D* 376
Forenote: Philanthropic and religious activities in cities, p. 376. —Rescue work of recent origin, yet "Missions" are already planted in all the great cities, p. 377.—North End Mission, Boston, p. 377.—"Water Street" and other missions in New York City, p. 378.—Missions in other cities, p. 379.—The National Florence Crittenton Mission, p. 380.—Mile-End Road and Regions Beyond Missions, London, p. 381.—The sort of qualification needful for this task, p. 381.—Personal contact, p. 382.—Rescue is prevention, p. 382.—Society's lowest elements must be reached and raised, p. 383.

W. C. T. U., *Katharine Lente Stevenson* 385
Forenote: Condemnation of the liquor traffic, p. 385.—History of the temperance movement in America before the W. C. T. U., p. 386.—The origin and organization of the "Union," p. 390.—Dr. Dio Lewis' part in its origin, p. 390.—The Ohio crusade, p. 391.—Early conventions and officers, p. 392.—Expansion and development of work, p. 393.—Miss Willard, p. 395.—Round-the-world missionaries, p. 398.—Lady Henry Somerset, p. 398.—The first world's convention, p. 399.—The "Do Everything Policy," p. 399.—The work and influence of the "Union," p. 400.—Miss Willard's death, p. 402.—The Washington convention, 1900, p. 403.—Two quotations, p. 403.—The lost boy, p. 405.

World-wide Student Movement, *John R. Mott, M.A* 407
Forenote: Religion among students in 1800 and at the present time, p. 407.—The importance of the student element, p. 408.—Student organization—in America, p. 409; Great Britain, p. 411; Germany, p. 412; Scandinavia, p. 413; Switzerland, Holland, France, Egypt, p. 414; India and Ceylon, p. 415; Australasia, p. 416; China, p. 417; Japan, p. 420.—Federation of students, p. 420.—What has been accomplished? p. 421.

Salvation Army, *Commander Booth Tucker* 423
General Wm. Booth, p. 423.—Early life and experience of Wm. Booth, p. 424.—The influence of the Nottingham revival, p. 425.—Enthusiasm and natural leadership, p. 425.—Catherine Mumford, the army's mother, p. 426.—Ecclesiastical restrictions drive Booth out of "regular" work, p. 428.—Persecution, p. 429.—Evolution of the army idea, p. 429.—The army's wonderful progress, p. 431.

Social Settlements, *Robert A. Woods* 432
Forenote: The meaning of religion and life taught by action, p. 432.—The motive of first settlements, p. 432.—Institutional development and personal influence, p. 433.—Toynbee Hall the first, p. 434. —Oxford and other houses, p. 435.—First American settlement, p. 436.—Dr. Stanton Coit and the Neighborhood Guild, p. 437.—Hull

CONTENTS.

House, p. 438.—Prof. Taylor's efforts in Chicago noteworthy, p. 439. —Other settlements throughout the country, p. 439.—The influence on the community and on the church, p. 440.—Bibliography, p. 441.
CHRISTIAN ENDEAVOR, *Francis E. Clark, D.D*.................... 442
    Forenote: Enthusiasm for Christian Endeavor, p. 442.—Origin, character, and aim, p. 443.—Pledge and service, p. 444.—Fidelity and fellowship, p. 445.—First twenty years of C. E., p. 446.—"News-Tribune" of Detroit on the convention of 1899, p. 447.
BROTHERHOOD OF ANDREW AND PHILIP, *Rev. C. E. Wyckoff*............ 448
    Origin, aim, and growth, p. 448.
EPWORTH LEAGUE, BROTHERHOOD OF ST. ANDREW, KING'S DAUGHTERS AND SONS, *Rev. Wm. D. Grant, Ph.D*..................... 450-453

CONTENTS.

VOLUME I.

AFRICA................................*Frederic Perry Noble, Ph.D.*
ARABIA AND PERSIA............................*Rev. W. A. Shedd*
AUSTRALASIA........................*Rev. H. T. Burgess, LL.D.*
AUSTRIA.................................*Albert W. Clark, D.D.*
CANADA........................*George M. Grant, D.D., LL.D.*
CHINA...........................*Prof. Isaac T. Headland, S.T.B.*
DANUBIAN STATES.......*Rev. Marko N. Popoff* and *Rev. Stephen Thomoff*
ENGLAND AND WALES................*Rev. J. Arthur Meeson, LL.B.*
FRANCE AND BELGIUM........................*M. Eugene Réveillaud*
GERMANY...............*Count A. Bernstorff* and *Pastor P. Pieper, D.D.*
GREECE AND MACEDONIA......................*Socrates A. Xanthaky*
HOLLAND..............................*Rev. Wm. Thomson, B.D.*
HUNGARY..................................*Andrew Moody, D.D.*
INDIA, BURMA, AND CEYLON...................*James Mudge, D.D.*
IRELAND..............................*R. McCheyne Edgar, D.D.*
ITALY..................................*Alexander Robertson, D.D.*
JAPAN...............................*Rev. Sidney L. Gulick, M.A.*
KOREA..............................*Rev. George H. Jones, M.A.*
MALAYSIA........................*Rev. H. L. E. Leuring, Ph.D.*
MEXICO AND CENTRAL AMERICA......................*J. W. Butler, D.D.*
OCEANIA................................*Rev. Joseph King*
RUSSIA...........................*Prof. Fred. Kattenbusch, D.D.*
SCANDINAVIA..............................*C. F. Lundin, Ph.D.*
SCOTLAND.............................*Prof. John Herkless, D.D.*
SIAM...........................*President Chalmers Martin, D.D.*
SOUTH AMERICA..................................*Elsie Wood*
SPAIN AND PORTUGAL........................*Rev. Wm. H. Gulick*
SWITZERLAND.....................*Prof. J. Martin Vincent, Ph.D.*
TURKISH EMPIRE..........................*Prof. Edward Riggs, D.D.*
UNITED STATES—
 Lyman Abbott, D.D., LL.D., and *Rev. Wm. D. Grant, Ph.D.*
WEST INDIES..............................*Margherita Arlina Hamm*

LIST OF ILLUSTRATIONS.

VOL. II.

	PAGE.
Charles G. Finney	64
Charities Building, New York	72
Theodore L. Cuyler, D.D., LL.D.	120
James Martineau	128
Pope Leo XIII.	176
Group of Greek Clergy	200
Protestant Memorial at Spire-on-the-Rhine	216
General Neal Dow	328
John B. Gough	336
Robert Raikes	352
Sir George Williams	360
William Patton, D.D.	368
Jerry McAuley	376
S. H. Hadley	384
Frances E. Willard	392
Lady Henry Somerset	400
John R. Mott	408
Sir Wilfrid Lawson	416
General William Booth	424
Mrs. William Booth	428
Arnold Toynbee	432
University Settlement, New York	432
Francis E. Clark, D.D.	440
Y. P. S. C. E. Memorial Tablet in Williston Church, Portland, Me.	448

NEW PROBLEMS OF CHRISTIANITY IN MODERN SOCIETY.

MANCIUS H. HUTTON, D.D.,

NEW BRUNSWICK.

[Sometimes there is no good in going to church. It depends principally on the church. It is often claimed that church attendance is on the decrease. I do not know, but even if it is it may possibly be as much due to the debility of the churches as to the depravity of the people who stay away from them. People are not going to be drawn in by being scolded for staying out. Nor are they going to be drawn in—in a way to hold them—by being coaxed in by artificial seductions. The average man is too keen-scented to be caught in an ecclesiastical trap. A good deal of money is put into the artistic trimmings of sanctuary service. There is no objection to the artistic if it is wrought into the body of the service, and not availed of simply as so much millinery put on to make the service more presentable. The multitudes are not hoodwinked. They know how to crowd in for the music, and then how to crowd out in time to escape the Law and the Gospel.

The advertising of sensational topics is another way the pulpit takes to worry truth into reluctant hearts of advertisement-captured congregations. It does not hold the people, but it does cheapen the pulpit and set the house of God in the same row with the dry-goods stores, millinery shops and other institutions that put big headlines in the newspapers, and flaming placards in the front windows. We may call the rank and file of people very godless, but they are able to distinguish remarkably well between fact and fiction in matters of religion. I believe that ninety people out of a hundred would respect God's house if they were sure that it is God's house more than it is man's. It takes a good deal besides a pulpit, a choir loft and a spire to make a church.

The sanctuary is only playing with its opportunities and groping along the frontiers of its proper domain until it becomes in truth the very house of God, the temple which He fills with His presence, a meeting-place between God and man, and until the preacher becomes himself an apostle made competent by a direct Divine inspiration to speak God's truth into the hearts of men that are tired, troubled and sin-sick.—CHARLES H. PARKHURST, D. D.—ED.]

* * *

IT is a very obvious reflection that it would be vastly less difficult to write this paper with authority at the end of the twentieth century rather than at its beginning. It is always easier to be a prophet after the event. You go out on a spring morning to discern the probabilities of the weather of the new and still approaching day, to find that it is not easy. There are clouds in the sky, but the sun is struggling with them. The winds are variable and breathe from all quarters one after another, but from no one of them long and steadily. Under such circumstances one hesitates to say whether it will be a day of showers or of sunshine. But to-morrow it will take only a faithful observer to report what the weather was. At present, with the long day still before him, it takes a prophet to say what the weather will be. In the year 2001 we shall know what the problems of the twentieth century really were. Until that time one predicts at his peril. Clouds now black and threatening may dissolve before they are fairly overhead. Clear spaces all blue and pellucid to-day may be the centres of cyclonic convulsion before the centurial day is over.

The consideration just mentioned leads us on to observe that society itself varies from generation to generation, and from place to place. Problems which are pressing in one country may not be worth considering in another. For example, the early part of the eighteenth century, whether it be taken in Great Britain or in the United States, witnessed a totally different spiritual condition of the average population from that which obtained at the opening of the nineteenth. The work of the Wesleys and of Whitefield would hardly have had such welcome and such effectual activity in any other age than the one in which it fell. The problem which it met and solved so blessedly was one whose conditions lasted for only a decade or two. In the same way it is now impossible to foresee distinctly the problems of an approaching era. Christianity must indeed be alert to see them when they come and to solve them as they stand before its face. But there are doubtless oncoming problems in the bosom of the twentieth century which no one can treat or is competent to discuss at present. It was not until Œdipus had arrived at Thebes and actually stood before the Sphinx that he so much as guessed what her riddle would be. Its solution was entirely hidden until after she had spoken.

It may be further remarked that the survey of such a paper as the present one is limited. The new century will cover the whole globe. Probably countries which can hardly now be said to have any "society" will develop one, and each its own. But it is impossible to predict what particular problems Christianity will have to grapple with in societies which are yet to be. Even if we restrict ourselves to actually existing social conditions it is evident that the problems to be met in modern Italy are totally different from those in Australia, and that those in the regions of the Evangelical Church in Bohemia are not at all like those in the United States. To deal with the social conditions of the whole globe and the distinct problems which Christianity and its pulpit are likely to encounter in each during the impending century would require the study of a lifetime, and would be to write not a paper but a volume.

These three limiting conditions must control the course of the present discussion. Perhaps it ought to be added that, on the very terms of the topic, satisfactory and full solutions are not to be expected. A solved problem is no longer a problem.

The problems which confront the new century are largely those of form. Human nature is the same in every age. Revelation has ceased for the present, at least in that aspect of it in which "men spake from God, being borne along by the Holy Ghost." No voice since that of St. John fell silent at Ephesus has spoken with the self-evidencing authority of those others to which Christendom has so long bent unquestioning. Accordingly, so far as can be now foreseen, there is no forthputting of new material to be expected. We are left to readjust our conceptions of the old and to modify that which is on hand rather than to invent new. Neither David nor the Sibyl testifies in these days to anything absolutely hitherto unknown. It is not, therefore, to be expected that the questions which are to arise as we go onward should be entirely novel, but that they should be rather problems of the *forms* with which, and in which, the Christianity of the twentieth century appears likely to be required to meet the new forms of opposition and the exigencies of the approaching days.

These new problems of Christianity and its pulpit in modern society seems to be of its form of application to that society itself— to worship, and to doctrine. To their consideration we now turn.

I. The problem first to be studied, then, is that which relates to Society itself as an organism. With what is technically called sociology and socialistic questions the present paper is not especially called to deal, because they are handled by another writer in this series of papers. In that more exact sense, no doubt, the "Housing of the Poor," and "Capital and Labor," are two problems which press most heavily on the heart and conscience of awakened Christendom in general. These are essentially modern. In the days of serfdom no one cared, not even the serf, about the rights of labor, and no one was comfortably housed, not even the mediæval baron. But now, before society—not in the limited sense of the rich and cultured, but in the wider and nobler sense of the brotherhood of man—can rest in comfort and satisfaction, those great problems must be settled finally and rightly. Somehow the Golden Rule will settle it for both; but we shall have to wrestle with it far on into the new century to all appearance. It is not yet a solution: it is a problem.

But turning from these aspects of the question as having been discussed elsewhere in this series of "Timely Papers," there are other and perhaps even wider problems which Christianity has to meet before the year A. D. 2001 shall dawn. As an example of one whole class of these we may cite the mission problem.

We start out in the twentieth century with new conceptions of the Brotherhood of Man. It is quite true that these conceptions lie implicitly, or even more than implied, in the Christian Scriptures. The opening words of the "Lord's Prayer" have the whole idea folded compactly in them, ready to unfold until it fills the whole earth. But never has the duty and enthusiasm of missions been so widely recognized or the sense of human brotherhood as compelling to missionary effort been so greatly felt. The late great Ecumenical Conference on Missions, held in the city of New York, in 1900, is a signal testimony to that fact. A century ago such a conference would have been literally impossible; but the very progress and triumph of missions has brought us face to face with new problems which the new century must at least try to solve.

How long are we to keep converts from heathenism in leading-strings? It is an exceedingly difficult question to decide. When the Apostles and apostolic men went forth on their early mission errands, as recorded in the Acts of the Apostles, they seem to have labored a few weeks, or at most months, in a given city, and then passed on. This was true not only in towns where they preached among Jews who had some previous training in revealed religion, but also in those where, after they had "turned to the Gentiles," the community was wholly heathen. As they left they "ordained elders in every city," and with only an occasional re-visit to "confirm the churches," or a rare epistle, they were left to their own devices. No missionary residences were built; no colleges or academies founded; no hospitals were provided—other than "the handkerchiefs and aprons from his body" by which St. Paul seems to have done some healing work. Everybody knows what form our modern mission work has taken and how unlike it is to the primitive method of church-planting. No doubt our way was the best for the last century; was necessitated by the conditions, and has justified itself by its success a hundred times over. But now, when the work proceeds essentially in heathen lands, as it does in those already Christian, is it not possible that the impetus of the nineteenth century has spent its useful force? It does not follow that we are to revert to first century methods: judging by analogy we are not. But may it not be that the twentieth calls, or will call, for a new method? If it does and the question is put, What shall it be? one can only say, "The twentieth century must solve it!"

There are other problems connected with missions over which thoughtful men are puzzling, but they must be dropped here to pass on to speak of some quite other ones which are likely to press on the practical religious life.

II. The shapers of the forms of Christianity for the coming century and the modern church pulpit have at least three pressing and imminent problems to solve. Perhaps all might be reduced to the one immeasurable problem of counteracting the indifference which prevails at the opening of the new epoch. When Christianity began it had to contend with violent physical opposition. Even in the book of the Acts there are signs of persecution beginning to set its knees on the new religion to break its ribs by violence. Not only at Jerusalem, where, as the headquarters of Jewish prejudice and wrong judgment, bigoted cruelty might have been expected, but also abroad in heathen but civilized cities, Paul and Silas and Barnabas woke by their evangelical preaching a storm of bitter and active opposition. Under Nero, Trajan, Decius and Diocletian the violence culminated in the "great persecutions" wide as the Roman Empire. The second great era of opposition was that of "Free Thought," the age of the infidels, the era of spiritual opposition. The press poured forth a black flood of literature scoffing at the ideas which generations of Christians had found most grave and venerable. Those were the two eras of active opposition. In these days all that violence, physical and intellectual, has subsided like retiring floods, and the opposition which confronts the Church of God to-day is that of indifference. Men do not care for, have no interest in, religious things. They no longer blaspheme the name of the Christ and fling filth at Christians. They just go their ways as if there **were no** Christ. We sometimes sadly say that the church has lost its **grip on** the masses; we might more truly say that the masses have **let go** their grip on the church!

But let us look a little more in detail at the conditions which it is our problem to overcome. Perhaps we might legitimately put the re-setting of the Bible as the first problem of the Christianity of the twentieth century.

That Book has never been so studied as in the closing years of the nineteenth century, but it has been studied in a peculiar way. This is not the place to discuss the question of the higher criticism, nor is it much to the present purpose whether its pending views are to be permanent conclusions or not. Without at all touching on that aspect of the matter there can be no doubt that the study lately bestowed on the Scriptures has either loosened the popular faith in them as the final and indisputable Word of God, or else has made the study of them principally a critical exercise. It is easy to see why this is so; but no one mixing with his fellow men throughout Christendom can fail to see that the result has been that the general feeling is that there is no standard of absolute authority in either doctrine or social ethics whose word is accepted as the end of controversy.

No doubt this state of things will right itself in time. The Christian mind will re-adjust itself to such new decisions about the outward form of revelation as shall ultimately be fixed beyond dispute and transferred conclusively from hypothesis to fact. Many things now in suspense as between the old and new views will settle back on the old foundations when once the rocking of the passing wind is over.

Meantime the problem of the new century will be to secure a deeper study of the Word than that which has agitated the old one; to induce a spiritual treatment of the great Book as soon as the critical treatment of it is settled so as to stay settled. Somehow the new era must manage it or the Bible will be gone as a force making for Christian living. It needs no prophet to say how disastrous to all earnest and Christ-like religious conditions it would be to have the race virtually without a line from its Father in Heaven.

The next point to be noted relates to the new problems of worship. There are two elements to be considered, viz., the Day of worship, and Worship itself; the latter falling apart into two subdivisions.

First comes the Sunday problem. Historically, the observance of the Lord's Day among Jewish Christian converts began, no doubt, as a voluntary addition to the Sabbath. The latter, received from Moses, was still considered binding on the ancient covenant people, even if they had become disciples of Jesus the Jew. For His sake they added to the faithful observance of the seventh that of the first day of the week in memorial of His resurrection. Among heathen Christian converts the Lord's Day was the only sacred day, of course, but it was wholly voluntary as among the Jewish ones. In the next stage its observance became a sort of badge of Christian discipleship, and popular sentiment soon made it virtually obligatory on all who professed to walk in "the way." Then came Constantine, with his enlargement of Christian obligation along civil and governmental lines, and Sunday observance became a civil as well as religious law. The mixture of the two sentiments by mediæval times, and indeed long before, made the observance of the day both enforced and formal. The Reformation, with its new and deeper spiritual impulse, made its subjects eager for the religious opportunities of the Lord's Day, emphasizing Sunday observance as a privilege. In Great Britain, for reasons so familiar that they need not be recounted here, the Puritan Sabbath came in with its stringencies, voluntary at first, but soon made obligatory when Puritanism had the power. Even after Puritanism had lost its initial force as a spiritual movement, ingrained habit stamped deeply into the consciences of the communities where it had once held undisputed sway the custom of the outward observance of the Lord's Day. Long after the laws on the matter ceased to be enforced, it was not quite respectable not to go to church.

That feeling has about disappeared. The old Sabbath has gone. Multitudes of men and women have no conscience about it any longer. It is not simply the abandoned, heaven-defying old "Sabbath breaker" of the Sunday-school library books of a generation or two ago, but it is respectable, decent, moral people who now deliberately arrange to travel on Sunday trains to save business time; who throng the Sunday roads with automobiles and bicycles; who give dinner parties and play golf on the first day of the week without a prick of their consciences. Not long since the summons of a cycle club to a "run" on Sunday, in an American city, brought together by actual count seven hundred wheelmen. How many congregations of that number assembled in the churches of the town that day?

And yet God's Fourth Commandment has never been revoked any more than any of the other nine of the Decalogue. We need not sigh over the vanishing of the Puritan Sabbath; there is no passage of the Scripture which ever enjoined it. But God's Word does put a difference between His Day and ours. How are we going to get the Fourth Commandment on its feet again? *That* is a problem the new century must not only grapple with but solve, or the curse solemnly pronounced on the wilful desecrators of the day which God has "hallowed" will fall on those nations which will not "reverence My Sabbaths." It is too early in the century to say how the end shall be gained and the solution wrought safely out. All that can be done now is to blow a solemn trumpet of alarm.

Turning next to consider the new problems of worship, we come first on that of family religion.

There is a solemn doom pronounced in the Bible on "the families which call not on My Name." There are certainly few families left who do it in the old-fashioned way. The "family altar," as the elder religionists used to call it, has been rent in two like that of Jeroboam, and its ashes poured out to grow cold. Of course it can be accounted for. Modern life, with its haste and drive, its thousand new interests, shortens the available time in a way of which our more leisurely fathers never dreamed. The old opportunities and facilities for parental religious instruction, for the assembling of the household around the parental priest, are all gone. It does not seem as if they ever could return. It was a beautiful observance in its day. Men who made no religious profession, like Burns in his "Cotter's Saturday Night," felt the charm. Long after the voice of the parent-priest was silent in death, the children grown to maturity testified to the beneficent effect of family worship. But while the present pace keeps up and even augments, with the old habit thoroughly broken up and the old facility of immemorial practice gone, how can it be reinstated? Yet something must be done to replace it, or individual religion will perish with that of the family. Some new form must be found into which the old life can be poured or it will perish from the earth. With that problem, too, the twentieth century must grapple and solve it as the condition of its spiritual life.

But turn again from that to public worship. All over Christendom, with few exceptions, the nineteenth century has seen a notable diminution of attendance on public worship. Few churches are thronged at any time, and the "second service" has become the despair of most pastors. For a while the latter service may be filled up by special music, or sensational topics of discourse, or by the magic lantern. Yet not only do these things soon lose their power to draw a crowd, but even while their attraction lasts it is the gravest of questions whether any real spiritual benefit or upbuilding in consecration and depth of spiritual life accrues.

So the problem challenges the new century, and asks what it will do about it. If Christ's own people have lost their interest in the "assembling of themselves together," it can hardly be expected that those who are not in covenant will attend. Add to it all the facts that outside of the ranks of professing Christians the vast majority of the people hold an attitude of absolute and unfeigned indifference, and yet that by virtue of living in Christian lands they are sufficiently instructed in religious truths for them to have lost all their novelty, and how prodigious is the problem for which Christianity and its pulpit in the twentieth century have to find a solution.

One does not have to search far to account for this prevalent indifference. Life is harder than it was, and people are fagged and wearied. They crave either rest or excitement—mostly the latter. In former times the pulpit was the lyceum and university of the masses. It refreshed the latter to come in contact with a trained mind dealing with topics on which they might stretch themselves for intellectual as well as spiritual gymnastics as they eagerly listened. Nowadays books, newspapers, periodicals, these keep men overwhelmed with new facts and intellectual interest. Besides all this, the age is material, and things which are spiritual are remote from their "hearts and bosoms." Perhaps, too, in explaining the neglect of the "second service," we may note that men weary of monotony. To repeat the morning's process at night is unattractive. Breakfast is good, but who wants two breakfasts exactly alike in one day?

This much, however, we may say toward the solution: God does not intend that the church of His dear Son shall run out by self-limitation. He has said that the gates of Hades shall not prevail against it. The church is not to grow less and less effective and efficient, and run down like an electric lamp whose battery has polarized. Nevertheless, the details of its operation He has assigned to His co-laborers on the earth. The new century must find out for itself what to do. That is its problem. Shall it be by some widespread outpouring of the Holy Spirit? Shall it be by the personal work of each present Christian taking the careless by the hand and "compelling him to come in" by sympathetic love for his soul? Shall it be by throwing away entirely our present time-worn forms of public worship, and initiating a wholly new departure? Or is it to be along lines now utterly unthought of, but which the twentieth century shall reveal?

The twentieth century will have to answer. But one thing is sure: It will be the *form* and not the essence of worship which will change, if there is to be change at all.

There remains still another problem which will have to be solved, and which must be discussed here with only a few closing words. It is that of doctrine.

Here, too, one may safely venture to predict that it is going to be a change of form rather than of content. It was Carlyle who spoke of the changes of views of religious truth as the laying aside of worn-out garments. "Hebrew old clothes," he called the system which gave place to Christianity, and he thought the latter—as the nineteenth century knew it—was already mostly rags soon to be discarded for brand new outfits of Christian doctrine. Most of us do not agree with him, but certainly there has been much in the religious discussions of the later years of the vanished century which has looked as if Confession and Creeds might soon be either in the waste-basket or the fire.

But discussions never alter truth. Glass is hard, but it scratches no diamonds. When John Robinson, speaking to the Pilgrims as they started from Leyden for Cape Cod, said that he had no doubt "there would be more light breaking from God's Word," he was not saying, as he has too often been interpreted as saying, that new truth obliterating the old, or new facts at variance with older ones, would be discovered. He meant only that which he actually said, namely, that new *light* would break, and at that not from new revelations, but from and on the old, well-searched Word. There are no new doctrines or new facts or new revelations lying perdue there. The content of dogmatic revelation will not ever change. Even if new books shall be added to the sacred canon—of which there is no sign either from within or from without the volume at present—no contradictory or annulling doctrine can be introduced.

But that is not to say that the *form* of the now familiar truth may not be modified. The new century may find that dogmas which fallible theologians have deduced from Scripture by fallible logic may have to be dropped entirely. At all events, "the Word of God standeth sure," and has His seal. No doctrine unmistakably set down therein will grow obsolete.

Yet men do grow. They grow wiser and broader and more mellow. So do generations. It is quite within the range of possibility that before the twenty-first century begins to dawn on the then darkening eastern sky of the twentieth, a new light may rise. It will be the task of the twentieth before it passes on to "prove all things, to hold fast that which is good." If the doctrines and dogmas of Christianity have to be modified, as some predict, it will be the solemn duty of the now new century to change the form, and hold fast the substance of the teachings of the Holy Spirit. It is too soon to say what changes may be necessary, or even that any will be. If the latter, it is equally too early to suggest what shape they ought to take; above all, what shape they will take. But of one thing we who are not to survive the new era may be sure as we lie down to rest and wait with Daniel—the twentieth century will not itself go down with its setting sun looking out on the wrecks of truths on which God's saints have stood to fight His battles, and on which they have pillowed their dying heads in every age. Uzzah will have no need to steady the Ark.

SOME GAINS OF CHRISTIANITY IN THE NINETEENTH CENTURY.

President John Henry Barrows, D.D.,
OBERLIN.

CHRISTIANITY means, in the treatment given by this essay, the interpretation and realization by Christendom of the teaching of Jesus Christ. There has been progress during the last hundred years along many lines—theological, ecclesiastical and practical. The Christendom of to-day is a larger and completer realization of the spirit and doctrine of Jesus Christ than was the Christendom of the year 1801, when the century began. This will be apparent to all minds not blinded by theories of the world's increasing degeneracy. It is not claimed that the church is approaching perfection, or that, in every particular, Christendom has advanced a long step during the last ten decades. Still, a comprehensive survey of the changes of the century will reveal the fact that Christianity has made notable gains.

The Christian Church, taken as a whole, is more aggressive in its effort to reach all men with the heavenly Gospel; it is more generally imbued with the missionary spirit, which is the essential Christian spirit. It may be that we have only played at missions in the last hundred years, but it has been the most inspiring and beneficent play which the race has ever seen. In America the domain of a Christian civilization has been expanded to a continental area. Many savage tribes have been evangelized. The Bible has been distributed by hundreds of thousands of copies in Mexican, Central American and South American lands. At the beginning of the century the entire slave population of the South was excluded from a reading knowledge of the Scriptures. At the beginning of the century only a small beginning had been made in what is now the world-wide movement of Christian evangelism. Church after church has been enlisted in the Foreign Missionary Crusade. Millions of dollars are now annually contributed for that cause, which Dr. Wayland pronounced "the sublimest that ever awakened the hopes and called forth the moral energies of mankind." The Young Men's Christian Associations, the societies of like spirit for young women, the great Christian Endeavor movement, and the Student Volunteer movement, are imbued with missionary enthusiasm, and probably fifty persons stand ready to-day to undertake service in non-Christian lands where one could be found at the beginning of the century. In the churches of Great Britain, Germany, Switzerland, Scandinavia and France there has been growing, to large proportions in some cases, a sense of responsibility to the unevangelized world. Christendom to-day is more cosmopolitan than ever before. Our religion for the first time presents the aspect of a world-wide faith, and this is due to the out-reaching efforts which have sprung from missionary zeal.

No one can return from a careful inspection of the moral and spiritual conditions of the great continents without a new conviction that Christianity is an aggressive and elevating force in every part of the world. Japan owes the beginning of her industrial, commercial, political and moral regeneration to Christian influences, and Japan is likely to be one of the dominant Christian forces of Asia. Korea is passing through a similar transformation. The Chinese Empire is rapidly being leavened with influences of Christian origin, and the advent of America into the Orient as an Asiatic power means much more for the future enlightenment and uplifting of the greatest of the continents. The Pacific Ocean, which is to dominate the future of the world, is surrounded and crossed by Christian forces. It is something to have made a difficult, magnificent, historical beginning. No other religion presents any such world-wide aspect to-day as Christianity. The nineteenth century made the cosmopolitanism of the Christian Gospel apparent to the leading minds of all nations. On every shore to-day Christianity is a vital and progressive force. The world has been made ready through international communication, through a friendlier feeling toward Christians, through a new knowledge, which discriminates between a true and a false Christianity, through a better understanding of the living spirit of the time—for a universal faith.

Parallel with this out-reaching activity, which has marked the hundred years now past, has been an in-reaching effort to get closer to the heart of Christianity. There was large dissatisfaction at the beginning of the century with many of the forms and statements of the historic churches. This dissatisfaction has increased in a measure. Theological controversy and the coming in of new light have not only led to skepticism, but have also led to more careful study of the sources of Christianity. The result has been a return to Christ. Never before have there been so many means of getting truly acquainted with the Founder of Christianity. The lives of Jesus Christ belong, almost all of them, to the present century. The study of manuscripts of ancient contemporary history, and of that fifth Gospel, the Holy Land itself, has thrown a dazzling light upon the person of Jesus Christ, making the Gospel records more living and luminous. It may be truly said of the latter part of our century that it has lived with Jesus of Nazareth. In some respects we knew Him better than did His early followers. There is a growing conviction that He is God's last and best manifestation of Himself; that in His light we see light for all the chief problems of human existence; that knowing Him we know Christianity; that He is the Way, the Truth and the Life.

It is inevitable that the Bible should be better understood than it was a hundred years ago. No other book has received such prolonged and such profound investigation. It has been attacked as untrustworthy and even as immoral. Science has been arrayed against it, but the period when controversy over its claims has been sharpest has been the period when its true Divinity has become most apparent. To-day it is not only not outgrown or obsolescent, but it is a force of Divine life more penetrating and pervasive than ever before. When understood as the ripest Christian scholarship of to-day understands it, the Bible is not exposed to many of the objections which skepticism has made. It is seen to be the spiritual literature of a Divinely guided people, which has come to us under a variety of forms, expressed in language which can be translated into all languages, universal in its adaptations and permanent in its influence, because it is a book of dynamics, a literature of life speaking through object-lessons to the deepest needs of the human soul. Its comparison with Sacred Books of other nations simply reveals the supremacy and sufficiency, the uniqueness and authority of that revelation which came to Israel and was completed in Jesus Christ.

Another gain of Christianity in the century, springing very largely out of the return to Jesus Christ, has been the discovery of Christians that He binds them together in spiritual fellowship. Christianity has been found to be larger than any creed or church, because it is identical with Him who is the fullness of knowledge, of light and of love. Churches which have been kept apart by the memory of old-time divisions, by masses of ecclesiastical and theological rubbish, by an unintelligent conservatism, ill-founded fears and a lack of brotherliness, have been drawing closer together. They have been educated in those higher truths, living by which men are caring less and less for minor distinctions. At the beginning of the century how far apart, in America and Great Britain, were the various churches, how strong was the antipathy of churchmen and nonconformists, of Congregationalists and Methodists, and how wide was the antagonism between Protestants and Catholics! The chasms have not been filled up, but they have been here and there bridged over. Among Protestant churches, to a hopeful degree, the noises of discord are being drowned in the notes of concord. The centrifugal forces which have wrought a good work are dying down and giving way to centripetal forces. One may discover no single church on the face of the earth to which all disciples acknowledge allegiance, but there is a rapidly increasing unity in Jesus Christ. When Dean Stanley was a young student at Oxford, he walked one day with another student, a High Churchman, and passed by a Dissenting Chapel. Seeing it, his High Church friend said: "How could it have been built here? I wonder that they did not pull it down long ago." The Christians of to-day who are anxious to have the churches of other forms and faiths pulled down are not alarmingly numerous. In some communities they will soon be so few as to seem like curiosities.

Most thinking men have come to realize that tolerance is a word representing an imperfect spirit in regard to the rights of the human mind. Governments which may tolerate, would seem to reserve the right to persecute. "The most despotic governments are tolerant toward the subjects who are too numerous or too useful to be killed or exiled." But toleration is a stepping-stone to liberty. No sensible man, acquainted with the facts, can fail to realize that the wide growth of toleration is one of the most important facts of the century. Wherever we look, whether to Russia or to Italy, to Germany or South Africa, to Great Britain or China, to France or Austria, we behold the area of toleration, and hence of religious liberty, widening. In the German Empire the progress of toleration has been conspicuous, so that, according to Dr. Schaff, the great Teutonic realm "is committed to the principles of religious liberty and equality as much as the United States, and can as little interfere with religious convictions and the exercise of public worship, or deny to any citizen his civil and political rights on account of his religious opinions."

In Austria the history of religious progress, beginning in 1848, culminates with the law of 1868, which granted full liberty of religion, but a liberty limited to the churches recognized by the Government. Whether that freedom is enjoyed or not depends largely upon the sentiment of local authorities. Toleration and freedom have still other victories to be won in Austria. In Italy the Waldenses were emancipated in that year, 1848, which marks a new era of religious progress throughout Europe. The constitutions granted at that memorable epoch guaranteed the free exercise of divine worship. Since 1870 the Free Italian churches and many others have sprung into life, and a new leaven is working for the emancipation of the Italian mind. In Spain religious liberty dates its feeble beginnings from 1869. Concessions are neutralized by certain restrictions, for the constitution of 1876 limits the liberty of those who are not Catholics to worship in private houses. Switzerland comes nearest to America in religious freedom. In France the Catholic, Protestant and Jewish churches have been placed on a level before the law. The right of assembly and teaching is legally unquestioned, and the Protestant missionaries are able to go everywhere in France and carry on their zealous propagandism.

Professor Bonet-Maury sums up his history with the statements that, "Since the Edict of Toleration of Louis XVI, in spite of some offensive returns to the gloomy idea of religion in the state, the spirit of tolerance, or better, of respect for liberty of conscience, has grown." "Violent procedures by civil powers against individuals or societies on account of their philosophical or religious beliefs have become more and more rare."

In Holland and Scandinavia, even with church establishments, perfect religious equality is enjoyed. And by the treaty of Berlin, 1878, the Sultan's Government was forced to this position, that in no part of the Ottoman Empire shall differences of religion be alleged against any person as a ground for exclusion or incapacity as regards the discharge of civil and political rights, admission to the public employments, functions and honors, or the exercise of the various professions and industries.

The British Empire—I am now speaking of what lies beyond the British Islands—is the widest domain of tolerance on which the sun shines. That empire has been called "the hugest outstanding parliament of religions now existing in the world." In Australia, New Zealand, South Africa, the Dominion of Canada and throughout the broad and populous peninsula of India, full liberty of conscience and all the rights of spiritual freedom are enjoyed. When we look at England itself, we are compelled to remember that her great act of religious freedom is the Act of Toleration of 1689, and that this was not an edict of liberty. Englishmen at that time did not believe in religious freedom. But inevitably that Act of Toleration led to a large enjoyment of the rights of conscience, and during our century its benefits have been extended to Unitarians, Catholics and Jews. The disestablishment of the Church of England in Ireland was a great step in the right direction, and with the surely coming disestablishment of the church in Scotland, Wales and England, the area of liberty will be enlarged.

The idea of toleration has been enlarged by the official action of China in granting to the different European nations the right of sending Christian missionaries, not only to the port cities, but to the interior of that vast empire. The Chinese Government has given repeated assurance of its belief that the doctrines of Christianity and the practice of them were for good. The recent fanatical uprising of those who hate all foreign influences will not permanently diminish the area of religious liberty in the Far East. No sensible man believes that the Christian nations will permit any abrogation of rights guaranteed by international treaty. In Mexico religious toleration is a part of the new life of that prosperous republic; even in priest-ridden South America, the rights of non-Catholic citizens have received new guarantees, or have been acknowledged for the first time—in Ecuador, Bolivia, Peru and elsewhere.

America is the great home, not so much of toleration as of true liberty. In the United States the Government has no authority to interfere with religion. The fullest liberty is possible only where the church and state separate. From the beginning of our organized national life this separation has prevailed and been the fundamental law and practice of our country. Here the Jews have had freedom, and have been treated with a friendliness never elsewhere shown them. America is the standing reply to those who believe that religion needs the support and guidance of the state. Christian progress in our country has been more rapid than the progress of the population, and it is as true to-day as when De Tocqueville wrote that: "There is no country in the whole world in which the Christian religion retains a greater influence over the souls of men than in America."

When complete religious liberty exists, toleration becomes not a legal but a mental and moral condition. It is a state of mind, and the most remarkable advance has been in the kindlier feelings between men of various faiths and various divisions of the same faith. James Grant Allen, in his "Reign of Law," recalls the time in the last century when Christians used to throw live snakes into the assemblies of other Christians of whom they disapproved. Snake-throwing has disappeared. Occasional acts of intolerance occur, but they are opposed to the almost universal sentiment of the country. Bigotry, or the worship of one's own opinions, is giving way to charity. Pulpits are exchanged to-day by representatives of various denominations. Eighty years ago such interchange was scarcely known. The Unitarians have accomplished a large work for the spirit of true tolerance. Men who are pronounced in their church preferences are pleading with more earnestness for the co-operation of denominations. Church comity is coming to be a fact. Men are seeing that Presbyterianism, for example, is much smaller than Christianity; that Congregationalism is not the Holy Catholic Church. With Christian large-mindedness we are learning to love the virtues and achievements of other denominations. The next great step of progress will resemble the political change which came over our country when the colonies having common interests became federated. Federation precedes either unification, or wide and generous co-operation in many things.

Those who have contributed to the world's progress in religious liberty during the century now closing are a noble army, working in various ways and in different lands. He who writes the story of the century in this realm of progress must tell of James Madison, the chief advocate of the first amendment to the constitution, declaring that "Congress shall make no law respecting any establishment of religion, or prohibiting the free exercise thereof." He must tell of the work of Channing, Theodore Parker, Emerson, Lyman Beecher, Phillips Brooks, Charles A. Briggs, Francis E. Clark and John Henry Vincent. The historian will not forget Max Müller, and his great work for comparative religion, and the humanizing of the churches in their attitude toward non-Christian faiths. He will tell of what Gladstone, Macaulay, Tennyson and Dean Stanley wrought in England for the enlargement of mental freedom. Coming to France, he will speak of Madame de Stael, Guizot, Athanase Coquerel and Jules Simon. He will not forget John Frederick Oberlin, the model pastor, the friend of Catholics and Jews, and the champion of love as greater than zeal.

Probably in no other country than America could such a Congress of Religions have been held as that which was the crowning feature of the Columbian Fair. By that remarkable gathering the bounds of brotherhood and of true toleration were enlarged. Catholics and Protestants for the first time, in a great assembly, sat together for seventeen days in the spirit of fraternity and kindliness. The representatives of the great non-Christian faiths were treated with perfect courtesy, and illustrated the spirit of courtesy themselves. Many Christians learned a new lesson, following the teachings of Sir Monier Williams, not to shut their eyes to any truth or virtue which may be found in non-Christian characters and non-Christian writings. Mr. Mozoomdar has recently written with great appreciation that the attitude of Christian missionaries toward Hindoo prophets and Hindoo faiths shows less and less of the old-time polemic intolerance. It may take generations before the other peoples reach the height which America reached in 1893, but no one doubts that such a height, which now looks lonely, will yet become a table-land on which the nations of the earth will assemble.

One of the gains which has come from a truer knowledge of Christ, and hence of Christianity, has been a better understanding of the true church. It must be both high and low and broad. It is high enough to meet what is loftiest in man; low enough to reach down with helping hands to all the burdened and suffering, and broad enough to include all the disciples of Christ. It loves and venerates every manifestation of truth and righteousness. It includes in its affection every devout layman, artist, singer, reformer, seer and humble servant of Jesus Christ. It is a church in which there is room for every style and form of ordinance which the individual may prefer. It has room for the various theories of man's origin. It is a church where the intellect and heart are not set over against each other. It is a temple not only of larger liberty and larger truth, but of closer fellowship and greater outwardly manifested unity.

There has been a simplification of theology; that is, its reduction, so far as co-operation is concerned, to the common denominator of all evangelical Christians. When asked their beliefs men are more apt to say that they believe in Jesus Christ, in what He was, in what He said, in what He taught. Resulting from this is the more earnest co-operation of believers in the greatest work which Jesus gave to His followers; namely, the evangelization of the world. A leading denominational paper of our country has recently made the editorial confession that there was a time when the writer was slow both to recognize and to report the excellences and good deeds of other denominations. It may be truly said that there was a time when many Christians shut out of their minds thoughts of what other churches were doing for Christ, lest thereby they should become less zealous for their own sect. How the field of loving thought and fraternal fellowship has been widened during this century, and how many are happy in feeling that Baptist piety, Methodist piety, Anglican, Presbyterian, Lutheran, Armenian, Greek and Roman Catholic piety are not only praiseworthy, but are a part of our spiritual riches! Perhaps this is, after all, the greatest gain of the century —the drawing together of Christian hearts about the person and work of the historical Christ, about His cross and broken tomb.

The century of Christian history in America has brought the various Protestant churches somewhat close to the position which the American colonies occupied at the close of the Revolution. In those colonies there was much of individual liberty; they could choose their own magistrates and governors, and frame their own laws. There was also much local pride, and there was also a degree of jealousy. Furthermore, there was a consciousness of national weakness. This became a burden to the great heart of Washington. Finally, under his guidance and the pressure of necessity, the Constitution was adopted. The thirteen colonies became a nation. The adoption of the Constitution did not destroy differences, it did not abridge liberties, but it did make America. Under the guidance of Washington and Hamilton, what was disintegration and weakness was transformed into unity and power. We have in this historical example the key to the changes which have taken place in the church. Broken into fragments, while it has been able to work wonders, it has not accomplished its full mission. Through co-operation and through such a measure of organization as may be needed, the church will begin its grander life. The changes already wrought in the temper and convictions of Christians are such as to presage a marvelous degree of unity. There are few events of the nineteenth century more significant than this drawing together of the disciples of Jesus Christ. Christians of various names and peoples are coming, with increasing joy in the unity of the faith, into nobler convictions and to ampler service. The gains of Christianity in the nineteenth century have been so large and vital as to prophesy for the twentieth century the unification of Christendom and the evangelization of the world.

Whether there have been losses as well as gains in the Christian history of the last hundred years is a question which deserves a passing notice. Religion as a preparation for the eternal life is not to-day so pressing and solemn a question as it was a hundred years ago; that is, with those who believe in religion. But faith in the supernatural has a wider domain at the present hour than it had at the beginning of the last century. Skepticism is not so prevalent in the colleges and among educated people. It may be said that religious men are not so intensely religious as they were a hundred years ago, but this seems to be true largely because religion is more diffused, covering a larger area of human life at the present time. Christian men are sincerely anxious to-day that the principles of the Gospel shall be applied to modern social conditions, and, as Bishop Potter has said, there has been a "growth of candor as to the defects of present systems of ecclesiastical life and work." The last century has been one during which a great variety of noble and mighty efforts have been tried. Some of the evangelistic methods of Finney and Moody may not be repeated in the coming century with similar results to those of the past; but the church is getting ready for a new and wiser, a wider evangelism; the social conscience has been touched and quickened by the words of Ruskin and Wendell Phillips, and by the lives and teachings of those who are giving their strength to Christian social settlements. Christianity has identified itself with the temperance reform, and with the work of municipal reform.

The century has been largely one of experimentation. All sorts of panaceas have been proposed and tried. Many promising efforts outside of the church have proved themselves futile, and, therefore, a chief gain of Christianity has been the acknowledgment by many social reformers and scientists, and even by non-Christian thinkers, of the necessity of such a scheme of spiritual teaching and power as that represented by the Christian Gospel. The adequacy of a true Christianity, rightly applied, to meet all the individual and social needs of humanity, has been proved in the nineteenth century as in no other. Two of the hopeful tendencies of recent times may be mentioned as among the Christian gains of the century. One is the acknowledgment of leading educators in our colleges and universities that Christianity is a vital force needed in the shaping and perfecting of human character. The insufficiency of an intellectual training for the fashioning of manhood and womanhood is very generally conceded. The other hopeful tendency, which I deem perhaps the chief gain of the century, is the disposition of the Christian Church to take a world-view of all problems. We are getting to the view-point of Jesus Christ Himself, in whom there was nothing local or limited. Christianity is a world-religion, and Christ is not lifted up anywhere in the fullness of His purpose and power until, as one has said, he has been lifted up everywhere. The missionary enthusiasm which burns in the hearts of so many men and women in Christian lands may not always fully understand itself, but it is a prophecy of a world-conquest, the beginnings of which lie very largely in the century now closed. The insufficiency of all other religious has become apparent by the discussions and contacts of the last hundred years. The non-Christian faiths have been stirred by the collision of Christianity with them. Some of them are absorbing Christian truths and claiming them as a part of their own religions. It may be truly said, in spite of the divisions and imperfections of Christendom, that the nineteenth century has brought Christianity to the front and placed it on the mountain-top, where it shines today with wider and purer light than in any previous century.

CONTRIBUTIONS TO RELIGIOUS THOUGHT DURING THE NINETEENTH CENTURY.

GEORGE T. PURVES, D.D., LL.D.,

NEW YORK.

THE twentieth century has opened with Christianity in a far more prosperous condition than it was at the beginning of the nineteenth. This is true not only in regard to its outward expansion, and the many practical applications which have been made of it in the social life of Christendom, but also in regard to its power in the realm of thought. Its right to the control of man's whole moral life is very generally admitted by philosophy and science; and this could not be if it were not recognized that religion represents a reality with which philosophy and science in some sense must deal. In fact, there is no more potent intellectual force to-day than Christianity. It cannot be and it is not neglected in any serious discussion of questions pertaining to man's deepest interests. Sociology, psychology, metaphysics alike give heed to it. Books which deal with it, or into which its problems enter, are the ones most widely read. The spirit of reverence toward it characterizes the attitude of all serious minds. Even scepticism, except in a few coarse examples, commonly strives to preserve the essence of religion while rejecting its dogmas. It is no longer possible for culture to speak of it in terms of derision or contempt. Christianity has made a long advance toward the day when "Every thought" shall be brought "into captivity to the obedience of Christ."

This result could not have been reached if the nineteenth century had not witnessed important contributions to religious thought. It has unquestionably been a century of religious revival; and revivals, to be permanent, must affect the intelligence as well as the emotions. The past century has been a stirring one. The activity of the human intellect has been very great in all departments of thought and action. Ambitious philosophies have assumed to give the final interpretation of the universe. Science has revolutionized our modes of thinking about Nature and life. Discoveries have illuminated our views of ancient history. Society has realized with far-reaching effects the rights and limitations of the individual, the nature of the social unit, the defects of the social organism which should be rectified. Inventions have transformed our modes of living, brought the whole world together, modified our thoughts concerning foreign peoples by familiarizing us with their ideas. Amid this stir of thought religion could not but be affected. It certainly has been, and since the result has been the increased power of religion, we must believe that some contributions of real advantage have been made to religious thought.

It is the purpose of this paper to mention briefly some of the contributions which appear to the writer to have been the most important. They have indeed often been abused, carried to extreme positions, allied with movements prejudicial rather than beneficial. Yet a just discrimination will recognize that they have entered widely into the Christianity of the nineteenth century, and have added largely to its power.

1. In the sphere of purely religious thought, or of theology proper, mention should be made first of the new emphasis which has been laid on the immediateness of the Soul's relation to God in the experience of Christian life. This of course has not been a new truth. It is biblical teaching. It was one of the keynotes of the Protestant Reformation. It has been realized by devout souls in all the centuries. Nevertheless, it marks a notable contrast between the nineteenth century and the preceding, so far as its recognition by philosophy, and its wide dissemination in popular teaching, are concerned.

This contribution to religious thought has had, also, a complex history, has sprung from a variety of influences, and has been followed by varied consequences.

It appeared in the first place as a strong reaction against the cold deism and vulgar rationalism with which the eighteenth century closed. It has been like the substitution of fire for frost in the religious life; of the sense of life for the conception of a mechanical relation of God to His world. On its intellectual side its origin must doubtless be referred to the philosophical movement led by Kant, which led thought to the inspection and criticism of its own processes. The rise of the critical philosophy turned the mind in upon itself. The conditions and the possibility of all knowledge became the subject of investigation, with the result of creating an intellectual scepticism which gave to the superficial rationalism of an earlier period its death-blow. But with this scepticism concerning the mind's ability to know aught beyond itself, there came, it would seem of necessity, the assertion of the worth of the affirmations of man's moral consciousness. This appears in ethics in Kant's own "Critique of the Practical Reason." In religion it appeared in Schleiermacher's Discourses. Schleiermacher has undoubtedly been the most influential personality in the sphere of past religious thought which the century has produced. He voiced the Soul's longing for a direct justification of its religious consciousness amid the scepticism to which the intellect seemed doomed, and the current dissatisfaction with the church. As is well known, he found the origin and indestructible cause of religion in the universal sense of dependence. But his influence was not limited by his particular theory. He initiated a movement of the religious spirit, which took various forms and became associated with the most diverse theological views; but which has been characterized by the assertion that religion is the life of the spirit in immediate relation with God. By this affirmation of the validity of the religious consciousness, a valuable contribution has been made to modern thought. In it many have found rest to whom sceptical objections created serious difficulties. The essential contribution, however, ought to be distinguished from many of its accompaniments and developments. It ought to be maintained earnestly that the scepticism which denies the ability of the intellect to attain to that which is beyond itself, and in particular in religion to lay a rational basis for a knowledge of Divine things, is unjustifiable. The intellect can and does know transcendental truth. It cannot indeed comprehend the Divine; but it can know it. In like manner scepticism concerning the historical basis of Christianity is unjustifiable. The evidences for the historical reality of the Christian revelation amount to a moral demonstration. Nevertheless, the strong affirmation which the nineteenth century has witnessed of the intrinsic validity of the religious consciousness, and the recognition of the Soul's own testimony to its relation to God, as given in the experience of Christian life, have formed a distinct contribution to religious thought, and have been one of the chief reasons for the admitted power of religion which, as has been said, marks the beginning of the new century.

In connection with this, it is also to be noted that a new emphasis has been placed on one phase of the relation of God to the world.

This has been the Divine immanence. The very phrase itself has become almost a characteristic of modern religious thought. It seldom appears in the writings of the older theologians. It has in a great measure replaced the term Providence. It is not, however, synonymous with the latter. The providence of God implies His control over the finite universe, both as being superior and external to it, and as working through or with its second causes. The doctrine of the Divine immanence conceives of God as in the creation, manifesting Himself through it, and unfolding His will and power by means of its operations. To complete the doctrine of Providence, therefore, the Divine immanence must be supplemented by that of the Divine transcendence. The emphasis, however, during the past century has been upon the former aspect. God is in the world. Its laws are the manifestation of His activity. Nature is "the life-garment of Deity." This, again, is the very opposite of the deistic idea which prevailed widely a hundred years ago.

Much might be said in criticism of some of the forms in which the idea of God's immanence has been presented. It is perhaps true that it has been allied with, and in some instances has grown out of, a monotheistic and even pantheistic philosophy. Often, also, has it been emphasized so exclusively as to result in a denial of the Divine transcendence. Yet, in spite of these errors, the truth itself has been a positive gain to religious thought. It is certainly a Biblical idea. In God "we live, and move, and have our being." As Jehovah dwelt in the temple, so does He in the universe of which the temple was in one view a type. It is also a conception which accentuates, as we have seen, one side of the doctrine of Providence, and by doing so prevents the latter from being conceived in a mechanical and purely external way. While it must be admitted that the idea, when pressed to an extreme, has tended sometimes to obliterate the distinction between the natural and the supernatural; yet, when combined with a proper view of the Divine transcendence, it has given a religious value to the natural which we would not willingly lose. The world now seems to us vitalized by deity. Its laws appear more than ever the expression of His will. Men feel him to be nearer than they used to do. He will never again be conceived of as a *deus ex machina*. He is the "universal soul" of Nature, as well as its Creator and Ruler. The life and growth of the universe, of which we are a part, is the unfolding of the purpose and power of Him who ever dwells within it.

Now, there is evidently a close affinity between the idea of God's immanence and that sense of the Soul's immediate relation to God of which we have spoken. It is not surprising that the two conceptions should have appeared and moved together. They may both, as already remarked, at times have been pushed into extreme and onesided forms, and so have served error rather than truth. But that they have affected profoundly our religious thought cannot be questioned; and, when they are supplemented properly by other truth, they constitute a contribution which has supplied the corrective of other grave errors, and has made religion more vital and real to the mind of man.

2. The next contribution to be mentioned is the strong emphasis which has been placed upon the love of God. We should do gross injustice to the theologians and Biblical students of former ages if we supposed them not to have taught the love of God. But it must be confessed that often they were more concerned with His other attributes; and the strong emphasis laid to-day on God's love for the world as a whole must be reckoned a real addition to religious thought. It is also a complete statement of the teaching of revelation on the subject.

It is difficult to say how this contribution has come about. It appears to have sprung from practical rather than from philosophical causes, and to have been a reflex product of tendencies which were themselves born of Christianity. Thus the conviction that the Gospel was to be given to the whole world, naturally brought the love of God to all mankind into prominence. Again, the progress made within Christendom in the realization of the humane duties of man to man, the spirit of social helpfulness thus engendered, the growing conviction that Christianity is a religion of service and benevolence, has opened the mind to the unutterable goodness of God as He has revealed Himself. It has often happened that revelation has been reinterpreted through the effects which have been produced by it; and such seems to have been the case in this instance. We may add, also, that the attention directed to the Incarnation, with the emphasis laid on the humanity of Christ, and the perception that in His life of love the revelation of God was brought to its highest point, has added to the emphasis. But be the causes what they may, their feature has been a marked contribution to religious thought. It has become the central principle of some of the most influential theological teaching. It has transformed the preaching of the age.

It has brought forward the Fatherhood of God. It has beautified our conception of the Almighty. It has restored the integrity and proportion of the Biblical teaching on the subject. Of course, like all great truths, it has been pushed too far, and illegitimate inferences have been drawn from it. It has been used to destroy the co-ordinate truth of God's justice and righteousness. It has been perverted to the extent of denying that He will punish. It has led men to say that St. John's language, "God is love," is a complete definition of God, instead of a description of Him. But in spite of these errors, the emphasis placed on the intensity and breadth of the love of God has been a proclamation of truth which Christendom needed to realize and the world to hear. The other truths of His righteousness and sovereignty are equally precious, and must not be let go. But His love must shine out with the lustre which Christ gave to it, and that it has been made to do so during the past century is an immense gain.

It should be remembered also that the emphasis on the love of God has led to a more ethical conception of the revelation which He has made. This is another of the marked features of modern religious thought. Men have come to feel that metaphysical conceptions in the sphere of religion need at least to be clothed in the living flesh and blood of ethical reality, in order to be apprehended aright. Thus the unity of the Father, Son and Spirit is a moral unity of affection and purpose, as well as a unity of substance and of attributes. So the Fatherhood of God, because He is love, has become an intense, realistic idea, endowed with all the highest beauties of fatherhood with none of the defects which appear among ourselves. In short, theology has been, as one has said, "ethicized." The tendency has, like the others, been pushed to injurious extremes. The ethical has been in some cases substituted for the metaphysical, thus resulting in a body without a frame. The foolish attempt has been made to deny the value of doctrinal concepts, when stated in an intellectual or logical form. Nevertheless, the stress on the ethical aspect of doctrine has been a real advance beyond the dry statements of scholasticism. It has given impressiveness and practicality to doctrine. It has made dogma seem a living reality. In particular has the love of God, the realization of which has been the chief root of the ethical reclothing of theology, brought into religious thought an element which has seemed to many like a new revelation of the Gospel.

3. Turning next to quite a different direction, we mention the contribution to the religious thought of the century which has been made by historical criticism.

This science has made for itself a special place. It has sought to ascertain, without prejudice, the actual facts of the past. It has applied its instruments of investigation to both secular and sacred history. Casting aside all prepossessions, it has endeavored to read afresh the origin of nations, societies and institutions, and to trace their developments. It has brought to the task an untiring spirit of research, and has accumulated an immense mass of information. It aims to see things in their historical connections, to trace their mutual relations, to discover the forces which generated them, and the influences under which they advanced. The result has been, in many instances, that history has been rewritten, and, of course, the new conceptions have affected the thought of the present.

In the sphere of sacred history this criticism has been busily at work. It has studied afresh the origin of Christianity. The first three centuries of our era have been re-examined with the closest scrutiny. The origin of the books of the New Testament, and the rise of Christian institutions and dogmas, have been the particular objects of investigation. Apart from special results, the effect has been to create a lively sense of the historical character of Christianity, to show the actual circumstances of its origin, the phases of its early development, and the extraneous influences to which it was subjected. In regard to the Old Testament, likewise, a similar criticism has arisen. With a boldness hitherto unimagined, the whole course of Hebrew history has been revised, and the contest is still being waged between the old views and the new.

It must be confessed, however, that criticism in the sphere of sacred history has not been able to escape from the control of philosophical prepossessions, however much it may have thrown aside dogmatic ones. It has too often been pursued under the influence of rationalism. The supernatural has been discredited and the effort made to represent the history of religion as a purely natural evolution. Hence there have appeared the most diverse schools of historical criticism. In regard to the origin of Christianity, there has been the mythical school of Strauss, the "tendency" school of Baur, the "Hellenic" school of Ritschl; while, in the sphere of Hebrew history, Prof. Kuenen and Wellhausen have entirely overturned the Biblical narrative, and placed the ritual attributed to Moses at the close, instead of at the beginning, of the national development of Israel. This has often been done with the open declaration that the supernatural cannot be recognized by the historian; and where the avowal has not been made, it has more frequently been assumed. Such a method is, of course, as prejudiced as that of the older dogmaticians. It really violates the canons of historical criticism. But it may be expected to cure itself. Already in the study of the Christian origins the cure has begun to work. The authenticity of nearly all the books of the New Testament is now acknowledged. The theories of Strauss and Baur are dead. A like result may be expected in regard to much of the current criticism of the Old Testament. Out of the long debate evidence is accumulating which is sure to buttress the essential facts of the history as given in the Bible, and to sift the final result down to the underlying question of the supernatural itself—a question which philosophy and experience must solve.

While, however, historical criticism has succumbed frequently to alien influences, its contribution to the religious thought of the century has been very valuable. Through it, for example, the Bible has become almost a new book, so fresh has been the light thrown on its original meaning and the relation of its parts. Systems of theology are no longer formed by the arbitrary selection of proof texts from any part of the inspired Word. The progressive character of revelation, as presented in the Bible, is fully recognized. The beginnings and the unfoldings of the religious and moral teachings of revelation have been carefully studied. What is known as Biblical Theology has gained a place as a definite branch of theological science, and its purpose is to set forth the historical process of revelation. On its results theology has come to rest. The result has done much to preclude mere speculation and to obtain a fairer conspectus of Biblical truth, even when put in the categories of a theological system. Meanwhile, the original signification of Biblical terms, and the relation of the parts of the Bible to one another, have been studied anew. Then, too, the historical development of Christian institutions has been made more clear. The rise of forms of church government, the observance of the sacraments, the more or less alien ideas which attached themselves to the original usages of the first disciples, the influence of pagan philosophy and customs on the thought and life of the early church, have been reinvestigated. The effect has been, even when the supernaturalness of Christianity has been frankly accepted, to give a new sense of the historical movement in which the supernatural power operated. Ultradogmatism has thus received a severe blow. Revealed religion has been shown to be not unnatural, even though it be not a merely natural process. It came in accordance with historical needs, and under intelligible conditions. In the many books devoted to the history of Hebraic or Christian religion which have appeared during the century, we may see the profound influence of historical criticism on religious thought; and it may be maintained with confidence that, in spite of the speculations which philosophy has introduced under the guise of criticism, the issue has been a great gain in the apprehension of revelation and in the conception of the Word of God.

4. Still another contribution to the religious thought of the century has been made by the progress and results of physical science. This contribution, also, has been a profound one, for it has affected our whole thought concerning the relation of God to the universe. It has, moreover, been obtained after a prolonged conflict. During the first three-fourths of the century, religion and science were in a constant attitude of hostility. It has been only of late years that peace has been in some measure secured, and the real harmony of the two widely perceived.

The contribution given by science has not lain in the particular discoveries in the realm of Nature which science has made, but in the establishment of a certain view of the world and of the processes which are taking place in it. Science has observed that Nature is force under the control of fixed laws. These laws she has partly discovered and classified. She has found, also, that the forces of Nature are capable of transmutation one into another. The changes of the natural world are known, at least in most instances, to have proceeded slowly, and by the adaptation of objects, organic or inorganic, to new conditions. Geology has ascertained that the earth was gradually formed through vast ages into its present state. Biology has discovered a like history in the forms of living creatures. Kindred sciences have found evidences of similar processes operating elsewhere. In short, the scientific conception of the universe has become that of an unknown power, called force, or energy, evolved in accordance with ascertainable laws into the various objects and beings which now present themselves. Whether this evolution has been ever interfered with by a power from without is a mooted question. The purely scientific observer is apt to feel, indeed, that he has no call to raise the question. It is his business simply to observe phenomena. But it must be admitted that science has not proved the spontaneous origin of life, nor the development of mind from lower forms of intelligence, while at the beginning it can only posit the great First Cause. Yet in general the scientific conception of the universe has obtained control of men's thoughts, and the relation of God to the world has been conceived very differently from the ideas current in former times.

It is not surprising that the new conception at first should have appeared to be in entire conflict with religion. It seemed to make Nature a Godless manifestation of force. It appeared to substitute natural law for Divine control. It was in opposition to the traditional interpretation of Scripture. Science often treated the religious view of the world with scorn. Many scientists openly repudiated religion or took an agnostic attitude with regard to supersensual truths. The conflict became the more bitter when science essayed to enter the field of human history, to reduce man to a higher form of animal, to explain the origin of his intelligence and conscience on the basis of natural development, and his subsequent history as a more extended evolution of the same kind.

In course of time, however, mutual concessions have been made. On the one hand science has come to realize that it is not and cannot be an ultimate interpretation of the universe. It is only the ascertainment of observed phenomena. The ultimate nature and reason of things it cannot learn. It cannot say why the evolution should have moved upward and onward to higher goals. It confesses itself, at least in its best forms, in the presence of a Power which, for reasons lying beyond the discovery of science, has led the course of the world in a given direction. Many of the ablest students of Nature acknowledge that life and mind are beyond scientific explanation. Others find the supernatural in the natural processes themselves. But the spirit of hostility has largely changed for one of reverence, and in the study of Nature the scientist finds it possible to worship God.

On the other hand, the scientific view of Nature has still more powerfully modified religious thought. It has been found that the old interpretation of Scripture was too crass and literal, a real misunderstanding of what Scripture meant to teach. It has been felt, also, that it is no less religious to admit that God has operated through natural laws, which He Himself impressed on the creation, than to suppose that He frequently set them aside. In fact, the discoveries of science have given a larger sense of His immensity, infinitude and immanence. This need not mean that He has never set aside natural laws, and has never given fresh starting points for the life of the world. But religious thought, under the influence of science, has come to reduce these exceptional acts of God to a small number. Between them it recognized God in the processes of His laws. The latter now appear more sacred and inviolable than ever. In matters of detail, likewise, the scientific influence has been great. Religious thought is less tainted with superstition than it used to be. It depends more on intelligence and less on emotion. It has observed more carefully, and in the spirit of science, its own phenomena. That it will be able to maintain the integrity of its faith and the fervor of its life in the face of science, there is no doubt. It is even certain that science will become more and more the handmaid of intelligent religion, and that the two will combine in the worship of Nature's God and of the Incarnate Creator. That science has profoundly affected already the way in which God's relation to the world is apprehended by thoughtful, religious men, and that this has already proved a benefit, can hardly be questioned.

5. We should not fail to mention in the next place the influence exerted on religious thought by the idea that Christianity is a social force.

The eighteenth century was extremely individualistic. Its watchword was personal liberty. The individual asserted his rights, and revolted against tyranny in state and church. The result, however, was disorganization, making room at times for the restoration of tyranny. The nineteenth century, on the other hand, has felt the need of social reconstruction. The duty of the individual to society has claimed attention; the limitation which free society puts upon its members has been realized; the nature of the social organism itself has been studied; the socialistic tendency has replaced largely the individualistic; and in the study of society the place of religion has been widely recognized.

It has been perceived that only a religious sanction can bind society permanently into an orderly community, and redress social wrongs. Christianity, also, it has been seen, contains in itself the power of social progress. It aims to determine the relations of different members of society. It assigns to all both rights and duties. It is, in short, not merely a Gospel for the individual, showing him how to be saved in the next world, but an uplifting and renewing power in the life of man under present conditions.

Under the inspiration of this idea the Christian activities of the century have been directed toward social betterment to a degree never before attempted. The redress of the grievous evils inflicted by human slavery, the amelioration of the lives of the wage-earning classes, the enactment of legislation in the interest of the poor and oppressed, prison and factory reform, are but illustrations of the movement. Christianity has become humanitarian. It has given rise to innumerable organizations for the improvement of life; it has revolted against the selfish assumptions of current political economy; it has created innumerable reforms. The stream of thought is moving in this direction more vigorously than ever. There is even danger that the message of Christianity to the individual may be forgotten in the zeal with which its social message is being proclaimed.

Now there can again be no question that this has been a real contribution to the religious thought of the century, as well as to its activities. It is quite true, indeed, that society is but the aggregate of individuals, and that the way to mould society is primarily and necessarily by the regeneration of its members. But this is so because the social aggregate is not a mass of distinct individuals related to one another merely by juxtaposition, but is an organism. The parts are vitally bound together. "The eye cannot say to the ear, I have no need of thee." The rich and poor, the capitalist and the laborer, the rulers and the governed, the healthy and the sick, are mutually dependent. The regeneration of the individual affects society as the restored health of any member of the physical body brings health to the whole. Conversely, the health of the whole reacts on the parts. Religion, therefore, has its social message and is so represented in Scripture. In past ages Christianity has been used to uphold the social fabric by the maintenance of monarchical institutions. It would have been a fearful loss if, with their dissolution, it had been identified with them. It was an unspeakable gain that its spirit was found to be in reality accordant with a free democracy, providing the sanctions by which such a society could hold together and the altruistic sentiments by which it could exist in health and vigor. This discovery has been made. The religious thought of the age has received from the social idea the occasion for another fresh interpretation of Christ's Gospel. Thereby it has found the adaptation of Christianity to the new conditions of the modern world. The result has also been an immense enlargement of the conception of the mission of the religion of Jesus. No gain has been greater, whether we view it as manifested in thought or in life; for while the social message of religion has been re-announced and applied as never before, the message to the individual has not been, and is not likely to be, forgotten.

6. Finally, mention should be made of the contribution made by the comparative study of the various religions of the world. This has been possible only during the nineteenth century, because previously the non-Christian religions were not accurately known. In fact, such knowledge first became possible with the unification of the world by modern commerce and the spread of foreign missions. The religions of the world have now, however, been closely studied, their sacred books and customs investigated, and their ruling ideas reduced to system. Out of this has arisen the science of comparative religion. Religion is considered by it as a phenomenon of human life. Its rudimentary forms have been examined. The phases through which it has passed have been described. Christianity has been brought into the comparison, and its resemblances with and differences from other religions have been noted.

The effects of this comparison have been, as was to be expected, quite various. Many have been impressed chiefly by the resemblances between Christianity and other religions, and have inferred that all are manifestations of the natural religious instincts of humanity, and differ only as better from worse. A syncretism in religion has been created. The whole phenomenon has been explained on the basis of naturalism and naturalistic evolution. Christianity has been robbed of its uniqueness, though not of its preëminence. Others have seen into the facts more deeply. They have recognized in the resemblances between Christianity and other religions only what was to be expected, if Christianity was a real religion at all; and they have been more impressed by the differences. Christianity has appeared by the comparison to be the perfect and absolute religion, achieving what others failed to do. Its idea of God, its disclosure of a universally applicable way of salvation, its satisfaction of the yearning of conscience for peace, its regenerating power in the individual and in society, have appeared more brilliant than ever when contrasted with heathenism. To such observers the comparative study of religions has been fruitful in fresh zeal for the spread of Christianity throughout the world. But, whichever of these specific impressions have been made, the knowledge of the religious life of humanity has deepened the consciousness that religion is an essential factor of human nature. Whatever theories of its origin have been held, it is seen to be a persistent, indestructible, fundamental fact in the life of man. It is imbedded in the very structure of his being. It can never again be regarded as the arbitrary creation of priests, nor as a political device. Neither science nor political economy can leave it out of consideration. The only thing that can be done with it is to purify it. It has taken its place as a constituent factor in the world's life, because arising out of the relation in which man finds himself to the universe, as well as out of the requirements of his conscience and intelligence. Thus, again, the thoughts of men have deepened concerning the very nature of religion; while more and more is it being felt that Christianity alone realizes the idea of religion and is itself the only absolute one.

Such appear to be the most important contributions which have been made to religious thought during the nineteenth century. They assuredly attest the fact that great progress has been made. They partly explain the revival of the religious spirit and give ground for hope that it will prove permanent. Through them all must we not recognize the working of the Spirit of Christ, supported also by the providence of God, who is steadily, though slowly, taking of the things of Christ and showing them unto men? For certainly the result has been to glorify Jesus Christ. At the beginning of the new century He, more than ever, stands before the world's thought as the supreme object of veneration. Religious thought sees, as never before, that in Him all truth centres and from Him all real life flows. He is plainly to be the Omega, as he was the Alpha, of the religious life of the centuries. The process, whatever it may be, by which Christ is becoming Lord of All, must certainly be the true progress of humanity toward the final goal.

THE SOCIAL ASPECT OF CHRISTIANITY.

J. H. W. Stuckenberg, D.D., LL.D.,
NORTH CAMBRIDGE.

A NEW spirit has entered the Christian Church, effecting a transformation of its character, its relations, its energies and methods, and its influence. This spirit is social, and in marked contrast with the individualism which has so often been dominant. The effect is felt in the relation of the individual Christian to society, and of the church to secular affairs and all social enterprises. This paper seeks to indicate briefly the causes, the nature, the purpose and the methods of the new Christian social movement; to describe the newly awakened Christian social conscience and its operations.

Modern life is so complex, and its social forces are so inextricably interwoven, that the religious factors cannot be absolutely separated and treated as isolated. They affect, and are affected by, economics, politics, æsthetics, the intellectual trend, and the general situation. The social forces constitute an organism in which each is for all and all are for each. Therefore the sociality of the church can be understood only in its connection with the general tendencies in thought and life. These very tendencies which influence the church may have had their origin, in a measure at least, in Christian faith.

The Christian thought and life of the present are culminations of long processes; but their more immediate causes are found in recent epochs. The growth of associations, the increase of their power, and the prominence of society are significant features of modern times. Once politics dominated society; now society seeks to dominate politics. The revolutions of America and France in the eighteenth century, and of other countries in the nineteenth, have brought the people to the front, and made the demand for liberty and equality a striking characteristic of present tendencies. The people have become conscious of themselves and their needs; their condition and possibilities have been studied; and their rights have been demanded with persistence, and even with violence. Personal and social duties have not kept pace with the insistence on privilege. In many cases the sovereignty passed from one man, or a privileged few, to the people; while its full responsibility was not realized. But the prominence and power of the masses now made them objects of interest and study; and history, formerly concerned chiefly about monarchs, statesmen, generals and scholars, began to take account of the common people. The conception of society was enlarged; it included entire communities, not merely court circles and the aristocracy of birth, wealth and intellect.

The French revolution proposed to right the wrongs of centuries of corruption and oppression. Human affairs were treated as if wholly subject to human will, and it was forgotten that historic processes involve necessity as well as freedom, and that to remedy evils may require as long time as it took to develop them. Since that revolution the exposure of evils, particularly the ills of the poorer members of society, has become a mania. During the revolutionary agitations communism appeared, and began the spread of its doctrines throughout the enlightened nations. Socialism, a name invented in 1835, was a broader term and covered a larger variety of social tendencies. Men and systems were called socialistic which opposed the prevailing individualism, and were intent on improving the social condition, especially that of laborers. The situation of the poorer members of society was investigated, the sufferings and inhumanity to which they were subject were exposed, and measures of relief advocated. The socialistic agitations, at first most active in France, soon passed to England, Germany and other Continental countries, differing in aim and labors according to locality and nationality, but always aiming to benefit the toilers. The means proposed were various, such as self-help, co-operation, for which in some instances state help was asked, the organization of laborers to gain their ends from employers, and to promote their general welfare, and to exert political influence. The Social Democracy, now the largest and most powerful socialistic organization, aims at a total economic and social revolution, in order to turn private and competing capital into non-competing social capital.

The socialists aim at practical results, but have developed economic and social theories and systems as the means of attaining them. Sociology differs from socialism in that its immediate aim is not practical but scientific. It wants to construct the science of society, whose application can be left to practical reformers. Comte, who invented this term, as well as altruism, and gave an impulse and valuable directions for the development of the social science, came from the school of St. Simon. As is usual, the new science received its inspiration from practical needs and tendencies. Sociology aims to interpret society, to show how it is related to nature and the individual, to explain its various processes, especially its evolution, and thus prepare for inferences respecting what it ought to be. Numerous subjects have been discussed under this name, and only tentatively can sociology as yet be called a science, there being no consensus regarding its scope, its method, and the system itself. But on whatever social phases and phenomena sociologists have specialized, they always aimed to penetrate the mysteries of society, and have produced profound and valuable results. Sociological study brought society before thinkers and investigators as an object of supreme importance, made individuals and associations more fully aware of their relations, powers and duties, and intensified the interest in societies and humanity. The claim by scientists that the nineteenth century belongs to natural science has been disputed; history has made marvelous progress, anthropology, ethnology and sociology were born, economics and politics were transformed and much advanced, human interests in general were greatly developed, and now the concerns of man and his associations are dominant. It has even been claimed that the nineteenth ought to be called "the socialistic century." Men eminent in natural science, who claim last century for their specialty, admit that the twentieth belongs to sociology. It is natural that man and his relations should be the chief concern of man; and present tendencies indicate that sociology is becoming increasingly the study of the age, and that henceforth unprecedented attention will be devoted to social affairs.

The church breathed this atmosphere, and felt the effect in its life; and the environment in which it lived, as well as its internal development, must be taken into account in order to understand the church of to-day. A relation of co-operation and mutualism has existed between the practical and scientific social tendencies and Christianity. The church itself is a social institution, and as such has at all times felt the molding influence of society, and even in its most individualistic periods has affected social affairs as well as individuals. Christianity has a part in all the extensive movements of society, and is a powerful factor in the nations and the world. But whether its sociality is what it ought to be is another matter. It is a Christian axiom that before God all men are equal, that believers are one, that to each other and to the worldly, whether friends or foes, they owe love and its fruits, and that they are called to transform society by means of the Gospel. However derelict it may have been, something of this fundamental Christian spirit and work has always been found in the church. Christianity possesses humanitarian and social principles which affect even such persons as are not attracted by its spirituality. But in the realization of its social mission and power, and in the effort to infuse the Christian spirit into all the social relations, we are justified in claiming that a new epoch has begun for the church.

Powerfully as the church has been affected by sociology and socialism, these have also been powerfully affected by the church. Christianity is not the only factor in the soil from which the modern social tendencies have sprung; but there is truth in the claim of Laveleye, of Belgium, Todt, of Germany, and of English and American writers, that socialism, in spite of its perversions, strikes its roots in Christianity.

Wherever Christ has been preached the personality has been emphasized as made in the image of God, and therefore possessing inherent dignity and rights. The demands for the rights of man, urged so vehemently and even fanatically at the close of the eighteenth century, have their basis in the Gospel. Properly understood, the watchwords of the French revolution—liberty, equality, fraternity—are a Christian requirement. The pulpit, in teaching that God is no respecter of persons, that men must be judged by their hearts, not by position, wealth, or any other outward circumstances, prepared for the revolt against the external and fictitious distinctions according to which men, regardless of personal ability and character, were usually estimated.

Much in the trend of modern times also exalts the significance of the present life and temporal interests. The older Christian literature has more to say about the next world, and less about the value of earthly things and relations. The modern view was promoted by the study of natural science, the great progress in economic pursuits, and the growing interest in secular affairs. Materialism, philosophical and historical criticism, and the effort to substitute science for religion, reason for faith, made the future world recede, occasioned doubt, and concentrated attention and hope more on present actualities. While agnosticism gained favor with some scientists, the belief spread among the masses that religion was used to make hope in the next life the means of robbing the toilers of the enjoyments of the present. German socialists were incensed when it was affirmed among scholars that while they themselves did not need religion, it was serviceable in keeping the masses quiet. Even where religion held its own, or made advances, it could not retain its former dominance, on account of the marvelous progress in secular learning and worldly interests. The conservative tendencies in the church made theology comparatively stationary, while in every department of natural and human studies great advances took place.

The religious life was also profoundly affected by the change from metaphysical speculation and theological dogmatism to practical affairs. Since the time of Hegel speculative philosophy has lost ground and yielded the supremacy to facts, experiments, and the direct investigation of reality. Becoming suspicious of subjective notions, men demanded objective realism, by which they were apt to mean what appeals to the senses and can be handled, weighed and measured. Even in the church the cry of religion versus theology was raised, overlooking the fact that all deeper thinking demands a reduction of religious phenomena to principles, causes and system. But the emphasis on practical religion promoted the tendency to concentrate the attention on this life and its immediate concerns. No other century has equaled the nineteenth in the radicalness, severity and scholarship of the attacks on dogmatic theological systems. Those who could not investigate the profound questions involved turned to the more evident practical teachings of religion.

The attacks on theology directed Christians to its source, the Scriptures; and the attacks on the Scriptures led to a more thorough investigation of their contents. When Strauss attempted to overthrow the authenticity of the history of the evangelists, the church was aroused and made a vigorous defence. The very study of the Gospel augmented the conviction of believers that Christ is Himself the substance of His preaching. The increased study of the Bible by means of numerous helps is characteristic of modern times. Laymen wanted to investigate for themselves, and they were aided by Sunday-schools and other associations, and by evangelists. The study was influenced by the general social movement. Christ's attitude toward social problems became an important question; and it was found that His teaching and that of the Apostles are exceedingly rich in instruction respecting the social relations and duties of Christians.

That the social actuality did not correspond with the Christian ideal was as evident as that the church seemed indifferent to the realization of the ideal. The evils revealed in Christian lands by social students and socialists were appalling. Carl Marx and Friedrich Engels made astounding revelations respecting the brutality with which women and children were treated in the mines and factories of England during the first half of the nineteenth century, and how laborers were exploited and undergoing a process of gradual degeneration. Similar or even worse horrors were exposed in other lands. Public attention was still more aroused when communistic socialism grew in power, and threatened the throne and the altar, and the whole social structure, in order to establish an entirely different social organization on a new basis, and when anarchism actually began the work of destruction. The consternation caused in Europe by an extreme socialism and a brutal anarchism was not appreciated in America, where economic conditions were different, and greater freedom was less favorable to extreme measures. Radical socialistic and anarchistic theories began to prevail later in the United States than in Europe, and flourished chiefly among foreigners who had learned them in the Old World. The same views have recently, however, spread also among Americans.

A survey of the history of the century which has just closed thus shows that the origin of the modern Christian social movement is due to a variety of causes both religious and secular. It is the culmination of numerous practical and scholarly tendencies, special influence being due to the new interest in social studies and the uprising of the masses. As is usual in such movements, the development which pushed society and its concerns to the front has been gradual and often imperceptible, so that it is impossible to say just when it began and what agencies promoted it. There are, however, well-defined landmarks, epochs we might call them, when the Christian social movement received a special impulse, or took a new start. It was about the middle of the nineteenth century that certain popular tendencies culminated and became the occasion of a specific and continuous Christian social activity in Europe.

The indifference and even apathy of the clergy and churches of England to the welfare of the poorer classes before this time would seem incredible if the same were not still common to some extent in all Christian lands. Appeals for justice and mercy, on the plea of Christianity, were made by Lord Ashley, afterward Earl of

SOCIAL ASPECT OF CHRISTIANITY. 43

Shaftesbury, and his associates, for the improvement of the legal status of laborers. Their miserable situation was exposed by committees, and fully discussed in Parliament; yet the Earl of Shaftesbury complained that the Christians were indifferent to the matter. Even the wretched condition of the children did not move them. Men of the world were with him, he said, while the saints stood aloof and were silent. But the exposures were not without effect. Some Christians were at least made aware of the situation, and this was a preparation for arousing their consciences. Near the middle of the century Chartism had practically failed. It had demanded universal suffrage and Parliamentary reform, and devised plans for the relief of workingmen; but it also became involved in socialistic and revolutionary agitations. In 1848 a new movement was started, with some of the reformatory aims of Chartism, but based on Christian principles. The conviction that something must be done for the masses was strengthened by the revolutionary disturbances throughout Europe during that year. The term socialist was at that time, as it has been since, deemed a reproach in the church and among the wealthy. But Maurice, Kingsley, Ludlow and others started what they called "Christian Socialism." They published the "Christian Socialist," and "Tracts on Christian Socialism," to aid the laborers in their efforts to rise, and to Christianize socialism and socialize Christians. Their peaceable aim was misinterpreted, though they declared that they wanted to prevent rather than to promote revolution. Maurice said, respecting Christian Socialism, that it is "the only title which will define our object and will commit us at once to the conflict we must engage in sooner or later with the unsocial Christians and the unchristian socialists. . . . We believe that Christianity has the power of regenerating whatever it comes in contact with, of making that morally healthful and vigorous which, apart from it, must be either mischievous or inefficient. We found, from what we knew of the workingmen in England, that the conviction was spreading more and more widely among them that law and Christianity were merely the support and agents of capital. We wished to show them both by words and deeds that law and Christianity are the only protectors of all classes from the selfishness which is the destruction of all."

Since that time a great awakening of the Christian social consciousness has taken place in England. What is now known as Christian socialism has been modified by the views of Carl Marx,

Henry George and Edward Bellamy. The present society of Christian socialists is small, liberty is advocated respecting theological views, they seek "the union of all men in a real universal brotherhood," and aim at the gradual "public control of land and capital." This is its religious position: "Christian socialism aims at embodying the principles contained in the life and teachings of Jesus Christ in the industrial organization of society."

The St. Matthew's Guild in the Established Church unites radical social views with High Church principles, aims to remove prejudices against the church and her institutions, and "to promote the study of social and political questions in the light of the Incarnation."

More powerful is the Christian Social Union, which urges upon the church "the necessity of careful and painstaking study of the social question, and to take the lead in establishing branches for such study." Books are to be suggested for this study, and lectures on social subjects to be delivered. The "Economic Review," containing valuable economic and social discussions, is published by this society. The "Church Army" aims at the same kind of work as the Salvation Army, but on a much smaller scale.

The Rev. R. A. Woods, in "English Social Movements," says: "On the whole, and in its main features, the Church of England exerts a larger and more salutary influence on general social life than any other Christian body in the world. . . . Most of the churches are well supplied with paid workers. In addition to the rectors and vicars, there will be found curates, lay readers, members of lay brotherhoods and sisterhoods, deaconesses, Bible women, and trained nurses, besides the usually well-organized volunteers from the church membership."

Excellent social work is also done by the Congregationalists, Methodists and Baptists, but not so much by means of special organizations. Their churches are reaching out after the masses, and trying to aid them in temporal and spiritual matters. In this connection the London Congregational Union, Dr. Barnardo, F. N. Charrington, and Rev. Hugh Price Hughes, deserve special mention.

Rev. Mr. Woods states that Christian Socialism is spreading, but that as yet it has not collected much of its strength into organization. "In the dissenting churches, while many of the younger ministers hold very radical views, the number of avowed socialists is comparatively small. But, in the Church of England, one might fairly say that there is a strong socialistic movement. A group of forty

London clergymen, nearly all socialists, meet during the winter to consider what attitude they shall take toward specific labor troubles. A good part of the young High Churchmen, often the best representatives of the university and of the upper social class, are facing the problems of poverty in London and other towns. This experience, together with the new enthusiasm of humanity, which is running so strong in the High Church party, is making many of them socialists."

About the same time as in England, the modern Christian social movement began in Germany. At a religious congress held in 1848, in the Reformation city, Wittenberg, John Henry Wichern directed attention to the condition of the masses, and zealously urged that with respect to the poorer classes the church has a *special* mission. It was generally recognized that it owes them duties as well as other men; but sight had been lost of the fact that the poor and suffering are committed to the church as objects of peculiar care and helpfulness. This was involved in their very needs. Spiritually as well as in economic affairs, they were the neglected classes. The church was viewed as an organ of the state, even as a clerical institution for political ends, where respectability, wealth and aristocracy ruled; but in which the common people had little interest except to receive religious instruction. It was too exclusively an institution for worship and the exercise of clerical functions to be in an exalted sense sociable, to promote lay activity, or to uplift the masses. Wichern's earnest appeals had the more effect because Germany had just been appalled by the revolution, which revealed deep discontent, threatened the existing institutions, and resulted in much bloodshed. The revolution was no more significant in revealing the feeling of the masses than in testifying to the neglect of the needy by the church. Not only were many of the workingmen alienated from the church, but infidelity, materialism and agnosticism prevailed among them to an alarming extent. To win back to the church and Christianize the masses now became the problem. Great as the difficulty then was, it was still greater when an extreme socialism developed its power, enlisted millions under its banner, and either avowed atheism or at least opposed the church because conservative and an ally of the state in preventing its revolutionary schemes.

The state church, as an institution, had too little freedom, and was too unwieldy to accomplish the work of social reform; but it was deeply affected by the socialistic agitations. The sermons paid more attention to the social condition; preachers drew nearer the laborers, and in many parishes special efforts were made to help the poorer classes. The new spirit, however, found the best expression in what is called "Inner Mission." We have no corresponding English term, home mission and evangelization being more limited. In distinction from foreign mission the Inner Mission works among people in Christian lands, and nominally in the church, but not full participants of its spirit and in special need of temporal aid. The term is not limited to purely spiritual efforts, but is intended to include all the work outside of the regular ministrations of the church undertaken in Christ's spirit, whether it be for the individual or society; for the soul, the body, or the surroundings. The Inner Mission was the sphere in which Christian individuals and voluntary organizations promoted the cause of Christ among the neglected such as the church did not reach. It includes the works of mercy by thousands of deaconesses, who, in institutions and homes, minister to the sick, the suffering, and the poor; the brotherhoods trained to take care of orphans and neglected children, to provide religious instruction and services in destitute regions, and to undertake whatever reformatory work may be needed; Christian hotels for the traveling public, and homes for young workmen and for servant girls; and efforts in behalf of particular classes, such as cabmen and waiters, who are unable to attend religious services, the unemployed, released prisoners, fallen and abandoned women. It therefore embraces every department of Christian effort in behalf of the needy. Christ's regenerative mission is interpreted to apply to the whole man, physical, mental and spiritual, and the whole world so far as it sustains human relations. The cause enlists the energies of many preachers, and it presents a sphere for Christian laymen to exercise the gifts for whose development the church affords too little opportunity. Laymen are often the managers and most efficient workers. Formal organizations are not necessary; any Christian can undertake the work wherever needed. There are general conventions of workers in the Inner Mission, but each department is independent and supported by voluntary contributions. The work is extensive, thoroughly Christian, and fruitful of good, and one of the most significant evidences of the social power of Christianity in our day. The Inner Mission reaches all the Protestant cities of Germany, extends to country districts, and even to foreign lands where Germans reside, and contains twenty-five or more distinct departments.

SOCIAL ASPECT OF CHRISTIANITY. 47

It is a general rule that the church which is in the minority in a region is apt to be more zealous than the one which has the ascendancy. The zeal of the latter seems to be affected by the fact that without special effort it has things its own way. The Protestants are most energetic in Catholic and the Catholics in Protestant lands. However the Catholic clergy may neglect the masses in countries where their church has undisputed sway, they reveal much energy in their behalf when they have Protestant rivals. In Germany, parts of Austria, in Holland, Scandinavia, England, Scotland, and the United States, the Catholic priests display much concern for the workingmen. German Socialists declare that in Germany the Catholic Church has shown more interest in behalf of laborers than the Evangelical Church. Protestants are charged with individualism and disintegrating tendencies, while in its very nature Catholicism is more united and more socialistic. The Pope's encyclical on the labor question has made special attention to the workmen a duty of the priesthood. Before it appeared, however, men like Bishop Ketteler, of Mayence, Moufong, and their co-laborers, had directed attention to the demand made on the church by the needy classes. The priests, under the guidance of the bishops, and these under the direction of the Pope, have made vigorous efforts to keep the masses in the church. In this respect they have been more successful than the Protestants. It is evident that the interest in labor and the spiritual welfare of the church were not the sole considerations of the priesthood. The *Culturkampf* united the Catholics into an Ultramontane political party, known as the Centre, the strongest faction in the German Parliament. Votes were eagerly sought to secure the political aims of this party. But whatever motive prevailed, large Catholic labor organizations have been formed among miners, railroad employees, workers in iron, textile industries, and other trades. These organizations are made auxiliary to the church, and the priests have been active in establishing and promoting them. They are on a positive Christian basis, and therefore oppose the anti-religious tendencies of revolutionary socialism; but on this basis they labor for the promotion of the general interests of the workingmen. Capitalists and employers are often invited to their meetings. The numerous eleemosynary institutions of the church and its emphasis on deeds of charity have kept it in touch with the suffering masses. Most of the revolutionary socialists have come from the ranks of Protestantism. Protestant labor organizations have also been formed, but they are less numerous than among the Catholics. Court Preacher Stoecker, Rev. Naumann, Rev. Eoehre, and many others, preachers and laymen, have tried to arouse the Evangelical Church to a deeper and more active interest in the labor problem, and their efforts have not been in vain. But under the plea that they might aid the Social Democracy they have met with opposition from the court and the moneyed aristocracy. The Christian social leaven, however, cannot be checked; and in many instances the inner mission surpasses in efficiency the eleemosynary institutions of Catholicism, and at the same time promotes Christian freedom and a healthy Biblical piety.

In the United States the beginning of the modern Christian social movement is less clearly marked than in Europe. It is not surprising that so long as slavery existed, public attention should be but little concerned with the problems of free labor. Even before the civil war, however, labor had its grievances, formed organizations, and carried on agitations for better conditions. America was called the paradise of laborers. The country was large and rich in resources that needed development; labor was abundant, food cheap, while wages were high, and the political advantages of workingmen the greatest in the world. Even then their favorable condition was, no doubt, generally over-estimated by the other classes, because not carefully investigated. A great change took place when the slaves were freed and became competitors in the labor market, when hundreds of thousands of emigrants landed from Europe and Asia, when the best arable and the most accessible land was taken by actual settlers, corporations, or speculators, and when laborers found it difficult to become employers or capitalists because the existing opportunities were seized by men of means, and also because business enterprises became so extensive as to require large sums of money. Discontent increased in labor circles; yet long after socialism had gained prominence in Europe Americans boasted that the United States had no social problem. The singular apathy of capitalists and employers toward the situation of laborers is largely due to a failure to perceive that organic connection of society which makes the interest of one class the concern of all, and to that false individualism which adopts the theory "Each one for himself," and leaves it to every man to work out his own destiny as best he can. Heathenism prevailed under the guise of a Christian freedom which totally lacked the brotherly element of Christianity. Crises came

SOCIAL ASPECT OF CHRISTIANITY. 49

when labor was scarce and multitudes were out of employment and in need. At such times there were vigorous manifestations of imported socialistic and anarchistic theories. The poorer classes drifted into the slums, the abode of vice and crime, of filth and misery. The vast accumulations of wealth, the increase of luxury and extravagant display, and the influence of money in social and political and ecclesiastical affairs, made the contrast the more striking, because in theory all men were regarded as equal. In Europe, as well as in America, the view spread that the American laborer had lost his former advantages and was gradually sinking to the European level. With a theoretical training in political and religious independence and equality the American workingmen felt that in respect to the church, to culture, and in courts of justice, they were at a great disadvantage. They were embittered, denounced existing social conditions, and charged the church with being an institution of the rich and respectable classes. Ministers came in for their share of abuse as slaves of the wealthy, on whom they depended for their salaries. The growing alienation between the classes, and of laborers from the church, was gradual and even imperceptible until too marked any longer to escape attention. It was discovered that America has a social problem of great magnitude and peculiarly dangerous. The laborers are in the majority, and by union can exert the strongest political and martial force. Every one knows what this means in a free state where the majority rule, the people are sovereign, and no large standing army exists to coerce them. The freedom, intelligence, traditions, and ideals of the laborer increase his demands as well as his power of realization.

It is not more strange that slavery could exist in a land otherwise the freest on earth than that in the same land the labor movement should so long be left to laborers, as if of no interest to the other members of society. Frequent reference was made to the sacredness of property, for the protection of which the strictest laws must be enacted and all the powers of the Government exerted; but it was often ignored that property has value only for man's sake and that it is wrong to exploit men for the sake of property. Gradually, however, it became apparent that the labor problem is a *social* problem, that it affects capital and the rich as well as labor, and concerns the church, the state, civilization, itself, and all the relations of man to man.

The church in the United States naturally partook of the views generally prevalent respecting labor. Prosperity was supposed to be so universal, or within the reach of all, that there appeared to be no need for a special consideration of laborers. The man who spoke of *classes* as actually existing in American society was liable to be branded as a demagogue, until the class consciousness of laborers and their conflicts with capital left no doubt on the subject. Class distinctions were attributed to churches themselves. Down-town was left to the poorer people, often foreigners and Catholics, and the Protestant churches moved up-town. Large districts, densely populated, were neglected or provided with mission chapels which lacked the attractions of the elegant churches in the wealthier parts of the city. The separation of the wealthy and middle classes from the laborers is neither universal nor always desired by the churches; but it is too common among Protestants and contrasts painfully with the union of all classes in the same Catholic service. Recently many Protestant churches have been more ready to welcome laborers heartily than laborers were to give a favorable response. Often the prejudice of workingmen against the church is fostered mainly by a few churches of peculiar prominence, where the dominance of wealth and love of display prevent laborers from feeling at home. The charge that the pastors and the people do not study the labor problem, and fail to advocate impartial justice in labor conflicts, has truth in it, but is by no means universally applicable. Great progress has been made within a few decades; but in interest in the social problem and in efforts for its solution on Christian principles, America is still far behind England and Germany.

The pulpit here, as elsewhere, promoted the labor movement by preaching liberty, equality, the worth of man, the value of character, and Christ's law of human brotherhood. The hope that in America the realization would come first deepened the despair as the ideal seemed to recede. Preachers always existed who were the best friends of laborers and sought to apply the whole Gospel of Christ to them and their situation; but it cannot be claimed as characteristic of American Christianity that pastors and churches regarded it as their supreme call to seek the needy classes to which Jesus was most drawn and who responded most favorably to His message. The smaller denominations, doing extensive missionary work, and such as are composed chiefly of foreigners, have, of course, a large percentage of laborers, and in all denominations there are congregations in which workingmen are prominent.

SOCIAL ASPECT OF CHRISTIANITY.   51

The religious social movement in the United States was mainly inaugurated and carried forward by individuals. Their pioneer work often isolated them; not only were they without sympathy from their brethren, but even subject to denunciation and persecution. During the sharp and bitter conflicts between capital and labor, sympathy expressed for workingmen was liable to be interpreted as hostility to capitalists. With no state church, with numerous denominations as competitors and rivals, with organizations often loose, scattered over a great extent of territory, and with little union between them, it is not strange that the movement should be more individualistic than in Europe. Here, however, as in England, the Episcopal Church has special organizations for the laboring classes, such as the Church Association for the Advancement of the Interests of Labor and the Christian Social Union.

Communistic experiments, some on a religious basis, are old in the United States. One of these, American in origin, shows that an effort was made to introduce Christian socialism about the same time as in England. In 1854, a work entitled "Practical Christian Socialism" appeared. Its author, Adin Ballou, was a Universalist preacher and founder of the Hopedale Community. The large volume seems to have fallen still-born from the press. The Community, founded in 1841, existed only seventeen years, was near its end when the book appeared, and this may have contributed to the neglect of the volume, which deserved a better fate. Many of the discussions are able and contain valuable expositions of society. The author proposes to give a "true system of human society," basing it on the teaching of Jesus Christ. The book reveals a sublime faith in the social righteousness to be established by the Christian religion, and in the help of God. Theological dogmatism is avoided; practical Christianity is advocated; the importance of the individual is emphasized, and stress placed on his freedom and individuality; and mind, heart and conscience are exalted about the external surroundings. Love and the spirit of brotherhood were to dominate society instead of the worldly methods of force and competitive rivalry.

It is indicative of the neglect of the social aspect of Christianity that no attempt was made by Christian scholars to give the social system involved in the teachings of the New Testament. There is little hope of uniting Christian social workers until a definite idea is formed of the Biblical conception of the nature, relations, responsibilities and agencies of Christian society. In order to direct attention to the importance of the subject and to give hints for its development, a volume entitled "Christian Sociology," by J. H. W. Stuckenberg, was published in 1880. As this was the first time that the term Christian sociology was used, it became the occasion of much discussion then and since. It has now been permanently established, stands for an extensive literature, and designates a specific sphere of Christian inquiry. It makes no claim to supersede, or dictate to, general sociology, but holds that the principles of Christian society are found in Scripture and can be formulated into a system. The volume defines Christian sociology "as the science of Christian society, or as the science of that society which is controlled by Christian principles. Its aim is to describe this society; to explain its origin, nature, laws, relations and purposes. This science will be perfect in proportion as it gives the distinguishing characteristics of Christian society and indicates the relation of this society to other societies." While Christian socialism is practical in its aim, Christian sociology aims at a science of Christian society in the same sense that theology and Christian ethics are called sciences.

Numerous other Christian social works of a later date have appeared, such as those of R. Heber Newton, Herron, Gladden, Abbott, Hodges, Bliss, Lorimer, and others. The interest awakened in the subject is evident from the space given to social matters in the religious press, and from the prominence of the theme in conventions, in the pulpit, on the platform, and in schools. Numerous special journals have also been established to promote the social work of the church. In America, as well as in England and other countries, the Salvation Army is doing valuable service in meeting the needs of the poorer members of society; its labors are too well known, however, to require extended notice.

A general survey of the social activity of the Protestant Church in different countries does not enable us to claim that as an institution it has anywhere given a dominant place to the social aspect of Christianity. The subject has frequently been discussed and resolutions on social work have been adopted, but as a body the church has not committed itself. No platform exists on which all the workers stand, and no uniform method has been adopted. Individuals and associations undertake different kinds of work, but there is no union of Christian reformers or of Christian reforms. The lack of a definite understanding and of organized coöperation is a hindrance to success. But everywhere the social spirit has been developed and the social conscience quickened. The social factors of Christianity, the character, power, and mission of Christian society, and the methods of Christian sociality, receive an amount of attention in the church and religious literature altogether unknown a few decades since. Many pastors are students of sociology, of social conditions, and of the means of removing social ills and elevating the masses. Churches are more intent on attracting laborers, and in a number of instances the pews have been made free and services specially adapted to the masses. Workingmen also speak more kindly of the church since they find it more friendly to the cause of labor. The Christian social movement is here to stay. It is only in its initiatory stages, is making progress both in extent and in power, and promises to gain a controlling influence in the future. Its character and purpose are, however, frequently misunderstood, and therefore it is necessary to explain them.

It aims to socialize the churches, to create an interest in all that pertains to social welfare, and to substitute for the perverted conceptions of society, so often prevalent even in churches, the social aspect contained in Scripture. In spite of the extensive literature on the subject, a complete Biblical conception has not yet been attained, which accounts for the conflicting notions respecting the social requirements of the Gospel. The diversity regarding what is required is due to the fact that the investigation is new, the material is extensive, investigators come with preconceived views, and on the burning social problems prejudice is easily excited. Much and profound research is still required in order to appropriate, systematize, and apply the social wealth of the Bible.

The economic theories adopted by social thinkers and workers must not be confounded with the Biblical aspect of society. Scripture does not propose to teach the laws of production, exchange, distribution, and consumption of wealth, but establishes certain fundamental principles as the guides of men in their industrial relations. With the same Christian motives different economic theories may be adopted, if not in conflict with Scripture, the choice being determined by questions of expediency. Neither can the effort to make society communistic according to the model at the close of the second chapter of Acts be regarded as a law. Under the inspiration of the day of Pentecost the religious fervor and brotherly love of the believers established a species of communism, so that they "had all things in common, and sold their possessions and goods, and parted them to all men, as every man had need." This was wholly voluntary, did not become a rule for the Apostolic Church, was no doubt soon abandoned, because impracticable, and might work well in a particular community under special circumstances and fail in others. What believers actually hold in common and share with each other is a profound problem which that early experiment could not settle for all Christians and all times. Frequently some kind of coöperation is far more expedient than communism, and Christian socialism in England has been promotive of an extensive coöperative movement, especially in the form of distribution. According to the Gospels and Epistles, charity and helpfulness are to be exercised for the relief of need and suffering, but the methods are left to Christian freedom and wisdom.

Even among those called Christian socialists different economic theories may be adopted for the reform and reconstruction of society. That, from a Christian standpoint, the present social condition, with its unjust distinctions, its vice, crime, and misery, is intolerable and demands a radical transformation cannot be questioned. The tares are ripe for the burning. So many things are involved in the reconstruction on Christian principles that the problem can only be solved tentatively and progressively. The Rev. W. D. P. Bliss defines the essence of Christian socialism as "the application to society of the way of Christ. It believes that Christ has a social way, and that only in this way are there healing and wholeness for the nations. * * * Christian socialism follows from, and is involved in, personal obedience to Christ. It is first Christian. Its starting point is the Incarnation.

The new social gospel of Christian thinkers and workers is simply an effort to restore the original Gospel to its proper place in the church and to make it effective by means of the spirit of Christ. Whatever differences exist, this is the heart and the purpose. The social aspect of Christianity makes a specialty of the teachings of Christ and the Apostles respecting society. Many of these teachings are plain and oft-repeated, but they have been overlooked by the individualistic tendencies, or have at least not been fully appreciated and properly embodied in life. Christian society recognizes God as its spiritual Father, Christ as its Founder and Elder Brother, love as its essence which constitutes the members of real brotherhood, with the Gospel as its basis, with the spirit of Christ as its guide, and with humanity and the world as the sphere of its activity. Children of the same Father are, of course, brothers; but this ideal relation is to be made a living actuality. As God must be loved supremely, so the neighbor is to be loved as self. The old and narrow particularism of Jews and Gentiles is to be overcome by making neighbor mean especially one in need, regardless of nationality and creed. Humanity constitutes neighborhood. The Golden Rule is the Christian law: "All things whatsoever ye would that men should do to you, do ye even so to them: for this is the law and the prophets." We must forgive others if we want God to forgive us; that means we are to do to our fellow-men what we want God to do to us. By his royal law of service Jesus overthrows the Oriental heathenism which made greatness consist in being served, while He begins a new world by making him greatest who serves most. "But whosoever will be great among you, let him be your minister; and whosoever will be chief among you, let him be your servant; even as the Son of Man came not to be ministered unto, but to minister, and to give His life a ransom for many." Men ordinarily seek such as can help and exalt them; Jesus is unique in that he seeks those who need Him most, and thus He gives a new law for His followers.

As distinct from His teaching by word of mouth, Jesus must Himself be taken as the Word and the social model. He lived His doctrine and made His life the doctrine for His Disciples. No dogmatic system can give full expression to this personal element; the command is to go and do likewise. Christianity is a spirit, and that spirit is Christ. An important factor in the mighty revolution He wrought consisted in the infinite tenderness with which He sought the most needy and embraced them in His compassionate heart, becoming the friend of the friendless, the helper of the helpless, preaching to them, and then illustrating His preaching by feeding the hungry, healing the sick, comforting the distressed, and receiving sinners and eating with them. He saved those whom we call abandoned, and to the man who fell among thieves He is the Good Samaritan. His mission is to the surroundings of men as well as to men themselves; therefore He denounces the mammonism of His day with its fiendish covetousness, the ceremonialism with its displays before men as a substitute for religion, the tradition of the elders put in place of the decrees of God, and that entire religious and political degradation which made Him weep over Jerusalem.

Christ's social work can be a mystery to such only as will not see.

It is inner and spiritual, but at the same time penetrates and pervades the entire human cosmos, touching and transforming all of man's relations and conditions. The Disciples are commissioned to preach, to heal the sick, cleanse the lepers, raise the dead, and cast out devils. He regenerates men, and with them the world.

The new emphasis on the study of Scripture, on practical religion, and on sociality gave prominence to these neglected Biblical teachings. It was discovered that the Bible is marvelously rich in teachings applicable to the social agitations and miseries of our times. The possibilities which our Lord opened up to the neglected masses have a meaning in relation to the insistence of the poorer members of society for recognition, for better culture, for greater opportunities. If in Christian lands they were content with a degraded condition, it would prove Christianity, so far as they are concerned, a failure. Men looked at the abject heathenism in the centres of our most Christian civilization and asked, "Were Christ to come, what would He do?" Christians truly alive insisted that the time had come for judgment to begin at the house of God, for worldliness to be scourged out of the temple, and for a restoration of the spirit and work of Christ and the Apostles to the church.

While men of the world looked to the church to take the lead in the social regeneration, objections were raised by the pulpit and laymen. The effort to extend religion to all human relations according to the New Testament model was opposed by professing Christians, who said, "Preach the Gospel." By the Gospel they meant individual salvation, doctrines in a narrow sense spiritual. "Preach the Gospel" was said to those who advocated political purity, temperance, honesty in business, mercy for the needy, and a Christian humanitarianism. The very preaching they wanted had, however, prevailed all along, and in the midst of it the existing social wretchedness had developed. Another objection was that social affairs are determined by nature, and therefore inevitable, or by God, and therefore can be opposed only in defiance of His will! Since then some have learned that social affairs are largely of human creation and subject to human volition.

The social awakening of Christians led to an apprehension of the teachings of the New Testament respecting the socializing and organizing influence of Christianity. It became evident that Jesus gave a prominence to the Kingdom of God which had been lost sight of by the Christian consciousness. In Germany, Ritschl laid great stress on the Kingdom as a dominant factor in the teaching of Jesus, and, however viewed in other respects, the wide influence of the new theology concentrated attention again on this neglected doctrine. To identify God's Kingdom with a church and with the limited sphere of its organized labors was recognized as a perversion. It means the spiritual dominion or reign of God, and the Kingdom exists wherever this dominion is found. It thus includes all true spiritual activity on earth, whether inside or outside of the organized church. The revival of the doctrine of the kingdom socializes Christianity and overcomes the old individualism which is intent only on saving the individual and embodying him in the church.

The oneness of believers is likewise indicated by representing them as a family by Christ and the Apostles, as a household of faith and a brotherhood; as an organism, either as a vine and its branches, or as a body with its organs; as a flock under Christ, the Good Shepherd; as a temple or building of God; and as a church. Christ prays that between believers the same unity may exist as between Himself and the Father, and that this unity be made evident to the world. This oneness of Christians has significance for the world as well as for their own sake. Through their labors humanity is to be discipled.

The social awakening of the church also gave a new meaning to this life. The importance attached by Christ to society and the blessings He offered in this world made it possible to defer all the glories of the Christian to the life to come. Jesus reveals a passion for humanity. We have seen that His teaching respecting man includes all of man and all his relations and surroundings. This truth is enforced by the fact that the physical and intellectual life, the natural conditions and secular social relations, exert a marked influence on spirituality. There are environments whose atmosphere is pollution, and only by changing them can religion flourish in them. Hence the concern of Christianity for the home and whatever affects family life; its relation to politics, to sanitation, to slums, the saloon, to recreation and amusement, to the schools and charitable institutions. To neglect them is suicidal. In this world a spirit without a body is a ghost; and an isolated spirituality is ghostly.

This religious extension has brought the church into spheres of activity formerly but little regarded. It has a new message to capital and labor; to municipalities, states, and nations; to women and children that should be at home but wander into factories; to sweatshops and palaces; to culture and ignorance. Just as in the heathen world missionaries seek to transform the total physical and mental condition, together with the moral and religious, so in lands called Christian the church is learning that it has part in all that is organically connected with the church, and that all ought to be spiritualized. Hence the church is changing—we live in an era of transition respecting its relations and methods. The problem has been seized, how to enter this wondrously complex modern life, with its enlarged range of thought, feeling and activity, with its denial of authority and culture of anarchism, and to leaven every part of it with the Gospel. Churches are even socially transformed which do not formally change their methods. More attention is given to questions of social justice and mercy in economics, politics, and human intercourse in general. Churches are inquiring how far, by their neglect or example, they are responsible for the abandoned and outcasts; for Dives and Lazarus; for the corruptness in government; for the prevalence of vice, crime, and illiteracy; and for the social shams which have taken the place of mind and heart. That a new Christian world has been entered is proved by the tone of the pulpit and the character of religious literature.

Besides this change in the church in general, many churches are instituting special means for meeting the social demands. They are becoming in a fuller sense eleemosynary institutions. Agencies are also established for various kinds of instruction. Civic leagues and good citizenship classes are formed, the neglected are taught and trained in industry and thrift, and Christians are prepared for undertaking social work among the needy. Settlements have been established for the purpose of bringing the different social grades together and giving opportunities for refinement and culture to the poorer classes. They are also valuable aids in purifying the external environment, and in increasing the vigilance and efficiency of the police and other public authorities. Institutional churches have been organized in cities and also in country districts, for the purpose of applying the principles of Christ to every species of individual and social need. They differ according to locality and requirements, the aim being to make an application of the Gospel to all the relations and necessities of men. The Sunday services are made attractive and popular so as to win all classes; life is studied with a view to discovering and meeting its needs; classes are formed for promoting various studies or for instructing in the evening such persons as are engaged during the day; agencies are established for advice and relief; and offices at the church are kept open day and evening for consultation and service. In this way the church is made in the truest sense a missionary and social institution. It can recommend and circulate the best literature, establish societies as needed by the community, furnish profitable recreation and entertainment, and can become the centre from which light radiates in every direction. Many Christian societies are also organized, in various places, without direct connection with the church, which aim to carry on works of reform, that of temperance being specially prominent. It is evident that there is much religious effort which is not in the organized church, but flourishes in the Kingdom of God.

The fear that this religious extension into regions formerly sharply separated as secular or worldly, common and unclean, might rob the church of its spirituality is proving groundless. That in the first reaction against false traditional methods there should be extremes is not surprising. With time and experience these evils will be corrected. A religion which thoroughly penetrates every phase of social life is immeasurably more valuable than a religion which isolates itself. The pulpit occupies a larger sphere in this religious extension; it applies its message to all the human actualities, and thus attains that reality which is an urgent demand of the age. Suddenly a vast field has been opened up to Christian effort, and in entering it new life, new power, and greater influence may be expected by the pulpit and the church.

Thus far the social movement has considered the social problem chiefly as it involves the workingmen. But there is also a social problem among the rich—how they can maintain themselves amid growing discontent, the increasing power of the masses with the ballot, and the determination to overthrow all unjust inequalities; what the duties of wealth are to the less favorably situated; and how the power of wealth can be consecrated to the highest leadership in religion, politics, economics, and culture. As no other institution, the Church of Jesus Christ rises above class distinctions and class prejudice, and has the means for uniting, on the basis of the Gospel, all the social grades and conditions. This will be a matter of course so soon as the prevailing worldly tests of society yield to those of Christian love and brotherhood. Some pastors and laymen despair of the prospect of Christianizing the churches sufficiently to enable them to seize this glorious mission, and therefore they organize churches especially for laborers. Whatever demand may exist for them amid present conditions, the Christian ideal tolerates no distinctions according to external circumstances which ignore the claims of character. The time has evidently come for the letter of James, which has been called the sociological Epistle.

The Christian sociality already attained promises well for the religious spirit and labors of the new century. It will no doubt grow in knowledge and efficiency, and thus prepare for the fuller coming of the Kingdom of Christ. The church will become all things to all men for the purpose of making them the children of God. In this great Christian social movement and religious extension believers have the hope of realizing the words of the Apostle: "All things are yours. . . . The earth is the Lord's, and the fullness thereof."

REVIVAL MOVEMENTS IN THE NINETEENTH CENTURY.

J. WILBUR CHAPMAN, D.D.,
NEW YORK.

[A revival presupposes a condition of deadness from which a spiritual resurrection is desired. The ideal condition would naturally be that in which a continuous state of religious efficiency is maintained. Some have even ventured to coin the word "vival" as expressive of that ideal state. A "revival" is etymologically therefore a making an individual or church to live again, after a lapse into spiritual lethargy. But while the desirable condition would be that in which the church is always animated with the intensest zeal and enthusiasm, as a matter of fact, as we look back in history, we note a periodic recurrence of seasons of spiritual ebb and flow. The kingdom of God in its visible unfolding has experienced a series of retardations and accelerations.

Surely the supreme need of the church of Christ in the opening years of the twentieth century is a revival of spiritual power. Without being unduly pessimistic, we are compelled to admit that the tendencies of the times are grave enough to call for the most serious consideration. Many things that ought to be very sacred to Christians are imperiled. The fundamental truths of the evangelical faith, the loyalty of the people to that righteousness which exalteth a nation, and even Christianity itself as an authoritative revelation of God to our race—all are exposed to a storm of controversy which grows more vehement every day. The condition of the churches themselves is far from satisfactory. They abound in activity, but their fruitfulness is scanty. Statistics that have a lurid prominence in newspaper reports emphasize a widespread and growing conviction of spiritual impotence and sterility. The machinery is ample enough, but "the spirit of life is not in the wheels." The cry for years has been for an increase in the number of effective preachers, for an improvement in the organization of our Sunday-schools, for a better financial system, for larger accommodation for public worship, and for more attractive services in the sanctuary. Cheering progress has been made along these lines; but something more is needed, and the need was never felt more keenly than now. That something more is a fresh baptism of the Holy Ghost and of fire, which alone can vitalize congregational machinery and activity. Its necessity has always been acknowledged in petition and meditation, but of late the acknowledgment has grown in many hearts into a longing of passionate intensity.

But critical as is the condition of the church in many respects, there is much to inspire every believer in the vital forces of Christianity with confidence. Men who have a knowledge of the times express the conviction that we are on the edge of a great manifestation of the presence and power of the Spirit of God. Already signs of a more intense spiritual life are making their appearance in our churches. The fire has been kindled, and it is silently but surely spreading. The prayer of many is that it may flame up into a great revival which shall sweep the continent from ocean to ocean. For the sake of the churches, for the sake of the irreligious multitude, for the sake of the struggle with unbelief and with the paralyzing forces of indifferentism —the worst of all isms—may God grant the fulfillment of the prayer so that the whole nation may become conscious of the presence and power of the Holy Spirit! Prayerful expectation justifies hopefulness.—Unidentified. —ED.]

* * *

THE nineteenth century, though born in a religious revival, passed away, apparently, in a state of apathy and indifference such as have not been known in the church for years.

Not apathy, let it be observed, regarding benevolence, for the giving of the members of the church has been most generous, and hundreds of thousands of dollars have in recent years passed through its treasury for the betterment of society and the honor of Christ. Certainly, never in the world's history have there been so many benevolent works carried on through the inspiration and under the guidance of the church as at the present time.

Nor is indifference to religion so manifest in the matter of attendance upon church services; while here and there may be found churches where the attendance has greatly decreased, yet, as a matter of fact, the morning service at least continues to be well attended, and the interest in prayer meetings, as a rule, encouraging.

But so far as conversions are concerned, the close of the nineteenth century leaves ample room for discouragement; and, since it is our business to win men to Christ, and to preach in such a way that sinners may be converted, there is certainly, as shown in the reports of the various churches, recently made, an indication of a serious defect somewhere in the effectiveness of our services.

But our discouragement is evidently to be our encouragement, for already we hear the sound of a going in the tops of the mulberry trees, and in many quarters there are not wanting signs of abundance of rain.

The modern Christianity presents us with a glorious series of revival movements, a résumé of which is as follows:

First—The great Reformation, properly beginning in the fourteenth and extending into the sixteenth century.

Second—The work of God in the seventeenth century in the days of Owen, Bunyan, Baxter and Flavel.

Third—The great awakening in the eighteenth century in the days of Whitefield, Wesley, Edwards, Brainerd and the Tennents.

Fourth—The revival of the nineteenth century, beginning about 1790 and reaching to about the year 1840.

Fifth—The revival of 1857 to 1860.

Sixth—The special work of grace as carried on under the leadership of Mr. Dwight L. Moody.

The work of grace which ushered in the nineteenth century began about the year 1790. In the old country the fearful inroads of French infidelity had sapped the foundations of faith and hope in God, till the hearts of the faithful began to fail them for fear. This aroused such men as Bishop Porteus, Andrew Fuller, Rowland Hill and kindred spirits in England to such noble efforts as greatly blessed the world; a simultaneous work in Scotland being carried on under the Haldanes and others. This work of grace was the direct cause of the formation of the Religious Tract Society, the British and Foreign Bible Society, the London Missionary and the Church Missionary societies; also the first society for evangelizing the heathen, and the Baptist Foreign Missionary Society. In the north of Wales, also, under the labors of Charles of Bala, the Apostle of North Wales, a great revival occurred in the beginning of the year 1791.

The influence of French infidelity, aided and represented by Paine's "Age of Reason" and Voltaire's assaults upon Christianity, was felt in America, until it became fashionable for the upper classes to sneer at the Bible and ridicule the foundations of the faith of the people. But when the enemy was thus coming in like a flood the Lord lifted up a standard against him. In different parts of the country God began to manifest Himself in the outpouring of His Spirit, as, for example, in western Pennsylvania about the year 1790; also in northern and western Virginia, and a little later in the Eastern States. These awakenings introduce us to the names of such men as Bellamy, Griffin, the younger Edwards, Backus, Mills, Dwight, Livingston, Nettleton and Lyman Beecher, besides many others who in their day did not shun to declare the whole counsel of God.

In 1792 began the unbroken series of American revivals—in Maine, in Massachusetts, in Connecticut, and, indeed, in all the New

England States. By 1802 remarkable revivals had spread through most of the Western and Northern States, while Dr. Ashael Nettleton has left on record the fact that, commencing with 1798, not less than one hundred and fifty churches in New England were favored with the special effusions of the Holy Spirit, and thousands of souls were translated from the kingdom of darkness into the Kingdom of God's dear Son.

In 1812 Ashael Nettleton began to preach as an evangelist and continued his labors for upward of twenty years. Dr. Nettleton's life was marvelously forceful and his ministry signally helpful. He was a most Godly man, serious, circumspect, discreet, and gifted with rare discrimination, enabling him to know and read men, and greatly aiding him to adapt himself in his instructions to men's various moods. He preached and labored in revivals in so wise a manner as to render religion and revivals real and respected. The converts, with very few exceptions, were eminently intelligent and sound, and proved by their subsequent lives that they possessed the power as well as the form of Godliness. For seven years he labored in Connecticut, accomplishing remarkable results, then made a short tour into the State of New York and back again to Connecticut; visited England in the spring of 1831; returned to America for subsequent labors, and died May 16, 1844, his last words being, "While ye have the light walk in the light."

REVIVALS IN COLLEGES.

Perhaps nowhere have revivals of religion been oftener or better illustrated than in colleges.

In Oberlin College, from 1836 to 1841, was a period which was regarded as almost a continuous revival. Meetings for inquiry were held every Sunday. From 1836 to 1838 there was a season of refreshing never to be forgotten. Occasionally the theological recitation or lecture hour would be spent in fervent prayer and earnest supplication. When students met in the most casual way, before they parted they sang and prayed together. Oberlin still feels the power of those days.

In Amherst College, from 1827 to 1831, under the presidency of Dr. Heman Humphry, there was a great awakening; for several weeks there was a manifest increase of concern for those who were ready to perish; then there came a great outpouring of the Holy

CHARLES G. FINNEY.

Ghost, and in a very few days the students began to press into the Kingdom, and the influences upon the institution were visible and salutary.

In Dartmouth College, in 1805 to 1815, there was a great revival. Suddenly, without premonition, the Spirit of God descended and saved the greater part of the students. The chapel, the recitation room, every place of meeting, became a scene of weeping. Most of all those who were converted at this time became ministers of the Gospel or missionaries of the Cross.

In 1814 there was a great *awakening in Princeton.* Every religious service, both on secular days and on Sundays, was attended with a solemnity that was very impressive; then, suddenly, without any special instruction, deep searching of heart began and lasted for about four weeks, until there were very few left in the college that were not impressed with the reality and importance of spiritual religion. It was said that there was not a room that was not a place of earnest and secret devotion.

Revivals in Yale College have been of frequent occurrence. They began with the presence of Edward Beecher, who was a tutor in Yale. He was burdened for the condition of the students, and one Sunday night chose for his text, "If the Lord be God, then follow Him; but if Baal, then follow him." From that Sunday service in Yale College dates a new era. Many impenitent were awakened and converted, and the whole college was transformed. These are but a few of the many tokens of Divine favor which have been shown in the educational institutions of the land. Since then, under the direction of the Young Men's Christian Association, there is not a college in all the land but has been visited by some special manifestation of the power and the presence of God.

THE PRINCE OF EVANGELISTS.

Charles G. Finney was born in Litchfield County, Conn., August 29, 1792. Neither of his parents professed religion. While pursuing his profession, the practice of law, he was brought under conviction by the preaching of Rev. George W. Gale, of Adams, N. Y. One Sunday evening in the autumn of 1821 he determined that he would be a Christian, but he could not bring himself to the point of public confession. During Monday and Tuesday his conviction deepened; early Wednesday morning, leaving his office, he passed a piece of woods, just over the hill from the town, and throwing himself upon his knees and then upon his face, God met and gave him peace and joy. In 1825 he started out upon his wonderful career in evangelism, and his power and success easily made him the Prince of Evangelists. In western New York the most remarkable evidences of the presence of God accompanied his preaching. Mr. Finney would spend days without eating and nights without sleeping, and as he would begin to preach the power of God would fall upon the people so that frequently he would be obliged to stop his address in order to give them an opportunity to find peace. In 1831 there was a special work of grace in the city of New York; thousands of Christians assembled for prayer, conversions occurred in all parts of the city, the churches were crowded to overflowing. An old theatre on Chatham Street was purchased, and here Mr. Finney began to preach, taking as his first text: "Who is on the Lord's side?" For seventy successive nights he preached to immense crowds. The bar-room was changed into a prayer-room, and the first man who knelt there poured out his heart in these words: "Oh, Lord, forgive my sins. The last time I was here I was a wicked actor on this stage. Oh, Lord, have mercy upon me!" For three years this building continued to be used for revival meetings.

The period commencing with the year 1792 and terminating with 1842, was a memorable period in the history of the American church. Scarcely any portion of it but was graciously visited by the outpouring of the Spirit. It has been estimated that from 1815 to 1840 the Spirit was poured out upon from four to five hundred churches and congregations annually, and from forty to fifty thousand were added by profession in a single year.

THE REVIVAL OF 1857.

It is an interesting fact in revivals, that they frequently succeed some great calamity, a prevailing epidemic, a general financial embarrassment or something of the sort. It was so with the wonderful work of grace which began in 1857; men seemed crazed with the desire for gold, speculation was at fever heat, and as a natural result there were failures everywhere. In a twinkling of an eye millionaires became bankrupts. In such a mood they were ready to listen to the voice of God. A little room in the lower part of New York belonging to the Reformed Dutch Church, Fulton Street, was thrown open for a public noon-day prayer meeting. The City Missionary, Mr. Lanphier, who made the appointment, first met there with three persons, then six, then twenty, and thus the business men's prayer meeting began to attract attention. A call was made for a daily meeting, and very soon three crowded meetings for prayer were held. Such meetings sprang up in other parts of the city also; the example spread to Philadelphia, to Boston, and to other cities, until there was scarcely a town of importance in the United States in which the business men's prayer meeting was not a flourishing institution, and the leading agency in awakening public interest in religion. One day there came into the New York meeting a gentleman from Philadelphia who read with thrilling effect a hymn, one verse of which is here given:

> "Where'er we meet, you always say
> What's the news? What's the news?
> Pray what's the order of the day?
> What's the news? What's the news?
> Oh! I have got good news to tell;
> My Saviour hath done all things well,
> And triumphed over death and hell.
> That's the news. That's the news!"

The telegraph wires frequently carried messages between Philadelphia and New York concerning the progress of this work of grace.

ENGLAND AND ELSEWHERE.

Abroad the work was also extensive and powerful. The services in Exeter Hall, and the opening of Westminster Abbey, together with other prominent places of worship, meant the leading of thousands of souls to Christ. In England and in Wales it is estimated that the number of conversions in the various orthodox denominations was from thirty to thirty-five thousand. In Ireland, too, the work was remarkable. It has been said that in Belfast, then a city of 30,000 souls, there were 10,000 conversions. America, however, was the most favored in this gracious visitation, and such a time as that which was ushered in with 1857 was never known since the days of the Apostles. The results, of course, cannot be recorded certainly, nor the number of conversions. In New York State 200 towns were reported as having revivals; in New York City all the churches were largely increased in membership. It was estimated that there were 10,000 conversions in the city of New York alone in that year.

DWIGHT L. MOODY.

This revival of 1857 was a layman's revival. God singles out from among the men of the church those who are to accomplish His will; such men as Mr. George H. Stewart, of Philadelphia, and Mr. Dwight L. Moody. Mr. Moody's work may be roughly divided into three periods; the first, growing out of the revival of 1857 and 1858, was largely carried on under the inspiration and direction of the Young Men's Christian Association. The second period, Mr. Moody wrought only at the united request of the churches and pastors, with their organized co-operation. The third period of his work was largely educational. It was while he was in the midst of this that God called him home.

Dwight L. Moody was born in Northfield, February 5, 1837. He was converted in Boston, and afterward removed to Chicago in 1856. His Sunday-school work in that city was phenomenal. The great revival of '57 and '58 led to the formation of the Young Men's Christian Association of Chicago. About this time Mr. Moody began attending the meetings, and by his personal efforts induced more than one hundred persons to join the praying band, and it was then that he decided to give up all his time to God's work. His first evangelistic work was really done in Chicago.

It was in connection with the Young Men's Christian Association work that Mr. Moody became acquainted with Mr. Sankey, who was to occupy so prominent a part with him in subsequent revival work. A sentence dropped by Mr. Varley, a British evangelist, to the effect "that it remains for the world to see what the Lord can do with a man wholly consecrated to Christ," was used of God to arouse Mr. Moody; he could not get away from the thought throughout his entire career; it largely helped to shape his life and work. In 1873 Moody and Sankey went to Liverpool. Their reception was not cheering, and their work was not in any way remarkable. In November of that year they arrived in Edinburgh; here was the beginning of the great meetings. Thousands of people attended their ministry, and all classes were reached with the Gospel. Their great success in Scotland opened the way for them in Ireland, and in 1874 the work was inaugurated in Belfast. As the meetings proceeded the interest became more and more apparent; thousands of

REVIVALS.

people were led to Christ. For ten weeks the evangelist labored in Ireland; wherever one went the topic of conversation was the revival services. Think of a man coming a hundred miles with his son fourteen years old, that he might come under the influence of the preaching. In 1874 they returned for work in the larger cities of England. After an address by Mr. Moody in Oxford Hall, to young men, along the line of Christian service, a campaign was planned, the results of which were most wholesome and encouraging. Services were conducted in Manchester, Sheffield, Birmingham, and then a second visit, on February 7, 1875, was made to Liverpool. Thousands of people were unable to hear the evangelist because of the crowds; the tide of enthusiasm rising with every added hour of their visit. On March 5, 1875, the work was inaugurated in London. A gathering of 1,500 ministers of all denominations had been called to confer and make and adopt plans. At the close of the first month's work in London it was said that the success of the meetings was marvelous, and in its way quite unexampled within the memory of living men, or in all that has been recorded by the pen of the English historian of the Christian Church.

On his return from Great Britain, Mr. Moody went to Northfield, there to spend some little time resting at his old home. The Gospel Campaign in America began at Brooklyn, on Sunday, October 24, 1875. The skating rink on Clermont Avenue, with its seating capacity of 6,000, was secured for the services. The very first meeting brought together enormous crowds; the rink was filled. Overflow meetings were held; still, there was no falling off in the crowds, who could not find even standing room. At least 15,000 people attended the services each day. The effect of the Brooklyn meetings was an awakening rather than the conversion of non-churchgoers. The meetings closed November 19th.

From Brooklyn Moody and Sankey went to Philadelphia, and began their meetings in the old Pennsylvania Railroad Depot, at Thirteenth and Market streets, now occupied by the great store of John Wanamaker. About $40,000 was spent in the reconstruction and equipment of the building; chairs for 10,000 people were secured. The regular meetings ended January 16th, with thousands of people converted and the whole city stirred as it had never been before nor since. The meetings in Philadelphia established Mr. Moody's leadership of the Lord's active army in the United States.

Following the Philadelphia meetings the great campaign in New

York was entered upon. The meetings in the Hippodrome began February 7, 1876. At the first meeting 7,000 were present in the main hall, and 4,000 others attended the overflow meeting; while several thousand were left in the streets. The service was fittingly opened with silent prayer; what that moment inaugurated for New York can never be estimated, both in time and extent, and in the results accomplished. The campaign in the New York Hippodrome was perhaps the most important ever conducted by Mr. Moody. In moving New York God moved the country, and the voice of the evangelist was heard throughout the entire land.

The great meetings in Chicago were held in October, 1876. The Boston meetings began the last of January, 1877, and both of these engagements, like those in other cities, were a wonderful demonstration of God's power. From this time Mr. Moody's activity soldom ceased, one tour was followed by another, and hardly a city or town of any great importance in this country failed to receive through his help a revival of interest in spiritual affairs. The meetings in Baltimore, in 1878, were marked by notable results; they began in October, 1878, and continued until May 16, 1879. It is not possible to speak of the work in other cities and towns, but everywhere Mr. Moody's name has been an inspiration and his life a benediction.

No one can study the history of revivals and not be impressed with their mighty influence upon the destiny of the race.

First. Society at large has been uplifted by revivals. When Divine grace is abundantly poured out it is felt at the very springs of society, and there cannot but be a corresponding elevation; the foundations of life are purified, and a social and civil renovation is the result. What would our own land, as well as Great Britain, have been but for the revival period of the seventeenth century?

Second. Missionary movements came from revivals; all those great benevolent enterprises which are the glory of this age originated just there; all the first foreign missionaries—Hall, Newall, Mills, Judson, Nott, Rice, Bingham, King and Thurston, and others who entered the field a little later—were converted and received their missionary baptism in revivals.

Third. An efficient ministry has come from revivals. "We hardly dare to lift the curtain to see what the ministry was previous to some of the great historic revivals, as in the days of Wiclif, Huss and Luther, or when Whitefield began his career. The character of the English clergy of those times is but too well known. Of the clergy even as late as 1781, Cowper could write, without fear of contradiction:

> "Except a few with Eli's spirit blessed,
> Hophni and Phineas may describe the rest."

It must be remembered, too, that revivals mightily increase the number of ministers. It has been said by some one that nine-tenths of the ministry were the children of revivals.

Fourth. Institutions of learning owe much to revivals. Many originated directly in revivals. The founding of Princeton College is but one case of many where the beginnings were in revivals.

Fifth. Many of the strongest churches in the world have come from revivals. This is suggestion enough, and but faintly shows what we owe to revivals of religion. Blot out what God has done by revivals, and the sun would be shrouded in gloom, our churches would be vacant, missionary agencies would be things unknown, and distress would be on every side of us. "Oh, Lord, revive thy work."

The nineteenth century has truly been a marvelous one. It has witnessed among many others the birth of the following notable great movements: The enlarged work of Foreign Missions, the Bible societies in all lands, the Young Men's Christian Associations everywhere, the Young People's societies of Christian Endeavor, the Rescue Missions in cities, the inauguration of Bible Conferences, such as Keswick in England, and Northfield and Winona in America. God's grace to His people in days that are past was truly remarkable, and since He is the same yesterday, to-day and forever, there is no reason why the future may not be better than the past. The age of revivals then is not yet past. No man dare stand up and assert that such times of refreshing as those to which reference has been made, will be not again vouchsafed to the Christian Church. The question for the individual to ask himself is: Am I right with God? Am I in a receptive mood? Am I absolutely consecrated to His service? Am I myself ready to be revived and willing to be used in any way God may please? Thus the duty of the individual man is perfectly simple and plain, viz.: to surrender himself unconditionally to God for spiritual uses. When many individuals in the churches do this, a rich spiritual blessing not only will come, but has come. God will be inquired of, and when He is inquired of in the spirit of entire submission and of earnest, importunate faith, He will not say His people nay.

THE PHILANTHROPY OF CHRISTENDOM IN THE NINETEENTH CENTURY.

C. H. D'E LEPPINGTON,
ENGLAND.

[To have only a superficial acquaintance with the benefits conferred by Christianity would be, in fact, to know nothing of the subject. We must consider the ingenuity with which it has varied its gifts, dispensed its succors, distributed its treasures, its remedies and its intelligence. In soothing all the sorrows of humanity it has paid a due regard to man's imperfection, consulting with a wise condescension even his delicacy of feeling, his self-love and his frailties.

During the few years that we have devoted to these researches, so many acts of charity, so many admirable institutions, so many inconceivable sacrifices, have passed in review before us that we firmly believe that this merit alone of the Christian religion would be sufficient to atone for all the sins of mankind. Heavenly religion, that compels us to love those wretched beings by whom it is calumniated!

In order to form a just idea of the immensity of these benefits, we should look upon Christendom as a vast republic, where all that we relate concerning one portion is passing at the same time in another. Thus, when we treat of the hospitals, the missions, the colleges of France, the reader should also picture to himself the hospitals, the missions and the colleges of Italy, Spain, Germany, Russia, England, America, Africa and Asia. He should take into his view four hundred millions of men at least, among whom the like virtues are practised, the like sacrifices are made. He should recollect that for nineteen hundred years these virtues have existed and the same acts of charity have been repeated. Now calculate, if your mind is not lost in the effort, the number of individuals cheered and enlightened by Christianity among so many nations and during such a long series of ages.—CHATEAUBRIAND; "The Genius of Christianity," pp. 619-20.—ED.]

* * *

NO PHASE of our modern civilization is more deeply indebted for its inception to the spirit and teaching of Christianity than is that vast expenditure of energy and wealth in the service of distressed humanity which is characteristic of the century just closed.

Not that the altruistic sentiment inculcated in the New Testament solely or directly inspires all the charitable work of the present day, nor that that sentiment is not also traceable in the doctrines

UNITED CHARITIES BUILDING, NEW YORK.

of pre-Christian thinkers. The humane character of the tenets of Buddhism has caused that religion, more frequently perhaps than any other, to be compared with Christianity. Cicero, in *De officiis,* expatiates on the virtue of benevolence. Seneca and some others of the later Stoics likewise reckon the rendering of services to others as among the virtues to be cultivated by the good man. Not only so, but classic civilization was not entirely devoid of a practical application of such tenets. The enactment of the *frumentariæ leges* and the *alimentarii* of the latter republic and the early emperors, which decreed the periodical distribution of corn and oil, either gratis or at prices below the market rate, to needy citizens, not only of Rome but of some of the leading provincial cities also, may indeed be attributed chiefly to considerations of political expediency, but isolated acts of liberality among the Greeks, as well as among the Romans, are mentioned by Plutarch and some other pagan writers, which would seem to be hardly open to this charge.

Tacitus, describing the widespread misery and loss of life occasioned in the city of Fidenœ by the giving way of a "jerry-built" amphitheatre, adds: "However, immediately upon this destructive calamity, the doors of the great were thrown open; medicines and physicians were furnished to all; and at that juncture the city, though under an aspect of sorrow, presented an image of the public spirit of the ancient Romans, who, after great battles, relieved and sustained the wounded by their liberality and attentions."* Orphanages and funds for giving dowries to girls on their marriage are known to have been established by the younger Pliny, and other private persons, as well as by several of the Cæsars. Even in the remote and barbarian North, the claim of poverty seems to have met with some recognition, for the law of Iceland is said to have inherited usages for the prevention of destitution, in vogue in Scandinavia before the introduction of Christianity, and in some respects, perhaps, superior to those of the rest of Europe during the Middle Ages.

While we may not, then, refuse to paganism the credit due to it for acts of beneficence such as these, a sharp contrast is to be found between its achievements in this respect and those of primitive Christianity. As the author of "Ecce Homo" has observed: "Though there was humanity among the ancients, there was no philanthropy. . . . Exceptional sufferings had therefore a chance of relief, but

---

* "The Annals," Book IV, c. 63, Oxford Translation.

the ordinary sufferings, which affected whole classes of men, excited no pity, and were treated as part of the natural order of things; providential dispensations, which it might even be impious to counteract." In the words of the historian, Lecky: "There can, however, be no question that neither in practice nor in theory, neither in the institutions that were founded nor in the place that was assigned to it in the scale of duties, did charity in antiquity occupy a position at all comparable to that which it has obtained by Christianity. Nearly all relief was a state measure, dictated much more by policy than by benevolence." *

Already, before the era of persecution had closed, the colonies of Christians scattered over the vast area of the Roman Empire were knit together in a bond of mutual aid, administered by the deacons, under the direction of the bishops. When at length Constantine's accession put an end to the time of trial, they were ready to extend their charity to their pagan fellow citizens, until the Emperor Julian had bitterly to complain that the Galileans supported not only their own but the heathen poor as well. There is a general, if not unanimous, consensus of opinion that public hospitals were unknown until they were established by the Christians. It appears to be a question in dispute whether Fabiola, a Roman lady of the fourth century, or St. Basil the Great, at a somewhat later date, is entitled to be regarded as the founder of the first of these institutions. At all events, what are known as the Arabic Canons of the Council of Nicæa enjoined that Xenodochia, or refuges for the sick and needy, and for strangers, should be erected in every city.

On the whole it may be confidently affirmed that the benevolence of the primitive church far exceeded that of even the noblest pagans, not only in extent but also in intensity, since its members alone were ever ready in times of pestilence—at Carthage and Alexandria, for example—to tend the sick and to give decent burial to the dead. If, reverting for the moment to the modern world, we compare the charity of Islamism with that of our own faith, the same phenomenon is again traceable. The Koran does indeed impress on its followers their obligation "to show kindness unto . . . orphans and the poor," and "not to oppress the orphan, nor to repulse the beggar"; and among the objects of the Wakoufs, or ecclesiastical endowments, found in Mohammedan countries, are enumerated Imarets, or places for the distribution of food, almshouses, and lunatic asylums. Yet

---

*"History of European Morals," Vol. II, p. 78. (4th Edition.)

in the Constantinople of to-day, where Mussulman and Christian dwell side by side, as heathen and Christian lived in ancient Rome and Alexandria, all the Mussulman charitable institutions which Mr. Jerningham, of the British Embassy, could find to enumerate, in reply to an inquiry on the subject made some years since by his Government, were one Imaret and one lunatic asylum. "The principal effect," he sums up, "of the actual system of relief carried on in Turkey upon the comfort, character, and condition of the Mussulman inhabitants is to disturb the one, sour the other, and impoverish the third." The Greeks, on the contrary, he tells us, have a hospital, a hospice for aged men, an orphanage, and a lunatic asylum. Each of their congregations has a committee for seeing to the relief of its own poor.

Thus, when the test of positive experience is applied, we find that long centuries of Christian example and training have evolved in the keen and active Aryan intellect an ideal of practical beneficence which, at the present moment, exerts a marked influence upon the whole thought and life of Western civilization, reaching by repercussion far beyond the boundaries of the avowedly religious world. To quote once again the gifted author of "Ecce Homo": "We are advanced by eighteen hundred years beyond the apostolic generation. . . . Christ commanded His first followers to heal the sick and give alms, but he commands the Christians of this age, if we may use the expression, to investigate the causes of all physical evil, to master the science of health, to consider the question of education with a view to health, the question of labor with a view to health, the question of trade with a view to health; and while all these investigations are made, with free expenditure of energy and time and means, to work out the rearrangement of human life in accordance with the results they give. Thus ought the enthusiasm of humanity to work in these days, and thus, plainly enough, it does work. . . . But perhaps it is rather among those who are influenced by general philanthropy and generosity—that is, by indirect or secondary Christianity—than among those who profess to draw the enthusiasm directly from its fount, that this spirit reigns."

Christianity, it has been said, inculcated, perhaps, no more effectively than the older religions, the economic virtues of industry, thrift and courage, but it produced a more elevated way of viewing the different social relations, preaching with quite a new emphasis the claims of the poor. In the words of the late Professor Amos

G. Warner: "Charity, as we know it, gets its chief religious authority and incentive from Him who gave as the summary of all the law and the prophets the co-ordinate commands to love God and to love our neighbor; and who, in explaining these commands, pronounced the parable of the Good Samaritan." To put it briefly, Christianity has shown itself more dynamic as an incentive to philanthropy than other creeds. Where it has superseded them—those even which have accentuated the duty of alms-giving—its effect has been analogous, if a simile drawn from mechanical science may be permitted in such a connection, to the substitution of anthracite for brown coal, or lignite, in the furnaces of an ocean steamer.

To the influence of Christianity as a moral doctrine was added that of the church as an organization charged with the application of that doctrine to men's daily transactions. The canonists styled the relief of the necessities of the poor a "debitum legale." The Council of Tours, in 597, recommended that "every city should support its own poor and needy." Indeed, the obligation to relieve the destitute, at the present day, to a greater or less extent, is admitted by the leading nations of Christendom as a collective duty of the community; was recognized as incumbent upon the church, and especially on the clergy, by one of Charlemagne's capitularies. As quoted by Egbert, Archbishop of York in the ninth century, it was to the following effect:

"The priests are to take the tithes . . . and divide them in the presence of them that fear God. The first part they are to take for the adorning of the church, but the second they are in all humility to distribute with their own hands for the use of the poor and strangers." The remainder the priests might keep for themselves.

As the church in England had already been organized by Theodore of Tarsus, Archbishop of Canterbury in the seventh century, upon the parochial principle, we have here the rudiments of a system of parish relief for the poor. In the later Middle Ages, a kind of fund appears to have been instituted in some parishes known as the "church stock," or "church store," the principal of which was lent out and the interest derived from it applied to assisting the more needy parishioners. The disendowment of the monasteries, under Henry the Eighth, and the consequent cessation of the alms they dispensed, hastened on a remodelling of public beneficence in England, which Professor Ashley and some other authorities have argued would in any case have been eventually necessitated by the agrarian and other social and economic changes in progress during the sixteenth century. At all events, a number of laws on this subject were passed during that period, culminating in an enactment by Queen Elizabeth's last parliament, which made it the duty of the church wardens and overseers in each parish to provide material for "setting the poor on work," those, namely, "having no means to maintain them, and that use no ordinary and daily trade of life to get their living by; . . . and also competent sums of money for and toward the necessary relief of the lame, impotent, old, blind, and such others among them being poor and not able to work."

The above short summary has been thought necessary in order to trace the connection between the charities of the early church and those of the state in later times. On this account, as well as for reasons suggested above, it seems desirable to include in the present survey some reference to those agencis which, although secular in their origin, would yet in all probability never have been called into existence in a pagan community, and not to confine ourselves to considering those forms of philanthropy alone which have been inspired by motives of a directly religious character.

Moreover, the statute of Elizabeth, just now cited, lies at the root of American, as well as of British, systems of public relief. It had been in force nearly thirty years when the Massachusetts Bay Company was formed, and immigration under John Winthrop and others set in in earnest on the coasts of New England. When the growth of population in the new country compelled its citizens to take order for assisting their poorer brethren, they retained the machinery already in operation in England when they embarked.

In both countries, however, the present system of legal relief has departed widely from the Elizabethan model, though in different directions. Indeed, there are wide variations of method even between the several States of the Union themselves. In those of New England the centre of administration is the town, but in those of the interior and the West it is the county. In the former, and also in Pennsylvania and Virginia, the law fences in the right of settlement—that is, the claim to legal relief—with various qualifications, as, for example, length of residence, or the exercise of a trade, to a far greater extent than applies in the latter. Destitute persons without a settlement become chargeable to the state instead of to the locality. The forms of relief most generally met with are, admission to an almshouse, or poor-house, as it is called in some places, of which there is one in every town or county; and relief in money or in kind, distributed to the dependent classes in their own homes. As a set-off to the maintenance they receive from the community, the labor of dependents is farmed out in several states. In a few cases, in some of the counties of Oregon, for instance, their maintenance itself is also contracted for by private individuals. Further still, vast sums of public money (money, that is to say, raised by taxation) are also expended by state and city authorities in grants-in-aid of hospitals, orphanages, and other charitable institutions under private management, as well as in payments toward the support of state and city dependents who are accommodated in such institutions. During the year 1899 the United States contributed to charity and education the sum of $80,000,000. This is the high-water mark of benevolence reached in that country. According to Professor Amos G. Warner, the public expenditure on medical charities in ten American cities was $1,034,000. The amount spent under the former head by the city of New York alone, in 1890, was $1,845,872. Of the twenty-seven cities of the Union having in that year a population of one hundred thousand and upward, twenty-two gave out relief totaling $952,500. Boston is one of these. Between six and eight per cent. of her population receive grants of about twenty dollars each in the course of the year. In most of the states the placing of children in private families forms a very important part of the assistance rendered to indigent families. No general estimate of the number of dependents chargeable to the public funds for the whole of the United States is possible, because several of the states issue no complete returns. The census of 1890, however, records the population of the almshouses throughout the states as 73,045. The poor-houses of seventeen states, having a total population in 1890 of 33,500,187 souls, contained 68,110 inmates in 1898.

Nineteen states possess Boards of Charities, whose duty it is to inspect, and in some instances to control (for they are not all entrusted with equally high powers), both the institutions owned by the state itself, and also those under independent management to which it entrusts the care of its dependent poor. The State Board of New York is one of the ablest and most energetic of these bodies. It has under its supervision sixty-four almshouses belonging to counties, cities or towns, twelve institutions belonging to the State of New York itself, eight institutions for the deaf, one for the blind, and one for juveniles, all mainly supported from the public funds; and, in addition, upward of a thousand hospitals, dispensaries, orphan asylums, day-nurseries, relief agencies, and other institutions, having in all a population of 71,013 persons on October 1, 1898, maintained at an outlay of twenty million dollars a year. The State Board is assisted in its duties by a voluntary and unpaid body entitled the State Charities Aid Association, whose members are authorized to visit the above-mentioned establishments, and who report upon them to the State Board at frequent intervals.

It is claimed that the joint influence of these two bodies has raised the standard of treatment in every poor-house throughout the state; has entirely eradicated the ancient custom, still adhered to in a few states, of farming out the care of the poor to the lowest bidder, and has led to the separation of the insane from other paupers, besides rectifying many other abuses which would otherwise have continued unreformed. Surely such results constitute a remarkable testimony to the self-denying energy on behalf of others' welfare of which humanity of the higher type is capable.

Turning now to national provision for the poor in foreign countries, we find that in England a uniform system of administration prevails, carried out by public bodies entitled Boards of Guardians of the Poor, elected *ad hoc* by the inhabitants of every parish (or group of parishes termed a poor-law union) in the kingdom. Each board has a work-house (answering to the American poor-house) and enjoys unfettered discretion in admitting applicants for relief. But relief can be dispensed in the applicants' own homes only under the conditions set forth in various statutes of the legislature. and it is one of the functions of the Local Government Board, a department of the central government located in London, to see that these conditions are complied with, as well as to supervise the establishments belonging to the Guardians, which frequently include infirmaries and schools, as well as work-houses, and to correct abuses. A staff of inspectors is maintained for this purpose, and the accounts of the Guardians have also to be audited and sanctioned by the officials of the Local Government Board. The total annual cost of public poor relief, including the maintenance of establishments, is about fifty million dollars, or $1.62 per head of the population, and the proportion of the population at a given time in receipt of such relief is about 2.7 per cent.

Similarity in point of social, geographical, and industrial status causes the systems of relief in operation among the several junior nations comprised in the British Empire to develop along much the same lines as in the United States. In the boldness of some of their ideals one or two of them may, perhaps, be said to be somewhat in advance of the latter country; just as in the practical realization of those ideals they are, no doubt, behind it. This remark applies more especially to Australasia.

Germany also recognizes the principle of national responsibility for the support of her poorer citizens. One of the earliest enactments of the new-born empire expressly declares that every necessitous German subject has a right to suitable and gratuitous food, shelter and clothing at the expense of his place of settlement, to attendance in sickness, and to burial. The Gemeinde (parish or commune) is the unit of administration. A characteristic of the German system which distinguishes it from those of France, England and America is that every citizen (with certain exceptions) is liable to be called upon to assist in local affairs for three years without remuneration on these Gemeinden. For making provision for the insane, blind, and epileptic the Gemeinden are grouped together into Ortsarmenverbände. What is generally known as the Elberfeld system, according to which a certain number of cases of distress are placed under the care of an honorary almoner (styled Armenpfleger), who combines the very dissimilar functions of the American friendly visitor and the English relieving officer, operates with modifications in many of the cities of the empire. The almoners are frequently men of very good standing in the community. Among them may be found lawyers, professional men, merchants, and persons of private means, as well as tradesmen, and, here and there, artizans. The employment of women in the administration of relief is increasing, but up to the present time they have acted only as lieutenants of the regular male almoners. A law enacted last summer will place them on a footing of greater equality with the opposite sex. Relief is most usually dispensed to recipients in their own homes, rarely in institutions, except in case of sickness or infirmity, and the legislature has left to the almoners a much wider discretion in the choice of modes of relief than have the Boards of Guardians in England. These unpaid almoners number nearly three thousand in Berlin alone. All relief is by way of loan, so that if a recipient's circumstances improve, he may be called upon to reimburse what has been expended upon him from the public funds. As in America, orphans and children of destitute parents are placed out in families in the rural districts. In 1885, the most recent date for which figures for the whole empire are accessible, 1,592,386 persons were recipients of public relief, the latter amounting to $21,495,739. Since then the scheme of state-subsidized pensions for illness, accidents and old age, which has attracted such keen and general interest among all civilized nations, has come fully into operation. The magnitude of the scheme may be judged from the fact that, from 1885 to 1899, it has cost the imperial revenues $36,750,000; and that, at the end of 1896, 202,015 pensions for old age, and 154,745 pensions to disabled persons, were being paid. Yet inquiry has proved that these old-age pensions are in many cases insufficient to render the recipients independent of poor relief.

Other nations which recognize the principle of state responsibility for the indigent are the Scandinavian kingdoms and Russia. In the latter country, the responsibility of giving assistance rests with the General Councils of the Provinces, and with the committees of public charity established at the beginning of the century; but there is no central control. A commission was recently appointed to revise all laws relating to relief, but it has been compelled to recognize the practical impossibility of collecting information from the whole of Russia. The expenditure on municipal and private charitable institutions (schools included) in St. Petersburg, in 1889, has been estimated at $6,267,750. Omitting the schools, these institutions were 431 in number. The city of Moscow celebrated the accession of the present Czar by establishing twenty-three *bureaux de bienfaisance* for the domiciliary relief of the poor, and obtained from the Czar and Czarina on their marriage the grant of an annual subvention of thirty thousand dollars. More than fifteen hundred persons are now enlisted as visitors by the council of the bureaux, which are erecting orphanages and almshouses.

Although the broad principle of national responsibility is not expressly admitted to its full extent by the laws of the remaining nations of Christendom, yet in some among them a very active part is played by the central and local authorities in directing and subsidizing relief in certain channels. In France, provision for the insane and for destitute or neglected children, as well as for the sick poor, is made under the supervision of the Ministry of the Interior, and of the Administration de l'Assistance Publique. The administration of public relief of the aged and infirm, the homeless, and of the valid poor is entrusted to the communes (townships) and departments, and to the *bureaux de bienfaisance*. The latter, of which there are about sixteen thousand (and, according to some authorities, more) all over France, form a kind of connecting link between official relief and private benevolence. They have an official status, but may appoint volunteer helpers to act as almoners. They distribute money, food, fuel and clothing among the indigent (of whom each bureau keeps a register) in their own homes, to the value, in 1895, of eight million dollars. About half the revenues of the bureaux are derived from ancient endowments, many of them dating from monarchical times. The residue is made up of legacies, receipts from the tax on theatrical performances, and grants made by the communes. Since 1893, a scheme has come into operation and is being gradually applied throughout the country, by which the sick poor may be supplied with medical care and medicine in their own homes. The accommodation provided in institutions belonging to the communes and other public bodies, in the year 1889, was 65,204 beds in hospitals, 60,800 beds in hospices for the aged and infirm, and 14,921 beds for children in hospices. The Department of Public Assistance places many thousands of destitute and ill-treated children in the families of the peasantry, and maintains a staff of inspectors, whose duty it is to visit the children from time to time in the homes of their adopted parents. No less than 130,000 children are under the care of the department. One consequence of the wide discretion entrusted to local authorities in providing and organizing the machinery of relief is that they exhibit all degrees of adequacy in the provision made by them for the poorer strata of the population. Both the state and the local authorities subsidize the numerous provident associations established among the working classes.

The Belgian legislature, in 1891, decreed that the communes must provide medical treatment for their sick poor, adding: "Public relief will be furnished to paupers by the commune in which they are found." It also ordained the provision of disciplinary institutions for tramps and beggars. These already exist in the agricultural labor colonies at Merxplas and Hoogstracten. The Dutch law declares that—"The relief of the poor is left to the charitable institutions of the different churches, or to private institutions. No municipality is authorized to give relief to the poor until satisfied that they cannot be relieved by the charitable institutions of the different churches, or by those under private management, and then only in case of absolute impossibility." The law of Holland appears to be the harshest of all in its attitude toward the poor. Nevertheless, the municipalities of Amsterdam and some other towns expend considerable sums in relief, and that of Amsterdam maintains a poor-house and other establishments of a similar character. Holland, like Belgium, has labor colonies for tramps and beggars, which are supported by the state. A reform of the poor law is being agitated at the present time by a section of public opinion. Religious and philanthropic agencies are active, and Holland possesses no fewer than 7,476 benevolent institutions of various kinds.

There is no general poor tax in Italy, but there are a vast number of benevolent associations and institutions of every description, many of them extremely ancient. It has been estimated that in 1880 these numbered in all 21,769, of which 3,582 were hospitals, asylums, schools, asylums for the insane, blind, and dumb, orphanages and refuges, enjoying a revenue of $27,026,770, including the subsidies frequently made by city and provincial authorities. The Italian Statistical Department reports that, on January 1, 1899, Italy possessed hospitals, hospices, orphanages, lunatic asylums, institutions for the blind and for deaf-mutes, poor-houses, and other similar institutions numbering in all 3,188, and containing at that date 274,848 inmates. A very large proportion of the income is drawn from real estate, the charities having been liberally endowed. If the charges of administration and taxation, both of which are heavy, and also the expenditure upon worship and religious ceremonies, be deducted, only $16,903,256 are left for directly beneficent purposes. In 1887 nearly 770,000 persons received alms. Almost every city has a body styled the Congregazione di Caritá, a kind of Associated Charities, the administrators of which are appointed by the civic authorities in order to supervise minor endowments. By force of certain laws passed in 1862 and 1890, all charities must send in financial statements to the authorities every year, and the Minister of the Interior, as well as the local authorities, have a general power of oversight over them. It has been the task of the legislature of unified Italy not so much to prescribe ways and means—the accumulated benevolence of centuries provides these already—as to regulate and control the administration of them, and it has aimed at achieving this task by means of the two statutes just referred to. It is to be observed that Italy's position, owing to her possessing the oldest and the least broken record of civilization of any country, is unique. Her government has simply to control the administration of private beneficence, not to supplement it with a system of its own.

From what has already been said, it will be seen how vast a field is covered in most of the countries of Western Europe, as well as in the United States, by systems of public relief; by relief, that is to say, to which all citizens have by law to contribute, whether it be controlled by the township, the city, the county, or by the central government. This fact should never be left out of sight in attempting any comprehensive estimate of the forces engaged and the results achieved in the world-wide struggle to elevate the lower or less fortunate strata of humanity. As far as the community relieves the individual of the task of caring for the distressed, so far it also deprives him of the opportunity of exercising the virtue of charity (in the restricted sense of that word). At the same time, however, this very action on the part of the community at large testifies to a higher tone of public opinion. As in so many other departments of life, so in that of charity, undertakings at first attempted only by individuals, or by voluntary associations, or by religious bodies, have been adopted and absorbed by the state, either directly or by devolution.

Experience shows that this competition of the state does not entirely oust voluntary initiative. An instructive investigation from this point of view has recently been published by Mr. Frederick Almy, of Buffalo, N. Y. Taking the forty cities of the Union having a population, at the census of 1890, of a hundred thousand and upward, he compares the relative proportions of public (*i. e.*, municipal) relief and of private relief. He concludes, from the data at his disposal, that large grants of public relief do tend to check the flow of relief from other sources. But some support may be found, even in the returns he himself gives, for an opposite inference. In Boston, for example, relief from both sources is abundant. It is notorious that the same era which witnesses the enhanced activity of the public powers in coping with distress is also prolific in new forms of private beneficence.

The greater difficulty of obtaining complete and adequate information of non-official than of official charity impairs the conclusiveness of Mr. Almy's argument. The same cause obviously tells with redoubled force against any attempt to deal exhaustively with the amount and extent of the spontaneous beneficence, whether individual or associated, of the countries of Christendom. Still, while any endeavor of so ambitious a character within the limits of the present volume could only result in failure, the following review of the many and varied forms assumed by philanthropy, those especially of more recent growth, will, it is hoped, be found fairly comprehensive.

The altered social conditions which have followed in the wake of advancing civilization have effected considerable changes in the functions of philanthropy. Some classes whose claims the mediæval church urged upon the attention of the faithful no longer exist; others no longer stand in need, their necessities being met through the ordinary channels of commerce. Of the former, the lepers, for whom no less than nineteen thousand lazar houses are estimated to have existed in Western Europe, and the prisoners captured by the Turks, for whose ransom large sums were subscribed, are examples; of the latter, the ordinary peaceable travelers, for whom the monasteries regarded it as a sacred duty to furnish hospitality.

A vast number of new outlets for charity have, of course, taken their place. The care of the sick, the aged, and the young has descended to us, as we have already seen, from the age of primitive Christianity, in the shape of hospitals for the first, hospices for the second (and the older institutions usually served both purposes), or schools and foundling asylums for the last. Frequently all three were combined as departments in the same conventual establishment. The asylum founded for three hundred blind at Paris, by St. Louis, in the thirteenth century, known as the Quinze-Vingts, still subserves its original purpose. St. Bartholomew's, the oldest and next largest hospital in London, was founded in 1123, as part of a vast monastery, and several of the principal public schools for secondary education in England have had a somewhat similar origin. Since the imparting of elementary instruction, and the support of the indigent in old age, have become almost everywhere the business of the state, the provision of education alone, apart from maintenance, will probably cease to be a function of charity; and in England, at any rate, a tendency may be observed to limit philanthropic provision for the aged to those who can show some further claim on public sympathy than is presented by destitution alone.

In three directions the improvement in the institutional care of the sick has been specially remarkable of late years. The accommodation has been greatly improved. Separate infirmaries have been erected for sick paupers, instead of retaining them in almshouses and workhouses. Further, better sanitary precautions have been taken in erecting hospitals, such as thorough ventilation and drainage, and the use of glazed tiles for lining the walls of wards and passages. Thus the atmosphere inside the hospitals is purer, the chances of septic infection and of general cachexia are lessened, and the chances of ultimate and complete recovery proportionately increased. Indeed, the new pauper infirmaries are sometimes superior in this respect to the older endowed hospitals. Then, the standard of nursing has been raised, and the use of anæsthetics and antiseptics introduced in the performance of surgical operations. Trained nurses are being gradually substituted for pauper, or at best untrained, attendants, even in establishments intended for the pauper class. The State Charities Aid Association of New York has the credit of having initiated this reform in America, by founding a training school for nurses in the Bellevue Hospital. Between 1879 and 1893 more than fifty thousand patients were nursed by its alumni, many of whom have since held very responsible posts as heads of institutions. The same movement has long been in progress in England, owing largely to the influence and initiative of Miss Nightingale and Miss Louisa Twining. And, lastly, there has been the establishment of isolation hospitals for infectious diseases, combined with by-laws for the notification of such complaints to the authorities, and for the transport of the sufferers to these hospitals. According to German writers on the subject, the most conspicuous achievement in this direction has been the system devised by the Metropolitan Asylums Board of London, within the area under its jurisdiction.

The improvement which has taken place in the treatment of the insane within the last hundred years, and even less, has amounted to an absolute revolution. The special disability of the blind has been alleviated by the invention of the Moon and Braille types, and that of the deaf and dumb by the introduction of the lip-language.

The numbers of associations for personal philanthropic service having an expressly religious origin are legion. They include certain of the conventual orders in the Roman and Anglican communions. In other churches, also, there are communities the members of which devote themselves exclusively to definite branches of work of a philanthropic character. Five such communities are especially conspicuous for both the extent and the diversity of their operations. Each is the outcome of the talent and devotion of one man. St. Vincent de Paul, of whom it has been said that a mixture of ardent charity and practical sense was the hallmark of his work, died in 1660. Besides raising and dispensing enormous sums in alms-giving and establishing various hospitals, he founded the order of Sisters of Charity, with whom beneficence was to be the business of the religious life, instead of being only a by-product of it. Its members were to find their vocation in the streets and homes of the poor; "their only convent the houses of the sick, their cell a hired room, their chapel the parish church." At the present moment the order is said to number twenty thousand members, spread over Protestant as well as Catholic countries. Equally extensive is the sphere of the Society of St. Vincent de Paul, which enlists the services of laymen of the Roman Church, locally organized into Councils and Conferences. Besides visiting and alms-giving, these bodies carry on schools, savings banks, soup-kitchens, employment bureaus, and similar philanthropic works.

Pastor Fliedner, of Kaiserswerth, in Rhenish Prussia, who died in 1864, was the founder of an order of deaconesses for the purpose of visiting, nursing, and teaching the poor, which now not only has a network of branches extending throughout the German Empire, but maintains establishments in Italy, Palestine and elsewhere. Their educational work is not confined to the working classes. Fliedner subsequently became the originator of a kind of training college in philanthropic work for young men who intended to become pastors, and also for those of a rather lower social grade, who should fill such posts as superintendents of almshouses and labor colonies. At the same time, a somewhat similar work was being carried on by Dr. Wichern, of Horn, near Hamburg. Having first established a number of cottage homes on a farm for street arabs and young thieves, who were there taught agriculture and handicrafts, he utilized it for training young men for work in philanthropic institutions by setting them to live with the boys, and to teach and influence them. From these young men was recruited the band known as the Rauhe Haus Brotherhood, the members of which were sent into whatever fields of work Dr. Wichern and his committee should think fit, whether as teachers, city missionaries, or officials of prisons, reformatories and asylums, and wherever men of the German race have settled. Thus members of the brotherhood are engaged in Russia, America, England and the Turkish Empire.

The Salvation Army is the growth of the last thirty years. Originated in England by Mr. and Mrs. William Booth, simply as an evangelizing movement, it has bred a varied host of philanthropic institutions—hospitals, refuges for women, shelters, workshops and farm colonies and labor bureaus for tramps and the unemployed throughout the English-speaking world, as well as in several continental countries. Japan and India attest its manifold activities, which, indeed, even include life insurance. A very important feature in its operation is the Women's Social Section, which runs 125 institutions of its own. In the United States alone, the Army possesses homes for children and shelters in fourteen states, and farm colonies in California and Colorado and at Cleveland, while its officials compute the total value of its property throughout the country at $600,000. The income recorded by its head office in London considerably exceeds this sum, and it has thirteen shelters in that city alone, besides a farm colony at Hadleigh, and institutions of various kinds in several of the provincial cities of England. The Church Army to some extent follows in its social work in the track of the Salvation Army. It also has extended its field of operations into the States, as well as throughout the British Empire, and its undertakings are as ambitious and all-embracing as those of its predecessor and ante-type. It has an emigration test farm at Ilford, near London, an emigration agency at Montreal, homes for inebriates, for rescue cases, tramps and boys, and employment registries. Its income in 1896 was $465,000.

These five societies have been selected for separate notice because they are distinguished both by the many-sidedness of their work and by its international character. All of them, it is believed, include evangelization among their functions.

Turning now to the general field of philanthropic effort, we find that it has pushed forth many fresh shoots in quite new directions during the past century; and especially within the last thirty or forty years. The social changes entailed by the rapid strides of civilization within this period, adding to the complexity of life, are largely responsible for the unfavorable conditions—such as overcrowding, for example—which have necessitated such action. But without the immensely enhanced ease and rapidity of intercourse, which is one of the most remarkable features of the present epoch, several of our latest enterprises, such as the fresh-air movement, would be utterly impossible.

The rehabilitation, as self-supporting citizens, of the able-bodied unemployed and of tramps and liberated prisoners, is a difficult problem, evoking the expenditure of much energy. The Salvation Army and the Church Army, as we have seen, are both grappling with it. The sphere of labor colonies, which should be primarily reformatory agencies, instead of penal settlements like those already existing in Holland and Belgium, was inaugurated in 1882 by Pastor von Bodelschwingk, with the opening of the colony at Wilhelmsdorf, in Westphalia. Similar colonies, styled "Arbeiterkolonien," have since spread throughout Germany, until at the present moment they number thirty-two, and have in the aggregate accommodations for 3,514 inmates. The stay of each man does not exceed four months, but is often much less. Of 7,065 men who left the colonies in 1899, 1,548 went to work which they had found for themselves, or which the authorities of the colony had procured for them; 3,895 left of their own accord, and the rest left through illness or misbehavior. Nearly two-thirds of those admitted during the year had been in one or other of the colonies before. In connection with the latter are 457 "Herbergen zur Heimath." These are a combination of wayfarers' lodges and workmen's boarding-houses. They receive both paying and non-paying guests, who numbered in 1899 no less than 2,066,544 persons. Labor bureaus are carried on in connection with them, which find employment for about 6.6 per cent. of the men. Local authorities, as well as the benevolent public, subscribe to the support of these institutions. Committees for providing the unemployed with temporary jobs, and sometimes with shelter, are numerous in France. Fifty of them are affiliated together under a central committee in Paris, and there is at least one farm-colony, that at Chalmette, although the treatment of the unemployed in settlements like the Arbeiterkolonien has not met with general adoption.

Although a state of belligerency is, fortunately, not chronic between the nations of Christendom, it is well that the machinery for succoring the wounded in battle should be permanently organized in time of peace, as it is in the Red Cross societies of most nationalities. This form of charity is especially associated in the States with the name of Miss Clara Barton, as it is throughout the British Empire with that of Miss Florence Nightingale. Germany has a trained staff of at least 15,670 male and 25,000 female attendants at disposal for Red Cross purposes.

Of late years there has been a marked recrudescence of the practice of nursing the sick poor in their own homes. It was carried on long ago by certain conventual orders, and is so still, as also by the deaconesses of Protestant sisterhoods. The formation of staffs of trained lay nurses for this purpose is, however, of recent date. It was first introduced in the States in 1877, by the Woman's Branch of the New York City Mission and Tract Society. We have already seen that domiciliary nursing has a place in the public care of the poor in France. Local societies for home-nursing are numerous in London and other English towns, and congregations frequently support nurses in their own parish or neighborhood.

Agencies for procuring change of air and scene and suitable nourishment for those recovering from sickness constitute another feature of the latest philanthropy. Convalescent treatment is, of course, a form of after-care following upon a sojourn in the sick-room or the hospital, but, when offered in time, it may prove to be a prophylactic against illness. Poor women and children are sent to the seashore or into the country in thousands from New York during the summer by the Society for Improving the Condition of the Poor, the Children's Aid Society, the Society of St. Vincent de Paul, and other agencies, and the same kind of work is being carried on in Boston, Chicago, and probably most other big cities of the Union. Some of the English hospitals own branch establishments by the sea and in the open country for their patients when convalescent. There are some 350 institutions for this purpose in England. The Children's Country Holidays Society has boarded out in the country over thirty thousand children attending the public elementary schools of London since it was established fifteen years ago. Germany has 162 associations for providing poor children with change of air and other convalescent treatment, all federated together, with a central bureau in Berlin. They dealt with 37,479 children in 1898, sending some to convalescent homes,, others to sea-bathing places, and lodging others, again, with farmers in the country.

Day-nurseries, or crêches, in which mothers who have to go out to work can place their infants during the daytime, are a special feature of French philanthropy, though they are to be met with in other countries also. There are nearly a hundred in Paris and its environs alone, many of them being subsidized by the municipality, and a few belonging to it.

Not only has the treatment of the insane been reformed, but attention is being bestowed on the after-care of persons convalescent from insanity—that is, on obtaining for them change of air and scene on quitting asylums, and subsequently employment, thus aiding them to resume their place in society. Societies having this object in view exist in the States, France, and England.

Within the last ten years much attention has been directed toward providing suitable institutions for two classes of defectives who, till quite recently, have been herded with ordinary paupers in poorhouses or else left to be a burden upon their relatives. Epileptics are seriously handicapped in the struggle for existence by their constant liability to a malady which not only temporarily disables them, but may also render them dangerous to others, and yet does not incapacitate them for the ordinary duties of life in the intervals between its attacks. Experience has shown that epileptics are capable of working together and of giving mutual assistance on the occurrence of seizures. Accordingly, colonies for this class are springing up in several states of the Union, including New York, Pennsylvania, New Jersey, and Massachusetts. Of these the Craig Colony, in New York, comprising 620 patients, is perhaps the most widely known. The same movement is in progress in England, which has a colony at Chalfont, besides several homes. Pastor von Bodelschwingk, who has been already mentioned in these pages, has introduced the system into Germany, where, besides the colony founded by himself at Bielefeld, that of Wuhlgarten accommodates nearly a thousand, and is maintained by the municipality. The second class is that of the feeble-minded. The term is sometimes used to include the imbecile, but properly it should be limited to those only who are above the latter class, though mentally deficient and incapable of holding their own in the battle of life. It is now generally recognized that such persons, especially when females, ought to be under guardianship, both for their own protection and for the public welfare, since they are extremely apt to have illegitimate offspring, although it has not yet been deemed necessary to place them under compulsory restraint. New York possesses a Custodial Asylum for Females at Syracuse, but the feeble-minded are most commonly grouped with imbeciles and epileptics in the same institutions. There are a few voluntary homes for girls and young women in

England, and separate public elementary schools have been established in London, where feeble-minded children receive special attention in the expectation that a large number of them may thus be enabled eventually to take their place in the community as normal citizens.

Although prisons are in themselves by no means charitable institutions, yet the spirit of charity has inspired a great reform in the treatment of prisoners during their term of sentence. With regard to discharged prisoners, the practice in Minnesota, and probably in other states, is to appoint a prison official to supervise men released on probation and to obtain employment for them. In England a somewhat similar function is performed by voluntary associations in connection with each of the sixty-one English prisons, aided by a grant from the Government. Societies for the same purpose exist in France and in the great towns of Germany. Large numbers of discharged prisoners in the latter country resort to the Arbeiter-kolonien.

A very different department of government which has none the less been influenced by philanthropy is the housing of the poor, although action, as well public as private, has also been undoubtedly stimulated by the selfish consideration that diseases originating amid the squalor of extreme poverty are apt to spread among the families of the respectable and wealthy. The Tenement Exhibition held in New York in February of last year, and organized in order to show how much remains to be done, as well as how much has already been accomplished, will be fresh in the minds of readers. Dr. Gould, of the City and Suburban Homes Company, has stated that more than a hundred million dollars have been invested in the big cities of Europe and America in improved dwellings. The movement has now proved a commercial success, but it began as philanthropy, and, in the case of model dwellings founded by the late George Peabody, it continues to be so still, since all profits are devoted to erecting new dwellings. In some tenements of this class the rent is collected by ladies, who combine the functions of landlords and friendly visitors. In many instances, benevolent persons, following in the steps of Miss Octavia Hill, of London, buy up and endeavor to improve old tenements and their tenants at the same time. The movement has spread to Berlin. Some of the capital of the celebrated governmental insurance institutions of Germany is being applied to the erection of improved dwellings. The Tene-

PHILANTHROPY. 93

ments Commission in New York and the Mansion House Council on Dwellings of the Poor, in London, promote the passing of sanitary legislation and stimulate its enforcement, and this introduces us to a fresh phase of philanthropy, namely, the protection of the feebler classes of the community against particular forms of oppression or against their own failings. While the above-named associations protect tenants against unscrupulous landlords, the well-known Societies for the Prevention of Cruelty to Children in New York and England, and the Association Protectrice de l'Enfants, in France, protect children against unscrupulous parents, and there are others which aim at protecting the interests of married and other women in various ways.

Again, there is the form of philanthropy which seeks to raise the status and character, while adding to the happiness, of its protégés through the medium of kindly social influence. It is of quite modern growth and it assumes a large variety of shapes. Perhaps the vast amount of house-to-house visitation of the poorer quarters of American and English towns, set on foot and controlled by the clergy of the principal religious denominations, may be referred to most appropriately at this point. The practice obtains also in Berlin. In these and many other cases the rendering of material assistance is not excluded. Opening evening clubs for young men, young women and boys is one of the examples of this kind of benevolence most frequently met with. Here classes for instruction, books and games are provided, and opportunities for conversation are afforded. Accommodation for social gatherings is occasionally included in the construction of model tenements. Institutions such as these are designed to appeal to very different social grades, ranging from street arabs and "hooligans" to clerks and shop-assistants. In planning a club, regard has to be paid to the class for whom it is intended. The more intelligent and respectable the class, the greater the share in the management of the club, which may be, and ought to be, entrusted to the general body of its members. Evening amusements are often provided in public elementary schools for the scholars attending them in the daytime.

In some instances societies which were originated for evangelistic purposes have developed an educational and recreative side. The Young Men's and the Young Women's Christian Associations are examples of this expansion. Formed in the middle of the century, with the expressed object "to endeavor to bring young men from a life of sin to a life of righteousness," these twin societies have now educational classes, libraries, gymnasiums, meeting-rooms, and boarding-houses, and convalescent homes in connection with their headquarters in the chief cities of the United States and the British Empire. In Great Britain alone the Young Men's Society has 1,471 centres, and 103,420 members. The sphere of activity of both societies is co-extensive with the English-speaking world, as is also that of the Girls' Friendly Society, which is controlled by members of the Protestant Episcopalian Church, and which makes a special feature of its establishments for training girls for domestic service. Neighborhood guilds and college settlements are agencies of very recent origin, carrying on an analogous type of work. Of these, Hull House, Chicago, and Toynbee Hall, London, are notable examples. Members of these settlements do not confine themselves to direct work among the sections of the community whom they desire to benefit, but by also serving upon city councils and other public bodies they endeavor to infuse wisdom and honesty into the conduct of public affairs. Hull House has exerted itself notably in promoting the efficiency of the sanitary service of the quarter of Chicago in which its headquarters are located. There are at least two societies in Berlin which arrange lectures, concerts, and theatrical representations for the working-classes. In Dresden and several other towns in Germany there are associations of a somewhat similar character, called "Vereine für Volkswohl." That of Dresden holds classes in English, cookery, arithmetic and book-keeping, lectures on hygiene and choir practices, besides recitations and entertainments. All classes mix together at these assemblies, a very gratifying feature of which is that those who help to entertain are equally drawn from all classes.

It would be impossible to overestimate the social service rendered by these settlements and clubs and drawing-rooms in constituting a common meeting-ground where mutually helpful acquaintanceships may be, and very often are, formed between persons belonging to very different sections of the community, because the intercourse which takes place in them is untainted, or at least may and ought to be untainted, with the giving of relief or with the adoption of a tone of authority.

A form of benevolence especially characteristic of American cities is the system of "friendly visitors." Boston is the home of this movement, and there are no fewer than a thousand of these visitors working in that city. It is their business to give advice, and to act as go-betweens, when the case requires it, between the people they visit and hospitals and relief agencies, but not to give money or any other kind of relief themselves. They are organized into sixteen district committees, each with an agent and an office where they can meet periodically for consultation. This scheme has been adopted in several other cities, though not everywhere with as much success as in Boston. In Newport, R. I., it has been discontinued. On the whole, the opinion seems to be gaining ground that those opportunities of exercising a beneficial influence on the poorer and less educated classes are the happiest which occur naturally in such relationships as exist between teachers and their scholars' parents, or lady rent-collectors and tenants. Collecting from house to house for money to put in the savings bank has frequently been found to gain a ready welcome for visitors in the houses of the poor. Where such relations exist, the visiting can take place on a footing of friendly equality which can scarcely exist when the sole and obvious object of the visit is to give relief or even good advice. Accordingly, a tendency is observable among the clergy to avail themselves of these relations as a basis on which to organize the district-visiting in their parishes.

Friendly visiting is, nevertheless, one form of a new departure in philanthropy which has made vast strides on both sides of the Atlantic within the last thirty years. This is no less than the co-ordination of charitable workers and institutions into an organic whole, which shall, by basing the administration of material relief of all kinds upon certain definite principles, and by making it subservient to and an agent in the moulding and strengthening of character in the recipients themselves and in the social strata from which they spring, build up the national life instead of exercising upon it the prejudicial influence which experience has shown to result from injudicious benevolence.

The first Charity Organization Society was founded in 1869 in London, and was succeeded within the course of a few years by those of Buffalo, Boston and New York. There are now 128 in the United States and 103 in the British Empire. Paris has its Office Central des Œuvres de Bienfaisance, and associations discharging similar functions exist in eight other towns of France, and also in Berlin. The leading principles of the organization of charity, that the giving of relief must be preceded by adequate knowledge of the recipient and his circumstances, that it must not deteriorate character, and that there must be a free interchange of information between philanthropic agencies, are thus steadily gaining ground in all directions.

Thus far we have been principally engaged in considering activities instigated actually, or at least professedly, by the motive of philanthropy. Those workmen's dwellings companies referred to a few pages back constitute a connecting link with another phase, less tangible, indeed, but not a whit less real, under which the genuine spirit of beneficence asserts itself, and which must not be overlooked.

The commercial and industrial world, as a rule, preserves a very clear line of demarcation between its business and its charity. It permits its right hand to ignore what its left hand is doing. Indeed, its left hand—that is, its charity—is partly engaged in rectifying, or at least in mitigating, some of the evil consequences resulting from the deeds of the right hand. Fortunately, this is not true of all business men. Some there are, for instance, who refuse to regard the remuneration of their employees as the very first item of their working expenses to be reduced in order the better to meet the competition of rival producers, and who prefer to run their factories at half time during a depression of trade rather than to subject their workpeople to the demoralizing effects of intermittent employment. Action of this kind is frequently, but somewhat unjustly, attributed to enlightened selfishness. It is alleged that the practical advantages of promoting a good understanding with one's hands are so obvious that self-interest by itself demands that it should be attempted. In practice, however, there is always an element of risk attending the adoption of such a policy. This is especially the case in commencing a new undertaking, for then the business man is voluntarily handicapping himself, at least for the moment, in his race with strenuous competitors already in the field.

To respect the claims of employees while planning how to earn gross profits is benevolence of a higher type than to regard such claims for the first time, if at all, when deciding how to spend one's net profits. On this higher plane must be placed, among others, the efforts of men like the late Charles Robert, of Paris, and his imitators, who introduced the practice of entitling employees to participate in the profits of their employers' undertakings, and of those captains of industry and representatives of labor who have sought to supersede the appeal to the rude test of strikes and lock-outs by conciliation and arbitration. The same may be said of the achievements of founders of industrial communities such as those of Lowell, Mass., and Dayton, Ohio, in America; Saltaire and Bournville, in England, and the Carl Zeiss Stiftung, in Germany.

Immense as is the total output of the charitable activity of Christendom, there is a reverse side to it. Unwary benevolence is the natural prey of the designing promoter of bogus institutions, and even sometimes of the authorized solicitor on behalf of *bona fide* undertakings, as well as of impostors who feign poverty. Then, there is the temptation to which ministers of religion and others engaged in evangelistic work not infrequently yield of availing themselves of the alleviation of material wants as a kind of bait to attract "the man in the street" to their services, although not a few far-sighted clergymen have recognized that such practices do in reality impair their spiritual influence. Charity bazaars are becoming recognized as not unmixed blessings, and as sometimes no more excusable than the "Wohlthätige Skatabende" (benevolent card-parties) of Germany.

A graver evil lies in the mischief unintentionally wrought by unintelligent or uninstructed philanthropy. In the words of Miss Louisa Twining, "The shortcomings of the inexperienced and sympathetic district visitor are well known, and I have no hesitation in saying that, by the visits of those who will not take pains to obtain the training necessary for the most difficult of all social work, more harm than good is done; begging, imposture, and an appearance of poverty are encouraged that help may be largely given, and tickets and doles are expected as a right, though utterly inadequate to meet the needs, if they really exist, even for one day." In the analysis of the causes of poverty, given us by Amos G. Warner in his standard work on American charities, is enumerated as the last item, "Unwise Philanthropy," and he quotes with approval the words of the philosopher, Walter Bagehot: "Great good, no doubt, philanthropy does, but it does also great harm . . . and this is entirely because excellent people fancy that they can do much by rapid action, that they will most benefit the world when they most relieve their own feelings, that as soon as an evil is seen 'something' ought to be done to stay and to prevent it."

At this point the charity organization societies before alluded to step in and supply the much-needed machinery for education in the intelligent practice of charity by holding conferences of charities and correction, of which the twenty-seventh annual National Conference was held last year at Topeka, Kan. In these assemblies progressive reforms are advocated, the latest views of the best and most advanced thinkers and workers are ventilated, and difficulties are discussed. As the conference is an itinerating body, meeting each year in some fresh city, its educative influence on local opinion must be considerable. In addition to these conferences, summer schools in philanthropic work are held in New York and probably elsewhere. Besides attending lectures, the students are shown over hospitals and other charitable institutions, and are also afforded opportunities of acquiring practical experience in visiting among the poor. In England, also, the greatest stress is laid upon training workers on the charity organization committees in practical thoroughness and in width of view. The need for such training is being recognized, too, in Germany. Classes of instruction for almoners have been held in Berlin by Stadtrath Dr. Münsterberg, a prominent official in the administration of public charity in that city, with the result that the students attending the classes have induced him to publish the substance of his lectures. It may be added that very comprehensive directories of both official and voluntary charities are published by the Charity Organization Society of London, the Gesellschaft für Ethische Kultur, in Berlin, and the municipality of Amsterdam.

To sum up the conclusions suggested by the above survey, there are three traits which appear especially to characterize the benevolence of the closing years of the nineteenth century. One of these is the growing recognition of the fact that the intricate and mutually independent conditions of modern civilized life necessitate the most careful research into the indirect, as well as the immediate, results of his liberality on the part of every wise philanthropist, if he would not undo with one hand more than all he can succeed in achieving with the other. And, if this be true of the individual, it is tenfold truer of the association, the city, and the nation. Witness the results of reckless subsidizing of private charities from the public purse without a proper system of public inspection and control in America, as chronicled by the late Professor Amos G. Warner and Mrs. Josephine Shaw Lowell, or the lavish expenditure in out-relief for which some English towns are even now distinguished, notwithstanding the trenchant exposure of the abuses to which public assistance is peculiarly liable embodied in the Poor Law Commissioners' Report of 1832.

The second is the tendency to develop social service and social intercourse between the extremes of society, so as by elevating the tone of life among the poor to eliminate some, at any rate, of the causes of poverty, and therefore of the necessity of almsgiving.

And, lastly, in philanthropy as in commerce, the city or the state displays a tendency to take over, or else to compete with, the undertakings due to private enthusiasm or enterprise when, the initial difficulties having been overcome and the experimental stage having been passed, their utility and feasibility have been satisfactorily demonstrated. This is a phenomenon more especially, perhaps, noticeable in England, where, until well on in the century just closed, whatever educational and medical care the poor received was due least of all to the state. But it may also be met with on the western side of the Atlantic Ocean.

ART IN ITS RELATION TO RELIGIOUS AND SOCIAL WELL-BEING.

Francis E. Marsten, D.D.,
NEW YORK.

[In the ruder stages of national and individual life, men are educated religiously by and through the aid of sensuous imagery, either in outward embodiment or in those ceremonial observances which suggest and typify the inward and recondite truths aimed at—which paganism everywhere uses, which, with a nicer application and a wiser forelook, made up the Hebrew polity, and which the Church of Rome now so largely retains in her ritual—or in those less gross and ideal forms which make the staple of our modern creeds and practices; and it remains yet a profound problem whether, dispensing with them, society could have attained the spiritual culture and intellectual elevation which now characterizes it. Yet, with all the admitted advantages which have flowed from such a machinery, it has been liable to the most serious abuse, when not closely watched and guarded by divine counteractants, in landing the devotee into the depths of a degraded and besotted idolatry. The reason is apparent: Between the idea of truth aimed at and the human mind on which it is to be impressed stands the symbol, the rite, the agency, the instituted means; by ceremony, by picture, by cross, by altar, by temple, by whatever of sensuous appliance designed to aid the imagination and impress the sensibilities, which tradition or custom may have introduced and sanctioned. Here intervening as by authority, they gain for themselves a lodgment which gradually obscures the truth they were originally designed to symbolize; and so the agency supplants the principle, and what was intended as the scaffolding comes in process of time to be regarded as the building. And by a degeneracy easily understood, the imagination dominates every other faculty, and leads to the worship of the altar instead of God; the cross, instead of Him who died thereon; or wastes the sensibilities in an absurd flutter of robes and tippets of sacred millinery, and the ritualistic posture—putting of head and hands and knees to ape the external form of a devotion which has wholly escaped the heart.—"Renascent Christianity," page 165.—Ed.]

*   *   *

The relations of art to religion and social progress may hardly be exhibited in justice to so large a subject in the brief pages devoted to the present essay.

The century just closed has witnessed a wonderful development in this regard. Indeed, it is quite beyond all the dreams that the most sanguine entertained at its beginning. Plato in his treatment of ideas discussed art on its ethical side. The greatness of his mind is shown by the subtility and depth with which he treats this theme. His masterly delineation has never been surpassed. But before Plato art was. For man is an artistic as well as a religious being; and art has an ethical and spiritual mission, so stoutly denied in certain quarters. God predominates in the idea of religion; man in in the idea of art.

Religion and art have thus a common root in the constitution of the soul, a relation real and never to be broken.

There are different systems of æsthetics, it is true; but in all of them it is acknowledged that the mind has that quality, or sensibility, which is the mind's power of receiving impressions from the outside world. We may call it feeling, but not of the senses. We see supremely magnified in artists this instinct for form, by which the mind must and will express itself in art, just as truly as it must and will express itself in the domain of knowledge. For the work of the exalted imaginative faculty may not be excluded even in the investigation of truth. If it is, we must eliminate the preachers and prophets of the Church of Christ. Even Kant, writing of the validity of our æsthetic impressions, says that the meaning and mission of Beauty is to symbolize moral good.

Ruskin, in his "Philosophy of Art," classes the æsthetic faculty among spiritual powers that typify the Divine attributes—infinity, symmetry, repose, purity, moderation and holiness. Art may really be said to be the interpretation of the soul in its loftiest thoughts which rise toward God and set forth his qualities.

In seeking to trace the history of art for any period we must begin with the relation of art to the human mind. For art belongs to man as religion belongs to him. So its manifestation will be seen in his religion, and have its effect upon it just as well as upon his intellectual life.

The relation of art to religion is revealed under three aspects: In education, as a great factor in social well-being and progress; in morality; in worship. In making up the record of the age and reviewing the sweep of the century closed, our survey would be very imperfect unless we took into account the effects of art. It is one of the great underlying facts of human history, and it has been well said that the history of art is the history of man.

John Stuart Mill, Utilitarian that he was, wrote: "Science consists in knowing, art in doing; what I must do in order to know is art subordinate to or concerned in science; what I must know in order to do, is science subordinate to or concerned in art."

A study of what we owe to art may well be begun in some such way as this. Let us try to take away the fine arts from life. How much of human advancement do we lose at a stroke! The spirit and character of every nation from the dawn of history has been reflected in its art. What would be left of their history if art was swept out of that which remains to us of the life of Assyria, Egypt, Greece, Rome, to say nothing of the mediæval peoples, the renaissance of learning in Europe, the rise of Protestantism?

Art lies near the heart of humanity as an instructor. Poetry and art nestle close to the religious affections. Herman Grimm declares, in his "Life of Michael Angelo," "there are three means of instructing mankind as to what has happened or is happening—plastic art, poetry, and history. Of the earliest Egyptian traces all knowledge is wanting of deeds and personalities; we have only names and works of art, but the latter so eloquent, so convincing. . . . And there is another example: we are accustomed to look upon the Reformation as a movement growing chiefly out of literary antagonisms. The political and moral incentives whose combined workings brought about the final great result have often been analyzed; but what rôle art played will be generally known only when the influence of religious art in Germany, and its peculiar nature up to the time of Dürer, has been thoroughly examined and its historical connection demonstrated." Prior to the Reformation the ideas of religion and the contents of the sacred writings were familiarized to the people mainly through art. When we touch on the relation of art to morality, we may notice that art occupies a middle place between Nature and morality; while it is neither, it cannot be false to either. Nature is filled with God. Art's chief arena is the soul of man, so art must have a moral and religious expression.

If one says that the chief aim of art is to be true to Nature, is not the cry of realism that goes up so fiercely in certain quarters just this? Reproduce Nature? Why? Because Nature is the ultimate truth. To demand fidelity to Nature, then, is simply demanding fidelity to truth. If this fidelity is the aim and mission of art, the chief end of art, then, must be moral. Art is dead without morality. For there is no such thing as a work of art without an ethical element in it.

And still further, art cannot be immoral and last, because it is essentially social. Art cannot live alone. It is not good for it to be alone. Its aim is to please all. Hence it must eliminate whatever is low, ugly or bad. For it is the essentially good alone that can afford lasting pleasure to the multitude of humanity. It is affirmed by many that the ends of art are not good. It is even said that immorality hangs upon her garments; that great art centres are places of abounding vice and corruption and bad government. It may be replied that there is bad art as well as bad literature. A gross and vulgar picture will not afford moral and spiritual uplift any more than a vulgar and indecent book.

There are elements of evil that abound in all life. But because there are bad books in the world, is any one so daft as to advocate the destruction of all printing presses, and allow printing to become one of the lost arts? No one is so foolish. There are many good things in the world whose abuse has wrought damage and destruction. The excessive use of the lawful and proper may work harm. Shall we abandon or destroy what is liable to be used improperly? What would become of society? Chaos would tread on the heels of progress. The iconoclast has not always proved the world's saviour. Far from it. To hear the warning cries and acrid criticisms of some, one would imagine that art ought to be cast into limbo for the salvation of the world and in the interest of progress and virtue. But is art at fault for its abuse? Does not the blame lie at the door of a defective education, that makes art something that it is not? Is not the remedy in Christian education that will lead to Christian art?—an art redeemed and sanctified for the love of humanity.

So we may easily trace the relation of art to worship. It is a help, teacher and inspirer of true religion. But art is not religion. The attempt to make it so would be as abortive as the attempt to enthrone impersonal force in the place of the personal Lord God Almighty. It is the personality of the Redeemer, the authoritative personal will, that moves to obedience, the mother-heart beating in love that awakens yearning affection. Impersonal art cannot take the place of transcendent personality in worship. One breath of trust in the Cross "towering o'er the wrecks of time" avails more for salvation and Godlike character than multitudes of crucifixes, gold-chased and fastened by the æsthetic taste of a Benvenuto Cellini.

Thus without prejudice we may see the real relation of art to religion. What has been the case in the past has been demonstrated with unmistaken brilliancy in the nineteenth century. A good illustration of the helpfulness of art in moral and religious progress is witnessed in the times of the Reformation. Painted walls took the place of books in the Middle Ages. Poetry without words, speaking out from mural decorations, was quite as effective and intelligible as written poems. God's temples, filled with the masterpieces of sculpture and painting, were eye-speaking manifestations of religious ideas and symbols of the devotional spirit.

Then came in Luther and his co-workers the resurrection of simple Gospel truths. The teachings of the Reformation began soon to find expression in art. Dürer, who was a disciple of Luther, in his pictures of scenes from the sacred writings, made his compositions at once picture and text. They were full of the spirit and life of the new movement. These engravings were scattered all over Germany by the thousands of copies, and reproduced even in Italy. And these life-like, speaking pictures, with their wealth of evangelical truth, prepared the people in a most wonderful way for Luther's translation of the Bible.

Has art in its broadest sense accomplished anything for social well-being? The term has been defined as a state of life which secures or tends toward happiness. If we begin by thinking along right lines it must be evident that social welfare means social morality. If the ethics that inspire life are pure and the laws that spring out of them are obeyed, the simple joy of existence will be supreme.

The century reveals that art has relations to social development. It has affected society in four different ways. It may be truly stated that it has stimulated the ethical nature; awakened intellectual activity; drawn out the slumbering possibilities of man's nature; aroused a deep religious life through inculcating the ideas of worship, immortality, love, self-sacrifice and brotherhood, by touching the soul with tongues of living fire at the contemplation of the loftiest efforts of creative skill. Studied sociologically, we must consider the whole sweep of art as it touches with its divine fervor the industries and amenities of human life. It is, after all, in the last analysis, man's spiritual nature that is ever expressing itself in social activities; and here art comes in contact with social well-being. In the progress of the American nation, in the struggle with the gigantic forces of Nature and the effort to subdue them to human needs, art has had positive relation to the development of character. It has actually done much to render life sweeter, better, broader.

In no other century has art held such close relations to the everyday life. Physical science and multiplied industrial inventions have made this possible. The offspring of purely creative genius is not the only source of its mighty influence. Industrial art, in all its strivings for the beautiful in fabrics, wall hangings and furniture, has had an ameliorating influence that has somewhat of the moral and religious in it. So, without making any distinctions as to degrees of artistic merit, or attempting to classify technically, we may say, all things in art which in any sense stimulate the good emotions are beneficial in their scope.

Wright affirms: "There is nothing progressive that does not come from some form of art, or from some expression of the creative power." The simplest forms of art or of artistic expression may be helpful.

What a change has come over the world in two particulars, in respect to art, since the nineteenth century saw its birth! Protestantism, especially in its Puritan simplicity and austerity, repelled the aid of art as accessory in church architecture and worship. Its symbolisms were shunned as tainted with Popery and the devil. Now Protestant temples of worship are the product of the most artistic skill. Neither are painting and sculpture avoided as aids to the devotional spirit.

The resources of modern invention have sent the works of the world-famous masters into the humblest cottages and scattered them broadcast over the land.

Half a century ago, Cardinal Wiseman, addressing an English company of eminent artists, spoke of the wealth of power and influence that they possessed among educated people. And speaking reverently of the old masters, he announced: "Nor are we ever likely to see their marvelous and multiplied works within easy access of the people." Only ten years later a French Jew, traveling on foot from city to city, sold fac-simile reproductions of sketches of the old masters termed auto-types. Then came photography, and processes of quick and cheap multiplication, like the heliotype process. So invention went on. Every new stroke added to the readiness and perfection with which the art treasures of the world have become in reality the property of all humanity. Now, by aid of electricity in the hands of such men as Edison and Tesla, one need not journey away from his own village to have the wonders of the world pass in life-like procession before his eyes.

The world's masterpieces in painting, sculpture, architecture, scattered broadcast over the land, are helpful in lifting a man above the mere drudgery of a humdrum existence. The poetry and beauty of life thus come within our ken. The weary toiler may transport himself into a finer atmosphere, and keep company with the great artistic geniuses of all time. Such influences cannot but elevate. By such contact men and women are taught to demand that in their home surroundings and daily life there shall be somewhat to refine, elevate and inspire. So it is a vastly good thing for the well-being of society that one result of inventive art has been to bring into the possession of common folk these beauties of the world. This sort of education leads people to insist on having not only utility but beauty and artistic expression in the ordinary environment. Formerly in our architecture, utility, almost to the exclusion of everything else, was consulted.

In the early part of the century Dr. Timothy Dwight, president of Yale College, visited New York City. He has left his impressions of its buildings, society, and public works in his "Travels." He found at that date the City Hall "the most superb edifice" in America, and the new Presbyterian Church in Wall street possessing a handsome front. But what a spirit of change has swept over the land since then! It is as true of art as of letters—

> "A little learning is a dangerous thing;
> Drink deep, or taste not the Pierian spring."

Now the taste for nobler things has become so widespread in this land that it is the æsthetic spirit that demands that our libraries, public halls, colleges and churches shall be works of art; and under this régime the hideous effects of mere striving for utility are passing away. Amid deformities innumerable art is beginning to lift its majestic and tranquil presence among us. We have the Washington Monument and have had the Naval Arch in New York, the latter some day, we trust, to be done in enduring bronze or stone; such models as the Boston Public Library, the Corcoran Art Gallery, and that chef d'œuvre of American architecture, the Congressional Library at Washington. So everywhere in our higher schools and colleges the effort is made to surround the pupils with the æsthetic and refining. Environment is made to include those elements of culture that appeal to the artistic sensibilities and awaken purity of taste. It was argued, however, by some, that to take young girls out of the ordinary American home, plain as it often must be, and send them to such institutions as Wellesley College, where they could spend four years amid the creations of art and the refinements of creative genius, would work a positive injury in making such people discontented with their lot, and unhappy because they could not always have just such elevated surroundings. But the real result has been that graduates of these schools have taken the artistic spirit with them, and to the extent of their ability made their surroundings in humbler spheres conform to their artistic impulses. Low discontent has been changed into noble emulation. To such an extent, under the fostering care of religion, has the requirement for an inner and outward beauty of life spread that we may see its effects everywhere.

Prof. A. D. F. Hamlin, in "The Forum" for July, 1901, aptly says: "The century which has recently closed was preëminent for its marvelous widening of man's intellectual horizons and for its summoning of the multitude to share in this beneficent enlargement of the human outlook. The summits of learning are no longer walled about by insurmountable barriers.

"Until lately, however, our people have been too absorbed in their vast industrial activities and the solution of the grave political and social problems of their destiny to give much thought to the finer amenities of life. Only in recent years have they begun to discover the extent of their artistic destitution and to realize the immaturity of many features of the national life. This consciousness, once awakened, has aroused a new interest in artistic and historical studies. Yet, with all the progress of the last quarter of a century, it is surprising to note how many people of fair education think of art as a wholly extraneous thing, which it is quite permissible to ignore. People who entertain such ideas as these have had for the most part no opportunity to learn what art really is. They have seldom seen a beautiful building, or looked upon a fine picture, or stood before a noble statue. Their lives and surroundings have been barren of beauty. Through lack of occasion for exercise, and by reason of mental pre-occupation with practical, social, religious, political, and other interests, their æsthetic sensibilities have become atrophied. Given sufficient contact with beautiful things, however, and these æsthetic capacities spring into life like flowers in the sun."

The cry of the wage-worker of to-day is not merely for the bare necessities of physical living. His demand does not stop at give me better shoes, better clothes, better food, but it rises into the files of those spiritualizing influences that are superior to the craving of a paltry animal existence.

When Frederick Arnold was writing the life of F. W. Robertson, he went to Brighton to talk with Robertson's friends, to find incidents for his biography. Among other places he went to a bookseller's shop, and learned that the proprietor had been a constant attendant upon Robertson's ministry and had in his parlor a picture of the great preacher. The bookseller said to Mr. Arnold: "Do you see that picture? Whenever I am tempted to do a mean thing I run back here and look at it. Then I cannot do the mean thing. Whenever I feel afraid of some difficulty or some obstacle, I come and look into those eyes, and I go out strong for my struggle."

Man wants to realize that his intellectual and spiritual nature is being nourished and strengthened. He sees the ideals and possibilities all around him and is eager, in some measure at least, to make his life conform to them. Hence the demand, not only for utility, but for beauty.

The workman has been educated and his æsthetic perceptions developed so that in the matter of a kitchen stove, if you please, a mere ugly utility must give way to something that shall not be a glaring offence against good taste. For this reason, we were told, not long since, by a writer on social themes, that a certain stove manufacturer gave a prominent sculptor $5,000 to perfect for him a design for kitchen stoves that would embody the elements of grace and beauty. That manufacturer caught the spirit of progress that breathes in the century. He knew that people were educated enough to appreciate such things and to recompense him for his outlay.

In England, more than in this country, the poster is becoming a fine-art work. The highest talent is employed in its production.

If men live long in an atmosphere that is artistic and refined, they must naturally come to have a taste for such things, and be ill at ease and unhappy when deprived of them. But it may be argued, Is not this very demand for higher things causing the discontent and unrest characteristic of our times? If by the use of the word discontent one means that a man is dissatisfied with himself and his surroundings, and seeks to make himself better and to improve his opportunities, this is the way Nature and religion, in its highest expression in Christianity, have ordained to secure progress. If it were not for reasonable discontent the world would be nothing short of a stagnant pool. The desire for better things has in itself created new industries. Men say we should improve our lives in this direction. New articles to meet the demand are invented. Soon a new child of industry is born. Work begets work, and the general weal is improved to some extent.

Dr. Carroll Wright tells of a conversation he had with Pullman after his new town had been in operation for some time. "It has been my aim," he said, "to elevate the working people. I have provided refined and artistic surroundings for their homes—parks, fountains, gardens, public libraries, in short, everything that was possible within the scope of my scheme, that might prove helpful for the moral, intellectual and æsthetic betterment of the people." "Has the plan worked?" asked his listener. "Do improved surroundings really help to elevate taste and character? Have the rough and ill-mannered been benefited?" "I have noticed this," he replied— "when people move into Pullman with broken, shabby and ill-kept furniture, influenced by their environment they begin to see how incongruous it is. The broken and ugly stuff gradually disappears, and the dwelling by and by is furnished with the good taste prevalent in the neighborhood."

The time has passed for the political economist to reckon as wealth only material goods, or what can be actually expressed in a dollar-and-cent valuation. A young American college man has led the way into a wider and truer generalization. Intellectual accomplishments are wealth. Character in its spiritual essence is wealth. The value of a collection of art works to the community cannot be expressed in the figures that that number of fine-art works will bring in the market when exposed for sale to the highest bidder. The spiritualizing and refining influence on the community provoking to higher living, and inciting demands that find expression in progress, is reflected in the creation of new industries. More brains and hands are kept busy to gratify the exalted taste for something better, and this is again helpful in the better moral tone of society.

How foolish to say that the æsthetic perceptions do not produce anything that can be of value to social well-being! No shallow thinking can perceive the thousand ways in which they minister to human good. To the extent that public art becomes an educator, it is contributory to the well-being of the community. What the poor man cannot buy for himself he yet may be joint possessor of as a citizen of the state. The best works of the best masters thus come to be public property. And one marked tendency of the age is to keep every good thing easy of access to the people at all times. Let the good things be open all the while, and more and more, and let the bad things be closed. This is good philosophy and good common sense as well. The public mind seems to be directed along this wholesome line of thinking with increasing earnestness.

The popular verdict appears to be that there is no time too good in which to cultivate those finer tastes whose bent is in the direction of refinement, spirituality and religion. The divinity of beauty appeals to the divinity that is in the souls of men. It is this finer sense that has in it the very essence of worship. It is this that leads a man to ask, Whence comes all this spiritual beauty and longing for betterment? So beauty of outward form leads up to that temple wherein dwells the Author of all loveliness. Hence it is a good thing that our museums and treasures of art and literature be accessible to the masses every day in the year. It is acknowledged that man's latent moral and spiritual nature needs all the help it can get. The struggle between the good and the bad is so intense that no wise efforts to present to him the highest ideals ought to be scouted as unprofitable. Thus art has been a help to religion and a direct factor in social progress.

Though past ages have been such rich treasure houses of art and poetry, the direct offspring of religion, we observe that the nineteenth century has been far from being a barren period in this regard. Who can estimate the direct value to religious growth and training that the Scriptural studies of our great artists have been. The stained-glass window has told its story to the eye and so carried some loving and holy message to the heart that has ripened in loving deed and divine character.

For ground glass, or unsightly windows, where attempt at coloring was simply hideous, all over our land, we have the harmonious and finished work of such artists as Tiffany, LeFarge or Wilson, not to mention a host of others who have done more or less creditable work.

Among the many things that have been done by artists whose themes, in cheap, yet praiseworthy prints, have been the constant delight of youth and age, may be mentioned certain notable creations like the nineteenth century art serials of the life of Christ. Religious art in this age has assumed the form of illustrations of Bible scenes and incidents. Scarcely a scene or minor incident in all the

Bible story that has not been the inspiration of some art creation. Among those that should come within the scope of this review are the works of Johann Frederich Overbeck, who produced, from 1842 to 1853, some forty compositions. His work has in it much of the spiritual simplicity of Fra Angelico. Overbeck admired very much the early Tuscans, and caught much of their spirit. Gustave Doré is the best-known Bible illustrator of our time. With all his peculiarities his attitude toward religion and the person of the Redeemer was one of reverence. His popularity among the masses may be from his intense dramatic power, which now and again verged on the theatrical. His illustrated Bible, as first published in 1865, contained two hundred and thirty drawings. It was received with such enthusiasm that it some time since reached its third edition. It would be hard to estimate the multitudes of Christian folk that have received their conception of Bible life and story from his skilful pencil.

Another Bible delineator, not so well known, is Alexandre Bida. His "Les Saints Evangeles" was published in 1873. The text of the four evangelists was enriched by him with one hundred and twenty-eight etchings. Bida brought to his work a truth and genius that made his Christ reverent, refined, dignified, if not strong.

The century has produced some pictures in the realm of sacred art destined to live. The last of a series that we will mention here are the works of James Tissot. He labored for ten years in producing his New Testament illustrations, from 1886 to 1896. They number three hundred and fifty aquarelles and a great many pen drawings. His first exhibition was given in Paris in 1894. In 1887 he had already issued lithographs illustrating texts of Scripture in important full-page plates. Tissot's distinct purpose, with which he set out under the spell of a high religious enthusiasm, was to reconstruct the Palestine of the Christian era. He seeks to revive a picture of the Jerusalem of the Jews and of Jesus of Nazareth. His effort is to bring back the scenes that Jesus really knew. His are the only series of pictures attempting to be strictly archæological in accuracy of detail. That his efforts have been crowned with a certain amount of success, thousands bear testimony. They certainly have attained to the remarkably picturesque. Effective they are in teaching the great lessons the artist has set before his genius. Their mission is the exaltation of religion. Its lessons they vividly convey to mind and heart. If the figure of the Christ that moves through them is not as commanding a Presence as we have been taught by former masters to look for in the divine Personality that moves through sacred art, but simply one of a company portrayed with vivid Oriental realism, we may remember that the artist has sought to bring back to us the Son of Man as he really was in the days of His ministry in the flesh, and not as ages of adoring worshippers have imagined that He ought to be to claim humanity's paramount love, reverence and worship.

It is this exaltation of religious themes in art that has inspired man with religious sentiments. In a world of sin, moral and religious beauty has been uplifted. By this we are not saying that art is to save a world of sin. It takes a mighty personality to do that. It takes a blood-red cross, and righteousness and love triumphing in the light of God. But art may be the handmaid of religion, as it is certainly a formative power in social progress. To accomplish great results the latent æsthetic taste must be cultivated, however, just as the slumbering moral nature must be awakened. The ugly and commonplace look out upon every hand. They seek to mar human life and drag it in the mire. By artistic surroundings we may hope to counteract the dangers of ugliness, and by the Gospel of Beauty make moral deformity hateful. Most men of our time feel that there is some Power above us that has brought into being all the loveliness that crowds in countless forms Nature's atelier. Coleridge was inspired with something more than poetic afflatus when he sang in the Valley of Chamouni, gazing upon the wonders of the Alps:

> "Who made you glorious as the gates of Heaven,
> Beneath the keen, full moon? Who bade the sun
> Clothe you with rainbows? Who, with living flowers
> Of loveliest blue, spread garlands at your feet?
> God, let the torrents, like a shout of nations,
> Answer, and let the ice plains echo 'God.' "

God is a God of beauty. Love, truth and goodness are beautiful. They demand beautiful settings for their own perfection of being. The creation of a taste for the beautiful, education in art, means the awakening in the soul of a sense of beauty that lifts it to an appreciation of moral and spiritual beauty as well. Then, one step further, comes an acknowledgment of Him who is the Author of it all.

Our homes and public buildings, our streets and parks, ought to be made the embodiment of beauty. Have we not here the elements for a crusade against the hideous deformities that abound in so many of our American communities? Ghastly ugliness looks out on the right hand and left, shocking all budding æsthetic taste. What shall we say of the effect of such things on social well-being in our towns and cities? Filthy streets, unseemly collections of cast-off material of all sorts and in all conditions of degeneration, unsightly telegraph poles, fences and rocks, with the abomination of satanic advertising in all stages of putrefaction, and ill-shapen, crumbling buildings, offending every rule of architecture—what purpose do such as these serve but to lower the moral tone and blunt the finer sensibilities? Men who live in dirt and filth, whose daily vision is feasted on the ugly and misshapen, will hardly be moved by sentiments of brotherhood, or by a religion of love, good-will and beauty.

SOME OF THE PAST CENTURY'S RELIGIOUS LEADERS.*

Charles Simeon.	James Martineau.
Friedrich Schleiermacher.	Albrecht Ritschl.
Horace Bushnell.	Phillips Brooks.
Dwight L. Moody.	

[When the man dies, all life's scaffolding falls away. Then only the name epitomizing the life remains. For it stirs our wonder that names alone survive the shock of time. Cities become heaps and empires ruins, bronze tables and marble monuments are ploughed down in dust, the seven wonders of the world perish, but not the names of their creators. The marble of the Acropolis wastes, but Phidias' name abides. God has ordained the names of great men as the enduring monuments of civilization.

Most wondrous, that the prophetic eye, searching out the candidate for universal fame, should turn to a captive nation, to a degraded province, to a village into which had run all the slime of creation, to an obscure peasant's cottage, and therefrom select an unschooled youth, born into poverty, bound to coarsest labor, doomed to thirty years of obscurity, scorned by rulers, despised by priests, mobbed by common people, by all counted traitorous to his country and religion, in death stigmatized by a method of execution reserved for slaves and convicts.

Our wonder grows apace when we remember that he wrote no book, no poem, no drama, no philosophy; invented no tool or instrument; fashioned no law or institution; discovered no medicine or remedy; outlined no philosophy of mind or body; contributed nothing to geology or astronomy; but stood at the end of his brief career, doomed and deserted, solitary and silent, utterly helpless, fronting a shameless trial and a pitiless execution. In that hour none so poor as to do him reverence. And yet could some magician have touched men's eyes, they would have seen that no power in heaven and no force on earth for majesty and productiveness could equal or match this crowned sufferer whose name was to be "Wonderful." The ages have come and gone; let us hasten to confess that the carpenter's son hath lifted the gates of empires off their hinges and turned the stream of the centuries out of their channels. His spirit hath leavened all literature; He has made laws just, governments humane, manners gentle, even cold marble warm; He refined art by new and divine themes, shaped those cathedrals called "frozen prayers," led scientists to dedicate their books and discoveries to Him, and so glorified an instrument of torture as that the very queen among beautiful women seeks to enhance her loveliness by hanging His cross about her neck, while new inventions and institutions seem but letters in His storied speech.

---

* The names are arranged chronologically.

To-day His birthday alone is celebrated by all the nations. All peoples and tribes claim Him. He seems supremely great. None hath arisen to dispute His throne. Plato divides honors with Aristotle, Bacon walks arm in arm with Newton, Napoleon does not monopolize the admiration of soldiers. In poetry, music, art, and practical life, universal supremacy is unknown. But Jesus Christ is so opulent in His gifts, so transcendent in his words and works, so unique in His life and death, that He receives universal honors. His name eclipses other names as the noonday sun obliterates by very excess of light.—Newell Dwight Hillis; "The Influence of Christ in Modern Life;" pp. 92-94.—Ed.]

* * *

CHARLES SIMEON: Samuel Macauley Jackson, D.D., LL.D.

Among the great religious leaders of the first half of the nineteenth century in England and America there is surely to be reckoned Charles Simeon. His title to fame is made in what is known as the "Evangelical" movement. This movement really dates from the time of Wesley and Whitefield, but the followers of those revival preachers had left the Church of England, and left it very dead. It was Simeon's work to reanimate it and to deepen the spiritual life not only of the members of the Established Church, but as his influence crossed the Atlantic, also of that of the Protestant Episcopal Church in this country. He also had an important bearing upon the church life of other denominations, and so, although the Evangelical movement as such is now a matter of history, we owe a great debt to the man who transformed the clerical life in his own church and outside of it.

Charles Simeon was born at Reading, in England, on the 24th of September, 1758. His early training was not pious, but formally religious. His family belonged to the gentry and were wealthy, and so were part of the Establishment in full communion. He was sent to Eton and afterward to Cambridge, where his life was that of a boy and young man of his class. He himself confesses to having lived upon a low plane; sometimes indulging too freely in wine, but compared to his associates, his life was quite decent. It was not until 1781 that his conversion took place, and this was of such a thorough character that he never relapsed into his former mode of life, but was from that hour an Evangelical Christian of the most pronounced type. He entered the ministry, and through the influence of his father and of King's College, of which he was a Fellow, he obtained the very desirable living of Holy Trinity, right in the heart of Cambridge, and remained to his death its rector. His early experiences in the church were rather remarkable and certainly very unpleasant. His congregation did not want him, but somebody else who was not appointed by the patrons, and as in those days it was the custom to put locks upon pew doors, they adopted the efficacious device of locking the doors so that nobody should be seated in the church. Simeon endeavored to meet this move by putting settees in the aisles. They then went further and locked the doors of the church, and he had to meet this move by hiring a hall in the neighborhood of the church. This opposition also showed itself in personal forms. He was jeered at on the streets and his assistants came in for the same treatment. All of which conduct strikes us now as being the more extraordinary when we learn that Simeon was a very popular preacher and his services were in constant demand outside of his own church. The opposition seems to have been based simply upon resentment of the snub which the congregation had received and not to have been due to any very violent objection to the matter of his preaching. But it was so bitter that at first he was afraid to visit his congregation, and it caused him for years a great deal of suffering. He lived it down, and after a while he was welcomed by them and they were proud of his connection with them.

He was an indefatigable preacher, a great Bible student, a born son of consolation, a man of most thorough consecration to his church, a man to whom religion was not a part of life but the whole of life—the great subject of conversation and of private thinking. He also had the true missionary instinct to impart these views to others, and so by means of his university lectures, unpublished and published sermons, innumerable letters, and by means of weekly gatherings in his rooms, which he called "conversation parties," but the topic of which was always and only religion, he moulded the university life and educated large numbers of ministers in his way of thinking.

His theology would be considered in this day narrow and rather unreal. It has been described by Rev. Dr. A. V. G. Allen, in his biography of Phillips Brooks, as that phase of religious thinking which presented the Gospel of Christ "as consisting in deliverance from sin and penalty through the atonement upon the cross. It was not primarily an intellectual movement, whose aim was the adjustment of theological tenets, but rather an intensely practical purpose. Its adherents alike agreed in teaching the necessity of conversion as the first step in the religious life. It enforced also the cultus of an inward experience of the Divine life of the soul, magnifying the person of Christ as the motive power of Christian development, through conscious union with whom alone could salvation be secured."

In incessant preaching and lecturing, letter writing and talking upon the subject of religion, Charles Simeon passed his days, and when he died on the 13th of November, 1836, the event produced a world-wide sorrow. Those preachers at home and abroad, those private persons whose lives he had affected, rejoiced in the great work he had done, while mourning over his departure. He had surely well served the religious world and fell asleep at last in the sure hope of immortality.

FRIEDRICH SCHLEIERMACHER: Prof. Samuel Macauley Jackson, D.D., LL.D.

As a man of altogether different type, but of no less usefulness in his lifetime, and of a far more likely permanent worldly fame, was Friedrich Ernst Daniel Schleiermacher. The ordinary English reader has probably as little acquaintance with his name as with the former's, but every student of theology and of philosophy and of German history of the modern period knows at least that Schleiermacher was a person of consequence. He was born at Breslau on the 21st of November, 1768. His father was an army chaplain and connected with the Reformed Church. He seems to have been a very good man, but not to have known what to do with a son who was a genius. However, he sent him to be educated by the Moravians, and there Schleiermacher received his first religious impressions. He turned to God as naturally as the flowers turn toward the sun, but he did not in his mature years advocate Moravian ideas. On the contrary, he said a great many things which would have shocked the simple people among whom he had lived. Like many another earnest man the idea of God first took on the form of Pantheism, and so when, after passing through the University of Hallé, and having an experience of a private tutor, he came to Berlin in 1796 as a preacher, he held forth the idea that God is not only everywhere, but that man is in some sense an embodiment of God.

Schleiermacher was at that time a highly educated, independent, fearless young man, living in the society of scholars and poets and philosophers—and, in fact, the best literary set of Berlin; but though with them he was not of them, because he was gazing upward, for to his soul had come the voice of God, while the eyes of the company were fastened upon the ground. The fire of zeal to describe the heavenly vision burnt in his bones, and in 1799 he delivered those remarkable "Speeches upon Religion" which are the basis of his fame and the best piece of work he was destined to do. The object of these speeches is to present the claim of God upon the educated man. Their very first words show precisely the situation. He says: "It may be an unexpected and even a marvelous undertaking that any one should still venture to demand from the very class that have raised themselves above the vulgar, and are saturated with the wisdom of the centuries, attention for a subject so entirely neglected by them. And I confess that I am aware of nothing that promises any easy success, whether it be in the winning for my efforts your approval, or in the more difficult and more desirable task of instilling into you my thought and inspiring you for my subject." As we look back upon those speeches through the vista of one hundred years we find that their importance has not been lost. They are reprinted and read at the present time, and only so recently as 1893 an English translation of them appeared. As to their estimation by his own generation the testimony of Neander may be accepted. He says: "Whosoever participated in the religious movements at the beginning of the nineteenth century will recognize how a pantheistic enthusiasm can be for many a thoughtful and profound spirit a starting point for faith in the Gospel. Specially important, as a stepping stone to the theological and religious development, was the appearance of the 'Speeches on Religion' by the late Schleiermacher. This book was the occasion of a great revival and mighty stirring of spirits. Men of the older generation, adherents of the ancient Christian supernaturalism or earnest Rationalists, whose living faith in a God above the world and a life beyond was a relic of it, rejected the pantheistic elements in the book with anger and detestation. But those who were then among the rising generation know with what might this book, that testified in youthful enthusiasm of the neglected religious elements in human nature, wrought upon the heart. In opposition to one-sided intellectualism, it was of the greatest importance that the might of religious feeling, the seat of religion in the heart, should be pointed out. It was a mighty impulse to science that men were directed from the arbitrary abstract aggregate called the Religion of Reason to the historical significance, in the flesh and blood of life, of religion, and of Christianity as part of religion. This accorded with the newly-awakened interest and sense for research."

In 1810 Schleiermacher became professor of theology in the new University of Berlin, and was also a preacher in Trinity Church, and from that time until his death, on the 12th of February, 1834, he was recognized as the greatest theologian, as well as the greatest preacher, in German Protestantism. Schleiermacher was an old-fashioned German professor, having his say about everything, but his fame rests upon the "Speeches on Religion," already mentioned, and on his lectures on theology. Along with his deep thinking and speculations went a very simple religious life, and the scene about his deathbed was so touching and so indicative of his piety, that it may well be repeated here. Shortly before he died he said: "Lord, I have never clung to the dead letter, and we have the propitiatory death of Jesus Christ, His body and His blood. I have ever believed and still believe that the Lord Jesus gave the Supper in water and wine." Then raising himself he said: "Are you also at one with me in this faith, that the Lord Jesus blessed the water in the wine?" On the assent of the bystanders, he continued: "Then let us take the Supper; you the wine and me the water. Let no one be troubled about the form." After the words of the institution he said: "On these words of the Scriptures I rest; they are the foundation of my faith." Then turning to his wife he said: "In this love and communion we are and remain one." A few moments more and he had departed.

It may be that the evil that men do live after them, but the good does also. And although Simeon and Schleiermacher were in entire ignorance of each other's existence, and the one in his literal Biblical views, and the other in his speculative and philosophical views, were probably as far apart as persons could well be, they had one point of contact, which makes them essentially one, and that is, they were ardent lovers of the Lord Jesus Christ. Schleiermacher was always ready to turn aside from his profound lectures and sermons to say a few simple words of loving admiration and profound gratitude toward that Heavenly Being who had come down to earth to be his Saviour. Like Simeon, he clung closely to the essential Christ, and in this all-compelling name he called the people back from their wanderings in the paths of rationalism and atheism to God and to the

Son of God, and for this service he deserves to be held in perpetual remembrance.

HORACE BUSHNELL: THEODORE T. MUNGER, D.D.

It is getting to be generally recognized that next to Jonathan Edwards, no theologian in England has exercised so deep and permanent an influence as Horace Bushnell. As the sun of one was descending, that of the other rose, but has not yet set. The contrasts between them are many, but none is so striking as that between the gradual decadence of the influence upon theology of Edwards and the growing influence of Bushnell, which actually unfolds to meet new phases of thought. The reason for the difference is plain. Edwards' work clustered about the *will*, taken at the point of its evolution from necessity into freedom, where he rendered great service. But the factor ceased to be important, and the theology built upon it shared the same fate. Bushnell hardly touched the will, assuming its full freedom, and laid hold of themes that are permanent by their very nature. His contentions were spread over life in all its breadth, and his treatment of it was drawn from Nature and from the world of the Spirit. Themes taken from such a source will never lose their interest so long as they are treated by a great mind.

It is almost a hundred years since Horace Bushnell was born in Litchfield, Conn. Three years later his parents moved to New Preston, nearby, where he was reared upon a farm, supplemented by a wool carding and dressing factory. He shared in the labor of each until he was twenty-one, winning meanwhile a good common school education and a preparation for college. The influence of his home was deep and lasting. His father was a Methodist and his mother an Episcopalian, but both became sincere members of the Congregational Church—there being no other in the town. The Puritan influence, without doubt, predominated, but it was softened and qualified by the other strains. There was more of the Arminian than of the Calvinist in his theology; and as he said of himself, "I always had it for my satisfaction, so far as I properly could, that I was Episcopally regenerated." The beauty of the region about him, the moral earnestness of the community, the purity and intelligence of his home, the drill of work, the play of his own mind—believing, yet always full of question—such were the influences that followed him

THEODORE L. CUYLER, D.D. LL.D.

to Yale College, where he entered at the age of twenty-one, a man in years, and beyond his years in the maturity of his character. He was the leader of his class physically and intellectually, a good student, too earnest for much play, but no recluse, and living a college life out to the full. After graduation he studied law, but was made tutor, and while in that relation he threw off a latent scepticism that had come over him, and found himself, after much struggle, in the peaceful exercise of a faith which he stated in a phrase that underlay one of his main contentions in theology: "My heart wants the Father; my heart wants the Son; my heart wants the Holy Ghost—and one just as much as the other." Bushnell's life and work were based on that experience.

He had studied theology in the Divinity School while a tutor, where he came under the instruction of Dr. N. W. Taylor—last, and by no means least, of the New England theologians of the Edwardian school. His reaction from the theology of the day, which began in college, increased rather than lessened while in the seminary, but it moved in circles and forms of thought that kept him aloof from the fierce controversies that were going on between the two schools in theology, which were chiefly over the will. Bushnell waived them or rose above them, and fell to meditating on the nature of language itself, and so delivered himself out of the contentions that turned mainly on close definition of words. Under such a cover—honestly taken, however—he found a settlement, unchallenged by either party, over the North Church, in Hartford, though not without suspicion, because of his association with the new Divinity School.

Thus he entered upon a career untrammeled by adherence to any party, with the freedom that a Congregational pastor can claim whenever he sees fit. Dr. Bushnell needed all the sea-room he could gain, for he was to sail far and wide upon seas then unknown, or known only as full of danger. He is to be regarded as a preacher and a theologian. For a period of twenty-six years—1833-59—he filled the pulpit and pastorate of his church with incessant labor, except when forced to rest by illness. From the age of forty he was an invalid until his death, but never did he rest from his labors. He spent a year (1845) in Europe, a winter at the West (1852), and another in Cuba (1855), and a year in California (1856). They by no means were periods of inaction. Bushnell was a thinker of the meditative order—not, as is often said, a restless one; rather was he a steady and incessant thinker, and always, after the New England fashion, on great subjects. His larger works were conceived in his sermons and carried out in these periods of search for health, but in not a line of them is there a trace of invalidism.

This brief sketch must assume a knowledge of the theological condition in New England in the middle of the century.* It might briefly be described as a transition from the dogmatism of the Edwardian system to those methods induced by modern thought and science. It was a period of confusion and hot debate—one order passing away and another coming on; a

> "Wandering between two worlds, one dead,
> The other powerless to be born."

What was needed was not an ecclesiastical leader, but a great thinker; not a critic nor a destroyer, but a prophet and an upbuilder. It will not be claimed that Bushnell made no mistakes, but—looking back—it is difficult to imagine how the work that was needed could have been better done. Even in the light of present thought it can be seen that his shortcomings and wanderings served to win the attention and sympathy of one party and to mitigate the antagonism of the other party.

Bushnell did not seek the rôle of a reformer. Whatever he undertook came to him as a pastor. He met his questions in the way; but once seen and felt, they were searched to the bottom, when utterance became a necessity. The audience he found and holds is a sign, but not the measure of his greatness.

It was in this natural way that he approached his most significant and moving book, "Christian Nurture." It was, in its present form, ten years in preparation, having been called out, at first, by a request of his Ministerial Association, in order to explain more fully what he had already said in a review article. Its specific aim was to show that "the child is to grow up a Christian, and never know himself as being otherwise." This apparently innocent statement of what seems to be a most desirable thing shook New England theology to its foundation. The book with difficulty came into being, its first issue having been recalled by a timid publication society. Though charged as heretical, it was in fact a return to an older and never questioned orthodoxy. The New England churches, under the influence of de-

---

* For a fuller statement, see "Horace Bushnell; **Preacher and Theologian,**" *passim*, but specially Chapter III.

bates over the will and the rise of democracy, had drifted into an individualism that practically excluded children from the church in which they stood by virtue of baptism.

Individualism favored the revival system, which also necessarily ignored children. Hence Bushnell set himself to limit and define the place of individualism in the church, and to plead for the Christian nurture of the young, in place of reliance upon revivalism as it then was.

It is enough to say of this treatise that it not only prompted that return of the churches to the nurture of their children which had been obscured and almost buried under other theories, but it undermined a good part of the Calvinism that had shut it out. The greatness of this achievement has not yet been duly recognized. Not only did "Christian Nurture" recall the churches to ancient and, I might say, eternal orthodoxy, and re-established in the church the proper law of its growth, but it no less turned thought to the future and prepared the way for those conceptions and methods of training the young which now prevail and have the sanction of psychology and of impartial human nature. No better handbook on the subject has ever been produced. When first read it seems to be a wise and fervent appeal for a careful and intelligent training of children; and here, indeed, is its chief value. But it reaches into other fields. Looked at theologically, all its implications are opposed to Calvinism—old or new. If regarded ecclesiastically, its implications are in favor of the historic churches.

While "Christian Nurture" was the first serious work of Bushnell, it was not his first volume; that was "God in Christ," prefaced by a "Dissertation on Language." The key to a right understanding of Bushnell is always to be found in this brief essay on language, nor is it fair to judge him otherwise than by it. He faced a theology that was based on and defended by definitions. It was, therefore, narrow and human, rather than Divine. To escape from this world of literalism and hard deduction was a prime necessity for Bushnell. He could neither breathe nor find room to move about in a world so shut in.

"God in Christ," a volume made up from three sermons enlarged into treatises, had its genesis in the prevailing conception of the Trinity. The Unitarian movement had led many of the churches to recast their creeds—as Congregational churches have a right to do, each for itself—in such a way as to imply tritheism; and the popular defenses of the doctrine all verged in that direction. Bushnell's book is a protest against this over-orthodoxy, and puts in its place what he calls an "instrumental Trinity"; the three persons are *forms* or *modes* in which God manifests Himself.

He was charged with Sabellianism—if, instead, the term semi-Sabellian had been used it would have been correct. But whatever it is called, it saved the churches of New England from a general lapse into deism, for the Arian view, then prevalent, had no retaining power and was not long after discarded under the lead of Theodore Parker. Tritheism was too near polytheism to be endurable. Bushnell's theory of an *instrumental* Trinity, despite much criticism and almost persecution, gradually worked its way into acceptance, but with a steadily increasing pressure on the humanity of Christ and the doctrine of the Spirit.

This volume was soon followed by another—supplementary and explanatory—under the title of "Christ in Theology." Though one of his most brilliant productions, it is no longer in print, for the reason that it is a vigorous—at times more than vigorous—defense against accusations of heresy and bitter attempts to bring him to trial. These efforts were kept up for more than five years—Congregationalism, though sensitive to divergence in theology, is not favorable to conviction of heresy.

Bushnell's next volume was "Nature and the Supernatural." Like his previous works it was an attempt to deliver the churches from a definition of miracles as a violation or suspension of natural laws. This generally accepted view was working havoc in faith and feeding infidelity just in the degree in which it was urged. The conflict between creed and science had begun.

A great argument cannot be put into a word, and all we have space to say of it is—that it contends that Nature with its laws, and the supernatural, which is a spiritual world, over but not contrary to Nature, together form our system of God. The old view, however plausible in one stage of human thought, and however consonant with the accepted theory of inspiration, was no longer tenable. Modern thought and foregleams of the conservation of energy demanded some unity in nature. Bushnell gave it in liberal measure, and in such a form that faith no longer rested on confusion. His treatment may be summed up as referring the subject to the general problem of Jesus—the miracles do not prove Him; He proves the miracles.

Perhaps none of his works was more eagerly welcomed or brought so great relief to troubled minds as this. While singularly at fault in certain respects, it is regarded as the most carefully wrought of his treatises.

His fourth treatise pertains to the Atonement and was published in 1864 under the title "The Vicarious Sacrifice." Late in life (1874) he published a supplementary volume, "Forgiveness and Law"; after his death the two were combined in one book, and now issued as such with a modified sub-title. Again we must confine ourselves to a word. Bushnell's aim in this great work is to supplant the expiatory theory of the Atonement as it is stated in the Westminster Confession and the Grotian or governmental theory—generally held in New England—by what came to be known as the "moral view." In all his writing there is nothing so revolutionary, and so at variance with prevailing orthodoxy, as the following quotation will show: "Christ is a mediator only in the sense that, as being in humanity, he is a medium of God to us." That is, he is not an expiatory sacrifice laden with the sin of the world, but a revelation of God's love and power set to work in humanity for its deliverance from sin by a moral process. I have elsewhere spoken of its methods as follows: "Bushnell domiciled it in the religious thought of the day, and saved it from utter loss by recasting it in the terms of human experience. It is a view of the Atonement that deepens and strengthens life at every point. Its central idea is that it puts the believer directly into the very process by which Christ became a redeemer, and is saving the world; that Christ does nothing for a man beyond what the man himself is required to do for other men, and that it is exactly at this point that the world is redeemed—the principles underlying salvation are of 'universal obligation.' "*

Briefest mention must suffice for Bushnell's work in other forms than these four treatises. He published three volumes of sermons which reached a circulation surpassed by few preachers in the country. "They are to be found on the shelves of every manse in Scotland," said Prof. George Adam Smith, adding that "he is the preacher's preacher." Even to-day no preacher of standing dares to confess that he leaves them unread. Taken as a whole, they reinforce the general purport of his four theological treatises, and translate their main contentions into everyday life. They reflect and aug-

* "Horace Bushnell; Preacher and Theologian." By Theodore T. Munger. Houghton, Mifflin & Co.; 1899.

ment the transition that was going on in the world of thought and discovery. They strike straight into life and the heart of things— as though dogma had no existence. They deal with the unchangeable factors and conditions of humanity. For weight of matter they have no superior. "They are timeless in their truth, majestic in their diction, commanding in their moral tone, penetrating in their spirituality, and are pervaded by that quality without which a sermon is not one—the Divine uttering itself to the human. There is no striving and crying in the streets, no heckling of saints nor dooming of sinners, no petty debates over details of conduct, no dogmatic assumptions, no logical insistence, but only the gentle and mighty persuasions of truth, coming as if breathed by the very spirit of truth."*

Four volumes of essays and addresses, with those already named, fill out the work of Bushnell so far as it has been put into permanent form. It is in these volumes that one realizes that he belongs to the world of literature as well as to theology. It is there we see him as a poet—well defined by his Cambridge address on "Work and Play." In others—as "The Growth of Law," "The Founders Great in Their Unconsciousness," the "True Wealth and Weal of Nations," and "Barbarism the First Danger," we find a civilian of the first order. "The Age of Homespun" will perhaps be the longest read of his writings, as an unequaled picture of a phase of New England life, photographic in its accuracy and idyllic in its form.

The volume, "Moral Uses of Dark Things," while at fault on some matters of science, is a series of profound psychological studies of certain phases of human life—as correct as if written to-day, and masterly in their unraveling of the ethical as it is interwoven with human experience—"tearing the disguise of a curse from many a blessing."

Two essays on preaching touch the high-water mark of all discussions of the pulpit, and should be the *vade mecum* of every preacher.

We have mentioned but eleven of his volumes, but a full bibliography would indicate more than fifty titles, consisting chiefly in addresses and magazine articles. He followed the nation from the beginning to the end of its conflict with slavery, with discussions of its phases profound in their statesmanship and enlivening in their patriotism. When the war ended he pronounced a funeral oration

---

* Quoted from "Horace Bushnell; Preacher and Theologian": p. 288.

over the Yale alumni who had fallen, on "Our Obligations to the Dead," which might serve for all the dead in that and later conflicts. Like Lincoln's address at Gettysburg, it is keyed not to heroism and bravery but to sacrifice. Bushnell always aimed at the deepest in his subject, and struck its highest note.

In closing, we can offer no better sign and index of the man than that made by the city in which he lived for almost half a century. He was the ideal citizen. He had fed its life from the first, breathed his own strong spirit into its people, guided it by his counsels, honored it by his achievements, labored for its welfare in all ways, beautified it by securing, through his untiring, personal efforts, a public park, now crowned by the State Capitol. On the day of his death he was told it had been offcially named for him. It was the grateful voice of the entire city.

And so, at Hartford, Conn., on February 17, 1876, he ended his great, and at times stormy, but always successful, career, at the age of almost seventy-five years, having been born at New Preston, Conn., April 14, 1802.

JAMES MARTINEAU: Rev. Wm. D. Grant, Ph.D.

The subject of this sketch came of Huguenot stock, and was the seventh of eight children of Thomas Martineau, of Norwich, and Elizabeth Rankin, of Newcastle-on-Tyne, England, being born at Norwich, April 21, 1805, and dying in London, January 11, 1900.

His native town was not without its people of culture and distinction and places venerable with age and endeared by association. His father, having met with business reverses, left the family with fewer advantages than otherwise would have been enjoyed had prosperity continued. Young Martineau attended the grammar school of his native place from his eighth to his fourteenth year; thence he was sent to Bristol to the school of Dr. Lent Carpenter, where he remained for two years. To no other of his mental helpers does Martineau confess a larger debt of gratitude than to this preceptor, who communicated both goodness and learning; while teaching his pupils how to decline *virtus,* he taught them at the same time to love virtue.

It was decided in the family councils that James should become an engineer; accordingly, he was sent to Derby to master his profession. But, to his father's disappointment, he remained there but a year, having in the meantime decided to enter the Christian ministry. The historical universities of England had not as yet become liberalized, as they still required subscription to the Thirty-Nine Articles of the Church of England by those who would enjoy their advantages. So our dissenter entered in 1822 as a student at Manchester College, then located at York. This was a college of divinity and general culture, with a course of five years, the last two being theological. Having completed the full course, Mr. Martineau, at the age of twenty-two, with thoroughly furnished mind and disciplined faculties, was prepared to serve his age in the Christian ministry; but though admitted to preach he did not for a year enter upon formal work.

His former instructor, Dr. Carpenter, of the Bristol School, having become ill through excessive toil, Mr. Martineau was invited to take his place. Though urged to continue as principal of the school, and though he was fully qualified and found the duties pleasant and fairly remunerative, he preferred to follow the calling to which he had dedicated himself. He therefore accepted an invitation to become co-pastor of the Eustace Street Presbyterian Church, Dublin, in the autumn of 1828. This congregation was more allied in its doctrine to the Presbyterian Church in England than to that of Scotland—the Bible being regarded as the sole rule of faith and life. Shortly after his settlement in Dublin he crossed to England and was united in marriage to Helen Higginson. Here he labored and grew and was happy in his work for three years, and finally severed his connection with the congregation only because he refused to be a party with them in accepting state aid—*regium donum*—of one hundred pounds. Shortly afterward he was invited to become a colleague of Rev. John Grundy, Paradise Street Chapel, Liverpool. Mr. Grundy, however, dying in 1835, left Martineau in sole charge.

Through a public controversy in 1839 between Evangelical Episcopacy on the one hand, and Mr. Martineau and two clerical associates representing Unitarianism on the other, not only did the trend of his mind toward full-fledged Unitarian belief become manifest, but he emerged from the contest with a consciousness of power unknown before either to himself or to others.

In 1840 he received an appointment as Professor of Mental and Moral Philosophy and Political Economy in Manchester New College—his alma mater. Here for forty-five years he was to toil at the deep problems of the sages. In connection therewith, however, he continued his duties as pastor at Liverpool. In 1841 the attitude of

JAMES MARTINEAU.

his mind toward Unitarianism further appears in his "Five Views of Christian Faith."

In 1848, his congregation having undertaken the erection of a new church edifice, he took advantage of the opportunity to go to Germany for rest and study. In Berlin he attended the lectures of Trendelenburg—who expounded the Stagirite—in logic and the history of philosophy. Martineau himself acknowledges that this experience in Greek philosophic studies brought him to a "new intellectual birth." Necessarianism now reached complete and conscious repudiation. His study and travel having exercised a marked influence upon his thought and life, he returned to his congregation in October, 1849, after fifteen months' absence. He was invited to America to give the Lowell lectures, but the civil war prevented him carrying out the engagement. In 1853 Manchester New College was transferred to London. This made Martineau's task more laborious, as it increased the distance which he constantly required to travel. He continued his double labors, however, four years longer, when he was invited to London in order that he might devote his entire time to his college work. He reluctantly severed his pastoral relationship with his church in Liverpool after a ministry of twenty-five years. In 1858 he became joint pastor with Dr. J. J. Tayler, of Little Portland Street Unitarian Chapel, while still continuing the duties of his professorship. This chapel, it is said, was plain almost to rudeness, and had accommodation for about five hundred people, yet it soon became a centre for some of the most thoughtful and cultured people in London, attracted thither by the intellectual power and spiritual vision of Professor Martineau. In 1869 Martineau became principal of the college and sole preacher at the chapel, where he continued to minister till 1872.

She who for so many years had been the partner of his struggles and triumphs, of his sorrows and joys, faded and died in 1877, leaving him to face the remaining years alone. Having served his alma mater so faithfully and acceptably for five and forty years, at the age of eighty he desired to be released. His request was reluctantly granted, yet for three more years he remained on the Board of Direction. His retirement from public office, however, was in no sense due to enfeeblement of mind or lack of interest in public affairs; rather was it that he might have greater leisure for the completion of those literary tasks which, when eventually finished, made him at once the wonder and the hero of the public.

An incident characteristic of the large tolerance of Martineau occurred in connection with the formation of the Metaphysical Society, of which he was a member. Shortly before his death he was visited by a correspondent of "The Westminster Gazette," to whom he spoke, among other things, of the famous Metaphysical Society. He said that the formation of the society was indirectly due to Tennyson, who, in 1869, had expressed a wish to the present editor of "The Nineteenth Century" for the formation of some society which would put down agnosticism. Mr. Knowles thereupon went in quest of men whom he thought likely to join, Dr. Martineau among them. But Dr. Martineau objected to the militant character of the proposed society, and said that he did not believe in putting down theories, however he might differ from them. He suggested that certain well-known men with agnostic views should be asked to join, and that the society should thus consist of men of different types of thought, who, by interchange of opinion and mutual criticism, might possibly help one another. As a result of this the Metaphysical Society was formed, and ultimately numbered about fifty notable names, including Tennyson, Huxley, Tyndall, John Morley, F. D. Maurice Manning, W. G. Ward, Gladstone, R. H. Hutton, Frederic Harrison, and many other illustrious men.

Professor Huxley remarked regarding this society: "We thought at first it would be a case of Kilkenny cats. Hats and coats would be left in the hall before the meeting, but there would be no wearers left after it was over to put them on again. Instead, we came to love each other like brothers. We all expended so much charity, that had it been money we should have been bankrupt."

We are told by his biographer that in his figure Dr. Martineau was tall and spare. Of adipose tissue he had no superfluity. One meeting him in later years would observe a slight stoop, though it seemed rather the stoop of the scholar than that of the octogenarian. His features were thin, his complexion was delicate. His eyes, which were changeful blue, were not particularly noticeable until he became animated; then his very soul seemed shining through them. His head was not much beyond the average in size, but compact and perfect in its poise. His perceptive organs were large; his hair, always remarkable for abundance, was, in later years, bleached almost to whiteness. The soul of neatness himself, he could not endure untidiness in others. He had no artificial appetites; tobacco he never used; without being pledged to total abstinence, he seldom used wines or liquors, except for medicinal purposes. Intemperate he may have been in work, if that may be called intemperate which, though vast in amount, was sustained to extreme age. All his pleasures were of a rational and ennobling sort. Good art he appreciated; he enjoyed music and sought it for its solace; he delighted in conversation with the wise and good. He had a fondness for mountain scenery, and a favorite diversion of his was walking. In his seventy-eighth year he wrote of the "annual delight" not yet forbidden him of "reaching the chief summits of the Cairngorm mountains."

His biographer tells us that it was his privilege to form acquaintance with James Martineau in extreme age. "Of course, I expected to meet a scholar, but a scholar may be a Johnson; I knew I was to confront a thinker, but a thinker may be a Schopenhauer; I held him a man of genius, but a genius may be a Byron or a Carlyle." These examples only serve for contrast. "Over against the coarseness of Johnson one saw in Martineau refinement refined. In contrast with the selfishness of Schopenhauer, one saw in him consideration for others that was almost self-effacement. In place of the cynicism of Byron one met in him the serenest charity; instead of Carlyle's rudeness, the soul of courtesy and grace." The biographer adds: "The happy discovery was made that Martineau's greatness was of the kind that lifts, but does not overpower. Of the quiet hours spent with him I need not tell. Suffice that they fixed in my mind the impression of a sage, a hero and a saint; of one who might converse with Plato and dare with Luther and revere with Tauler, an habitué of the academy, who thrilled to the Categorical Imperative and who knelt at the Cross."

Some one has designated his as a grand life, which seemed to have realized almost perfectly our modern conception of a wise and a good man; a man who, "unhasting, unresting," pursued the truth, with unreserved fidelity and humility, from early youth to the extremest verge of mortal years; a calm, steadfast, loftily devoted teacher and example of righteous living without asceticism, and of piety without a shadow of superstition.

Francis Power Cobbe says of his preaching: "The general effect, I used to think, was not that of receiving lessons from a teacher, but of being invited to accompany a guide on a mountain walk. From the upper regions of thought where he led us we were able—nay, compelled—to look down on our daily cares and duties from a loftier point of view; and thence to return to them with fresh feelings and resolutions. The exercise of climbing after him, if laborious, was to the last degree mentally healthful and morally strengthening. To hear one of his wonderful sermons only, a listener would come away deeming the preacher *par eminence* a profound and most discriminating critic. To hear another, he would consider him a philosopher, occupied entirely with the vastest problems of science and theology. Again, another would leave the impression of a poet, as great in his prose as the author of 'In Memoriam' in verse. And lastly and above all, there was always the pious man filled with devout feeling, who, by his very presence and voice, communicated reverence and the sense of the nearness of an all-seeing God. Martineau no more assumed the tone of a prophet than of a priest; not even that of a didactic teacher; but only, as said above, of a guide. He seemed always to say to us: 'Come with me and I will show you what I have seen from the mountain tops.' Of preaching he said, 'It has been my life.'"

Some idea may be gathered respecting Martineau's literary activities by reviewing the following list of publications:

In the first place he issued three hymn-books—one in Dublin, 1831; a second in Liverpool, 1840; a third in London, 1874. He published in 1836 his "Rationale of Religious Inquiry"—concise, strong, earnest and elevated. Here he treats familiar themes with the freshness of original thought; pleading, with something of prophetic boldness, for rationalism in distinction from orthodoxy. In 1843 appeared the first series, and in 1847 the second series, of "Endeavors After the Christian Life." These two volumes were selections from his pulpit discourses—far above the regions of controversy, he brings God's message to the faiths and hopes of men. In Boston, in 1852, appeared a volume entitled "Miscellaneous"; in 1858, a second entitled "Studies of Christianity." In 1866-67 Spencer, of Boston, brought out two volumes under the title "Essays Theological and Philosophical." In 1876 and 1879 Martineau published the first and second series of "Hours of Thought on Sacred Things." In 1882 his volume on Spinoza appeared, "embracing the pleasantest account of his life, and the toughest analysis of his doctrine." In 1885, when eighty years of age, "Types of Ethical Theory" was issued in two volumes. In this work ethical systems are shown to take their origin either from the study of the universe or from the study of man. In 1888, at the age of eighty-three, he published his

"Study of Religion" in two volumes, which proved to be one of the strongest defences of fundamental truth. If his "Types of Ethical Theory" had brought him to a leading place among moral philosophers, this last work placed him in the foremost rank of philosophers of religion. Religion is here defined as, "Belief in an Ever-living God, that is, a Divine Mind and Will, ruling the universe, and holding moral relations with mankind." With the publication of this great work it was supposed his literary labors would cease; two years later, however, in 1890, to the astonishment of his friends and the public, he issued the "Seat of Authority in Religion." This, "in range of knowledge, in keenness of insight, vigor of statement or nobility of feeling falls behind its predecessors in no particular."

The seat of authority in religion he finds not with the Roman Catholic in an infallible church, nor with the Protestant in an infallible Bible—both these seats of authority being outward—but he finds the seat of authority *within*. It is not enough that a dictum be true, in order that I may receive it; it must be true to me. Martineau does not claim, however, for all men the ability to find this warrant within. He finds it in what he terms the "summit minds" which, through the unity of the race, represent the unfolded possibilities to all—the dimmer being dependent upon the clearer vision; the child upon the parent; the pupil upon his teacher. Eventually, however, the child gives up parental guidance, the pupil outstrips his master. In science, Agassiz may be exchanged for Darwin, and Compte for Spencer. But not thus are we permitted to treat the church or the Bible, which speaks from above reason and demands its surrender rather than seeks its persuasion. Undoubtedly the predilection of most men is for an *outward* authority, a voice that speaks to them a decisive word. "As the non-use of any faculty or power, however, means its enfeeblement and decay at last, the revelation that should supersede the hard exercise of reason and conscience, in the determination of ultimate truth, were not God's blessing, but his curse."

Still there followed further literary efforts, though of a less arduous character; four goodly volumes of selected papers under the title of "Essays, Reviews and Addresses," and lastly came a volume of "Home Prayers"—his *pax vobiscum*.

James Martineau's life had yet other years before it. But here the story of his labors ends. He lived, as we have said, until January 11, 1900, and even the last decade of his life was not a period of idleness. When Balfour's "Foundations of Belief" was published, Martineau, although at the great age of 90, contributed to the "Nineteenth Century" an elaborate discussion of the new book's contents, which showed clearly that "his eye was not dim, nor his natural force abated."

As may be supposed, Martineau was a remarkable worker, both in amount and variety; a man of diversified capacities and exceptional acquisitive power; at home alike in the departments of mathematics, science, history, political economy, religious institutions, biblical criticism, ethics and philosophy. Before me is a record of more than twenty distinct volumes to which his name is attached, any one of ten of which would have made him noteworthy. "He had many a teacher, but never a master." He was a logician rather than a divine, a Mill rather than an Emerson, yet his intellect combined the power of both the telescope and the microscope, equal to solar systems of thought and the finest reticulations of argument. "To apply a fundamental truth to diverse problems of human interest, to prove systems by their congruity with it, to build by it so that his structure in all its parts should be like the tree whose roots, trunk, branches, twigs, leaves, are informed by one life, was the aim by which his noblest labors were accomplished."

A preacher for 73 years, a professor for 45 years, a professor and pastor for 32 years, an author for 64 years, whose last work appeared when he was 83, and whose last review was penned when he was 90 years of age, has some right to be called remarkable.

His theological bent was always Unitarian, though he refused to be identified with Unitarianism ecclesiastically. He was early influenced by Channing. Though so commonplace in our day, to the contemporaries of Channing his thought came with the force of a fresh inspiration. Writing to his friend Thom regarding Channing, Martineau says: "Others had taught me much; no one before had unsealed the fountain itself, he was the first to touch the spring of living water and make me independent even of himself." To Martineau the Scriptures were perfectly human in their origin though recording superhuman events; inspiration being, not mechanical, but "illumination of the spirit in direct contact with God." He drew his religious faith from the words of Christ—a "unique" personage—who was the central orb of his system and to whom his heart was fixed in loyalty and love. To him the Christianity of Christ is without priest and without ritual.

He viewed God as both immanent and transcendent, making possible His full communion with the spirit of man—mind responsive to mind, affection answering to affection; and though the one be infinite and the other finite, the disparity makes the grace no less possible. Nay, he would contend *of all persons in the universe, God is the most easily accessible.* He would therefore make love to God the basis and the bond of fellowship and not opinions either Trinitarian or Unitarian. "It is the conscious sameness of spiritual relation that constitutes a *church*; it is the temporary concurrence in theological opinion that embodies itself in a creed and makes a *sect* in the proper sense. The former is unity in spite of difference, the essence of the latter being in the accentuation of difference amid unity.

"Be faithful to your intellect; seek the truth with all earnestness, and proclaim it with all fervor. But building a church, the central figure of which should be an altar, not a doctrine, make basal and prominent the truth that unites, not the speculation that divides. You hold to the Love of God and the Divine Unity; hold fast to the Divine Unity, but rear your church on the love of God. Let the doctrine be your personal conviction; let the love be your public confession. In the one you hold to a theory in which a few shall agree with you, in the other to a sentiment in which Christendom is at one with you. Others by dogmatic barriers keep you away from them; see to it that by no dogmatic barrier do you hold them away from you."[*] Noble words! noble words! The fathers may conceive that they are building for the sons, but the sons will excommunicate the fathers. Others would build upon a doctrine, he upon a reverence and a love.

In responding, upon his eightieth birthday, to the greetings of the National Conference of English Unitarians, he declared his belief that "the true religious life supplies grounds of sympathy and association deeper and wiser than can be expressed by any doctrinal names or formulas, and that free play can never be given to these spiritual affinities till all stipulation, direct or implied, for specified agreement in theological opinion, is discarded from the bases of church union."

Dr. Martineau himself, however, did not expect any realinement of ecclesiastical organizations in his day, but his teachings have had a profound effect on the thought of organized Christianity, sweetening, humanizing, and, if we may say so, Christianizing it. So that, while the old forms are still retained, and perhaps wisely, the

[*] Jackson's "Life of Martineau," page 215.

spirit animating them is less mechanical and less intent on merely perpetuating the ecclesiastical machine as the supreme function of religion.

Academic honors were slow in coming to Mr. Martineau, but they came. In 1872 Harvard University conferred upon him an LL.D. degree. Two years later the University of Leyden gave him an S.T.D. degree. Somewhat later Edinburgh made him a D.D. Later still, Oxford honored him with a D.C.L. Last of all, Dublin University bestowed upon him a Litt.D. In 1872 there came to him a worthy testimonial of esteem. At the close of the college session, as he was about leaving London, a check for 5,000 guineas was placed in his hand, with the intimation that there was more to come. The sums that flowed in later swelled the amount to £5,900, a portion of which was devoted to the purchase of two pieces of silver plate on which was engraved a suitable inscription. Accompanying the gift was an address, to which Mr. Martineau replied:

"You speak of mingled motives of this splendid gift. So far as it springs from personal friendship and generous affection it can bring me, however I may wonder at it, only the sincerest joy. But to accept it as an arrears of justice overdue would be to charge a wrong upon the past which I can in no way own. Far from having any claim to plead, I am conscious that, in account of services exchanged, I am debtor to the world, and not the world to me; and am half ashamed to have escaped so many of the privations on which I reckoned when I quitted a secular profession for the Christian ministry. My deepest disappointment has been from myself and not from others, from whose hands I have suffered no grievance I did not deserve, and received kindness far beyond the measure of my boldest hopes. Whoever dedicates himself to bear witness to divine things is the least consistent of men, if he does not lay his account for a modest scale of outward life, and a frequent conflict with resisting interests and opinions. Such incidents of wholesome difficulty attending the study and exposition of moral and religious truth are an essential guarantee that its service shall be one of disinterested love."* A little later, on his retirement from the Little Portland Street Chapel, the congregation to which he ministered presented him with the sum of £3,500, described as a token of "gratitude, respect and admiration."

We should here note that soon after the publication of the "Study

---
* "James Martineau"; A. W. Jackson, M.A., page 101.

of Religion," a movement was set on foot under the guidance of Prof. William Knight, of the University of St. Andrews, to greet the author on his eighty-third birthday with an appropriate tribute. The form decided on was that of an address signed by leading scholars and thinkers of Europe and America, without distinction of sect or party. The address, drawn up and sent to various friends for criticism, received its final revision at the hand of Benjamin Jowett. After the introductory paragraph it went on to say: "We thank you for the help which you have given to those who seek to combine the love of truth with the Christian life; we recognize the great services which you have rendered to the study of the philosophy of religion; and we congratulate you on having completed recently two great and important works at an age when most men, if their days are prolonged, find it necessary to rest from their labors. You have taught your generation that, both in politics and religion, there are truths above party, independent of contemporary opinion, and which cannot be overthrown, for their foundations are in the heart of man; you have shown that there may be an inward unity transcending the divisions of the Christian world, and that the charity and sympathy of Christians are not to be limited to those who bear the name of Christ; you have sought to harmonize the laws of the spiritual with those of the natural world, and to give to each their due place in human life; you have preached a Christianity of the spirit, and not of the letter, which is inseparable from morality; you have spoken to us of a hope beyond this world; you have given rest to the minds of many."

The address bore between 600 and 700 signatures of those whose praise was fame. The first signature was that of Tennyson; the next was that of Robert Browning; then followed the names of Benjamin Jowett, G. G. Bradley, Dr. E. Zeller, of Berlin; F. Max Müller, W. E. H. Lecky, Edwin Arnold, E. Renan, Otto Pfleiderer; a long list of professors of St. Andrews, Edinburgh, Glasgow, Aberdeen, Oxford; of the universities of Jena, Berlin, Gröningen, Amsterdam, Leyden; of Harvard University, the Andover Theological School and Johns Hopkins University; a long array of Members of Parliament; among distinguished Americans, James Russell Lowell, Oliver Wendell Holmes, Frederic H. Hedge, Phillips Brooks and Philip Schaff; a great number of clergymen of England, France, Germany, Holland and the United States; in fine, the leaders of all schools of Protestant Christian thought. The only names conspicuously absent are those of men of science, especially of those of agnostic tendencies; even some of these, unable to subscribe to all the terms of the address, sent him their personal acknowledgments.*

It has been said: "England is likely to see another Gladstone, Tennyson, Ruskin or Arnold before she sees another Martineau." This may be not because Martineau so greatly surpassed any of these in intellectual acumen, spiritual vision or true virility, but, perhaps, because his was such a "unique personality," so powerful and so unique that whoever once came under its spell was never afterward quite the same person; he had met a revelation of character and power, a higher order of man, whose touch had disclosed heights and depths of being before unknown.

Martineau occupied a unique and noble pre-eminence among the master minds of his age; he was easily the peer of a Mill, a Darwin, a Spencer, a Newman, or a Carlyle in the keenness of his intellect and the width of his learning. Though liberal yet was he profoundly religious; the high priest of tolerance and considerateness, yet swayed by the deepest convictions; commanding respect where he could not compel agreement. Certainly, "no man in the England of the last century did more to liberalize the religious thought of the nation." He represented not only a new school of learning, but a new school of piety as well. Not the least singular is his almost ascetic piety with a bold and increasingly radical criticism of the canon of Scripture. But this radicalism was counterbalanced by his spirit of reverence and enthusiasm for God and righteousness.

Whatever may be the value of Martineau's philosophical writings, it was in the spheres of morals and religion that his most valuable work was done. And though most of us may not be able to follow him in his views of the Divine Unity, all of us may do so in his love of God and loyalty to Jesus Christ. Some minds may not accord with his respecting the recognition that should be given the doctrine of evolution, or the social side of man's nature, yet none of us can fail to wish that the church at large might not limp so far behind him in his spirit of tolerance and basis of Christian fellowship. In these respects his greatest influence in Christian leadership is yet in the future.

To him who will undertake to read and digest the voluminous writings of James Martineau—or, to a measurable degree, Mr. Jackson's admirable biography and study—may be guaranteed a liberal

* Jackson's Martineau; page 119.

education in ethics and philosophy, in the arts of criticism and literary grace; may be guaranteed a clearer understanding of the value of and what constitutes religion, an enlarged spirit of tolerance, faculties greatly disciplined by the exercise and heart expanded by communion with one of the choicest spirits which God has given to modern times.

ALBRECHT RITSCHL: REV. ALFRED E. GARVIE, B.D.

DURING the last quarter of the century just closed no name was so well known in German theological circles as that of Albrecht Ritschl; none was used with either so warm praise or so severe blame. In the last decade of the century his fame reached the English-speaking world. It is admitted alike by those who fear and those who welcome this influence that we have much to learn from German theology, and that in it at the present moment the most vital and vigorous force is Ritschl, who "though dead yet is speaking" through the living voices of his disciples. It is, therefore, not only of supreme interest, but also of urgent importance, that we should try to understand the man and prove his worth.

Born in Berlin, March 25, 1822, his grandfather, a pastor and professor, and his father a pastor and then bishop, Ritschl was by birth and breeding dedicated to theology as his vocation. Although a man of thorough independence and marked originality, he showed himself in his student days, which began in 1839, receptive of, and responsive to, many influences in his intellectual development. His mental history was an epitome of the course of contemporary German thought. First of all influenced at Bonn by Nitzsch, and at Hallé for a short time by Hengstenberg, Tholuck and Müller, he was won for Hegelianism by Erdmann, and then became a disciple of Baur at Tübingen. But in the later phases of his thought he owed most to Schleiermacher, Kant and Lotze. After seven years spent in varied and diligent study, he began his career as a university teacher, first as a *privatdocent* at Bonn, in 1846; then he became a *professor extraordinarius* there in 1852; and lastly he removed to Göttingen in 1864 as *professor ordinarius*. There twenty-five quiet but busy years were spent, and there he died, March 20, 1889. One of his disciples, Herrmann, gives us a glimpse of what manner of man he was. "In religious intercourse Ritschl observed an extraordinary severity toward himself. How he lived in the world of thought of the Christian faith certainly was made so clear in his conversation that a less powerful disposition could be wearied thereby. In his house and here in Marburg I have been whole days together with him, without his ever having interrupted our occupation with the highest things by a longer conversation of lighter content. Herein *appeared* his being deeply possessed by the subject. But seldom did this impel a feeble emotional word; but he spake austerely and severely about what moved his heart."

Ritschl's first important work, "The Rise of the Old Catholic Church," published in 1849, showed that he had ceased to be a disciple of Baur. His greatest writing, "The Christian Doctrine of Justification and Reconciliation," the publication of which was completed in 1874, marked the formation of a Ritschlian school. Another great book, "The History of Pietism," was completed in 1886; but it had no such decisive significance. Among his minor works there need to be mentioned only his "Instruction in the Christian Religion," a brief but clear summary of his theology, and his "Theology and Metaphysics," a controversial writing in defence of his own position. Since his death his son has published two volumes of his "Essays" and his "Life." The first volume of his "Justification and Reconciliation," containing the history of the doctrine, was translated into English in 1872; but the third volume, giving his own constructive effort, appeared in English dress only a few months ago. His "Instruction" has just been translated. An understanding of his theology need not now be confined to those who can read his difficult German.

Ritschl's religious individuality explains both his mode of thought and his style of writing. He constructed his own ideas as he criticised the opinions of others. When apparently most dependent on others, he is actually asserting his own originality. His three most prominent characteristics are *a practical tendency, a historical positivism* and *a philosophical scepticism.* Moral action for the Kingdom of God, based on religious conviction of justification by God, finding its support in the historical facts of the Christian revelation, and not in the philosophical ideas of a speculative theism—that is a brief description of his distinctive position. Although he does sometimes yield to a speculative impulse, yet he generally remains faithful to this practical tendency to admit into theology only what is directly serviceable for the religious life. Intense and sincere in his own convictions, he was inclined to exaggerate the difference between himself and his critics, and so involved himself in controversy far more than was at all necessary. Suspicious of all sentimentality and mysticism, he misunderstood and held aloof from many forms of genuine and active piety in the churches, which he summarily condemned as *pietism;* and so greatly restricted the range of his influence, which was practically confined to academic circles, and which has only through the more systematic attitude of his disciples now begun to affect religious thought and life generally.

In 1874, on the publication of his greatest work, he began to gather disciples around him. Harnack, Herrmann and Schürer were at this time drawn to him by (1) his return to the historical revelation of the person of Christ; (2) his claim for the independence of theology from philosophical tendencies; (3) his attempt to put Christian faith beyond the reach of historical criticism; (4) his practical tendency. For several years there seemed to be a fundamental agreement between the master and his disciples. With the adhesion of Häring and Kaftan in 1880 a second period in the history of the school began, marked by growing divergence within and gathering opposition without. Since Ritschl's death in 1889 two tendencies in the school have begun to assert themselves. The one, represented by Harnack, is more critical; the other, expressed in Herrmann and Kaftan, is more positive; and it is uncertain how much longer we shall be able to speak of a Ritschlian school. As the agreement in the school is rather in theological method than in dogmatic propositions, it is difficult to define precisely the common principles, but the following may be said to be the distinctive features: (1) The exclusion of metaphysics from theology; (2) the rejection, consequently, of speculative theism; (3) the condemnation of ecclesiastical dogma as an illegitimate mixture of theology and metaphysics; (4) the antagonism shown to religious mysticism as a metaphysical type of piety; (5) the practical conception of religion; (6) the consequent contrast between theoretical and religious knowledge; (7) the emphasis laid on the historical revelation of God in Christ as opposed to any natural revelation; (8) the use of the idea of the Kingdom of God as the regulative principle of Christian dogmatics; (9) the tendency to limit theological investigation to the contents of the religious consciousness.

Ritschl gathered around him so many disciples, and these have become so popular and influential, because he reproduced in a vigorous original personality the tendencies of his age, and thus was able to minister to its necessities. His theology is "so living and fruitful," because it "answers to the needs of the present generation," which distrusts philosophy, believes in science, has been troubled by historical criticism, and seeks a social ideal, and so demands a Gospel, independent of philosophy, consistent with science, unaffected by historical criticism, and sympathetic to social ideals. Temporary and limited as may be the justification of these tendencies, yet, as "the faith once delivered to the saints" must be spoken to each age in language which it will hear, understand and welcome, it is not a defect, but a merit, of Ritschlian theology that it is seasonable and opportune. It has not a merely ephemeral value, for the tendencies it shows and the necessities it meets are not fleeting fashions and wayward whims, but are rooted deeply and firmly in the soil of thought and life of the age. The older dogmatism, which at one time was just as seasonable and opportune, has lost credit and influence among most thoughtful men, and the pressing need of the present moment is a reconstruction of Christian theology. Because Ritschl and his followers have attempted this with large intelligence and deep sincerity, we may confidently claim for him the place of a religious leader.

The merits of the Ritschlian theology are these: In its method it recognizes the authority of the New Testament as a witness to the contents and character of the Christian faith; it assigns to Jesus Christ the central position and the supreme value in the revelation of God to man; and it insists on religious experience as the essential condition of theological construction. In its opposition to speculative rationalism, on the one hand, it asserts the personality of God, the reality of sin and guilt, and of grace and miracle, the unique value of Christ as revealing God, and the essential significance of the Christian community. It has, on the other hand, legitimately exposed and condemned what is unsound in some forms of pietism. Its defects, briefly stated, are as follows: It does not recognize the necessity for unity of thought, and thus the legitimacy of philosophy as an ally of theology. Consequently, much of its criticism of ecclesiastical dogma is misdirected. In condemning what is unsound in religious mysticism it seems to set itself in opposition to the essential necessity of the religious life—intimate and constant communion with God. It fails to appropriate all the contents of the Christian revelation, being led by its too narrow conception of religion, and its undue restriction of the range of Christian experience, to neglect or reject facts or truths that do nourish and exercise faith. In avoiding a speculative treatment of Christian doctrine it often refuses to give the rational explanation which completes the empirical account of the objects of faith, and so arrests theological inquiry at an earlier stage than the interests of religion even demand, as notably in the doctrine of the person of Christ.

While Ritschl himself seriously modified or entirely rejected some of the generally accepted evangelical positions, many of his disciples have not followed him in this; and for the most part are in closer contact and more vital sympathy with the common religious life of the German churches, in which the Ritschlian school is a reviving influence. The hope may be cherished that the more positive tendency in the school will be so developed as to give us a theology which, while not less receptive of, and responsive to, contemporary phases of thought, will yet preserve more completely, and exhibit more adequately, the Christian revelation in its permanence as divine and its adaptability as human.

As a number of English-speaking divinity students visit the German universities, and many British and American theologians read German theological literature, the Ritschlian influence was felt in the British Isles and the United States before English translations of the Ritschlian literature began to attract general attention. The translation of the first volume of Ritschl's "Justification and Reconciliation" seems to have made no impression. A criticism of Ritschl, Stählin's "Kant, Lotze and Ritschl," ineffective through its violence, when translated in 1889, stirred no interest. Only when translations of Kaftan's "The Truth of the Christian Religion" (1894), Herrmann's "The Communion of the Christian with God" (1895), and Harnack's "History of Dogma" (1894-1900),) appeared, did the interest in the movement become more general. Probably Professor Orr has done more than any other writer to spread knowledge about Ritschl, and the wide range of his influence makes it all the more regrettable that his judgment is so unfavorable. The adverse criticisms of the Ritschlian theology in so popular a work as Professor Denny's "Studies in Theology" has still more widely extended the prejudice against this school. The writer of this article has endeavored in his book on "The Ritschlian Theology" to show Ritschl in a more favorable light, and so to win for him the attention which he deserves. Professor Swing, in a brief study of the theology of

Ritschl, recently published, goes much further in unqualified praise. Articles for and against the movement are becoming common in theological magazines. The translation of the most important of the three volumes of "Justification and Reconciliation," which appeared some months ago, is greatly stimulating the interest in what is increasingly being felt to be a timely and helpful influence. When the intellectual conditions of the age are estranging so many thoughtful men from the faith of the Christian Church, what seeks to be an apologetic "in relief of doubt" and in help of faith, demands at least patient and unprejudiced study. It is not probable, nor is it desirable, that theology in English-speaking countries should be dominated by Ritschl; but it will be profitable for all theologians to get suggestion and stimulus from contact with so vigorous a personality, so original a thinker, and so genuine a Christian.

PHILLIPS BROOKS: Alexander V. G. Allen.

Phillips Brooks was born in Boston in 1835, and on both sides of his family was the heir of a long line of distinguished Puritan ancestry. When he was four years old the family became connected with the Episcopal Church. He graduated from Harvard College in 1855, whence he went to the Theological Seminary in Virginia, graduating there in 1859, and at once entering upon the ministry as rector of the Church of the Advent, in Philadelphia. In 1862 he was called to the Church of the Holy Trinity in Philadelphia, and in 1869 he became rector of Trinity Church, Boston, holding this position until his election as Bishop of Massachusetts in 1891. He died in 1893 at the age of fifty-seven. His published writings include eight volumes of sermons, the Bohlen Lectures on the "Influence of Jesus," lectures on "Toleration," etc. Since his death his miscellaneous writings have been collected in one volume with the title of "Essays and Addresses." His biography appeared in two volumes in 1900.

The distinctive work of Phillips Brooks was mainly done in the pulpit, which he occupied as a conspicuous throne for more than thirty years. His place in history is among the few greatest preachers whom the Christian Church acknowledges from its beginning. In his preaching he resorted to no sensational methods, either of voice or matter, in order to arrest attention or enforce his message. He followed the conventionalities of the pulpit, turning them into sources of strength. He was pre-eminently a preacher to his own age, an age which had become doubtful in regard to supreme spiritual verities and found the formulas of the church irrational or distasteful. To such an age he commended Christianity and the religious life, faith in God and in man, with an almost irresistible power, compelling attention to his utterance by a singular gift of eloquence and by personal fascination. He became known, revered and loved throughout America, in England also, which he often visited, and, indeed, by his printed sermons his fame and influence extended throughout the world.

He could not have accomplished so great a result had he not been peculiarly adapted to his task. He understood his age; he was profoundly versed in literature which is the expression of the soul of humanity; he knew even the secret springs of the discontent which was undermining faith. His mind was as capacious as his heart, embracing with its comprehensive grasp the range and significance of all human interests. His natural preference would have been for the life of the scholar working at the world's problems, or the literary man uttering in the best forms the convictions and instincts of man. But his gifts in these directions he subordinated or held in check and reserved himself for the work of the preacher, a task whereto he was appointed not only by formal ordination, but by the voice of the world about him, which refused to allow him to abandon the pulpit.

While he was alive the world wondered at his mysterious power, exerted apparently by no effort; many also were the attempts made to fathom the secret of his strength and fascination, felt alike by cultured and uncultured people, by those of the highest education and by the lowest and poorest. Now that he is gone, the secret still baffles the inquiries into its sources. But at least it is possible to determine the distinctive, predominant character of his message. And in describing his work as a leader of men we need only fall back upon phrases familiar, so familiar that they might seem to have lost their meaning. Phillips Brooks was an instance of the constraining love of Christ, as with St. Paul; and he had the love of human souls. These two qualifications were his in an extraordinary degree beyond any other man of his generation. To these two endowments every sermon that he preached bore witness, never obscured by the literary charm with which he enveloped his theme.

In the preaching of Christ as the Saviour of the world he followed the evangelical method and was true to whatever was essential in its spirit. And yet he differed also, for he placed the supreme stress on the person of Christ, not upon any doctrine regarding him, although he held the traditional doctrines as true. Christ to him was the one towering personality in the world's history, who had given effect to his teaching by the power of his personality, and had thereby implanted in humanity the seed of spiritual life. To come into contact with Christ as a still living personality, whether in the church or in Scripture, or in the lives of faithful disciples, in all ages, was to be born again and to be alive unto God. To be in Christ was to fulfil all the rich purpose of manhood, the varied scope of regenerated humanity; to achieve the end of life. Although every sermon was devoted to setting forth this truth, yet so diverse were the variations upon it that his preaching never became monotonous, but was perennially fresh and absorbing. We must go behind the preacher, therefore, to the man himself, in order to get any comprehension of the secret of his power. When we do so we find a soul aflame with the love of Christ, in a faith simple and yet with the intensity of devotion which recalls the "ages of faith" before yet men had learned to doubt regarding spiritual realities. Although living in the modern world and himself a modern man, conversant with the best of modern literature, enjoying life as only a man with his rare endowments could do, yet we can easily think of him as at home in the age of the crusades, when the great ideal was to do something for the honor and glory of Christ, when a man gladly gave up his life in the effort to retrieve the Holy Sepulchre from disgrace. The man whom he most resembles in history is St. Francis of Assisi, who illustrated devotion to Christ in such personal and practical ways, to an extent never seen before, that it almost seemed as if he were a "second Christ." Such was the type of Phillips Brooks. We may see affinities in him to other great leaders in the church, but he differs from them in that he does not aim to establish a new doctrine or a new order. He proclaimed no renovation in theology as essential before the great work of salvation could begin. He simply showed men who Christ was, entering into His spirit and making Him live again in the modern world.

All this seems so simple and familiar that one might fail to see beneath it the evidence of profound thought and observation, a deep philosophical purpose, the intention to bring back the world again to its natural centre, or to the orbit from which it had wandered. The journals and notebooks of Phillips Brooks reveal an intellectual constitution capable of deep, clear insight into truths not obvious to the many—a subtle mind with a capacity for fine distinctions, a poetic mind finding in poetry the truest interpretation of life, but above all a man forever brooding on the mystery of life. Conjoined with this was his gift of incessant observation of life, whether in books or among living men. His well-trained mind, his classical culture, his wide reading, combined with his other gifts to fit him for a judge of what the world of his time needed and unconsciously demanded, was, indeed, waiting for, without knowing the sources of its unrest. He came to his age and pointed to Christ as the consummate personality in whom was the way, the truth, and the life. What all men wanted and needed was a leader whom they could follow, whose personal influence would reach every man in the ranks, and not only give the example, but the power to accomplish righteousness and salvation. Phillips Brooks did not enter much into argument, but he pointed to the one solvent for the difficulties of his time. In New England and wherever the transcendental philosophy had gone, there had resulted an over-intellectualism, whose influence in the end was spiritual bewilderment and loss. There had been an attempt to accomplish too much, so that the pinions of the soul had grown weary and men were falling again to the earth in disenchantment.

In his book on "The Influence of Jesus," Brooks pointed to the reality, tracing the power of the personal Christ, in history or in individual experience; for apart from the character and the person of Christ, his teaching would be of no avail. It was life, not thought or speculation, for which the world was hungering, and in Him was life. A certain spirit of fatalism had worked its way into the consciousness of men, and he presented Christ as the embodiment of human freedom. With the agnostic, who thought that nothing could be known or demonstrated as true in regard to these things, he did not reason, but he pointed to Christ, who believed them—God and immortality; and there he left them under the influence of One who must have known. He was in sympathy with the "New Theology," as it was called, but he maintained that no mere change of opinion in theology would make men better or more religious. He was a sturdy realist in an age confused by the multiplicity of ideals. At a time when intellect was overrated as a means of reaching the truth he maintained that the whole man, with organic totality of his powers, was appealed to by Christ, and that the intellect alone did not suffice. The weakness of the hour called for a reassertion of God as the commanding will in the universe, so that the highest glory of man lay in obedience, in the possession of a responding will.

With such a message it is not strange that the world responded to Phillips Brooks in an unusual way. The devotions of countless thousands went forth to him as to a heaven-sent leader. More particularly was this feeling manifested among the various denominations of Christians. He seemed to break down every barrier which divided men from each other, till nothing seemed more real than Christian unity. He had no faith in ecclesiastical expedients or adjustments as means by which the prayer of Christ could be fulfilled in order to the one fold and one Shepherd. But in the personal Christ and in allegiance to Him, so far as it was progressively realized, lay the reality of the brotherhood of men in church or state. In all this he was breaking down no creeds, nor forswearing the formulas of his own church. He saw beneath the creeds to their essential meaning, recognizing in them all a spiritual purpose, not for the disfranchisement of men, but toward their larger freedom. He was at home in the theological distinctions and refinements of controversy, nor did he scorn them as futile or meaningless, but he also simplified what had become to many a picture of confusion and hopeless contradiction, by the presentation of Christ as in Himself His religion. "Christ was Christianity," to use his own expression. When he died there was, as an observer of his funeral remarked, a more signal manifestation of Christian unity than the world had ever seen before.

DWIGHT LYMAN MOODY: A. C. Dixon, D.D.

[Dwight L. Moody would easily have reached the first rank in any vocation in life. In business he would have been a Vanderbilt or a Rockefeller; in politics, a senator, cabinet minister or president; in the army or navy, a Grant or a Farragut. He was born to command. He swayed an audience of ten or twenty thousands of people as by magic—not alone by his eloquence, but before he began to speak, by his personality. His judgment was as nearly infallible as seems ever given to man; his poise, common sense, instinctive grasp of a situation, foresight of results, were simply wonderful. In the technical or scholastic sense he had never been educated; but if education means gaining the best use of all one's powers, Mr. Moody was a superbly educated man. He made no false motions. Every blow that he struck carried its whole weight. Every sentence that he uttered counted for the full value of his great personality. Though most widely known as an evangelist, a preacher of power equal to the best traditions of the pulpit in any age, yet how far-reaching were his activities! The schools of Northfield and Mt. Hermon and Chicago—possibly his best monument—testify to his zeal for education. The valuation of the grounds and buildings is as follows: Seminary, $376,010; Mount Hermon, $450,932; Bible Institute, $195,301, a total of $1,021,243. How wisely and indefatigably he used the press! How eagerly he labored to put good reading into the cells of all our prisons! How his voice rang out for a pure patriotism! How prudently he encouraged every genuine reform! And how sweetly shrewd he was; how quick to penetrate every sham; how righteously intolerant of hypocrisy! If one characteristic more than any other marks Mr. Moody and his work, it is perfect genuineness. —TEUNIS S. HAMLIN, D. D. "The Congregationalist," Jan. 11, 1900.—ED.]

* * *

DWIGHT L. MOODY was born in Northfield, Mass., February 5, 1837, and died at the same place December 22, 1899. The Rev. Dr. H. G. Weston, president of Crozer Theological Seminary, in his address at the funeral of Mr. Moody, said: "I would rather be D. L. Moody dead in his coffin than any other man living on earth." And Dr. Weston, over seventy years of age, is known to be very careful in the use of words. Such men are not given to exaggeration.

Let us see what there was about D. L. Moody which justifies so conservative a man in making such a radical statement.

D. L. Moody was honest. He hated shams. He could not bear pretense. The first question he asked about everything was, "Is it right? Will Christ approve it?" He would do nothing that he did not believe to be right before God, and when he decided that a course was right, the consciousness of its righteousness caused him to throw all the energy of his great soul and vigorous body into it.

D. L. Moody was humble. He never boasted of his own powers. In early life he was informed that he had none to boast of. When he talked in prayer meetings his friends approached him and urged him to remain silent, for they thought he had no gift of public speech. This early discouragement may have had something to do with his self-depreciation, but I think that the secret of his humility was largely in the fact that he always had on hand great enterprises for God. He was not easily satisfied. What had been done was only the stepping stone to greater achievement. When a man becomes satisfied with what he has done in life, he is apt to grow proud of it. But Moody always stood in the presence of a great unfinished work. The magnitude of it made him look away from himself to

God. His great heart took in the United States and the world. He prayed for a revival in the nation. When he came into a city its millions of souls burdened his heart. He loved crowds because crowds gave him a great opportunity for doing good. A thousand conversions filled him with joy, but he could not be content with a thousand when there were hundreds of thousands still unsaved. Great preacher as he was, he was never satisfied with his sermons, because there was in his mind an ideal higher than anything he had ever reached.

D. L. Moody was practical. It was truly said of him, "He hitched his wagon to a star," but he kept the wheels on earth and its axles well oiled. He never made the mistake of the philosopher who, while gazing at the stars, fell into the ditch at his feet. He worked out his own salvation with fear and trembling, while God worked within him to will and to do. Enthusiasm never ran away with his judgment.

D. L. Moody was hopeful. I never saw him discouraged; if he was he never mentioned it. To him better times were always ahead. His face was toward the sunrise. He looked not at the darkness, but at the stars. He gazed not at the clouds, but on the rainbow. His hope was in God, and there was nothing too great for his God.

D. L. Moody was brave. God said to Joshua while he stood in the presence of danger, "Be of good courage," and the same God said to Solomon while he stood before great difficulties, "Be of good courage." It takes as great bravery to meet difficulties as danger. D. L. Moody would doubtless have been a brave soldier, going wherever duty called, but he was not called upon to do this. He did stand, however, frequently in the presence of great difficulties, and they never made him quail. He could stand alone with God. He delighted to consult with his brethren, and had an ear open to counsel, but his final decision was reached upon his knees, and when he took a stand nothing could move him. His denunciation of sin in high places brought upon him severe criticism, but he did not flinch; he simply repeated his charges with greater emphasis. He sought the favor and the praise of no man at the expense of conscience. He was popular with the rich and with the poor, because in his preaching he sought to please no one but God.

D. L. Moody was tolerant, but not through indifference, and "his tolerance was not the least of his remarkable characteristics," says "Zion's Herald." "Though a man of clear and decided religious tenets, and though he held his convictions with tenacity, yet he was comprehensive and considerate of variant theological opinions. Conservative in his opinions of the Bible, yet he was so large and so tolerant that he could 'find' Prof. Henry Drummond and give him Northfield for a pulpit, sending him forth as a 'son in the Gospel.' And later, when terror-stricken defenders of the faith were affrighted at the utterances of Prof. George Adam Smith, Moody invited him to Northfield to preach and to lecture. He was a robust, expulsive, apostolic disciple, a combination of much of the best of Peter and Paul, having Peter's burning zeal and consecration, but without his infirmities, for he never did nor could he have betrayed his Lord; not possessing Paul's culture of philosophy, but having his charity, brotherliness, and largeness of outlook for the Kingdom of Christ, and, like Paul, 'abundant in labors.' The world is inexpressibly richer for the life which he has lived and the work which he has done."

D. L. Moody was great in the Christly sense. Jesus said, "If any would be great among you, let him become the servant of all"; and the mission of Moody was to serve. His love of Jesus was a passion, and he loved people because Jesus loved them. All he was and had was on the altar of sacrifice. He never spared himself. No one who knew him ever accused him of seeking money for himself. He lived and died a poor man, while he raised and passed on millions for the uplifting of others. The fact that he was without early educational advantages led him to sympathize with poor young men and women, and to establish colleges where they could secure education at small cost. A large book might be written on Moody as a builder. There is scarcely a great city in Christendom which has not some building erected with money raised in response to his prayer and work.

"D. L. Moody," says "The Outlook," "was a religious preacher, not a theological teacher; and the character of his work is to be measured, not by its theological structure, but by its religious power. The difference ought to be as self-evident as it is simple. The theological questions are such as these: What was the nature of the influence exerted by the Spirit of God on the minds of the writers of the Bible? What is the relation of Jesus Christ to the Infinite and Eternal Ruler of the universe? How do the life, passion, and death of Jesus Christ effect a saving influence on the character and destiny of mankind? The religious questions are: How can I best use the Bible to make better men and women? What is Jesus Christ to me, and what can He be to my fellow men? What can I do to make available to myself the influence of His life and character in securing a purer character and a diviner life for myself and for those about me? It would be difficult to name any man in the present half century who has done so much to give the power of spiritual vision to men who having eyes saw not and having ears heard not, to give hope to men who were living in a dull despair, or an even more fatally dull self-content, and to give that love which is righteousness and that righteousness which is love to men who were before unqualifiedly egotistical and selfish. With him the theology was never an end, always an instrument. If any liberal is inclined to criticise his theology, let him consider well with himself whether he is doing as good work for humanity with his more modern and, let us say, better instruments."

D. L. Moody was a prophet. He spoke for God. His message was the whole Bible. He believed it to be the Word of God. It was easy for him to accept its miracles, for the God who wrote the Book was equal to anything that it claimed for him. Like Spurgeon, he was never ordained by the laying on of human hands. His ordination was of God. "The hand of the Lord was upon him." He had no sympathy with the critics who tear the Bible to pieces. There were among them some of his friends, whom he loved in spite of their errors. But his friendship for them never made him swerve from his loyalty to the Bible. He believed in God the Holy Spirit, who inspired men to write the Book, and who is with us ready to endue with power in preaching it. Moody did not despise other books, and he read more widely than some people suppose. But all other books compared with the Book were weak things. He was emphatically a man of one book, and because he honored God's Word, God honored him.

D. L. Moody had a message of salvation by grace. He believed that sinners are saved, if saved at all, by the unmerited favor of God. He magnified mercy. His was a gospel of blood. I heard him say that he once went to a place in Great Britain where he was told by one of the prominent preachers that it would never do for him to say much about blood in that place. Moody told him without hesitation that he would preach it in every sermon, and he magnified atonement through the blood until the whole town was shaken by the power of God. He frequently said that when a preacher ceased to preach the blood, he began to be powerless in his ministry. The great effort of his life was to induce sinners to take shelter under the blood. His sermons on the blood have won thousands to Jesus. He denounced as a fatal error the illusion that men can be saved by character without the blood of Christ.

D. L. Moody brought to the world a message of regeneration. He magnified the work of the Spirit in the new birth. He was not a reformer; he thought little of the efforts at reforming society by programme or law. With him the regeneration of the individual was everything. When men are saved, they will become good citizens and good fathers. He believed with all his heart in instantaneous conversion. He declared that somewhere between the top of that sycamore tree and the ground Zaccheus became a Christian. He emphasized the sudden conversion of the jailer, the eunuch, the three thousand on the day of Pentecost. Indeed, he believed in no other kind of conversion than that which comes suddenly; that it is not possible to cultivate the old nature into a state of grace; we must receive the Divine nature by an act of faith. The proof of this reception and the evidence to the individual consciousness may come gradually, but every one accepts Jesus at some definite time.

D. L. Moody brought to the weary, burdened toilers of earth a message of heaven. He looked forward to its rest and its righteousness. He cared little for this world, because he looked for "the city which hath foundations, whose builder and maker is God." His citizenship was in heaven. He loved his home, and made it a little heaven on earth. His wife and children could hardly think of him as the great man that he was, he was so loving and gentle and tender. The home on earth he prized, but the home in heaven he prized more. The fallacy so prevalent that we should make the best of this world and leave heaven to take care of itself received no sympathy from him. His real world was "the building of God, the house not made with hands, eternal in the heavens." As friend after friend passed through the gates, he became more attached to the "Father's House." The death of his little grandchild broke his heart, while it brightened heaven and made him more willing to go.

His last words will be immortal: "Earth is receding; heaven is opening; God is calling me. Do not call me back." What a commotion his entrance into heaven must have made! While on earth he preached with his voice to millions of people, and through his pen to millions more. How many millions have been saved through his words and life no one can tell, but certainly he received an abundant entrance into the city of life and light. He has seen the King in His beauty. The yearning in his soul that he might be like Him has been satisfied.

MOVEMENTS CRITICAL AND ETHICAL.

Prof. George H. Schodde, Ph.D.,
COLUMBUS.

[Freedom to criticise and reconstruct the text of Holy Scripture; freedom to re-investigate traditional opinions concerning the dates and the authorship of the sacred books of the Old and New Testament; freedom to revise and amend the traditional interpretation of their contents; freedom to revise and amend definitions of great Christian doctrines by whatever venerable authorities the definitions may be sanctioned; this must be conceded—conceded frankly, not under compulsion, but with the full consent of the judgment, the conscience and the heart. The public opinion of the church should be friendly to intellectual integrity in its theological scholars. It is better that they should reach a false conclusion by fair means than a true one by foul. Truth itself is not the truth to the man who has been disloyal to his intellectual conscience in the formation of his belief.

We have learned much from the saintly theologians of past generations; we may learn much from the saintly theologians of our own time; and we must be willing to learn, or God will not give us new teachers. Yet the fathers were not infallible; and modern theologians are but men. We have it on excellent authority that even general councils "may err, and sometimes have erred, even in things pertaining to God;" nor can exemption from error be claimed for great critical scholars brilliant with genius and learning; they must consent to have what they confidently proclaim as "the final results" of criticism, examined, tested, controverted, and sometimes rejected by their successors.—R. W. Dale, LL.D., "Fellowship with Christ," p. 109.—Ed.]

* * *

The critical movements in the theological world during the nineteenth century all find their common bond of unity in the noteworthy facts that they concerned themselves not about any particular doctrine or doctrines of the Scriptures, but that the Scriptures themselves constituted the debatable ground between the various trends and tendencies. Essentially the purpose of critical inquiry has been to answer the question: "What are the Scriptures?" These have been the cynosure of all eyes, and it is no exaggeration to claim that never before has the Written Word been the object of such penetrating and subtle investigation as has been the case during the past ten decades. The canonical books of the Old and New Testaments have been the central problem of research as never before.

Not indeed is this to be understood as though the Bible had never before been a chief concern of theological investigation; but it is a fact that never before have the Scriptures been examined so minutely from the historical and literary point of view as has been done in our day. In the Reformation period, too, they were the subject of the most vigorous debate, but the issue at stake was not the origin or the literary character and development of the Biblical books, but the authority of the Bible as a whole over against the principle of tradition as taught by the Roman Catholic Church. The outcome of the whole discussion was the formal principle of the Reformation, which has practically controlled Protestant thought ever since, namely, that the Scriptures and these alone are the source of Christian doctrines and morals. That the discussion of that period should take this course with reference to the Scriptures was the most natural and necessary thing in the world. Protestantism needed a sure foundation to take the place of the authority of the Roman Catholic hierarchy, which had been rejected, and found this authority and basis for its very existence in the Scriptures as the sure revelation of God. Then, as now, the fundamental fact was recognized that these Scriptures are the joint product of two factors, a divine and a human, but the former was regarded as the all-controlling element in the composition of the Biblical books, that the presence and activity of the human element was practically eliminated. In other words, the Reformation and the Reformers saw in the Bible only the Word of God, which because it was such could be trusted absolutely, as its very character of inerrancy made any appeal to other sources unnecessary and impossible. The practical interests of the Reformation prevailed also in its conception and ideas of the Scriptures. Even of the question of the Old Testament Apocrypha, contained in the Greek or Alexandrian, but not in the Hebrew and Palestinian canon, which the Protestant Church of that period rejected as not belonging to the real Word of God, there is found in the literature of the period practically no formal discussion. Luther's works in the Erlangen edition fill one hundred solid volumes, yet we nowhere have from his pen anything like critical or historical discussion of the Apocrypha or other literary problem of the Scriptures.

The characteristic peculiarity of the Bible work done by the scholarship of the nineteenth century is that it has for the first time emphasized to the fullest extent the human side of the Scriptures.

The fact has been recognized as never before that although holy men of God wrote as they were moved by the Spirit, they nevertheless were men; that the books of the Bible indelibly show the impress of a human as well as a divine authorship; that these books all have a history. To determine these factors and to do justice to them in formulating any definition or description of the Biblical books has been the leading ideal of the critical research of our times. This spirit of historical inquiry stands in the closest possible touch with the general trend and tendency of the learned research of the day. Without doubt the most potent agency in the character of modern scholarship has been the idea of historical development. Essentially we are living in the era of Darwin. For good and for bad this trend has made itself felt in the Scriptural investigations of the century as never before and has given these their distinct character. It is not at all accidental that among the new sciences in theology, probably the most important is that of Biblical theology, the gradual unfolding of the truths of revelation and the different phases and forms which these truths assumed in various periods and in the hands of different exponents. The historical side of the Scriptures has been studied and understood by no generation of scholars as thoroughly as at present. The earlier Protestant Church, beginning with the Reformation era, had no interest in this problem, as the Scriptures were to them chiefly a codex of proof passages; but the historical spirit of modern scholarship compelled the church to investigate this phase of the Bible problem too; and the emphasis, greater or less, that is laid upon the human and historical side of the Written Word really causes the difference between the various Biblical schools of the times. For, quite naturally, from this new point of view taken of the Scriptures, some teachings concerning them, which were based on the traditional method of regarding these books as a whole, have been more or less modified. Among these teachings are the doctrines of inspiration, of inerrancy, of the unity of Scripture, of the absolute uniqueness of its contents, of the hermeneutical principle of the analogy of the Scriptures, and others. Just in proportion as any school or class of Bible students emphasize the human element over against the divine, even to the extent of allowing the failings and weaknesses of the human to appear in the contents of the Scriptures, to this degree, too, is the radicalism of a school marked. The differences and distinctions between the various schools of the day do not consist in this, that the one or the other has a greater abundance of facts at its command, but solely in the methods and manners in which these facts are interpreted. All schools have essentially the same knowledge of the contents of the Scriptures, but the one in interpreting these contents will ascribe to human agency and understand accordingly what another will ascribe to the divine. Thus Delitzsch and Wellhausen both were thoroughly at home in reference to the actual contents and literary history of the Old Testament; yet the former saw in these and behind these facts the special workings of Jehovah educating Israel for the fullness of times and the reception of the Messiah, while Wellhausen makes such a combination and interpretation of these same facts that the result is to all intents and purposes a naturalistic reconstruction scheme of the whole Old Testament historical development. The difference between these two eminent representatives of the opposing clans is one of "standpoint," of underlying principles, and not one of learning, critical acumen or knowledge.

This great work of studying the human side of the Scriptures rather than the divine, has been done in the two leading departments of Lower and Higher Criticism, both of which have fully occupied the attention of the learned world during the entire century. Historically and logically the Lower or textual criticism precedes the Higher or literary and historical criticism. The first of these disciplines, so-called merely because it naturally precedes the second, aims at a restoration of the text of the books of the Bible to a form nearly as accurate as scientific methods can bring it to the autographs as these come from the hands and the pens of the Prophets and Apostles. The object is the same that a good classical scholar has when he edits a Thucydides or a Livy. The problem itself is entirely the same whether a scholar edits a Latin or Greek classic, or the New Testament books, and substantially the principles and methods in both instances are identical. Only in the case particularly of the New Testament is the task more difficult, partly on account of the importance of the matter itself, where sometimes a single letter may change the reading of a whole verse, as in Luke ii, 14, and partly on account of the "embarrassment of riches" which are at the disposal of a New Testament editor, who, in addition to a mass and multitude of other excellent aids, has, as Gregory, in his new "Text-Kritik der Neuer Testaments," page 3, states, no fewer than three thousand Greek manuscripts alone, no two of which are absolutely alike throughout, but together, as Schaff, in his "Companion to the Greek Testament," page 177, shows, have about 150,000 variants. Lower Criticism has for a century and more been trying to select from this immense number those which, according to acknowledged canons of literary criticisms, are probably the original readings of these books.

It is a singular fact that the application of this science to the Bible text has all along met with more or less opposition, although in almost every particular textual criticism has rendered conservative scholarship excellent services. A scrupulous examination of these tens of thousand of variants has demonstrated the fact that only about four hundred of them materially affect the sense; that not more than fifty are really important for one reason or the other; and that even of these fifty not one affects an article of faith or a moral precept which is not abundantly sustained by other and undoubted passages and by the whole tenor of the Scriptural teachings. Ezra Abbot, the greatest textual critic of America, and as a Unitarian certainly not hampered by orthodox bias, declares that "no Christian doctrine or duty rests on those portions of the text which are affected by differences in the manuscripts; still less is anything essential in Christianity touched by the various readings." Even if the textual criticisms of the nineteenth century had only rendered this negative service of demonstrating that the New Testament is invulnerable from what seemed to be to many in former generations its weakest side, it is entitled to a high rank among the useful theological discipline. But its greatest service has been the positive work of furnishing what is practically a critical *textus receptus* and of having given us the New Testament books in a better and more trustworthy shape than any other century since the Apostolic period possessed them.

The names that stand out prominently in this department of Biblical research during the present century are especially those of Tischendorf, Tregelles and Wescott-Hort, although there are others who deserve mention, such as Scrivener, von Gebhardt, Gregory, Weiss, Nestle and others. Nor has the work been entirely done during these hundred years. To a certain extent textual criticism, at least of the New Testament, is an inherited problem from preceding ages, which in men like Bengel have representative scholars in this respect. But the real work, and especially the development of scientific methods in this work, has been done in the nineteenth century, and in the combined efforts and practically uniform and almost unanimous resultant text of the Tischendorf, the Tregelles and the Wescott-Hort editions, we have the ripest and richest fruits of the century in reference to the New Testament text. It is true that not all of this work has been constructive in the sense that it has led in everything to a retention of the old but uncritical text of former generations, but it has been constructive in this, that everywhere it has sought to restore what were really the *ipsissima verba* of the Biblical writers. Textual criticism has indeed eliminated the doxology of the Lord's Prayer, the closing verses of the Gospel of St. Mark, the pericope of the woman caught in adultery, in the fourth Gospel, the Trinity passage in John's Epistle; but also these have been dropped simply because they are not in harmony with the contents of the best manuscripts.

In the prosecution of this discipline, it is remarkable that the practical work has almost entirely crowded out the theoretical. It is only now, in the new book of Textual Criticism, by the famous American representative in the Leipzig Theological Faculty, Professor Caspar René Gregory, that we are receiving a perfectly complete and satisfactory exposition of the facts, the principles and the practices of New Testament textual criticism, although the Plain Introduction of Scrivener and the smaller work of Warfield are good as far as they go. It is this lack of perfect clearness of the underlying principles that has to a greater or less extent given the results of the practical work in this department the appearance of some uncertainty. In the English school headed by Dean Burgon, the attempt was made, but in a very arbitrary manner, to undermine the principles and the results of the textual criticism of the times in favor of the old traditional readings throughout, especially attacking the authority of the leading older manuscripts, such as the Vaticanus, and the methods in vogue in estimating the weight and character of the variant readings of these sources. This school has virtually ceased to exist, but a new tendency has sprung up, advocated especially by the classical philologian, Blass, of Hallé, who, on the basis of the peculiar readings of the famous Codex Bezæ, or D, in Cambridge, representing, with some Latin translations, a certain Oriental type of readings, maintains that Luke himself published two editions of both the Acts and of the third Gospel. This view concerning the prominence to be assigned to this codex has been expanded, particularly by Nestle, in his "Einführung in das Neue Testament," and elsewhere, to the proposal that the entire New Testament text should be revised in accordance with the D group of manuscripts. While some few, such as Zöckler, of Greifswald, have in part at least expressed their agreement with the two-edition theory of Blass, the demand for a revision of the entire New Testament text along new lines has found very little favor. Gregory (*l. c.,* p. 47) declares it to be his judgment that "there is no justification for this tendency." The fact that the textual criticism of the century has produced tangible and satisfactory results in the shape of a critical reliable text—at any rate, as reliable as the vast abundance of facts and data at the disposal of modern learning can possibly make—this is manifestly the rich fruits of investigation in this department, which is not the least rendered doubtful by the independent action of a few acknowledged scholars in reference to the New Testament text, notably the veteran and venerable Bernhard Weiss, of Berlin, who in an eclectic manner has recently, after continuous labor of ten years, published a new edition of the entire New Testament canon.

In the textual criticism of the Old Testament the object has been the same, namely, the restoration of the original readings as far as possible, but the means and methods of attaining this end have been different and the results attained have not been as substantial and successful as was the case in the New Testament field. In this latter department the chief critical helps were the manuscripts; in the Old Testament textual criticism the manuscripts occupy a most subordinate position, and the first position in the critical apparatus of the text belongs to the old translations, especially the Septuagint or old Greek version. The reason for this lies in the singular fact that we have no manuscripts of any part or portion of the Hebrew text of the Old Testament earlier than the ninth or tenth Christian centuries, so that between the close of the Jewish canon and the oldest form extant of the written text a period of thirteen hundred and more years intervenes, while in the New Testament department the time between the Apostles' autographs and the earliest manuscripts is three hundred years or less, and the hope of some time discovering these autographs themselves has not altogether been discarded. Accordingly, the solution of the textual problem in the case of the Old Testament became something quite different from that of the New, and respecting the former the old versions, at least the Greek of the Seventy, brought the text up to a few hundred years from the time that the latest books of the Hebrew canon were penned. But in this unique character of the problem lay also its difficulty, as nothing could be done for the Old Testament text until the old versions themselves had been critically examined and edited. This is a peculiarly difficult task in the case of the Septuagint, as there are three recensions of this version, and the determination of which is the original form is as yet unsolved, although it has engaged the acumen of a Lagarde. On account of the immature shape and condition of the critical helps that must be depended upon for work in this department, the critical work on the Old Testament text has been done rather tentatively and experimentally, and in many cases subjective reasonings have produced radical proposals not justified by any objective data in the sources. In most circles the conviction prevails that the Old Testament text, as it has been handed down to us traditionally by the Massoretic school, is substantially correct and requires little or no emendations; and nothing that has been discovered in any literary source is hostile to this position. The changes that have been proposed in the Old Testament text are almost entirely those of conjectural criticism and have the common faults and failures of subjective methods of research. This is both the strength and the weakness of the text of the so-called "Rainbow" or Polychrome Bible, edited by Professor Haupt, of the Johns Hopkins University, and prepared by an international company of savants. In so far as it amends the text there is rarely any ground except the convictions of the editor as to what the text ought to be. Even more radical are some of the efforts made at a revised text of particular books by some other scholars, especially by Cornill in his edition of Ezekiel, but much less by Workman in his Jeremiah. Wellhausen's emendations of the text of Samuel is a work of rare scholarship on one of the most difficult textual problems of the Old Testament. But, taking all the researches together that have been made in reference to the text of the Old Testament, it can be fairly stated that no substantial reasons have been discovered for making any material changes in this text. Negatively, at least, the Hebrew Massoretic text stands firmer now than ever. This is substantially the outcome of the textual researches in the Old Testament department.

But the nineteenth has been eminently the century of Higher Criticism, and no theological movement has aroused an interest equal in depth and width to that called forth by the methods and results of the higher critics. It has become the international problem that vexes and perplexes Christianity. In marked contrast to

Lower or textual criticism, the claims and teachings of the higher critics have penetrated the masses and the congregations, and there have met with favor or disfavor that is pronounced in its expression. Textual criticism has all along remained essentially the work of the theologian and the specialist, and it appealed but to a limited degree to the concern of the rank and the file of the ministry or the laity, who knew practically nothing of its workings except as some evidences appeared in new translations and especially omissions in the Revised Version. On the other hand Higher Criticism affects directly the vital interests of Christianity at large. Such fundamentals as the inspiration and inerrancy of the Scriptures, the unity of their teachings, their reliability as sources of history and even of religious matters, are all more or less influenced by the spirit and the results of the Higher Criticism of the day. As a result, this science is a sign that is spoken against and in many cases its very right of existence is called into question.

And yet all this opposition is really directed against the abuse, but not against the use, of the Higher Criticism. This discipline, rather, is an important and indispensable tool in the workshop of the student of God's word. Every thorough student of the Scriptures is and must be a higher critic. It is very unfortunate that this name has been popularly selected as a term of reproach, at least of distrust, for a theological discipline that belongs to the oldest sciences in this department. In reality it is no "higher" than textual criticism; these two auxiliaries of Bible study are co-ordinate, and not one the superior or inferior of the other. The term itself is rarely if ever applied to it by its friends or by those who cautiously or carefully make use of this discipline as the best interests of Biblical research demand. A much better term would be historical or historico-literary criticism, as this name would express the leading functions of the science. It is not a science with esoteric principles and processes for the discovery of truth not accessible to the ordinary Bible reader, but merely the application to the Scriptures of the critical canons that prevail in the interpretation of other literary works of antiquity or even of modern times. If, *e. g.*, the student of Herodotus examines the writings of this historian in the light of what is known of their author, his times and surroundings, his literary methods, and the records of the nations he describes, such a process is nothing but Higher Criticism. If, again, the student of Cicero's letters studies the historical surroundings of these writings, as also their style, contents, etc., for the purpose of understanding all the better their real lessons, this again is nothing but Higher Criticism. The scholar who, like the late Professor Green or like Professors Hengstenberg and Keil, defends the Mosaic authorship of the Pentateuch on internal grounds is just as much a higher critic as are those who from data drawn from such an analysis of these books maintain that they are productions of the post-Mosaic period. That which made the work done in this department so obnoxious to the great bulk of conservative Christians is the fact that this science has been handled not according to objective facts or principles, but that certain philosophical ideas and ideals have been injected into its application. In this way the New Testament school of Baur, of Tübingen, which made the Christianity of the later books of the New Testament and of the Apostolic period the result of a compromise between two antagonistic principles or schools, the Jewish of Peter and the Gentile of Paul, that prevailed in the earliest church, was really nothing but the Hegelian philosophy of history applied to the New Testament records, the facts and contents of which were forced into the Procrustean bed of this philosophical scheme. In the same way the Wellhausen-Kuenen reconstruction of the Old Testament religious development, which is now the battle ground of the contending hosts in Biblical science, is practically little more than the application of Darwinian natural selection in the interpretation of what the Old Testament books teach. It is this injection of philosophical subjectivism into the higher critical methods and manners that has aroused the antagonism which modern Higher Criticism, in its more or most radical phases, amply deserves. But the course of investigation has demonstrated that this Higher Criticism, when prosecuted along legitimate lines and in a sober and reasonable spirit, can be productive only of good. The history of the Baur or Tübingen movement shows this beyond a doubt. A generation ago the New Testament was the field in which the higher critics operated, and where Christianity was attacked in its very essentials and fundamentals. Baur accepted only four of the Pauline Epistles as genuine, namely, Romans, the two Corinthians and Galatians; all others were in his eyes spurious and forgeries, and on the basis of this readjustment of the literary sources of early Christianity he erected his theological scheme that virtually brought Christ's teachings and original Christianity in pronounced conflict with that of the New Testament literature and of the Christian Church. The most extreme radicalism of this school found its expression in the famous or rather infamous book of Strauss, "The Life of Christ," which practically reduced the records concerning the life and the teachings of Jesus to a myth. It was this school of higher critics that forced Christian scholars to investigate the sources of their creed and faith as never before. The New Testament itself, as the entire body of Patristic and early Christian literature, had to be examined anew with a detail investigation and research that had never obtained in theological science. And the result has been more than beneficial to the church and its faith. The credibility and authenticity of the New Testament books now stand firmer than ever before; the renewed examination of this field led to a gradual reaction against the radical proposals of the Tübingen school and, above all, to a better knowledge of the real character of New Testament books and the grounds for their claim to be Apostolic and authoritative writings. What this counter movement and reinvestigation has led to can be best seen in three magnificent works that have appeared within the last few years, namely, the "Chronology of Early Christian Literature," by the brilliant Harnack, of Berlin; the "Introduction to the New Testament," by the recently deceased Professor Godet, and the massive work of Professor Zahn, of Erlangen, with the same title. The latter two defend the New Testament books throughout and substantially as the church has believed in them for centuries, and particularly does the splendid work of Zahn deserve mention in this regard. Such a mastery of the original sources and such an abundance of data and details from the earliest sources, and all confirmatory of the traditional views of the church in general, have never been equaled in theological lore, and stamp this grand work as one of the most learned that the world has ever produced. Harnack is generally regarded as an exponent of critical theology, and this estimate is correct. Yet he accepts the entire New Testament collection of books as authentic with the sole exception of Second Peter, although he does not regard the fourth Gospel in its present shape as the work of John, nor the Pastoral Epistles in the form in which we now possess them as penned by the Apostle Paul. Yet what a wonderful change there has been in this respect within recent years! The tendency has been steadily and persistently in the direction of the older views, and the radical phases of New Testament Higher Criticism have been eradicated by the more moderate claim of scholars in this department. Not, indeed, in the sense that nothing of

Baur's teachings has been left. In all radical movements that show the least vitality and life there is an element of truth, the exaggeration and misinterpretation of which constitute the stock in trade. This element of truth always remains as a residuum when the radicalism has been thoroughly filtered, and becomes a fixed fact in theological science. The Tübingen school emphasized as had never before been done the different tendencies that prevailed in the early Christian Church, and the fact that there were in existence a Pauline theology, a Petrine theology and a Joannine theology in primitive Christianity is now admitted on all hands, but not in the sense of the Tübingen school, as antagonistic tendencies, but as expressions of the one common faith, but from different points of view. There can be scarcely a doubt that when once the Old Testament discussions shall have advanced to the stage which the New has attained, that then, too, the element of truth in the Wellhausen theory will be acknowledged and become a permanent possession of Christian theology. That this controversy and debate has already been productive of much good in certain directions is an undeniable fact. The historical side of the Scriptures; the fact that they are not only a revelation, but also the history of a revelation; the gradual development of this revelation through various historical phases and stages; the connection of the Old Testament books with the thought and the life of the times that produced them, and especially the understanding of the externals of the Scriptures, such as history, chronology, archæology, etc., in the light of the recovered treasures from the ruins of the former civilizations of the Nile and the Tigris-Euphrates valleys—all these and many more things are better understood concerning the Old Testament now than ever before. A proper estimate, however, of this additional knowledge can only be made when it is remembered that all the new sources that the Higher Criticism of the times has made available cannot and do not touch what must be for the church the main and the chief things in the Scriptures, namely, the revelation of the mysteries of God, the Trinity, the Personal Work of Christ, the Plan of Salvation, Atonement, Justification, Sanctification, etc.—all these have gained nothing through the external sources to which Higher Criticism appeals, and only to a limited extent by the internal criticism and investigations as conducted by this school.

In both the New and the Old Testament Higher Criticism, much stress has been laid on the literary analyses of the various books, and, indeed, this has been made the basis for the different theories that have been advanced. The father of this tendency was the French Roman Catholic physician, Astruc, who in his work on the "Sources Which Moses Seems to Have Employed in the Composition of the Pentateuch" sounded the keynote of the whole modern criticism. This principle of an analysis of a book into parts of which it is claimed to have been composed has been applied in the Old Testament much more than in the New. In the latter, serious attempts in this direction have been made only in the case of the Acts and the Apocalypse, although a similar process is advocated for Second Corinthians and a few other books. In the New Testament department the chief literary question is the Synoptic Problem, which seeks to determine the literary dependence or independence of the three Synoptic Gospels. The outcome has been this, that the largest consensus favors the older form of Mark—Ur-Markus—and the "Sayings" of Matthew, a Hebrew collection of quotations from Christ's teachings, as the basis of the three Gospels as we have them now in their canonical form. In the Old Testament the analytical method has been applied to almost every book, and in some cases, as in the Pentateuch, the Book of Isaiah, the Psalms, has led to entirely new adjustment of the contents of these books and their place in Hebrew literature and their teachings concerning the development of the Old Testament religion. In the Wellhausen scheme the Levitical system is the last element in the literature of the Old Testament, this scheme thus literally turning topsy-turvy the common and traditional view of the church as founded on the position taken by the Jews of the New Testament period and by the Christ and His Apostles.

The nineteenth century has thus brought to a certain and satisfactory close the work of investigating the New Testament, although naturally much yet remains to be done in details and particulars. It has given us an excellent critical text of the New Testament on the basis of the best sources extant; and it has given us the best defence of the New Testament books that the world has ever seen. In the Old Testament such progress has not yet been made, neither in Lower nor in Higher Criticism. The latter is still the great debatable land between the conservative and the advanced scholar, and the twentieth century will have much work yet to do in this field, notwithstanding the fact that the advocates of the more or less radical type of Old Testament research are accustomed to claim that their teachings are the "sure" result of accurate scientific methods. They are constantly being attacked by those who favor older views, and it can fairly be stated that a reaction against them has set in. As yet this reaction is—at least in Germany, which has been the headquarters of all innovations in this department for decades—confined to the rank and file of the church, and has not yet reached the universities. At these centres of thought there are indeed many opponents of radicalism and friends of evangelical and positive Biblical science; but none of these is willing to defend the old positions, such as the verbal inspiration of the Scriptures, the Mosaic authorship of the Pentateuch, the composition of Isaiah xl-lxvi, by the prophet of that name, etc. But even at the universities the sober second thought is beginning to exhibit itself in connection with detail researches, and the prospects are that it will prove contagious and spread, as was the case among the New Testament men.

Outside of the purely Biblical department, no critical movement of the nineteenth century equals in importance that which is connected with the name of Albrecht Ritschl, of the University of Göttingen, Germany. This is the new theology in the systematic field and has become practically an international school. Ritschl is the only theologian in Germany who, since the days of Schleiermacher, has managed to found a distinct "school," his only possible rival in this regard being Von Hofmann, of Erlangen. At bottom there is a deep-seated connection between the tendencies of modern theological thought as seen in the Biblical sciences and the new liberal theology of Ritschl. The greatest difference is this, that the former is based largely on the philosophy of the Darwinian school, while the latter is founded on the system of Kant. The great Königsberg philosopher wrote three leading works, namely, his "Critique of Pure Reason," his "Critique of Practical Reason" and his "Religion Within the Limits of Pure Reason." These three books complete and round off his whole system. The aim of the first work is to prove that all knowledge through perception (Erkenntniss) is confined to the range of our experience; and that consequently the doctrines of our religion, since these belong to a supernatural domain, cannot thus form the objects of knowledge proper. At the same time, Kant maintains that we are thus compelled to look to a subjective source for the fundamental conceptions of religion. To find these is the purpose of the second book, where it is maintained that in our natural consciousness we have immediate and imperative conceptions of a duty to observe a moral law, to accept God, freedom and immortality, not as objects of knowledge, but as moral postulates, *i. e.*, as the necessary preconditions of the moral law. The actual results of this theoretical standpoint Kant gives in his third book.

These fundamental positions of Kant, who holds in history the position of a father of rationalism, especially of that type of ethical rationalism which seeks, in a moral system demanded by consciousness, a substitute for the doctrines and dogmas of the Scriptures which the adherents of this school decline to accept—these positions have been adopted and applied to systematic theology by Ritschl, who has thus developed the leading ethico-systematic school of the century. His fundamental positions are these: (1) Metaphysics, being the science of things in themselves, are to be excluded from theology proper. We can know an agent only by its actions, and theology has to do only with *Werturtheile, i. e.*, judgments as to what a fact is worth to us practically, not with *Seinsurtheile, i. e.*, judgments of what the thing actually is. We can know what the benefits of the life and work of Christ are, but the real knowledge as to His superhuman being and character we cannot know. In this way the common definitions of theological science become something entirely new in the Ritschl system, the Divinity of Christ, *e. g.*, being only an expression for this idea, that He completely revealed God to the world according to the ethical purposes of God, and that He exercises ethical world supremacy. It is on this ground that the common charge is made against this system that it "empties" the central doctrines of Christianity of their positive and objective contents and puts in its place a moral system after the manner of the Kantian "Categorical Imperative" without the necessary Biblical and dogmatical substructure. But it is just this feature that makes it so attractive to younger minds who would like to accept the negative teachings of modern criticism and not discard the positive elements of the Christian system. This system seemingly solves the anomaly of much of modern advanced theology, which, as the German philosopher Jacobs says, demands that its adherents "must be Christians in their hearts, but unbelievers in their heads." The Ritschl system has captured the younger element in the theological world, not only in Germany, but also in French Switzerland and France proper (where it appears in the form of *la theologie de la conscience,* or the theology of consciousness), and to a certain extent in

England, America and the Scandinavian countries. Its second thesis is equally attractive, viz., (2) Religion and religious knowledge are based exclusively on ethical principles, which decides the fundamentally *ethical character* of this new theology.

With the sole exception of the Ritschl school, the nineteenth century has produced no distinctly ethical movement of a theoretical character that can claim to have made a decided impression on the thought of the age as such. Ethical problems have indeed engaged the attention of the theological and religious world, but usually in the shape of practical work. In this respect the nineteenth has been a century of progress in every direction, but in all such cases the actual work precedes the theoretical discussion of its principles. Thus, *e. g.*, this has certainly been the greatest missionary century since the days of the Apostles and the mission literature has been simply enormous, but it has only been in the last year or two that we have received the first systematic presentation of the principles and practices of missions as a science, this three-volume work being from the pen of the greatest living authority in this line, Professor G. Warneck, of the University of Hallé. In a similar manner the actual problems of Christian Sociology are receiving marked attention everywhere, in America, in Germany, in England, and that by all the leading churches, the Roman Catholic included; but a system of Christian Sociology has not yet been forthcoming and the movement has not yet attained the dignity of an independent phase of international modern theological thought. Other movements, such as that of Tolstoi in Russia and Nietsche in Germany, which aim at a change in the estimate of fundamental Christian ethical values, by that very fact are excluded from the category of Christian ethical agitations. Indeed, the work in this department has been nearly all of a practical kind, and in this respect the nineteenth century has a good record. Its chief work has been in the line of Biblical science, in which it has accomplished excellent results, but still leaves some leading problems, especially of Old Testament criticism and Biblical theology, for the twentieth to investigate.

THE RELIGIOUS PRESS.

WM. C. GRAY, Ph.D., LL.D.,
CHICAGO.

[The religious paper, however its methods may be modified, is a permanent form of journalism. The secular paper may pay increased attention to news of the churches; but, even though it should ultimately publish a weekly religious supplement—some day a newspaper proprietor will open his eyes and discover that there are as many people interested in religion as in literature—it can never make the definitely and aggressively religious organ unnecessary. For it is not a mere matter of news, but a question of tone and of standpoint. As Dr. Dunning puts it: "The great interests of the church, ethical, sociological, educational and missionary, have become essential elements of national life." These cannot be understood except by men who have given them careful study. Then it is impossible for any one paper to present the creedal distinctions which prevail. Still less could it deal adequately with theological problems, or supply devotional reading that would be acceptable in all quarters.

There is no reason, however, why there should not be a further grouping of literary effort among churches that are nearly allied. For example, the churches in England federated in the Free Church Council have enough in common to make such a union possible. The vast distances in this country will always prevent any Eastern weekly paper from circulating all over the United States to the same degree that a London paper circulates all over the United Kingdom. But if at Chicago, for example, there were published one strong, well-endorsed and well-equipped religious weekly, representing these various churches in the Middle West in the same way that "The Christian World" represents the Nonconformists of England, would it not exert a far stronger force in the promotion of righteousness than is at present exercised by all the religious papers of that city put together? The facility with which a minister in America passes from one denomination to another suggests the possibility of a larger union in literary enterprise than at present exists. This further appears possible in view of the growing tendency for denominational papers to be less destructive than formerly. As Henry Ward Beecher put it: to regard such differences as lines instead of walls.

Yet the denominational periodical, whatever may be its future, has made in the past a valuable contribution to popular education; not only giving an intellectual and a religious stimulus to its readers, but also in affording a literary training to its contributors.—H. W. HORWILL; "The Forum," July, 1901.—ED.]

THE first printed sheet taken off movable types was a text of Scripture, and the first printed book was the Bible. Therefore the press belongs to religion by right of discovery and occupation.

The beginnings of all literatures are wholly religious. The first poems were inspired by religion. So, also, the first traces of painting, the first outlines of sculpture, first masses of architecture, were inspired by religious longings. And so I might proceed with the whole round of the activities and achievements of the mind of man. So, also, I might show that the highest reaches in all the conquests of knowledge over the earth, over the seas and amid the starry heavens, were inspired and nerved by religion. I am justified in believing a truth which can be arrived at by other paths of thought, that the crowning triumph of the journalistic art is to be the religious newspaper.

The periodical press is a development out of the pamphlet. The pamphlet was originally a weapon of polemics. But as polemics and politics were intimately blended, so the pamphlet was an admixture of politics and religion. John Milton was the king of pamphleteers. His theme was God first, and then human rights. The first periodical newspaper, whatever may have been its character, was called the "Acta Diurna," and was published in manuscript in Rome, 1438-40. The first secular newspaper was either the "Frankfort Journal" or the "Neuremburg Gazette." They first appeared almost simultaneously, in the year 1457. The name "Neuremburg" suggests the fact that the topics which occupied the "Gazette" were not only religious, but religion in helmet and cuirass. The chief secular interest in Neuremburg was soon after the battle of the Reformation. But the newspapers, as time progressed, became more and more secular, and religious topics were left to the pulpit.

The first conception of a distinctly religious newspaper occurred to the mind of a secular journalist, Mr. Nathaniel Willis, of Boston, editor and publisher of the "Argus." Willis happened to hear a sermon preached by Rev. Edward Payson, in the year 1808, which convicted him of sin, and brought him to Christ. In those times the battle between the Federalists and Republicans was very truculent and bitter. Willis was a Republican, and when it came to political lying and vituperation he took a back seat for no man. But on confessing Christ, he promptly reformed, refused to lie or to engage in blackguardism, and made the "Argus" an honest and a gentlemanly paper. The result was general dissatisfaction in the ranks of his party. They told him that he was milk and water, that he was either priest-ridden or turning Federalist, and that if he did not make a more spirited paper they would start another.

He did not know what so many yet fail to perceive, that religion and stupidity are not conditions precedent of each other; so he sold out to them; and rightly thinking that it would require money to make a success of his new enterprise, went into the grocery business for a time. But here his conscience again defeated him. The principal profit of the trade then was in the staple of New England rum, and Willis would not sell rum. At that time if there was a minister in that region who did not buy and drink rum, he kept his blue light under a bushel. I suppose that Willis must have been regarded as a religious crank and fanatic. He had an idea that lying would form no part of the spirit of the religious newspaper. But he was doomed to disappointment, as many a man has since been. He was maligned to the day of his death, and the attempt made to wrest his honors from him.

Willis did not realize his idea till eight years after he had laid the plan before his spiritual adviser, Dr. Payson. His first issue was dated January 3, 1816. The paper lived till the year 1871, when it was merged in the "Boston Congregationalist," but the name of the "Recorder" is still kept at the mast-head. Willis died in 1870.

While Willis was trying to make money enough to float his proposed "Recorder," strange to say his seed thought had been blown across the woody wilderness, hundreds of miles, and fallen in the rich alluvium of the Scioto. Ohio was then mostly a dense forest. The deer, the wolf, the bear, the panther and the wild turkey everywhere abounded. It was the paradise of the hunter and the fisherman. No wonder that the first religious paper, amid surroundings so congenial, was a success. The irons for a wooden Ramage press had been packed across the mountains for the Territorial Government, then located at Chillicothe, and on this old press—now, I believe, in the "Gazette" office in Cincinnati—Rev. John Andrews printed his "Christian Recorder." This was in 1814, or nearly two years before Willis was able to get out his "Christian Recorder." Andrews not only took Willis's idea, but the name, also. The "Recorder" was moved to Pittsburgh, and became the "Presbyterian Banner." The two "Recorders" were quickly followed by a brood of religious papers, and many hundreds have since been born to die—to die in sweet, confiding infancy:

> Happy infants, early blest,
> Rest in peaceful slumber, rest;
> Early rescued from the cares
> Which increase with growing years.

The religious newspaper is the form in which journalism is to achieve its highest and finest development. It is highly interesting to notice the changes which have already taken place in its character. The early forms were wholly sermonic. They were hortatory, homiletic, polemic—simply the pulpit of the times in print. The names indicated their character. They were the Recorders, Observers, Expositors, Evangelists, Presbyters, Advocates—the whole line of names expressive of ponderosity was exhausted. Then came the Presbyterian, Baptists, Methodists, and other denominational newspaper names. In every instance they were edited by ministers, and in no instance evinced journalistic skill. They were heavy and solemn. Anything like levity was regarded as inappropriate as it would be in the pulpit. There was plenty of good thought in them, but no vivacity. The two departments of heavy leaders and long obituaries fitted them for the solemn and penitential hours of the Sabbath.

The general character of the religious press will be more and more of the popular kind. Competition has become so intense, and popular taste has become so appreciative and refined, that higher journalistic skill will constantly be in demand.

The day for doing editorial work as a side issue has passed forever. The religious press hereafter will seek for the best brains, the finest training, and the best natural aptitude, and with these a capacity for endurance and intense application. Tennyson says that he has applied himself closely for two hours to write one line. George Eliot wrote but sixty lines per day. The successful religious journalist of the future will put in work something like that. The rising culture will demand it, and it will get what it demands. The higher-class English journals are working for this degree of excellence. The "London Times" allows members of its editorial staff only three hours of working time per day. They are required to come fresh from sleep, and with only a glass of tea or claret, to their desks, and at the end of three hours they must hand over their work and leave the office. The result is those editorials, impressive as a thundercloud, but instinct with lightning, which gave the great paper its name. Now, contrast with these the editorials of the

"London Spectator." They are almost equal to the essays of Addison in the old "Spectator" in classical finish, and yet in materials and force they are, if anything, superior to those of the "London Times." The difference lies in this, that the "Spectator" is a weekly, and after these editorials have been poured red-hot into their sandy molds, they are allowed to cool, and then subjected to careful polishing. The "Spectator" is not a large paper, and it is plainly issued—the cost of manufacture not being half what it would be in Chicago, and yet they charge thirteen cents per copy for it—nearly seven dollars a year. The work is not magazine or review writing, but newspaper writing of the highest class. There is nothing approaching to this in religious journalism, but there will be, and there ought to have been before now.

The religious press is often spoken of as a means of great influence, but he who regards his paper as a means for giving him personal influence is a politician, not an editor; and in seeking to save his life thus, he is dead sure to lose it. The editor has no time, nor ambition, for anything but his art. He seeks to make a first-class paper in every particular. He sees nothing beyond the four walls of his sanctum, and he works for excellence, not for influence.

An established paper, like any of the first-class religious journals, is a creation of slow growth, but it is practically indestructible, and it is very foolish for an individual, or any number of them, to make a crusade against it. Fortunately the tendency of the work is to make the editor teachable, if he be a man of true piety and honesty.

I asked my neighbor, Mr. Edward Goodman, proprietor of "The Standard," what his object was in newspaper work. "First," he said, "to promote spiritual life; and, second, to advance the interests of the denomination. I never think," he said, "of the moneyed revenue, except to that end."

Editor Major Robinson says: "The object of a religious newspaper is to stimulate the piety and elevate the morality of its constituency, and to furnish the family with wholesome and instructive reading."

Editor Dr. Smith says: "We should make it an object to provide a complete family paper—to furnish all the kinds of reading most needed in the family. It should be first of all religious, because 'Religion is the chief concern of mortals.' While it should give its denominational intelligence freely, it should have all the religious intelligence which tends to teach, stimulate and guide."

ROMAN CATHOLIC CHRISTIANITY.

Rev. A. P. Doyle, Paulist Fathers,

NEW YORK.

[The following is the profession of faith made on joining the Catholic Church. It is received by a priest before the altar, though not necessarily in presence of the congregation. It is omitted when the convert has not previously had any form of baptism:

I, ——— ———, having before my eyes the holy Gospels, which I touch with my hand, and knowing that no one can be saved without that faith which the Holy, Catholic, Apostolic Roman Church holds, believes, and teaches, against which I grieve that I have greatly erred, inasmuch as I have held and believed doctrines opposed to her teachings—

I now, with grief and contrition for my past errors, profess that I believe the Holy, Catholic, Apostolic Roman Church to be the only and true Church established on earth by Jesus Christ, to which I submit myself with my whole heart. I believe all the articles that she proposes to my belief, and I reject and condemn all that she rejects and condemns, and I am ready to observe all that she commands me. And especially, I profess that I believe:

One only God, in three divine persons, distinct from, and equal to, each other—that is to say, the Father, the Son, and the Holy Ghost;

The Catholic doctrine of the Incarnation, Passion, Death, and Resurrection of our Lord Jesus Christ: and the personal union of the two Natures, the divine and the human; the divine Maternity of the most holy Mary, together with her most spotless Virginity;

The true, real, and substantial presence of the Body and Blood, together with the Soul and Divinity, of our Lord Jesus Christ, in the most Holy Sacrament of the Eucharist;

The seven Sacraments instituted by Jesus Christ for the salvation of mankind; that is to say, Baptism, Confirmation, Eucharist, Penance, Extreme Unction, Order, Matrimony;

Purgatory, the Resurrection of the dead, Everlasting life;

The Primacy, not only of honor but also of jurisdiction, of the Roman Pontiff, successor of St. Peter, Prince of the Apostles, Vicar of Jesus Christ;

The veneration of the saints, and of their images;

The authority of the Apostolic and Ecclesiastical Traditions, and of the Holy Scriptures, which we must interpret and understand only in the sense which our holy mother the Catholic Church has held, and does hold;

And everything else that has been defined and declared by the sacred Canons, and by the General Councils, and particularly by the holy Council of Trent, and delivered, defined, and declared by the General Council of the Vatican, especially concerning the Primacy of the Roman Pontiff, and his infallible teaching authority.

HIS HOLINESS, POPE LEO XIII.

The common welfare urgently demands a return to Him from whom we should never have gone astray: to Him who is the Way, the Truth and the Life—and this on the part not only of individuals but of society as a whole.—*Leo XIII.'s Message to the Twentieth Century.*

With a sincere heart, therefore, and with unfeigned faith, I detest and abjure every error, heresy, and sect opposed to the said Holy, Catholic, and Apostolic Roman Church. So help me God, and these His holy Gospels, which I touch with my hand.—Mass-Book for Non-Catholics, pp. 71, 72.—ED.]

* * *

IN ORDER to fully appreciate the doctrinal life of the Roman Catholic Church to-day, it is necessary to comprehend certain fundamental principles. While the revelation of Christian truth was closed with the ascension of Christ into Heaven, still there has been a development in the doctrinal system. The many truths and precepts which He gave us that are now recorded in the inspired writings of the Evangelists are not mere lifeless facts, but are rather germ-ideas capable of development and were intended to be developed.

The revelation of Christianity was not the passing to men of a system of dogmas to be compared only to a bag of stones, each one of which is a solid, cold, lifeless fact with no power of growing or of being anything but a stone. It was rather giving to mankind a package of seeds which were designed to grow and develop into a beautiful garden. This garden to-day is the doctrinal and devotional system of the Roman Catholic Church. The Catholic Church, with all its magnificent ritual, with its systematic codices of laws and precepts, its enchiridions of clearly defined dogmatic truths, its hierarchical orders and grades of offices, its complete and sometimes puzzling devotional life, to the casual observer, is different from the simplicity of the Gospel Church where the truths were enunciated by the wayside, where the only ritual which surrounded Christ was a profession of faith in His Divinity, no matter how awkwardly made, and where the only act of devotion that was asked was "Lovest thou Me?" and yet in reality it is identical with the church formed by Christ.

There is nothing in the Catholic Church to-day that was not contained in germ in the words that Christ spoke or the revelation which he made. The garden is the outgrowth of the seeds; the church is the development of the seed-ideas which Christ gave to the Apostles. It is necessary to fully appreciate this theory of development before any one can approach a comparative study of the doctrines and practices of the Catholic Church.

The Catholic idea of a "church" is not merely the truth affixed in the individual heart by the operation of the Holy Ghost, though this is a part of the work of the Holy Spirit, but it is an existing, corporate entity whose body consists of all the faithful scattered throughout the world, of whatever tribe or people, believing all the teachings of Christ and living in obedience to the lawfully constituted bishops with the Pope at their head; and whose soul is the Spirit of God who descended on the Apostles at Pentecost, animating the body, giving life to all the members, guiding the teaching authority in the ways of truth, and enabling all to grow to the fullest stature in Christ Jesus.

The Catholic Church is not so much an organization as it is an organism. When this distinction is fully appreciated, one can far more readily understand what the church is and what she is destined to do for mankind. An *organization* is a gathering of individuals in which the whole possesses what is contributed to it by the parts. Apart from the individuals which make it up, it possesses nothing of itself. The individuals may separate from the whole and they will take away all the innate life that is their own. Not so is it with an *organism*—a human being is an organism, in which all the organs and members depend on their junction with the body for their life. Cut off a hand or a leg, the life does not go with it; it is "lifeless," it decays. So, too, is it with the tree; a branch cut from the trunk withers away.

In this sense the church is not an organization that has its existence through a number of people who believe in interpreting Scripture in the same way and are ready to make public profession of their concurrent interpretation; but it is an organism in which the Holy Ghost is the animating principle, and by establishing the proper relationship one may partake of that Divine life which flows from the soul throughout the entire body. To be cut away from this body is spiritual death. It follows from this exposition of the "Church Idea" that the Catholic Church must of necessity, in appearance at least, be entirely different to-day from what she was a century or ten centuries ago, though in reality she is the same church, teaching the same essential truths. Growth and development necessitate change. It follows, also, that though she changes, still, because the active principle of the church, the Holy Ghost, is the same God who founded her, she cannot depart from the truth that was enunciated amidst the Judean hills; and as Christ destined her to be the means of salvation for all time for all the world, through all time, she will never depart from that truth.

There will be, as time goes on, a clearer enunciation of those truths, a practical exemplification of them as it becomes necessary to apply them to the ever-changing affairs of men and a more accurate definition of great principles when they are assailed by misguided antagonists. But in all, the teaching authority of the church will be guided by the Spirit of Truth so that the world will not be led into error, and mankind will know where are to be found "the way, the truth and the life."

Having premised these things, we are ready to come to the consideration of her distinctive teachings. The operation of the Holy Ghost is twofold—one through the corporate body as is indicated by the words of Christ: *I will ask the Father and He shall give you another Paraclete, that He may abide with you forever* (John xiv, 16); *He will teach you all things* (John xiv, 26): and the other on the individual mind and heart, convincing it of the truth and personally bringing it unto sanctification—*You when you were dead in your sins He hath quickened together with Him, forgiving you all offences* (Col. ii, 13).

It sometimes may happen that the belief of the individual may be allowed to drift into opposition to the teaching authority of the church. It may become impossible for one to persuade himself that such and such teachings are true. But as we know truth is one and the same at all times and all places, the same spirit of truth cannot teach the church one thing and the individual the opposite thing. If there be an opposition between the teaching church and the believing individual, the church must be right and the individual wrong. For on the church alone has Christ bestowed the gift of inerrancy. She is *the pillar and the ground of truth* (Tim. iii, 15). *The gates of hell shall not prevail against her* (Matt. xvi, 18). It is, therefore, the duty of the individual to yield his own conviction to the infallible teaching of the church, and that not in any slavish submission or self-stultification, but on the reasonable principle that the church is an infallible guide and cannot err. *As my Father hath sent Me, I also send you* (John xx, 21). *He that heareth you heareth Me, and He that despiseth you despiseth Me* (Luke x, 16). *He that believeth and is baptized shall be saved, he that believeth not shall be condemned* (Mark xvi, 16).

On this reasonable basis the church secures a marvelous unity of belief. She is everywhere one in her teaching and in the complete, whole-souled acceptance of her teaching by her children. She presents to the world a wonderful homogeneity, and in these days of free-thinking and independence of mind there is no more marvelous spectacle than the fact that two hundred and sixty millions of people, some of whom are of the highest intelligence and the utmost freedom of will, accept her teaching and bow in submission to her voice as the voice of God.

In order that there may not be any doubt as to what the teaching of the church is, Christ has constituted a living voice to speak for Him. In order to yield our conviction to the teaching of the church, as indicated above, there must not be any danger of our misinterpreting or misunderstanding the sense of established formulas. Mere written statements in a book, no matter how accurately formulated, can never preclude the possibility of this danger. They cannot correct one if he does misunderstand or misinterpret the genuine sense. Hence a living voice is necessary so that when one does misunderstand he can be corrected; when he does drift away he can be called back. He who speaks for an infallible church must himself be infallible if he would command the assent of the children of men. When he teaches the whole church on questions of dogma and morals he must be preserved from leading the church astray. Hence the Catholic Church has always believed, from the very beginning, through the nineteen hundred years of her life, that the Pope, when teaching *ex cathedra,* cannot teach error. It was in the Vatican Council, when this traditional belief of the church was assailed, that it was clearly defined and incorporated into the formulas of the church. It was no new doctrine, but merely a new formulation of a doctrine as old as Christianity itself. *Simon, Simon, behold Satan hath desired to have you that he may sift you as wheat. But I have prayed for thee that thy faith fail not, and thou being once converted, confirm thy brethren* (Luke xxii, 32).

It may be useful to quote here the exact words of the decree of the Vatican Council: "Wherefore, faithfully adhering to the tradition received from the beginning of the Christian Faith, for the glory of God our Saviour, the exaltation of the Catholic religion, and the salvation of the Christian people, we, the Sacred Council approving, teach and define that it is a dogma divinely revealed, that the Roman Pontiff, when, discharging the office of Pastor and Teacher of all Christians, by reason of his supreme Apostolic authority, he defines a doctrine regarding faith or morals to be held by the whole church—he, by the Divine assistance promised to him in Blessed Peter, possesses that infallibility with which the Blessed Redeemer willed that His church should be endowed in defining doctrine regarding faith and morals, and that therefore such definitions of the said Roman Pontiff are of themselves unalterable and not from the consent of the church." (IV Sess., Chap. IV.)

It is needless to explain that this doctrine of Papal infallibility does not include Papal impeccability, nor does it include Papal inerrancy in politics, or in science, or in any matters save those of faith and morals; and one can readily appreciate what a compactness this doctrine gives to the whole system of Christian teaching. It is not only the broad and solid and unshakable foundation, but it is the cement that gives the bond to the whole superstructure. Catholics do not waver in their faith, they are not tortured with doubts, their spiritual life is not blighted by the withering blasts of infidelity, and the appeals to them do not consist in exhortations to faith, since the faith is never shaken, but they are appeals to better living and to higher spirituality.

The indwelling of the Holy Spirit in the church is not only the source of her doctrinal inerrancy, but it is the active principle of the holiness of the church, that is manifested by the practice of heroic sanctity by many of her children, by the standards of morality which she sets up and by the influence of her teaching in the social order. Whatever there is of Christian civilization is the work of the Roman Catholic Church. The long bead-roll of the saints, from the martyrs who died in the Pagan Coliseum to the Father Damiens of to-day, who leave all the world holds dear and sacrifice themselves in order to care for the sick and the unfortunate—these are the fruit of the Holy Spirit, who is ever with His church. Undoubtedly, there are many instances of sublime sanctity outside the pale of her membership, and these, too, are stimulated to heroism by the same Holy Spirit; but the natural and ordinary channels of the grace of God are the sacramental channels of the Catholic Church. As it is through the teaching authority personified in the Holy Father that the pastures of truth are preserved from contamination by the poisonous weeds of error, so it is through the sacramental system that the streams of Divine grace are sent to impart fertility and virility to the practical living of Christian men.

The sacraments are the seven channels instituted by Christ, and they are filled with the Divine graces from the reservoir of the Redemption. They each carry to the soul a saving grace.

The grace of (1) *Baptism* regenerates. By means of it the child is born again into the newness of the supernatural life. There are established between the soul and God relations of adoption whereby we cry *Abba*, Father! (2) *Confirmation* is a strengthening grace, imparting vigor of spirituality that one is led to fight for, and, if necessary, to die for, the faith that is in him. (3) *Penance* is the forgiving grace; when one going down from Jerusalem to Jericho falls amidst the robbers of temptation, who despoil him of the mantle of purity and leave him naked of God's friendship, and cast him aside from the pathways of righteousness, Penance, like the good Samaritan, comes along and picks him up, binds up the wounds sin has made, cares for him during the periods of convalescence, until he is finally restored to spiritual health. (4) *Holy Eucharist* is the nourishing grace. It is the real Body and Blood of Christ, which unless we eat thereof we cannot have life. *Amen, Amen, I say unto you: Unless you eat the Flesh of the Son of Man and drink His Blood, you cannot have life in you, and he that eateth my Flesh and drinketh my Blood hath everlasting life, and I will raise him up the last day* (John vi, 54). It is the manna which has come down from heaven to support us spiritually while we wander through the deserts of this life into the Promised Land. (5) *Extreme Unction* is the sustaining grace in that last fierce conflict with the Evil One. When the weakness of dissolution has come and cold sweats of death are on our brow, the enemy of our soul makes a last determined effort to seize us, the grace of Extreme Unction fortifies us against his attacks and guards the soul in its upward flight until it gains its home in heaven. Then, for the special states in life, there are assisting graces—(6) *Holy Orders,* to enable the priesthood to guard the sanctities of their office; and (7) *Matrimony,* to help the married pair to consecrate the love they have for each other and enable them to bring up their children in the fear of God. Like a good mother the Catholic Church takes the child in infancy, watches over him as the years roll by, strengthens him to meet life's conflicts; if he falls, picks him up again; ever places before him the ideals of perfection, consecrates the great love-passion of his heart, follows him to the end, and when his eyes are closed in death she lays his body with her blessing in the grave to await the resurrection day, while by her prayers and her suffrages she follows the soul into its place of purgation, and does not leave it till the last traces of sin are washed away and it is prepared for admittance in the realms of the blest. The continual flowing of these graces all through life, from the cradle to the grave, creates among Catholics types of sanctity that are known only to those whose eyes are so spiritualized that they can read the inner secret of hearts.

The lives of the saints constitute a literature rarely known outside the Catholic Church, and one that is replete with multiplied marvels of heroism. The continual flowing of these graces elevates the general average of holiness, so that in convent and in cloister, among all ranks of society, under the mantle of the king and the rags of the beggar, there flourish the most beautiful flowers of sanctity.

The Catholic Church maintains the standards of holy living by placing as conditions for admittance to holy communion a profession of profound sorrow for sin committed, joined with a determination never to sin again and a willingness to repair whatever injury has been done by sin. This is the very least that is exacted for full membership; though if the sinner does not possess this he is not cast out. In the church there are both good and bad; the cockle grows with the wheat; in the net there are both good and bad fishes. But like a good mother, she is patient and loving with her disobedient children. Though they do bring disgrace on her at times, still she claims them as her own and waits till the time comes when they are ready to meet her standards of holy living before she admits them to the Sacred Table. But beyond these simple conditions of repentance there are no heights of sanctity and union with God to which she does not urge her children to aspire.

Finally, by the influence of the church's teaching in the social order she is the very saviour of society. She guards and protects the family by affirming the indissolubility of the marriage tie; she sets herself, with all her mighty influence, against the divorce abomination which is prostituting domestic virtue in our modern life; she interprets strictly the precept of Christ that *What God hath joined together let no man put asunder.* She has in this way saved the Christian home and all that it means of education and preservation to the growing child. Moreover, she has maintained the highest ideals of chastity by singing the praises of the state of virginity, by encouraging her priesthood and her thousands of cloistered men and women to the highest practice of it. Thus, in a most forceful way, she says to the world that men and women may live without yielding to sensuality. The practical effect of this is felt throughout the entire married state, where people are taught restraint of passion and that a life of continence is among the easy possibilities.

The church has in her hand the key to the labor problems which harass us. In this country particularly the scramble for wealth is going on with all its intensity. In the strife for preëminence many are thrown down and trampled to the earth; others are cast by the wayside. The fierce striving for the biggest prize has made men disregard all human rights. Classes have been set over against the masses. Men have climbed to prominence over the backs of their fellow-men. The result of this social strife has been the reducing of thousands to a slavery more galling than the negro slavery of a century ago. Life is to many a child born into it but a damning fate. The segregation of wealth into the hands of the few has left the many in the grasp of a most distressful poverty, so that with all our wealth there is abroad the gaunt figure of want; and with our teeming markets the pitiful hand of beggary is stretched forth.

There is only one remedy for all these terrible social evils, and that is the religious one. The root of the social evil is the cruel spirit of greed and of grasping avarice. No law can legislate this out of existence; no policeman's club can subdue it. To conquer it there is needed a power which reaches the heart. It must be a force which can turn men's minds away from the pleasures of life and bid them fix the desires of their souls on the greater riches beyond the grave. It must be an agency that spans the gulf that avarice has created between the rich and the poor; that can teach both the great principle of the brotherhood of man, the trusteeship of wealth, the dignity of labor and the common destiny provided by a Heavenly Father for all. Religion alone can do this. But to do it effectually a religion must be strong and thoroughly organized. It must be one that is down among the poor, commanding the love of their hearts. It must be one whose precepts can be enforced by spiritual penalties, if need be, by the sick bed, or even by the open grave. The Catholic Church can do all this in a most effectual way. She therefore is able to give the *social pax vobiscum* to the age. The Encyclical of Leo XIII, "The Condition of Labor," has been pronounced by noted publicists to be the *Magna Charta* of the rights and responsibilities of the wage-earners of the world.

The Catholic Church, by the indwelling of the Holy Ghost, is, then, the very salt of the earth, saving it from the corruption of vice and preserving it sweet and pure from the degenerating and decomposing action of evil. The presence of the Holy Ghost with her makes her the world-wide religion, at home amidst every nation and tribe and people, no matter how much they differ in language, manners and genius. The Latin language gives her a universal means of interchange of thought. The spiritual authority which the church possesses enables her to bring all minds into a complete unity of belief, so that wherever one finds a Catholic he is the exact duplicate in doctrinal life of every other Catholic. Ask a child in the Philippines the questions in his catechism and one will get exactly the same answers as one would get if he had the patience to go through and ask every one of the 200,000,000 Catholics scattered throughout the earth. In these days of crumbling creeds and of drifting away from old-time dogmatic moorings, the spectacle of a united church, homogeneous in its belief and uniform in its ethical exactions, is something to charm the soul of man and gladden the heart of God. Nothing but the compelling influence of the Divine Presence can bring it about.

Not only is the church everywhere the same, but she is perpetual in her life. She is to-day the only thing that goes back to classic civilization. She can affirm the inspiration of the Gospels, for she was present when they were written. The church can assure us of the conversion of the European races, for she it was who brought it about. She can point to all the artistic treasures of the ages, to the great cathedrals of Europe, to the famous Madonnas of the art galleries, to the masterpieces of poetry and song, for it was she who inspired them all.

She has borne through the ages the Apostolic privileges of the remission of sin in God's name—*As the Father hath sent Me, I also send you. When He had said this He breathed on them, and He said to them, Receive ye the Holy Ghost. Whose sins you shall forgive they are forgiven them; whose sins you shall retain they are retained* (John xx, 23)—and that other Apostolic privilege of consecrating the bread and wine in the sacrifice of the Mass and changing it into the Body and Blood of Christ (John vi, 52-56; Matt. xxvi, 28).

These two essential practices in the life of a Catholic, auricular confession for the purpose of receiving the forgiveness of sin, and sacramental communion, in which not bread and wine but the real

Body and Blood of Christ are received, are sustained by the exercise of the sacerdotal power which was given to the Apostles by Christ and handed down in an unbroken succession through the generations of duly ordained bishops and priests unto their legitimate successors of the present day. The possession of these Divine gifts establishes the identity between the church of the nineteenth century and the church of the first century, and constitutes, in the Catholic Church of to-day, the Apostolic succession.

I have endeavored in the foregoing to make a simple exposition of the Catholic Church, and to explain what her doctrines and her practices are as they arise out of her very nature, as a world-wide and perpetual institution destined to carry the effects of the Redemption through all ages even to the consummation of the world, and make them operative in the hearts of men. There are many other distinctive beliefs of Roman Catholics which it is only possible to hint at. The common beliefs of all Christians—the existence of one God in three Divine Persons, the Divinity of Jesus Christ, the fall of man from the state of original righteousness, his redemption and regeneration through the vicarious sacrifice of the God-man, the ultimate resurrection of the body, the particular as well as the final judgment, and the various states of being in the world beyond the grave—are enshrined in the formulas which have been adopted by all Christian churches. There may be some difference in the explanation of details. In Catholic theologies all these truths are delineated with all the exactness of a scientific study, and reasons given from the authority of Sacred Scripture, the writings of the fathers of the church, as well as the rational basis. But the few distinctive beliefs which I may touch on are the devotion to the Virgin Mary, the custom of praying for the dead, the belief in Purgatory, the intercession of the saints, and the celebration of the Divine Mysteries.

In the devotion to the Virgin Mary, we honor her only with the honor due a creature. We believe that her influence with her Divine Son is still powerful and may be exercised in our behalf. She is the mother of the God-man. She conceived through the overshadowing influence of the Holy Ghost; she was always a virgin, and in view of the aforesaid merits of her Divine Son she herself was preserved from all stain of original sin which is the common inheritance of all the children of Adam. By this latter privilege we understand the Immaculate Conception.

Purgatory is a place where they go who die with some lesser stain on their souls, and where by suffering it is purged away, preparatory to admission into Heaven. The church teaches, concerning Purgatory, two points: First, that there is a Purgatory, and second, that souls detained there are helped by our prayers. Hell is a state of eternal separation from God. There are no definitions of the church concerning the character of the punishment. It is of Catholic faith, however, that hell is eternal.

The Saints are they who have fought the good fight and are now reigning with God. Owing to their intimacy with God on the one hand, and their sympathy with us on the other, they become powerful pleaders with the Divine Majesty. There is, however, but one mediator between the soul and God, and He is Jesus Christ. Nothing is farther from the Catholic mind than to supplant Him by any one else. The Mass is the clean oblation foretold by the Prophet Malachi, that would be offered up from the rising of the sun to the going down of the same (Mal. i, 10, 11). It is the sacrifice of the Cross offered through the ages as a constant propitiation for sin, in which Christ is immolated again, though in an unbloody manner, and by means of which the justice of God is condoned and the sins of men are atoned for.

All these various dogmas are parts of, yet essential to, the complete system of Catholic teaching, and they are the framework of that beautiful organism which derives its life from the indwelling of the Holy Ghost, and has been the ark of salvation to myriads of the children of men.

MISSIONS IN THE ROMAN CATHOLIC CHURCH, ANNO DOMINI 1901.

Rev. A. P. Doyle, Paulist Fathers.
NEW YORK.

[Long and far was this church the sole vehicle of Christianity, that bore it on over the storms of ages, and sheltered it amid the clash of nations. It evangelized the philosophy of the East, and gave some sobriety to its wild and voluptuous dreams. It received into its bosom the savage conquerors of the North, and nursed them successively out of utter barbarism. It stood by the desert fountain from which all modern history flows, and dropped into it the sweetening branch of Christian truth and peace. It presided at the birth of art, and liberally gave its traditions into the young hands of Color and Design. Traces of its labors, and of its versatile power over the human mind, are scattered throughout the globe. It has consecrated the memory of the lost cities of Africa, and given to Carthage a Christian as well as a classic renown. If in Italy and Spain it has dictated the decrees of tyranny, the mountains of Switzerland have heard its vespers mingling with the cry of liberty, and its requiem sung over patriot graves. The convulsions of Asiatic history have failed to overthrow it; on the heights of Lebanon, on the plains of Armenia, in the provinces of China, either in the secluson of the convent or the stir of population, the names of Jesus and of Mary still ascend. It is not difficult to understand the enthusiasm which this ancient and picturesque religion kindles in its disciples. To the poor peasant who knows no other dignity it must be a proud thing to feel himself a member of a vast community that spreads from Andes to the Indus; that has bid defiance to the vicissitudes of fifteen centuries and adorned itself with the genius and virtues of them all; that beheld the transition from ancient to modern civilization, and itself forms the connecting link between the Old World in Europe and the New; the missionary of the nations, the associate of history, the patron of art, the vanquisher of the sword.—James Martineau.—Ed.]

* * *

It is difficult to measure by a short statement of facts, or even by long tables of statistics, a century of heroic missionary endeavor; nor is it fair to other churches to place in contrast to their noble efforts to bring the Gospel to the peoples who sit in darkness and the shadow of death the world-wide efforts of an enormous organization which claims the whole earth as its inheritance.

Whether the contrast be made or not, it is well to differentiate the categories in which various Christian denominations are working in the mission field.

Protestant churches are more or less national; hence there is for them a foreign mission field where different methods are employed or specialized work is carried on. For the Catholic Church there are no foreign missions, because she is not the church of one people or of any country, but, as her name implies, she is the catholic or universal church, and her language, her service, her preaching and her doctrines are the same in Africa as in Rome, in China as in Jerusalem. She is the great tree grown from the grain of mustard seed which a man took and cast into his garden. It grew and waxed a great tree and the fowls of the air lodged in its branches. (Luke xiii, 19.)

An account, therefore, of the Catholic missions would be a story not of planting new seed, nor of the strengthening of the trunk and limbs of the old tree, but rather of the putting forth of new branches. This particular work is assigned to the *Congregation de Propaganda Fide* in Rome. A mere tabulated statement of its activities fills a large volume.

Some idea of the progress made during the last century may be had by making a few contrasts: The year 1800 was full of forebodings for Catholics and of triumphs for the enemies of the church. The French Revolution had just swept over France. The doctrines that it stood for were an attack on organized Christianity and had inoculated the best thought of the active-minded men of every nation. The Catholic Church was down in the Valley of the Shadow of Death. The wise men seemed to see in her a hoary, worn-out institution, bearing with some dignity, to be sure, the laurels of the past, yet feebly tottering to her ruin. Judged from worldly standards there did not appear to be any elements of recuperation within her bosom; her strength was sapped and in her face were the wrinkles and in her frame the emaciation of old age. England and Germany, who had been nourished at her breast, had gone out from under her roof-tree. Russia and the East were in decadent schism; Austria, like a spoiled child, attempted to rule the household; Italy and Spain defended the old home, but it was with many insults to their feeble mother. France had rebelled and had enthroned the goddess of reason on the high altar of Notre Dame. Humanly speaking, there was but little hope that the church would ever rise from her bed of prostration and defeat.

The ways of God, however, are not the ways of man. "Why have the Gentiles raged and the people devised vain things? . . .

Ask of me and I will give thee the Gentiles for thy inheritance and the uttermost bounds of the earth for thy possession." What a wonderful change the hundred years of this greatest of all centuries have brought! In North Germany ninety years ago there were but 6,000,000 Catholics, and they were steeped in apathy; but the flail of persecution came to them and awakened them from their torpor, with the result that to-day they number 13,000,000. In the German Empire to-day there are 18,600,000. In Switzerland, the home of Calvin, as late as 1880 the Catholic population numbered but one-third—now they are over two-fifths. In Denmark and on the Scandinavian peninsula the church practically had no existence. To-day there are a re-established hierarchy with a completed organization and a fast-increasing clientage which already numbers many thousands. In Holland, where the Reformation had a profound influence, the growth of Catholics has been from 350,000 to 1,854,346. And among the English-speaking peoples, who lead the world in commercial enterprise and who possess in a marked way what is known as the Spirit of the Age—it is among these that the undoing of the Reformation has been the most thorough. In 1800 England and Scotland had 120,000 Catholics and only 65 priests, and they were absolutely destitute of churches, schools and institutions. To-day there are 1 cardinal archbishop, 2 archbishops, 18 bishops and 3,000 priests who care for the spiritual interests of more than 2,000,000 Catholics. In Australia there is a commensurate increase. A century ago the church did not exist there; to-day there is a well-organized and thoroughly established hierarchy with a cardinal archbishop at its head; 6 archbishops, 31 bishops, nearly a thousand priests and a Catholic population that numbers nearly a million souls.*

Great as all these increases are, they are not a moiety of the phenomenal growth within the United States. A century ago there was little organization; Catholics were a mere handful scattered throughout the thirteen states, with no civic life and with very little hope for the future. The forces by which public thought and sentiment are moulded were antagonistic to the Catholic faith. How the church has grown since then in spite of the most adverse circumstances may be indicated by the following figures: In 1800 there were 40 priests; in 1830 the number increased to 232; in 1850 to 1,800; in 1900 to 11,636. The Catholic population during the same

* Mulhall is the authority for the figures.

period has grown from 100,000 to 12,000,000. A comparison with other churches in point of view of aggregate wealth shows that in 1850 the wealth of Baptist, Methodist, Presbyterian and Episcopalian churches was greater than that of the Catholic Church. In 1870 the Catholics had taken second place, and now they are easily the first.

Besides the external growth indicated by numerical strength and worldly wealth, the internal growth indicated by evidences of maturing organization, as well as by signs of increasing spirituality, is none the less remarkable. The best flowering of the inner life of the church is the vocations to the religious orders, through which men and women leave the lower ranks of the ordinary Christian and consecrate themselves in poverty, chastity and obedience to the perfect life, following the higher call of Christ when he said to the rich young man who had kept the commandments from his youth up: "If thou wilt be perfect, go sell what thou hast, give to the poor and come and follow Me." (Matt. xix, 21.)

In 1800 there was but one convent in the United States, with less than 10 religious; in 1900 there are 44 distinct orders of men, with 5,500 members devoted to the sacred ministry, Christian teaching and social work, and 118 communities of women with over 50,000 nuns. This army of men and women devote themselves. without hope of worldly gain to the alleviation of the ills of humanity in the hospitals by the sick-bed, in the tenements of the poor, in the slums among the depraved, in the asylums caring for the orphans, and among the aged who have been stranded on the shore waiting for the merciful hand of death to release the spirit for its upward flight. They spend and are spent in the close schoolroom instructing the young and leading them up the rugged heights of virtue, without one cent of salary; contenting themselves with meagre fare, with short hours of sleep on a hard bed, and long hours of work and prayer and devotion to the sick and the poor and the wretched.

While this marvellous growth of the church throughout the so-called missionary countries may be ascribed to many causes, still there is this much to be said about it—it is perfectly healthy; it has been sound in doctrine, compact in organization, united in spirit and homogeneous in its expansion. The church has not consumed, nor retained any waste products, but has been ready to lop off any diseased or decayed members, so that her life-blood is pure and her organic life is wholesome. Another item of statistics is valuable, for it is a pledge of the continuance of this growth: There are in the United States 109 seminaries for the education of priests, training 4,728 students for the sacred ministry. Moreover, there are over 1,000,000 children being educated in the Catholic religious schools of the country, at an expense of $15,000,000. This sum is the voluntary contribution of the Catholic people to good citizenship; for the sole purpose of this system is not to derogate one jot or tittle from the effectiveness of our magnificent system of public instruction, but to add an element that will develop conscience, increase respect for law, make people more honest, give them a respect for the sanctity of an oath and inculcate in their hearts a keener sense of the obligations of man to man.

So much for the growth of the church among civilized peoples. One would imagine that these branches had outgrown their missionary state, but they are included within the purview of the great missionary department of the church—the Propaganda.

If we go farther afield we shall find evidences of the same vigorous growth. The pagan world is mapped out between twenty missionary societies, some composed of the regular clergy, others of the secular clergy, all of whom are affiliated with and under the direction of the Propaganda. The islands of Japan, the Corean peninsula, the steppes and forests of Manchuria, are an appanage of the *Mission Etrangères* of Paris. Kansu and Mongolia offer a vast and difficult field to the labors of the Belgian missionaries. The Middle Kingdom is divided between five orders: in the north and centre are the Lazarists and the Franciscans; in the west are the Dominicans and the Jesuits; in the east and south, again, are the *Mission Etrangères*. Passing on to the Indo-Chinese peninsula, we find the latter society in almost exclusive possession of its vast block of territory; only a seventh part is occupied by the Dominicans and the Milanese Foreign Missionary Society. In Hindustan the high ground at the foot of the Himalayas is occupied by the Capuchins, while at the three angles of the peninsula, at Calcutta, at Madurè and Mangalore, the Jesuits are established, with the Mill Hill missionaries and the Irish priests at Madras, the Salesians of Annecy, Fathers of the Holy Ghost, Carmelites, Benedictines, Foreign Missionaries of Paris and Milan in the centre and at certain points along the coast. In Ceylon the Oblate Fathers make headway against three enemies at once: the gurus of Brahma, the bonzes of Buddha and the marabouts of Mohammed. Persia belongs to the Lazarists; Mesopotamia to the

Dominicans; Syria and Armenia to the French and Italian religious—Jesuits, Franciscans, Lazarists and Carmelites.

Coming back to this continent, the Indian tribes of North America were evangelized during the middle decades of the century by Father De Smet and his companions. Senator Vest bore testimony on the floor of the Senate to the wonderful results the black robes had achieved among the Indians of the Rocky Mountain regions. No less fervent and heroic were the zeal, indomitable energy and self-sacrifice of the Oblate Fathers, who during the last half century have carried on the work of evangelization throughout the ice-bound Western territories of the Canadian Dominion. Between the Oblates and the Jesuits the territory of Alaska is divided.

In India the statistical returns for the present year show that for the first time in three centuries the number of Catholics exceeds two millions. What is a singularly interesting feature of this mission, full of hope for its future fruitfulness, is its complete organization. Its 36 dioceses have 826 European missionaries and 1,580 priests. There are more than a thousand religious men engaged in the work of teaching, and 2,400 nuns. There are 42 seminaries, with 2,200 students; 162 orphanages, with 9,874 orphans; while in its 2,562 primary schools there are 145,500 pupils.

I need no more than mention the great continent of Africa. At the beginning of the century its teeming population was almost everywhere seated in darkness, while impassable barriers shut out every approach of missionary zeal. Explorers, led on by love of fame, backed by powerful newspaper enterprises, plunged into the heart of the black country. They blazed the way for missionary effort; the missionaries were not slow to follow up the opportunities. They immediately parceled out the country among themselves so as not to overlap territory or to neutralize each other's efforts; and to-day there are 60 dioceses with as many bishops, each with a well-equipped corps of missionary workers and an estimated number of 3,000,000 Christians, though under the immediate supervision of the Propaganda there are only 458,170 souls.

The eyes of all the world are now turned to China. The lust of empire and the greed for gain are sure to parcel it out among the European nations. Spheres of influence will inevitably become subjugated provinces. The old way was—the peaceful missionary went first and then followed the military conqueror. The way of the modern world is the search for the golden fleece. The first step is to locate commercial enterprise and then back it up by the army or the navy. For three centuries China has resisted all missionary effort. From the days when the longing eyes of St. Francis Xavier looked at it from afar, down to the middle of this century, little or no progress was made with the Chinese masses. It was not for lack of effort, God alone knows the heroic sacrifices; and the bead-roll of martyrs who have shed their blood in an attempt to evangelize the yellow race is not by any means insignificant. Among those who thus sacrificed everything that the world holds dear, emulating the heroism of the early martyrs, we meet with the young and the old of every sex and class and condition in life, even some of the highest-rank military officers, magistrates, teachers and princes of royal and imperial dignity. And of such, as of the martyrs of the early ages, it may be said: "It was not their sufferings and death alone, but the cause for which they suffered, that merited for them the martyr's palm."

Two instances may be selected to illustrate the growth of the church. In the vast kingdom of Anam, now occupied by France, religious peace at present remains undisturbed. There are 700,000 Christians, 20,000 children in the religious schools, 355 priests (native), besides the European missionaries; and what is characteristic of this field is the large number of native nuns, of whom there are over two thousand. The church here has been swept over and over again by the fierce outbreaks of Anamite fanaticism. In 1885 the outbreaks reminded one of the Roman persecutions. There was a wholesale massacre in which 15 priests, 60 catechists, 270 nuns and 2,700 Christians spilled their blood to be the seed of a more vigorous Christianity. In the same year, in the northern vicariate, 10 native priests and 1,200 Christians shared the crown of martyrdom.

The frightful massacres of the Christians in China which have startled the civilized world during the past few months are but the repetition of what have been going on during the past two centuries. Nevertheless, in spite of sword and fire and tyrannical law, the church in China has grown from 200,000 at the beginning of the century to over a million at its close. In one diocese last year there were 20,000 Chinese inscribed on the roll of those who were awaiting instruction, and in another diocese the number of catechumens were no less than 50,000.* Through an agreement entered into

---

* On Nov. 21, 1901, Rt. Rev. Adolph Favier, Bishop of Peking, reported more than 1,400 baptisms and 4,200 placed under instructions in the Vicariate of Peking since the siege.

with the French Government, the missionaries hold the rank of mandarins, so that they may have access to the viceroys.

As to the type of man the Catholic missionary is, and the way he does his work, I can do no better than quote a witness who cannot be accused of any partiality to the Catholic Church. Captain Younghusband writes in his book, "The Heart of a Continent," of a visit to a missionary station in Manchuria as follows:

"On our arrival we were cordially welcomed by two priests, Père Litot and Père Maviel, and introduced to the Bishop, a noble-looking, kindly gentleman, who had lived for over thirty years in this country, and who has since died there. A noticeable feature in this village was that the inhabitants were all Christians. The mission had begun by educating and training children as Christians. These had grown into men and had sent their children in turn; and in the course of time the whole village had become Christian. We attended the services on Sunday and were very much struck by the really sincere and devout character of the converts. Brought up from their childhood as Christians and under the kindly, genial influence of these good priests, the people of this village seemed like a different race from the cold, hard Chinamen around them.

"It was indeed a pleasure to see these French missionaries and to have that warm-hearted greeting which one European will give another, of whatever nationality, in the most distant corners of the world.

"Except the French Consul, who had been sent to inquire into the outrage on Père Conroux in the previous year, no European has ever visited these different mission stations, and we on our part had not met a European for several months, so the delight of this meeting may well be imagined. But apart from that, we were very deeply impressed by the men themselves. Few men have made a deeper impression on me than these simple missionaries. They were standing, transparent types of all that is best in man; there was around them an atmosphere of pure, genuine goodness which made itself felt at once. We recognized immediately that we were not only with *good* men, but with *real* men. What they possessed was no weak sentimentality or flashy enthusiasm, but solid human worth. Far away from their friends, from all civilization, they live and work and die; they have died, two out of the three we met in these parts, since we left.

"Their strong yet gentle and simple natures, developed by the hardships of their surroundings and the loftiness of their ideals, and untainted by the contact with worldly praise and glamour, impressed itself on us at once and, as we saw evidenced in the people around, had affected the Chinese likewise.

> 'Great deeds cannot die.
> They with the sun and moon renew their light;
> Forever blessing those that look on them.'

"Others may bring discredit on the missionary cause and produce the feeling of hostility to it which undoubtedly exists, but these are the men who are a true light in the world and who will spread the essence of Christianity—the doing of good to others—abroad.

"This remote mission station, established here where no other Europeans had ever penetrated, was a source of the greatest interest to us and fulfilled our highest ideal of such a station. There was here no elaborate, costly house, no air of luxury such as may be seen in many missionary establishments elsewhere, but everything was of the most rigorous simplicity. There was merely a plain little house, almost bare inside and with stiff, simple furniture. Under such hard conditions and with such plain surroundings, and shut off forever from intercourse with the civilized world, it might be supposed that these missionaries were dull, stern, perhaps morbid, men. But they were precisely the contrary. They had a fund of simple joviality and were hearty and full of spirits." ("The Heart of a Continent. A Narrative of Travels in Manchuria." By Captain Younghusband. London, 1896.)

This story of the Catholic missionary's effort will not be complete without a sketch of the organization which supplies to a large extent the sinews of war. In 1822 a young woman of Lyons conceived the idea of collecting the pennies from the poor, through the children, for the support of missionaries in heathen lands. The work rapidly spread throughout the churches in France and ultimately it was organized for a world-wide effort. From small offerings at first the work grew until in 1891 the Central Direction of the Society of the Propagation of the Faith was able to report that the sum of $58,994,925 was contributed to this work since its inception in 1822. In the year 1899 there was distributed throughout the missionary dioceses by this same organization $1,362,854.74. It also publishes an item of statistics which is very valuable in this connection:

"At the beginning of the century, before the founding of the Society of the Propagation of the Faith, of Lyons, the Propaganda numbered scarcely five million Catholics under its jurisdiction. For the present century the number has risen to about twenty-six millions. Generations of missionaries have spent their lives in bringing about this happy result. In 1896 alone 112,318 converts were officially reported."

So much for the financial side. As a type of the twenty societies associated with the Propaganda Fide that supply the men for the arduous labors of the Apostolate, I select the *Société des Missions Etrangères* of Paris. A comparison of its work in 1822 with the results achieved in 1899 is made in the following table:

	1822.	1899.
Number of missionaries	33	881
Number of students preparing for its work	250	1,760
Number of chapels and churches	10	3,575
Number of conversions from heresy	3	464
Number of adults baptized	800	72,700
Number of catechumens receiving instruction	100	60,000
Number of dying children baptized	4,500	175,000
Number of native priests in Society	120	500

These figures speak for themselves. I will only add that during the past half century this Society alone has sent out 2,000 missionaries to enlighten the heathen and it counts 86 on its roll of martyrs.

For those who desire to investigate the statistics of Catholic missions I submit the following tables, which have been taken from the reports of the Propaganda of 1898 and as far as I know are now for the first time published in English.

In conclusion, after mature consideration of the figures, it is evident that the old church which has been the exponent of Christianity for the last nineteen centuries has not passed into the barrenness of old age, but she possesses rather the virility of youth. Though she stands to-day the most ancient institution in the world, going back to the days of classic civilization, still she is the most vigorous.

In the religious world we see not a few crumbling creeds and disintegrating systems. Religious bodies are drifting away from the old moorings. What was taught a generation ago is repudiated now. In the face of all this there is no more fascinating sight than to see the grand old church steadily pursuing her course unmindful of the attacks of enemies and undeterred by the antagonisms of the world. She serenely moves on, bearing the Gospel to all who sit in darkness and the shadow of death. The words of Gladstone have the deepest meaning: "Since the first three hundred years of persecution, the Roman Catholic Church has marched at the head of human civilization, and has driven, harnessed to her chariot, as the horses of a triumphal car, the chief intellectual forces of the world; its genius, the genius of the world; its greatness, glory, grandeur and majesty have been almost, though not absolutely, all that in these respects the world has had to boast of."

Official statistics from "Missiones Catholicae cura S. Congregationis de Propaganda Fide descriptæ Anno 1898":

Missions.	Catholics.	Priests.	Churches & Chapels.
England	1,362,489	2,674	1,492
Scotland	373,500	432	299
Ireland	3,547,079	3,445	2,707
Norway			
Sweden	9,750	74	57
Denmark			
Holland	1,854,340	3,168	1,826
Balkan Peninsula	686,210	890	684
Greece	34,710	109	189
Turkey	129,680	310	297
Persia	7,650	11	4
Arabia	1,500	11	6
India (Eng.)	1,478,325	1,080	3,995
Chino-Indian Peninsula	827,680	823	3,379
Malay, Borneo, Java and Siam	57,890	89	113
Chinese Empire	532,448	1,168	3,930
Corea and Japan	84,410	772	247
Africa	458,170	1,015	1,649
British America	2,187,480	2,766	2,716
United States	9,479,250	10,049	10,922
West Indies	339,200	195	257
Patagonia	99,500	70	89
Australia	704,170	736	1,280
Polynesia	196,850	348	684
	24,352,232	30,135	36,822

ROMAN CATHOLIC MISSIONS.

The American Statistical Association publishes the following returns as to the number of Christians (excluding Greeks and Kopts) in the various MISSIONARY COUNTRIES in 1893:

	Catholics.	Protestants.	Total.
India	*1,199,000	534,000	1,733,000
China	1,116,000	88,000	1,204,000
Siberia	70,000	20,000	90,000
Japan	30,000	—	30,000
Syria, etc.	663,000	20,000	683,000
Total in Asia	3,078,000	602,000	3,740,000
Total in Africa	2,660,000	1,740,000	4,400,000
Manila, Java, etc.	5,720,000	220,000	5,940,000
Totals	11,458,000	2,622,000	14,080,000

* The English Catholic Register for 1898 gives the number as 1,870,000.

GREEK CHRISTIANITY.

Prof. Andrew C. Zenos, D.D.,
CHICAGO.

[Replying to the encyclical of Pope Leo XIII addressed to the Greek Church, July, 1894, on the subject of reunion, the Greek ecclesiastics, after specifying the "dangerous inovations" which the Roman Catholic Church has introduced, say:

Overlooking, however, many material and weighty differences in the beliefs of the two churches—differences created, as we have seen, in the West—His Beatitude [Pope Leo XIII] represents in his encyclical that the question of the supremacy of the Roman bishops is the decisive and only cause of discord, and refers us to original sources wherein to seek what it was that our forefathers thought thereof, and what was the tradition of early Christianity. But when we do refer back to the Fathers and to the ecumenical councils of the first nine centuries, we find that the Bishop of Rome was never regarded as the supreme authority or as the infallible head of the church; but that every bishop was the head and president of his own particular church, subject only to synodical decrees and to the decisions of the church at large, which alone is infallible. From this rule the Bishop of Rome was in no wise exempted, as ecclesiastical history shows, since the sole eternal Chief and the immortal Head of the Church is our Lord Jesus Christ. Peter, whom the Papists—basing themselves on the apocryphal pseudo-Clementines of the second century—have purposely imagined to have been the founder of the Roman Church and its first bishop, Peter is seen in Scripture discussing as an equal with equals in the Apostolic Council of Jerusalem. On another occasion he is bitterly rebuked by Paul, as it is manifest in the Epistle to the Galatians. The very Gospel text to which the Roman pontiff refers, "Thou art Peter, and upon this rock I will build my church," was interpreted during the early ages of the church, both by tradition and by all the divine and sacred fathers without exception—as the Papists themselves well know—in an entirely different manner, and in an orthodox spirit; the immovable fundamental rock on which the Lord built His church, and against which the gates of hell shall not prevail, was understood metaphorically to signify the right confession which Peter had made concerning the Lord: "Thou art Christ, the Son of the living God." On this confession of faith rests firmly the saving message of the Gospel preached by all the apostles and their successors. Therefore the heaven-soaring apostle Paul refers manifestly to this Divine sentence when he declares, by Divine inspiration: "According to the grace of God which is given unto me, as a wise master-builder, I have laid the foundation, and another buildeth thereon. But let every man take heed how he buildeth thereupon. For other foundation can no man lay than that is laid, which is Jesus Christ."—"Reply of the Holy Cath. and Apo. Orth. Ch. of the East to the Ency. of Pope Leo XIII on Reunion," page 7.—Ed.]

From "Constantinople." Copyright, 1901, by FLEMING H. REVELL COMPANY.

GROUP OF GREEK CLERGY

GREEK CHRISTIANITY.

THE name Greek Christianity should be employed in strictest accuracy to designate the type of thought and life developed under the influence of the Gospel, among those peoples which had been previously molded by Greek civilization. As a matter of fact, however, the expression is used as the equivalent of the Greek Church, whose full name is *The Holy Eastern Orthodox Catholic Apostolic Church.* This church includes the Greeks of Turkey, under the Patriarchs of Constantinople, Antioch, Jerusalem and Alexandria, the National Church of the Kingdom of Greece, under the National Synod of Greece, and the National Church of the Russian Empire, under a Holy Synod of its own. It embraces a population of 100,000,000 souls. The Christian Church finally divided into the Eastern and the Western, 1054 A. D., by Pope Leo IX, of Rome, and the Patriarch Cerularius, of Constantinople, solemnly excommunicated each other.

Of all the forms of Christianity, the Greek claims to be the most ancient and primitive. This claim is made, it is true, by the Roman also; but there is a difference. In order to account for the apparent difference of their type from the Apostolic as pictured in the New Testament writings, the representatives of the Roman Church have resorted to a theory of development.[*] The adherents of the Greek type, on the other hand, have always stood by the theory that the whole of Christian truth and law of practice was once for all delivered in its final form to the Apostles, and by them in part committed to writing, and in part redelivered to their successors[†]. Thus while Roman Christianity is based on the three-fold ground of Scripture, tradition and development, under the care of a living and

---

[*] We accept here as correct the theory of Romanism expounded by Cardinal Newman in his essay on "Development" (published 1845), according to which the original teaching of Christ and the Apostles only implicitly contained the full doctrinal development of the later ages. The opposite view, set forth in Father Clark's "Theory of Catholicism," "that the subsequent development of dogma was contained in the deposit which Christ handed to His Apostles; that Christ Himself instructed Peter in the doctrine of the Immaculate Conception of the Virgin, the Infallibility of the Pope, the doctrine of transubstantiation and the system of penance," we regard as more nearly a correct exposition of the standpoint of Greek Catholicism.

[†] According to the "Orthodox Confession of the Eastern Church," put forth in 1643, the standards of the Greek Catholic Church are "partly the Holy Scriptures and partly the ecclesiastical traditions and teachings of the synods and of the Holy Fathers" (*Quest.* 4). In the Confession of Dositheus adopted by the Synod of Jerusalem, 1672, substantially the same view is put forth, but with less clearness (*Decr.* 2). The church as a whole seems to be regarded as the interpreter of the truth given in the Scriptures, rather than as an original source of truth.

infallible church, Greek Christianity is built on the two-fold foundation of Scripture and tradition, infallibly preserved and interpreted by the living church. The task, however, of formulating for preservation and interpretation was a simple one; and according to the adherents of the Greek type, it was fully and finally accomplished during the ancient period. The standards were, in fact, fixed during the first eight centuries of the Christian era by the first seven ecumenical councils, the only ones recognized as ecumenical. Among these, it includes the so-called Quinisext, held in Constantinople in 892—*i. e.,* during the interval between the sixth and seventh centuries. Naturally, the Council of Nicæa, as the first in order of time, and as dealing with the question of all questions, that of the mode of the Divine subsistence, stands out above the others in importance; and its creed and decisions are esteemed in a special manner as valuable and authoritative.

To understand and appreciate the true genius and character of Greek Christianity, it is therefore not necessary to trace its history beyond, at the most, the end of the ninth century. By its theory of the Gospel, it sets the limit of its own growth within that period.

We may conveniently group the distinctive features of Greek Christianity under the familiar rubrics of doctrine, polity and worship.

I. The first and most striking element in the environment which the Gospel encountered as it touched Greek soil was a definite system of philosophy. The Greek-speaking Fathers of the Church, who flourished between the second and fifth centuries, were not able to resist the power of this philosophy. This philosophy at first took the field against Christianity, and in the persons of some of its most strenuous representatives, such as Celsus and Porphyry, it bitterly fought the new system. But from the very opening of the second century a movement was inaugurated toward their conciliation, a movement which began in the very bosom of the Christian Church. The Christian apologists, who were for the most part philosophers of the Platonic type, studied to show the inner harmony between true philosophy and the Gospel. Thus, by the time of the founding of the Alexandrian School, by Pantænus, a distinct and strong tendency had set in toward formulating the truth of Christianity in the terms of the Greek philosophy. Alexandria naturally furnished a favorable soil for the growth of this tendency. It had already witnessed a powerful effort to harmonize Judaism with

GREEK CHRISTIANITY.

Greek philosophy in the person of Philo. It is true this effort had not proved entirely successful. It had found no adherents among the Jews, at least of Palestine. But it had at least opened the way for the reconciliation of the newer and more flexible offshoot of Judaism—Christianity—with Platonism.

Of the four names with which the School of Alexandria is identified, that of Pantænus represents a comparatively unknown quantity. Clement, however, who succeeded him, was evidently a man of vigorous and well-versed mind. He is believed to have been an Athenian, and his works abound in quotations from the classical writers which, though fragmentary in themselves, have a value entirely independent of the history of Christian thought. With his antecedents and equipment, it was natural that he should gird himself to the task of casting the truth of the Gospel into the mold of philosophy. Perhaps it would be more accurate to say that he performed this task without the consciousness of doing something that no one else had done before, or of taking a view of the Gospel destined to result in a great development of thought. In any case, he began with the definite assumption that philosophy was as direct a preparation for the Gospel as the Old Testament was. "To the Jews belonged the law, and to the Greeks philosophy, until the advent; and after that came the universal calling to be a peculiar people of righteousness, through the teaching which flows from faith brought together by one Lord, the only God of both Greeks and barbarians, or rather of the whole race of men." (*Strom.* v. 17). "Philosophy was a schoolmaster to bring the Hellenic mind, as the law was of the Hebrews, to Christ." (*Strom.* l, 19). In this view of philosophy lies the germ of Christian theology. If philosophy may be used as a regulative principle of thought in the sphere of religion, it follows that through it the facts of the Christian religion as given in the Scriptures may be molded and interpreted into a system. This was a considerable contribution to the development of a Christian system of thought.

Clement, however, did more than open the way for doctrinal construction. He used philosophy in the specific elaboration of the Christian view of God. As against a prevalent tendency in the heathen systems of his day, he asserted with emphasis and amplitude the Christian idea of immanence in the world, and in humanity through Christ. Without denying the mysterious and unknowable aspects of God, or attempting to reconcile the transcendence involved in it, he unqualifiedly set forth the truth that in Christ God dwells in the world and in man. Thus he imparted to the Christian doctrine of God its first though vague form. He constructed the bridge that was to span the distance between the notion of the incarnation, as held in solution in Christian experience, and the doctrine of the incarnation as formulated in the creeds.

But to the Christian conception of man also, Clement gave a form which, though not universally accepted by Western Christendom, served as the immovable basis of all further thinking on the subject in the East. This contribution consists in the working out of the Biblical idea that man is in the image of God, which image is a moral and spiritual one. It is the ability to express the inmost essence or character of God. Man's spiritual constitution is constructed, so to speak, after the Divine type. And it is for this reason that he responds to the call of God. The law is written within his heart. He is possessed of the spontaneous power of working out his destiny. He has freedom of will, and is able to follow out the Divine purpose, which is the law of his being. But his freedom is not that of a being independent of God; but of one linked into and holding a vital relation to God, and thus retaining the capacity, through all the vicissitudes of a sinful career, of fulfilling his appointed destiny. This view, so emphatically set forth, becomes a constant factor in the Greek theology from the day of Clement onward. The Oriental Church, without wavering or hesitation, has incorporated it in its standards, and holds it to the present day. It is the doctrine stoutly advocated and reasoned for in the Confession of Dositheus (Deci. 3) and in the Orthodox Confession (Quest. 27).

Together with this anthropology, and in fact necessarily related to it, is Clement's doctrine of redemption as a process of education. The indwelling God is the instructor. (Pædag 1, 9). Sin is not minimized in this scheme, but the power which is to eliminate it from the world of humanity is conceived of as working within human nature itself as a constant process rather than as a pure historic fact once for all. The work of Christ in redemption is not so much that of securing the reconciliation of God alienated from man, or of man alienated from God, as that of informing man of a relationship with God which has always existed but was likely to become ineffective on account of ignorance and sin.

We have given so much space to these positions of Clement, because, on the fundamental points of thought regarding God, man and redemption, Greek Christianity has never left the ground occupied by him. It would be a mistake, however, to suppose that he stamped his impress upon that type in every particular. First of all, his system is not full and well rounded. His influence, vast as it must have been, did not extend into many regions of religious thought. His attitude toward the sources and standards is essentially different from that of the leaders of Greek Christianity who followed him. So is his view of the church and of eschatological questions.

But what Clement left imperfect was measurably completed by Origen. It is hardly necessary to say that Origen was the first thinker who took a universal and comprehensive view of the whole sphere of Christian thought, and proposed to himself the task of a complete, systematic theology. Building on the foundations laid down by Clement, he worked out a doctrine of Scripture without departing from the philosophical basis of his predecessor. He carried the principle of philosophic construction so thoroughly into the realm of Christian doctrine that he conceived it possible to build a cosmology out of the Gospel. He may fairly be called the father of systematic theology. He did not claim to have solved all the problems of the Universe, but he swept the horizon in his universal gaze for the truth, and harmonized what he found into a system. As was natural in a first effort in this direction, his system failed to satisfy all the varying types of Christian thinkers who came after him. But his influence was incalculable. His so-called heresies did not deter men from employing his methods and accepting most of his conclusions. In the West, it is true, he was unappreciated, one might say almost altogether ignored; but in Alexandria, which became the centre of ferment in thought during the Arian and Christological controversies of the fourth and fifth centuries, his principles were a potent influence. The theology of the Greek Church followed in the main the lines laid down by him. Leaving out the objectionable elements in his system, the great councils of the church elaborated and formulated his thoughts into canons and creeds.

This process of crystallization was naturally fomented and even directed by great minds like that of Athanasius, the three Cappadocians (Gregory of Nazianzus, Gregory of Nyssa, and Basil of Cæsarea), and John of Damascus ("the last of the Greek Fathers"). The first of these occupied a special position of the guardian and preserver of the Christian notion of the tri-personality of God. In the well-known controversy with Arius and the Arians, he laid down the lines beyond which the Christian idea of God could not be carried without danger of being lost in heathen polytheism. But he never swerved from the philosophical basis of treatment employed by the first of the Greek theologians. And when closely considered, his doctrine of the Trinity, as distinguished from that of Augustine, bears the marks of a freer, less mechanical, and more rational—*i. e.*, philosophical—treatment.

The same may be said, with somewhat less emphasis, of the theology of the three great Cappadocians, who closely followed Athanasius. They centre and move within the sphere of philosophy as opened for them by their Alexandrian predecessors. The Trinity, as defined in the Creed of Nicæa, occupied their minds almost to the exclusion of every other doctrinal topic. And it is under their influence, and as a result of their discussions, that the doctrine received its final touches and passed into the amplified and perfected form given it in the second ecumenical council. Even to sketch in outline their work would be not to show the distinctive features of the Greek theology, but to trace the history of the common orthodoxy of Christendom. It is enough to notice that in them all, as in the last great theologian of the East, John of Damascus, philosophy is the vehicle and the solvent of all religious thought.

But with John of Damascus, synchronizing as he does approximately with the last of the seven ecumenical councils, progress in the philosophical formulation of Christian truth reaches its end. Christian theology becomes in a sense a *philosophia ultima*. And the results gained are, first of all, a distinct body of recognized sources and standards which include the Scriptures and the Catholic traditions. The latter with some of the Fathers, at least, is supplementary to Scripture, filling up its gaps and perfecting its incompleteness. Secondly, a clear conception of the church as the ark of safety without which salvation is impossible. Thirdly, a definition of the personality of God as subsisting in three hypostases but one essence. Fourthly, a representation of the person of Christ as including a Divine and a human nature existing together in one person, without confusion, without change, without separation and without division. Fifthly and finally, a doctrine of the intermediate state, which is opposed on the one hand to the Roman idea of Purgatory (Cf. *Orth. Conf. Quest.* 66. *Conf. Dos. Decr.* 18); but opposed on the other hand, also, to the idea generally current in Protestantism, that the condition of believers is finally fixed at death. Accordingly, prayers, alms-givings and sacramental services are enjoined upon the living on behalf and in the name of the dead. (*Orth. Conf. Quest.* 64 and 65; *Conf. Dosith.* 18).

How firmly the very form of these doctrines was fixed in the ultimate philosophy may be seen from the flint-like resistance offered by the Eastern Church to the addition in the West of the *filioque* clause to the creed. The Nicæno-Constantinopolitan symbol closes abruptly with the article: "and in the Holy Spirit." As enlarged and finally adopted in the East it reads: "and in the Holy Spirit, the Lord and Giver of Life, who proceeds from the Father." This form of expression was confirmed in the council of Chalcedon in 451, and prevailed both in the East and in the West until 589. In the third provincial Council of Toledo, held that year, out of zeal for the deity of Christ, which was assailed by the Arians in the West, and without the slightest intention to alter the sense of the creedal statement, the words "and from the Son" were added to the article above cited. The addition passed unchallenged, and was universally accepted throughout the West. But in the East it was regarded as tampering with the fixed standards. Photius, the Patriarch of Constantinople, called attention to it, and protested against it in his controversy with Pope Nicholas I. Ever since, in all discussions regarding the relations of the Eastern and Western churches, the *filioque* has been the principal ground of contention in the sphere of doctrine. All efforts to re-unite the two churches have stumbled upon it as upon an immovable rock. It has often been said that the doctrinal difference between the Greek and Roman Catholic churches is only of secondary importance; that the political rupture between the Oriental and Occidental branches of the old Roman Empire was the chief and primary cause of the division. But the tenacity with which both sides to the controversy hold to their views would indicate something more than a political line of division. The conviction had evidently been deepened and fixed that the conceptions of truth held under the name of Christianity were capable of only one formulation, and once reached that must abide unalterable.

II. A second main feature of Greek Christianity is its oligarchical polity, as distinguished from the monarchical polity of Roman Catholicism and the predominantly democratic polity of Protestantism. It may be safely asserted that historical scholarship has put it beyond question that all the forms of church polity under which Christianity is organized at the present day are developments of certain tendencies or principles given in the New Testament. The polity of Greek Christianity is not an exception to this generalization. In the New Testament the leaders, and if we may use the term in an accommodated sense, the officers of the church are presbyters or elders. These presently become, still within the New Testament period, pastors or bishops. Later the bishop assumes the place of president over a circle of elders and bishops of less important churches, and thus there arises the episcopate of the hierarchical type; still later the metropolitan is singled out and placed above the diocesan bishop; then the patriarch appears above the metropolitan. And all along the church is represented in its entirety in councils, synods or convocations. Greek Catholicism stops with this stage of development in polity. Romanism takes one step further in establishing first, one patriarch above the others as the first among equals, and second in ascribing to the one thus singled out (the Bishop of Rome) absolute supremacy and infallibility. Greek Catholicism is organized upon the basis of a regular hierarchical system of patriarchs, metropolitans, bishops and presbyters and lower clergy, all supervised by national or provincial synods. It has never gone the length of recognizing one supreme head of the church upon earth (Cf. *Orth. Conf. Quest.* 85; *Conf. Dosith. Decr.* 10). On the contrary from the earliest days it has strenuously resisted the claim of the Pope to supremacy, and consistently held the ground that such claim was contrary to the Scriptures and the traditions of the church.

Furthermore, having thus planted itself upon the ground of opposition to the monarchical system, it has also declined to put the authority of the church over that of the state. On the other hand, it does not believe in the separation of church from state, but adheres to the standpoint reached in the adoption of the church as a branch of the state by the Emperor Constantine; and thus it is practically upon an Erastian basis. It subordinates the government of the church to that of the civil ruler. It is hardly necessary to say that this feature of it, like those already named, represents a half-way stage of development. It is beyond the primitive and simple attitude of the New Testament, in which the church is a community of itself and by itself within the secular world, having no connection whatever with civil government; but it is not advanced to the position of the eleventh century Western Church, in which the Church of Jesus Christ, as a spiritual and eternal organization, is above all secular governments, and has a right to control and direct them. But on the church as a spiritual body the Greek doctrine is neither uncertain nor rudimentary. It is explicitly declared to be an infallible body, to which the light of absolute truth is forever and inalienably entrusted from above (*Conf. Orth. Quest.* 96; *Conf. Dosith. Decr.* 2).

III. The third general distinctive feature of Greek Christianity is its form of worship. Historically it has imported two essential features to the worship of the New Testament. One of these it takes from the Old Testament, and the other from paganism. The first is the setting of the sacrificial idea in the central place in worship. This, of course, it does in common with Roman Catholicism. Both look upon the Lord's Supper as embodying the chief and central act of worship in the Christian Church; and both view the Lord's Supper as a sacrifice requiring a priesthood for its proper administration; both regard the sacrifice as a sacrifice of Christ's real body and blood by way of transubstantiation; and both finally consider all other parts of worship accessory to this sacrifice. Yet in details even here the position of Roman Catholicism is further advanced than that of Greek Christianity. First, Greek Christianity insists on a more primitive way of offering the sacrifice, in that it calls for communion in both kinds. The communicant is, according to its doctrine, entitled and enjoined to participate both of the body and of the blood of the sacrifice. Roman Catholicism has come to limit the laity to the participation of the body alone. Secondly, the Greek Church insists on the use of leavened bread in the ordinance (Cf. *Orth. Conf. Quest.* 107); Latin Christianity, on the other hand, has since the tenth century used unleavened bread (Cf. Bingham, *Orig. Eccles.* XV, ii, 5). But apart from these details, which show simply a fixity in custom in the Greek Church which was not reached until later in the Roman, the basis of doctrine on the nature of the sacraments as well as on their number is identical in both churches. Both of the churches proceed upon the assumption that the Old Testament idea of sacrifice is carried into and adopted by the New.

The element which Greek Christianity imported into its worship from paganism is the veneration of saints and images. We speak of these two subjects as one, because the latter is simply the sequel of the former. The worship of saints was not strenuously objected to in the ancient church. It was so natural to yield to the instinct of honoring the departed; and there was so much stimulus and guidance in the examples of men respected and honored that a protest was not to be expected to anniversaries and celebrations having this object in view. But such celebrations soon led, especially in the popular conception, to the idealization of those honored, and through stages which it is unnecessary to trace, saint worship arose as a counterpart of the worship of heroes and demigods among the heathen peoples of antiquity. It was inevitable that in the quasi-Pantheon thus constituted the place of prime importance should be given to the Virgin Mary.

The introduction of images was not as easy. The second commandment of the Decalogue appeared to positively exclude the use of sculptures and paintings, even as means of worshiping the true God, lest they should become objects of worship in and for themselves. Yet representations of the Virgin, of the saints, and of the angels seemed to have been quite early introduced into the churches both of the East and of the West. When this practice reached considerable proportions, a controversy arose which proved to be one of the bitterest in the history of the church. For over one hundred years the question whether images should or should not be used in worship was not only discussed by theologians and church dignitaries in vigorous rhetorical sentences, but also fought over by emperors and generals upon the battle field. The issue was the complete triumph of image worship. And in the celebration of All Saints' Day the church to the present day commemorates the permanent establishment of this feature of its cultus. Here once more the difference between Eastern Catholicism and Western must be noted. Romanism, developing with rigid consistency the principle of the use of images, allows all forms of art as permissible means of worship. Greek Catholicism, looking back on the second commandment, and aiming to reconcile her practice with the apparent prohibition of artistic representations of God and divine beings, excludes "graven" images—*i. e.*, sculptures and carved works of all kinds—from the churches, but allows sketched or painted images.

In the main, then, in the doctrinal sphere the characteristic of Greek Christianity is the early closing of questions for discussion which in the West were held open much longer; the acceptance of certain conclusions as final which to the Western mind represent only intermediate stages of development in the erection of a fixed and ultimate orthodoxy upon a philosophical basis. In the sphere of church government, the characteristic is the formation of a fixed and unbending hierarchical system of the oligarchical type. In the sphere of worship it is the development of a fixed cultus bringing together Old Testament, Judaic elements, and purely natural and pagan forms, and fusing them into an elaborate ritual. In one word, in all the spheres it is the cessation and exclusion of progress.

PROTESTANT CHRISTIANITY.

Rev. Wm. D. Grant, Ph.D.,
NEW YORK.

[Rome alone has presented her theology to the world in a thoroughly institutional form. What Protestants believe, Rome embodies in a visible organism. While they derive the life of the church from their faith, Rome derives her faith from the life of the church. Romanism was a vast organization almost before it was a distinct faith. Rome did not so much incarnate her dogmas in her ritual as distill her dogmas out of her ritual.

Contemplating her conquests, she did not hesitate to affirm that God was in her institutions; that He was acting through her agency; that He was really placing His divine influence at her disposal. With her, faith is nourished from the divine institution, not the divine institution from faith. Every rite which other Christian sects regard as suggesting and shadowing forth the spiritual life of faith, Rome regards as itself the shrine of divine power. The Roman theology claims for the entire ritual of the church that it is one vast transubstantiation. She believes that the church's ministrations impart more grace to her ministers than her ministers can impart to their ministrations. God's power is held to be in the church's actions, and from that centre it flows out to the whole church.

It was characteristic that the Roman Christian should look rather for a divine *administration* than for vivid, conscious communion with the spirit of God. Hence a sacramental system was of the essence of their religion. They did not so much seek to be spirit to spirit with God as to adore Him in His acts. In this respect the Catholic Church has never changed since first the ancient world began to suspect that the lost sceptre of the Cæsars had passed into a Roman bishop's grasp.

Thus the Roman Catholic Church, though beginning in humility, early passed into incredulity and arrogance, followed by a passion for social and political ascendancy. In her judgment, she became necessary to God. She was willing to recognize her own dependence, but most unwilling to believe that God could ever choose any other instrument. It was natural for her to believe that all real power could be organized, codified and reduced to a system, and to claim exclusiveness for her own acts. After proclaiming that a divine influence attended her ministry, irrespective of moral and spiritual conditions, she fell into the snare of prizing her own instrumentality as if it had been the very centre of that influence, and so gradually forgot the essence of her former faith. She now dreams that she holds a monopoly of ecclesiastical instrumentality. Reliance is no longer had on the person of the living Christ, but in powers which she claims have been exclusively delegated to her. Thus the more she believes in herself the less likely is she to rely on her Lord. The vicious principle then becomes established that the church means the priesthood. Therefore, the fulness of divine action is denied to any outside of her institution and sacraments. Human agency everywhere appears on behalf of God.

The Protestant faith is a protest not merely against the abuse of this machinery, but against the machinery itself. Isolate the mind from visible agency and the Roman Catholic has hardly a religious life to live. But the religion of Protestantism is, in its original nature, separated from visible agencies; springing up in secret struggles, it is matured by thought, watered by personal devotion, and rooted directly in God. It has been the child of Conscience, the pupil of Philosophy, the companion of Poetry, the parent of Freedom, and the discoverer of the Bible.—R. H. HUTTON, "Essays I," page 354.—ED.]

* * *

IT SEEMS to be universally assumed by our Roman Catholic brethren that, since they can, in their judgment, establish a right to claim for their church historical priority and tactual continuity; since they were originally entrusted with the Revelation of Jesus Christ and the establishment of His kingdom, therefore, all mankind, on pain of eternal damnation, must unite with and adhere to their communion; and all must do so, let the moral character of the institution be what it may. Said Pope Boniface VIII: "We declare, say, define, and pronounce that every human being should be subject to the Roman Pontiff, to be an article of necessary faith." The institution must be maintained in its historical integrity, regardless of consequences, as though historical continuity were the all-important matter, and the possession of which would atone for every other defect, no matter how great or serious. Even though recreancy to trust, wide departure from original simplicity in Christian teaching and practice, viciousness in administration and corruption in morals may be shown, yet the institution must continue to lay claim to its original commission. This is surely an application of the doctrine of "the perseverance of the saints" applied to the perseverance of sinners.

It may not be a difficult task for the Roman Catholic Church to establish its claim to historical priority and tactual succession, but let all Christians remind themselves that there are matters, relating to doctrine and life, which are infinitely more important. We remember that the Jews of Christ's day (John, viii) laid claim to special, divine consideration because they could say, and say truthfully: "We be Abraham's seed." But though they might be able to mislead others by their high-sounding claim to historical descent from such a distinguished ancester, Jesus Christ clearly sees through their subterfuge, and pierces the thin disguise of their specious pretensions, and tells them that such a distinction, however true, counts for nothing unless they do the works of Abraham.

That it is a religious institution does not guarantee exemption from a condemnation which would be the merited desert of any secular organization guilty of the same offence. Nay, more, God Almighty *must* chastise, if He does not utterly reject, an institution, even of His own appointment, which has manifestly failed in its trusteeship as witness to His grace and representative of His righteousness. Whoever else may, He cannot afford to condone or continue to recognize such as His representative. His promise and warning are in such words as these: "If ye be willing and obedient, ye shall eat the good of the land; but if ye refuse and rebel, ye shall be devoured with the sword; for the mouth of the Lord hath spoken it." (Isaiah i, 19, 20.) They did "refuse and rebel"; therefore He who saw at once their spiritual pride and poverty said to them: "Behold your house is left unto you desolate"—God, their covenant God, had forsaken them, and had done so notwithstanding He had chosen them as the channel and custodian of His own revelation. "Ye pay tithe of mint, and anise, and cummin, and have omitted the weightier matters of the law, judgment, mercy and faith; therefore, *the kingdom of God shall be taken from you, and given to a nation bringing forth the fruits thereof*" (Matt. xxi, 43; xxiii, 23). This prophecy became history in the year 70 A. D. Our Lord teaches this same principle in the parables of the talents and of the vineyard. Indeed, the principle applies to sacred and secular history alike—to churches and nations, as well as to individuals the world over and for all time. It is the voice of history, of reason, and of God. And not even His own church, when it has become degenerate, can claim immunity or be allowed to escape. Why were the seven churches of Asia Minor allowed to perish, think you? What is the significance of the rise and rapid advancement of Islam in the seventh century? Was it not sent with its drawn sword to scourge an idolatrous church? Were not John Wesley and his associates in the eighteenth century amply justified in the course which they pursued, when the Anglican Church of that day had failed to administer its trust in the interests of righteousness and the kingdom of God? Or in 1843, under the oppressive power of an arrogant church in Scotland, were not Thomas Chalmers and his 470 fellow-protestants fully justified in seeking freedom by withdrawal? Is there no moral and religious significance in the recent loss to Spain of her American possessions; and, in recent times, too, what about the loss of Roman Catholic religious and political power and prestige in Mexico and Central and South America? And, in a still more recent instance, and one nearer home, the application of this principle may be clearly seen, viz.: the overthrow of Tammany Hall in New York City, November, 1901. Official corruption, fostering of crime, and political oppression having been proven against the institution, were not all those who united for its overthrow amply justified in the course which they pursued?

May not an institution, then, be called to account—even though that institution claims to be the true and only church of Jesus Christ—when it has violated common, moral decency, has lorded it over God's heritage, and has manifestly proved recreant to its trust? Is withdrawal from such permissible under no circumstances whatever? And can anything be lost by leaving an institution, whatever its claims to divine sanction and recognition, when in spirit and purpose it has manifestly left its Lord and Founder?

Now, who can doubt that the Reformation of the sixteenth century was another application of this same principle, even though the institution in this case was the Church of God itself?—God's time and method it was for scourging a thoroughly corrupt church.

It were a thankless task, however, to beat anew the oft-threshed straw of this epoch in church history; enough to say a state of things did exist in the Christian Church—in doctrinal innovations, in moral laxity, and in maladministration—at the beginning of the sixteenth century, which, in the eyes of all right-thinking and unprejudiced men, not only amply justified the course taken by the Reformers, but which made reformation a moral necessity.

Luther himself, while on a visit to Rome, 1511, was deeply shocked at the profane levity of the priesthood, while they were equally astonished at his solemn credulity, and jeered him as a dull German who had not genius enough to be skeptical, or cunning enough to be hypocritical. Rome itself was full of mocking hypocrisy, defiant skepticism, jeering impiety and shameless revelry. This is not to be wondered at, since the reigning Pope, Leo X, himself regarded Christianity in the light of a "profitable" fable.

I may be told, however, that this was Rome as seen through the eyes of prejudice and bitterness of spirit. Not so! Remember, it was but the year 1511—six full years before the appearance of his famous ninety-five theses. Martin Luther had come to Rome neither to spy out the land nor to secure ammunition to bombard the Roman citadel, but on a special mission for his monastic order; had come believing the Eternal City to be the abode of all the sanctities; for when once in sight of its walls he exclaimed, "I greet thee, thou holy Rome!" He went the rounds, too, of all the churches appointed for pilgrims, and climbed, on his knees, the holy stairs of Pontius Pilate. And, wonderful to relate, he wished his father and mother had been dead, since, in the Holy City, he was afforded such a rare opportunity of delivering their souls from purgatory. Such was the spirit and such the belief which animated Martin Luther when he visited Rome. But after he returned home he said: "Never would I have believed the statement, had another told me, of what I saw with my own eyes and heard with my own ears in the Holy City." But we have witness other than that of Martin Luther.

Some years ago the sensational historical work of the late Dr. J. Janssen, entitled "History of the German People Since the Close of the Middle Ages," published in a half-dozen volumes, kept the Protestant and the Catholic reading public of the Continent on the *qui vive* for half a decade, as the work aimed to demonstrate, on the ground of authentic sources and in accordance with correct historiographical principles and methods, that the Reformation was the greatest misfortune that ever befell Europe and was really the source and fountain-head of all the ills of later generations, politically, socially, and religiously. A counterpart to this attempt has been undertaken by the Innsbrück Roman Catholic historian, Dr. Louis Pastor, in his "History of the Popes Since the Close of the Middle Ages." With indefatigable industry the author has been at work since 1889 along Janssen's lines in method and manner. In the third volume, recently issued, he comes to consider the crucial period of papacy, the period of 1484 to 1513, and to his credit it must be said that he has not, as did his predecessor, forced historical truth into the Procrustean bed of dogmatical prejudgments. In fact, he acknowledges the direful condition of the papacy of that period in a manner even exceeding that of such model Protestant writers as Ranke, Gregorovius, Brosch, and others.

Pastor does not try to save what can not be saved. He acknowledges that with the sole exception of the short reign of Pius III, in 1503, the highest office of the Roman Catholic Church was occupied by men who represented the acme of unworthiness of the dignity.

PROTESTANT MEMORIAL CHURCH, SPIRE-ON-THE-RHINE.

The leading characters, Innocent VIII and Alexander VI, are depicted much as this is done by Protestant writers. Innocent's wicked life before his ascent to the papal throne is not ignored, nor the fact that he had at least two illegitimate children, and that for one of them, Francheshetto Ciob, he prepared a grand wedding in the papal palace in Rome, the same son being the one who in a single night lost in gambling 14,000 ducats, the winner being Cardinal Riario. Such nepotism and favoritism was shown that in 1492 the Pope appointed to the office of cardinal a fourteen-year-old boy, Giovanini Medici, who afterward became Leo X.

In Alexander's case the author adopts the dictum of Möhler, the great Catholic theologian of Munich, who declared that "the curse of this Pope was his family." The horrible deeds of his son, the infamous Cæsar Borgia, are openly discussed in this volume. In the case of Alexander it is not denied that before and after his appointment to the clerical office he led a very immoral life. On the occasion of the marriage of his daughter Lucretia in the Vatican carousing and dancing was the order of the day, or rather of the night. His nepotism is soundly condemned. In agreement with A. de Reumunt's judgment, Pastor regards the reign of Alexander as "a misfortune," which brought great discredit on the whole institution of papacy.

Thus "Rome has lost her power," as Mr. Hutton says, "not so much by doctrinal blunders as by moral and spiritual failure. She lost it because the corruptions of the church made her moral fallibility patent, and because the just moral instincts of men perceived at once that a church which had, for a time at least, lost all her pre-eminence in righteousness over the world which she was leading, could not by any possibility be competent to interpret infallibly spiritual truth."

But, some one may say, though the Roman Catholic Church in the sixteenth century was as bad as you have made it appear; yea, though it may have been a great deal worse, by what right or authority has any one to call her to account for her conduct? True, if we must abide by her deliverances, we have no right to question her course in any respect whatever. We have no redress from moral turpitude the most shameful, or deliverance from administration the most oppressive. Should this statement be questioned, let us hear what Mr. Gladstone says: "The Pope demands for himself the right to determine the province of his own rights, and has so defined it in formal documents as to warrant any and every invasion of the civil power. Against such definition of his own power there is no appeal to reason, that is, rationalism; nor to Scripture, that is heresy; nor to history, that is private judgment."

But should it be said Mr. Gladstone speaks as a Protestant, and may be either biased or misinformed, then let us hear Cardinal Manning, who says: "The church herself is the divine witness, teacher and judge of the revelation entrusted to her. There exists no other. *She is her own judge respecting the faithfulness of administering her trust.* There is no tribunal to which appeal from the church can be taken; there is no co-ordinate witness, teacher or judge who can revise or criticise or test the teaching of the church. She is sole and alone in the world * * * it belongs to the church alone to determine the limits of her own infallibility."

Thus, you will observe, the Roman Catholic Church is as immutable in her nature as her pretensions are arrogant—neither modern science, historical criticism, nor loss of temporal power has led the Pope to modify in the least his astounding claim to be sole lord of the individual conscience and arbiter of human destiny. Rome has modified neither her doctrine, her purpose, nor her spirit—she has frequently changed her methods—since Luther's day; nor is she now more amenable to Scripture, reason or lay suggestion than she was then. If I should be mistaken in this respect it would be a great gratification to learn of Rome's conversion.

Her deliverances at the Council of Trent were Rome's answer to the Reformation, and the Pope's promulgation of his infallibility in 1870, on the loss of his temporal power, was his answer to the world that he would be supreme at least in his own house.

It was against this spirit of consummate arrogance, which was responsible for a state of evil that had passed beyond endurance, that Luther threw the whole weight of his majestic personality and moral enthusiasm; it was against this spirit that the representatives of Evangelical Christianity in Germany entered their solemn protest at Spier, April, 1529; and it is against this same spirit, imperious now as ever, that, after four hundred years, nearly 150,000,000 of people protest, and, with ever-increasing numbers and vehemence, shall continue to protest.

Could the Reformers have brought the church round to their way of thinking, respecting the supremacy and sufficiency of Scripture, respecting the right of private judgment, regarding justification by faith alone, regarding the privilege of the individual to treat directly with God, they would have been glad, no doubt, to have remained within the bosom of Mother Church. But history had taught them that any efforts they might put forth to secure such reforms within the church itself must prove a fruitless task. It was well known to them that for more than two centuries before the historic protest was entered, there were those who had sought, by every fair means in their power, to introduce and carry through reforms within the church, but everywhere they met defeat, and not a few of them a violent death at the hands of the ecclesiastical machine. The principles of the Reformation had already been represented in men like Arnold of Brescia, and Savonarola, Huss and Jerome, Wiclif and the Lollards, Tauler and the Mystics; in the minorities at the Reformatory Councils of Pisa, Constance and Basle, and in the reform efforts made by Peter d'Ailly and John Gerson in the University of Paris. Long before Luther's day, therefore, there were those whose souls wept in secret on account of corruptions which they could not cure. It was not till now (1529) that men felt strong enough and bold enough to lift up their heads and make public profession of their faith and demand their religious freedom. It mattered not that their protest was unheeded and their demand denied by both the civil and the ecclesiastical authority. "If God be for us," said they, "who can be against us?" But in thus breaking away from Roman Catholic control it was necessary that the Reformers should give a reason for the faith that was in them.

To go back to the creeds and confessions then adopted and say, Here are Protestant faith and practice defined, would be an easy way of settling what, in the course of centuries and the multiplication of sects, has come to be a very difficult matter to secure—a definition of Protestantism. For in common parlance, a Protestant means anybody who is not a Roman Catholic, and Protestantism is thus a sort of drag-net that "gathers fish of every kind," from the believer in the Trinity and Incarnation to the Mormon and the agnostic, and even the avowed atheist. What, then, is "the Protestant faith"? What, or whose Protestantism, then, shall be defined?

It may be proper to state here that the definition of a system is its poorest part. It is the weakness and not the strength and glory of a system that its real power and distinctive character can be organized and codified and reduced to a finality. Most certain is it that the strength of Christianity itself is not found in any elaborate definition that may be given of it. Its Founder Himself nowhere defines it—unless in the suggestive statement, "The words that I speak unto you, they are spirit and they are life." Or does St. Paul define Christianity when he says: "The law of the spirit of life in Christ Jesus has made me free from the law of sin and death"? Certainly "spirit and life" distinguish Christianity.

A Divine truth, however, is not a truth intelligible to all as a matter of mere definition and intellectual exposition; that it may become intelligible it may require to be translated into terms of life, clothed with flesh and blood, and warmed with a tender heart. Mere definition may not demonstrate anything; deeds alone insure demonstration. So the "spirit and life" of Christianity are embodied in Him—"He went about doing good." Christ is Christianity. And since Christianity is pre-eminently a personal religion, establishing the most intimate and solitary relations with God, its essential features are more forcefully presented through life than through logic. In the measure, therefore, in which Protestantism is allied to Christianity, in that measure does it elude definition, save as "spirit and life" may be defined.

It is not difficult to define an institution whose characteristics and powers reside in its organization, its ceremonies and its rites; a system whose every doctrinal deliverance is logically consistent with every other part, and whose vast machinery is directed by a single, infallible head; a system which demands the unconditional surrender of the intellect, the conscience and the will; a system which constantly calls attention to itself, and as constantly reminds its adherents of their entire dependence upon it for their salvation, since it possesses all the treasures of Divine grace and forgiveness. It must be quite apparent that Protestantism is not such a religious system—it makes a very different claim and has a very different aim. So far from the Protestant Church calling attention to itself and asking its adherents to entrust themselves to it for salvation, impressing upon them their entire dependence, it is its constant endeavor to direct them to the ever-living and the ever-present Christ, who Himself says, "Come unto *Me*." But, more than this, it is the aim of Protestantism to make man, as far as possible and as speedily as possible, independent of the church, and this end is attained just in the degree in which its members advance to the "measure of the stature of the fulness of Christ." The distinguishing feature, therefore, between Romanism and Protestantism is this: While the former magnifies the church and endeavors to persuade men to entrust themselves to her for pardon and guidance, the latter magnifies the living Christ and endeavors to persuade men to entrust themselves to Him for forgiveness and guidance. There follow, naturally, two seats of religious authority: The seat of religious authority for the Roman Catholic is the church—what does the church say?—while the seat of religious authority for the Protestant is the Christ—what does the Christ say?

It is quite apparent, also, that the office of the Christian Church, as conceived by a Roman Catholic and as conceived by a Protestant, is considerably different. The former is taught to regard his church as a necessary means, through appointed rites and ceremonies, of mediation between himself and God; while to the Protestant the office and value of the Christian Church are found in the opportunity which it affords for:

(1) Social worship and the administration of the two sacraments.
(2) An opportunity to voice and witness to a divine revelation.
(3) An opportunity for religious instruction.
(4) An opportunity to receive inspiration for service through communion with the ever-present Christ, and with those who are animated by a common faith in Him and a common purpose—the realization of His kingdom in the world.

It would be a wearisome and fruitless task to attempt to define the creedal position occupied by each of the numerous branches of Protestantism, even though we were to confine our discussion to the main bodies. Our task, therefore, is reduced to a statement of those foundation principles of Protestantism, the enforcement of which has made such glowing history during the last four hundred years; principles which, broadly speaking, are common to all Protestants.

THE SUPREMACY AND SUFFICIENCY OF HOLY SCRIPTURE.

Protestantism, whatever may be said to the contrary, still stands for the supremacy and sufficiency of Holy Scripture in doctrine and life. True, this doctrine is as old as the Reformation—better still, it is as old as Jesus Christ. Were it not for a converted Luther and a rediscovered Bible, the Reformation could never have taken place. The Scriptures became to Luther what the church had formerly been—the seat of authority, the court of final appeal. Said Calvin: "If Scripture, as the only religious authority, and salvation by grace through faith, were yielded, it would not pay the cost to contend about other matters in controversy"—all other differences were but eddies in the main stream.

Tell me, ye who say the Bible alone is not sufficient to guide man into the way of peace and spiritual freedom, have you anything better to offer? Tell me, have the fathers, or the councils, or the voice of the "living church" added a single sentence to the sum of essential Christian truth? Have they not one and all had to resort to the same source of divine truth, which is open to us all alike? True, the living church can interpret, exemplify and enforce the truths of Scripture, but can she *add* anything thereto? If the New Testament does not contain a sufficiently clear announcement of God's mercy, we will look in vain for a fuller revelation of it elsewhere.

Some timid Protestants, however, have been greatly disturbed by the announcement that their seat of authority, the Bible, has been wholly discredited by the physical sciences, evolutionary philosophy and higher criticism, and, in consequence, are disposed to conclude that our Roman Catholic brethren occupy the only tenable and safe position, in possessing an infallible head whose word makes the Bible unnecessary. But let any who may thus be alarmed turn to the paper of Professor Schodde, in this collection, and read it carefully. If he will do so, there will not remain a ghost in sight to disturb his peace.

That the Bible, and the Bible alone, is sufficient to guide man to peace of heart and righteousness of life is fully confirmed by the testimony of Heinrich Heine, the great German Jew, who said at the close of his life: "In truth it was neither a vision nor a seraphic revelation, nor a light from heaven, nor any strange dream, nor other mystery, which brought me into the way of salvation. I owe my illumination entirely and simply to the reading of a book. A book? Yes, a homely-looking book, modest as Nature, and also as natural as she herself—a book which has a workaday and unassuming look, like the sun which warms us, like the bread which nourishes us; a book which seems to look at us as cordially and blessingly as the old grandmother who reads it daily with dear, trembling lips and with spectacles on her nose. And this book is called quite shortly *the Book*—the Bible. Rightly do men also call it the Holy Scripture. He who has lost his God may find Him again in this Book, and toward him who has never known God it sends forth a breath of the Divine Word." And he says also, "Why do the British gain foothold in so many lands? With them they bring the Bible, that grand democracy wherein each man shall not only be king in his own house but also bishop. They are demanding, they are founding, the great kingdom of the spirit, the kingdom of religious emotions, and the love of humanity, of purity, of true morality, which cannot be taught by dogmatic formulas, but by parable and example, such as are contained in that beautiful, sacred, educational Book for young and old, the Bible."

But, it may be said in reply, while the Bible is sufficient for the individual's guidance, the nations—the world, true and permanent civilization—require more than the Bible, require the Roman Catholic Church to furnish them with the fundamental principles of social order and political permanency. This is virtually the contention of Archbishop Ireland in the "Catholic World" of September, 1871: "Protestantism, like the heathen barbarism which Catholicism subdued, lacks the elements of order, because it rejects authority, and is necessarily incompetent to maintain real liberty or civilized society. Hence it is we so often say that if the American Republic is to be sustained and preserved at all it must be by the rejection of the principle of the Reformation and the acceptance of the Catholic principle by the American people."

And in his sermon at the centenary of the establishment of the Roman Catholic hierarchy of the United States in 1889, the Archbishop said: "That the work which Roman Catholics in the coming century were called to do in the United States was to make America Catholic, and to solve for the church universal the all-absorbing problem with which the age confronts her. Our work is to make America Catholic . . . . Our cry shall be, 'God wills it,' and our hearts shall leap with Crusader enthusiasm. We know the church is the sole owner of the truths and graces of salvation . . . . The Catholic Church will confirm and preserve, as no human power or human church can, the liberties of the Republic . . . .The church triumphant in America, Catholic truth will travel on the wings of American influence, and with it enrich the universe. . . As a religious system, Protestantism is in hopeless dissolution, utterly valueless as a doctrinal or moral power, and no longer to be considered as a foe with which we must count. . . . The American people made Catholics, nowhere shall we find a higher order of Christian civilization. It can be shown to the American people that they need the church for the preservation and complete development of their national character and their social order. The Catholic Church is the sole living and enduring Christian authority. She has the power to speak; she has an organization by which her laws may be enforced."*

How men equally good, perhaps, differ respecting Roman Catholic ability to accomplish the best results for mankind becomes apparent when, after reading the above, we turn to a writer like Adam Smith, who says: "The Church of Rome is the most formidable combination that ever was formed against the authority and security of civil government, as well as against the liberty, reason and happiness of mankind."

Or, if we turn to Mr. Froude, the verdict is practically the same: "So much only can be foretold with certainty, that if the Roman Catholic Church anywhere recovers her ascendency, she will again exhibit the detestable features which have invariably attended her supremacy. Her power will be once more found incompatible either with justice or with intellectual growth, and our children will be forced to recover by some fresh struggle the ground which our forefathers conquered for us, and which we by our pusillanimity surrendered."

How clearly that fine spirit, M. de Lavelaye, saw the necessity for the Bible in his country, Belgium; how clearly one of the greatest Frenchmen of this century, M. Guizot, saw it in France! Being asked one day what, in his opinion, was the cause of the moral, political and social evils of France, the historian of European civilization answered, "Want of faith. Nothing can stand, nothing can prosper, without faith." "What, then, is the remedy?" said his interlocutor. "The Gospel! Preach the Word! Circulate the Holy Scriptures!"†

Return to Holy Scripture, therefore, on the part of the Reformers, was a return to primitive Christianity—a return to Christ; it was a return to the only authority that could emancipate the conscience, give spiritual freedom, produce national regeneration and world-wide evangelization; a return to the only judge that could authoritatively condemn and cast out the multiplied innovations and novelties in doctrine and practice that had been introduced by the church during the previous thirteen centuries.

The Bible still remains supreme among the world's sacred books,

---
*Jas. M. King, "Facing the 20th Century," page 199.
†R. F. Horton, "England's Danger," page 123.

and is in itself the safest guide in life and the greatest consolation in the hour of death.

RIGHT OF PRIVATE JUDGMENT.

But, though the Bible in itself is a treasure of supreme value to man, what were it worth to him if he were refused access thereto, if he were denied the right to read and interpret it for himself? Instead, he must allow an ecclesiastical institution to read and interpret it for him. But who ever refused to any one the privilege of reading Holy Scripture or the right to go to the fountain-head of divine truth and learn for himself what *the Book* teaches?

When told by Roman Catholics that they, too, accept the Scriptures, but that only the church can interpret them, and that the Bible is not a safe book for the people, Luther rose, more powerful, more eloquent, more majestic, than before; he rose superior to himself. "What," said he, "keep the light of life from the people; take away their guide to heaven; keep them in ignorance! What an abomination! What treachery to heaven! Besides, your authorities differ; what would Gregory I say to the verdicts of Gregory VII? No, the Scriptures are the legacy of the primitive Christian Church, and are the equal and treasured inheritance of all peoples. O, ye blind leaders of the blind, will you suffer the people to perish, soul and body, because you fear that, instructed by God himself, they will rebel against your accursed despotism! No, I say, let the Scriptures be put into the hands of everybody; let every one interpret them for himself; let there be private judgment; let spiritual liberty be revived, as in Apostolic days. Then only will the people be emancipated."

The denial of the right of private judgment as an article of faith at the Council of Trent was Rome's answer to Luther's demand. Thus it was the Reformers protested four centuries ago; it is against the denial of the same privilege that their children protest to-day.

Bishop Martensen, of Denmark, says: "All sciences were in the Middle Ages dependent on theology, and this was in its turn dependent on the Popish church as the external authority. With the Reformation the liberated human mind broke up for itself new paths, asserted the importance of the secular sciences and also the right of every one to read with his own eyes what is written in the book of Nature. Man's mind bowed to the authority of Scripture not only as the written Word, but because Scripture approved itself to the conscience by the inherent power of divine truth. Truth evidencing and proving itself to be such to the religious consciousness, and itself producing certainty in the heart of man, is the principle of the Reformation and of Protestant theology."

It may be thought, however, that refusal to allow the people to read and interpret the Scriptures for themselves is only a figment in the mind of some bigoted Protestant. Then let us hear what a recent Catholic writer named Maclauchlin says in a work which has circulated in England beyond a hundred thousand copies:

"The Catholic Church interdicts the use of private judgment in matters of faith; she has ever interdicted it, and she will continue to interdict it to the end of time. Free inquiry, individual preference, liberty of mind, freedom of thought, private judgment in the domain of faith, are words which she has no ears to hear. She will not, she cannot, listen to them; they would rend the rock on which she rests."*

The right of private judgment has a noble sound, but, alas! Protestants themselves have frequently failed to live up to the doctrine. An infallible Bible, a second pope, has been set up, together with the addition of creeds and confessions imposing restraints on the conscience and intellect, as rigid as those from which deliverance was supposed to be had. "The official organization of the church has, at various times," says Dr. Crapsey, "undertaken to do the thinking not only for its own age, but for all ages to come. The theory is that at a certain time God made a final revelation to man, and that the official organization of the church at another time officially interpreted that revelation; and that ever afterward the only thing the human mind has to do is to think what had been thought and to say what had been said."

"The Outlook," in commenting on a recent encyclical of the Pope to American Catholicism, takes occasion to state the advanced position of Protestantism respecting the right of private judgment: "We recognize the self-consistent attitude of the Roman Catholic Church, but not that this attitude is consistent with the liberty wherewith Christ makes free. Nevertheless, we are glad to have it stated with such explicitness, for it will help clear thinking. For between the position that religious faith is a dogma once for all delivered to the saints, and either transcribed in an infallible Bible

---

*R. F. Horton, "England's Danger," page 96.

or committed to the custody of an infallible church, and the position that every man is a child of God, may have direct communion with God, and may learn for himself by that communion what the will of God is; that no dogma can possibly state spiritual truth in a permanent form, that philosophical definitions of spiritual life must change with changing philosophy, as the language in which they are expressed changes with changes in language and literature; that truth is more than dogma and life is more than discipline; that neither truth nor life has been or can be ossified in a written record or a traditional ecclesiastical decree; that, in a word, the kingdom of God is like a seed planted in the ground, which grows men know not how, and that when it ceases to grow it ceases to live, and therefore ceases to be the kingdom of God—between these two attitudes there appears to us to be no middle ground. The Roman Catholic Church is the self-consistent exponent of an infallible, unchangeable dogma, an immobile, unalterable life. Protestantism will never be self-consistent until it stands with equal courage for the opposite doctrine—adaptability of religious institutions to changing circumstances, the mobility of religious life as a perpetual growth, and the continual change of dogmatic definitions, always inadequate to express the ever-enlarging spiritual life of the individual and of the race."

That the denial of religious liberty has proved fatal to the true development of the Roman Catholic Church many of themselves are happily beginning to recognize. For that the levels of Protestantism and Romanism are essentially different is a fact of which the more enlightened Catholics are just now becoming uneasily conscious. One of the most striking evidences of this is found in the remarkable work by M. Hermann Schell, rector of the Catholic University of Wurtzburg, on "Catholicism as a Principle of Progress," in which the author sets himself to answer the question, "Why German Catholics are so inferior to their Protestant compatriots." The fact itself he assumes as beyond question. He touches the nerve of the matter in his contention that the principle of ecclesiastical authority which lies at the basis of priestly education and of general church teaching is in direct opposition to that spirit of scientific investigation which is the basis of modern progress.

Many Catholics are thus beginning to recognize the truth of what Dr. Fairbairn states so well ("Religion in History," p. 176), that "the father is an excellent authority when his family are children;

but once the family is grown they must not be treated as infants. Papacy, making men spiritual infants, stands in the way of the realization of the highest Christian idea, which is essentially the religion of manhood, and speaks to men as men."

The more a man grows inwardly in thought and experience, the more self-reliant he becomes, the less is he disposed to be governed by external authority, and the less does external authority become needful. "The law of the spirit of life in Christ Jesus" makes every man free who surrenders himself to its domination.

That Roman Catholicism has not been disturbed as much as Protestantism, either by modern science or historical criticism, is due, first, to the fact that the discussion of such has not been brought to the attention of the Roman Catholic people, neither in the pulpit nor in the religious press; secondly, as the Roman Catholic does not depend so much on intellectual conviction as on the infallible head, therefore, were the entire Bible to become discredited or obsolete he would simply continue to rely on the voice of the living church, as to him, in any case, the Bible is not the first and final authority. If, however, the Protestant should have been so unwise as to set up the external Word as a second infallible pope, and should find that this object of his trust has become discredited, whither shall he go for religious light and consolation?

JESUS CHRIST THE ONLY MEDIATOR.

"The priest, as all cults present him, is the representative of man before God. He stands between the worshipper and his Deity; without his mediation there is no access to the mediation of heaven. His office no one else can exercise; there are intercessions which are only prevailing when he makes them; rites, ceremonies, incantations that are efficacious when he employs them; and their aim is not to superinduce a healthier state within the worshipper—a penitent heart, a surrendered will—but to win the favor of an unmindful or offended Deity. The system, indeed, is capable of great refinement as well as great grossness; yet in its better, as in its poorer, ministration, the same essential features cling to it." The above statement—Mr. Jackson's "Martineau," p. 176—may be taken as representative of what has been true of religion generally. But let us hear Dr. A. M. Fairbairn's portrayal—"Religion and History," p. 185—of how and when the priest appeared in the Christian Church.

"In the earliest Christian literature, apostolic and post-apostolic, no man who bears office in the church is called a priest. In it there was no official priesthood and none of the signs and rites associated with one. The men who held office were called either apostles, or prophets, or evangelists, or pastors, or teachers, or elders, or ministers, or overseers, but never priests. About the end of the second century, however, that fateful name begins to appear. A great Latin father, Tertullian, speaks of 'the sacerdotal order,' and calls the bishop priest, and even high priest, though he was far enough from allowing priesthood in any sense that denied the spiritual priesthood of universal Christian men. Half a century later another writer, Cyprian, makes quite a strong claim on behalf of an official priesthood, and show us, just beginning, the change of the Lord's Supper from a simple feast of love and remembrance into a sacrificial ceremony. Now, once a change like this begins it proceeds rapidly, and the further it proceeds the more disastrous it becomes. It forced into Christianity many of the limitations and much of the materialism of Judaism and paganism. In the apostolic days every Christian man was a priest, with the right to approach God when and where he pleased; but this neo-heathenism tended to give, and ultimately gave, the official priest the right to stand between God and man, distributing the grace of the one, granting or denying access or pardon to the other. In the religion of Christ, no place was sacred or necessary to the worship of the Father, the one thing needful was the pure and true spirit; but the renascent sacerdotalism created a whole new order of sacred persons, places, ceremonies, acts, which had to be respected if the worship was to be approved. The Christianity of the New Testament was a religion inward and spiritual, all its virtues were those of the believing, meek, true and loving spirit; but the Christianity of the priesthood and their church became outward and material, consisted in things the priesthood could prescribe and regulate, rather than the obedience commanded and approved of God."

In one of Luther's most pertinent and persuasive papers, the "Freedom of the Christian Man," or the "Priesthood of All Believers," he smites ecclesiasticism in one of its most vital and cherished features and thereby dethrones another of man's most dangerous enemies—spiritual despotism. Of all things most needful to man, in a religious sense, direct access to God is the most important—when, heart to heart and spirit to spirit, man may commune with his Maker as friend with friend. What were freedom of access to the Bible, liberty to read and interpret it, worth to me, were direct, personal intercourse with God denied? Consciously lacking this privilege, or failing to utilize it, I must remain to a very large degree impoverished and forsaken in spirit.

No one will deny that it has been Rome's policy, it still is, and, as at present constituted, it must continue to be her policy, to impress upon her adherents a sense of utter dependence upon mother church. When a Roman Catholic hears Scripture read, as he may, and the voice of Jesus saying, "Come unto me, all ye that are weary and heavy laden, and I will give you rest," or, "I am the door; by me if *any man* enter in he shall be saved," he does not understand the statements as meaning what, on their face, they seem to teach. If any untutored mind were to be asked to interpret these passages of Scripture, he would reply, doubtless: "Why, they mean just what they say; come directly to Jesus Christ, enter directly by Him into the enjoyment of forgiveness and life." But the church steps in and says no; "you are to come to the church; you can enter into the enjoyment and privileges of salvation only through the church; with me are the treasures of Divine grace—forgiveness, consolation, eternal life—and I am divinely delegated to bestow them on whomsoever I will."

How different from the finding of the Reformers! Everywhere in Holy Scripture they discovered entreaty, invitation and exhortation addressed to man, God's child, urging him, with a Divine insistence, to return *directly* to his Father, than whom no man was ever more easily approached. When man recognizes this cardinal truth of Holy Scripture, and enters upon the enjoyment of his birthright—personal fellowship with God—a sense of dignity and enrichment fills his soul of which no earthly power can rob him.

While, therefore, freedom to think for himself gives the Protestant his intellectual and political supremacy, direct intercourse with God gives him his moral and spiritual supremacy.

Schleiermacher reduced the whole difference between Romanism and Protestantism to the formula: "Romanism makes the relation of the individual to Christ depend on his relation to the church; Protestantism, *vice versa,* makes the relation of the individual to the church depend on his relation to Christ." In other words, a Protestant is not a Christian because he is in the church, but he is in the church because he is a Christian.

The Jews of Christ's day were still possessed with the belief that they held a monopoly in the favor of God. It required a special vision to drive this delusion out of the mind of St. Peter himself and teach him that "in every nation he that feareth God and worketh righteousness is accepted with Him." Paul's conversion to Christianity had taught him that, in the light of the Incarnation, all distinctions—class or racial—had practically disappeared, and that, henceforth, there was to be "neither Jew nor Greek, barbarian, Scythian, bond nor free." How slow the church of Jesus Christ has been in recognizing and applying this principle! Why, we are only now beginning to be taught that neither the peasant at his plough nor the painter at his canvas need be one hair's-breadth surpassed, in religious privilege and devoutness, by either the priest at the altar or the monk in his cell.

Men speak about advancing on the Word of God, as though already they had sounded all its heights and depths, and there were left no new discoveries to be made in its hidden treasures. Take the words of our Lord to the woman at the well, *e. g.,* "The hour is coming when ye shall neither at this mountain nor yet at Jerusalem worship the Father." Here is a Scripture whose importance to the religious world can scarcely be overestimated, yet whose import, after nineteen centuries of Christian history, is only beginning to be recognized and applied. Persons and places, seasons and services, are all one to him to whom every man is a priest, every day a Sabbath, all service a sacrament, and the universe God's temple.

JUSTIFICATION BY FAITH ALONE.

It is said that three several times the Scripture—"The just shall live by faith"—was brought home to Martin Luther's heart with peculiar power: once while lecturing in the university at Wittenberg; again, when ill at Bologna on his way to Rome; and lastly when, on his knees, climbing the Holy Stairs in the Eternal City. So that up to the time (1511) of his visit to Rome, this truth, that man is justified by faith alone, without the aid of good works, and without the promise of any—save as all good works are latent in penitence and faith in Jesus Christ—had not been experimentally recognized, as even then he hoped to ease a burdened conscience by making a full confession and performing all the penances prescribed for any ordinary pilgrim. From the time he had entered the monastery, in 1505, he had sedulously employed all the prescribed offices of the church in the hope of finding peace of conscience and assurance of salvation. Indeed, he tells us that, should any one win heaven by good deeds, he had determined to be that person. But when at length he saw that God forgives the penitent, freely and fully, without any good deeds whatever to commend him, it was as the bursting forth of the noonday sun in midnight darkness. How could he fail to convey the joyous fact of his emancipation to his fellow-men, whom he knew to be held in bondage to the same misconceptions which so long had enslaved himself? Is it any wonder that henceforth justification by faith alone became the central theme of his teaching and preaching? Had he not, in his efforts to secure soul-relief, conscientiously and diligently complied with all the methods prescribed by man, while this, the method of God, lay on the surface of His Word so plainly written that he who runneth may read?

It is difficult to see how the Reformation and Protestantism could have been possible without such an experience on the part of a Martin Luther, as the doctrine and its experience gave to the Reformation its spiritual power and moral enthusiasm, its undaunted courage and ultimate victory. And this doctrine of justification by faith alone is the truth which, more than any other, perhaps, is to-day making for the freedom of man and the establishment of the kingdom of God; it is the truth, too, which must be kept in the forefront of all our Christian teaching and preaching, or Protestantism will speedily become what it would deserve to become, and what, from more points of the compass than one, it is being said it has already become—a *failure*. But Protestantism is not a failure, as some good people would have us believe, nor is it a finality. It is a considerable distance just now from decrepitude, and it is a good, long step in the course of religious evolution toward finality. Protestantism is not as yet a failure, therefore, and will never become a failure so long as its four cardinal principles, to which reference has been made, are maintained and enforced. It matters little whether the terms employed in presenting these principles are the same as those employed by the men who begat them in agony and conflict, so long as we have the same fruitage—liberty of conscience and enthusiasm for righteousness.

As in some sense and to some degree Jesus was the child of the Jewish Church and the child of his own age, so the Reformation was in some sense and to some degree the child of the Roman Catholic Church and the child of its own age. The Jewish Church was no more blameworthy in rejecting Jesus Christ and His mission than is the Roman Catholic Church blameworthy in rejecting the mission and principles of the Reformation. Had the Roman Catholic hierarchy been consistent and carried its own theory of ecclesiastical and doctrinal development to its logical conclusion, it would have acknowledged the Reformation as a stage—and a very important one—in the evolutionary process.

Now, the principles which Jesus Christ taught and for which He gave His life have, as seen in their application through the centuries that are numbered from Him, amply justified His claim to recognition by His own people. And, shall I say, with equal reason, the principles which made the Protestant Reformation, as viewed in their application from the vantage ground of four centuries, have amply justified the historic protest and entitle those who maintain them to recognition on the part of Holy Mother Church?

Why is it, any one may well ask, that Romanism so heartily dislikes Protestantism?—a dislike which appears in language such as this: "Protestantism in all its forms leads the pilgrim astray. Protestantism is a siren; it sings to the seafarer and allures him to the breakers. Protestantism is the enemy of God; of God's truth; of God's church. It is not better than nothing, because good for nothing."

"Which of all the positions of Protestantism was new, or extra Biblical, that Romanism should have disliked it so? Was it the denouncement of indulgences?—which had never been heard of till the eleventh century. Was it the interdict which it pronounced upon the Pope's supremacy?—who dared not himself to claim this distinction till full six hundred years after the days of the Apostles. Was it the assertion of the people's right to search the Scriptures for themselves?—when for three centuries every father of the church, to say nothing of Christ and His Apostles, urged the same doctrine. Was it the rejection of tradition, as a co-ordinate rule of faith?—when no such sentiment was broached during the only period when apostolic tradition could have been satisfactorily identified. Was it the exposure of the monstrous pretension of Rome's infallibility?—which had never obtained currency until the Roman pontiff proclaimed himself universal head of the church, in the seventh century. Was it the contempt which Protestantism poured upon the celibacy of the clergy?—when the professed head of the Romish episcopate was married; when Paul expressly declares that 'marriage is honorable in all'; when one of the signs of apostate Rome is that she 'forbids to marry'; and when for three centuries the impure dogma was unknown to the Christian Church. Was it the denial of purgatorial fire?—when no trace of such a doctrine can be fairly discovered in the Word of God, or in the teaching of the fathers, for more than six hundred years. Was it the unsparing condemnation of the Mass and the adoration of the Host?—which had their distinct origin in the Florentine Council, early in the thirteenth century. Was it the stern denouncement of image-worship, of the invocation of departed saints, of prayer to the Virgin, of supplication for the dead?—none of which corruptions were known till the fourth century, and some of which were the offspring of the thirteenth. Was it the bold and determined stand made by the Reformers against priestly absolution and auricular confession, with the several abominations to which they led?—when these novelties were of no earlier date than the twelfth and thirteenth centuries. Was it the plea urged by them for public liturgies and offices of devotion in the vulgar tongue?—when the Latin ritual was never introduced till the seventh century. Was it the loud voice of remonstrance which sounded in Rome's ears for robbing the laity of the cup in the Eucharist?—when the impious proposal was never heard of till the eleventh century. Was it the caveat urged against the addition of five sacraments to those instituted by Christ and His Apostles?—when that addition was made by fallible mortals in the twelfth century. Was it the removal of the apocryphal books from the canon of Holy Scripture?—when they never found a place in it until the Council of Trent, in the sixteenth century, did this mighty dishonor to the living oracles of revealed truth. It may be fearlessly asserted, then, that *whatever Rome retains from antiquity, of any real worth, she holds it in common with the churches of the Reformation.* The leading points of doctrine against which the Reformers protested were pure innovations and novelties, the date of which may be distinctly marked on the page of history."*

The principle, to which reference has been made in the first part of this paper, has more than once been applied in the case of Protestantism itself, and may need to be applied again when the arrogance,

*John Morrison, D.D., "Protestant Reformation in All Countries," pp. 488-491.

engendered by growing wealth and influence, leads the Protestant Church into the same quagmire as has so foully besmeared Rome. Protestantism has no guarantee of immunity from an arrogant spirit, political ambitions, striving after national recognition and public favor, preaching a Gospel suited to the tastes and pleasures and extravagances of the rich, regarding wealth or numbers as power, despising the poor and the man of toil—when it comes to this with Protestantism, no matter against what it may protest in others, no matter what theories it may adopt for itself, God shall smite the institution with a blast that shall blight all its finest blossoms and turn its fairest fruits to rottenness, making Protestantism a stench and a hissing among the people. The Kingdom, the privilege of establishing and representing the Kingdom of God, shall be taken from the churches of Calvin and Luther, Canterbury and Wesley, and shall be given into the hands of the "weak things of the world," which shall confound the mighty; and these shall administer God's trust, not in the interests of a system, or of a class, or of a theory, but in the interests of man. This is an everyday lesson of history, both secular and sacred, a lesson confirmed both by Scripture and experience. God can do without Protestantism, if Protestantism refuses to co-operate with Him and serve His people with its best.

PROTESTANT FOREIGN MISSIONS: A RETROSPECT OF THE NINETEENTH CENTURY.*

JUDSON SMITH, D.D.,

BOSTON.

[The immediate hope of Christian unity seems, to "The Spirit of Missions," to lie in the foreign field, where there are closer relations between the different bodies of Christians than elsewhere. It is perfectly natural, and an experience in other walks of life, that those who feel the stress of circumstances most strongly are most closely drawn together. Those to whom life is labor, on whom the work to be done presses always insistent, have not time to divide the mint, anise and cummin of social or theologic distinction. Prosperity is very apt to beget self-satisfaction, and self-satisfaction is very likely to cause dissatisfaction with other people. In the mission field the Master's business is too absorbing for those who are faithful to it at all to allow jealousy to take root. A recent witness of this is the General Conference of Missionaries at Tokyo, who resolved "that all those who are one with Christ by faith, are one body," and then put their resolution into action in a letter just issued to all Christians in Japan, asking them to make "Our Lord's desire for the oneness of all who believe in His name an object of special prayer," of which the letter suggests a suitable form. They do not mince matters at all, these Christians in Japan. It is no indefinite bond between individuals at which they aim, but "a corporate oneness, a oneness of the churches as churches that shall be manifest to all the world."—"The Churchman," Aug. 17, 1901.—ED.]

* * *

THE nineteenth century has gone into history with an imperishable name and glory. During its progress, our knowledge of the world and of the people who live in it has been vastly expanded. The whole domain of physical science, if it has not been discovered, has certainly been explored and mapped out in the most comprehensive way. Inventions, and those of the greatest importance, have multiplied beyond all precedent. Steam and electricity have been applied to human needs in manifold forms, have revolutionized modes of travel and have brought the ends of the world together. Solid gains have been made in the possession of civil and religious liberty; the leading nations are coming to a mutual understanding

*Appeared in "The North American Review," March, 1901.

and combining in a league for perpetual peace. Time would fail to tell of the gains in Education, Literature, the Arts and Social Forces, which enrich life and enhance personal power. But if the nineteenth century is the *saeculum mirabile* in these respects, it is quite as much so in the development of the Foreign Missionary enterprise. There are but two other periods in the history of Christianity that can compare with it in this respect—the first three centuries, including the Apostolic Age, and the three centuries at the opening of the Middle Ages. In the former, the church was founded, the nations taught and the Roman Empire Christianized; in the latter, the peoples of central and northern Europe were converted and brought into the circle of Latin Christendom. At the beginning of the nineteenth century there were a few societies, scantly manned and equipped, prosecuting their work far apart, not without spirit and promise, but with very meager results. At the end of the century, we see an enterprise of wide reach, conscious of itself, experienced, wisely drilled and led, attempting great things and winning splendid victories. It is like the Parliamentary army in the Puritan Revolution, at first not without merit, of high purpose, but not united, not effective, which at last became the Ironsides that won at Naseby and Dunbar and Worcester, sweeping everything before it, entering no battle but to conquer.

The Modern Era of Protestant Foreign Missions set in decisively with William Carey, and the formation in 1792 of the English Baptist Missionary Society under his leadership. The London Missionary Society, in which many Dissenting churches united, followed in 1795; a Scotch Society, and one in the Netherlands, in 1797; the Church Missionary Society, within the Anglican Church, in 1799. One fact should be premised. As there were heroes before Agamemnon, so there were Protestant missions before Carey's time; and foreign missionary work had been done on this side of the sea before the days of Mills and Judson and Hall. In some proper sense, the discovery of this western world was in the interest of the wider spread of the Gospel; Columbus sought to enlarge the jurisdiction and blessings of the Roman Church. Plymouth Colony was designed to gain a free field for the reformed faith, and a foothold whence to spread the Gospel into new parts of the world. John Eliot's work among the Indians to the west of Roxbury, from 1646, was a fine instance of foreign missionary enterprise; and it was only one among many. The Mayhews and Sargents wrought on the same plan. The great work of the Moravians, from 1732, in Southern Africa, in Labrador, in the West Indies, is a noble instance of pioneer effort in hard places.

Let us take a brief survey of the state of Foreign Missions one hundred years ago. Carey is just beginning his wonderful work as translator at Serampore; the first labors of the London Missionary Society are enduring the "night of toil" on Tahiti before any fruit appears; the Moravians are bearing the Word to darkened souls in remote parts of the Eastern and Western hemispheres. The churches are scarcely awake to the call, or to their privilege in responding to it; the enterprise is known by few and believed in by fewer still. There are few converts on foreign soil, here and there a feeble band; no schools for training native laborers; the Bible speaks as yet in few vernaculars. Goodly beginnings have been made, the church is awakening, and all is hopeful; but it is the gray dawn of the day, and it is faith only that can take in the greater things that are at hand. Scarcely a dozen missionary societies, all in Great Britain and Germany, a few scores of missionaries scattered through many lands, a handful of converts and pupils, a total expenditure of a few thousands a year—this is the scene which presents itself at the opening of the century. From this point the growth has been slow but continuous, and accelerating through the successive decades; until we reach the facts with which all are familiar to-day.

The expansion of the fields occupied by foreign missions is one of the most striking facts of the century. Where Carey stood alone at its opening, more than two thousand missionaries, representing fifty different societies, now occupy nearly every strategic point in the vast peninsula of India and in Ceylon. And Burma and Siam and China and Japan, not even explored as missionary ground at that time, are studded with mission stations and teem with a vast volume of missionary labors. Africa was then touched only by the Moravians in a few points; to-day thousands of missionaries, from nearly fifty societies, are at work around all its vast seaboard, and among many tribes in the interior, then wholly unexplored. The pioneers of the London Missionary Society had just arrived among the islands of the Pacific, where now well-nigh every group has its missionaries, and not a few have become active centres of a wider Christian propagandism. And, in short, there is scarcely a country, or tribe, or island on the earth where missionaries are not at work, and where the Christian Church does not already exert its uplifting

PROTESTANT MISSIONS. 239

influence. There is no recorded march of military conquest that is more resistless, significant or inspiring, than this steady expansion of the foreign missionary enterprise.

The most reliable statistics enumerate 449 different Protestant Foreign Missionary organizations to-day, 249 of them directly devoted to missionary work, 92 indirectly co-operating in such work, and 102 engaged in special lines of work. There is scarcely a Protestant denomination that does not have its society, its field, and its laborers. This is a new and significant fact in Christian history. For the few scores of missionaries at work in 1800, at the close of the century we have 13,607, with an army of 73,615 native helpers by their side, distributed in over five thousand central stations through all the unevangelized peoples of the earth. In this single fact we have the promise of final victory. In these fields are 10,993 organized churches, with a membership of 1,289,289 souls, increasing at the rate of 83,895 each year. The annual income of the major societies has reached the noble sum of $17,161,092, and the yearly gifts from native Christians aggregate $1,833,981. The educational work presents like noble proportions. There are 93 colleges on mission fields, with 35,414 students, of whom 2,275 are women; of theological and training schools, 385 are reported, with 11,905 students. Boarding and high schools number 857, and 83,148 pupils; industrial and medical classes count 197, and enroll 6,998 pupils; while in common or day schools, the pupils reach the number of 904,442. The grand total of those under instruction is 1,046,309, one-third of them girls. The Bible, entire or in portions, has been translated into 421 different languages or dialects; a work of incalculable labor and value, of itself alone sufficient to challenge for this great enterprise the profound respect of the civilized world. Add to this the products of mission presses—364,904,399 pages of Christian literature annually, and 297,435 copies of periodical literature—and the significance of this fact becomes majestic in proportions and influence. Besides all this, bear in mind the 355 hospitals and 753 dispensaries, with 2,579,650 patients treated every year, to every one of whom the Gospel is preached, many hearing it for the first time; and the Foreign Missionary enterprise that includes all these varied agencies assumes the dimensions and character of the greatest single force for the uplifting and regeneration of the world which we know or of which we can conceive. All this is the achievement of the century which lies behind us, and is a just index, but by no means the full proof, of the progress of missions in this period. And when we consider that the rate of advance has been accelerating with every decade, that this century has been marked by pioneer work, and that now the forces that co-operate here are working at their best, who can measure the significance of the animating scene that rises before us in the new century, or fail to exult in the nearing prospect of Christ's universal sway among the nations of the earth?

It is instructive to note the great names that mark these decades, and lift the service they represent above all petty criticism and thoughtless ridicule. Among them are such as Carey, Marshman, Duff, Hall and Ballantine in India; Judson and Vinton in Burma; Moffatt, Livingstone and Lindley in Africa; Dwight, Hamlin and Riggs in Turkey; Morrison, Bridgman and Parker in China; Pattison, Williams, Bingham and Gulick in the Pacific Islands. And what shall we say more of Ashmore and Griffith, John and Blodget, of Davis and Verbeck and Hepburn, of Chamberlain and Clough, of Logan and Paton, who, through faith, have "subdued kingdoms, wrought righteousness and obtained a good report."

There are many particular facts included in this general description of progress, which may well detain our thoughts for a time. Note first the growing enlistment of the church in this great work. How difficult Carey found it to draw the Baptist churches of England into the effort of supporting a mission in India! Recall the indifference which the London Missionary Society had to encounter, the animosity which missionary proposals evoked in Scotland, the opposition which the chartering of the American Board called out. But little by little the atmosphere changed, the trickling streams became rills, and rills deepened and multiplied and formed brooks and rivers; till now the winter is vanished and it is springtime everywhere. It is no longer good form for any Protestant Church, or for any Protestant Church members, to have no share in mission work. The Woman's Boards, which began their work only thirty years ago and now number 120, with an annual income of $2,500,-000, are both cause and effect of the widening hold of this enterprise; the Student Volunteer Movement, with an organization which reaches thousands of colleges and seminaries, and belts the globe, with its grand apparatus for the study of missions and the awakening of enthusiasm for missionary work, is a noble proof of its deepening sway in all the schools for higher education. And, though we are still far from what is ideal in condition, the progress is so prodigious as to call for the deepest gratitude.

The dimensions and influence of the native agency in the field constitute another fact of peculiar significance and glorious hope. It is all the product of the nineteenth century; and no part of mission work is of greater value. Every native pastor becomes an apostle to his own people, and does more to make the Gospel permanent in the land than any missionary can do. Multiply them sufficiently, and the missionary is needed no longer; they themselves become the leaders and bulwark of the native church. It is by them that every land is to be evangelized. And the fact that to-day 73,000 native helpers are co-operating with the 13,000 foreign laborers, that there are as many native pastors as there are ordained men from all Christian lands, is a noble proof how far the work has advanced, a glorious promise that it is presently to be complete.

A notable evidence of the progress which missions have made is found in the character and deeds of the native Christian communities in many lands. This is a demonstration beyond all question or cavil. Instances may be brought from many fields; I mention but three.

After a period of remarkable growth, the Christians of Madagascar were subjected to the fiercest of persecutions under the wicked Ranalavona, through a series of years, with their foreign leaders all expelled from the island. They perished by the score and by the hundred, till they wearied out their persecutors, but kept their faith and enriched the martyr hosts of the Christian Church.

When missionaries went to the Fiji Islands, in 1835, the people were heathen and cannibals, the terror of their neighbors and of all mariners. After a period of fifty years, cannibalism had ceased; all idols had vanished; Christianity was in possession of the islands; as many people, in proportion to the population, attended church there as in Massachusetts; and their gifts for religious purposes ranked with the most generous in the world.

Until very recently China has been deemed one of the most difficult of missionary fields, the converts being few and progress slow. Morrison began in 1808; in 1840 there were but six converts; in 1860 they hardly reached a thousand. To-day they exceed a hundred thousand, and, until the recent anti-foreign disturbance broke out, they were doubling in less than ten years. And now their character has been tested in the fierce flame of persecution; hundreds and thousands, for their faith, "have not loved their lives to the death." And the Chinese Church is the martyr church, Christian faith and love casting a celestial radiance upon the horrors that have filled the land. By the side of Polycarp, Ignatius, Cyprian, whom we sing and praise forevermore, stand now these Chinese believers, who have renewed the deeds and heroism of those early martyrs before our very eyes. And in a thousand homes in many climes, the virtues that bespeak Christ's transforming power even more clearly than a martyr's death, blossom in beauty and fill the land with a glorious light.

When the century opened, the great religions of the East seemed to stand untouched and strong, firm in their hold upon the people, stout in the opposition they offered to the entrance of a new faith. This was one of the serious obstacles which missions had to encounter as each new field was entered. Many things, doubtless, have contributed to the change which we witness: the extension of commerce; the wider reach of England's influence; the internal decay of the old faiths; the demonstrated power of Christianity to give comfort, courage, an aggressive spirit, a noble style of life and thought. To-day these religions have ceased to be formidable opponents of the Christian faith. Hinduism, Buddhism, Confucianism, are but the shadows of their former strength, and seem on the point of extinction. In nothing have we a surer proof of the progress of missions, the resistless growth of the Kingdom of Christ. What Milton saw, in poetic vision, of the power of Christ in the presence of the ancient faiths, is becoming reality:

> "The oracles are dumb;
> No voice or hideous hum
> Runs through the arched roof in words deceiving;
> Apollo from his shrine
> Can no more divine,
> With hollow shriek the steep of Delphos leaving."

The message of the missionary has not changed; indeed, it cannot change until the errand of Christianity in the earth is finished. Differences of methods there have been; variations in the place of emphasis may be noted; diversities of gifts will always exist. But the vital message of the missionary is the same to-day as that of St. Paul in Macedonia and Athens, the same as when Carey and Judson began; the same in China and Japan as it is in India and

Africa. Its great theme is the living God, Maker of heaven and earth, revealed in Jesus Christ for the redemption of man, speaking to the conscience and heart of man through His written word, and supremely by the Holy Spirit, and opening the Kingdom of heaven with peace on earth and a glorious immortality to all believers. The missionary proclaims the God of love and salvation, and opens the door of hope to all the children of men. This message can never change while sin exists and human nature remains the same. It is redemption that men need, it is redemption that Christ brings, it is redemption that the missionary preaches wherever he goes. This is his single theme, his ample message, his persuasive story. All else may change; tongues may cease, knowledge may vanish away; but this remains the supreme word of life to a hopeless world. Civilized nations, refined peoples, these later days, need it, wait for it, will perish without it, as truly as barbarous nations and savage peoples and the ancient days.

The century has been a period of beginnings, of pioneer work in many lines. It is not reasonable to demand completed results. Much time has necessarily been given to exploration, to the discovery of lands and peoples and opportunities for work. This has already been carried so far that it is a simple statement of fact to say that the unevangelized world is fully opened and accessible to missionary labor. It is the first time in the history of the world when this could be truthfully said. This work will not need to be repeated. The mastery of the vernaculars of the people among whom the work is to be done was an imperative prerequisite to the success of the enterprise. In many cases the languages had never been reduced to written form, and this was the first duty awaiting the missionary. To-day this herculean task is far advanced toward completion, and the fruits of this vast labor are the inheritance of the new century.

Like permanent foundations have been laid in many other ways. The good will of the people has been won; schools have been organized and are in successful operation; churches have been gathered and are in training under native pastors for an increasing share in the work; the Bible, wholly or in parts, has been translated into hundreds of languages or dialects, and is accessible to the vast majority of the unevangelized peoples of the earth; text books for schools and a Christian literature are provided in large measure, to aid in the development of the Christian body. These things will not need to be done again, but they stand ready for continued and more effective use—the splendid apparatus of a vigorous and world-wide campaign. There is in many lands a strong, well-trained and experienced body of missionaries, surrounded and aided by seven times their own number of native helpers, prepared to take advantage of all these vast facilities, and push the work of Christianizing the world in the most energetic and effective way. We have already observed a constant acceleration in the rate of increase in the positive results of mission work; and we have every reason to expect that this rate of increase will steadily rise throughout the coming century. Probably in no respect is the progress of this work during the nineteenth century more marked or significant than in the accomplishment of all this vast preliminary and pioneer work. It took three years to marshal and train the armies of the Union; but when that had been done, it required but another year to bring the war to a victorious end. But the progress in those years of preparation was as real and significant as in that one year of resistless advance.

But even the nineteenth century has recorded signal successes, foretastes of the final victory. Witness the conversion of Tahiti, of the Society Islands, of Samoa, of the Friendly Islands, of the New Hebrides, of the Sandwich Islands and so many other islands of the Pacific. Recall, also, the inspiring progress in Madagascar and Uganda, among the Telugus and the Karens, in Japan and in the older missions in China. Enough has been achieved to prove the possibility of universal success. It is no experiment in which we are engaged; it is a supremely successful work. There are no backward steps in Christ's march down the centuries and across the nations to universal victory. This imposing work, with its impregnable foundations, its powerful and growing array, is beyond the reach of cavil or sneer, is confessedly the one resistless, triumphant force in the enlightenment of the nations and in the uplifting of the world. We do not now celebrate the triumph, but we are on the march; every foe flees before us, every year makes the cause more resistless; and the end is both certain and near at hand.

ESSENTIAL CHRISTIANITY.

Rev. William D. Grant, Ph.D.,
NEW YORK.

The man who began one of the greatest religious movements of modern times, John Wesley, said: "I want life; I am tired of opinions." A follower of Wesley, however, a century after, not only expresses the desire that Methodist opinions shall be sharply defined and tenaciously adhered to, but even exclaims, "Oh, the pity of it, that John Wesley did not clearly specify the cut and color of the coat and the style of the hat to be worn by the Methodists for all time and in all lands!" So much smaller was the disciple than the master. Yet, this is not an extreme or isolated case; it is only an indication of what has taken place in the history of all religions and religious movements. Martin Luther did not lay claim to the prophetic office, yet he uttered no word that has proved more true than "that the very people who in his lifetime would not touch the kernel of his teaching would be greedy after the husks of it when he was once dead." That every fresh stream of religious influence should be purest at its source is no more than to say that the first ages of a faith must exhibit most plainly the tendencies and characteristics of the system when the emotions are stirred rather than the intellect, and when fervor has not given place to formalism and machine-rule.

The history of institutions and systems shows that they have not long remained in the original simplicity which characterized the purpose of their founders, and which satisfied their earliest disciples. As conceived by other minds less capable of distinguishing the non-essential from the essential, and when applied in other circumstances from those in which they were originally introduced, to those who are observant, soon a system, however divine in its origin and intent, is seen to indicate accretions, which, like the barnacles on a ship, may require heroic measures for their removal.

But if the system is of Divine appointment, and, like Christianity when first introduced, meets the deeper needs of the human heart, we may believe, when it has departed from its primary purpose and purity, God will take pains to see that voices shall not be wanting—though at first these may be despised and discredited—to summon men to apprehend anew the simple evangel freed from the mass of dogmas and rites which have hidden it from view.

Christianity, though divinely given, has, no more than other religious systems, been able to escape the corroding influences of time; human ambition and lack of spiritual insight having caused deterioration. It is no depreciation of its Divine origin, however, that such should be the case. The waters of the stream take their coloring from the soil through which they flow. It is no more than voicing history to say that with the outward progress of Christianity and ecclesiastical development corruption has kept pace.

That the essential character of Christianity changed from a system of religious living to a system of metaphysical belief; to right thinking rather than right doing, was largely due to the influence of Greek thought, human reason, philosophical speculation, and human ambition. Men became satisfied with belief in certain doctrines instead of demanding that these doctrines should be realized in their action and intercourse with their fellow-men; satisfied with accepting certain opinions about Christ for fellowship with Christ himself.

It is the unique distinction of Christianity, however, that it can be revived and largely restated without altering its essential character. Such has been the task of all true reformers from Tauler to Luther; from Luther to Wesley, and from Wesley to William Booth. Because true Christianity is "spirit and life," it possesses an inherent power of self-renewal, a reconstructive vitality. The Reformation of the sixteenth century was such a revival and reconstruction; an attempt, in a measure at least, to return to the simplicity of the Gospel, to be satisfied with the original requirement of Jesus Christ—personal loyalty to Him. It was the mission of Luther and those associated with him to recall men from the hardened dogmas of the church to the living experience of St. Paul; from paganized Christianity to Christianity itself. It is more than we should expect, however, that those who had been schooled in the principles of scholastic theology could instantly and in every particular break away from the traditions, customs and authority to which they had been so long subject. While individually enjoying the peace and freedom of the Gospel, yet the Reformers permitted much to remain in their reconstructed system of doctrine that was anti-Scriptural;

much that lacked utility and which became a standing menace to the future peace and progress of the Evangelical Church. In self-defence they were required to state what they believed and why they believed it. They were, in a sense, compelled to place a new set of doctrines over against those from which they disagreed. Hence it comes to pass that men are now doing what should have been done four hundred years ago, stripping off the unessential garb of ecclesiastical Christianity; going back of doctrinal systems, back of councils, confessions, tradition, the fathers; treating all such practically as though they never had been; going back to Christ Himself, asking themselves and asking Him what was His mission; what did He bring to and do for man that man could not have done for himself; and what must we do in order that He may regard us as His disciples?

In pursuing this course the difficulty has always been to determine where fundamentals end and where circumstantials begin. Where is the seat of authority to be found to which an appeal may be taken to guide us in the settlement of such a difficult problem? At first, in attempting to settle this question, many will insist upon the "belief of certain opinions as being necessary to salvation, though these, it is admitted, must be strictly confined to a few essential doctrines; then follows an earnest effort, comparatively easy at first, but always more painful as the process of compression proceeds, to reduce the fundamentals of religion to the lowest possible denomination. This involves, as you will observe, the necessity for drawing a line which shall separate essential opinions on the one hand from non-essential opinions on the other; a line which in practice it is found impossible to keep permanent or clear." For instance, a man who at one period of his life draws an imaginary line, say at the doctrine of the Bible's infallibility, may afterward remove it to some special form of opinion respecting the divinity of Christ.

Now, if we turn to the Gospels themselves and interrogate them, we will find that Christ gives his disciples neither creed, liturgy, nor rule for perfecting an ecclesiastical organization. He defines nothing; He systematizes nothing; though doubtless there are in the Bible the materials for the science of theology, as there are in the heavens materials for the science of astronomy, but He did not combine them, and His disciples, in doing so, have been far from infallible. There is in the Bible, however, a constant insistence upon clean hands and a pure heart; a forgiving spirit; an enthusiasm for righteousness, but nowhere are you asked to believe—in order to be saved—a proposition, or assent to formulated opinion regarding Christ Himself. The reason is plain; belief of dogma respecting a person does not necessarily bring man into vital union with that person, while, on the other hand, refusal to assent to this or that dogma respecting a person does not necessarily hinder man from entering into the closest and most blessed fellowship with him. The acceptance of theories respecting the Son of God, therefore, are not needful in order to fellowship with the Son of God. He Himself is the life, and not some opinion about Him. And, fortunately, this life that He is "cannot be patented, or shut up in the keeping of any ecclesiastical corporation, or bench of bishops, or infallible Pope, nor can it be squeezed into any sacrament, rite, catechism or creed." For agreement in doctrine, at best, is but a bond of union between the *understandings* of men, while agreement in affection is union between the *souls* of men; and this is the essential thing in Christianity, whether man thinks of his relation to God or thinks of his relation to his fellow-men. To maintain, therefore, that Christians must think alike on any point, save self-evident or axiomatic truth, is as absurd as to maintain that they must think alike on all points without exception.

But the fellowship of the church is a fellowship of persons—not necessarily agreeing in opinions—and must have a person as its ultimate bond; therefore in the Gospels the person of Jesus is central and not some fine-spun theory regarding Him. His first disciples and evangelists, recognizing this fundamental distinction, became heralds of a person rather than the framers of a code of rules for the regulation of conduct, or a creed for the regulation of faith. But when the church, degenerating, could no longer point to the living epistle and say, See, here is Christianity, in its impotency and pride the church pointed to its doctrinal deliverances, saying, See, this is what we believe Christianity to be, and what, if you are to fellowship with us, you, too, must believe. It is very much as when the Pope, pointing to a treasure of gold, said to Thomas Aquinas, "See, Thomas, the church of to-day can no longer use the language of St. Peter, 'Silver and gold have I none.'" "True, your holiness," Thomas replied, "but neither can she say, 'Rise up and walk.'"

Ever since Christianity ceased to be expressed in terms of life, the church has been too well satisfied with assent to its doctrines, regarding the belief of such as tantamount to being a Christian.

If we would learn what essential Christianity is, surely it cannot be needful to go to the Old Testament to find out, for Jesus Christ at once embodied, interpreted and exemplified all that was essential in the teachings of Moses, and the prophets, and the Psalms. Nor is it needful to go to the Acts and Epistles of the New Testament to learn the essential elements of Christianity, for these do no more than illustrate, develop and apply the principles latent in the Gospels; at best they are secondary, derivative and dependent. St. Paul differs from Christ only by amplification, illustration and application, not by addition, much less by opposition. Much less, in order to learn the character of essential Christianity, do we need to go to the church fathers, to the councils, or to the creeds and confessions of Christendom, for the fathers and the framers of the creeds and confessions were themselves dependent on the same sources, which lie open to all alike.

I assume that we are as capable Anno Domini 1901 of examining and determining the content of Christ's teachings as the church was in any previous period of Christian history, and we are fully justified in returning and confining ourselves exclusively to the Gospels themselves, when we would know what essential Christianity is. Did the Gospels constitute the whole of our Bible, could not man find therein, without much difficulty, the words of eternal life?—if he could not, then the teachings of the Christ are fatally deficient. Time was when man had to be satisfied with a very much dimmer measure of light concerning God and duty than has been given him to-day. What body of doctrine, do you suppose, Abraham, Moses, Isaiah, Socrates, Epictetus or Plato adopted?

It is highly desirable, of course, that Christianity should be stated historically, doctrinally, philosophically, ecclesiastically, experimentally, etc., especially if we understand that the thing itself, that which gives value and meaning to history, doctrine, and the like, cannot be expressed by intellectual formulas or syllogisms; neither does spiritual truth make its finest conquests by the force of logical processes, nor by the removal of intellectual difficulties, for few men receive the truth simply because it is made clear and commends itself to their judgment and logical understanding. But it is all-important that Christianity should be stated, too, in terms of life, as when introduced it was exemplified and commended by a life.

"The words that I speak unto you, they are spirit and they are life"—not limping logic or a cold creed. "He that hath the Son hath the life, he that hath not the Son of God hath not the life."

The essential and distinguishing feature of Christianity, therefore, is *life in Christ,* had by union, and fed by communion, with Him; or, in other words, essential Christianity is life in and fellowship with Jesus Christ in spirit and purpose—the reign of God in the human soul, commanding the conscience and the will because possessing the affections. "In the strictest sense of essential," says Coleridge, "this alone is the essential in Christianity, that the same spirit should be growing in us which was in the fulness of all perfection in Jesus Christ." Whoever is thus united to Jesus Christ is freed from and superior to all externalities; creeds may crumble, the Bible become discredited, theologies change, good men differ, the church itself degenerate; he is disturbed by none of it; he is superior to all of it, for his dependence is upon Him "who is the same yesterday, to-day and forever." It is inevitable that theories and opinions, and systems and views should change, for man—the growing man, in view point—is ever changing. But he need give himself little concern about the curious questions of the intellect to whom all the vital questions of the heart have been answered.

We are of Dr. Parkhurst's mind: "I am not making light of creeds nor belittling orthodoxy, but all that creeds and orthodoxy are worth is in what they can do toward making a man to be in his heart what Christ was in His heart, and if they are that, I don't care whether they get it by being orthodox or by being heterodox, by being Lutherans or Wesleyans, by being Calvinists or heretics. The best doctrine is that which does most to make men God-like, and the best denomination is the one that will graduate the finest saints and the most of them."

But how does the soul enter into this secret place of the Most High? Surely, neither subscription to Christian creeds, acceptance of doctrinal standards, nor agreement with theological systems is needful, when fellowship with a person is the question at issue. Besides, were there not those who enjoyed the unspeakable boon of fellowship with Jesus—spirit to spirit and heart to heart—before the creeds and the systems and the standards of the Christian faith were thought of? What a man *may* know and believe, and what a man *must* know and believe, in order to enter into life in Christ, may be as wide apart as the intellect of a Newton and that of a Hottentot. It is not absolutely needful—it is not needful at all—that man should believe, know, and acknowledge certain well-defined doctrines in order that he may enjoy any benefits which flow from them; just as a man may hold erroneous views regarding the sun's relation to our planet and yet enjoy all the benefits of sunlight. It is not needful to discuss the whole science of botany that you may win the admiration of your neighbor to the beauty and fragrance of your rose-bush. Jesus Christ said a good many things in His teaching that are pertinent here—and we are trying to confine our discussion strictly to the teaching of the Gospels. It was of little children that Jesus said, "Of such is the kingdom of heaven," and "Whosoever shall not receive the kingdom of God as a little child, he shall not enter therein." And again, "I thank Thee, O, Father, because Thou hast hid these things from the wise and prudent and hast revealed them unto babes." It is said a Chinaman who had applied for membership in a Christian church was put back on the ground that he had not sufficient knowledge of the faith to be received. He was among the number seized by the Boxers, and technically might have been justified in denying that he was "one of them," but when he was questioned with a sword at his throat, he boldly answered: "Yes, I am a Christian." To his surprise, he was allowed to escape. It is worthy of note that the man who had not enough knowledge to be a member of the church had enough courage and fidelity to be a martyr.

All of which goes to show, conclusively, that the amount of *knowledge* of the Christian faith needful, on the part of one who would enter into vital union with the Son of God, is not so great as to afford him alarm or keep him waiting. How much, think you, did the man referred to in John ix know about Jesus Christ when he believed and worshipped Him?

"It will be proper, then, to say," to quote Dr. Parkhurst again, "that the thing Christianity is here to do is to make men right in their feelings. It may not always make people wise; it may not give them correct understanding of things, nor attempt to. That quality of heart that Christianity aims to induce is something that correct understanding has almost nothing to do with. We know how much a child can love his mother without understanding his mother, without having ever in any way thought nicely and accurately about her. Indeed, it is his love for her that helps him to understand her a great deal more than it is his understanding of her that makes him love her."

But it may be replied to the foregoing statement of essential Christianity that such a weak and emasculated system might do very well in the imagination and for the kindergarten, but it would never endure being brought out into open day; so what is the use of discussing a theory that can have no practical value?

I have been attempting to present neither a system nor a theory, but a statement of fact. It may not be known to some people that in Neuchâtel and Geneva, Switzerland, as shown in Professor Vincent's paper on "Switzerland," the responsibility for doctrine rests entirely upon the conscience of the minister. The constitutions declare that "the liberty of the conscience of the ecclesiastic is inviolable; it shall be restricted neither by regulations, nor by oaths, nor by engagements, nor by disciplinary punishments, nor by the articles of a creed, nor by any other measure whatever." In the city of Calvin, Geneva, "every pastor teaches and preaches freely upon his own responsibility; this liberty shall be restricted neither by confessions of faith nor by forms of liturgy."

It would seem, therefore, that, measurably, essential Christianity is more than an emasculated creation of the fancy in Switzerland. "It is certainly not true," as some one has said, "that to fix the mind upon the central objects of faith—God, Christ, love, truth—instead of on the Thirty-nine Articles, or the Westminster Confession, or the canons of the Council of Dort, or other denominational standards, makes religion weak and flaccid. The experience of many, if not of the most, of the greatest minds, has been that they have tended, as life goes on, to think more of the former and less of the latter. I appeal to the experience of Richard Baxter, than whom no one was more qualified to speak, having lived through the seventeenth century and taken a prominent part in all its disputes. 'In my youth,' he says, 'I was quickly past my fundamentals, and was running up into a multitude of controversies and curiosities. But the older I grew, the smaller stress I laid upon these controversies and curiosities, as finding far greater uncertainties in them than I at first discovered, and finding less usefulness, comparatively, even where there is the greatest certainty. And now I value most highly and find most useful for myself and others the Apostles' Creed, the Lord's Prayer, and the Ten Commandments; they are to me my daily bread and drink, and I can speak and write of them over and over again, so I would rather read and hear of them than of any of the school niceties which once so pleased me.' And thus I observe that it was with old Bishop Usher and with many other men. I believe that the tendency described by Baxter is that of our own age. The great central truths of religion are being made the objects of thought and faith."

In saying that life in and union with Christ is essential Christianity, we are reminded that life alone is the creative power. Life is the originating, organizing and unifying principle in the organic sphere. Given life—"the spirit of life in Christ Jesus"—and you may have a Paul, an Augustine, a Savonarola, an Assisi, a Neander, a Fénelon, a Channing, a Spurgeon, a Martineau, a Whittier, a Brooks, a Wesley, or a Moody; men too large to be bound by any system of doctrine. And as each of several cities of Greece would fain have claimed Homer for its citizen, so each denomination would fain claim the right to call these Christian saints its own. The relation which these men sustained to one system of doctrine rather than to another was mainly accidental. Given the same men and the same spirit of life, and you would have had the same results under any system; that is to say, identification with a particular system of doctrine did not make them what they were—it was "the spirit of life in Christ Jesus." This spirit was common to them all alike—Roman Catholic, Protestant, Unitarian. They claimed kinship with all men and have their reward in all men wishing to claim kinship with them. "The weakest part of every man's creed is that which he holds alone, the strongest part is that which he holds in common with the whole of Christendom."

To him who is looking for metaphysical subtlety, doctrinal completeness, ecclesiastical impressiveness, or æsthetic attractiveness, the statement of Christianity just made may seem radically defective. But he must remember we have been trying to present essential Christianity, "spirit and life," that which gives to all forms and rites their significance, and without which they are of little avail.

Is this, then, to be the issue of all that our fathers fought for in bygone theological conflicts? Are all their labors to go for naught? Far from it; our position and outlook to-day is due to the battle for truth, as they saw it, which they so courageously waged. Their reward is in the advanced position which we to-day are enabled to occupy. Jesus Christ Himself was the issue, the fulfilment of the incompleteness of Judaism as a religious system, as a finality.

CHRISTENDOM.

O, friends, with whom my feet have trod
   The quiet aisles of prayer,
Glad witness to your zeal for God
   And love of men I bear.

I trace your lines of argument;
   Your logic, linked and strong,
I weigh as one who dreads dissent,
   And fears a doubt as wrong.

But still my human hands are weak
   To hold your iron creeds;
Against the words ye bid me speak,
   My heart within me pleads.

Who fathoms the Eternal Thought?
   Who talks of scheme and plan?
The Lord is God! He needeth not
   The poor device of man.

I walk with bare, hushed feet the ground
   Ye tread with boldness shod;
I dare not fix with mete and bound
   The love and power of God.

O, brothers, if my faith is vain,
   If hopes like these betray,
Pray for me, that my feet may gain
   The sure and safer way.

And Thou, O Lord, by whom are seen
   Thy creatures as they be,
Forgive me if too close I lean
   My human heart on Thee!

—WHITTIER.

THE COMPARISON OF CHRISTIANITY WITH OTHER RELIGIONS.

Professor Allan Menzies, D.D.,
SCOTLAND.

[Even those who shrink from any such notion as that the religious history of the world is the expression of a natural process of development, are not thereby precluded from recognizing in the earlier stages of that history a preparation and a propædeutic for the more advanced. Though there is an essential relation between Christianity and the pre-Christian religions, yet we cannot admit that the former is merely a combination of Jewish and heathen elements. If there are in the pre-Christian religions the germs of conceptions of God, and of His relations to the world, we find at once their unity and their explanation in our Christian faith. What the great monotheistic and pantheistic faiths of the ancient world were feeling after they failed to reach, because, apart from other reasons, their attempted solution of the problem of religion was in each case one-sided and fragmentary—the element of truth which each contained being rendered false because held in isolation from that which is its necessary complement. In other words, monotheistic religions are imperfect because they exclude the pantheistic element, pantheistic religions because they lack the monotheistic element. It lends a new force to our appreciation of the nature and spiritual value of the Christian faith if we can discern in it that which at once comprehends and transcends these earlier religions, embracing what is true, and supplying a complement of what is imperfect, and the corrective of what is false in both.

Whilst, therefore, we may hold that Christianity is neither a reproduction nor a natural development of the imperfect notions of God in which the religious aspirations of the Old World embodied themselves, it is possible at the same time to maintain that the study of the old religions sheds new light on the Christian religion, and gives to it a new and deeper sense of its spiritual significance and power.—"The Faiths of the World," pp. 2, 3.—Ed.]

* * *

How can we profitably compare Christianity with other religions?

The question is one which is constantly occurring to us; and the answer to it is not quite obvious. It is easy enough, indeed, if we can still intrench ourselves in the position that our religion is the only true one, and that all the others are false religions and doctrines of demons. But this few can do; and if this plan is abandoned, how are we to proceed?

The missionary naturally wishes to compare the Christian Gospel which he bears to other lands with the faith he finds prevailing in them, and if he is a good missionary, and loves truth and justice, he desires to carry out his comparison in the right way and to reach a result which can defend itself at the bar of reason, where Jews and Buddhists and Chinese are judges as well as Christians.

And those who send missionaries abroad are also under a moral obligation to understand what they are doing when they seek to substitute Christianity for the indigenous religions of distant lands. We do not now believe that the heathen are perishing, so many hundreds of them every hour, because they do not know Christ. But if this motive for missions is defunct, we do not, therefore, give up our missionary enterprises; no earnest Christian can think of such a policy. We must seek to approve ourselves in a new way, worthy of the knowledge of the age we live in, that Christ is the desire of all nations, and that it is not only love of our own creed, but love of mankind, that prompts us to bring all men to Him.

The question is a pressing one for missionaries and for missionary societies. But it is urgent for all who wish to occupy a satisfactory position in their own minds. If we are Christians at all, we most wish to know that in being Christians, and not Mohammedans or pagans or followers of Confucius, we are in the right position. The doctrine has been very much preached of late that every religion bears truth in it, and that it is good, first of all, that a man should be true to that religion which he professes. We have also heard it much insisted on that all religions are, at the root of the matter, one, and that God is present in them all, that they may all save if heartily believed and faithfully obeyed. No doubt there is much truth in these contentions; but on the other hand, if all religions are true, then how, we cannot help asking, is one of them better than another, and what does it matter to which of them any man belongs? The popular science of religion has brought home to us these perplexities, and it is only by the comparison of the various religions together that we can hope to unravel them and to arrive at some clearness on a great and important subject. Most men who have ever thought of the matter at all believe that Christianity is the best religion, but few can prove it or define how the religion of Christ is the best. And so not only is our missionary practice vague and confused, but we want, to a lamentable degree, the clear and enthusiastic conviction which ought to inspire us in our personal and social attachment to Christ. What, then, we ask again, is the right and proper way to compare our great religion, say Christianity, with another?

That there are many wrong ways of making such a comparison few, perhaps, will deny. It is not fair to compare a lofty and pure example of our religion with a degenerate and unworthy example of another, say the Christianity of the Protestant lands in this century with the decadent Hindooism now to be seen in India, or with Buddhism as now found in China. If the comparison is to be done by samples, then the flower of each religion must be taken, or the average product, if it can be obtained, and the abuses of which each is capable, the mischief to which it is apt to give rise, must also be taken into the account. The missionary, who requires to make up his mind without any long delay, must judge by samples. He will naturally compare what he brings with him with what meets his eye and ear when he lands on the foreign shore. But on reflection he will see that the idolatrous Buddhism of China is not true Buddhism, and that the barbarities of modern Hindooism do not belong to the essential faith of India, any more than the superstitions of Italian villages are to be laid to the charge of essential Christianity. The good missionary, when he sees that the heathen he is dealing with are not acting up to the true spirit of their own religion, will tell them so; he will remember that Christian cities also have their slums; that Christian peoples also are apt to give way to materialism of thought and action, that cruelty and strife, that superstition and fanaticism, that disobedience to the teaching of religion are not unknown to Christian lands.

If the missionary must act there, so must the Christian at home, who is not bound to make up his mind on the subject at once, but has time to think of the best way of arriving at the truth. If we are to compare religion by the samples we meet with of their respective fruits, we must take care that the samples we employ are really representative and well chosen. We must not judge of the heathen religions by the samples we happen to meet with in conversation or in the newspapers, or even in missionary reports. We must compare the best fruits of one religion with the best fruits of the other, and no doubt also the worst with the worst, and must avoid the appearance of judging the religion of the heathen by one standard and our own by another.

All this shows us that a religion which is believed in by multitudes of men is a thing with many sides which it is by no means easy to sum up in a single statement for the purpose of comparison. Who will draw up the character of Christianity in such a way as to embrace all its legitimate existing forms, not to speak of its aberrations and abuses? Who will define Christianity in such a way as to embrace in his definition both the Roman Catholic and the Protestant form of the faith, both the religion of the Unitarian and that of the Anglican, to say nothing of the faith of the negro or the Scottish highlander? And then we have to remember how much Christianity has altered with the centuries. Like everything that has life it has had its periods, on the one hand, of vigor and expansion, and on the other of contraction and decay. What is true of it in one age may have been untrue of it in the preceding age, and in the next age may again cease to apply to it. If we are to compare Christianity, then, with other religions, it may well be asked, What Christianity? The average faith and life of all Christians? But who can possibly define what these are? Is it the original faith of the Master and the Apostles? But to multitudes of Christians that constitutes a very meagre portion, as they think, of what they profess. Is it the ultimate purified Christianity aspired after by the pious and the thoughtful? But where, we may ask again, is this religion to be found, and how many will agree in such a description of it?

And what is thus true of Christianity is true of other religions also. True, the differences are less with them; none of them has put forth so many and so various forms of creed and worship as it has. Yet with them, also, the forms and manifestations in different countries and ages are so manifold as to make it very hard to state the essence of the religion in a form suited for the purpose of comparison. Who can define what is common to all the branches of Buddhism, north and south, at the present day? Even Mohammedanism, with its short creed and simple practice, covers with its name on the one hand whole forests of primitive superstition, and on the other systems of advanced speculation in which the practical purposes of religion are to a large extent lost sight of. And what unity can be predicated of the Hindoo religion, with its rapidly succeeding generations of new gods, its old gods changed beyond recognition from the appearance of their vigorous youth; its monasticism, its mystical speculation?

It appears, indeed, as if the multiplicity of forms which is found in every great religion must forbid any effective comparison of one of them with another. What comparison can there be between systems which have so little internal unity? We can compare a sample of one with a sample of another, or a whole set of samples of each; but this method can never be satisfactory unless it goes all the way, and sets the whole history and the whole present condition of each religion side by side with that of the other. The comparison of religion by samples leads, in fact, to the demand for an exhaustive and complete statement of each. The only satisfactory comparison of religions in their outward features lies in their history. This the science of religion has clearly acknowledged at the present day by the titles it has adopted. Students of religion do not now call their works by the name of "Comparative Religion"; they call them the "History of Religion," a change of title which implies, along with other things, that in order to understand the relation to each other of the various religions of the earth, it is necessary to study each of them thoroughly, and to trace to their root in the far past the various manifestations each of them exhibits.

And along with the historical methods the statistical has to be mentioned. To compare two great religions is as if we should undertake to compare the Atlantic and the Pacific oceans. That could only be done by the aid of maps and of tables of figures, in which all the main facts of each, so far as they admit of exact statement, should be set forth. In the case of a religion also, after we have studied its history, and seen how each of its modern developments is related to its primary form, and how the differences in its form arose, we can proceed to count and measure what in it admits of such processes.

The number of adherents in each country can be given, and the total number of adherents, its geographical distribution, the dates of its festivals can be given, its places of pilgrimage can be stated, the arrangement of its temples. The statistics of the world's religions are of great interest, and in any complete statement are, of course, essential, and they afford standards of comparison which can be readily applied.

Yet at the same time it cannot be denied that one may know a good many statistical facts about two religions without being able to institute any effective comparison of them; neither history nor statistics will avail for this, in the absence of insight into their genius and character. We may know all about their history and may have command of the facts of their present condition, and yet be very far from knowing what, after all, is most important and interesting, *i. e., their comparative value for the human spirit and for human society*. This, every one will acknowledge, is the central part of our problem. The comparison of religions means, first of all, the comparison of their respective characters. How do they compare together with respect to the yoke they impose on their adherents, and the inspiration they afford; with respect to the action they bring to bear on individual character, or the family, or the state? This surely is the question.

And when we attempt to compare religions from this point of view, as instruments of human welfare and advancement, we find that science does not refuse its aid. There are two methods by which the ethical values of religions may be compared. There is, in the first place, the consideration of the outward form of different faiths, and of the place in the general development of religion which the outward form of each shows it to hold. In the second place, there is the method, less capable, perhaps, than the other, of strict scientific application, and more liable to be misdirected by subjunctive bias, but still legitimate and necessary, viz.: the comparison of religions according to the central principle or idea which they embody. The former method may be called the morphological; it judges religions according to their structure, and it will be found to grow less applicable as we advance to the higher stages of religious growth. The second may be called the moral, or practical, method; it judges religions according to the end and aim they set before believers.

The Morphological Method of Comparing Religions.—The student of the social arrangements of mankind can arrange the various types of society in which men have lived together in some sort of a scale, which rises from the lowest social or unsocial state of man and ascends to the most highly organized, the best governed, the most refined communities. To name some of the principal steps, the nomadic condition is succeeded, in the case of our own ancestors, by that of settled pastoral life, and that again by the agricultural. Then comes the life of towns and cities, with their advancing industries, their ever-increasing division of labor; their arts, their new social distinctions. Or, again, the system of slavery gives way to feudalism, and feudalism in turn to the democratic state, in which all are equal before the law. With such a scale of development before him the student can readily assign to its proper place in human progress any society he is examining; and thus he is in possession of an objective standard by which to compare different societies together with precision. A more familiar instance of this procedure is that of biology, where the structure of a plant or animal at once locates it in the scale of the development of living organisms.

In the case of religion also this procedure may be applied. Human religion also has developed and has passed through various well-marked phases on its way toward its higher and its highest forms. It is true that no single religion exhibits the whole of the development of man's relations with God. It is religion as a whole that develops, not merely this or that particular religion. It often happens that a particular religion falls back to a lower stage, but the religious growth of mankind is not thereby arrested. Now, if we can make out what the steps are by which religion advances from its earlier to its higher forms, then we have a standard by which it is possible for us to assign to any given faith its proper place in the scale of human religion as a whole. And this can to a certain extent be done.

What are the steps by which mankind has advanced, and is advancing always, to a worthier faith? That question is carefully answered in the Gifford lectures of Professor Tiele, in "The Elements of the Science of Religion," Vol. I, "Morphological." It has also been answered, though never quite so systematically, by other writers. The result of the inquiry may be briefly summed up as follows: The lowest stage of religion—whether or not it is always the first in time, we need not here consider—is that of Animism. Here men believe in the existence of numerous spirits; whether spirits of ancestors or not, spirits at any rate without organization or fixity or definiteness. Where such beings are believed in, the service of the unseen objects of devotion is apt to be in the form of magic rather than of anything that we call worship. Charms and spells are sought after, by which the spirits may be kept at a distance from man, or may be compelled to do his bidding. Religious acts are occasional rather than stated or regular in their nature. Human life is at the mercy of capricious beings, and every kind of device is resorted to with a view to some small security. Of this lowest religion, many a survival, or, to use a word which is often abused in its strictly correct application, many a superstition, is to be found even among the most civilized people and in the presence of lofty and pure faith, with which it is in reality quite incompatible.

This religious stage, however, is succeeded by that higher one in which the gods acquire fixed character and came to receive a stated and regular worship. There is a settled place in which the god resides, and where he is to be approached, and he comes to have a definite clientele of worshippers, who approach him in a customary method of service at fixed intervals. These gods are at first very numerous; each tribe will have its god, if not each family. It is by no means an exaggeration when the prophet says: "According to thy cities are thy gods, O Israel."

It is a further step when, out of the multitude of petty local deities, the great gods by degrees lift up their heads; gods who are worshipped in more towns than one, whom several tribes acknowledge in addition to their own particular deities, or who are even common to a race or to the whole of a great country. In this way we come to what is called national religion; a god is believed in who is greater, wiser, better, holier than were the local gods before him. As the people grow stronger and more refined and civilized, the god grows also and becomes the representative of its proud self-consciousness and of its high ideals. He is the father of his nation, the giver of its laws, its just judge and the defender of its poor and unregarded members, the rewarder of its favorite virtues, the inspirer of its arts. At this stage, at the same time, there are still many gods; each people has its god, but believes also in the existence and the power of those of its neighbors. Or a people has several gods, each having been in its own place and time supreme, but not having destroyed the faith placed in his brother gods, so that the people think of a Pantheon in which a family or a system of gods is seated; and all the contradictions and confusions of Polytheism disturb the mind and chill the heart.

Here a very momentous change is to be noticed which, when the figures of the gods are once firmly defined, takes place, in religions of adequate vitality, in their character and their relation to man. The national god is primarily a natural phenomenon, made personal and living; he is fire, he is the storm in its beneficent or in its overbearing aspect, he is the bright heaven, he is the sun, he is the ocean. But as the tie between him and his people grows more close and familiar, he puts on human qualities, and becomes such a being as the people desire to have in their ruler—just, impartial, generous, kind and merciful. And in some happy instances the time comes when this side of the divine character prevails over the earlier natural features; and the deity becomes a moral being. Instead of continuing, like the ocean or the stars, neither good nor bad, or, like some of the Greek gods, continuing to represent human nature in its non-moral, natural side, the God comes to represent essential moral goodness. Now he is in the first place good and holy, he is not to be bribed by sacrifice or turned aside by any weakness in himself from being good and holy. What is now most prominent in him is that he favors what is good in man and is the power by whose aid man can hope to rise above his lower self to a life of purity and reason and love. The instances are, no doubt, few in which this change in the character of deity has quite realized itself; where it has done so it has proved the most momentous change of all.

Again, a step closely connected in some instances with the last, and a religion comes into view which is not for one nation only, and is not confined to the soil of one country, but is capable of appealing to men of different races, and of uniting them in a community wider than that of country or of language. Here we come to the wonderful phenomenon of the fellowship of believers, or the church, which is capable of binding men together by a bond in which there is nothing political or national. They are one, not because they dwell in the same land or came of the same stock, or speak a common tongue, but because they think alike and are filled with the same ideals and hopes. Now we find religion grown so strong that it can make a man forsake his family to seek his spiritual kindred, and his nation, if need be, to seek the spiritual kingdom which has laid its commands upon him. The religion of which we now speak springs, in most instances, out of the spiritual experience of one gifted individual, an experience which all can understand and feel to be drawing them also near to the divine; and thus it is able to spread from land to land, and to gather into its fold nations and kindreds and tongues.

This, then, is in rough outline the morphological scale of religions in which it is possible to determine the place of any particular faith. Animism comes first, then the worship of local or tribal gods, then that of great gods who preside over a conquering race and a wide territory. Up to this point religion is polytheistic; a plurality of gods is believed to exist, each being entitled to recognition on his own soil and at the hands of his own people. As these gods grow more human and more ethical in their character the belief is prepared, which if reason is to prevail in religion must come some day, that only one God exists, and that the other beings called gods are not gods at all, and ought not to be worshipped; and from this point it is but a step to the universal religion in which it is discovered that religion, instead of separating men, is capable of bringing them together, since the way of salvation which has been opened up in a great human experience is fitted for all and ought to be presented to all and received by all.

If this scale of the religious progress of the world is, so far as it goes, a true one--and this will, I think, be generally recognized--then one religion may be readily compared with another by marking what place each holds upon the scale. And when we consider Christianity in this way we find, in the first place, that with many religions which have prevailed and many which still prevail in the world, Christianity can scarcely be compared at all. They belong to stages of the religious growth of mankind which, even among the people among whom it had its birth, had been outgrown for centuries. The Animistic position, the worship of indefinite numbers of spirits, and the dealing with such beings by magic and incantation, has been outgrown, though many of its traces long remained in Israel, if not by the patriarchs, at least by the generation of the Exodus. The relation of Christianity, therefore, to Shintoism, to the Chinese worship of spirits, to the religion expressed in most of the Babylonian hymns, or to the fetishism of tribes now living, is that of the vertebrate to the mollusc, that of the grown man to the infant, that of the modern civilized state to the social arrangements of the Red Indians. They are all, no doubt, Christianity and spirit-worship in these various forms, they are all alike to be called religion; in all there is a seeking after God, a cultivation by man of a higher unseen power. All alike, therefore, are to be sympathized with by the man of insight; they are all in their degree good and holy, all evidence of the power which works within man and leads our race forward to full manhood. But Christianity is in no degree parallel with faiths like these; it comes long after them in the scale of human growth, and is not to be compared with them except as the full-grown animal may be compared with the infant it once was.

And in the same way Christianity cannot be compared, to any profit, with the local worships of Greece, though these were often so beautiful; nor with the worship of Rome, though its organization was so stately; nor with the national worships of Assyria and of Egypt, though they have left such imperishable monuments; nor with the state religion of China. These all were for the state, the nation; but Christianity is not limited to any nation. These were regarded as instruments of national well-being, and were so administered that the individual found little provision made in them for his private wants or griefs, however great. They addressed the individual not as an immortal being of infinite value in himself, but as a citizen whose part it was to share in the national cult, even when it had nothing of any use to give him. They even laid fetters on his spirit from which, when his mind and conscience awoke, he felt it necessary to seek deliverance. They offered him no help to grow to his full stature as an intellectual and moral being, but rather, as Paul says in his great comparison of pre-Christian with Christian religion (Galat. iv, 1-7), kept him in bondage and prevented him from realizing his true nature. In these old cults there no doubt are many features which we are disposed to envy; but in their quality as religions they are far below our own. They were more closely in alliance with the arts of their respective states, and so to the outward eye were far more richly equipped and entitled in their service, far more than our religion in general does to all the various efforts of the national mind. But they did not encourage or inspire the heart as Christian worship did, nor draw men together as it does in mutual regard and helpfulness. While we regret their vanished charm, we cannot but see that it is better that they are left behind.

Of great religions which are strictly to be called national there are at least two now flourishing in the world. The Chinese religion does not extend its regards beyond the Chinese nation; while tempered by a system of ethics in which the individual finds his account, it contemplates as its direct aim the welfare of the state and does not seek the conversion of foreigners. The other national religion presently existing is the Jewish. This is not meant to suggest that there is any similarity between the Jewish and the Chinese religion in their inner character, but only that each is limited to its own nation. How much we owe to Judiasm we all know; though we have departed from its fold, we carry its treasures with us in our worship and in our heart. But Judaism in its creed, though not, no doubt, in the belief of most of its adherents, restricts the blessings of the covenant to the posterity of Abraham, and so stands morphologically on a less advanced position than Christianity. Our own religion represents more fully than the Jewish what the world has attained and what the world craves.

So much, then, of our task we have discharged. The religions of custom and tradition, such as all the faiths of the old world were, and those which are and remain identified with a single nation—these cannot properly be compared with religions which have sprung from the spiritual impulse of a personal founder, and address all who sympathize in the founder's struggles and experiences. They belong to an earlier stage of the growth of the human race. No doubt a great part of the human race is still living in that earlier stage; even in the most enlightened lands the religion that is customary and traditional still flourishes. Christianity itself has become the national religion of many nations, and has put on some of the narrowness and stiffness which is inseparable from national worship. But the vital or growing or missionary element of one of the higher religions is not to be sought in its traditions or in its national form. The thoughts of the founder, the nearness he suggests to us of the spiritual world, the hopes he bids us cherish for ourselves and for mankind, the view he bids us take of our own nature and of that of other men—these are the characteristic elements of religion of the most advanced type. And because it has blessings of this kind, which all men can share, consolations applicable to all, hopes which appeal to all, therefore we cannot seriously compare it with a religion where all is tradition and routine inherited from a shadowy past, or where everything is regarded as subserving the interest of one particular state.

Now there are three great religions, as all know, for which the claim is made that they have this character of universalism. It is certainly true that Buddhism, Christianity and Islam, to name them in the order in which they entered the world, have spread far beyond the countries of their origin. Buddhism, which arose in India, is now the principal religion of Ceylon and has spread over the southeastern lands of Asia. In India itself it has become almost extinct, but to the north of India it has its second and much larger realm of northern Buddhism, embracing China, Japan and Korea, not to speak of Thibet and Manchuria. Its total of adherents rises to five hundred millions. The religion of the Prophet, too, spread with immense rapidity from Arabia, the country of its birth, to the lands of Eastern Asia and along the north of Africa, from which it crossed over to Spain; and it is now spreading rapidly in the Indian Empire. Its adherents are thought to number two hundred millions. The spread of Christianity is to be read in the church histories, and it now sends missionaries to every land. Its fold is not so numerously filled as that of Buddhism.

How do we compare these three religions together? The morphological standard will not serve us here, for all three of those claim to belong to the highest stage in the morphology of religion. The claim, indeed, is in some respects disputed. It is said of Islam that it is not a universal religion, because it is not universal. It has been planted, no doubt, in various lands, but its spread was forced and artificial. It did not spread by its inner force, and is not in its own nature a universal one, but rather a limited and narrow one, and tied to a particular shrine and land. And of Buddhism it may be said that it is not a universal religion, because it is not in its full sense a religion; it has no object of worship properly belonging to it, and cannot properly meet the needs of a society of men for common religious acts addressed to higher beings and bringing to the community the sense of higher guidance and blessing.

But not to press in the meantime these objections to the classification of Islam and of Buddhism as universal religions, let us ask in what way a comparison may be made of the three systems which have spread themselves over by far the greater part of the human race. To compare them together fully, we should have to study each of them historically; we should have to examine the stories of their respective founders, to analyze the leaven thus introduced in each case into the human mind, and to trace its action subsequently and at the present day. The task is one which has never been performed as it deserves, and cannot, of course, be attempted here. All we can do is to throw out a few hints as to the respective principles of the three religions, and as to the way in which each of them might be expected to operate on human character and on human society. The reader who is interested in the subject will be able to satisfy himself by reading the history of the three religions and studying the condition of human life in countries where each prevails, whether or not our forecast has been rightly made.

Buddhism was originally a mendicant monastic order, which sought to communicate to the world, and bring all men to adopt, the deeper insight into the problems of life which had been discovered in its own circle. The founder and his associates had no doctrine of God to preach, no heavenly message to make known, no heaven or hell to set before men's eyes, no system of worship either to set up or to pull down. But on the other hand they had found out the secret of dealing with the sorrows of life, and believed themselves to be able to offer the true remedy for the universal suffering by which they considered mankind to be tormented. All life is suffering was the axiom from which the teaching of the founder set out; all suffering is due to desire, he held, not in this differing very much from Jesus Christ; and the cure for all suffering is to be sought in the eradication of desire, in this differing from Christ, who taught men how to control desire by directing it into higher channels of service. By withdrawal and self-absorption, the Teacher held, desire could be got rid of in the end, while a man could not be saved at once from being born again to another life, and still another and another, all of them made up of suffering, yet by strenuous effort the goal might be brought a little nearer. The man might get upon the road to retrieve the errors of his past existences and to travel toward the final state in which desire should be quite gone, and with it suffering also.

Applied to a large number of adherents or made into the religion of a country, this system, of which this is the keynote, has obviously great defects. It puts before the believer no god to worship, but directs him to try his own efforts as the source of success in the higher life. For select souls, or for a monastic community, or a set of such communities, the method perhaps might serve; in the state of belief that existed in India when Gautama taught, it may have been the highest possible; but as the faith of a people it was too full of blanks and of negatives not to be quickly altered from its original character. In practice Buddhism has been filled up with heavenly beings who have no right to be where they are. Gautama Buddha himself soon came to be worshipped, as well as other Buddhas or Revealers who came before him; and in Chinese Buddhism a whole system of gods, saints, sacrifices and prayers flourishes greatly, so that the religion came to appear not very different from the others which existed beside it, and its original motive and intention were to a large extent obscured. In this case, therefore, its inherent evils are not so manifest; but wherever this religion travels it must necessarily carry with it much of the sadness of its birth. Rising out of the bankruptcy of Hindoo thought as to the gods and as to human destiny, and out of the mortification of the monkish life in which compensation was sought for the loss of direct and natural religion, Buddhism must tend, wherever it goes, to darken and unnerve. It calls to sacrifice and self-mortification, which do not issue in the glory of God or in strenuous action for the good of society, but are taught to be good and desirable for their own sake; it therefore checks rather than encourages action and enterprise, it builds up no healthy social fabric, and holds out no hope appealing to the general mass of men, either for this world or for any other.

In Islam, on the contrary, we find a faith which is highly practical and energetic, with extremely precise and definite beliefs, and clear and unmistakable injunctions for conduct. If in Buddhism the aim of the believer is found in his own life, and the working out of such redemption as is possible to him, here the believer is bidden to subordinate himself entirely to the will of God and to accept without hesitation what is fixed for him from above, to do or to endure. He is not encouraged to think of his own redemption, but to devote himself unhesitatingly to the following of God's law and the execution of the divine purposes, secure that if he does so God will take care for him, and give him, if not what he would choose, at least what God deems to be best for him. This great religion sprang into being through the experience of one who is rightly called the Prophet, since he heard with perfect clearness the voice of the supreme and only God and handed on to others with uncompromising faithfulness what was thus revealed to him, and acted the part assigned to him from above with overwhelming vigor and unshakable conviction. A religion so simple and so forcible, laying hold of men with so clear a voice and calling so imperatively for obedience to its behests, could not fail to produce an immense impression in the world. For races full of vigor and not yet arrived at the highest levels of culture, it is an admirable rule. It provides them with a code of duties they can understand, holds out sanctions which readily appeal to them, calls them to action, restrains some at least of their passions, and makes the spiritual world real and present to them. It is a drill which lifts them above many of the vices of barbarism and forms them into a life of discipline and effectiveness. To many nations which have embraced it, Islam has proved highly tonic and elevating, and among races at a certain stage of civilization it no doubt has still a great future to expect.

On the other hand a stream may not rise higher than its source, and the source from which Islam set out was in many respects not the most lofty. The defects of Islam are to be seen in its origin. The greatest is that Allah, the god who spoke with such vehemence through the Prophet, is an abstract being, with little history, little definite character, and therefore somewhat remote from men and an object of fear rather than love. The faithful cannot recite his mighty works in the past as the Jew can those of Jehovah. He is the negation of the false gods, the idols, whom Mohammed found receiving the worship of his countrymen, but in himself he is merely an abstraction of the qualities of deity as conceived by the South Semitics; power, impetuosity, strictness in judgment, jealousy, and also a certain mildness in some directions, mercy, without which men would scarcely worship him. He is a moral god, but not equally so in all matters; some indulgences he allows and even holds out as part of the blessedness of the future, and his religion is for men and does not encourage a high view of the nature or of the rights of woman. The civilization, therefore, which this religion fosters will be very defective on this side, and this is a defect from which Islam can never free itself. It has also to be said that Allah is a local god and has taken up into his worship various local superstitions connected with Mecca which are not of an elevating character, and belong to the "beggarly elements" of religion much more than to its spiritual and emancipating tendency.

We should, therefore, expect to find that if this religion spread quickly, its extension was due not wholly at least to its own inner character causing it to be eagerly adopted, but to the policy of the virile race who were identified with it and whose highest duty lay in promoting it. Local and narrow, and carrying along with it unimprovable relics of heathenism, it was spread by force, and while it proved a valuable discipline to the peoples who accepted it, it could not lead them to any high level of civilization.

When we come to speak of Christianity we find ourselves, of course, in a difficulty. We have spoken of Buddhism and of Islam from the outside and have pointed out their merits and defects from the position of a disinterested observer; but we cannot speak of Christ's religion in the same way. Living in the religion we feel its blessings too strongly and are too unconscious of its drawbacks to speak of it as a Mohammedan or a Buddhist might. Perhaps it is not to be desired that a Christian writer should do so. One who could write on the subject of this paper without feeling or showing any enthusiasm for his own religion would surely be wanting in one of the chief qualifications demanded by his task.

That is not to say, however, that the writer is not to have his own views of what Christianity is, nor to be at liberty to discard views of its nature which he thinks one-sided or untrue. Christianity has been a monastic system like Buddhism, and has preached withdrawal from the world and the modification of all desire; but we at least could not defend it in that aspect. To us it is a doctrine which inspires action—action in the world and for the world—and makes for the free development of human nature, for the salvation both of the individual and of society. Christianity, again, has been, like Islam, a system of discipline imposing itself from without upon the people, and requiring outward conformity to its creed and to its moral code. But in this aspect, also, as a system of weak and poor elements, we could have no heart to defend it except as a yoke which may have been necessary at certain times and among certain barbarous peoples. What, then, do we regard as the essential part of Christianity, as that which constitutes its life and force, and is present more or less in all its multitudinous and most widely different forms? Surely there can be no doubt that its essence is love. That God loves man and would have him to know it, and to take that love to his heart and live in the power of it—that is the essential Christian Gospel. In this message lies its energy to call men back from evil ways, to give them a higher view of their own nature and destiny, to emancipate them, to inspire them, to lead them forward in an unending course of self-realization and development. A religion of which this is the central thought cannot but send missionaries to all the world to tell men who do not yet know it what their true nature is, and what God and those who already know themselves to be God's children would have them to become. Where this belief is held all the institutions of human life must be so moulded as to allow God's children to come to their true position and enjoy their rightful heritage. All men must be considered entitled to be treated with the utmost respect, for their own sake; no man can be the chattel of another; all must be encouraged and assisted so far as the framework of the world permits; to grow up to the full stature of their being, and to enjoy as far as possible the gift God has bestowed on his children.

If this is Christianity, then it is an instrument of the greatest possible efficiency for the redress of human evils, the unsealing of human energy, and the improvement of human society, and neither Buddhism nor Islam is at all to be compared to it in point of value for the world.

THE DISUNION OF CHRISTENDOM.

Rector Algernon S. Crapsey, D.D.,
ROCHESTER.

Lines of progress and unification as indicated by the present state of the church:

First. The subordination of the official organization of the church, from the highest to the lowest of its members, to the church itself, as practiced in the primitive church, as decreed by the Western church in the Council of Constance, and as affirmed by the principles of the Protestant Reformation.

Second. The pastoral rather than the priestly conception of the ministry. It is the office of the ministry to bring the people to God, rather than to be to the people instead of God.

Third. The statement of Christian doctrine so that it will be in accord with the facts of the visible universe, as these are discovered and formulated by the processes of inductive thought. The earth's form and motion, man's place in the earth, his past history and present condition, are matters for scientific investigation and settlement.

Fourth. The statement of Christian doctrine so that it will not conflict with the great primal instincts of the human heart; the instinct for justice, mercy and truth. No man will be compelled to believe such a doctrine as that of everlasting punishment as taught by S. Augustine in "The City of God," or the doctrine of predestination as taught in "The Institutes of Calvin."

Fifth. Absolute intellectual freedom within the church, so that every opinion shall have a hearing, and be taken for what it is worth; to have the force of its author's personal character, learning and wisdom; and to establish itself by its own truthfulness or not at all.

Sixth. The submission of the entire content of Christian tradition, both oral and written, to the trained intelligence, that the content, meaning and value of the whole and of each part may be ascertained, correctly estimated and set forth, "that those things which are not shaken may remain."

Seventh. The restoration of the church's moral discipline as the only true basis of her spiritual life.

* * *

No one can read the prayer of our Lord and Saviour Jesus the Christ, which He prayed in the upper chamber of Jerusalem, on the night before His death, without a feeling of compassion for Him. So far as we can see, one great petition in that prayer has never been answered: The last wish of the heart of Jesus has never been gratified and, if that heart be living to-day, it must, we think, be bearing the grief of a great disappointment.

DISUNION OF CHRISTENDOM.

At the close of that great prayer recorded in the seventeenth chapter of the Gospel according to St. John, Jesus prayed that His followers might be one in Him as He was one in and with the Father.

He placed all His hope and expectation on this unity of His people. It was to be His witness to the world. He was about to lay down His life that He might by His death reconcile men to God and to one another. The world in His day was a world of disunion and discord. Men were at odds with God and at odds with one another.

The only unity existing at the time was the outward political unity of the Western World in the Roman Empire. Men were at one, only in so far as they were, by physical force, compelled to obey the will of one man.

But this forced accord only made more acute the inward discontent. Within the Roman Empire there was a chronic condition of disorder. Society, besides the ordinary divisions of rich and poor, of great and small, was separated into the two irreconcilable classes of master and slave; with cruelty on the one side and treachery on the other.

Nor did the political organization secure for the world over which it tyranized the poor boon of political union. The Emperor himself was the centre of disorder. He was the object of envy and of fear, and was again and again the victim of conspiracy in his own household.

Nor could men in those days find any centre of union in their religion. Their very gods were at war with one another. There was no common faith in any Divine Being. Religion was largely a matter of national custom and tribal tradition. Every city had its own god; almost every street its own cult. Our Lord and Saviour was of the Jewish race and as a Jew He felt most keenly the evils arising from the disorder of the world. The Jew had for ages lived in lonely and bitter isolation, separated from the nations of the earth by impassable religious barriers, and this separation had been the breeding cause of hatred. "It was unlawful for a man that was a Jew to keep company or come unto one of another nation," and among the Jews themselves there were sects and parties which hated each other even more bittrly than they hated the Gentile.

So both at home and abroad Jesus saw men hateful and hating one another; saw human society in a state of dissolution, as if about to resolve itself into its original elements.

OUR LORD'S PLAN OF UNIFICATION.

To save the world from the awful calamity of relapsing into a hopeless barbarism was one object of the mission of Jesus Christ. He came to give mankind a principle of unity; He came to break down middle walls of partition, to make of Jew and Gentile, of Greek and barbarian, of clean and unclean, of male and female, of bond and free, one united people.

And his method was very simple. If we may say so reverently, He adopted the fundamental principle of the Roman Empire. He set up a kingdom with its absolute King, in obedience to whom men were to find peace, and in communion with whom they were to find a common life.

But the King who was thus made the centre of unity was not some wretched mortal, some man whose kingdom might fail, set up to-day, cast down to-morrow, but it was the infinite and eternal God whose Kingdom is everlasting and of whose government there is no end.

The King of the Kingdom of Heaven differs, however, from the Roman Emperor in the nature of His government. He does not rule outwardly and formally over the actions of men, but inwardly and really over their affections and motives. He is in personal touch with each man and each man is in personal union with Him, and it is this personal relationship with their common King which is the bond of union among the citizens of the Kingdom; they have fellowship with Him, therefore they have fellowship with one another.

Jesus conceived of Himself, as being in such close and personal union with God that He could say of Himself, "I and the Father are one," and "whosoever hath seen Me hath seen the Father." It was this consciousness of His absolute union with God which has given the Lord Jesus His place in human history. Men have seen in Him the revelation of God to themselves; in coming to Him they believe that they are coming to God.

And this was the thought of the Lord himself. He prayed for them, saying, "That they may all be one as Thou, Father, art in Me and I in Thee, that they may be one in Us, that the world may believe that Thou hast sent Me."

This principle of unity in God is the only principle that can unite all sorts and conditions of men, all nations and generations. There can be no class distinctions in this Kingdom, for before God all men are necessarily equal. God is so far above men that He can look upon them with perfect impartiality. He has no court favorites and is no respecter of persons. Then, as He is unchangeable, His government does not change, and each generation, as it is born into the world, finds itself under its beneficent rule.

SUCCESS OF THE PLAN.

Our Lord gave practical effect to this principle of unity by making it the organic principle of a distinct society of men. He called out of the world such as could hear Him, and them He constituted the new people of God.

The first consequence of this preaching of unity was a greater disunion. A few men separated themselves into a distinct company, which company had for its unifying principle the union of each with God and of each with all; they were saints, set apart to God; they were brethren, living with and loving each other.

This society was open to all; any one, no matter of what race or condition, could come into it, provided he would conform to its fundamental principles. This society was the creation of Jesus the Christ; His history was its history, and His life its life. He was the centre of union to His church, as His church was to be the centre of union to the world.

And what Jesus expected did actually come to pass. His experiment at unification is successful beyond all experiments in human history. No other principle has unified so many men for so long a time.

We can say with safety that the Christian Church was the centre of moral unity to the Roman Empire. Within two centuries of its foundation it had gathered to itself and given organic form to what was left of the moral and spiritual life of that decaying people, and saved society from utter dissolution.

And when the Roman Empire fell, we know, as a mere matter of history, that the Church of Jesus the Christ was the only centre of unity left in the Western World; and the church organization the only one strong enough to resist the disintegrating forces that were resolving human society into its tribal elements.

It preserved for future generations all that was vital in the old civilization, and it received into its communion the new life, as in tribe after tribe it came down from the North. It baptized that life and disciplined it, and reduced it to a certain order, and gave to it a common character, so that the Goth and the Frank, the Dane and Saxon, were united in a great common life, which modified, and in a large degree took the place of, the tribal and national life of each people.

The result of this action of the Christian organization, and of the Christian principle upon the world, has been the creation of the highest, the greatest, and, as it now seems to be, the most permanent form of human society which the world has ever seen.

The great fact of present history is the domination of Christendom over the rest of the world. That civilization, in the midst of which we live, is Christian in history and Christian in character; it is over two thousand years old, and it seems to be just entering upon its life. In its early days it suffered the assaults of the pagan world, which put forth its whole power to destroy this new principle of life. But the Christian Church not only survived these assaults, it prevailed over them, and it was the pagan world that died. Six hundred years after its organization the Christian civilization was subjected to an attack by another civilization, based upon a bastard form of its own principle of unity; and for seven centuries it had to fight for its life. In that warfare Christendom lost its original home, and some of its fairest provinces. But it survived the struggle, and has been growing younger with the passing years, while its ancient enemy, Mohammedanism, has grown old and decrepit, and is simply waiting the sentence of Christendom to die a dishonorable death. And we cannot see in the far future any power that can destroy and supplant that which the Christian forces have organized and preserved in the world.

THE FAILURE OF THAT PLAN IN THE CHURCH SINCE THE FOURTH CENTURY.

It may seem strange, considering what has just gone before, that we should speak of the disappointment of the Lord Jesus Christ; as if He were looking down from Heaven upon the failure of His hopes.

Surely He to whom the ages belong, who has given name and form and substance to the last and greatest era of human history, can have no reason to be dissatisfied with that short, earthly life which has been productive of such wonderful and lasting results.

DISUNION OF CHRISTENDOM.

It is not, however, the world, over which, we reverently believe, our Lord is, at this present moment grieving; with the world at large He has every reason to be satisfied; it is the church which has disappointed him.

There is at this moment a Christian world, which has a certain rude, available unity, but within that Christian world the distinctive Christian organization, to which it owes its origin, has gone to pieces.

The church is no longer a centre of unity to the world, because it has no unity in itself. There is no sadder sight now to be seen by God or man or angel than that scene of discord and disunion, which is, almost without shame, presented to the public gaze by the Christian Church. Christians seem to be acting in open scorn of their Lord's last earthly wish. They who profess and call themselves Christians seem to have lost all desire to keep the unity of the faith, in the bond of peace. The followers of our common Lord are separated one from another by almost impassable gulfs of prejudice and hatred. And to-day the Christian religion seems to be the one disintegrating force in the world. Not only have we the great churches and denominations set off, one against the other, in battle array, watching each other with jealous suspicion, but within each church and denomination we have party strife and factional discord. There would seem to be nothing too trivial for Christians to quarrel over. A light too little or a light too much will bring about a crisis in a great national church. Multitudes of men and women tired of the ceaseless bickerings which appear in these days to be a necessary adjunct of all church life are finding peace outside of every Christian communion. The necessary result of our present condition is waste of force, loss of efficiency and decay of moral influence. Neither at home nor abroad can the church fulfill its mission. Men will not believe where the witnesses do not agree together. They will conclude that an institution that does not know its own mind can hardly claim to know the mind of God.

The millions in heathen lands and the still sadder millions in Christian lands are waiting, and have been waiting for centuries, for the church to settle her quarrels, that she may have time and strength to preach to them the blessed Gospel of the Lord and Saviour Jesus Christ. The Lord Himself is waiting for that unity that He may manifest Himself more fully to the world.

Any contribution, therefore, to the cause of Christian unity, even if, like some bitter draught, it for the moment intensifies the disease, should be welcome by all who have the good order of the church at heart.

In what follows some things will be said which will not be pleasant to all hearers. The only excuse for saying them is that they are believed to be true.

CAUSE OF FAILURE.

The present unhappy divisions of Christendom are in a great measure owing to two inadequate, if not false, ideals of Christian unity, which up to this time have had almost entire possession of the Christian world.

The first of these is: That the unity of the church is an outward, formal unity in a visible political corporation; and that the centre of unity is to be found in the official organization of that corporation. That there are certain officials who by right of their office are clothed with plenary power to organize and govern the church.

This theory is that the church centres in its own official organization. As Louis XIV said of himself: "I am the state," meaning that the state centred in him, deriving from him all its political rights and even its political life; so the official organization of the church has said of itself, "I am the church," meaning that the church centres in it, and derives from it all truth and life.

This theory holds that the authority of the organization, though derivative, is absolute, vested forever in the persons who hold office in the organization. The doctrine is that God gave all power in heaven and earth to His Son Jesus the Christ, that Jesus, in turn, delegated his power to St. Peter, that St. Peter went to Rome and centred the church in that city and in himself as the bishop of that city. And St. Peter, according to this theory, is not so much the head of the church as he is the church; the church derives its life from him, and out of him has no existence. Then St. Peter in turn handed on his power to his successor, and so it has come down from the first Bishop of Rome to the last, and whosoever happens for the time being to occupy that office is, *ex-officio*, clothed with Divine wisdom and Divine power. His will is law and his word infallible.

This theory is the one upon which the Roman Church is based and which found its last expression in the decrees of the Vatican Council.

But it would be a mistake to suppose that this theory is not to be found outside the pale of Rome. It is to be feared that this is the theory of many an Anglican prelate and many a Protestant minister.

Indeed, the extreme High Church theory is only a modification of the Roman theory. In this theory the ministry is the church, so much so that when a man goes into the ministry he is said to go into the church. The Lord Jesus, according to this doctrine, delegated His power not to one man, St. Peter, but to twelve men, of whom St. Peter was only one; that these twelve men handed their power on to their immediate successors and so on down to our day. And many a man has lurking in his heart the thought that when, by the accidents of an Episcopal election, he is chosen to a bishopric, he is clothed in his own person with awful and mysterious powers, that his personal will is law and his personal word infallible.

Nor is the Protestant world free from this conception of the Christian ministry. When a man stands in a pulpit, looking down on a quiescent congregation, he can hardly help thinking that he is greater than they—that he is to them instead of God.

This theory that the church centres in its official organization is the natural theory of officialism the world over.

Both in church and state office-holders magnify their office, and are apt to think of themselves (to use a pregnant current phrase) as the "whole thing." The few officials are so important, in their own eyes, and in the eyes of the world the unofficial multitude is so unimportant, that the office-holder naturally thinks that the people exist for him, rather than he for the people. This theory of official life did not begin with the Christian ministry in its Papal or any other form. It is as old as human society. The divine right of kings is a doctrine dear to every absolute monarch, and all that the Papal theory has done is to carry that doctrine to its highest point, and to give the spiritual monarch and his assistants absolute power over the inward as well as the outward life of man.

We can safely say of this theory that it is a false and inadequate theory, because it has utterly failed in practice, both in church and state. In the long run such a system does not preserve unity, it destroys it. A despotism either in church or state is always a destructive and not a creative force. Such a form of government is excusable only in times of violent disorder and possible only in low stages of human development.

The history of man's progress is the history of his painful deliverance from under the hand of his rulers, and the last outcome of his age-long struggle has been to make his rulers his servants instead of his masters.

In barbarous times, when men are for the most part thieves and murderers, a strong central government is necessary to preserve order. Such times are the opportunity of despotism, which, having once taken hold, keeps hold. And when better times come and the mass of men are honest and peaceable, they find that their government is an incubus, which, if they would live and thrive, they must throw off. So a despotism is the breeder of revolution, and in revolution society is disordered, if not destroyed.

So, we see, that a personal official despotism, in one man or a few men, is not conducive to, but destructive of, unity. And this its logical is also its historical consequence. The history of the theory of Christian unity which we are now considering is the history of the disruption of Christendom. The schism between the East and the West was occasioned by a quarrel among the officials of the church for precedence. And to this day the only real question between the East and the West is which shall be greater, the official head of the Latin, or the official head of the Orthodox communion. The Pope excommunicated the Metropolitan of Constantinople and the Metropolitan of Constantinople excommunicated the Pope upon a matter in which the Christian people at large were not at all concerned, and for a thousand years the people of the East and the West have been isolated from each other, to the great loss of both.

And the great disruption of the sixteenth century, which shattered the outward organization of the church in Europe, was a religious revolution, rendered absolutely necessary by the intolerable abuses and corruptions of the official organization of the church.

There is no better way to describe the official organization of the church at the time of the Reformation than by giving it a name familiar to every American politician. It was a machine. Now a machine is a political organization which gets control of a great party and uses that party for its own purposes. And the purpose of the machine is not the advancement of any political principle; the sole purpose of the machine is plunder. And there existed in Rome, at the time of the Reformation, a machine, beside which Tammany is a very harmless thing.

The official organization of the church was bent solely upon its own earthly aggrandizement and enrichment. The dream of the older and greater Popes of ruling the world for the world's good had passed away; and the Popes of the sixteenth century were content to tax the world for the Pope's good.

It is impossible here to enter into details. It is the thrice-threshed straw of history. It can only be said that it was absolutely necessary for the Christian world to break that machine, if Christianity was to live in the world, and to do this great violence was required, and this violence destroyed not only the machine, but also for the time being the outward unity of Western Christendom. But the loss of unity was a small price to pay for that great deliverance.

In that great upheaval the theory that the church's life centres in the official organization of the church received its death blow. Like all great ideas that have once possessed the human mind it dies slowly, but it is dying; it is no longer in Papal, Episcopal or Presbyterial form a living, workable theory. The theory which is gaining ground every day is the theory expressed in the prayer of the Lord Jesus Christ, which is that the unity of the Christian people centres in the Christian's God and Lord, and that on earth the power of the Christian Church centres in the Christian people.

But I hear some one cry all this is mere moonshine. Such a unity is no unity at all. It is without power to control the disorderly elements of the world.

But take care! this theory of unification has been in the world for four hundred years, and it has accomplished more for the advancement of real Christianity than the other theory did in all the thousand years of its existence. It has banished the stake and the gibbet from the church. It has declared the equality of all men before the law of God and secured their equality before the law of man. It has driven official cruelty from the world. It stands to-day an awful power; the power of Christian public opinion; behind every Pope and every bishop and every priest, holding him to a strict account for his acts.

It may be asked: Is this unofficial power to utterly destroy the old official life of the church? Certainly not. It will not destroy, but it will control. And it is our part to hope and work and pray, not for a revolution, but an evolution. "The greatest disaster that can happen to any life or institution is an utter break with its past." Let the church give back to every bishop his pastoral staff and send him forth to seek the lost sheep of Christ; let her touch the lips of every priest or elder with a coal from off the altar, that he may speak burning words of love and warning to the people; let her reconstitute her diaconate and send it forth upon its errands of mercy. And for my part, I pray that the church may yet save the Papacy; that the Pope, at her bidding, may yet come forth, from his voluntary prison in the Vatican, and be once more a shepherd, in the midst of his sheep; and as Queen Victoria sat with dignity, as constitutional Queen over a great constitutional empire, so in time may the venerable Bishop of Rome come to sit as a constitutional primate over a great constitutional church.

But let him know, and let every bishop and priest and deacon and minister and synod and general convention know, that the theory that the unity of the church centres in him or in them has perished.

The unity of the church centres in God and in the people of God. And whatever form the outward organization of the church may take in the future it will be a form in which the Spirit of God can work and the voice of the people be heard.

For the present mere officialism is dead. What the people are seeking is not St. Peter's successor, but St. Peter. If they do not find him in St. Peter's chair they will look for him in the darkest street of Rome. And the great need of the church is not an apostolic succession, but a succession of apostles. If it does not find these in settled apostolic sees it will seek for them in the wilderness.

DOCTRINAL UNITY.

The second theory of Christian unity, which up to the present day has been of universal acceptance, is that the unity of the church centres in her doctrine; that her members are made one by their agreement in certain intellectual statements concerning the facts and principles of their religion.

This theory asserts that it is the great duty of the church to set in order propositions concerning the absolute nature of God; His attributes and final purposes; His relations to creation and His relations to man. It is also the duty of the church to define with scientific accuracy the inner nature of Christ, the cause and effect of His death, and the content of His teaching.

She has also the duty of defining the nature of man; of setting forth his relations to God and to the world, and of describing his past history and declaring his future destiny.

These various departments of the church's doctrine are arranged with all the formality of an exact science under various heads, such as Theology, Christology, Anthropology and Eschatology. And

DISUNION OF CHRISTENDOM. 283

when the church has formulated a statement of doctrine, it becomes, as the theologians say, *de fide,* and its acceptance the highest duty of every Christian. To question, much more to deny, any formula set forth by proper authority is the greatest crime a Christian can commit. Even if a man were but to whisper such doubt or denial in his heart, he is *ipso facto* excommunicated in this world and damned in the next.

And for ages there has been no greater act of daring possible to man than to question or deny received doctrine. He braved the fate and he met the fate of one whose life is supposed to be dangerous to the good order and peace of the community. He was hunted from house and home, and if taken suffered a violent and shameful death.

This theory of the church's unity in a common doctrine was not in conflict, but worked together with the other theory that the unity of the church centred in her official organization.

It has, since the fourth century, been considered the chief duty of the official organization of the Christian Church to formulate and enforce doctrine. Indeed, so long has this theory held possession of the Christian mind that to doubt or deny it is, in the popular judgment, to doubt or deny the existence of the church itself. Christian history seems to prove that it is a chief function of the church to philosophize upon the faith, and the chief duty of the individual Christian to accept the conclusions of such philosophy.

From the councils of the fourth century down to the synods of the seventeenth, and the councils of the nineteenth, the whole Christian world has spent its main strength in an effort to secure intellectual agreement concerning the most abstruse and difficult subjects that the human mind can entertain.

Before the fourth century the main purpose of the church was to discipline life; to make men pure and just and kind. Since the fourth century the main purpose of the church has been to discipline intellect, to reduce the intellectual conceptions of humanity to a common form, so that they can be accepted ready-made, and thus lead all men to say the same words and think the same thoughts. Indeed, it was the church's task and purpose to render thinking unnecessary to the great mass of men. It was, and in the minds of many to-day it is, the duty of the official organization to think for the rest of the people.

Now, great as is this task of intellectual discipline, it is an infinitely easier one than the task of moral discipline that preceded it.

CHRISTENDOM.

When the church made her peace with the world in the days of the Emperor Constantine, when she became the established church and the popular religion, she suffered the consequences of her establishment and popularity. Membership in the church was an easy way to favor with the court and popularity in the world, and millions sought the communion of the church and many the dignity of the episcopate for what there was in it, by way of honor and ease, for themselves.

The consequence of this influx from the world was a relaxation of the church's moral discipline. She found it impossible to regulate the morality of this mixed multitude, as she had regulated the moral life of the select few, who were hers, in the days of her exclusion and seclusion.

The moral discipline of the church was, in a large measure, destroyed by the worldliness consequent upon her popularity, but more by the diversion of the mind of the church from the moral to the intellectual sphere. She had a great discipline after the fourth century, but it was the discipline of the mind, rather than of the soul and the spirit.

And this last is, as we have said, a much easier task than the first. Few men care to think; all men love to sin.

To secure intellectual conformity it is only necessary to silence, discourage or kill the few thinkers. But to secure moral uniformity on the high plane of Christian morality requires a radical change in every human heart.

It is not a matter of wonder that when the church lost her moral zeal in consequence of her worldly prosperity, she sought to make up for it by an increased intellectual zeal. And until this day the zeal of the church for her own corporate greatness and for her own intellectual formula has been as great, if not greater, than her zeal for the moral purity and the spiritual advancement of her people.

And when the church entered upon this task of regulating by formula the thoughts of men, she continued in it until her formula covered every region of human thought.

There was, as some think, a gradual development of Christian doctrine, or, as others think, an encroachment of Christian dogma, until everything about which a man could think was a closed question; settled by the decisions of the Christian official organization.

This organization was terribly successful in its enforcement of intellectual uniformity. For ages it held the mind of man in thrall.

For ten centuries the Western Christian mind did nothing but mark time. It was in motion but like Gehazi, the servant of Elisha, "it went no whither." It was active, but its activity was without result, because it was forbidden to inquire into fundamental principles, to look facts in the face or to question the validity of received opinion.

It could only discuss its own discussions and define more nicely its own definitions.

The modern world differs from the Byzantine and mediæval, because in it two great regions of human thought have been delivered from under the hand of the Christian official organization, and a third is in process of deliverance. In that historical movement known as the Renaissance, art and letters escaped from under the control of the official organization of the church. The heads of that organization gave freedom to artists and to men of letters. By their permission and encouragement men were permitted to paint the human form as it is, rather than the old Byzantine symbol of that form; and they were at liberty to apply to the remains of ancient learning the principles of scientific literary criticism, and so to acquire an accurate knowledge of the thoughts and life of the ancient world.

This freedom of art and letters was won easily, because this freedom did not interfere with the domination of the official organization of the church, and more because Popes and cardinals dearly loved a good picture and a good story; and were wise enough to see that only by leaving each man free to follow his own fancy could a good picture be painted or good stories be written.

The next great region of human thought did not win its freedom without a struggle. When men began to use their own eyes and ears; to look at the sights of the outward world and listen carefully to its sounds, they began to see that the facts were in conflict with received theories. So these men began to put forth new theories more in accordance with the facts. They began to speak of the earth's motion, to say of it that it was only one in an infinite number of worlds; to speak of the world's great age, to number its years by the million instead of by the thousand. These statements as they came forth, one by one, created the greatest consternation. They were supposed to be not only in conflict with, but utterly destructive of, Christian truth and Christian life.

The official organization of the church put forth its whole power to crush these new opinions. And we know the result. Again, it is not necessary to go into details. The official organization was beaten at every point. Scientific thought has won for itself absolute freedom. No one to-day dreams of looking to the official organization of the church to settle any question of astronomy or geology, of biology or chronology; such questions are settled in these days by scientific men and by scientific processes.

The only thing we have to fear for science is that it will, by the great power which its freedom has given it, create a new tyranny. But however he may use his power, to-day the man of science is free. The whole visible world of nature and the inward world of man is open to free investigation and speculation.

The only region of human thought which is now, in any respect, dominated by the official organization of the church, is that which has to do with man's relations to God and the world to come.

This region the official organization claims as its own and warns from it every intruder. It claims the right to define with the utmost precision just what each man shall think, and it asserts for its decisions infinite consequence; except a man believe them he shall perish everlastingly.

Scientific theology is supposed to be separated from all other sciences. It is admitted that they are progressive, but asserted that theology is not progressive. The official organization of the church has at various times undertaken to do the thinking, not only for its own age, but for all ages to come.

The theory is that God, at a certain time, made a final revelation to man, and that the official organization of the church, at another time, officially interpreted that revelation; and that ever afterward the only thing the human mind has had to do is to think what had been thought and to say what had been said.

There is, of course, a certain truth in this theory. There is in the intellectual, as in the moral world, such a thing as settled questions —without this no progress is possible. But the integrity of the human mind requires that every intellectual question shall be settled by intellectual processes, not by knocking the other side down with a club, or voting him out by a majority, but by convincing his reason. The law of the intellect also requires that even every settled question shall always be an open question.

There is no received opinion that is not by this law required to come, at any moment, into the court of human inquiry and show the proof of its right to exist.

The official organization of the church has attempted again and again to act in conflict with this law of the human reason. It has made its statements of truth and denied the right of man, under the pains and penalties of eternal damnation, to ever question these statements.

Two consequences follow. A certain number of men question and the official organization condemns them and casts them out; the vast unthinking mass do not question, and to them the statements are as dead letters—they are received, but they are not assimilated.

The attempt of the official organization of the church to make its statements final is, historically considered, a failure. It has again and again put forth statements of doctrine which it claimed were the final utterances of the Holy Spirit, from which nothing was ever to be taken away, and to which nothing was ever to be added; but before the ink was dry with which the writing of these statements was made, some new question, deeply affecting the whole problem, rose up and would not down until a new settlement was made.

The effort of the official organization has been to cover the whole ground of possible theological opinion by statements *de fide*. In consequence we see the creed in a constant state of elaboration and enlargement. When we compare the simple statements of the Lord Jesus and even of St. Paul with the statements of the councils of the fourth century, and these with the confessions and articles of religion of the Reformation period, we can see how steady has been the encroachment of official authority upon the region of free opinion.

The Reformation, in its ecclesiastical aspect and in its intellectual life, was really a reversion. The Reformers broke the Papal machine, only to put a machine of their own in its room. They established an intellectual tyranny even more galling than that of the Pope. One might with dignity submit his intelligence to a great and venerable church, but not to a conventicle of fanatics or to a self-appointed dogmatist. To-day the official organization of Presbyterianism, and Lutheranism, and of Methodism, and of the Baptists, is as inimical to intellectual and spiritual freedom as the Roman organization.

The only official organization that seems to-day at all friendly to freedom is the organization of the Anglican Church, and, perhaps, the only reason for this is that the Anglican machine is out of order and won't work.

And for this reason also that machine is at the present moment the safest. For, if machines are dangerous, the less you use them the safer it is.

It is both the strength and weakness of the Anglican Communion that the various forces of her organization are so balanced that no one can control the others.

REUNION OF THE CHURCH IN GOD AND IN HUMANITY.

We may conclude by saying that the effort to centre the unity of the church in her own intellectual statements has failed even more signally than the effort to centre her unity in her own official organization. And the hope of so centering the unity of the church has gone forever.

The mind of man has emancipated itself and it will never be re-enslaved.

You can to-day, by petty persecution, drive the thinking man from one Christian communion to another, you may drive him out of all Christian communion, but you cannot drive him from thinking.

And in this fact I see the hope of the church and the hope of humanity. God has a word to say to us, as He has had a word to say to our forefathers. And who can tell to whom that word will come?

In all the history of the world it has never come to an official organization. Truth is never discovered in committee. The word of God comes to the prophet in the wilderness, truth is the reward of the lonely watcher. Let us not stone the speaker of the word, lest we be stoning the messenger of God; let us not kill the watcher, lest, with him, we kill the truth of God.

It is my belief that the twentieth century will see a great unification of Christendom, a merging of all present forms into a higher form. The movement will come from below, not from above.

Official organizations may be standing still, but the people are moving. Already there is a great unity in which all Christians are one. It is a union in God. To-day men pass easily from church to church, and from denomination to denomination, and so are learning that the various Christian bodies are but the keepers of a common Christianity. And as the citizen of the smallest state in the

Union of the United States has his right to the larger citizenship in the great Republic, so the member of the most obscure sect, if he be really united to God, has his right to membership in that larger communion of which God is the unifying centre.

No one to-day would dare to question the essential godliness, Christianity and final salvation of Vincent De Paul or John Wesley, of John Henry Newman, or John Keble, of Savonarola, or St. Charles Borromeo, or St. Francis Xavier, or Michael Faraday, of William Wordsworth or Ralph Waldo Emerson.

These men, though separated from each other by difference of opinion and difference of outward Christian communion, or non-communion, were united in a grander union of life. They all loved the truth; and they all lived the truth. And he who loves the truth loves God.

Dear Dr. Pusey used to say that he hoped to die in the communion of the Catholic Church before its division into the East and the West. I have even a larger hope than this; by God's grace I hope to die in the communion of the Church of God; that congregation of God's people which began to be in the days of Enos, the son of Seth, "when men began to call on the name of the Lord," and will not have its consummation until all mankind are gathered into the presence of the Lord.

It cannot be that the love of the Father will forever disappoint the expectation of the Son. Unless all signs fail, a belief in Jesus Christ as the spiritual head and centre of the human race is the goal of human thought, and a union, through Him, with God, the end of human life.

CHURCH UNION MOVEMENTS.

Bishop John Fletcher Hurst, D.D., LL.D.,
WASHINGTON.

[Disputes and quarrels, dissensions and jars,
And the sound of fighting, and civil wars;
And, ere the morning, brother and brother,
Instead of the enemy, fought with each other.

* * * * *

Over the hill, the foe, in glee,
Listened and laughed. "Ho, ho!" quoth he.
"There is strife in the enemy's ranks, I see,
And the bright red beams of the rising sun
Will see a victory easily won.
It matters little how strong the foe,
This is a truth we all do know:
There is no success without unity,
However noble the cause may be.
The day is ours before it's begun.
Ho! for the triumph so easily won."

And on the morrow, the ranks of the Right
Were routed and beaten, and put to flight,
And the Wrong was the victor, and gained the fight.
—Unidentified.—Ed.]

* * *

DIVISION OF GREEK AND LATIN CHURCHES.

The iconoclastic dispute, which, beginning under Leo III, the Isaurian, in 727, lasted for about one hundred and fifty years, is enough to prove how widely apart the East and West were drifting, and how grave and irreconcilable were the points of discord. They had, indeed, been growing apart for centuries. The very type of mind in the East was contemplative, metaphysical, hair-splitting; the West was practical, legal, progressive. This difference of temperament was not in itself a sufficient cause of the separation, but, intensified by time, it was ample to overcome the natural bonds of sympathy, and thus prevent each from seeing the other's point of view.

The first element of difference was doctrinal. Originally, this chiefly centered around the doctrine of the Holy Spirit's procession from the Father—the *Filioque* controversy. The Nicene Creed ran simply, "I believe in the Holy Ghost." At the second general council, that at Constantinople (381), this clause was added, "Who proceedeth from the Father." The third general council, at Ephesus (431), ordered that it should not be lawful to make any additions to the creed. Some of the Western fathers, however, taught that the Spirit proceeds from the Son as well as from the Father. The *Filioque* clause had been, in fact, introduced into the creed in Spain and France, and recited in the churches. The Popes did not at first favor this. Pope Leo III (795-816) censured this departure from the original form, and, in order to emphasize the importance of the exact words of the true creed, caused the creed of Constantinople to be engraved on silver plates in Greek and Latin, and thus to be publicly displayed in the church. Pope Nicholas I (858-867), however, with the true infallible instinct, authorized the addition. For this the West was condemned in 879, at Constantinople, at what the Greeks call the eighth general council. This disregard of the ancient formularies of the church, which were to them as dear as life, mortally offended the Greeks, and they could hold no communion with a church which had thus added to the faith.

The extraordinary pretensions of Rome were reached in a letter by Pope Nicholas I to the Emperor Michael the Sot in the Photian controversy. The Pope dwelt with unbounded confidence upon the privileges of the Holy See, their eternal and unchangeable character, their divine origin, and their absolute independence of all human or even ecclesiastical ordinance. "The Roman Church," he wrote, "encompasses and comprehends within herself all the nations of mankind, she being in herself the universal church, the mirror and model of that which she embraceth with her bosom. To Peter, and to Peter alone, was committed the command to kill and eat, as in like manner he alone, of all the Apostles, received the Divine command to draw to the shore the net full of fishes. Unto us has been committed that identical commission to embrace in our paternal arms the whole flock of Christ." Nicholas was the first Pope to promulgate or formally recognize the forged decretals, and these gave to claims which had before been vaguely and tentatively held the authority of unbroken tradition. These novel and extravagant pretensions formed a deep gulf between the East and the West.

We pass over the intervening disputes and come to the final break in 1054. The high-handed bigot, the Patriarch of Constantinople,

Michael Cerularius, closed all the churches in the city where the Latin rites were used. In conjunction with Leo of Achrida, the metropolitan of the Bulgarians, he addressed an epistle to John, Bishop of Trani, in Apulia, which was also to be sent to the Western clergy and to the Pope himself. In this epistle, Luther-like, he drew up a formal accusation of heresy against the Latin Church. He charged the Latins with the use of unleavened bread in the Lord's Supper—azyma—the use of blood and things strangled, and fasting on the Sabbath (Saturday) in Lent, and called on the Western bishops to separate from the see of Rome. After various attempts at reconciliation the papal legates formally laid on the altar of the Church of St. Sophia a sentence of excommunication against the Eastern Church (1054), which Michael Cerularius and the other patriarchs solemnly returned.

FIRST ATTEMPTS AT REUNION.

Nevertheless, many attempts were made toward reunion, and some almost bore fruit. Latin theologians were allowed to argue their case before the Court of Constantinople. Political exigencies led the Emperor Michael Paleologus to offer terms of surrender to the Pope. At the Council of Lyons (1274), the Eastern delegates repeated the creed with the addition of the *Filioque,* and swore to conform to the faith of the Roman Church, and to recognize the supremacy of the Pope. They were allowed to use the creed without the addition, and to practice their peculiar ecclesiastical customs. The Greeks were thoroughly enraged at these measures, and to bring them to terms the emperor resorted to the usual punishments of these times—punishments which the iconoclastic and Photian disturbances made familiar, such as scourging, mutilation, blinding and imprisonment. But with the next emperor the Lyons union was thrown to the winds.

At the Council of Florence (1438) the last effort was made. The emperor, John VII, Paleologus, went personally with the cultured and able archbishop, Bessarion of Nicæa, and many bishops, to this council, called the eighteenth ecumenical by the Latins. Here everything was at last arranged satisfactorily. The Pope was acknowledged as the "successor of Peter, the chief of the apostles, and the vicar of Christ, the head of the whole church, and father and teacher of all Christians, to whom plenary power was given by our Lord Jesus Christ to feed, rule and govern the universal church in such a way as is set forth in the ecumenical councils and sacred canons," which the Greeks interpreted mainly as referring to the canons of Nicæa and Chalcedon, but which the Latins interpreted mainly as referring to the pseudo-Isidorian decretals. In most of the Greek texts of the Florentine articles the parts defining the primacy of the Pope are either wanting or essentially modified. It was admitted that the doctrine of the procession of the Holy Spirit, as defined by the Greek Church, from the Father through the Son, was really the same as the Latin formula, from the Father and the Son, but the Western doctrine was maintained in the explanation: "The Holy Spirit proceeds from the Father and at the same time from the Son, and from both eternally as from one principle and one spiration."

After long disputes the Greeks surrendered also on the doctrines of purgatory and the seven sacraments. On his part the Pope, Eugenius IV, promised that ships and men should be provided for the defense of Constantinople against the Turks, and that he would induce the rulers of the West to come to the rescue of the Greeks. The Pope, the emperor and the bishops subscribed to the edict amid wild rejoicings and shoutings, July 6, 1438. But once more it was all in vain. The promised supports from the West did not come. The people were bitter against their emperor and the bishops and clergy who favored the union. The churches where these ministered were deserted. On May 29, 1453, Constantinople fell before Mohammed II, and the last emperor, Constantine IX, went down in a brave fight against great odds. Mohammed confirmed the constitution of the churches, giving the primacy over the whole Eastern Christendom to the Patriarch of Constantinople. Many of the Greeks went into Italy, Hungary, Poland and other countries, and united with the Roman Catholic Church, or, under the name of the United Greeks, formed churches of their own, being allowed to keep their old liturgy and customs by accepting the Roman doctrine and the Papal primacy.

IRENIC MOVEMENTS SINCE THE REFORMATION.*

The Reformation had, in 1530, grown to such proportions that both the Emperor Charles V and Pope Clement VII felt it neces-

*Much of what follows is taken from an article on the same subject in the volume entitled "Church Unity," published by Charles Scribner's Sons, 1896, and consisting of five lectures delivered at the Union Theological Seminary, New York.

sary to proceed in a spirit of conciliation. The emperor now began his efforts for a reunion of the divided church. After all the reforms introduced by the Lutherans, they still claimed to belong to the Roman Catholic Church. The hopes of the emperor did not therefore seem unfounded. The Protestants succeeded in having the ecclesiastical differences considered first, and their efforts were directed toward a justification of their previous conduct. This harmonized, in spirit at least, with the purpose of the emperor to do away with the ecclesiastical schism and to unite the parties in a harmonious comprehension of Christian truth.

The pugnacious disposition of Eck, who laid before the emperor a bitter attack upon the Protestants of all schools, was at this point the only visible hindrance. The emperor himself made the Apostles' Creed the test as to correctness of doctrines.

Melanchthon strove earnestly to meet the emperor's conciliatory tone by carefully expurgating, from the confession which he prepared, all unnecessarily harsh expressions, by yielding all that he possibly could, and by omitting all mention of some of the principal articles of the Protestant faith; but in vain. He continued his efforts so long and with so many concessions that the Romanists had good hope of winning him back to their cause. All efforts at reunion failed, since, however much the reformers yielded, the Roman Catholic theologians still demanded more. Besides, the Pope's legate called the attention of Charles to the omission of several points of Protestant belief. This the Protestants would not deny. At length the emperor himself laid a confession before the diet, in which he declared the Protestants to be refuted, and which he required them to accept. This aroused the ire and spirit of independence of the Protestant princes, and proved how foolish had been the attempt of the Protestant theologians to satisfy the Roman Catholic demands.

THE FORMULA OF CONCORD BETWEEN CONTENDING GERMAN PROTESTANTS.

The attempt to make it appear that Luther and Melanchthon agreed in their doctrine was not pleasing to the strict Lutherans. Nevertheless, enough had been done to prepare the way for the more complete victory which was secured by means of the Formula of Concord. This was early encouraged by Duke Christopher of Würtemberg. He was at first aided by Duke Julius of Braunschweig and Landgrave William, the eldest son of Philip of Hesse. The theologian to whom, more than any other, the final adoption of the Formula of Concord is due, was Jacob Andreæ. The first efforts resulted in failure. In 1574, however, Andreæ prepared what is known as the Tübingen Book, or the Swabian Concordia. The views of the lower Saxon theologians were afterward incorporated with it, under the name of the Swabian-Saxon Concordia. This was now abbreviated and adopted, under the name of the Maulbronn Formula, by the theologians of Würtemberg and Baden, in council at Maulbronn, January, 1576. This work, which had been undertaken at the instigation of Elector Augustus, was sent to him, together with the Swabian-Saxon Concordia. He called a convention of theologians at Lichtenberg in February, 1576, and found them ready to make any reasonable concessions for the sake of peace.

A convention of theologians from the electorates of Saxony and Brandenburg, including Chemnitz, Selnecker, Chrytræus, Musculus, and Christopher Körner, met in Torgau, and, with the Swabian-Saxon Concordia as a basis, produced the Torgau Book in May and June, 1576. The Concordia had mentioned Melanchthon with honor, but in the Torgau Book this mention was omitted, while the whole work was more strictly Lutheran. Few, however, were satisfied. To some it appeared too severe against Melanchthon; to others the distinction between Lutheranism and Philipism was objectionable. Some wanted Melanchthon to be expressly condemned; others thought both the Melanchthonians and Flacians ought to be included in the condemnation. At the Convent of Bergen, near Magdeburg, the Torgau Book was revised into the Bergen Book, more in accord with criticism which had been made. This was in March to May, 1577. Andreæ had made an epitome of the Torgau Book, which the same theologians now revised and approved. In the Bergen Book the traces of Philipism almost totally disappeared. It was hastily signed by many. Objections which had been made known after the signatures of such large numbers had been attached could only be noticed in a preface, which was prepared at the convention in Smalcald, in 1578, and Jüterbock in January and June, 1579. In February, 1580, the final Formula of Concord was adopted at the Convent of Bergen, and on June 25, 1580, the fiftieth anniversary of the Augsburg Confession, it was solemnly published at Dresden by Elector Augustus. It had been signed by fifty-one princes and lords, thirty-five cities, and about nine thousand theologians.

There were, however, many who for various reasons declined to subscribe, including Schleswig-Holstein, Hesse, Pomerania, Anhalt, and Silesia, together with the cities of Frankfort-on-the-Main, Spires, Worms, Magdeburg, Nuremberg, Nordhausen, and Strasburg. Duke Julius of Braunschweig became offended and refused to sign because he had been censured for allowing his three sons to receive emoluments at the hands of the Roman Catholic Church. The King of Denmark refused to allow its publication in his realm, and with his own hand threw two richly bound copies, sent him by his sister, the Electress of Saxony, into the chimney fire.

The Formula of Concord became an apple of discord. Its adoption and promulgation, though enacted with good intentions, was a high-handed act. It violently interdicted free thought, and gave the Lutheran Church for a long time to come a direction as truly dogmatic and uncharitable as the Roman Church, from which it had sprung. But the worst feature of all was the confirmation of the division between Calvinism and Lutheranism. The predestinarianism of the Formula of Concord and of Calvinism were but slightly different, but the divergence was found in the doctrine of the Lord's Supper, and in the practical features of church life. Yet the Lutherans openly professed themselves more favorable to Romanism than to Calvinism.

EFFORTS FOR THE UNION OF THE REFORMED AND LUTHERANS.

The Reformed Church was ever willing to effect a union with the Lutherans, and although the latter were generally bitter in their opposition to such a union, there were enough of a contrary mind to mark a distinct phase in the church life of the period.

In the same way it was, that from the Palatinate in which the Reformed tendency prevailed, came efforts at union. Francis Junius favored the cessation of strife about points which had been sufficiently discussed, particularly because of the dangers to which the Protestants were exposed (1592 and 1606). Still later (1614) David Pareus, professor in Heidelberg, declared that nothing should be held obligatory which did not necessarily proceed from the Bible, and that in fundamentals the two communions agreed. In 1628, under the pseudonym of Rupertus, Mildenius called attention to the losses which Protestantism was sustaining on account of theological strifes. This writer was probably the first to employ the expression: "In essentials, unity; in non-essentials, liberty; in both, charity." But it was of no avail. The Lutherans refused these offers of peace.

The colloquy at Leipzig, in 1631, in which Saxon, Brandenburg, and Hessian theologians discussed the question as to how far the two communions agreed, accomplished nothing. And the efforts of the Scotchman, John Durie (Duræus), who strove to the end of his life for union, were also fruitless, except that he aroused the co-operation of George Calixtus, professor at the University of Helmstädt, 1614-1656.

Durie first meets us at Elbing, Prussia, where he was pastor of an English factory. There he became acquainted with Godeman, a privy counsellor of Gustavus Adolphus. Godeman suggested to Durie that whoever should bring about a reconciliation between the great parties into which Christendom was divided would be the greatest peacemaker. This remark was the turning point of his life. In 1628 he addressed a letter to the Swedish king, "for the obtaining of aid and assistance in this seasonable time, to seek for and re-establish an ecclesiastical peace among the evangelical churches." The king gave his sanction, and gave him letters recommending him to all Protestant princes. Henceforth he devoted his life to this work. He went to and fro between England and the Continent, attending assemblies, receiving opinions, exhorting to union, trying to bring about reconciliation of differences, and looking for a common platform on which all could stand. Some English bishops—even Laud, then Bishop of London—looked with great favor on his work. Bishops Davenant, Morton, and Hall gave him their views on Christian union, which were published in 1634. Bishop Davenant's statement is one of the most valuable contributions to Christian union ever published. It contains this noble sentence: "True and genuine charity is no less necessary to salvation for all churches and members of Christian churches than the true and entire profession of sound and saving faith." Many of the most eminent divines in England gave a hearty God-speed to Durie. It is interesting to notice so early as this a sincere longing for Christian union on the part of many of the leading spirits both in the English Church and on the Continent. A meeting of the Protestant states at Frankfort, in 1634, passed a resolution indorsing Durie: "They did judge his work most laudable, most acceptable to God, and most necessary and useful to the church." In 1640 he presented a petition to the House of Commons, urging "that the blessed and long-sought-for union of Protestant churches might be recommended unto the publick prayers of the church, and that his majesty, with your honours advice and counsell, might be moved to call a general Synod of Protestants in due time for the better settling of weighty matters in the church, which now trouble not only the conscience of most men, but disturb the tranquility of publick states, and divide the churches from one another, to the great hindrance of Christianity and the dishonour of religion." And so he labored on through his long and restless life, having only one object—the pacification of the churches, and their restoration to ancient unity. He was charged by William Prynne with being "the time-serving Proteus and ambidexter divine"; but defended himself as "the unchanged, constant and single-hearted peacemaker." His principles were:

"1. A full body of practical divinity, which instead of the ordinary philosophical jangling school divinity, might be proposed to all those that seeke the truth, which is after godlinesse.

"2. To abolish the names of parties, as presbyterial, prelatical, congregational, etc., and to be called Reformed Christians of England, Scotland, France, Germany, etc.

"3. To discountenance controversial writings by private persons.

"4. It is the mind of Christ that His servants, in all matters merely circumstantiall by Him not determined, should be left free to follow their own light, as it may be offered, or arise unto them, from the general rules of edification, and not constrained by an implicit faith to follow the dictates of other men."

This great apostle of Christian union died in 1680, without seeing the fruits of his labors. The times were too turbulent and the age was not ripe for his pacific ideas. Many of the best spirits of his time gave him encouragement, and his numerous books and his tireless labors form one of the noblest legacies which church history has bequeathed us from the seventeenth century. His studies in church history had widened his intellectual horizon until he was ready to include Romanists, Reformed and Lutherans in one great Christian community. But his irenic spirit suggested a syncretism which the dogmatism of the period would not tolerate. He was no more successful in bringing about a union than others had been.

CHURCH UNION MOVEMENTS.

The great apostle of Christian union was George Calixtus. At the University of Helmstädt, where he was professor, 1614-1656, he became imbued with the Melanchthonian theology, and by his wide travels in England, Holland, Italy, and France, he formed a larger acquaintance with other churches than was common with either the Lutherans or Reformed of his day. This brought him to a breadth of view far in advance of his time. He was an earnest Lutheran, always maintaining that the Lutheran Church was the purest of all. But he saw the transcendent importance of those great doctrines on which all Protestants were agreed, and he laid down as a basis of Christian union the New Testament, as interpreted by the church of the first five centuries. He contended that the points on which the churches differed were unimportant by the side of the fundamental points of Christian theology, which they had inherited in common from the purest ages of the faith. The churches should work together in peace and harmony, paving the way for a possible union. Calixtus did not at first advocate a formal union. A conference for Christian union was appointed at Thorn in 1645, but nothing came of it except as a wise and pacific example. The strict Lutherans opposed him with intense bitterness. He was called by some a Crypto-Calvinist, by others a secret Papist. It is pathetic to read how the well-meant efforts of the Helmstädt peacemaker were frustrated and denounced by the vehement controversialists of that age. Walch called him (Calixtus) Cal(vino m)ixtus, and identified him with the number of the beast in the Apocalypse. It was a militant age, and the peacemaker's rôle was not popular.

Hugo Grotius, a contemporary of Calixtus, was also enamored of the idea of a united Christendom. He differed from Calixtus in this: that while Calixtus was a staunch Protestant, and made his concessions not toward Rome, but toward Geneva, and contented himself with trying to bring the Reformed and the Lutherans to a common understanding, Grotius turned rather toward Rome, and advocated a restored and purified Catholicism, as a common solvent of all sects, and a large fold for the peaceable meeting-place of all Christians. This strange reversion on Grotius's part to the Roman Church as the hope of Christendom may be explained from two facts: (1) Grotius was an Arminian. He was delighted to find, as he thought, that the stern doctrines of Calvin were absent from the ancient fathers, that Jerome and Chrysostom and the Catholic fathers knew nothing of these tenets. This led him to a passionate rebound in favor of antiquity. (2) The iron of the Protestant intolerance had entered into his own soul. After his escape from prison he had taken refuge in France, where he was received with open arms. The cordial attitude of the Catholic ecclesiastics softened the rigidity of his Protestantism. By ample quotations from his epistles, Hallam has proved this defection of Grotius. But it was in the interest of a large union. He thought the Swedish, the English, and the Danish churches might come together, under a revived and reformed Catholic banner. He was weary of dissension. He wanted peace. But he wrote rather as a statesman than a theologian. It was peace at the expense of truth; it was peace at the expense of the fullest liberty of private judgment. Grotius did not himself go so far as to make the last sacrifice of his own conscience by accepting the infallibility of the Roman Church. Whether he would have done so had he lived, it is useless to inquire. His scheme was a vision, an hallucination. The history of Roman Catholicism for the last three hundred years has proven that.

John Owen, the greatest of the Puritan divines, the Nestor of the Congregationalists, in his treatise on schism, lays down a liberal platform. He holds that the true and essential note of the Church of Christ is union with Christ, "and wherever there is a man, or a body of men, who are united to Him by living faith, and are keeping his commandments, he or they are in communion with the Church of God." "He belongs to the Church Catholic," runs his noble charter, "who is united to Christ by the spirit, and none other." He vindicated boldly the right of the Noncomformist churches to exist, and yet in an irenical spirit, and as one sincerely desiring the union of all Christians in England. Thus, in his vindication of the Noncomformists from the charge of schism, an answer to a sermon by Stillingfleet (1680), he deprecates religious controversy in the interest of Protestant union, and says that in the presence of the common danger of the Roman Church the sharp words of Stillingfleet are unseasonable. But he had no faith in artificial schemes of union. He says: "I should be very sorry that any man living should outgo me in desires that all who fear God throughout the world, especially in these nations, were of one way as well as of one heart. I know that I desire it sincerely. But I verily believe that when God shall accomplish it, it will be the *effect* of love, and not the *cause* of love. There is not a greater vanity in the world than to drive men into a particular profession, and then suppose that love will be the necessary consequence of it; to think that if, by sharp rebukes, by cutting, bitter expressions, they can drive men into such and such practices, love will certainly ensue." These are golden words, as true now as in Owen's troublous day.

Owen had his own scheme of comprehension. In his Tract on Union among Protestants (1680), he outlines a plan of a Larger Church of England by law established, which would include all dissenters, but exclude all Romanists. As a doctrinal basis he would have the articles of the Church of England as explained in the public authorized writings of the church in the days of Elizabeth and James, "before the inroad of novel opinions among us," to be subscribed, however, only by ministers. All spiritual affairs were to be left with the churches, and "outward rites and observances," which were not inconsistent with the supremacy of Protestantism, were also to be left to the free determination of the churches. But for such a large scheme as this England was not then ready. Owen anticipated the broad statesmanship of Arnold of Rugby.

Richard Baxter, the great English Protestant schoolman, was another prophet of Christian union. Living in a most stormy and trying age, when the spirit of faction ran high, when ecclesiastical fighting was the order of the day, he was the great peacemaker. He spoke in these terms of his disappointment over the result of the Westminster Assembly of Divines: "The Christian world, since the days of the Apostles, has never seen a synod of more excellent divines than this and the Synod of Dort. Yet, highly as I honor the men, I am not of their mind in every part of the government which they would have set up. Some words in their catechism I wish had been more clear, and, above all, I wish that the Parliament and their more skilful hand had done more than was done to heal our breaches, and had hit upon the right way, either to unite with the Episcopalians and Independents, or at least had pitched on terms that are fit for universal concord, and left all to come in upon those terms that would." Baxter's chief objection to the Westminster Assembly was (1) against their making presbyterial orders a matter of divine right. This, he saw, would form another separating barrier. Baxter was a Presbyterian, but would be now classed as a Low-Church Episcopalian. That is, he believed Episcopacy to be a convenient and very ancient form of polity, though without Scriptural authority. "As to fixed bishops of particular churches, that were superior in degree to presbyters, though I have nothing at all in Scripture for them, yet I saw that the reception of them was so very early and so very general, I thought it most improbable that it was contrary to the mind of the Apostles." Baxter would have had a modified presbyterial episcopate as a centre of union for all parties, and would have thrown overboard all "divine right" theories of the ministry as divisive and false. But more important still was his objection (2) to their doctrine of coercion. He saw that this would only accentuate church divisions and embitter all parties. He says: "I disliked the course of some of the more rigid of them, grasping at a kind of secular power. They reproach the ministerial power, as if it were not worth a straw, unless the magistrate's sword enforce it. What, then, did the primitive church for three hundred years? Till magistrates keep the sword themselves, and learn to deny it to every angry clergyman who would do his own work by it, and leave them to their own weapons, the Word and spiritual keys, and *aleant quantum valere possunt*, the church will never have unity and peace. I disliked also some of them that were not tender enough to dissenting brethren, but too much against liberty, as others were too much for it, and thought by votes and numbers to do that which love and reason would have done." This is as noble a testimony for toleration as it is for Christian union.

ENGLISH PRESBYTERIANS AND CONGREGATIONALISTS.

There was first the effort to bring together the Presbyterian or moderate party in the Church of England, and the Congregationalists. Baxter was one of a noble band who saw that underneath all differences there was a real unity.

"There is no such difference," said Thomas Hill, a Presbyterian, in 1645, "for aught I know, between the sober Independents and moderate Presbyterians, but if things were wisely managed, both might be reconciled; and by the happy union of them both together, the Church of England might be a glorious church, and that without persecuting, banishing, or any such thing, which some mouths are too full of. I confess it is most desirable that confusion (that many people fear by Independency) might be prevented; and it is likewise desirable that the severity that some others fear by the rigor of presbytery might be hindered; therefore let us labor for a prudent love, and study to advance one happy accommodation."

On the side of the Congregationalists Jeremiah Burroughs advanced these magnanimous sentiments. It is notable to see that the finest and highest of recent words for the universal peace of Protestant Christendom are but the echo of these proposals of the seventeenth century.

"Why should we not think it possible," says Burroughs, "for us to go along, close together in love and peace, though in some things our judgments be apparently different one from another? I will give you who are scholars a sentence to write upon your study doors, as needful an one in these times as any; it is this: *Opinionum varietas, et opiniantium unitas non sunt ἀσύστατα*, Variety of opinions and unity of those that hold them may stand together. There hath been much ado to get us to agree; we laboured to get our opinions into one, but they will not come together. It may be in our endeavors for agreement we have begun at the wrong end. Let us try what we can do at the other end; it may be we shall have better success there. Let us labour to joine our hearts, to engage our affections one to another; if we cannot be of one mind that we may agree, let us agree that we may be of one mind."

In answer to this flag of truce the Presbyterian ministers of the Provincial Assembly of London, in 1653, sent forth the following:

"A fifth sort are our reverend brethren of the New and Old England of the Congregational way, who hold our churches to be true churches, and our ministers true ministers, though they differ from us in some lesser things. We have been necessitated to fall upon some things, wherein they and we disagree, and have represented the reasons of our dissent. But we here profess that this disagreement shall not hinder us from any Christian accord with them in affection; that we can willingly write upon our study doors that motto which Mr. Jer. Burroughs (who a little before his death did ambitiously endeavor after union amongst brethren, as some of us can testify) persuades all scholars unto: *Opinionum varietas, et opiniantium unitas non sunt ἀσύστατα*. And that we shall be willing to entertain any sincere motion (as we have also formerly declared in our printed vindication), that shall farther a happy accommodation between us.

"The last sort are the moderate, godly Episcopal men, that hold ordination by presbyters to be lawful and valid; that a bishop and a presbyter are one and the same order of ministry, that are orthodox in doctrinal truth, and yet hold that the government of the church by a perpetual moderator is most agreeable to Scripture pattern. Though herein we differ from them, yet we are farre from thinking that this difference should hinder a happy union between them and us. Nay, we crave leave to profess to the world that it will never (as we humbly conceive) be well with England till there be an union endeavoured and effected between all those that are orthodox in doctrine though differing among themselves in some circumstances about church government."

Unhappily, the England of the seventeenth century was too stormy for the fruition of such lofty desires. But on this continent twenty-four years before the Presbyterian Assembly of London issued that remarkable paper, there had been realized exactly the union for which these men were praying. At Salem, in 1629, the Plymouth Congregational Church and the Salem Presbyterial-Episcopal Church were united in one blessed fellowship—a happy omen for this continent.

Robert Hall (d. 1831) was an earnest advocate of Christian union. His words are fully equal to those of the latest zealot in this matter. He says:

"Nothing more abhorrent to the principles and maxims of the sacred oracles can be conceived than the idea of a plurality of true churches, neither in actual communion with each other, nor in the capacity for such communion. Though this rending of the seamless coat of our Saviour, this schism in the members of His mystical body, is by far the greatest calamity which has befallen the Christian interest, and one of the most fatal effects of the great apostacy foretold by the sacred penman, we have been so long familiarized to it as to be scarcely sensible of its enormity; nor does it excite suspicion or concern in any degree proportioned to what would be felt by one who had contemplated the church in the first ages. Christian societies regarding each other with the jealousies of rival empires, each trying to raise itself on the ruin of all the others, making extravagant boasts of superior purity, generally in exact proportion to their departures from it, and scarcely deigning to acknowledge the possibility of obtaining salvation out of their pale, is the odious and disgusting spectacle which modern Christendom presents. The evils which result from this state of division are incalculable. It supplies infidels with their most plausible topics of invective; it hardens the conscience of the irreligious; it weakens the hands of the good, impedes the efficacy of prayer, and is probably the principal obstruction to that ample effusion of the Spirit which is essential to the renovation of the world."

This passage reveals Hall far in advance of the general sentiment of his day.

THE UNION OF 1817.

The early years of the nineteenth century were distinguished by an event of great importance. It was the formal union throughout most of Germany between the Reformed and the Lutheran parties, which had so long been in conflict. The union was first effected in Nassau, in August, 1817. On September 27th of the same year Frederick William II of Prussia issued an appeal to the clergy to strive for a union as one of the best means for a proper celebration of the three hundredth anniversary of the Reformation, October 31, 1817. The influence of this proclamation was great, but it could have effected nothing had not the progress of events been most helpful. Both the people and the theologians were convinced that the points of division, even with reference to the ritual observance of the Lord's Supper, were not clearly set forth in Scripture, and were therefore not essential. The king saw and embraced his opportunity, and accomplished what the Hohenzollerns had long been seeking. Many places celebrated the union by the solemn administration of the Lord's Supper, in which the two parties united. The terms "Lutheran" and "Reformed" were abolished, and the united church was called the "Evangelical." The union did not compel the relaxation of opinions previously held, but only provided for mutual toleration, and the admission that in each communion the pure word of God was preached and the sacraments duly administered. Nevertheless, the introduction of a new liturgy, in 1821, caused difficulty. To the Reformed it appeared too much like the Roman Catholic mass; to the Lutherans it was too plain that the underlying presuppositions were those of Calvinism. The desire for union prevailed, however, with the vast majority.

The first real difficulty occurred in Breslau, where Scheibel was professor and pastor. He refused to employ the new liturgy, claiming that it must lead to a fatal indifferentism to tolerate, for the sake of peace, errors of faith in the church. His persistence was so great that in 1830 he was deposed by the magistracy, and with him went about two thousand of his flock and a number of scholars. The beginning had been made, and although Frederick William III would not tolerate these so-called Old Lutherans, but forbade their assemblies, and punished their clergy for administering the sacraments, congregations arose in many parts of Germany. Vast numbers of them emigrated to America, while others remained at home and endured the persecution so unjustly inflicted upon them, and have perpetuated their branch of the church to the present day.

THE FRIENDLY RELATIONS BETWEEN PROTESTANTISM AND THE GREEK CHURCH.

When Western Christendom found itself suddenly cleft into two warring halves, it was natural that the Reformers, who had bought their freedom by a breach with the immemorial traditions of doctrine, ritual and polity, should consider the possibility of making these losses good by alliance with the Eastern Church. The orthodoxy of this was so indisputable that Orthodox had become a part of its very title; its succession was more certainly authentic than that of Rome; and every one of the undisputed councils of the whole church had been held in its territory. To the hierarchical arrogance of Rome it opposed a calm assurance of doctrinal and ritual superiority. Could the Reforming North and the Orthodox East join their forces, Rome would sink into relative insignificance. The scheme, however, was an impossibility from the beginning. However much the Eastern patriarchs and their dependent bishops might resent the pretensions of Rome, they recognized themselves as belonging to the same great system. The continental Reformers, on the other hand, had broken altogether, not with **Romanism** merely, but with the Catholic Church. With the martyrs and the early fathers they had the fellowship of a common Christianity, but not of a common Catholicism.

The learned Melanchthon and his scholarly fellows could not fail to see that their hopes were very slender of negotiating a union with the East. Indeed, the attempt was only an incidental matter, and the first occasion was given by the Greeks. In 1559, the Patriarch Joasaph II sent the deacon Demetrius Mysius to Wittenberg to inform himself as to the new doctrine. Mysius stayed at Wittenberg half a year, and on his return carried with him a Greek copy of the Augsburg Confession. This is exceedingly conciliatory toward Catholicism. Yet the patriarch did not even condescend to answer the reassuring letter which Melanchthon had committed to Mysius.

Fourteen years later Martin Crusius and Jacob Andreæ, of Tübingen, after writing three times to the Patriarch of Constantinople, obtained from him a disdainful answer, in which he simply summoned them to profess steadfastly the true faith of the Greeks, and not to deviate from the Bible, the seven synods, and the holy fathers, maintaining also traditions, written and unwritten. The two divines replied that they accepted the true faith as propounded by the seven synods, and only differed from the Greeks in some local usages of no great account. After about two years' delay Jeremiah returned a formal reply, rejecting everything in which the Protestants differed from the Greek orthodoxy, and accepting only those points in which the Greeks, too, differed from Rome. He closed with a solemn adjuration to the Protestants, as they valued their eternal salvation, to enter into the bosom of the true Oriental Church. The Lutheran divines now at last set forth more distinctly their points of divergence from the East. After long delays and repeated attempts of the Lutherans to conciliate the patriarch, Jeremiah at last returned a decisive and angry reply, showing the impossibility of reconciling Protestantism with Oriental Orthodoxy, and reproaching the Reformers with their arrogance in thinking themselves wiser than the fathers, whose faith had been attested by miracles; wiser than the churches of Old and New Rome together, while they divided among themselves into innumerable parties. He entreats, in conclusion, that they would importune him no longer with their theological correspondence. To a new dissertation Jeremiah returned no answer. Thus ended the second attempt to establish a good understanding between Lutheranism and the East.

Protestantism, however, was destined to have a temporary triumph in the East, and that in the predominant see, at Constantinople itself. Moreover, this victory was reserved, not for Lutheranism, whose attitude toward Catholicism, in externals at least, was comparatively conciliatory, but for the absolutely irreconcilable system of Calvin. The agent of this temporary triumph was the Patriarch Cyril Lucar. Lucar was born in 1572, at Candia, the capital of the island of Crete. He sprang of a Greek family of old nobility, akin even to the imperial house of Paleologus.

Cyril's long sojourn in Italy, while intensifying his hostility to Rome, had broken his prejudices against the West, and thereby predisposed him to view Protestantism favorably. And since, after his return East, in 1595, his patron, Meletius, who was just then

Administrator of Constantinople, sent him into Poland, to have a part in the repeated but always futile negotiations for reunion between Roman Catholics, Greeks and Protestants, he became more and more favorable to the last as allies against the first. He was yet only a boy of twenty-three, and, discovering in the course of the complicated disputations that his knowledge of theology was very insufficient, he resolved to visit Wittenberg and Geneva. He seems to have stayed there, principally at Geneva, for nearly three years. Geneva was then much more eminent than Wittenberg, and thus Calvinism made the deeper impression on his mind. In 1601 Meletius died. His cousin Cyril, not yet thirty, was chosen his successor.

Cyril, like his predecessor, does not appear to have been particularly devoted to the little flock of the Orthodox in Egypt. Constantinople drew them both to herself with irresistible attraction. Once, on allegations of intriguing against the chief patriarch, Cyril was banished to Mount Athos, and when released was forbidden even to say mass in Constantinople. He then retired to Wallachia, but finally returned to Egypt, where he issued a flaming admonition against the Roman emissaries. He now entered into a most intimate correspondence with the Puritan Archbishop of Canterbury, George Abbot. At Abbot's suggestion he sent to him as a student, to be supported by the king, a young Alexandrian priest of eminent descent, Metrophanes Kritopulos.

Cyril Lucar became Patriarch of Constantinople in 1621, and, with several mutations of banishment and recall, he maintained himself in this second bishopric of the Christian world until his violent death in 1638. His constant correspondence with the Reformed, while still at Cairo, shows a rapidly developing inclination to Calvinism, until at last he became in theory a Calvinistic Protestant out and out. This appears fully in his confession of faith, first published in Holland, in 1629. In 1633 he himself published it at home. He obtained for it the sanction of a small synod of his personal adherents, but never ventured to publish it, by an encyclical, throughout his patriarchate, or even in his immediate diocese.

The confession is completely Protestant and Calvinistic. It subordinates tradition and the church emphatically to the Scripture, declaring that the church can always err in doctrine, and must be set right by the Scripture. It teaches election and reprobation in Dominican and Calvinistic severity, against the more Arminian bent which has always distinguished the Greek Church. It describes Christ not only as the supreme but as the sole mediator. It explicitly teaches justification by faith alone. It virtually denies the hierarchical, though not the administrative, power of the bishops. It maintains that all the works of the unregenerated are sinful. It teaches two, not seven, sacraments, and implies that their efficacy is *ex opere operantis*. It explicitly denies transubstantiation, and allows only the spiritual presence of Christ in the eucharist. It denies purgatory explicitly.

This creed, so utterly contradictory at so many points to Catholicism, Eastern and Western alike, passed for five years without action by the bishops of the great Constantinopolitan patriarchate, or by the other Eastern patriarchs. An ultimate explosion, however, was inevitable. The Jesuits were indefatigable in calling attention to the new danger. The Pope himself wrote, adjuring his Eastern brethren, if they must be schismatics, at least not to disgrace themselves by turning heretics. For a while the influence of England and Holland kept Cyril in his place, but at last the much stronger influence of France, the special ally of the Turk, overcame theirs. The metropolitan clergy, in the end, however unwillingly, came to perceive that their patriarch was a thorough Calvinist, and was bent on giving over the whole East to Calvinistic Protestantism. Finally, by secret order of the Sublime Porte, Cyril, in the evening of June 26, 1638, having been already imprisoned, was put on board a boat, which was rowed out into the Bosphorus, where the executioners, allowing him a little time for prayer, strangled him and threw his body overboard. The corpse was cast on shore and reverently buried by friends. Thus perished the first and only Protestant Patriarch of Constantinople.

Since Canterbury has risen to be a world-wide patriarchate, having some two hundred and fifty bishops subordinate, or at least loyal, to it, Constantinople regards it less decidedly than once as a mere rebel against Rome. Anglicanism, too, now that it advances its Catholic elements of doctrine and worship more to the front, and remands its Protestant polemics more to the rear, is less offensive to the East than when it was simply a Calvinistic Episcopal Church. Whether the Orientals and the Anglicans will ever form a close conjunction as against Rome is wholly uncertain, but it is at least not an impossibility.

A beautiful irenicon was that of an American lawyer of the Reformed Church, Abraham Van Dyke, Esq., who in 1836 published a book entitled, "Christian Union; or an Argument for the Abolition of Sects." It was dedicated to the Rev. David Abeel, a missionary of the Dutch Reformed Church in the East. It is an earnest and pious plea for Christian union. Van Dyke had also the faith to believe that such a union would in fact soon be realized. This was a more daring faith sixty years ago than now. He considers every objection, and modern discussion has added but little to his systematic and large-minded presentation.

The irenic proposals of Van Dyke met with serious opposition from two influential sources. One was the opposition of the Protestant Episcopal Bishop of Kentucky, Dr. B. B. Smith. He welcomed the book as an evidence of dissatisfaction with the present position of Protestantism, but he had no faith in the peaceable and catholic plans of Van Dyke. These plans he ridiculed by calling them simply an "agreement that Christians shall not bite and devour one another." On the contrary, said Bishop Smith, it is futile to talk about Christian union until all Christians are agreed in one outward form of church organization. "What sort of union," says Bishop Smith, "among the followers of Christ should be proposed? Shall they be called upon to unite in some way or another as they now stand divided; or are they bound to agree in one outward form of Christianity? For our part we most explicitly avow our conviction that every attempt to put a stop to the dissensions and subdivisions which distract the church must forever prove futile, until Christians are agreed in one outward form of Christianity. To talk about union in feeling and spirit, whilst there is disunion in fact, is about as wise as to exhort those to love one another between whom occasion of deadly feud exists." Bishop Smith himself was a High Churchman. He considered "one of the grand mistakes of the Reformation a separation *from* the church instead of reformation *in* the church." This hostile reception of the Dutch Presbyterian layman's pacific propositions on the part of this prelate of the Protestant Episcopal Church was a distinct intimation on the part of that church that nothing could be considered on this subject unless the adoption of the Episcopal Church constitution was laid down as the first plank in the platform.

Another powerful voice lifted against the too hasty adoption of the peace propositions of Van Dyke was that of the "Princeton Review." In an article published in 1836, the "Review," then conducted by its founder, Dr. Charles Hodge, expressed hearty sympathy with the aim and spirit of Van Dyke's book, but could not go so far as the enthusiastic author, for these reasons:

1. Truth is greater than union. In such an amalgamation of Christians some would have to lay aside their convictions, or keep silent respecting them, and either course would be disloyalty to the God of truth. "Every attempt to reconcile differences among Christians which involves the relinquishment of truth, or a compromise with important corruption, either in doctrine or worship; or giving countenance to what is deemed an injurious departure from what Christ has commanded, is undoubtedly criminal and mischievous."

2. Such an amalgamation of the churches, on the principle that their diversities in doctrine and order, as long as they do not affect the fundamentals of religion, are of little account, and ought not to permit the most intimate union, would discourage that "searching of the Scriptures," and that earnest "contending for the faith" which is expressly commanded as a Christian duty.

3. But such union, even if attained without dishonest sacrifice, would do no good. It would not produce love, and without love it would be a curse. The nearer the Christian denominations come to each other, the more they would fight. This writer does indeed express the hope that all the Reformed churches in the United States holding the Presbyterian system will be united in organic union, and that some alive then (1836) would live to see the day, but he says that even such a union as that he would strenuously oppose, because the conditions of friendship and love which would make the union a blessing did not then exist.

In conclusion this able writer lays down the following principles:

1. All who profess the true religion in its essential characteristics belong to the church catholic, and ought to be so regarded by all who believe that Christ is one and His religion one.

2. Concurrence in some outward form of Christianity is not essential to Christian union, or to the communion of saints.

3. Yet everything that tends to divide the body of Christ or its members from each other is sinful.

4. The day is coming, and is not far distant, when the people of God will be so united, both in form and spirit, that they will feel that they are one body in Christ, and every one members one of another.

5. A formal coalition of all sects into one body under one name would not necessarily be Christian union.

6. The spirit of sectarism must first be slain, and the spirit of charity become triumphant in every part of the church.

7. Attempts to break down the barriers which now divide Christians before such baptism of the spirit of love is given are of no use.

8. Those churches which stand aloof from other churches on grounds not supported by the Word of God, are guilty of schism. This applies to the Roman and to the Episcopal churches.

9. There will be at length a pouring out of the Holy Spirit in a measure never known since Pentecost, which will prepare the world for a consummation devoutly to be wished—the formal and real union of all Christians.

MORE RECENT UNIONS AND NEGOTIATIONS.

An irenic movement which has affected the ecclesiastical life of Scotland, and thence of the world, was that which brought together the great churches—the United Secession Church of Scotland and the smaller and yet influential church, the Relief Church. The spirit of the Relief Church was eminently Catholic. Its founder, Gillespie, had been trained by Doddridge, and he, Gillespie, could say: "I hold communion with all that visibly hold the Head, and with such only," a sentiment which reminds one of the famous declaration of his great contemporary, Wesley, who said: "I desire to form a league, offensive and defensive, with every follower of Christ." In 1847 the union of these two churches was effected with great enthusiasm. The United Presbyterian Church of Scotland has been one of the most aggressive and spiritual churches of Scotland. In 1876 the congregations of this church in England united with the English Presbyterian Church, making the Presbyterian Church of England. In 1852 one of the Secession churches of Scotland—that in which Dr. Thomas McCrie was the leading light—united with the Free Church of Scotland, and in 1876 the Reformed Presbyterian [Cameronian] Church—or a large majority of it—also joined its fortunes with the Free Church. Although there have been strong counter-currents driving the Scottish Christians apart, there have been also strong centripetal movements bringing them together. For ten years negotiations were carried on by the Free Church between herself and the Reformed, the United and the English Presbyterian churches with a view to union. But a small minority threatened to secede from the Free Church if the project were carried through, and it was wisely abandoned. The General Assembly of the Church of Scotland has formally approached every Presbyterian Church in Scotland with the expression of her "hearty willingness and desire to take all possible steps, consistent with the maintenance of an establishment of religion, to promote the union of such churches." Her efforts have as yet proved fruitless, but we must echo the words of the Rev. Pearson McAdam Muir, in his admirable brief history of the Church of Scotland, that "it is hard to believe that it is impossible to find a basis of agreement on which, without abandonment of principle or compromise of honor on either side, the now opposing communions may take their stand, and thus avert a long, unhappy, and disgraceful strife."

The movement for the union of two of the Scotch Presbyterian churches, which began several years ago, reached a successful issue, and on October 31, 1900, the final legal and ecclesiastical steps were taken consolidating into one body the Free Church and the United Presbyterian Church of Scotland. The name of the new organization is the United Free Church of Scotland. Its ministers number 1,786, and its members 495,178. This union is very successful in the Lowlands, but encounters some opposition in the Highlands.

In speaking of Scotch Presbyterianism we naturally think of the daughter on this side of the water. In 1837 the Presbyterian Church of the United States was unfortunately broken into two divisions—commonly called the Old School and the New School. But it was impossible that churches having the same creed and discipline, and not divided by any profound sectional and political feeling, could remain forever apart. A new generation came that knew but little and cared less about the old causes of strife. Churches and pastors united in the ordinary ways of fraternal intercourse. Then the mighty struggle for the Union baptized the northern churches into a oneness of feeling. Patriotism became the handmaid of religion. Why should not the church be one as the nation is one? In 1862 the Old School Assembly proposed a stated annual and friendly interchange of commissioners between the two General Assemblies. This was met by a hearty response in the friendliest spirit by the New School Assembly. At a meeting of the Old School General Assembly at Newark, in 1864, a number of ministers and laymen met together to consider organic union. This non-official body adopted a statement in which, among other things, they said:

"It is believed that the great majority in each branch sincerely receive and adopt the Confession of Faith, as containing the system of doctrine taught in the Holy Scriptures, and approve the same government and discipline. On this basis we may reunite, mutually regarding and treating the office-bearers and church courts of each branch as co-ordinate elements in the reconstruction. There are difficulties in the way of repairing the breaches of Zion, which must be met and overcome by well-considered methods, and in a spirit of forbearance and prudence. Reunion cannot be accomplished, nor is it to be desired, without the restoration of a spirit of unity and fraternity. We believe this spirit exists and is constantly increasing. That which should first engage the attention of the friends of reunion should be to find out how far unity of sentiment and kindness of feeling prevail."

The same year, at Dayton, Ohio, that great scholar and irenic spirit of whom not only Union Seminary but the whole American Church has reason to be proud, Dr. Henry B. Smith, as retiring Moderator of the New School Assembly, preached a sermon in which he presented the subject of organic union "with singular felicity and power." In 1866 both assemblies met at St. Louis. There they mingled together in religious worship and in the sacrament of the Lord's Supper. Nothing could withstand the spirit that made for fraternity. The Old School Assembly passed resolutions looking toward organic union, and appointed a committee to act with a similar committee of the New School Assembly. It was a thrilling moment in the history of the Church of God when the Rev. Dr. Phineas D. Gurley, of Washington, and the Hon. Lincoln Clark, of Detroit, walked into the New School Assembly bearing these overtures. With equal cordiality and readiness the New School Church met the advances of the Old School brethren. In 1867 a plan for reunion was submitted by this committee to both assemblies for discussion during another year. At this juncture an ominous voice in dissent was heard. In the "Princeton Review" for July, 1867, Dr. Chas. Hodge objected to the plan, on the ground that the New School Church does not now receive and never has received all the doctrines of the Calvinistic system in their integrity, and that, therefore, union would not only be inexpedient, but morally wrong. This was met by an article in the "American Presbyterian Review" for October, 1867, by Dr. Henry B. Smith, denying this charge, and attempting to prove that the sense in which the New School Church received the Confession was precisely that claimed as the true one by Dr. Hodge, viz., the Calvinistic or Reformed. Both articles were published in pamphlet form, and scattered far and wide, and both, says the late Dr. Wm. Adams, "tended to the same result—the conviction of the substantial oneness of both bodies in the receiving and adopting the Confession of Faith in the true, honest, liberal, common-sense and Presbyterian significance of those words." The bases for reunion as amended were adopted by the assemblies in New York in May, 1869, and were submitted to the presbyteries. At an adjourned meeting of the two assemblies the next November, in Pittsburg, the returns from the presbyteries showed an overwhelming majority in favor of reunion, and in May, 1870, the first reunited assembly met in Philadelphia amid the rejoicings of innumerable saints and the congratulations of sister churches all over the world. Five years later, in 1875, the Presbyterians of Canada, who had existed in almost as great variety as those of the United States, all united in one body, called the Presbyterian Church of Canada.

Another great union movement is that which brought together all the Methodist churches in Canada. In 1873 there were six Methodist churches in Canada; the Wesleyan Methodist Church in the Eastern Provinces, the Wesleyan Methodist Church in Ontario and Quebec—two churches historically and organically separate—the Methodist New Connection Church in Canada, the Methodist Episcopal Church in Canada, the Primitive Methodist Church in Canada, and the Bible Christian Church. The note for the bringing together of these bodies was struck by Rev. Dr. E. H. Dewart, in 1870. In the fall of 1870 an informal meeting of representatives of different Methodist bodies was held at the house of the editor of the "Christian Guardian," Dr. Dewart, in Toronto. From the beginning this powerful journal threw the whole weight of its influence on this side. In 1873 a plan for union was adopted by the Wesleyan Methodist Conference of Upper and Lower Canada, by the New Connection Methodist Conference, and by the Wesleyan Methodist Conference of the Eastern Provinces. The first united General Conference was held in Toronto, September, 1874—the first time in history when laymen were accorded equal representation in the chief court of any large Methodist Church. The name chosen for the united church was the Methodist Church of Canada.

This irenic result was an object lesson which the other churches could not resist. The Ecumenical Conference in London, in 1881, intensified the desire for union. In 1883 the Methodist Episcopal Church in Canada, the Bible Christian Church, and the Primitive Methodist Church in Canada, merged themselves into the larger church. Thus, where there had been six, there was henceforth to be but one Methodist Church in Canada. A grand example has in this way been set for other Methodist churches to follow. England is looking in the same direction.

The union of the Methodists in Australia may be spoken of as a virtually accomplished fact, though some details of final adjustment still remain to be made before its full and formal consummation. The union in Canada has been very helpful to this similar movement at the antipodes. This union comprehends the Wesleyans in their six annual conferences in the different colonies—New Zealand, Queensland, Victoria and Tasmania, New South Wales, South Australia and West Australia, and the "Minor Methodists," a convenient group name for the Primitives, the United Free Church and the Bible Christians. The Wesleyans, the United Free and the Bible Christian churches in New Zealand united in 1896, the Primitives still standing aloof; the Wesleyans and the Primitives of Queensland united in 1898; and the South and West Australia bodies came together in 1900. Victoria and Tasmania have agreed to consummate their union in 1902, and the New South Wales Wesleyan Conference in 1899 voted in favor of union, which will doubtless be carried into effect about the same time that result is reached in Victoria and Tasmania.

Christian union is one of the most beautiful phases of our American ecclesiastical life. It is only with recent years that fraternity has predominated over denominational differences. The old theological controversies were so bitter, and men held to their convictions with such intense emphasis, that it was impossible for the churches to co-operate in the spirit of Christian love. The great revival of 1857-59 helped to dissolve these animosities. The Evangelical Alliance, founded in 1846, has been a powerful agency in bringing the churches into closer relationship. The Young Men's Christian Association, founded in London by George Williams, June 6, 1844, attracted a great number of young men of all denominations into Christian work, and furnished a broad platform on which all churches could stand for the furtherance of the Redeemer's Kingdom. The growth of this non-sectarian organization is one of the golden fruits of this era.

The needs of the unevangelized masses; the folly of intruding denominational rivalries into small communities in our own land and in mission fields already occupied; the helplessness of a divided church before any great and urgent call; the scandal to the Christian name of the spirit of division which has had free course in many parts of the country; the perpetual object lesson of the Roman Catholic Church in the massiveness and unity of its impression—these and other considerations have helped forward the conviction that the time has come when some kind of a Bund, or federal union, or alliance—some method of realizing an interdenominational fellowship—is imperatively demanded. The noble work of that best of all non-sectarian organizations, the American Bible Society, formed in 1816 in New York—a society which for nearly a century has been the meeting-ground of Christians of every name—has shown that such a communion of labor and counsel is entirely practicable. The growth of Christian union has been also helped by the formation of the Young People's Society of Christian Endeavor, organized in Portland, Me., by the Rev. Francis E. Clark, in 1881. This society emphasizes loyalty to one's own church as one of its cardinal principles. But it has interdenominational features which give it a unique and splendid advantage. This recent development of the Christian activity of America has had a marvelous growth in all evangelical denominations, and has contributed toward the realization of the sense of Christian brotherhood and of the oneness of all of Christ's followers.

The Protestant Episcopal Church has the honor of being the first to institute proceedings looking toward the reunion of Protestantism. In its General Convention, held in Chicago in 1886, the House of Bishops submitted a plan by which it was thought the churches might take initial steps toward organic union. This basis was endorsed by the convention, and it has been submitted to the other Christian churches for their action. It puts forward the Apostles' and the Nicene Creeds as an expression of doctrine, the Bible as the rule of faith, the sacraments of the Lord's Supper and baptism, and the historic episcopate. The overtures have received cordial welcome in many quarters, and in others only indifferent attention. The chief difficulty seems to be in the interpretation of the "historic episcopate." The consummation of some form of tangible and visible Christian union is the great need of the modern church. But there is no likelihood that this fruition will ever be reached on the basis of any definite form of ecclesiastical polity. A declaration identical in terms with that of the House of Bishops of the Protestant Episcopal Church was set forth by the conference of all the bishops throughout the world in fellowship with the Church of England, held at the Lambeth Conference, London, in the summer of 1888. But the almost unanimous report of the Committee on Christian Union, appointed by the chairman of this conference, the Archbishop of Canterbury, in which the acceptance of the "historic episcopate" was interpreted as not necessarily invalidating the ordinations of other churches, was voted down by a large majority and even its publication suppressed.

In 1895 twenty-one leading American ministers voluntarily joined themselves in a league for the promotion of Catholic unity on the basis of the four Chicago-Lambeth articles. Seven of these were members of Episcopal, seven of Presbyterial, and seven of Congregational polities.

In May, 1893, the Commission on Church Unity of the General Convention of the Protestant Episcopal Church sent to the General Assembly of the Presbyterian Church, at its session in Washington, a communication embodying the views of the commission, and inferentially of a large part of the clergy and laity of the Episcopal Church, to the effect (1) that the law relating to the episcopate is subject, if exigency arise, to modification or change; (2) that the Episcopal Church is willing to qualify, if necessary, the law regulating the episcopate, and many other things which it has held in high esteem; (3) that it now gives recognition to the validity of the Presbyterate as the Presbyterians of England, under Baxter's leadership, asked in 1660. This paper also contained other statements promotive of a better mutual acquaintance and comity of feeling in order to secure a "drawing together to the final attainment of corporate unity—the goal never to be lost sight of or in any way obscured." The reply of the Committee on Christian Unity of the General Assembly of the Presbyterian Church, couched in conciliatory language, declares a similar readiness to modify usages, laws or traditions, which, however highly prized and valuable, are not fundamental in their nature, provided the reunion of the two bodies could be thus secured. It also expresses the hope that the question of reunion might yet reach a full solution, and that the American Church might yet find, through wise and Scriptural methods, an effectual reorganization.

The validity of ministerial orders in the Anglican Church was ostensibly made the subject of a fresh investigation by a special commission of the Roman Catholic Church, and the decision of the hierarchical court, composed of cardinals, was given out by Pope Leo XIII in an apostolic letter on September 15, 1896, declaring the English orders null and void. The clear and unmistakable language of the Pontiff is: "Of our own motion and certain knowledge we pronounce and declare that ordinations carried out according to the Anglican Rite have been and are absolutely null and utterly void." Thus disappeared the hope of many of the High Church Anglicans that a basis of union with the Roman Catholic Church might be found in the historic episcopate as interpreted both at Canterbury and at Rome.

In February, 1888, a general meeting of all Protestant missionaries in Mexico was held, at which, among other important acts, the following plan of denominational comity was adopted:

1. Towns of 15,000 or more inhabitants, not now occupied, may be entered by more than one denomination. 2. In places of less than 15,000 population, occupied by more than one mission, the oldest mission shall have the right of sole occupancy, save in the case of private agreement between the interested parties. 3. A place formally occupied by a denomination, and abandoned for a year or more, may be occupied by another denomination. 4. The organization of a congregation and the holding of regular services constitute occupancy. 5. A committee of arbitration, to consist of one member of each denomination, was appointed to decide questions arising under this plan of arbitration, and its decision is final.

Dr. John Watson (Ian Maclaren), in his "The Mind of the Master" (1896), has set forth an ideal creed as a basis of union among all Christian believers. It runs as follows: "I believe in the fatherhood of God; I believe in the words of Jesus; I believe in the clean heart; I believe in the service of love; I believe in the unworldly life; I believe in the Beatitudes; I promise to trust God and follow Christ, to forgive my enemies, and to seek after the righteousness of God."

Conferences for the discussion of theological and practical questions have brought the various Reformed churches into fraternal communion, which has issued in the formation of the Alliance of

Reformed Churches throughout the world holding the Presbyterian system, which held its first general council in Edinburgh, 1877, and its last in Washington, 1899. A like friendly feeling of all the Methodist churches in the world has been consummated, of which the fruit is the first Ecumenical Conference in London, 1881; the second in Washington, 1891, and the third in London, 1901. It is to be devoutly hoped that these union meetings for discussion will lead to an organic union for work, as well as for an exhibition of that real brotherhood and unity of spirit which form one of the essential prerequisites to the conversion of the world.

CHURCH FEDERATION IN OLD WORLD AND NEW.

Rev. Walter Laidlaw, Ph.D.,
NEW YORK.

The Reformation was the inevitable result of irrational restraint upon the liberty of human thought. Mediæval Christianity attempted the folly of compelling men to think alike or not to think at all.

The thoughts of men on subjects so vast as God, responsibility and immortality, can no more coincide than can the orbits of the planets. All theological systems are variously illumined by the True Light that lighteth every man coming into the world, and any system that claims a monopoly of light from above, and such celestial eminence as to cast all others into the shade, forgets that the sun's light falls on Mars and Jupiter as well as on the earth.

The right of private judgment, for which Luther successfully contended, has been reasserted by the cleavages of Protestantism. Some Protestant communions, without doubt, have crystallized around charlatans seeking personal triumph rather than the perfecting of truth. Nevertheless, on the whole, the multiplicity of Protestant communions is a witness to the vitality of the principles of Protestantism rather than to their decay. As Rosenkranz wrote in 1831, "The premises of Christian theological study are: (a) The Christian religion, as the religion of essential truth and freedom, is the absolute religion; (b) Protestantism is not the dissolution and annihilation of religion, but rather its evolution into an affirmative self-consciousness of its future; (c) a reconciliation of Christian theology and philosophy is possible."

Protestant Christianity not only claims that it is in harmony with the Bible, but that its principles are in harmony with the highest order of the universe, and unity in thinking can no more be expected in religious matters than in scientific affairs, for the simple reason there can be no finality in religion until there is finality in science. The content of final science will be a content of final religious philosophy. Some of the bizarre Protestantisms of recent times, stripped of all unscientific accretions, may have enduring religious value, because they possess a scientific element as yet unrecognized by an exaggerated supernaturalism. Absolute unity in thinking is less and less a Protestant ideal as time goes on. Organic union of Protestantism, consolidating the many into one—who shall worship in one way, is giving place to attempts at organic union of many who may worship in many ways—witness the effort, renewed for many years, and almost successful in September, 1901, to unite, under Episcopalian oversight in America, congregations worshipping by Lutheran liturgies with congregations using liturgies of English and Reformed origin, and the advocacy, by Dr. Parker, in England, of the organic unity of the Baptists and Congregationalists. Unity in thinking and even unity in worshipping are not therefore instincts of the time; but increased efficiency in religious work is a demand of the time, especially in congested cities, and federation to effect it undoubtedly is inspired by that Spirit of Power without whom nothing good or lasting can be achieved.

The instincts of church federation, in the Old World and in the New, are therefore one in many particulars; nevertheless, Old World federation is as different from New World federation as is monarchy from republicanism. Their historical origins are absolutely alike, their surrounding conditions are entirely different; their methods have but a faint resemblance; and their future will have greater divergences than their past.

OLD WORLD—CHURCH AND STATE.

Church federation in the Old World is primarily a consolidation of Nonconformity for the purpose of displaying and employing its strength against the aggressions of a State Church. Those aggressions, between 1880 and 1900, had become especially irritating to English dissenters, and additional irritation was caused by the indiscreet utterances, in 1889, of some of the High Church Anglicans at the Church Congress of that year. There are adherents of Canterbury's orders whose claims to supernatural sanctions are not exceeded by the adherents of the Vatican; and the extent of Nonconformity in England proves that Englishmen are as hesitant to believe in the centering of truth around Canterbury as is generic Protestantism to make all truth centre around the chair of St. Peter.

Impelled by the utterances of the Church Congress, Dr. Guiness

Rogers contributed, February 20, 1890, to the "Methodist Times," an article entitled "A Congress of Free Churches." If there was a congress of workers under the State Church, why should there not be a congress of workers from the Free churches?

ENGLAND'S EARLY CONGRESSES.

Two years later the first Free Church Congress met at Manchester, in November, and a second was held at Leeds in the following year. In the interval between the Manchester and Leeds Congress several Free Church Local Councils had been organized. Most of these councils were a development from the "Ministers' Fraternals," which, in English usage, correspond with "Ministers' Association" or "Ministers' Union" in America. The development effected had extended the Ministers' Fraternals into "Church Councils" by adding to the clergymen lay delegates from the churches which they served, and by making the meetings of the Fraternals more positively practical in purpose. Prior to 1890 there were but four of these councils in all of England, but in 1895, when the third congress met at Birmingham, its membership was largely made up of representatives of the councils, which then numbered one hundred and thirty. The Leeds Congress had decided that the Birmingham meeting should be constituted on a territorial basis rather than a denominational basis; and at Birmingham a further forward step was taken by electing a president whose duties should not expire with the adjournment of the Congress, but endure to the convening of the next. Dr. Charles A. Berry, of Wolverhampton, who was the first choice of Plymouth pulpit after the death of Henry Ward Beecher, was elected to this new and important position, and continued, until his sudden and lamented death, to speak and labor for the movement on both sides of the Atlantic. Dr. Berry's elevation to the presidency was largely due to the vigor of the Wolverhampton Free Church Council, of which he had been founder and president, and the constitution of the Wolverhampton Free Church Council is a good illustration of the spirit and aims of the original movement.

It announces two general objects:

(a) To enable evangelical Free churchmen to take united action upon all matters that concern their common interests.

(b) To bring the united influences of the Free churches to bear upon all questions that relate to the moral, social and religious condition of the people.

CONTRAST WITH AMERICA.

A glance at these two objects shows that self-defence is as primal in the federation movement in the Old World as is self-devotion. Nowhere in the New World is there a federation of churches which includes in its constitution a clause committing it, even by implication, to combat with other Christian bodies. There are many people in America who are timid concerning the aggressions of Romanism, but no federation of churches in America would think of sounding a battle-cry against Romanism in the list of its objects, and still less, of course, would any American federation sound a battle-cry against any form of Protestantism, unless, indeed, it were Mormonism, in which case the casus belli would not be theological but sociological. The happy severance of church and state in America permits American federation to be much broader than the federations of the Old World; and, in the future of federation work, it is more likely that the Old World will learn from the New, than that the New will learn from the Old. When Dr. Berry visited America in 1896, he learned, to his great surprise, that the Episcopalian Church, which is excluded from the Old World federation, is heartily co-operant in federation work in the New World's largest city. At a meeting in New York City, which Dr. Berry addressed, Prof. Henry S. Nash, of the Episcopalian Divinity School, Cambridge, Mass., also spoke and, after listening to Prof. Nash's brilliant address on "The Need of Formulating Theology in the Midst of the Problems of Life," Dr. Berry said:

"I am not telling you what you ought to be and do; I am telling you what we have been forced to become, and what we are striving to accomplish. We, in our federation, have been compelled, not by any ideas of sentiment, but by the actual situation, to form ourselves quite independently of the Episcopal Church in England. I rejoice that it is not so in America."

ADDITIONAL CONTRASTS.

The Wolverhampton Free Church Council's objects deserve yet more detailed study as an exhibit of the peculiar conditions surrounding the Old World federations. The first group is listed in the constitution as follows:

1. The maintenance of New Testament simplicity in the faith and practice of the church.

FEDERATION OF CHURCHES.

2. The exposition and defence of Free Church principles by means of such agencies as may be deemed advisable from time to time.

3. The question of supplying the religious needs of hospitals, workhouses and similar institutions.

4. The education question.

5. The due representation of Free churchmen on municipal, county, district and parish councils, local boards, school boards, boards of guardians, and other public representative bodies.

6. The question of religious persecution and intolerance.

All of the foregoing detailed objects are specified under the first general object of the Wolverhampton Free Council, and it is plain that several of them would be anachronistic and useless in any American federation.

The first is an object which in America would be attained not by a federation, but by evangelical movements within any communion whose churches should depart from New Testament simplicity. High Church theory in America has not, in any communion, reached such disturbing proportions as to call for a federation of all churches to defeat its philosophy or its practical power.

From the second object of the Wolverhampton Free Church Local Council, the Constitution of the United States defends the nation as a whole, and every constituent state, though there are some efforts to connect the resources of state treasuries with particular communions which have in the past needed, and may again need, the defence of more restrictive enactment, in the periodical revision of state constitutions, for the practical severance of church and state. The education question is agitated by the Roman Church in America to the end of securing for parochial schools the assistance of public funds; but American churches do not need to be federated to deal even with that, for Roman Catholicism itself is not a unit on the education question, and there is not a single school in the United States where, as in England, Scotland and Ireland, catechetical instruction is given in school hours at the public charge. The question of supplying the religious needs of hospitals, workhouses and similar institutions, has been, and will continue to be, a concern of American federations, but the object of such federative effort is not to defend invalids from unwelcome Erastian instruction, but to secure, by a coöperative method, efficient and adequate religious and consolatory care for the unfortunate inmates of public institutions.

The fifth and sixth objects of the anti-Anglican constitution of the

Wolverhampton Free Church Council are happily unnecessary in America, and it would, in fact, be unconstitutional to strive for the realization of the fifth. There can be no direct recognition of any church or communion in the make-up of municipal, county, and parish councils in the United States, nor yet on local boards, school boards or any other public representative bodies.

There was a period in American religious history when persecution and intolerance characterized the relationships of religious bodies to one another, but no parallel can be now found in the United States to the tales which are told, in the English Federation reports, of the need of forswearing private faith in order to secure public office or industrial positions.

Any American who studies the detailed objects of the English Free Church Councils cannot but devoutly thank God for the larger opportunities for federation in America arising from the severance of church and state.

SOCIOLOGICAL OBJECTS.

The sociological scope of the Wolverhampton Council, as shown by the detail of its second general object, is exceedingly broad.

It calls upon the federated Free churches to bring their influence to bear upon the following questions:

1. The condition of the lapsed and lost, and how to reclaim them for Christ.
2. The suppression of sweating, overcrowding, social vice, gambling, betting and other evils.
3. The liquor traffic, licensing of public houses, music and dancing saloons, promotion of temperance.
4. The opium traffic, and prohibition of the liquor traffic with heathen countries.
5. The adoption of the principle of arbitration in international and industrial disputes.
6. The maintenance of a high moral standard in public men and institutions.
7. United evangelistic and other services.

With nearly all of the foregoing sociological objects American federations have expressed their sympathy, but one cannot read the list without a feeling that the English Federation movement would be very much stronger if the Free churches and State churches of Great Britain were federated for objects which are evidently common to all churches, whether Free or State. It may be that, in the future, the impossibility of meeting the sociological needs of English cities will compel the State and Free churches to federate; and that the first general object of the Wolverhampton Free Church Council, and all other similar councils, will be accomplished through an organization which will not seek to unite, in the same constitution, a declaration of battle against some of the Lord's servants and a sense of devotion to the whole community.

COUNCIL MEMBERSHIP.

The National Council of the Evangelical Free Churches of Great Britain consists of representatives of local councils similar to the Wolverhampton Free Church Council, and of district federations, which frequently are federations of the local councils of an entire county. There are about 700 councils and there are thirty-six federations.

It was at the Fourth National Congress of the Evangelical Free Churches of England and Wales, held in Nottingham, in March, 1896, that the present name of the English movement, "The National Council of the Evangelical Free Churches," was adopted. Hugh Price Hughes was the president of that year, and the change of the name of the organization has been followed by increasing emphasis upon its spiritual and sociological aspects, while the political aspects of the movement have been given secondary attention. "Council" sounds less combative than Free Church "Congress." In his presidential address at Nottingham, Hugh Price Hughes devoted considerable time to proving that the movement is "not political but distinctly Christian and ecclesiastical." The leaders of the movement are fond of reiterating this claim. At the Cardiff Council, 1901, the official report claimed that "The movement has been, from the beginning, first of all preëminently spiritual. The fear that the councils would meddle with party politics, and that the movement would, in consequence, be wrecked, has, we believe, entirely passed away. It is now seldom expressed at all. During the past year we have had the general election, and party feeling has, in many quarters, run high, but we quite confidently assert that never for a moment has the movement been in peril, and that not a single local council has even been temporarily paralyzed by the gravest differences in political opinion."

This has quite a reassuring ring, but American people are bound to perceive, even in the latest developments of the Council of the Evangelical Free Churches, an underlying purpose which is pronouncedly political.

CATECHETICS ON CHURCH AND STATE.

Through the coöperation of many leaders a catechism has been prepared, for use in religious and secular schools, with fifty-two questions and answers, a question for each week of the year. Four weeks of the year are, in this catechism, given to the consideration of the relation of church and state. That very fact is the proof of two things: first, that the Free Church catechism, unamended, will have no large circulation in America, where it is not worth while to give a whole month of the year to the discussion of a question which was settled over a hundred years ago; second, that the political question of the relationship of church and state is so important in Great Britain that a whole month of catechetical instruction can profitably be devoted to it.

A study of the results of the English work, as stated in the annual reports of the Organizing Secretary for 1900 and 1901, shows that the combating and curbing of the aggressions of the State Church bulk fully as large as general sociological results. This is true both in the work of the district federations and in the work of the local councils, which are the federations of particular towns and cities.

RESULTS—DEFENSIVELY AND DEVOTIVELY.

Some of the results especially mentioned in these reports, and here divided into two sections, namely, results connected with the combat between the Free churches and the State Church, and results connected with increased community service, are as follows:

I. *Results connected with the combat between the Free churches and the State Church.*

1. Lectures on Free Church topics, given under the auspices of district federations and local councils, on such subjects as "The Basis and Aims of Nonconformity"; "Rome, Reform, and Reaction"; "The Priesthood and Its Theological Assumption"; Oliver Cromwell's "Struggle for Liberty," and Ian Maclaren's sermon on "Apostolic Succession."

2. Classes in church history; the history of the Reformation, etc.

GENERAL NEAL DOW.

In many of these classes prizes are offered to the student who passes the best examination on subjects connected with the question of the proper relationship of church and state and on the Free Church doctrine of ministerial orders.

3. Pamphlets prepared and distributed on such topics as "The Strength of the Free Church," "pointing out the significance of the figures;" "Christian Citizenship," "showing the opportunities presented to Free churchmen to exercise their political rights in the interests of the Kingdom of God."

4. Attention to local elections where the interests of Free churchmen were at stake.

5. Watching the action of boards of guardians, etc.

6. Chaplains appointed to serve in workhouses, etc., where, heretofore, only representatives of the State Church had been employed, or in "alternation with the Anglican chaplain, who hitherto has had the monopoly."

7. Undenominational day schools established.

8. Oversight of boarding schools to secure, for Free Church boarders, rights of attendance at Free Church services.

9. United action to secure "a majority of Nonconformist representatives on school boards."

10. United action to secure Free Church cemeteries.

11. United action to enforce the Conscience Clause Act of 1870.

12. Initiation of a registry system for domestic servants, permitting them, without change of religious adherence, to secure domestic positions.

13. Appointment of a committee to investigate the administration of charitable and educational trusts, to see whether these are not being directed for the benefit of the State Church.

14. Free Church services established by guarantee funds at Grindelwald, Chamounix, Zermatt, Engelberg, St. Beatenberg, Geneva, Framnaes, Eide, Ullensvang, and other continental summer resorts. These services are said to be necessary to counteract the "offensive ritualism" of Anglican chaplains abroad.

15. Preparation of a Free Church catechism for use by the Free churches. About 300,000 copies of this catechism were in use in 1901, and the National Council refused the Liverpool School Board, which was under Anglican control, permission to use it, unless the questions relative to church and state, and to the sacraments, which had been changed by the Board, were restored to their original form.

16. Circulating libraries to increase acquaintance with Free Church literature and history. Three hundred boxes, containing from thirty to sixty volumes apiece, were in circulation in 1900.

II. *Results of increased community service.*

1. Union open-air services.
2. United missions.
3. House-to-house visitations.
4. Temperance conferences and legislation.
5. Secural of lists of volunteer Sunday-school teachers, ready on two days' notice to fill vacancies in village schools.
6. Overlapping "amicably disposed of." One instance of this deserves especial mention. At Bristol the Congregational Church Extension Committee served notice on the Church Extension committees of other bodies of its purpose to build six chapels. "To avoid overlapping, and also to secure the whole city being cared for, in any case of need, a conference shall be held between us and either of the denominations whose plans may in any way be touched by these suggestions as to localities as named above; and we shall hold our hand, as far as sites are concerned, until the end of this month, so that there may be proper brotherly consultation." As a result of this, one of the chapels yielded to the Presbyterians.
7. Cycling corps established for the distribution of tracts and the holding of open-air services.
8. United action against Sunday newspapers at Swinton and in London. In the former place the Romish priests joined in the movement. It was agreed, in order to suppress the Sunday newspapers: (a) That no advertisements should be inserted in papers issuing a Sunday edition. (b) That week-day papers issuing Sunday editions should not be purchased by Free Churchmen. (c) That newsdealers refusing to handle the Sunday papers should be given the preference by Free Churchmen. Mr. Cadbury coöperated with this movement by withdrawing all his advertisements of his food products from the Sunday papers, and the "Daily Mail" and other strong newspapers were forced out of the Sunday issue business.
9. Lectures on Bible study for the benefit of Sunday-school workers and local preachers.
10. Distribution of New Year greetings in all homes of some cities.
11. Appointment of district nurses.
12. Institution of a religious magazine adapted to localized use.

13. Institution of reading rooms to act as saloon substitutes, and of Sick and Dividend funds in opposition to Public House funds.
14. Rescue of children from the streets.
15. Stoppage of the sale of intoxicants at such festivals as the Eisteddfod, Cardiff.
16. Arrangements for the National Simultaneous Mission, covering all England.
17. Institution of a Nonconformist parish system. "Some churches visit every house in their parishes once every month, and have always special evangelistic services on hand. By such means the crowd of people outside the churches are touched as they are not touched even by united missions." For the extension of this parish system, Mr. George Cadbury offers $25 to every local council for the preparation of a map showing the coöperative districts adopted by it.

The above list of results certainly proves the vigor of the English Federation Movement, but shows at the same time how political it is, to American eyes. Dr. MacKennal, in summarizing his observations of the work in all parts of England, says: "In some places I heard mostly of missions, in others of philanthropic work. The influencing of town councils, magisterial benches, and police activity for the good of the community, has been the particular direction taken by others. I regard this local independence as another healthy sign of the hold our work has taken on our churches."

MISCELLANEOUS NOTES.

The National Council issues hymnals, tracts, and an official paper called "The Free Church Chronicle," and has lantern lectures on Free Church facts and theory for free use. It has in its service at least three evangelists, Mr. W. R. Lane, Gipsy Smith, and Rev. J. Tolefree Parr, whose character and capacity are abundantly vouched for, and who have brought thousands into fellowship with Christ, including many adherents of the State Church. "We have come together spiritually," says one of the leaders, "and we are prepared to unite for anything which means the frustration of the devil and the enthronement of Christ." But the English Federation movement, though covering the whole country, is not, and cannot be, a union of all the forces whose aim is "the frustration of the devil and the enthronement of Christ," because it excludes the auxiliary forces within the State Church, and the time must come when all of England's Christian forces will be united.

SOUTH AFRICA.

The council is by no means at one with itself on the question of the Boer war, but, in interest in arbitration, it has spoken more pronouncedly than the State Church, and this, perhaps, is what one would expect under the circumstances.

It is interesting to note, in the literature of the English Federation movement, how frequently Robert Browning is quoted. One of the leaders, indeed, calls him "The Poet of Nonconformity."

In South Africa there are federations which in some instances include the Episcopalians. This is true in Durban, where the Church of England works with the Wesleyans, Baptists, Congregationalists, Scandinavian Lutherans, Salvation Army and South African Mission. There is no union of church and state in Durban. This federation has fought the Sunday theatre, gambling, and the impurity of the town. There are federations also in Capetown, Maritzburg, Kimberley, Johannesburg, and Port Elizabeth, but in all of these, owing to the union of church and state, the circle of denominational inclusion is smaller.

JAMAICA AND SCOTLAND.

In Jamaica, as in England, action has been taken against the denominational schools, and the churches have united to enforce temperance law and to benefit the children.

There is at least one federation in Scotland in a town where the Established Church has no branch. It has conducted a special mission, prayer meeting, and house-to-house visitation.

DENOMINATIONAL INCLUSION.

Nowhere in the Old World is the circle of denominational inclusion as wide as in America, and this for two reasons:

1. Because in America all churches stand on an equal footing under the state.
2. Because in America, as in Durban, South Africa, the denominations have received large accessions from immigration.

A third reason might be added, namely, that the freedom of church and state in America has tended to an inventive increase of denominational division. There are many denominations, born in America, which have no representation in England, while, so far as is known, there is no denomination in England which is not represented in America.

The report on the English Council for 1901 says: "Very soon we shall have to report that no more councils are being formed, for the simple reason that in a comparatively short space of time the whole of England and Wales will be covered." When this stage is reached the Old World Federation movement will doubtless have a most powerful influence upon the political question of the future relations of church and state in Great Britain.

INTOLERANCE.

An American cannot read an incident recorded in the report of 1901 without sympathizing with the Englishmen who smart under the wrongs inflicted by the State Church, when its ministers or sympathizers depart from the principle of the Reformation, the right of liberty of thought. Lord Hastings last Michaelmas sent notice to Mr. Burrell Hammond, a farmer, to quit the place, and his landlord wrote him: "The reason you have notice to quit your farm is that I am anxious to have a tenant who would act on more friendly terms with his landlord, and also one not so hostile to the clergy and everything connected with the Church of England."

Every landlord in America, of course, has the right, and probably the habit, of securing tenants with whom friendly relationship can be cultivated, but there are few landlords, if any, in America, who would mention the fact, even if feeling it, that their tenants are unpleasant on account of their religious opinions. The instance reveals the tension of the state of feeling in England.

LONDON'S FEDERATION.

The Metropolitan Federation, which concerns itself with the city of London, includes sixty separate councils, and Dr. Joseph Parker, of the City Temple, is the president of the Federation. Last winter this Federation engaged in two great enterprises, one of which is unnecessary in America, while the other is a perpetual need of America as well as of all Christian lands.

The former was the participation of the London Federation in the School Board election, when the Federation sided with the Progressives as against the Moderates. The Moderates believe in the retention of catechetical instruction in the public school system, while the Progressives stand for its elimination. The last election "resulted in the return of the Progressive Unsectarians by a small majority." The Metropolitan Federation also concerned itself with the Borough Council elections, pointing out that "the new municipal arrangements provided a great opportunity, and laid a heavy burden of responsibility upon all Christian citizens."

SIMULTANEOUS MISSION.

The other great concern of the Metropolitan Federation was the Simultaneous Mission, whose opening was so shadowed, and yet sanctified, by the death of the Queen.

For London, as for all other parts of Great Britain, preparations had been made to make the Simultaneous Mission as successful as diligent and coöperative human effort could render it. All-day conferences, at which the mission was the sole subject discussed, were held throughout all the country. One hundred thousand copies of a pamphlet relative to the mission, by the Rev. J. Tolefree Parr, were circulated broadcast. The Rev. F. B. Meyer wrote two special booklets, entitled "To Missioners," and "The Direction of Inquirers," which proved of great practical service; and a pamphlet entitled "Preparing the Way" was also published. Material on house-to-house visitation, inquirers' cards, workers' cards, etc., etc., were published by the million pages, and Rev. G. Campbell Morgan wrote for converts a book of advice entitled "All Things New."

The first great public meeting in London was presided over by Lord Kinnaird, an evangelical layman of the Church of England, and an address was made by a clergyman of the Established Church.

This clearly showed the spiritual sympathy with a spiritual movement of many of the Christian people of Great Britain whom the constitution of the Council of the Evangelical Free Churches excludes, and proved that there is no barrier to unity in Christ which does not break down under the unifying Spirit of God. Hugh Price Hughes once claimed for the Council of the Evangelical Free Churches that it included the "Scriptural Catholics." "We are not one in the Pope," he said, "we are not one in the Crown; but we are one in Christ. The Roman Catholic stands for the supremacy of the Pope, the Anglican Catholic for the supremacy of the Crown, and the Scriptural Catholic for the supremacy of the Christ."

But the opening and the history of the Simultaneous Mission in London, and throughout the land, proved that all the Scriptural Catholics are not Free Churchmen.

The Mission proper opened with a service at the Guildhall on January 28, 1901. Never before had a Nonconformist service been held there, but the Lord Mayor and sheriffs attended "in state," and the famous, ancient building was crowded with a congregation representing all classes of society and all schools of religion.

Midday services were conducted for nearly a fortnight by the Rev. John McNeill in the City Temple, and by Dr. Clifford and Mr. Meyer at Bishopsgate Chapel and Exeter Hall, while Gipsy Smith preached at the Metropolitan Tabernacle.

In all of these places rich results were reaped, though throughout the whole country there was some disappointment that the results were not larger. It cannot be doubted, however, that this spiritual opening of the twentieth century history of London, and of the land, will bless the city and the nation through many years to come.

Mr. Meyer calculates that, in all, the missioners, each day of the mission, reached 200,000 people, and believes that the impression was greatly intensified by the sorrow over the Queen's death, which had smitten the nation. It is altogether likely that the movement for a similar mission in America will receive a special blessing, through the exhibition, in President McKinley's closing hours, of the calm and beauty and dignity of a Christian death. It is an augury for an even greater blessing in America that the Episcopalian churches are represented both in American federations and in the National Gospel Campaign Committee.

One feature of this great movement was the effort made for special classes, such as noonday meetings for laborers, services for policemen, etc., etc. There were efforts also to reach the Jews of the metropolis.

MISSION RESULTS.

One result of the mission, which is given especial mention in the official account, is its influence upon the pulpit style of many ministers. It is claimed that all traces of scholasticism disappeared, and that, as missioners, they were straightforward and simple, while as ordinary preachers they had been liable to be diffuse and complex. Mr. Meyer, however, concedes that the great outlying masses were "not largely influenced or induced to come to the meetings." "They are not to be convinced of our earnestness or desire to have them by one spasmodic effort. We must persevere with this kind of work." There is indeed a decided evidence of saving common sense in the comments, upon the success of the mission, which emanate from its leaders; and Mr. Meyer concludes that the next great Free Church Mission, "if we live to see it, must occupy the local public buildings, and, where possible, the places of amusement in which the people are accustomed to congregate."

MISSION ELSEWHERE.

Interesting special reports upon the Mission from Birmingham, Blackburn, Bradford, Brighton, Bristol, Cambridge, Cardiff, Halifax, Hull, Ipswich, King's Lynn, Leeds, Leicester, Liverpool, Manchester, Newcastle, Plymouth, Portsmouth, Sheffield, Swansea and York are contained in the report of the National Council which met at Cardiff in 1901.

In many of these centres, as in London, the Anglican clergy attended the mission, and at Portsmouth an Anglican clergyman assisted the Rev. G. Campbell Morgan at his meetings in the Town Hall.

THE CO-OPERATIVE PARISH IDEA.

The general conclusion upon the utility of the work emphasizes the fact that permanent effects can be accomplished only by the co-operative districting of the country. Mr. Cadbury, a member of the Society of Friends, says: "No great permanent effects will be produced on the country, except by each church taking its parish and working it vigorously. The country has suffered because Christian men and women have not been at work. The churches have suffered because work has not been found for them to do, and, like a limb unused, they have become helpless. That individual and that church only will be filled with all peace and joy in believing which unselfishly devotes itself to the good of others." Dr. Horton makes a comment which is quite startling, but yet perhaps sadly true. He says: "To reach the masses of the outsiders, the services should be held in neutral buildings. It is not the Christian truth or the Christian Church that repels the people, but the Christian building, and the conventionalities which have gathered about it." Dr. MacKennal says: "The churches have not caught and represented the ethical idea of the Lord. By discussing

JOHN B. GOUGH.

whether the Sermon on the Mount was a possible law on earth, instead of learning from it how to live, we have awakened the suspicion that our own belief in Christ is not thorough. I have not been surprised that, of the large congregations which the Mission has gathered, only a small percentage of 'outsiders' has been anywhere observed. If the desire becomes a purpose to follow Christ everywhere, to have no other rule than His, for personal, social and material life, there will be such a revival as England has never known."

FEDERATION EXTENSION.

The 1901 report of the council states that federation is being discussed in the churches of Scotland, and that leading representatives of the Scottish Episcopalian Church, the Established Church of Scotland, and the United Free Church of Scotland, have issued a call to prayer for visible unity. In the face, however, of this inclusive movement, the extension of the federation idea, on the part of the Council of the Evangelical Free Churches, continues to encourage the exclusion of the Episcopalian churches. In Sydney, New South Wales, for instance, the Rev. J. B. Meharry, B.A., is quoted as urging upon the General Assembly of New South Wales "the possibility, if only from an economic point of view, of all non-Episcopalian churches making a great federation." The Council of Churches in Victoria includes only the Presbyterians, Wesleyans, Congregationalists, Baptists, Lutherans, Primitive Methodists, United Methodists, and Bible Christians. It has been in existence for seven or eight years, and concerns itself mainly with the "overlapping" question.

Four Evangelical Councils have been formed in New Zealand, at Dunedin, Christchurch, Wellington and Auckland. The Free churches of Berlin have formed a council which will ultimately, perhaps, include all the Free churches of the German Empire, and serve as "a united testimony or action toward the very powerful, almost Imperial Lutheran State Church."

NEW WORLD FEDERATION.

The Federation movement in the New World is entirely independent, in origin, methods and purposes, of the Federation movement in the Old. It owes more to the Evangelical Alliance of the United States than to any other root influence.

There was a period in the history of the Evangelical Alliance of the United States when it itself promised to be a complete solvent of the problems of Christian coöperation in the New World. Not content, however, with increasing interest in the unifying of religious *work,* some individuals connected with the Alliance, in 1873, took a step, in connection with the World Congress of the Evangelical Alliance, held in New York in that year, in the direction of unity in *worship*—a matter which to federationists is not of immediate concern. The existing canons of the Protestant Episcopal Church of that time prevented a clergyman from celebrating the Holy Communion on terms of parity with the clergy of other churches, just as the customs of the Baptist Church of that period prohibited a clergyman of that communion from inviting all lovers of the Lord, without regard to the method of their original baptism, to join in celebrating the Lord's Supper.

As a result, therefore, of the criticism of the participation of an Episcopal clergyman in the sacramental service which was held in connection with the meeting of the Evangelical Alliance, the Reformed Episcopal body in the United States was created by decedents from the Protestant Episcopal Church, and the attitude of the Episcopalian body toward the Evangelical Alliance was thereafter inevitably less cordial. This effect would have been averted but for an unfortunate misunderstanding which attributed to the Evangelical Alliance an action which was taken by a few individuals on their own responsibility.

The effect remained, however, and in many quarters of the United States the federative efforts of the Evangelical Alliance thereafter were quite perceptibly affected. It was not until the Rev. Josiah Strong, the distinguished author of "Our Country," became, through the insight and liberality of Mr. William E. Dodge, president of the Evangelical Alliance, its field secretary, that the Alliance began again to receive expressions and accessions of Episcopalian sympathy. Dr. Strong's portrayal of the problems of America in that book was so forcible as to arouse a very widespread interest in coöperation.

A NATIONAL CHURCH.

Within the Episcopalian Church itself the Rev. Dr. William R. Huntington has been pleading for years for a unified American Church, and the "Church Idea" for which he stands is statesmanlike and tolerant. While the Episcopalian communion, as a whole, has not yet adopted it, the influence of Dr. Huntington is quite perceptible to all federation workers. His plan virtually concedes the regularity of non-Episcopalian orders, and advocates a National Church, under Episcopalian oversight, not because the church descends directly from the Apostles, but because a history of helpfulness, on the part of the churches in America, can best be made, he believes, in the future, under the executive oversight of bishops.

The need of increased efficiency in the present religious work of America is the foundation of Dr. Huntington's interest in his proposal; and, consciously or unconsciously, his activities have reinforced the literature and work of the Evangelical Alliance in convincing American Christians of the necessities and opportunities of federation in the United States.

POLITICAL FEDERATION.

The fact has been frequently pointed out, and it is a very important one, that the political framework of the United States is a parallel to a possible framework for the federation of its churches, and even of its communions. Just as the states are federated without the surrender of their entire autonomy, the churches and communions could be federated, for the achievement of purposes common to all, without the surrender of their individual autonomy.

Dr. Strong's book, "Our Country," was followed, after he had assumed the secretaryship of the Evangelical Alliance, by the "New Era," a most masterly proof of the need of coöperation to solve the problems which intimately concern the life of American churches, especially in cities. The book, moreover, concludes with a description of the method favored, and carried into operation in some localities, by the Evangelical Alliance.

It is hard to see why this book failed to produce a permanent effect upon New York City, in which the Evangelical Alliance had its headquarters. As a matter of fact, however, the Chickering Hall Conference, in the interest of coöperation in New York City, which was held in 1888, failed to produce a permanent federation of the church forces of New York. Two years before the English federation movement began, however, the Evangelical Alliance had already called attention to the need of coöperation in meeting the religious and social needs of the New World's metropolis. Elsewhere in the

United States the efforts of the Evangelical Alliance were more successful. In Boston there is an organization which is twenty-six years old, having been called into being shortly after the World's Congress of the Evangelical Alliance in 1873. The effect of the misunderstanding, already alluded to, however, has restricted the membership of the Boston Alliance, and it was at best only a federation of clergymen, little stronger than an English Ministers' Fraternal, until 1900, when its constitution was revised to provide for the direct representation of the churches by laymen, in addition to clergymen. This was the result of the experience of the New York Federation, whose methods are the most fully developed of all federations in the New World, and which had been organized in 1895.

AMERICA'S PROBLEM.

New World federation thus owes nothing whatever to the Old World movement. Its methods are entirely its own; and they are an expression of the fact that the problems of federation in America are different from those of any other quarter of the world, and that the federative needs of America, for the immediate future, at least, will be best met by the formation of federations in what the French call *les grandes villes,* or cities of 100,000 or over.

URBAN POPULATION.

There are several states of the American Union, notably in the North Atlantic section, whose percentage of urban population is higher than the percentage of urban population in England. This fact is most astonishing, but is nevertheless true. New York State alone has an area nearly equal to the whole of England, and its population is 77.6 per cent. urban, if all incorporated places be included in the tabulation, while if places of 4,000 and over are counted, it is 71.2 per cent. urban.

In 1891, England, including London, was but 70.4 per cent. urban, and included in the classification "urban" were all the sanitary districts of over 3,000 persons. But in 1900 Massachusetts was 76 per cent. urban, including in the classification only places of 8,000 persons and over, while Rhode Island was 81.2 per cent.; New York 68.5 per cent. on the same basis; New Jersey, 61.2 per cent.; and Connecticut 53.2 per cent. The latest statistics from England show that England of to-day, including the whole of London, is but 67.4 per cent. urban, including only cities of 10,000 or over.

There are in America thirty-eight cities of 100,000 or over, with an aggregate population of 12,208,347 persons, or 18.5 per cent. of the entire population of the United States, including Alaska and the remoter possessions of the United States in the Far East. The cities of 100,000 and over in New York State comprise 55.2 per cent. of the entire population of the State, but in England, the cities of 100,000 and over, in 1901, comprised only 35.3 per cent. of the entire population of England.

Astonishing as the fact is, therefore, the fact remains, nevertheless, that the more populous regions of the New World are more largely urban than England. There were in England, in 1896, only fourteen cities of 200,000 or over, while in the United States there are nineteen such cities.

ALIEN POPULATION.

The foreign-born in the United States in 1900 numbered 10,460,085 persons, or 13.7 per cent. of the entire population of the country. The population of England and Wales, in June, 1900, was officially estimated at 32,091,907 persons. The foreign-born in the United States are therefore the equivalent of almost one-third of the entire population of England and Wales.

The city of London, in 1901, is officially stated to be less than 10 per cent. foreign-born, but there are six American cities whose population is over one-third foreign-born. Fall River, Mass., has the largest percentage, viz., 47.7 per cent., and New York City is next with 37 per cent. The Borough of Manhattan, which comprises over half of the population of New York, is 47.2 per cent. foreign-born, while sixteen of its thirty-four Assembly Districts are above 40 per cent. foreign, six above 50 per cent., and one nearly 70 per cent. The foreign-born in New York City exceeded, in 1900, the entire population of Liverpool and Manchester, and was greater than the entire foreign population of Chicago, Philadelphia, St. Louis, Boston and Baltimore combined. In the year 1896, 17,108 aliens arrived in the port of London, and only 40,036 in all the ports of the United Kingdom. In the same year 343,267 aliens arrived in the United States, and 72 per cent. of them were destined for New York State, for Massachusetts, Pennsylvania and Illinois; in other words, for the states having the largest cities.

53.7 per cent. of the foreign-born living in cities of 100,000 or over in America live in cities of 1,000,000 or over, and 31.7 per cent. of the population living in cities of 100,000 or over live in New York City, leaving only 22 per cent. to Philadelphia and Chicago combined.

When the Federation of New York City, therefore, began its work in 1895, it was evident that the plan to be adopted should definitely address itself not only to the problems arising from New York's diversity of religious communions, but to the problems arising from the diversity of its nationalities, and this, from the first, has characterized the work of the Federation of Churches and Christian organizations in New York City.

CONGESTION.

There is another feature of the situation in New York which compels, in the New World, federation methods different from those adopted in London.

In London, in 1901, there was an average of only 7.8 persons to a house, but in Manhattan, in 1900, there was an average of 23.2 persons to a house. In 1890, only 6.3 per cent. of the families of Manhattan owned their own dwellings. As a matter of fact, the housing problem of New York City is a greater problem than the housing of London, and the plan which the New York Federation has adopted is as minutely adapted to the frequent migration of the people from tenement to tenement and from apartment to apartment as to the problems arising from the diversity of religious communions and nationalities.

CHURCH EXTENSION.

There is yet another fact which is of great importance in New York, namely, that the number of Protestant churches, relatively to population, has not been keeping pace with population. There is no district of New York which, in proportion to population, has as many churches as has London, if the Established Church and Free churches are added, and no New Yorker, of course, would look at the religious problems of London simply through Free Church eyes.

NEW YORK'S FEDERATION.

Hence the work in the New World's largest city has a scale and method which make it inclusive of anything and everything that could be attempted in any American city of 100,000 and over, and as a matter of fact, its influence has already been apparent by the formation of a National Federation of Churches and Christian Workers, which is endeavoring to reproduce the New York Federation in other American cities, as well as to introduce in rural communities the work of the Interdenominational Commission of Maine.

The membership of the New York Federation includes representatives of its churches and Christian organizations, as well as a considerable number of individuals who give to its support $50 or more annually.

It is controlled by a board of thirty directors, who represent the five boroughs of New York City, and who belong to the Baptist, Congregational, Lutheran, Methodist, Presbyterian, Protestant Episcopalian and Reformed Dutch communions. On its committees and in some of its sub-federations there are also representatives of the Friends, Moravians, Reformed Presbyterians, Unitarians, Welsh Calvinistic Methodists, Disciples, Primitive Methodists, the Evangelical Association of North America, United Presbyterians, Reformed Germans and the Free Baptists. The Hebrews of New York are not directly represented in the Board, but are committed to coöperate with the Federation in philanthropic matters, and friendly relationships are cultivated with them, by instituting inquiries which will be of advantage to such movements as the Baron de Hirsch Fund.

The Roman Catholics of the city also coöperate with it along philanthropic lines, but in the main concern of the New York Federation, namely, the development of a coöperative Protestant parish system, the Hebrews and Catholics will not, of course, coöperate.

CREEDS IN NEW YORK.

Statement was above made of the difference between English and American cities in respect of their nationality. It should be added that these divergences are accompanied by startling divergences in creedal conditions. In the last report of the Council of Evangelical Free Churches of Great Britain it was stated that, in 13,000 families visited in South Manchester, only 880 were Roman Catholics, or 6.8 per cent., but there are many districts of New York which are over 60 per cent. Roman Catholic. If the Protestantism of New York concentrated its attention upon proselytizing its Hebrews and Catholics, rather than upon the discovery and recovery of the Protestants who are lapsing from church attendance and interest, it would have a task truly colossal, and one which could never be discharged by any mere surface evangelism.

The recorded marriages in the city of London, for the year 1897, include only 1,391 marriages at which a Roman Catholic priest officiated, 885 at which a Rabbi officiated, while there were 30,094 marriages by clergymen of the Established Church, 1,777 by other Protestant religious bodies, and 5,725 civil marriages. The Roman Catholic and the Hebrew marriages combined are thus less than 2,300, while distinctively Protestant marriages are nearly 32,000. New York City possesses the facts for a similar tabulation, but such a tabulation has never been made. It is altogether likely, however, that the Roman Catholic and Hebrew marriages in New York are proportionately ten times as numerous as in London. There are said to be over 400,000 Hebrews in New York. There are nearly 200 synagogues.

The New York Federation is making a special study of the intermarriages among Protestants, Catholics and Hebrews, and of the changes of the children's creed from one to the other, and it is believed that the facts will prove that the changes from the Roman Catholic and Hebrew faiths are most numerous and genuine where the Protestant churches are directly ministering to the everyday life of the people, in addition to their announcement, whether overt or covert, of their conceptions of religious truth.

SOCIOLOGICAL BUREAU.

The Constitution of the United States forbids the establishment or prohibition of any form of religious belief among the people, and this, the First Amendment to the Constitution, is interpreted as a prohibition upon any inquiry, on the part of the nation, into the faiths of the people. Religious statistics were, indeed, gathered and published in connection with the census of 1890, but these facts were taken from the official publications of the various religious bodies of the country, or from replies to inquiries directed to such officials in their official capacity. No municipality of the United States has ever made, or ever can make, a religious inquiry among its population.

The New York Federation is, therefore, first of all, a sociological bureau, through which its churches and Christian organizations are put into possession of facts concerning localities, nationalities and religious communions which can be obtained in no other way, and which are especially important for the advancement of religion in New York, owing to the congestion of the city and the diversity of its nationalities and creeds. The work of this bureau has so grown in appreciation and experience since 1895 that the Board of Directors has authorized an appeal for an endowment of $500,000 for the conduct of a similar and enlarged work throughout all the future of the city's history.

The Federation has developed a system whereby it can cover one-fifth of the population of New York City in a minute sociological inquiry each year, besides handling in each year the population inquiries in the other four-fifths of the city, made by the churches having charge of co-operative parishes. The "minute sociological inquiry" referred to includes housing, educational, economical and racial conditions as well as religious conditions, and the inquiry is designed to equip the churches with those environment features which are both the limitation and the opportunity of their work, and to make this inquiry, in the name and for the sake of Christ, as frequently as the state makes inquiry for the primal purpose of apportioning representation in legislatures. In America, as in all other Christian countries, the censuses of the state are more than mere enumerations, but the facts which the state gathers are nearly always published on such a scale that they are of little avail to direct the work of particular churches or Christian organizations. In the Federal Census Bulletins concerning New York City, for example, the smallest area reported is an entire Assembly District, while in the inquiries of the Federation of Churches the facts, on the other hand, are given for each block in such Assembly District. Moreover, there is no means of connecting the State Census Bureaus, through directories of the people, with the practical work of churches and Christian organizations; but this the voluntary inquiry can and does effect.

Every church is, through the canvass and co-operative visitation, put into touch with the families that adhere to it, and the duplicate of the forms which are tabulated in the Federation's office directly acquaints them with all the environment conditions of their clientele. This information has in one or two instances revolutionized the methods of churches in the city.

The original canvassers' forms are translated in the Federation's central office into card directories of the population by blocks, nationalities and religious communions, and these directories, which are made on a pantagraph similar to those employed in the Federal Census Bureau, can be tabulated on electrical machines.

It is the application of this latest resource of statistical compilation that enables the Federation to be such an effective Sociological Bureau.

CO-OPERATIVE DISTRICT PLAN.

The Federation is gradually instituting a co-operative parish system. The lines of the districts are drawn as the result of its inquiries. It gives, for instance, blocks in which there are many Italians, to churches which are conducting work among the Italians. It gives blocks in which there are many Germans, who are Baptists, to a German Baptist church in preference to a Lutheran church. Among Americans it will give to an Episcopalian church blocks which are more largely Episcopalian than adjacent blocks which are largely Presbyterian, and which should, therefore, be assigned in preference to a Presbyterian church.

The Federation furnishes each church taking charge of a parish with a card directory of the population as at the time of the canvass. It furnishes each church, moreover, with cards of another color, but of the same size, on which the newly arrived population may be recorded. After the co-operative visitation, in reporting the results, the central Federation takes no account of the original cards yet remaining, for these families were reported, of course, in the process of the original canvass, but it does report the families recorded on the new cards.

It is the duty of the church which assumes charge of such a co-operative parish not only to visit its entire population at least once a year, but to oversee the district in moral matters. In some such parishes the churches have investigated the legality of the licenses of the saloons, and by co-operation succeeded in breaking the licenses of those whose permits had been obtained by false representation. These districts are to be watched also in regard to disorderly houses, and besides working together, on the district plan, to fight evil, the churches are beginning to combine in philanthropic matters. A summer playground has been carried on in one district by co-operative contributions from the churches, though, to their shame be it said, the largest gift was from a Jewess, and that in a district which is not very largely Hebrew. In another auxiliary the churches are considering the engagement of a physician for the district. In that same district, on the united petition of all churches, Catholic and Protestant, two blocks have been condemned for a public park. The house-to-house visitation of the Federation had shown the churches in this neighborhood that there are several blocks whose population is nearly 1,000 to an acre.

CO-OPERATIVE CALENDARS.

The New Year's Greetings of the Council of Evangelical Free Churches were anticipated in New York by a calendar, which is a good illustration of the difference between English and American conditions.

The English New Year Greetings, distributed in Birmingham, announce only the Free Church services, while the calendar of Auxiliary "A" of the New York Federation announces all places of worship—Catholic, Protestant and Hebrew—and brings to the attention of the people all the uplifting institutions of the neighborhood, such as schools, savings banks, libraries, etc., etc.

In England, where the Free churches are fighting the catechetical instruction given in schools, the greetings of the Free churches to their neighborhood could not, of course, make mention of the schools, except to their detriment; but in the New World universal education is esteemed so important that it is compulsory, and the day schools are supplemented by evening schools. The Federation, remembering that the recent immigration to New York has been from the illiterate sections of Europe, is glad to advertise the existence of these evening schools in every language spoken in a district.

INDUCTIVE CHURCH EXTENSION.

The studies of the population by the New York Federation have enabled it to suggest to the various churches' extension societies of the city suitable fields for their work, and, unlike the English Federation, it is just as glad to institute an Episcopalian as a Presbyterian or Baptist church. It has actually located two Episcopalian churches, a Lutheran church, a Moravian, and directed the Baptists in two important movements; while its sociological inquiries have located industrial and other settlements, kindergartens and similar philanthropic work. Its disclosure, in 1897, of the fact that the most populous tenement block in New York immediately adjoins its most favored residence section, was deeply influential upon the enactment of the improved tenement house legislation, which goes into effect in 1902. Its investigation of the bathing facilities of the tenements has led several of the churches to provide for this physical need of their neighborhood.

Thus, while the control of the New York Federation is Protestant, it is the friend of every church and charity that is ministering to the people, and its investigations are so comprehensive that it can aid civic religion as well as personal evangelism.

CHICAGO AND OTHER CITIES.

Chicago has a federation called the "Chicago Federation of Religious Workers." It is thus an association of individuals rather than of churches, and it will be noticed that its name is more comprehensive than that of the New York work. It does not yet appear, however, that the indefiniteness of the name has increased the vitality of the organization, which has, as yet, made no large history. Its prospectus calls for a Bureau of Information which shall do a work similar to that done in New York, and for the promotion of federative effort in various districts of the city. The president of the Federation is Prof. Graham Taylor.

The "Evangelical Alliance of Boston and Vicinity," which, as before stated, has become a practical federation of churches, as the result of the experience of the New York work, has conducted united open-air services and a ministration in the hospitals, and is moving, in the words of the report for 1900, "toward a work for the neglected sections of Boston, similar to the work in progress in New York."

Continuing the account of federation in American cities, in the order of their size, as they appear in the above statement, mention should next be made of the "Christian Federation of Cleveland," which is still in process of organization. It is not pronouncedly a federation of churches, but it yet designs to be such, and it began in January, 1901, by the distribution, in a section of the city, of a directory of church services. The organization is encountering a great deal of apathy, but may yet develop, especially if some defects in organization plan are remedied, into a strong federation.

In Pittsburg, Pa., and in Allegheny, there is a quite vigorous federation, which has instituted a house-to-house religious census, appointed a Tenement House Committee, and devoted attention to the problems for effective evangelization which arise from the Sunday and seven-day labor of that great industrial centre. It is quite apparent that the church will command the interest of laboring men in such a community in direct proportion to its interest in the adaptation of the Sabbatic code of the Hebrews, which originated among a pastoral and agricultural people, to the changed conditions of a manufacturing community. In Minnesota the state has discovered that over one-third of the workers in manufacturing establishments work on Sundays, some of them as many as fifty-two Sundays a year, and a Christian Church which shall meet the needs of workingmen must be willing to take its message into their midst, and must be the friend of remedial legislation to secure them their rights of rest.

In Detroit the Federation of Christian Churches restricts its membership to "evangelical churches," and has thereby lost the co-operation of some churches which are evangelical, but which believe that federation, on a Christian basis, is more likely to be effective if words which are shibboleths are omitted from the constitution. The federation, however, is moving slowly forward.

Jersey City has a federation which omits both the words "evangelical" and "Christian" from its constitution, but it in turn limited itself at the outset by declining to receive the negro churches into the movement.

Providence, R. I., is the centre for a federative organization which designs to cover the whole state, which is at once one of the smallest and the most urban of the states of the Union. The Federation is not yet fully under way, but it has powerful sympathizers and supporters, and the Universalists are interested, as well as the Baptists and other leading communions.

Rochester, N. Y., is having difficulty from the inclusiveness of its Federation's constitution. The Methodists have declined, as a body, to enter the work because the Unitarians are eligible for membership.

Toledo is moving toward a co-operative Protestant parish system on the lines of the New York work, and, in its religious census, is treating the Catholics and Hebrews precisely as does the New York Federation, though the constitution admits to membership only "evangelical churches."

Columbus, like Rochester, and unlike Detroit, has encountered complications because the Universalists are included, and Syracuse, on the other hand, which omits the word "evangelical" from its constitution, is progressing toward the districting of the city.

New Haven, Conn., has a federation which is four years old, and, under the oversight of the Connecticut Bible Society, which has for several years made religious tabulations in the cities of the state, but which, unlike the New York Federation, has not included sociological and educational problems in its inquiries, has already made a census of the city and divided it into sub-federations.

In Cambridge, Mass., there is an organization called "The Associated Churches." It is the creation, very largely, of Dean Hodges, of the Episcopal Divinity School. Dr. Hodges, in his book, "Faith and Social Service," has proved that co-operation is the patent duty of the hour in the church life of the nation, and the book concludes with a recommendation of the adoption, in all American cities, of work similar to the work in New York. Cambridge is divided into districts, and all churches, except the Roman Catholic and one Protestant, are in the movement.

In Methuen, Mass., the "Christian League" has been in existence since 1887, and is a result of the work of the Evangelical Alliance of the United States. It has conducted religious censuses, a successful "No License" campaign; removed objectionable illustrated papers from the news-stands; kept the theatrical billboards clean, and suppressed short-termed insurance. It is one of the earliest federations of churches, in the sense of providing, in its constitution, for church memberships. It antedates the English movement by five years.

Hartford, Conn., Winsted, New Britain and other towns of the state have federations which are operating district plans, influencing municipal administration, and carrying on various activities adapted to their varying needs, while in Erie, Pa., Easton and other cities there are organizations which adhere to the "Evangelical Alliance" title, but which are doing federative work.

The foregoing facts concerning federation in American cities prove that there is no patent plan which can be taken from one city to another and applied, without change, to meet the needs and possibilities of co-operation. One thing is certain, however, namely, that the principle called by sociologists "consciousness of kind" is a good working principle for the institution of federative work. A second fact is evident, namely, that there is not a single American city where it would be either courteous or judicious to institute a federation from which the Episcopalian churches should be excluded. Englishmen may say that this should be done, because there is not a free exchange of pulpits between the Episcopalian and other religious communions. The proper reply to this is that there are many Lutheran churches in which the same principle of exclusion obtains. It is difficult to see, however, how the needs of New York, for example, should ever be met by a federation which should exclude any auxiliary force of Christian righteousness.

Federation in rural communities has exhibited its possibilities most signally in the State of Maine. That state, in 1900, was 23.7 per cent. urban, and in 1890, when the work of the Interdenominational Commission began, was 19.7 per cent. urban. The Commission held its first meeting at Brunswick, Me., in that year, and by 1892 had passed the experimental stage. Five denominations are concerned in it, namely, the Baptists, Free Baptists, Christians, Congregationalists, and Methodists. The denominations concerned are committed to a practical co-operation in church extension in the new industrial villages. It is the custom to establish a union church through the co-operation of the missionary societies which recognize that there is an ultimate, if not an immediate, possibility of building up an independent work. Such churches continue to be union churches under the oversight of the Commission for a period of years, and then, by a vote, the churches determine to what denomination they shall thereafter adhere. The Millinockett church, which was founded among a new community on the borders of the Penobscot and Aroostook pulp region, is the historic and prophetic instance of such co-operation in church extension. The building was erected jointly, a minister was placed in charge, and it was agreed that the work should be a union work till one denomination should assume sole support by the consent of the majority. The principle is further applied by making canvasses of communities in which church extension is desired or projected, and the canvass sometimes determines the particular communion which is to enter.

The State of Vermont is even more rural than Maine, having but 11.2 per cent. of urban population. Its Governor has recently publicly bemoaned the decadence of its Christian institutions. This decadence, in the minds of many of the local Christian workers, is believed to be traceable to the lack of federative common-sense in the conduct of home mission work. One worker says: "We were forced into forming a committee on interdenominational comity by the fact that in many of our small villages some three or four denominations were at work, all weak, and demanding missionary aid, and none of them really doing much for the communities. In a few cases adjustments have been made and one has retired to make room for others. A weak body yields to a stronger one in a given locality, and that stronger one yields in another place where it may be weak. Practical men are beginning to feel that something must be done to prevent waste and give more efficient service." The Congregationalists, Baptists, Methodists, Christians and Free Baptists are here co-operating as in the State of Maine.

It is without doubt true that there are many states of the American Union which need commissions similar to that in the State of Maine and in Vermont. Massachusetts and New York and Pennsylvania already have committees on comity, but they are not in any instance inclusive of all of the strong communions of these states, and it is altogether likely that this particular aspect of federation work has a more hopeful field in the states which are less than half urban than in the states where the majority of the population is domiciled in cities. Even thus, however, federation can effect great economies which will be honored of Him who acquired His Messianic consciousness in the thickly settled Galilee of His time, and who, after working His great miracle, in the comparative desert across its lake, said to His disciples: "Gather up the fragments, that nothing be lost."

In these sparsely settled areas, as well as in the cities of alien population, federation in the New World must work out its own problems, emulating, but not imitating, the methods of federation in the Old.

ROBERT RAIKES.

THE SUNDAY SCHOOL.

A. F. Schauffler, D.D.,

NEW YORK.

[We are the chisel with which God carves His statues. The mother, the teacher, the Christian friend, must carve and mould the life of the child into the beauty of the Lord. The sculptor needs his chisel; but the chisel can do nothing, produce no beauty of itself. We must put ourselves into Christ's hands that he may use us. God will work through us only when we humbly, in faith and love and self-renunciation, lay ourselves into his hands. There is a hallowing and an inspiring influence in the thought that we are working beside God in what he is doing on immortal lives. Are we worthy to do it? Hawthorne, speaking of a block of marble, and the possibilities of beauty that lie in it, waiting to be brought out, said that the stone assumed a sacred character, and that no man should dare touch it unless he felt within himself a consecration and a priesthood. If this be true when it is only a block of marble that is to be wrought upon, how much more is it true of a human soul —a child's life, for example, laid in a mother's arms; any life laid in your hands or mine—that we may free the angel that waits within it? It is a most sacred moment when a life is put before us to be touched by us. Suppose that the mother—suppose that you or I—should not do the holy work well, and the life should be marred, hurt, stunted, its beauty blurred, its purity stained, its power weakened; think of the sadness of the result. How sweet the mother must keep her own spirit, how gentle, how patient, how pure and true, while she is working with God in nursing her child for Him! How heavenly must the teacher keep his temper, how quiet, how unselfish, how Christlike, when he is sitting beside the Master, working with Him on the lives of the scholars!—J. R. Miller, D. D. "The Building of Character," p. 54.—Ed.]

*   *   *

Modern Sunday-schools date from July, 1780, when Robert Raikes, moved by the spiritual destitution of the poorer class of children in the city of Gloucester, England, started a Sunday-school for their benefit. As early as 1787 there were in Great Britain as many as 250,000 pupils enrolled in these schools. Intended at the start for the more illiterate classes, they soon found favor among the better educated, until at the present time there is no community where they are not to be found. The result is that at the present day the Sunday-school army is numbered by the million. It is distributed as follows: In North America—Schools, 148,139; teachers, 1,482,308; scholars, 12,017,325; total, 13,499,633. Great Britain and

Ireland—Schools, 47,060; teachers, 676,151; scholars, 6,979,913; total, 7,703,124. Massing all other lands, we find that they have in their Sunday-schools a total of 3,330,547, making, with the above-named lands, a grand total in the Sunday-school army of 24,553,314.

For many years the Bible was studied with the aid of such lesson helps as teachers could secure, but in time there came to be prepared by various publishing houses regular "Question Books," which secured a considerable circulation. As yet, however, there was no such thing as uniformity in the parts of Scripture studied. Indeed, the stricter denominations, like the Episcopal and the Lutheran, used their own church catechisms for the instruction of the young. As the results of much thought, study and conference, in 1872 what is called the "International Lesson System" was adopted in the United States, and soon largely accepted in Canada, Great Britain and other English-speaking lands. The ruling thought of this system was that in all Sunday-schools, and all classes in the same school, the same portion of Scripture should be studied on the same day. Such favor did this system find, that at the present day a vast majority of Sunday-schools the world over have taken it up, and its adherents are numbered by millions.

One of the results of the wide adoption of the International Lesson System has been that many of the ablest divines and teachers in the church have been engaged to write "Teachers' Helps" of various kinds, so that now the average teacher has such assistance as those in the last century never could have secured.

For the further education of the vast army of teachers, summer schools such as that of Chautauqua, Framingham, Round Lake, etc., have been started, where in the summer season teachers could receive instruction as to not only the Book itself, but also as to principles of pedagogy, to better fit them for their work. Conventions—county, state, national and international—have sprung up, where those most competent are ready to give instruction and exchange views with regard to the Word and the work.

One of the latest additions to the Sunday-school has been the "Home Department." It was found that there were multitudes who for various good reasons were not able to attend the regular sessions of the Sunday-school, who yet were anxious to adopt some systematic line of Biblical study. This being the case, it was not difficult to enlist such persons in the study of the regular lesson of the Sunday-school, and so great has been the number of those joining the

THE SUNDAY-SCHOOL.

Home Department that (at least in the United States) an especial literature has sprung up for their benefit.

At first all the work of teaching and superintending the Sunday-school was done by volunteers. But the vast importance of the work to be done has so impressed itself on the mind of the church that it is now not uncommon to meet with regularly trained and paid Sunday-school superintendents, who in turn train their corps of volunteer teachers. In the primary departments of many of our Sunday-schools may be found paid teachers, who have had especial training in Kindergarten work.

Sunday-school work has modified largely church architecture. In former days there was no provision made for the right accommodation of classes. The conventional church edifice consisted of an auditorium (called the church) and an additional room called the prayer meeting room. Now no church can be considered "well-appointed" unless it has made especial provision for the wants of the Sunday-school. Primary rooms, adult class rooms, and well-adapted "forms" for the smaller classes can be found in every city, in great numbers of churches, and in some cases the Sunday-school appointments have cost the church as much as the main structure itself.

As between the Sunday-school at the beginning of the nineteenth century, and that at the close, there is a vast difference. About the only things that have remained the same are the prayers and the kindly relationship between teacher and scholar. All else has changed vastly. The music is better, the library has improved, the weekly papers are a great advance on what they used to be, the whole organization has made progress, and the grade of teaching is higher.

In spite, however, of all this encouraging progress, none knows better than the trained Sunday-school worker that we are still far from the true goal at which we should aim. "There is yet much land to be possessed." For while some noted Sunday-schools are very near the hundred per cent. mark, the vast majority are only fifty per cent., if not lower even than that. Every experienced worker needs but to go to almost any of our Sunday-schools, and to keep his eyes open, to see how far short they come in the matter of promptitude, order, good singing, and above all, good teaching. Teachers minus classes, classes minus teachers, disorderly classes, listless scholars—all these things will soon be apparent to the careful observer. And, if more careful investigation be made, many other defects will soon be discovered, such as loss of scholars, deficient grading, worn-out condition of the library, dilapidated state and insufficient number of hymn-books.

If now we pause and ask, "What is it that constitutes the difference between the good Sunday-school and the one that is deficient?" we shall, in the last resort, find it expressed in the one word *leadership*.

The secret of the excellence of our noted Sunday-schools is always to be found in the fact that some really able man is at the head and directs the various departments of the school. Given such a man and the success of the school is assured, in spite of any adverse circumstances that may surround the school. I have seen a very good school in most inadequate rooms, and a very bad school in palatial quarters. I have seen a most orderly school in the roughest tenement district, and a most disorderly school in a quiet New England village. Why this difference? Simply because of the difference in the leader. Put a John Wanamaker into any mob of a school, and he will before long evolve order out of chaos; or put a Frank A. Ferris into the most disorganized school, and in a year you will find it most highly and sensibly organized.

But such lay workers are like angels' visits, "few and far between." For one of these competent men we find a hundred that are incompetent. By far the larger part of the superintendents in our land are not even college graduates, and the vast majority of our teachers have no higher education than that given in our grammar schools. Here and there a man like those mentioned above has quite exceptional ability, which soon shows itself. But this is not the case with the majority. It must ever remain true that the average superintendent does not know how to fill his office successfully, and the average teacher does poor work from the pedagogical standpoint.

Must this remain the case through the whole of the twentieth century? Not necessarily. There is a remedy for all this paucity of competent Sunday-school workers.

In looking forward to the coming century, it seems to the writer that the main need of the Sunday-school is the more systematic preparation of the teacher for the work required. Of necessity, teachers must be recruited from the ranks of the laity. The vast majority of them are, and ever must be, more or less unfitted for the best work. In our public schools we employ only those who have been through a process of pedagogical instruction. The lack of any such instruction is a sore evil in the Sunday-school. When in addition to this it is remembered that the body of Sunday-school teachers is constantly changing, and new and utterly inexperienced teachers are coming to the front, the need of some systematic teaching of the teacher is more and more apparent. On an average, teachers change about once in four years. Merely to state this fact is to prove the need of such preparation. No adequate provision can be made for such instruction, unless it be found in the ranks of the ordained ministry. The minister of the church must, in the last resort, be responsible for the right training of his teachers how to teach. But for the average minister, as at present furnished by our theological seminaries, to do this, is not possible. He is not fitted for the important task. Therefore it would seem as though in all of our theological seminaries an especial department should be maintained in which pedagogical principles could be taught, so that the graduate should be the competent leader and instructor of his own corps of teachers. When the seminaries turn out ministers able to teach teachers how and what to teach, then, and not until then, will the force of Sunday-school teachers be thoroughly competent to do the work that is required of them.

So potent has been the influence of Sunday-schools that our Roman Catholic friends have been forced to establish such schools for their own children and youth in all Protestant lands. Otherwise they found that their children were largely lost to them, for they easily found their way into the attractive Sunday-schools of the various Protestant churches. This holds true only in those lands where Protestantism and Catholicism are brought into competition. Even Jewish communities have had to have recourse to something similar to the modern Sunday-school so as to keep their young people from seeking entrance into Gentile schools.

THE DEVELOPMENT OF THE YOUNG MEN'S CHRISTIAN ASSOCIATION.

PRESIDENT L. L. DOGGETT, Ph.D.,
SPRINGFIELD.

[The nineteenth century excelled all its predecessors in its extraordinary scientific discoveries and its ingenious and useful inventions. Among what may be called its religious inventions I would assign the highest place to the Young Men's Christian Association; for foreign missionary societies were started by William Carey in the closing years of the eighteenth century. If any man of our era was directly guided by the Holy Spirit to "rise up and build," it was our beloved friend Sir George Williams, who organized the first Young Men's Christian Association in June, 1844. He "builded better than he knew," for the "Grand Old Man" has lived to see more than six thousand associations, belting the whole globe, with half a million members, and ten times that number in some direct connection with the organization.

The Young Men's Christian Association is not a society on paper; it has housed itself in hundreds of solid structures (at a cost of many millions), each one a social home, a place for physical development, mental instruction and training for Christ's service. It has brought thousands of young men from impenitence to Christ Jesus, and made thousands of young Christians more like Jesus in their daily lives. The most effective lay preacher and organizer of the century, Dwight L. Moody, confessed that in his training for spiritual work he owed more to the Young Men's Christian Association than to any other human agency. To the world-known name of Moody may be added the names of William E. Dodge, Jr., Cyrus H. McCormick, Robert R. McBurney, William E. Shipton of London, John R. Mott, Richard C. Morse, John Wanamaker, and hundreds of others to whom our association has been both an inspiration and instructor in the Master's service. It has moulded the students of colleges and universities; it has put a Christian signal-light into the hands of thousands of railroad men; it has been a salvation to many a soldier and sailor; it has led many into the Gospel ministry; it has taught the whole world the beauty and power of a living unity in the Lord Jesus Christ. The Holy Spirit has set the divine seal of His approval and blessing on its world-wide work, and to the Triune God be all the praise and all the glory!—THEODORE L. CUYLER.

The Young Men's Christian Association, by its own work and by the work of the organizations inspired by it, has been the chief influence of the century in making Christianity a life to live instead of a theory to talk about. This means that it has helped to make it a reality to be reckoned with now, rather than an ideal to be aspired to some time. The effect of this influence upon the young manhood of the world is one of the modern miracles which attest to this practical age the truth of the Gospel of our Lord and Master, Christ, and is spreading His Kingdom mightily in the hearts of the strong men of this age of strength and power. Through it the educated men of our day are more strongly and sanely religious than ever before; through it the business men are more and more approving the business methods of the Church of God and conforming their own methods to its standards; through it we may well expect that the ever-increasing emphasis laid by the public conscience on our duty toward our neighbor will lead to a like increasing recognition of our duty toward God as a correlative and inseparable obligation. This influence is the great achievement of the century. The wonderful statistics of growth in numbers, equipment and efficiency are only hints of the significance of this achievement.—JAMES L. HOUGHTELING.—ED.]

*   *   *

THE task of the twentieth century will be the setting up of the Kingdom of God in the city. The most important element in the city population is made up of young men. The city will dominate the civilization of the new century, and the young men will dominate the city. The first achievement of the Young Men's Christian Association has been the creation of an agency for winning young men of the city to Jesus Christ.

In addition to work for young men in cities, the Association in America has reached out to all classes of young men. In America there are 5,000,000 young men in cities, 1,000,000 men employed upon railroads, 100,000 men in the army and navy, and 200,000 young men in institutions of higher learning. The most successful agency in carrying the Gospel to this unique and important body of men is the Young Men's Christian Association.

The history of the Association falls into two periods: the period of volunteer effort and the period of secretarial leadership. These are roughly separated by the year 1871, when the conference of the secretaries of North America was established. Prior to this time the leadership of the Association was in the hands of experts who were employed to give their whole time to work among young men.

The first achievement of this period was the founding of the Association under the leadership of George Williams. With remarkable rapidity the idea, which first took definite shape at London on June 6, 1844, spread to the continent and to the United States. In 1855, 97 representatives of 329 different associations, from nine different countries, from all Protestant denominations, representing a membership of 30,000 young men, assembled at Paris and announced to the Christian world the platform upon which the new organization would stand:

"The Young Men's Christian Associations seek to unite those young men who, regarding Jesus Christ as their God and Saviour according to the Holy Scriptures, desire to be His disciples in their doctrine and in their life, and to associate their efforts for the extension of His Kingdom among young men."

The second achievement of this period was the inaugurating of the international work in America, under the leadership of William Chauncey Langdon, of Washington. With prophetic eye, when there were but seven associations in the United States, he saw an organization of Christian young men touching every city in the land, bound together by ties of fellowship into a national union, moving toward one common end. The First International Committee was located at Washington in 1854, with Mr. Langdon as corresponding secretary. For twelve years the committee moved from place to place, until 1866, when, on the motion of Robert R. McBurney, permanent headquarters were established in New York City, with Mr. Cephas Brainerd as chairman. The American associations were the first to awaken to a national consciousness. This plan of administration under an executive committee was adopted by the World's Conference in 1878, introduced into England in 1882, and into Germany a year later. Thus an association polity was created which makes the local Association the original and independent unit of organization, and places the supervising agencies in an advisory relationship. It has proved elastic, adaptable and efficient.

It was through the Young Men's Christian Association that the great awakening of 1857 and 1858 touched American religious life. No preacher or evangelist stands out as the leader of this revival. It was characterized by meetings for prayer by laymen, usually at the noon hour, under the auspices of Young Men's Christian Associations. In this movement was developed the type of evangelistic work and Gospel music which has been dominant in the church under the leadership of Mr. Dwight L. Moody. This revival quickened the spiritual life of the associations not only in the United States, but in the British Isles, and stamped an ineffaceable evangelistic character upon them. At the same time it diverted many associations in America from specific work for young men by young men, and led a large section of the American movement for years into general evangelistic endeavor. It created for the Association the Men's Gospel Meeting.

SIR GEORGE WILLIAMS.

It was probably owing to the religious awakening preceding the Civil War that the Young Men's Christian Association for the first time undertook, in a systematic way, to carry the Gospel to soldiers under arms. The United States Christian Commission was an outgrowth of the Army Committee of the New York Association. It was organized at a national convention of the associations, held at New York City, November 14, 1861. The chairman of the International Committee, George H. Stuart, of Philadelphia, became chairman of the Christian Commission during the war. This commission raised $6,000,000 in money and supplies for the needs of the soldiers, and sent out 5,000 delegates, who served, without pay, an average of thirty-eight days each in the field. Thus was inaugurated a new form of Christian work.

While the Continental and British associations were tenaciously true to the evangelical faith, and while the American conventions had approved the Paris basis, it was not yet clear in America that the control of the associations would be placed solely in the hands of evangelical Christians. In 1868, 146 associations in America enrolled, as active members, only those who were members of an evangelical church, while 70 associations made no distinction in the membership. The American convention at Portland, in 1869, declared that in the future only associations which limited active membership to members in good standing in evangelical churches should be recognized as belonging to the Association movement. This identified the Association with the Evangelical Church.

At the close of this period there were in America 780 associations, with 95,000 members. There was about an equal membership in Europe. Under volunteer leadership the Association was founded, the international work established, a great revival promoted, work among soldiers carried on, and the Association placed on an evangelical basis.

The growing complexity of the Association, the fluctuating character of service by volunteers, and the multiplication of cities, created a demand for a new office—the secretaryship. The development of this office has resulted in the establishment of two schools: one at Springfield, Mass., in 1885, and one at Chicago, Ill., in 1890, for the special training of men for Association work.

The first achievement of this period in the United States was the bringing of the Association back to a definite work for young men by young men.

Already, under the leadership of laymen, the associations had conceived the idea of ministering to the intellectual and social as well as to the spiritual needs of young men, but it was under the leadership of Robert R. McBurney and other secretaries that the idea of an all-round work for young men was systematized and developed; first in New York city, and then elsewhere. It was through the leadership of the secretary that the Association, in addition to its evangelistic work, became also an agency for the culture of Christian manhood. It was this ideal which later created the physical and educational departments. To-day there are 77,485 members enrolled in the gymnasiums in the United States and Canada, and 27,000 students in the educational classes. It was this form of work for young men, developed in America, which was introduced into Germany in 1883, and later into non-Christian lands.

The third development during this period was the building movement. The first building which embodied the Association ideal of all-round work for young men was the building erected on the corner of Twenty-third street and Fourth avenue, in New York City, under the direction of Mr. McBurney, at a cost of $487,000. Under the stimulus of this example, slowly at first, but since 1885 with greater rapidity, these Association buildings have been erected in all parts of the world, until to-day there are 359 buildings in the United States and Canada, valued at $20,378,480; in the British Isles, 126 buildings, valued at $3,213,960; on the continent of Europe, 126 buildings, valued at $1,855,570; in other lands, 29 buildings, valued at $874,000; a total of 640 buildings, valued at $26,322,010. It is interesting to note that the American type of Association building has become dominant.

The fourth characteristic of this period was the extension of the work of the Association to various classes of young men. In 1872 work was begun for railroad men by the Cleveland Association. This became a department of the International Committee in 1877. To-day, in the United States and Canada, 37,000 railroad men are associated together in 159 associations, with $1,122,650 worth of property, either owned or set aside for their use, and to which the railroad corporations last year contributed $195,000. This is probably the most successful Christian work among workingmen carried on at the present time.

In 1887, under the leadership of the **American International Committee**, the intercollegiate work of the **Young Men's Christian**

Association, that had been inaugurated at Louisville, Ky., in 1877, was organized and carried to the students of the world. While this movement does not embody the all-round ideal of work for the whole man, it is the most successful example of directly religious work among young men in the modern church. From it has sprung the Young Women's Christian Association, the Student Missionary Volunteer Movement, and the World's Student Christian Federation. This intercollegiate movement enrolls under one management 65,000 young men, who are students in 1,400 institutions in 30 countries. It has fired the missionary zeal of the most intelligent youth of Protestantism, it has awakened an interest in the study of the Bible which has advanced that of the city associations. There are now 30 Student Association buildings, the value of which is estimated to be $1,000,000. In 1877, Mr. L. D. Wishard became the first secretary of this movement. There are now 75 secretaries, either local or international, devoting their whole time to work among students. In Bible classes there are 14,000 students enrolled.

In addition to the railroad and student departments, the American Association has extended its work to Indian young men, colored young men, foreign-speaking young men, and recently to men of the army and navy. A building for the use of the New York Army Branch has been erected on Governor's Island. Associations are being carried on with many of the regiments in the Philippines. During the past year the work has reached the troops in Alaska and China, and an attempt is being made to reach all the army posts. In the navy over 2,000 sailors have joined the Temperance League of the Association, and, through the generosity of Miss Helen Gould, a building at an expense of over $400,000 is being erected near the Brooklyn Navy Yard for the exclusive use of the naval Young Men's Christian Association.

In non-Christian lands work is being carried on among two classes of young men—students and young men in cities. Work among students was introduced in Ceylon in 1886, and Japan in 1888. In 1889, in response to an appeal from the missionaries of India, an American secretary was sent by the International Committee to become secretary of the Association at Madras. The American International Committee has now under its direction twenty secretaries in India, Ceylon, Japan, China and Brazil. This has already proved a most fruitful form of foreign missionary endeavor.

The Paris Convention defined the work of the Association as work for young men. For many years the field of effort was among young men of sixteen or eighteen years of age and upward. A desultory and limited work among boys was carried on with a view to supplying leaders for the senior department. But the American associations, stimulated by modern scientific study, have awakened to the consciousness that their work should begin when the boy is becoming a man—at the dawn of consciousness. There are nearly as many boys between the ages of twelve and eighteen as there are young men between the ages of eighteen and thirty. With the opening of the century the Association enters this new field of opportunity.

The chief agency in fostering the work in the United States has been the American International Committee, located at New York City. This committee, of which Mr. Cephas Brainerd was for twenty-five years the chairman, and of which Dr. Lucien C. Warner is now chairman, consists at present of forty-one gentlemen from different parts of the country, a quorum of which is located in New York City. The committee is chosen at the biennial conventions of the associations, and has in its employ 34 office and traveling secretaries in this country, besides 20 men in foreign lands. The International Committee's budget for 1899 for the administration of the home work was $129,825, and for the foreign work, $33,220. The World's Committee is located at Geneva, Switzerland, and supervises the work of the associations in all lands. The general secretary of this committee is M. Charles Fermaud.

The twentieth century opens with the Young Men's Christian Association organized at 6,192 points, in 50 countries, and enrolling a membership of 521,077. A survey of this field shows that by far the leading group of associations is found in America. While the North American associations number but 1,439, they enroll 49 per cent. of the members; they own 77 per cent. of the property.

What is it which has given the American associations this preeminence? It is chiefly due to the supervising agencies which are found in this country—the city secretaryship, developed and exemplified by Robert R. McBurney, and the secretaryship of the general agencies, developed under the leadership of Richard C. Morse. The Association secretaryship, including the physical and educational directorship, is perhaps the greatest contribution of the Association to modern religious life. Already there are 682 general secretaries employed in the United States and Canada, 79 per cent.

of those engaged in all lands. There are 99 international and state secretaries, and 262 physical and educational directors.

The two training schools in America enroll nearly one hundred students and have developed a thorough course of study for the training of men for this service. One in five of the secretaries and directors in America have had the preparation offered at these schools.

The Young Men's Christian Association enters upon this new century with the vigor of youth, with a well-defined aim, a widely extended organization, a trained leadership, and the hearty support of the Evangelical Church. We can say with the old Covenanter:

"He hath not caused us to trust in His name,
And brought us thus far to put us to shame."

When you come to view this work in all its departments, it is a remarkable grouping of agencies for the advancement of the Kingdom of Christ among young men. It has lived down prejudices and has won its way to the confidence of the Christian public, and its future place and continued usefulness are assured beyond dispute.

* * * * * * * * *

The founder of the Young Men's Christian Association, George Williams, was born at Asbury Farmhouse, near Dulverton, South England, in 1821. In 1841 he went to London and became a clerk in a dry goods house facing St. Paul's churchyard, of which he is now the proprietor. He became interested, when yet but twenty-three years of age, in the religious well-being of the eighty or more young men employed in this and other business houses in London. The movement took definite shape June 6, 1844, and was named by Christopher Smith, Mr. Williams' room-mate. The constitution provided that the Association should seek to promote the spiritual and mental improvement of young men engaged in the drapery trade. But a movement so manifestly of God could not be confined within such narrow limits; it speedily assumed important proportions. In a short time prayer-meetings and Bible classes were begun in fourteen different business houses, and a missionary to young men was employed as early as January, 1845. In 1848 apartments were rented in which a library, reading-room, restaurant, social parlors, and educational classes were provided. A lecture course was established, which soon became the most important lecture platform in London. Thus the Association was marked from its very inception by intense religious zeal.

Knowledge of this work, by and for young men, reached America in the autumn of 1851. On this continent, Montreal has the distinction of organizing the first Y. M. C. A., Nov. 25, 1851; while Boston followed on Dec. 29, 1851. As the Boston society gave character and direction to the American movement, it was fitting that the Jubilee Anniversary of the North American Young Men's Christian Associations should be held there. This jubilee took place June 11-16, 1901.

A truly great gathering it was, and unique in the history of the continent. The thought that perhaps most impressed itself upon us as we read was, what a revelation we have here of the growing sense of brotherhood among men of all nations in their efforts to extend the kingdom and work of Christ. Asiatic and African joined with Caucasian, Slav with Teuton, Frenchman with German, the Indian of Asia with the Indian of America, in a visible unity and in audible pledges of brotherhood, and an African ex-slave, Booker T. Washington, apparently received the greatest personal ovation of the entire session. Two priests of the Orthodox Greek Church of Russia were present as authorized delegates, and almost every Protestant country under the stars had its representatives. A personal message from King Edward VII was read by Mr. Howard Williams, son of the illustrious founder of the organization, and its reading was followed by the singing of "God Save the King," and three hearty cheers from an audience of six thousand people. A message from the Emperor William of Germany was read by Pastor Klug, of Berlin, and the King of Catholic Italy also sent a message wishing the organization God-speed. Surely such things speak of a growing catholicity of feeling, and also of the adaptability and usefulness of the Y. M. C. A. throughout the world.

"It is worth while once in fifty years to stop to celebrate a jubilee. This pause has been worth a hundred onslaughts. It has meant more for the young men of the world than a universal evangelistic campaign. The results in ten years will fully justify this statement, for in that time the number of the associations will not only double, but their efficiency will increase in a ratio that we do not venture to compute. The greatness of the value of this gathering to the Kingdom of God will not be realized even by its delegates within the year. A greater work for young men has been made possible—not only possible, but imperative—to the associations in every land, state, city and town. The universal usability of the Young Men's Christian Association is recognized because it has served in so wide a field. The jubilee revealed the Association's place in the world and its moral, social and economic value. The fallacy of the argument that it is tethered by its spiritual purposes has been thoroughly refuted. It has been examined by the public, business men, rulers of nations, and the church, and certified to, not as a visionist's theory, but as a fifty-year demonstration of serviceableness to men in the cities, towns, colleges, army, navy, mines, farms, railroads, in foreign lands and for all men, ministering to the man and conserving his entire well-being. In its work every man, poor or rich, in humble position or of royal rank, finds unlimited and unhampered place of service and personal benefit. This jubilee was not a brass band and tinsel parade of self-inflated egotists; the great evangelistic meeting of Sunday afternoon, with 4,500 men in attendance, held in Back Bay of cultured Boston, with 441 men registering as impressed to begin a Christian life, and the pledge of over $15,000 to extend Association work in foreign lands, proved the sincerity of a spiritual ambition to be well pleasing to God and of service to men. The Young Men's Christian Association in every place will be forced to elevate the standard of its work because of this jubilee. A higher grade of life and service will be demanded by the Christian public. The Association must be faithful to its great mission as a world organization. It can never again be content to simply hold its own. A larger name and place and field and work and ideals and obligations are given to it from this time on, and it must measure up to its new name and place. But the world will not care for the Young Men's Christian Association except as it continues to care for men."—"Association Men."—ED.

EVANGELICAL ALLIANCE.

Rev. William D. Grant, Ph.D.,
NEW YORK.

[Christ spoke of the church as His body. Where is there an organism so perfectly and exquisitely organized as the human body? Where is there such wonderful and beautiful and effective coöperation as between the members of the human body? It seems to me that the fact that Christ called His church His body is more than a hint that there should be perfect organization; that there should be perfect coöperation between members of that body. One hundred eyes do not make an organized body. One hundred hands do not make an organized body. There must be the different members having different offices, and each sustaining and aiding the others. My one pair of eyes makes my hands worth more than one hundred hands without eyes. Thus each organ, doing its proper duty, multiplies the efficiency of all the other organs. That is a truth that the Christian Church has yet to learn. These Christian churches are competing with each other as a matter of fact now. Different denominations are each watching the others, and vying with each other to get ahead of each other. The real principle, unconfessed, it is true, upon which the Christian churches are operating now in our cities and villages is the principle of competition. It is not the principle of coöperation. And in this competition they do not all move in parallel lines; they interfere, and they arrest and dissipate their energies, and neutralize one another. They have not learned, as the several organs of the body, how to coöperate, and hence multiply the efficiency of each other tenfold or fifty or a hundredfold.—Josiah Strong, D.D.—Ed.]

* * *

Near the end of the first half of the last century a spirit of Christian unity began to manifest itself in different countries, among the more prominent evangelical ministers. It was being more clearly seen and felt that the bonds which united them were vastly stronger than the questions which tended to separate them. There arose a longing, therefore, for an expression of a unity which already existed in spirit and in fact. Conspicuous among those who were desirous that some action might be taken which would give tangible evidence of the existence of such a spirit of oneness among Protestant Christians were Thomas Chalmers, of Scotland; John Angell James, of England; George Fisch, of France; Merle D'Aubigné, of Switzerland, and William Patton, Samuel H. Cox, Lyman Beecher and others, of the United States.

WILLIAM PATTON, D.D.

In the year 1843 a meeting of the Congregational Union of England gave large consideration to the question of greater unity among the various denominations of Christendom. In that year the Established Church of Scotland also appointed a committee to report on the same matter. The project afforded an important element of discussion in the Bicentenary of the Westminster Assembly, held in Edinburgh July of that same year. A conference of different denominations held in the Wesleyan Centenary Hall, in February, 1845, also gave to the movement mature consideration. At length a meeting, preliminary to organization, was held in Liverpool in October, 1845. At this meeting were assembled as many as two hundred ministers and laymen, representing nearly twenty denominations. The "British Quarterly" (Vol. III, p. 527) says of this gathering: "We speak advisedly when we say that we regard that meeting as presenting a more mature result of Christian judgment and of Christian affection than has been exhibited in the history of Christianity since the age of inspired teaching." At this meeting, after much conference and prayer, it was resolved to call a general conference to meet the following year in London. As much fervent prayer continued, and widespread discussion obtained through the public press, great enthusiasm was awakened, so that, at the meeting convened for organization in Freemasons' Hall, in London, August 19, 1846, there were present eight hundred delegates, representing fifty denominations. It was at this meeting, which continued in session fifteen days, that John Angell James, in an address, credited Dr. William Patton, of New York, with *having first conceived and suggested the idea* of the Evangelical Alliance. This conference and the preliminary gatherings included many of the most distinguished men, clerical and lay, in all the churches, and some of the noblest Christian leaders of their time. Thus it will be seen that the Evangelical Alliance was formed not more to awaken than to give expression to the spirit of Christian unity already existing. The object of the Alliance, as stated in its constitution, "shall be the furtherance of religious opinion, with the intent to manifest and strengthen Christian unity, and to promote religious liberty and coöperation in Christian work, without interfering with the internal affairs of the different denominations."

The motto chosen being: *Unum corpus sumus in Christo.* And the working principle of the association being: In essentials, unity; in non-essentials, charity; in all things, liberty.

More than a passing notice should here be given to Wm. Patton, whose name appears above. Born in Philadelphia, August 23, 1798, of Scotch-Irish descent, his father being Colonel Robert Patton, who came in his youth to this country, was an officer in the Army of the Revolution, and served under Lafayette. On the side of his mother, Cornelia Bridges, Dr. Patton could trace his descent from the family of Oliver Cromwell.

In his nineteenth year he united with the First Presbyterian Church of Philadelphia. He graduated in 1818, at the Middlebury College, and studied theology for about a year at Princeton, when he was licensed to preach by the Addison Congregational Association of Vermont, June, 1819. Shortly thereafter he married Mary Weston, of New York City. To this union ten children were given.

In 1820 he took up his residence in New York City, and at his own expense hired a small schoolhouse on the edge of the town, just north of Canal street, in which to begin religious services; having notified the community, services were begun on the first Sabbath in March, 1820. At his first service he had an audience of seven persons. Out of this humble beginning has grown the Central Presbyterian Church, whose history constitutes so important a chapter in the later religious annals of New York City.

The church was organized January, 1821, and young Patton installed as pastor. Here for twelve years with signal success he labored. During this period 564 persons united with the church on confession. Harlan Page was one of the elders of the church and superintendent of its Sunday-school.

That Dr. Patton's influence reached beyond his own congregation appears in the fact that he took a leading part in organizing the American Home Missionary Society, and later, in 1831, the Third Presbytery in New York. In 1834 he accepted an appointment as secretary of the Central American Educational Society. For the space of three years he gave himself up to the cause of ministerial education with characteristic energy and enthusiasm. It was at this time, when his whole soul was aglow with the thought of training laborers and sending them forth into the Lord's harvest field, that he suggested the location of a theological seminary in the city of New York. If not the first to suggest a theological seminary in the vicinity of New York, he was certainly the first to suggest one in the city itself, as a letter written to Dr. Edwin F. Hatfield in 1876 bears witness. And so enthusiastic was he respecting the founding of such an institution, and so influential among men of means, that of the $75,000 required for the maintenance of the institution for the first five years, personally he secured $50,000. Here was the origin of the Union Theological Seminary, in the founding of which, as is manifest, Dr. Patton took no small part. He was active in all the early meetings of the institution, and for many years (1836-1849) was a most efficient member of the board of directors.*

Dr. Patton was deeply interested also in the establishment of the University of the City of New York, in which his brother Robert, the eminent Greek scholar, was a professor.

In his fortieth year he accepted a call to the Spring Street Presbyterian

---

Vide Dr. George L. Prentiss: "Fifty Years of the Union Theological Seminary," pp. 12-14.

Church, being installed October 11, 1837. This second pastorate lasted ten years, and was not less remarkable for its fruitfulness than the first.

From New York he went to New Haven, where he served the Hammond Street Congregational Church, engaging at the same time in literary work.

He frequently crossed the ocean, and spent a good deal of his time in England, a warm friendship existing between him and John Angell James, of Birmingham, who once stated publicly that for the character and success of his ministry he had been more indebted to the early influence of his friend Dr. Patton than to any other human cause.

Dr. Patton was a firm believer in spiritual seasons of religious awakening, and labored earnestly, especially by republishing President Edwards' and Mr. Finney's writings on the subject, in order if possible to promote such revivals in Great Britain. That he was a man of strong catholicity of spirit, and took a deep interest in everything looking toward closer union among the followers of Christ, is witnessed to by a letter, of March 28, 1843, addressed to his friend John Angell James. In this letter Dr. Patton says: "It appears to me that the time cannot be distant when it will be most proper to call a convention of delegates from the evangelical churches to meet in London for the purpose of setting forth the great essential truths in which they are agreed. I know of no known object which would awaken deeper interest than such a convention. It would command the attendance of some of our strongest men from all evangelical denominations, and the result would be a statement of views which would have a most blessed effect." (See page 124 of Dr. Prentiss' book for entire letter.)

Mr. James, in publishing this letter, added: "The subject of this letter is of momentous consequence; it presents a splendid conception of the human mind." We have already seen that that letter was not without fruit, viz., the Evangelical Alliance itself.

Dr. Patton was in full sympathy with the reformatory spirit of the age. Strong anti-slavery principles came to him as a heritage from his father, who declined an offer from President Madison to make him Postmaster-General because unwilling to remove his family to a slave-holding community. He was a man of large and generous views, strong in his convictions of right and duty, as well as bold in asserting them; a natural enemy of wrong, oppression and intolerance, and one of the earliest and ablest advocates of temperance reform; an ardent patriot, whether at home or abroad, and a firm believer in the providential mission and destiny of the American people. In the days of his power, and this continued with him even into old age, Dr. Patton was a very earnest and effective preacher. The arguments, illustrations and applications of his discourses were alike fitted to make deep and lasting impressions. He was also a writer of considerable note. In 1833 he recast an English commentary called "The Cottage Bible," published in two volumes; of this publication nearly 200,000 copies were sold before his death. Then followed "The Cottage Testament," "The Christian Psalmist," "The Judgment of Jerusalem and Jesus of Nazareth," "The People's Bible Illustrated by Bible Characters," etc.

Dr. Patton died at New Haven, September 9, 1879, in the eighty-second year of his age.

The association thus established set before itself the task of promoting brotherly love, religious liberty, Sabbath observance, Christian education, and of being a bond of union between evangelical Christians of all churches and of all lands. This has been done through correspondence, coöperation, conferences, united action, and united prayer.

Branch national organizations since then have been formed in Scotland, Ireland, United States, Portugal, Canada, France, Switzerland, Germany, Brazil, Holland, Denmark, Italy, Spain, Turkey, Korea, Greece, Syria, Egypt, South Africa, Japan, India, China, Persia, East Indies, West Indies, Norway and Sweden, New Zealand, Australia, Palestine, Chili, Mexico, etc. Indeed there is now scarcely a country without its auxiliary of the Alliance. The British branch alone, however, owns a building for its offices, in London, and publishes a magazine, "Evangelical Christendom."

The organization of the United States branch took place January 30, 1867, in the Bible House, New York City. The Hon. William E. Dodge was made president and continued to devote wisdom, effort and financial support to the enterprise unstintedly till his death in 1883. The Hon. John Jay was elected his successor, but resigned in January, 1885, when William E. Dodge, the honored son of the first president, was elected, and has since then continued to perform the duties of the office with great efficiency and acceptance.

Many, more rash than wise, predicted a short career for the new organization, but it has far outlived those who prophesied its failure, and has accomplished for Christian liberty alone much more than its most sanguine founders could have hoped. "There is no doubt," said a shrewd observer of religious events, "that to the Evangelical Alliance is very largely due the improved relations now existing between the different sections of the Christian Church as compared with what they were fifty years ago."

The Week of United Prayer, in a sense, was begun by members of the Alliance shortly after the formation of the British branch. But in 1858 a few missionaries of different denominational schools held a three days' meeting for prayer in Lodiana, in India. Afterward they sent home the suggestion that all the Christian world be requested to unite annually in a week of prayer. The Alliance readily published the call, and ever since has prepared and sent forth the programme of topics to all Christendom. And not till eternity will it be known how much has been achieved for the Kingdom of God and the spread of evangelical truth through the general response to its yearly call to united prayer.

In all, ten international conferences of the Alliance have been held—in London in 1851; Paris, 1855; Berlin, 1857; Geneva, 1861; Amsterdam, 1867; New York, 1873; Basle, 1879; Copenhagen, 1884—though at that time there was no branch of the Alliance in Sweden, yet Dr. Philip Schaff remarked that the success of the gathering was the greatest triumph which the organization had so far achieved; Florence, 1891, and finally the Jubilee in London in 1896, June 29-July 4, at which there were 2,500 delegates present.

Besides guiding the currents of thought and quickening the exercise of faith throughout the world the Evangelical Alliance has been most practically useful in averting and ameliorating religious persecution and oppression from time to time in various parts of the globe. The Alliance found one of the most trying obstacles to its mission of good-will in the restraints placed upon religious liberty which fifty years ago were in force in most lands where the Roman Catholic or Greek churches were dominant, as well as in all Mohammedan, and even in some Protestant countries. To a very considerable extent that evil has been abated, and in certain countries wholly removed. Within the lifetime of the Alliance men have been imprisoned in Italy for possessing the Bible, their release being secured through the efforts of the Alliance. Now such a thing in Italy is impossible, as the King himself, during the great conference of the Alliance in Florence in 1891, sent a message of congratulation to the assembly. That gathering was in itself a complete demonstration to the Roman Catholic Church of the oneness of Protestantism.

Thus by united action in the way of remonstrance and petition, and by creating a wholesome and strong public opinion, religious liberty has been promoted in many countries, especially in Spain, Austria, Sweden, Turkey, Russia, Italy, Japan, Greece, Hungary, Egypt, Peru, Basutoland, Persia, etc. In making this relief effective a vast deal of labor has been needful, labor which, in the nature of the case, can never be tabulated. Indeed, the efforts put forth by the Association to free the persecuted from despotism and misrepresentation would fill a volume. The following statement by Mr. E. P. Field, general secretary of the Alliance in Great Britain, will be sufficient to show what course frequently it is needful to follow:

"His Majesty, the King of Portugal, yesterday received, at Buckingham Palace, a deputation of the Evangelical Alliance with reference to the invasion on religious liberty in Lisbon. Lord Kinnaird, vice-president, and Mr. John Paton, honorary treasurer, attended on behalf of the council, and presented a petition which stated that the Evangelical Alliance is a union, not of churches, but of individual Christians all over the world, allied together on the basis of a common faith in Christ and their common love to Him, and including representatives of all the churches; that this Alliance has been in operation since 1846, and that it has year by year, during the last fifty-four years, striven for the establishment of religious liberty in all parts of the world, believing that it is the principle established in our very nature and affirmed also in the Word of God, that each man should be at liberty to approach and to worship his Creator without hindrance; that early in the present year, while the various Protestant congregations in Lisbon were assembled in the Week of Prayer, arranged for all countries by the Evangelical Alliance, their representatives were summoned before the criminal judge in Lisbon, and were told that they must cease at once their religious meetings on pain of prosecution; that subsequently the Presbyterian native congregation, as well as the meeting of the Young Men's Christian Association, had been stopped by the police; that we have heard that some assurance has been since given by the Civil Governor of Lisbon that the interruption of the services by the police would not be persisted in; that the Evangelical Alliance would feel most grateful to the King if only he would consent to indorse such a promise for the future, not limiting its operation to Lisbon, and that he would of his free grace and sovereign mercy grant to all Christians throughout his dominions full liberty of religious worship in the same manner as has long been bestowed upon all Roman Catholics throughout the British Empire; that the Evangelical Alliance, in conclusion, desires earnestly to assure His Majesty of the sincere gratitude which exists in the hearts of all English Protestants for every indication of mercy and clemency which has been already evinced by His Most Gracious Majesty.

"His Majesty received the deputation most graciously. He said he was glad to welcome the council of the Evangelical Alliance, and to tell them that the matter had been brought under his notice by their letter. He also added that he at once ordered the authorities to cease further undue interference. He was very pleased to assure the members of the Evangelical Alliance that it was his distinct wish that religious liberty should be granted to all Protestant Christions throughout his dominions, and that it was his determination to enforce this rule. He also said that he had now given the necessary orders to ensure this.

"The deputation, on behalf of all Protestant Christians, expressed their sincere gratitude to the King for his kindness and the graciousness of his promise, and for the very friendly spirit which he had shown to the English."

The Papal newspapers in Portugal, of course, were angry that the King should have had anything to do with Protestants, and are denying that any such action took place.

Again, by emphasizing, in statements of doctrine, only essentials in which all are agreed, by collecting statistics which exhibit the religious condition and progress of the whole world, and by discovering the signs of the times in the discussion of advanced measures, these coöperating bodies have introduced ameliorating and unifying influences among widely differing churches, resulting in greatly increased coöperation and fraternity in Christian intercourse and work. There has been, therefore, throughout the history and work of the Alliance an ever-growing sentiment of comity among all the denominations, leading, gradually, to many important modifications, growing unity and mutual respect throughout all their ranks. The Association has thus accomplished in the cause of religious liberty and brotherly love much more than its early friends and promoters ever dreamed of accomplishing. But though much has been accomplished, never was there greater need for fraternity and coöperation on the part of all who hold the truth in simplicity and sincerity. For it is needful to-day, as, perhaps, in no former time, to seek to realize in actual intercourse that living and essential union which binds all true believers in one fellowship and in one service.

RESCUE WORK.

Kate Waller Barrett, M.D.,
WASHINGTON.

[In our time it is the habit to denounce the cities and to speak of them as the foci of all wickedness. Is it not time for some one to tell the other side of the story, and to say that the city is the heaven of practical helpfulness? Look at the embowered and fountained parks, where the invalids may come and be refreshed; the Bowery Mission, through which annually over 100,000 come to get bread for this life and bread for the life to come; all the pillows of that institution are under the blessing of Him who had not where to lay His head; the free schools, where the most impoverished are educated; the hospitals for broken bones; the homes for the restoration of intellects astray; the orphan home, father and mother to all who come under its benediction; the midnight missions, which pour midnoon upon the darkened; the Prison Reform Association, the Houses of Mercy, the infirmaries, the Sheltering Arms, the Bethesda Mission, the aid societies, the industrial schools, the Sailors' Snug Harbor, the foundling asylums, and the free dispensaries.

It would take a sermon three weeks long to do justice to the mighty things which our cities are doing for the unfortunate and the lost. Do not say that Christianity in our cities is all show, and talk and genuflexion, and sacred noise. You have been so long looking at the hand of cruelty, and the hand of theft, and the hand of fraud, and the hand of outrage, that you have not sufficiently appreciated the hand of help, stretched forth from the doors and windows and churches, and from merciful institutions—the Christ-like hand, the cherubic hand, "the hands under the wings."

There is a kind of religion in our day that my text rebukes. There are men and women spending their time in delectation over their saved state, going about from prayer-meeting to prayer-meeting, and from church to church, telling how happy they are. But show them a subscription paper, or ask them to go and visit the sick, or tell them to reclaim a wanderer, or speak out for some unpopular Christian enterprise, and they have bronchitis, or stitch in the side, or sudden attacks of grip. Their religion is all wing, and no hand. They can fly heavenward, but they cannot reach out earthward.

The highest type of religion says little about itself, but is busy for God and in helping to the heavenly shore the crew and passengers of this shipwrecked planet. Such people are busy now up the dark lanes of our cities, and all through the mountain glens, and down in the quarries where the sunlight has never visited, and amid the rigging, helping to take in another reef before the Caribbean whirlwind.—T. De Witt Talmage.—Ed.]

JERRY McAULEY.

It is but within the last half century that an attempt has been made in any degree commensurate with the requirements of the case to reach and to rescue what is frequently called the submerged classes. This rescue work, while receiving the cordial sympathy and support of the Christian Church, as it should, originated in the prayerful thought, as it is now in the hands and on the hearts, of those who themselves have known the bitterness and the foulness of sin.

It was recognized that the church through its ordinary services was incapable of reaching the very classes which most needed the sympathy and the support of Christian love and helpfulness. In order to gain their confidence and win them from their evil ways it was not enough that the church should open its doors and say "Come in"; the Master's call to "go out into the highways and hedges and compel them to come in" must be obeyed.

As Dr. Pierson says in his "Forward Movements," these brethren of ours "are in a pit so deep that the common means of grace do not avail; a special life-line let down to their level and fitted to grapple them fast, a special message and mission with peculiar love for the lost and passion for souls, seem needful for this sort of work. The church has often been charged with *indifference,* where perhaps the real difficulty is *inadequacy.*"

In the conduct of this work, the purpose has been not to set up a rival to the church, but to act as the church's auxiliary and representative; and, indeed, many of those who have been won from the paths of folly and sin, in the rescue mission, have become the church's most earnest and efficient helpers in its regular work.

Every city of any importance in the United States to-day has one or more rescue missions in its most unsavory localities. This is more particularly true, of course, of the larger centres of population, such as New York, Philadelphia, Chicago, Boston, Louisville, San Francisco, etc.

The missions of Boston deserve special mention, owing to the fact that the first mission for men and women, as well as the first rescue mission for women only, was located there. According to the official directory of that city, the Boston North End Mission was established in 1867; but from other sources we learn that a mission work was begun previously to that date. For the last forty years, we may safely say, this mission has played an important part in the philanthropic and rescue work of Boston. Besides the daily mission services it has a rescue home for women and another home for the care of dependent children.

During the history of this mission many notable men and women have been associated with it in various official capacities. In its infancy it received the active support of Eben Tourjee, who was president of the board of managers, and who afterward founded the New England Conservatory of Music. He was followed in office by Ezra Farnsworth; Silas Pierce, Jr., was president in 1878, while at the present time a member of the same Pierce family, and one who bears the same name, holds this office.

One of the earliest friends of the work was William F. Davis, who when a junior at Harvard in 1865 first became interested, and after being chaplain of the City Almshouse he was superintendent of the mission in 1875-78. The mission is still conducted on the original lines, and is prospering under the excellent management of the Rev. L. D. Younkin.

New York contains the greatest number of missions of any city in the Union. Missions for all "sorts and conditions of men," as well as women, have here been inaugurated. When one remembers that much of this wonderful rescue mission work, which is sufficient in itself to fill page after page of the Charities Directory, came from the inspiration of one man's life, and he an ex-convict, gambler and drunkard, we are impressed with the truth that God frequently takes the "weak things of the world to confound the mighty."

Jerry McAuley needs no other or better monument to perpetuate his work and his worth than the Water Street (opened in 1872) and the Cremorne missions. His consecrated life and methods of work continue to be the encouragement and inspiration and ideal of all who are engaged in similar effort; as what God did for him, and through him for the abandoned wrecks of humanity, may be repeated in the case of any other man who surrenders himself as fully to the service of God in the saving of men.

Space fails us to mention all the missions laboring in New York City, but one of the most important is the Bowery Mission, under the auspices of the "Christian Herald," attached to which is a restaurant and a lodging house for men. Some of the other missions are the Galilean, under the auspices of the Calvary P. E. Church; St. Bartholomew's, under St. Bartholomew's P. E. Church; the Florence Mission (on Bleecker Street), established by Mr. Charles N. Crittenton about eighteen years ago; the Doyer Street Mission, in the heart of Chinatown, under the auspices of the New York Rescue Band; the Seamen's Bethel, the Mariners' Church, and many others. There are also a number of Roman Catholic missions which are rendering excellent service.

One could not spend a week in a more profitable manner than in visiting the various rescue missions of New York City, especially if he were skeptical regarding what the grace of God is capable of doing for the men and the women who are morally and socially abandoned.

The Sunday Breakfast Association of Philadelphia was the father of the Breakfast Association movement. Its meetings are renowned among Christian workers as being the most successful and inspiring of their kind. Every Sunday morning a large number of tramps, homeless and outcast men, are served a comfortable breakfast, to which is added for the inner man helpful addresses and Bible instruction. This, with the Old Ship Mission and many other similar organizations, makes the rescue mission work of Philadelphia noteworthy.

The Central Union Mission occupies one of the most conspicuous locations in the city of Washington, and is well known to all visitors to the Capital who are interested in religious work. It has proved a veritable lighthouse for many a storm-tossed mariner on life's troubled sea. Among other means employed in ministering to and reaching the people it maintains a restaurant. and uses a Gospel wagon in the conduct of its street services.

Rescue work is carried on also in Atlanta, Cincinnati, Louisville, Richmond, Chicago, Jersey City and numerous other centres of population throughout the Union. Nothing need be said here respecting the rescue and slum work of the Salvation Army, as the work of that organization is presented in a separate paper.

A work that has been most successful in establishing branches not only throughout the United States, but also in foreign lands, is the Penal Mission, under the supervision of Mr. and Mrs. Ferguson. The headquarters of this movement is in Los Angeles, Cal., the various branches of which now number about twenty.

The medical rescue work, established by the Seventh Day Adventists under the direction of Dr. J. B. Kellogg, of Battle Creek, is accomplishing marvellous results. Of this mission there are about forty branches in the various states.

The National Florence Crittenton Mission is a movement which was begun eighteen years ago in New York City, designed particularly to reach and to rescue unfortunate and erring girls. Mr. Charles N. Crittenton, a wealthy business man of that city, having been led, by the death of his little daughter Florence, four years old, to consecrate his life and means to God, became especially interested in the apparently helpless condition of wayward girls, and was led to open a home for them in Bleecker Street, where gospel services are held every night in the year. While previously there had been a few small rescue homes, or refuges for first offenders, as far as known, this is the first home of its kind ever opened to welcome the depraved and abandoned classes. Under Mr. Crittenton's personal supervision the work became eminently successful, and so widely known that calls have come from all over the country for his services to aid in establishing similar institutions. So that the work begun in a very humble way and in dependence upon God alone has now branches scattered across the entire continent.

As the work developed, the need became manifest for some specific and central organization, under the guidance of which all these homes should be operated. The National Government was applied to for a charter, which was not only readily granted, but also an appropriation made to help maintain and enlarge the work. Under the stimulus of this generous coöperation on the part of Congress the work has grown to remarkable proportions. During the past year more than three thousand street girls have been resident in these homes under the saving influence and training of consecrated Christian womanhood. There are now about sixty such homes and missions in the United States; one in Tokio, Japan, and one is just being established in Marseilles, France. The fundamental principle in the conduct of these homes is that reformation of conduct is possible only through regeneration of character.

Besides the Florence Crittenton, there are a large number of institutions throughout the country that are doing a similar work in a most praiseworthy manner, having the confidence and receiving the support and coöperation of the Christian public. There are several such in New York City, such as the Magdalene Home, established 1833; the House of Mercy, established 1855; the Wetmore Home, established 1865, and the Door of Hope, established about fifteen years ago.

A number of such rescue homes have been opened under the auspices of the W. C. T. U. in different states and cities, and there is not a state in the Union where some sort of rescue work is not in operation. During the last quarter of a century a number of unique movements have been inaugurated for the purpose of reaching the non-churchgoing masses, some of whose methods may be regarded as sensational, and their efficacy questioned by the ordinary churchman, but they are sufficiently justified in view of the fact that they seem to be honored of God, and avail for the salvation of men.

Activity in mission work in the great centres of population is quite as manifest in foreign lands as it is in our own. While the McAll Mission in France was not founded with the purpose of reaching the same classes as are found in the slums of the great cities, but rather to restore the faith of those who had drifted from the Catholic Church into indifference or infidelity, yet the lines of work are practically the same.

Everyone who knows anything about the religious work being carried on in London for the unchurched masses, has heard of the efforts of Mr. F. N. Charrington, of the Mile-End Road Mission. Mr. Charrington is the man who gave up a lucrative business enterprise in order to engage in mission work, and when someone playfully asked him how much a year he received for wearing the "blue ribbon" he replied that he did not receive any money reward, but on the contrary paid £20,000 a year for the privilege. This amount he would have been able to make annually had he continued in the brewing business. There is another mission in London worthy of special note called the "Regions Beyond," the latter having several branches of work other than the daily mission services, such as sewing, educational and Bible study classes. This work has been successful in a large degree in the regeneration of the Whitechapel district. Time would fail us to mention the rescue work being done in Switzerland, particularly at Geneva, and also in the larger cities of Germany, where Le Société des Amies de Jeune Fille —which has branches all over Europe and America—does a noble work in directing friendless young girls when travelling from place to place, and aiding them in securing suitable employment or lodging.

Could any service be more honoring to our Lord, or more likely to win the indifferent and the wayward from their peaceless paths, than the self-sacrifice of those who, day after day and night after night, year in and year out, keep open house, give encouragement and counsel, and, frequently, provide food, lodging, work or clothing for those who have been battered and bruised by misfortune or sin? Such a work requires more than the artistic vision that sees an angel in the "dull, cold marble." To see the angel in the gnarled, the besotted, the drunken and the vicious requires a divine illumination—the Christ-spirit—and to bring that angel forth a faith unfaltering, a patience persistent and a love unwearying. May the good Lord give us such a vision as shall enable us to see Himself, not alone in the well-clad and refined, but in every man we meet, however degraded and begrimed! Only thus will our hearts warm to our work, and "the torrent that swept the valley shall be led to turn the mill."

When David, future King of Israel, had escaped to the cave of Adullam, those who joined him—besides his father's household—were such as were in distress, in debt or discontented; in all about four hundred desperate men, who had nothing to lose and everything to gain. By personal contact with the kingly son of Jesse they gained something of his greatness and eventually became sharers in and ornaments of his kingdom. Now, into the kingdom of "great David's greater Son" there have fled for refuge the harlot Rahab, the thief on the cross, the licentious Corinthians (1 Cor. vi, 9-11), the John Bunyans, the Jerry McAuleys; a host which no man can number has been gathered from the lowest slums and the deepest sinks of sin; these having adorned the doctrine of God their Saviour here, shall adorn His diadem yonder. "Perchance the convict from the galleys may stand above the hermit from his cell." How frequently in our rescue meetings do we hear such a testimony as the following, from Evansville, Ind.:

"In April, 1890, the Lord sent our brother, Yatman, here to conduct a meeting. At that time I was a poor, degraded, outcast drunkard, with no one to give a helping hand or a word of cheer. I had gone beyond all hope of my relatives, they had given me up as lost, as I was nothing but a barroom wall-flower, as I sat there from morning till late at night; all of my will power was gone and I would sell the clothes off of my back to get the soul-destroying stuff; but, praise the Lord, He sent Brother Yatman here as an instrument in His hands, to snatch me as a brand from the eternal burning, and to-day I am singing, in spirit and in truth, 'happy on the way, with a sorrow for sin I let Jesus come in and now it is glory in my soul.' The Great Physician healed me, and to-day I am a sober man, clothed and in my right mind, and trying to serve the Lord in all things, and praying daily that He will make me as clay in the potter's hand and use me to His honor and glory."

Thus the rescue mission is a work not alone of rescue, but of *prevention* as well. Every individual redeemed, from being the burden and the bane of society, becomes vice's enemy and crime's prevention—no longer preying upon others he now begins to pray for others. There is no more notable example of this than the case of Jerry McAuley himself. The very air is poisoned with vice, and it is contagious; obscenity and profanity are breathed with the atmosphere. You might as well think of standing in a closely confined room where there are fifty people, and yet not breathe the vitiated air, as to stand in a community where there is a multitude of the depraved, without being contaminated. Every city has its "Poverty Gap" and its "Damnation Alley," and though apparently hidden in some out-of-the-way street or corner, every inhabitant, especially our children, will be morally injured by the influence of the leprous life. But it is admitted that the ordinary agencies of the church fail to reach these abandoned classes. In that case the church ought not only to plant and sustain the rescue mission, as a simple matter of Christian duty, but as a means of self-defence as well.

We may labor never so earnestly in the upper strata of society without influencing the lower strata. If you placed screws under the roof of a building and raised that, you would never expect the walls and foundation to follow it up. But if you wish roof, walls, foundation and all to go up, place your screws under the entire structure, then every inch that your foundation goes up your walls and roof will go up also. It was Beecher who said that "in human society that system which is comprehensive enough to take care of the bottom will best take care of the top. You cannot boil a caldron downward with fuel, but you can upward. It is impossible to get a radiation from an upper class that shall enlighten a lower. The educated portion of a community is liable to be arrogant, exclusive and dominating; and in order to raise society as a whole, there must be a moral system whose genius is to exert its forces upon every class. Is it not reasonable to suppose that a system that is capable of taking care of the worst will be much more abundantly capable of taking care of the best? The Saviour came to the neglected, the despised and despoiled, the poor, the helpless. He was radical. He began at the root. He addressed Himself to the bottom. He preached a gospel that had regard, not to a few, not to the more prosperous, not to the wealthy, not to those who could make return for his efforts on their behalf, but to those who constituted the foundation of society, and who, if carried up, would be lifted by a system of moral influences that must carry up the whole of society."

S. H. HADLEY.

THE WOMAN'S CHRISTIAN TEMPERANCE UNION.

Katharine Lente Stevenson,
BOSTON.

[The first and most necessary effort, without which all others will be fruitless, must be to awaken the apathetic torpor, to scarify the dull callosity of the conscience of civilized nations on this subject. Oliver Cromwell said long ago: "National crime is a thing that God will reckon with, and I wish it may not be on the nation a day longer than you have an opportunity to find a remedy." Alas! the remedy has been pointed out with most earnest insistence for many years, but it has not been listened to because the greed of gain, the various pleas of self-interest, and the demon force of a self-created temptation have utterly drowned the voices of reason, of religion and of conscience. We need some God-inspired prophet to bring home the truth to us in words of flame. No prophet comes—perhaps because we are too much sunk in guilt and apathy to deserve one. One thing, however, is certain: Nations do not perish of their external disasters; they perish by their sins. I cannot speak from intimate knowledge as to the advance or stationariness of the temperance movement in America; but it is certain that in England, in spite of long-continued efforts, the liquor traffic is not only bloated with enormous wealth, but has managed, to our political infamy, so completely to terrify, hamper, sophisticate the Government as to leave us no immediate hope of real improvement. A short time ago our conservative Chancellor of the Exchequer warned us, not without a sense of astonishment, that—including hosts of total abstainers and millions of children—we are spending on drink every year no less than £3 17s. 6d. per head; and shortly afterward a Liberal ex-Chancellor proved, by statistics which ought to make us blush, that more beer, more stout, more wine, more ardent spirits of every kind, were consumed in England than in any other country on the surface of the globe. "It is a cheap device," said William Lloyd Garrison, "to brand the temperance movement as fanatical. I deny that it has a single feature of fanaticism, for it is based on physiological principles, chemical relations, the welfare of society, the laws of self-preservation, the claims of suffering humanity, all that is noble in patriotism, generous in philanthropy, and pure and good in Christianity." "Let us all carry deeply stamped on our minds." said Mr. Gladstone, "a sense of shame for the great plague of drunkenness which goes through the land sapping and undermining character, and breaking up the peace of families. This great plague and curse is a national curse, calamity and scandal."

If it be too much to expect consciences made impenetrable by custom that they should inquire at first hand into all this terrific evidence, is it a matter of indifference to them that all our judges, all our best divines, all our greatest physicians, even all our chief athletes, yea, our bravest generals, have united in condemning the pernicious influences of alcohol in every department of our national life? How utterly shameful, then, should apathy on this subject be in any patriot, in any Christian, in anyone who has the least care for or sympathy with his brother man!

"When Mercy has played her part in vain, Vengeance leaps upon the stage. She strikes sharp strokes, and Pity does not break the blow."—F. W. FARRAR. "Hom. Review," January, 1901.—ED.]

* * *

THE history of the Woman's Christian Temperance Union in America is so inextricably blended with the record of the temperance movements which preceded its organization that it is impossible to consider it as standing alone. It is true that, in its present manifestation, it sprang up with almost miraculous swiftness—full-armed, like Minerva, it seemed born in an hour—but the causes which led to that marvelous birth and equally marvelous growth lay far behind, and the organization is only the consummate flower of principles which long since took deep root in the soil of our common life. While we of the white ribbon believe our society to be the best and most efficient working force now in the field of reform, we are both glad and proud to acknowledge that it has been made possible only by all that went before us, and that we shall ultimately become but another contributing force to the greater all which is to come after.

Rev. Dr. Dunn, secretary of the National Temperance Society, contributed a luminous history of the temperance reform in America to the World's Temperance Congress which, at the call of His Grace the Archbishop of Canterbury, convened in London in June, 1900. From this paper, placed in my hands for this purpose, through the author's kindness, I glean the following facts with reference to the temperance history in America which precedes our own:

To the town of East Hampton, L. I., belongs the high honor of having passed the first restrictive legislation with reference to the sale of spirituous liquors. In 1651 this town passed a law forbidding any one to sell liquor except those deputed to do so. This law contained other clauses regulating the sale to youths, limiting the quantity to one half pint among four men, and positively forbade the selling to any Indian, unless he carried an order from his sachem. Other towns, in different parts of the country, passed similar laws—some much stronger—until, in 1676, the new Constitution of Virginia absolutely prohibited the manufacture and sale of spirituous liquors, thus antedating the Maine law by nearly two centuries.

It is evident, however, that this impulse toward temperance legislation was very speedily overborne by other matters which occupied the attention of the early settlers of our new country. As their power increased, their fear of the Indian seems to have diminished, and with it their fear of the enemy common to both white man and Indian—strong drink. A hundred years' lapse before any special temperance effort is recorded throughout the American colonies.

In 1760 the Friends united in a protest against the custom of furnishing drink at funerals.

On the 27th of February, 1777, the first Congress of the United States of America passed this significant resolution: "Resolved, That it be recommended to the several legislatures in the United States immediately to pass laws the most effective for putting an immediate stop to the pernicious practise of distilling grains by which the most extensive evils are likely to be derived, if not quickly prevented."

In July, 1789, we find the farmers of Litchfield county, Connecticut, pledging themselves to use no distilled liquors during their work the ensuing season.

The next temperance movement seems to have arisen among the physicians of the country, under the leadership of Dr. Benjamin Rush, of Philadelphia, and, on December 29, 1790, they petitioned Congress to "impose such heavy duties upon all distilled spirits as shall be effectual to restrain their intemperate use in our country."

In 1789 the Methodists of Virginia and the Presbyterians of Pennsylvania adopted, in their conferences, total abstinence resolutions, while *the first temperance society* in the country was organized in Morean, Saratoga county, N. Y., on the 13th of April, 1808. Several sections of the constitution of this society are interesting as denoting the slow growth of the principle of an absolute total abstinence, as the words are understood to-day. The drinking of liquor at public dinners was exempted from the provisions of this pledge, while wide latitude was given for possible "physicians' prescriptions." Other societies of a similar nature speedily followed this in the State of New York.

In 1811 the General Association of the Presbyterian Churches of Philadelphia appointed a committee to report plans for action with reference to temperance. On the 12th of February, 1813, the Temperance Society of Massachusetts was organized. The interest in this, however, speedily became lukewarm, but, in 1823, a strong appeal was issued by the society, in which, among other things, this prophetic statement may be noted: "Two things only appear certain; 1st, that a principal object must be to draw public attention frequently and earnestly to this subject; 2d, it seems at the same time equally clear that there is no man, nor body of men, who can strike at the root of the evil but *the Legislature of the nation.*" In that year Dr. Justin Edwards and Dr. Eliphalet Nott preached their strong, arousing temperance sermons.

The year 1826 was marked by the organization of the American Temperance Society, with its pledge of "Total abstinence from ardent spirits"; by the publication of "The National Philanthropist," and the wonderful temperance sermons of Dr. Lyman Beecher.

In 1832 General Lewis Cass prohibited the introduction of liquor into forts, garrisons and camps of the United States army; also its sale to the soldiers by sutlers.

The year 1833 marked the high tide of temperance sentiment in the first half of the nineteenth century. Five thousand temperance societies were reported in that year, with a membership of one and one-quarter millions; 10,000 of these were said to be reformed drunkards. Four thousand distilleries were reported closed; 6,000 merchants gave up the sale, and on over one thousand vessels the use of liquor was abandoned. On the 26th of February, in this year, the Congressional Temperance Society was formed in Washington, D. C., with General Lewis Cass as its president; while, on the 15th of March, Massachusetts formed a similar society, with the Governor of the state at its head. This memorable year also witnessed the first National Temperance Convention, which met in Philadelphia, May 24 to 26. Four hundred and forty delegates were present from nineteen states and territories.

In 1840 the famous Washingtonian movement, under the leadership of six reformed men, aroused the country with a new enthusiasm. In 1842 the Sons of Temperance and the Order of the Rechabites were organized; while, during the same year, one of the noblest heroes of the temperance reform, John B. Gough, dedicated his matchless and unique oratorical powers to the overthrow of the strong drink which had so nearly overthrown him.

The year 1845 witnessed the organization of "The Templars of Honor and Temperance," while, during the winter of 1845-46, the

"Grand Old Man of Maine," General Neal Dow, then in the prime of his manhood, came to the front, and, under his wise, magnetic leadership, the Pine Tree State passed the Prohibitory statute which has since been known as "the Maine law."

In 1847 the Supreme Court of the United States decided that any state had a constitutional right to regulate or suppress the sale of liquor. Under the incentive of this decision, New Hampshire passed a prohibitory law in 1849, while, during the same year, Wisconsin passed a law which obliged the seller of liquor to be responsible for all expense growing out of its sale, including the support of "paupers, widows and orphans," and the expense of all civil and criminal prosecutions growing out of or justly attributable to such traffic.

In 1849 Father Mathew began his work in this country. In 1851 the Order of Good Templars was instituted. During the same year the Prohibitory law of Maine was placed in the constitution of that state, by the overwhelming vote of the people, and from this vantage ground no effort of the liquor power has ever been able to dislodge it; the last attempt, in the Legislature of 1900 and 1901, having signally failed.

In 1852, Minnesota, Vermont, Massachusetts and Rhode Island passed prohibitory laws. In 1853 Michigan joined the goodly fellowship of prohibition states, and the law in Wisconsin was lost by one vote only. In 1854 New York passed a prohibitory law, which was vetoed by Governor Seymour. The candidacy of Governor Seymour was defeated the next fall, and his opponent, Myron H. Clark, gave his influence and signature to the Prohibition bill. In 1856 the first Juvenile Temperance Society was organized. As an offset to such rapid advance among the temperance forces it must be noted that, in 1862, the Brewers' Association was formed.

The year 1868 witnessed the organization of the National Prohibition Party; also of the Royal Templars of Temperance. In 1872 the Catholic Total Abstinence Society came into being, and during the same year the Prohibitionists placed a national ticket in the field, with James Black candidate for President, and Rev. John Russell for Vice-President. The twelfth Annual Congress of Brewers, which met shortly after, passed resolutions protesting against the action of temperance agitators, and pledging to oppose, at the polls, all candidates for office who were pledged to temperance legislation. In 1872 petitions against the sale of liquor in the Territories constituted the chief temperance activity, and in 1873 the Attorney-General decided that no liquor could be sold in the Territory of Alaska.

The winter of 1873-74 was marked by an uprising, in the interest of temperance, of the women of the nation, which soon came to be known as the Woman's Crusade. For despite all the temperance activity above recorded there had been a marked increase in the intemperance of the nation during the two preceding decades. The civil war, undoubtedly, must be held largely responsible for this fact, as well as the formidable combination which "the trade" effected at that time in its own interests. The nation's direct partnership in the traffic dates back to the taxes upon liquor imposed as a part of the war revenue.

The greed of gain, which is one of the many sad accompaniments of war, took possession of a large proportion of the people. The interests of manhood and of the home were largely lost sight of in the interest of money getting, and the country seemed in great danger of cutting loose from the traditions and ideals of its past.

The hearts of the Christian women of the land were sorely burdened. The passionate patriotism which they had poured out upon the altar of their country had grown rather than diminished with its giving. They longed to help redeem their nation from a foe, mightier and more inimical to righteousness than any which had hitherto assailed it; the foe of North and South alike—the organized, legalized liquor traffic. When the opportunity came it was small wonder that they availed themselves of it in such a spontaneous uprising as seemed little short of miraculous. The seed had fallen in prepared ground, and the harvest was both swift and sure.

Dr. Dio Lewis, of Boston, Massachusetts, was the man whom God used to incite the women of the nation. During a lecture tour through New York and Ohio, in the winter of 1873-74, he frequently told the story of what his mother had done, fifty years before, to close the one saloon in the little town in New York State where she had lived. As he told the story in Fredonia, N. Y., on December 15th, the women went out of the meeting and organized themselves into a *Woman's Christian Temperance Union*, the first organization in the world to bear that name. Mrs. Esther MacNeil was its first president. As he told the story in Hillsboro, Ohio, on the 23d of the same month, seventy women banded themselves together for prayer and effort against the liquor traffic. They chose as their leader Mrs. Eliza J. Thompson, wife of a judge of that town, and daughter of ex-Governor Trimball of Ohio, and the next day, after spending an hour in prayer at the church, they marched out upon the street singing:

> "Give to the winds thy fears,
> Hope and be undismayed;
> God hears thy cries and counts thy tears;
> God will lift up thy head."

They went to the drugstores on that first day, and pled with the proprietors to sell no spirituous liquors.

The same evening Dr. Lewis told his story to an audience in Washington Court House, Ohio, and there the most phenomenal results followed. Hundreds of women joined the praying band, which, under the leadership of Mrs. George Carpenter, began its work of visiting the saloons, praying upon the streets and "crusading" with such vigor that the eyes of all the world were speedily turned toward Ohio.

From this centre the flames of enthusiasm swept east, west, north and south, until the land was aroused in such a temperance revival as had never before been known. For six months this crusade lasted, and it is estimated that, during that time, many thousands of men gave up drinking and many hundreds of saloon keepers abandoned the traffic. The women met with much opposition, persecution, obloquy and contumely, as well as with much honest praise and noble encouragement from the best element in every community. In some instances they were prosecuted and even imprisoned, but the heart of the people was with them, since it was seen that they were standing for the home, and their victories were so signal as, in many instances, to seem nothing less than miraculous.

In the nature of things this method of work, though admirably adapted to awaken the public conscience, could not be continued as the normal method of temperance work. The homes of the land would have become disintegrated through the very efforts put forth to preserve them, if the mothers, wives and daughters had continued, from that time to this, their work through crusade methods. After six months had elapsed the enemies of temperance were able to point to the crusade as a thing of past history, and to say: "We told you it would not last." But by this very statement they gave proof of how little they had understood the significance of the movement. The women of that great moral uprising were not committed to crusade methods, but they were committed to the overthrow of the liquor traffic by any and all righteous methods which should appear feasible. Inevitably their thoughts turned toward permanent organization. Chancellor John H. Vincent, of the famous Chautauqua movement, now Bishop Vincent, of the Methodist Episcopal Church, issued a call for those who had been interested in the crusade to assemble at Chautauqua Lake, N. Y., in August, 1874. A comparatively large number responded to this call, and from this preliminary meeting a call was sent forth which resulted in the organizing convention, held in Cleveland, Ohio, November 18-20, 1874. At this convention, held in less than a year from the beginning of the crusade, the Woman's Christian Temperance Union of the United States of America was formally organized. Delegates from sixteen states were present and took part in the exercises. The officers elected were: President, Mrs. Annie Wittenmeyer, of Philadelphia; Corresponding Secretary, Miss Frances E. Willard, of Evanston, Illinois; Recording Secretary, Mrs. Mary C. Johnson, of New York; Assistant Recording Secretary, Mrs. Mary T. Burt, of New York; Treasurer, Mrs. W. A. Ingham, of Cleveland, Ohio. The spirit of the convention, throughout, was deeply devotional and intensely practical, and no wise onlooker could fail to see that the women were but putting into organized, concrete expression the motive and impulse of the crusade. Experience, even at that early date, had taught the women that to awaken good impulses in the heart of a man who had been a slave to intemperance, is by no means a sure guarantee of ultimate victory in that man's life. The mightiest strivings after reformation, they had found, were sometimes met by a seemingly overwhelming defeat; both because the habit had so crystallized that it had become a second nature, and because the legalized dram shop stood at well-nigh every corner, with its too alluring invitation to abandon self-control for self-gratification. It was seen that *society itself must be reformed,* reformed in its very organization; that the best way to reform the individual drunkard is to begin with him before he needs reformation, and that the best way to check the ravages of the saloon is to annihilate the saloon itself. Therefore, at the convention of 1874, plans were made to educate the children in the principle and practice of total abstinence, and to awaken public sentiment to the enormity of the evils growing out of and fostered by the licensed saloon.

FRANCES E. WILLARD
FOUNDER OF THE WORLD'S WOMAN'S CHRISTIAN TEMPERANCE UNION

The plan of work of this first convention reads like a prophecy of much that has since been accomplished; nor is this strange, when we remember that the woman who, almost from the inception of the society, was recognized as its God-given leader, was one of the members of that committee. I quote from the Annual Address of the President of the National Woman's Christian Temperance Union, Mrs. L. M. N. Stevens, at the Seattle National Convention, October, 1899:

"Miss Willard and Mrs. M. M. Brown were made the committee to prepare the address and plan of work of the National Union. Miss Willard wrote every word of the plan of work, and it is deeply interesting for us to note how much, then planned, has come to pass.

"The first section dealt with Organization, thus: 'Since organization is the sun-glass which brings to a focus scattered influence and effort, we urge the formation of a Woman's Christian Temperance Union in every State, city, town and village.' Then there were no auxiliary unions, now there are ten thousand, reaching over every State and Territory, and to our new possession of Hawaii.

" 'The careful selection of literature.'

"The demand for temperance literature by our unions, as soon as organized, has created the supply. Of late the Woman's Temperance Publication Association alone has turned out annually more than fifty million pages of temperance literature, to say nothing of the circulation of that already in stock and furnished from other sources, such as the National Temperance Society, etc., and nearly all the States have a State Woman's Christian Temperance Union paper.

" 'Teaching the children, in Sabbath schools and public schools, the ethics, physiology and hygiene of total abstinence.'

"To-day, as the outcome of this section of the plan of work of 1874, temperance instruction is given according to law in all the States save three, the District of Columbia and the territories, Indian, Naval and Military schools; there are also Quarterly Temperance lessons in the International Sabbath School series; the universal Temperance Sunday is widely observed; pledge signing is quite general in the Sunday-school; half a million children of the Sunday-school and Loyal Temperance Legion sent their autographs on the triple pledge to the World's Columbian Exposition in 1893.

" 'Offering prizes in these schools for essays on different aspects of these subjects. Organizing temperance Glee Clubs among the young people; enlisting the press in the temperance reform by securing columns, etc.; placing illustrative pictures in the school rooms.'

"Dear comrades, we know how truly all this has come to be a part of our work.

"Section third referred to the juvenile temperance societies; urging the formation and perpetual continuance of temperance societies to be composed of children and youth.

"As proof of the wisdom and utility of this recommendation, we have but to look away to the three hundred thousand Loyal Temperance Legion children of to-day.

"Section four referred to pledge signing; and section five recommended an effort to banish fermented wine from the communion table. Some of us remember the long discussion which was called up two years later, when a resolution to this effect was offered at the Newark Convention, which resolution was finally adopted by a rising vote of 52 to 21. Many true-hearted, conservative church women looked upon this resolution as sacrilegious; but these same women, after observation with eyes open to see the dangerous effects of wine, even though taken under the most sacred circumstances—especially upon those rescued from drink and brought to the church altar— were among the first at the next convention to declare that the resolution should be repeated and with renewed emphasis. And so it has gone on until some of the States are able to report the disuse of fermented wine in all the churches save the Episcopal and Roman Catholic, and in the latter communion the cup is received by the clergy only.

"Then, in this remarkable first plan, follow sections referring to anti-treating leagues, gospel temperance meetings, coffee rooms, homes for inebriate women, the erection of fountains, and a plan of finance similar to that under which we are working to-day; and lastly the trysting time with God, and the conclusion in these words:

" 'Dear sisters, we have laid before you the plan of the long campaign. Will you work with us? We wage our peaceful war in loving expectation of that day "when all men's weal shall be each man's care," when "nothing shall hurt or destroy in all my holy mountain"; and in our day we may live to see America, beloved mother of thrice grateful daughters, set at liberty, full and complete, from foamy King Gambrinus and fiery old King Alcohol.'

"Take up the Annual Leaflet of the National Woman's Christian

Temperance Union for 1899, and we will find that the plan prepared at the convention held twenty-five years ago, and the plan under which we are working to-day, are strongly similar, and the summing up of the whole matter means that the tree of intemperance is being girdled, the liquor system must be overthrown—the saloon must go."

Not even the briefest, most cursory history of the Woman's Christian Temperance Union could be complete without a short sketch of the life and work of its great leader. She, more than any and all other agencies, made it the power that it is to-day. Her far-seeing eye caught visions of the future; her all-inclusive mind was able to correlate this with other reform movements; her magnetic personality has placed its indelible impress upon the entire organization, from local to world's union, and the Woman's Christian Temperance Union is, in the truest sense of the term, her living monument.

Frances Elizabeth Willard was born at Churchville, near Rochester, N. Y., on September 28, 1839. Her parents were the Hon. Josiah F. and Mary T. Hill Willard, both a sturdy New England Puritan stock. Her girlhood was spent in Churchville, Oberlin, Ohio, and Janesville, Wis., whence the family removed to Evanston, Ill., where she came to be known for many years as the most distinguished citizen of that town filled with distinguished people. She graduated from the Northwestern University, and, in later years, received the degree of A. M. from Syracuse University, and that of LL. D. from Ohio Wesleyan. She was for four years Professor of Natural Science at the Northwestern Female College; one year preceptress of the Genesee Wesleyan Seminary, Lima, N. Y.; two years traveled abroad, studying continental languages and the Fine Arts; in 1871 became President of the Woman's College, and Professor of Æsthetics in the Northwestern University. When the crusade startled the land, Miss Willard recognized it as of God's ordaining, even before it had commended itself to the mass of Christian people. She longed to "help those women," but her hands were filled with the work of her position; so, beyond words of sympathy, both spoken and written, and prayer to the Divine Strength, she was not actively allied with the crusade. Suddenly and unexpectedly her hands were freed, and then she followed what all her after-history proves to have been God's voice, and gave herself in a splendid abandon of consecration to this new and unpopular cause. A fine position, as preceptress of a wealthy New York school, was offered to her; and in the same mail came a letter from the remnant of the crusade in Chicago, who were holding Gospel meetings and trying to carry on the work, asking her to be their president. She chose the cause which led away from ease and natural tastes, and gave herself to that handful of women, and the whole world justifies her choice.

From the Chicago Union, in the fall of 1874, she was sent as delegate to the organizing convention of the Illinois Woman's Christian Temperance Union. From this state gathering she was sent to the National Assembly at Cleveland, and there, even at that early stage, as has been already noted, her consummate genius for leadership was recognized. She was made Chairman of the Committee on Resolutions, and that famous, oft-quoted resolution, so prophetic of much that was to follow in our after-history—*Resolved, That, recognizing that our cause is and will be combated by mighty, determined and relentless forces, we will, trusting in Him who is the Prince of Peace, meet argument with argument, misjudgment with patience, denunciation with kindness, and all our difficulties and dangers with prayer*—was written by Miss Willard.

She was elected to the National Corresponding Secretaryship at the convention of 1874, which position she held three years. She was afterward elected to the presidency of the Illinois State Union, and, at the Indianapolis convention, in 1879, to the National Presidency. To this latter position she was elected at nineteen consecutive conventions, the last at Buffalo, N. Y., in 1897, the year preceding her death.

Concerning Miss Willard's connection with the work of the organization in its earlier years, I quote from the report of the National Corresponding Secretary at the Baltimore Convention, in the year 1895:

"In 1883, Miss Willard, in speaking briefly of her year's work, says: 'It will thus have been my good fortune to have represented the crusade movement in every one of the forty-eight States and Territories of the United States this year.'

"Mrs. Buell, Corresponding Secretary for fourteen years, in her report for the same year, says: 'In March last our president turned her face westward, and everywhere she went new organizations were formed and old ones received new life. Such a trip as this made by Miss Willard the world had never thought of. Going without money and without price, without advance agents except the messages Uncle Sam might have carried for any other, yet the enthusiasm of her welcome was more than anything ever before accorded to any other, not excepting the President of the United States.'

"In the President's Annual Address of 1884 I find this incidental remark: 'In the twenty State conventions in my itinerary this year I have urged plans of finance, etc.'

"In 1890, Mrs. Buell, in her admirable review of the ten years just passed, says: 'Since 1880 our president has made a tour of every State and Territory, and the Dominion of Canada; Alaska alone remaining as the sole bit of territory in which her voice has not been heard.'

"These things being so, is it any wonder that from the vast majority of the states to which I sent the question, 'By whom was the W. C. T. U. introduced into your State?' all the Southern and most of the Southwestern and Western—yes, and some of the Eastern—the answer has been, 'The work was introduced into our State by Miss Willard.' We know something of the history of those tireless years, in which her home was a railroad train and her inseparable companion a grip-sack. We know that not even those weary journeys were allowed to interrupt her labor of brain and pen, since the fingers might have been seen constantly flying over the writing-tablet, be the road rough or smooth. We know that many of the strongest bugle notes which have roused the world to action came into being under such conditions. . . . .

"But her marvelous work as an organizer is by no means all which has been made manifest to my mind through these yearly records. I have found that the tabulated suggestions of the past fifteen years contain, in prophecy, the history of well-nigh all our advance steps. Her eyes have seen the substance 'yet being unperfect,' and in her heart, and on her brain, department after department, advance plan and new method have been constantly written, 'when as yet there was none of them.' And what she has seen she has dared to do. Not alone the seer's vision, but the hero's courage has she shown through all these years. Who led in the struggle for the adoption of the Franchise Department as a part of our work? Who saw, almost alone, this new star in the east and followed it, so bravely, so truly, and withal so reverently, that we could not fail to see how, in very truth, it stood over each home?"

To Miss Willard's busy brain and far-reaching influence is due the organization of *the World's* Woman's Christian Temperance Union. She first conceived the idea of federating the women of the world together, and, by her persuasion and efforts, the first Round-the-World missionary, Mrs. Mary Clement Leavitt, of Boston, was sent out. Mrs. Leavitt spent eight years abroad, and visited nearly all the countries of Europe and Asia in the interests of the Woman's Christian Temperance Union. She carried with her the blanks of the Polyglot petition, itself an emanation of Miss Willard's thought, addressed to the governments of the world, urging that the traffic in alcohol and other narcotics be prohibited within the bounds of their jurisdiction. This petition, at its first formal presentation, before President Cleveland, in Washington, in February, 1894, had attained the gigantic total of 1,121,200 names. It has since been presented to Queen Victoria and to the Premier of Canada, Sir Wilfred Laurier.

Six Round-the-World missionaries have succeeded Mrs. Leavitt —Miss Jessie Ackermann, who has twice girdled the globe, who organized and was the first president of the Australasian Woman's Christian Temperance Union; Dr. Kate Bushnell and Mrs. Elizabeth Wheeler Andrew, who worked chiefly in the purity work of India; Miss Alice Palmer, who spent several years in South Africa; Miss Clara Parrish, who did most effective work in Japan and Burma; Mrs. J. K. Barney, who, having circled the globe, is now doing organizing work in Cuba and Porto Rico; Misses Vincent and Cummins, of Australia, who are now working in Great Britain, and Mrs. Addie Northam Fields, who organized the Woman's Christian Temperance Union in the Bermuda Islands, and is now working in Mexico.

One of the sweetest fruits which came into Miss Willard's life through the World's Woman's Christian Temperance Union was her friendship with Lady Henry Somerset, the gifted English noblewoman who—brought to the reform through a common sympathy —became Miss Willard's life-long friend. The later years of her life were spent, largely, in Lady Henry Somerset's beautiful home, either at Eastnor Castle or at The Priory, Reigate; here, together they planned largely for the great work, as well as took sweet counsel of personal friendship. Lady Henry Somerset, as Vice-President of the World's Union, became Acting President on Miss Willard's death. At the last convention she was unanimously elected to the presidency. Mrs. L. M. N. Stevens, President of the Woman's Christian Temperance Union of the United States, was elected vice-president; Miss Agnes Slack, of England, and Miss Anna A.

Gordon, of America, are the secretaries, and Mrs. Sanderson, of Canada, is the treasurer.

The first World's Convention of the Woman's Christian Temperance Union was held in Faneuil Hall, Boston, in the year 1891. Four conventions have since taken place—in Chicago, 1893; London, 1895; Toronto, 1897, and Edinburgh, 1900. At the Edinburgh convention delegates were present from forty affiliated countries, and requests were presented from six nations, that Round-the-World missionaries be sent them, to gather the women together in local unions, for more effective work. And this great and far-reaching work of the World's Woman's Christian Temperance Union is, even more fully than the work of her own National Union of the United States —since to her came its first inspiration—the work of and the monument to Frances E. Willard.

The chief advance of the National Union since 1874 has been along two lines; that of organization and increase of membership, and of enlargement of the scope of its work. One after another kindred reforms have been found to have such a close relation to the work of temperance, that room has been made for them in the society's programme. The "Do Everything Policy" came about by natural evolution. Purity, Woman's Suffrage, Prohibition, Antinarcotics, and other subjects, were seen to be in such vital alliance to the central thought of purified homes, and a saved nation, that they were recognized as legitimate parts of the main campaign.

To quote from the report of the year 1895:

"The 'Do Everything Policy' is a profoundly philosophical recognition of the Divine principles of evolution and solidarity. We have not left behind our first principles of total abstinence and prohibition, because so many other lines of work have been evolved. We could not leave them behind if we would. They are the foundation stones upon which our fair structure of the future is to be reared. But just as no building rises to its completion through its foundation stones alone, so we have found, not alone room for, but need of, many another material; and see with increasing clearness of vision that many others must be used before the cap-stone shall be laid with shoutings of 'Grace, grace unto it!' All that has been added has been by growth from within outward; it has been the natural unfolding of the seed planted twenty-four years ago. 'First the blade, then the ear; after that the full corn in the ear.' It surely does not lessen, but rather heightens the glory of the crusade, to believe that out of it has grown something infinitely grander, and that this outgrowth, too, is but the prophecy of a grander yet to come. 'Forgetting the things that are behind,' of achievement as well as of failure, humanity's only safeguard must lie in a continual pressing forward; and 'this one thing' we of the Woman's Christian Temperance Union will 'do,' God being our helper."

To-day, after twenty-seven years of existence, the National Woman's Christian Temperance Union of the United States is organized in every state and territory; indeed, it has outgrown the natural limits of states and territories, and inclusive of the colored unions of the Southern States, and the two organizations which, for convenience's sake, exist in California and Washington, we count sixty-two auxiliary unions; fifty-four are state, six are territorial, and the two others are the District of Columbia and Hawaii unions. Work is also being carried forward in the Philippines and in Porto Rico. There are at least ten thousand local unions in these several states and territorial unions, and, during the last year, an increase was made in membership of about fifteen thousand.

There are thirty-nine distinct departments of work, at the head of each one of which stands a National Superintendent, who has associated with herself a corps of associates, lecturers and helpers. There are twenty-two national organizers, fourteen national lecturers, and twenty national evangelists. These several classes of women include many names which have won a wide reputation—in many instances world-wide, for eloquence, executive ability and power of leadership. It would seem invidious to single out names where so many have won for themselves renown and where it is so manifestly impossible to mention all, but the story of the Woman's Christian Temperance Union of America would be incomplete without mention of Mother Stewart, the brave Ohio leader; Mother Wallace, Mrs. Mary A. Livermore, Mrs. Mary A. Woodbride, Mrs. Mary T. Lathrap, Miss Mary Allen West, who fell at her post in Japan; the Round-the-World missionaries; Mrs. Clara C. Hoffman, Mrs. Lillian M. N. Stevens, Miss Anna A. Gordon, for twenty-one years Miss Willard's private secretary; Mrs. Fry, the present Corresponding Secretary; Mrs. Helen M. Barker, the National Treasurer, and a hundred others. Indeed, there is hardly a state or territorial union which has not furnished names which will be forever remembered for the work their owners have wrought for humanity through the agency of this organization.

LADY HENRY SOMERSET.

"The results? Laws upon the statute books of every State in our Union save three [since changed to one], requiring scientific teaching to the pupils of our public schools of the effects of alcohol and other narcotics, and an ever-increasing army of earnest allies in the teachers of our land, who are eager to aid in the enforcement of those laws. The results? The raising of the age of protection for our daughters in nearly every State in the Union, and whole floods of light thrown upon the subject of purity in its relation to the home, and its relation to the individual. The results? Time and space forbid their enumeration. Listen to the tramp of three hundred thousand children of the Loyal Temperance Legion as they keep step to the inspiring words of our great leader: 'Saloons must go.' Go into the Sunday-schools of our land where temperance principles are taught; go into the houses of refuge, where hundreds and hundreds of poor, betrayed girls and heart-broken women have been lifted up into new life; go down into the mines, into our prisons, our jails, and our almshouses; up into the lumber camps, into our camps of war and our ships at sea; stop at Castle Garden, where our missionary meets the immigrant and puts literature into his hand, which in many instances has reached both head and heart; go into the sunny Southland and see the noble bands of colored women who are taking up our work and pledging themselves to the redemption of their race from a bondage far worse than slavery; enter our well-nigh numberless Gospel temperance and evangelistic meetings, in which so many prodigals are turning back to the Father's house; see our brave bands of organizers, lecturers and evangelists as they go patiently forth on their toilsome errands, daring summer's heat and winter's cold; see how the table of our Lord has been practically freed from the cup which means death; see how the press is responding to the call for a higher expression of the life of the American people; see how art and literature are being purified; principles of mercy taught and peace inculcated; read the Gospel of woman's enfranchisement, as it is written in literature, upon the pulpits from which she ministers and in the repealing of countless iniquitous laws, as well as in the four fair States in which full suffrage has been granted her. Read our advance as recorded in the treatment of diseases without the use of alcohol; read it in the healthful pages of the temperance literature sent forth, and in countless other forms which, for lack of space, cannot be mentioned, if you would know some of the results.

"But even in all these you can catch but a faint, fleeting shadow of the real substance, for, like the Kingdom of God, of which it is a vital part, the Woman's Christian Temperance Union 'cometh not with observation.' It is not a thing accomplished, it is the subjective state of mind and soul which must lie back of all accomplishment, and greater than anything it has done or can do must remain the fact that *it is*—an army of light-bearers, a company of seers, an exponent of the life-principle of love wrought out in divinest activities. Who shall set limits to the results flowing from such an organization?"

On the 17th of February, in the year 1898, came the saddest event which the Woman's Christian Temperance Union had ever known —to which allusion has been already made—the death of Frances Willard. Greater honors were paid to her in her death than had ever before been paid to any woman, unless to some queen. Her funeral journey extended from New York City to Chicago; and not this nation alone, but the entire world mourned.

At the convention in Cleveland, three years before, Miss Willard, through a constitutional change enabling her to do this, had appointed Mrs. Lillian M. N. Stevens, for more than twenty years the president of the Maine Woman's Christian Temperance Union, and for years one of the Recording Secretaries of the National Union, as vice-president at large. The wisdom of the choice was soon apparent. Mrs. Stevens brought to the difficult post to which she was so suddenly and so unwillingly elevated, all the accumulated wisdom of her long years of faithful and devoted service. She was very soon called upon to test her courage and fibre, and she stood the test in such a manner as to make all feel that the helm of the good ship W. C. T. U. was in safe hands. At the St. Paul convention, in the following October, she was elected, with a practical unanimity of choice, to the position of president of the National Woman's Christian Temperance Union. Miss Anna A. Gordon was at the same convention elected vice-president at large; Mrs. Susanna M. D. Fry was elected to the position of corresponding secretary, made vacant by the resignation of the writer, who had filled the position for four years; Mrs. Clara C. Hoffman and Mrs. Frances E. Beauchamp were re-elected as recording secretaries, and Mrs. Helen M. Barker, for the fifth time as national treasurer. The same women are holding these offices to-day.

The last National Convention was held in Washington, D. C.,

November 30 to December 7, 1900. It was the largest that has yet been held, and its results upon the organization throughout the country promise to be far-reaching and lasting. Twelve states— Iowa, New York, West Washington, Maine, Ohio, Southern California, Connecticut, Virginia, Vermont, Michigan, New Hampshire and West Virginia—had all made a gain of five hundred or more in membership. The convention pledged the union to work along the lines of organization and increase of membership; the instructing and building up of unions by means of courses of study and Woman's Christian Temperance Union Institutes; renewed efforts for the increased circulation of the official organ, "The Union Signal," and the circulation of other temperance literature; a voluntary thank-offering on the part of the unions and individuals, to be given on or near February 17th, of two dollars or more, as a Memorial Fund to Miss Willard, to be used in organizing and strengthening the work to which she gave her life; special work in our new national possessions, for young women, and in the promulgation of the truths of non-alcoholic medication; and for immediate action, petitions and personal influence in favor of the reform bills in Congress, especially all national and state bills looking toward the abolition of liquor selling. One of the most notable victories ever won by the organization was the second Anti-Canteen Bill, which passed the House of Representatives while the last convention was in session, the success of which is largely attributed to the influence of the Woman's Christian Temperance Union. The victory over polygamy, as represented in Brigham H. Roberts, is also, by common consent, attributed largely to the work of the women of the country, with the Woman's Christian Temperance Union at their head.

I cannot better close this necessarily imperfect sketch than by two quotations, the first from the Annual Address of Miss Willard before the Boston National Convention, in 1891; the second from the Address of Mrs. Mary T. Lathrap, before the first National Council of Women, in Washington, D. C., 1890:

"The hands that wave these snowy salutes of welcome have been placed on the heads of little children, of whom we have three hundred thousand in our Loyal Temperance Legion; they have given out total abstinence pledges to a million tempted men; they have pinned the ribbon—white, as a talisman of purity—above the hearts of ten thousand tempted prodigals; they have carried bread to the hungry, and broken the bread of life to those who were most hungry of all for that, although they knew it not. These hands have carried petitions for the protection of the home, for the preservation of the Sabbath, for the purification of the law, and during seventeen years of such honest, hard work as was almost never equaled, they have gathered not fewer than twenty million names to these petitions. These faces have bent over the bedsides of the dying, for whose souls no one seemed to care; they have illumined with the light that never shone on land or sea, many a dark tenement house in attic or cellar; they have gleamed like stars of hope in the slums of our great cities. These voices have sung songs of deliverance to the prisoner in ten thousand jails and almshouses; they have brought a breath of cheer into police courts, bridewells and houses of detention all around the world.

"These willing feet are more familiar with rough than with smooth pavements. They know the by-ways better than the highways. If their errands could be set in order they would read like the litanies of God's deliverance to those bound in the chains of temptation, sorrow and sin. Some touch of all that you have seen and done chastens each forehead and hallows every face. God has helped us to build better than we knew. If these women had their way (and they intend to have it), the taint of alcohol and nicotine would not be on any lip nor on any atmosphere of city, town or village on this globe. If they had their way (and they intend to have it), no gambler could with impunity pursue his vile vocation. If they could have their way the haunts of shame that are the zero mark of degradation would be crusaded out of existence before sundown, and the industrial status of women would be so independent that these recruiting officers of perdition would seek in vain for victims. If you could have your way, the saloon keeper would become, in every state and nation!—as, thank God, he is already in so many—an outcast, an Ishmaelite, a social pariah on the face of the earth; for you do not seek the regulation of the traffic, nor its prohibition even, but its annihilation. You stand for prohibition by law, prohibition by politics, prohibition by woman's ballot, and all these three are but parts of one tremendous whole."

"No association of philanthropic workers has touched so many springs of praise and blame, love and hate, and become equally distinguished for the friends it has won, and the enemies it has made, and the proof of the effectiveness of the mission it has undertaken is easy to find on the very surface of things. Cursed at the bar of the legalized dram shop; hissed on the floor of the Beer Brewers' Congress; scorned by conventions of political parties; misrepresented by the all-powerful press; denied its prayers in the halls of legislation; sneered at in palaces of fashion, where the wine-glass tempts to destroy; criticised by conservative pulpits, and unwelcome often in the Christian Church, it has been left to this organization of ballotless women to arouse all classes of opposers, and find for themselves the hate of hate. But, on the other hand, blessed by the fevered lips of the drunkard ready to perish; sought by the wandering feet of the boy or girl who went astray; hallowed by loving thoughts at thousands of firesides; baptized with holy tears by the mothers whose battles it wages; perfumed by the stainless prayers of little children; endorsed by the expressed principles of organized Christianity; sustained by the highest and freshest authorities in the scientific world; praised by lips grown careful through statesmanlike speech; believed in by the best, trusted by the most needy, it has been granted us, also, to find the 'love of love.' "

* * * * * * * * *

It was not on the field of battle,
It was not with a ship at sea,
But a fate far worse than either
That stole him away from me.
'Twas the death in the tempting dram
That the reason and senses drown;
He drank the alluring poison,
And thus my boy went down.

Down from the heights of manhood
To the depths of disgrace and sin;
Down to a worthless being,
From the hope of what might have been.
For the brand of a beast besotted
He bartered his manhood's crown;
Through the gate of a sinful pleasure
My poor, weak boy went down.

'Tis only the same old story,
That mothers so often tell,
With accents of infinite sadness,
Like the tones of a funeral bell;
But I never thought once, when I heard it,
I should learn all its meaning myself;
I thought he'd be true to his mother,
I thought he'd be true to himself.

But, alas! for my hopes, all delusion!
   Alas! for his youthful pride!
Alas! who are safe when danger
   Is open on every side?
Oh, can nothing destroy this great evil?
   Nor bar in its pathway be thrown,
To save from the terrible maelstrom
   The thousands of boys going down?

—Unidentified.—E<small>D</small>.

THE WORLD-WIDE STUDENT MOVEMENT.*

JOHN R. MOTT, M.A.,
NEW YORK.

[A few months before his death, Mr. Moody said to me that, from a religious point of view, he looked upon our colleges as the most hopeful field in all the world. The colleges and universities constitute, without doubt, the most religious communities in our country. Taking the young men of America as a whole, not more than one in twelve are members of evangelical churches. Some have placed the proportion as low as one in twenty. Among students, however, nearly one-half of the young men are members of evangelical churches. The proportion among the women students is larger. Among professors and instructors the percentage of evangelical Christians is far larger even than it is among the students. This is true in state and other undenominational colleges, as well as in denominational institutions.

A still more striking fact is that the proportion of Christian students in our colleges is larger than it ever was. An eminent clergyman has pointed out that, about a hundred years ago, there was but one professing Christian student at Yale. At that time, in a number of other colleges with Christian foundations, there were but small groups of disciples of Jesus Christ. It would be difficult to name half a dozen colleges of which the same thing could now be said. Six years ago a religious census was taken of more than three hundred American colleges, and it was ascertained that of the seventy thousand young men in these institutions over one-half were members of evangelical churches, whereas, a quarter of a century previous, not more than one-third of the male students in these colleges were professing Christians. Facts like these show that students in larger numbers relatively than ever before acknowledge Christ as Lord, and are identified with His church.

Generally speaking, it may be asserted that the type of religious life of American students is not traditional. They do not hold their present beliefs simply because they have inherited them. At the same time, they do attach great weight to the traditional facts and statements of the Christian faith. They are, as a class, loyal to the great verities of evangelical Christianity. Their religious belief is based upon a personal study of the Christian Scriptures and evidences. And not least helpful in establishing their faith has been the influence of the presentation and study of the facts of Christian missions.

Their religious life, therefore, may be characterized as intellectual, spiritual and practical; the typical American Christian student despises cant and hypocrisy, and desires, above all else, reality in his Christian experience. He is not satisfied to limit the Bible to the realm of thought and discussion; he

---
*Given at the "International Conference of Theological Students," Allegheny, Pennsylvania, November 1-4, 1900.

seeks to bring it to bear upon his life—to help him in his battle with temptation, to enable him to develop strong faith and a symmetrical character.

Moreover, he is not content to keep his religion to himself. He recognizes the force of Archbishop Whately's words: "If our religion is not true, we ought to change it; if it is true, we are bound to propagate what we believe to be the truth." Therefore he unites with his Christian fellow-students in an organized movement to make Christ known in his college, in his native land, and throughout the world.—JOHN R. MOTT; "The Sunday-School Times," January 19, 1901.—ED.]

* * *

ONE time when Charles Simeon, who was such a spiritual force in Cambridge University many years ago, saw an undergraduate entering Trinity Church at Cambridge, he said: "There come six hundred people." Not long since, Bismarck, a little before his death, struck off this remarkable generalization concerning the students of Germany: "One-third of the students of Germany break down as a result of dissipation; another third are incapacitated because of overwork; the remaining third govern the empire." We might multiply examples of this kind going to enforce the truth of the statement that the universities and colleges and seminaries teach the teachers, preach to the preachers, and govern the governors. They are, indeed, the pivotal points in civilization, and it is not putting it too strongly to assert that, as go these institutions of higher learning, so inevitably go the nations. All this attaches great importance to the attitude of the student class toward Jesus Christ. Is Christ, as some would try to lead us to believe, losing His hold on students, or are they year by year in greater numbers acknowledging Him as Lord and rendering unto Him a larger obedience? There could be no more important question for us to consider as men who are to become leaders in the church, for surely nothing more concerns the welfare of the church in the world and her ultimate triumph.

There are different ways in which we might attempt an answer to this question, but possibly one of the most satisfactory will be to view the various organizations of students in the different parts of the world, organizations which bear the name of Christ Himself. I say one of the most satisfactory ways of approaching the question and of attempting to answer it, because an organization puts in tangible form what men are thinking about and what they believe. That for which men are willing to go on record publicly, that to which they lend the weight of their influence, that to which they

JOHN R. MOTT.

give time and money and earnest advocacy, puts in concrete form what men are thinking about and what they believe. In this review I shall try to give an up-to-date statement of the tendencies and conditions in the universities, colleges and seminaries. What I shall now say could not have been said three years ago. Much of it could not have been said one year ago. I shall try to avail myself of the most recent information, as it was poured in upon us at the memorable conference held last August at Versailles, near Paris, the conference of the World's Student Christian Federation. I shall also ask your permission to view these movements somewhat in the order in which it was my privilege to study the conditions of student work in different parts of the world even before many of these movements came into existence.

AMERICA.

This necessitates our commencing on this continent, and it is fitting that we do so, because, strange as it may seem to us, on this continent—where we have not a few of the youngest universities, colleges and seminaries of the world—was planted and has been developed the oldest and largest Christian student movement of the world. I speak of the Student Young Men's Christian Association movement to which we belong. Twenty-three years ago, when this organization began, at the suggestion of the students of Princeton, there were only between thirty and forty Christian organizations of students in the United States and Canada. This included all that were in any sense worthy of the name. Now we have six hundred and fifty. This number includes our Seminary Section, as well as the sections in the medical colleges, in the state universities, in the three hundred and more denominational colleges and other higher institutions, in the normal schools, and in many of the fitting schools and high schools. I was at Yale a few days ago, and learned that they now have in the different branches of the Young Men's Christian Association in that university about one thousand members. It suggests to my mind that we only had a little more than that number in all the Christian Associations of North America twenty-three years ago, when this movement began. We now have not less than thirty-five thousand students and professors of these two countries who count it a privilege to identify themselves with this organization and to promote what it stands for in the world. We have a right to expect that such a combination of men in the name of Jesus Christ, fused together by His Almighty Spirit, will be used by Him in accomplishing great things for the Kingdom of Christ. We are not disappointed in our expectation. Under the influence of the Spirit of God, using these societies, very nearly fifty thousand students have been led to become disciples of Jesus Christ as their Saviour and Lord during these twenty-three years. The number has been steadily increasing, so that last year probably a little over three thousand of these men of the universities and colleges entered the Christian life as a result of the public meetings and the personal work in connection with this organization. Last year witnessed more remarkable and pervasive spiritual awakenings, even in some of the most difficult fields, than we have had any year within the memory of the most of us who have been connected with the colleges. The revival in Bible study also has been remarkable. I remember when I left college there were in all these institutions less than two thousand men in voluntary Bible circles. Last year we had over fourteen thousand. The number has been growing, and not only the number, but, even more important, the quality of the work has been constantly improving. It has become more thorough, more systematic, more progressive. It has related itself to the daily life, the doubts, the temptations, and the problems concerning life work of students as it did not do in the earlier days, except in rare cases. Something like sixty-two hundred men, according to our records, have been influenced by the Association to dedicate their lives to the Christian ministry. I suppose we would agree that if this organization had done nothing more than this—to turn the steps of over six thousand men into this most influential calling of men—it would have wrought sufficient to have justified all that has been expended upon it in supervision and money and time. But the missionary movement has been still more encouraging. Beginning in the form of the Student Volunteer Movement, it has related itself organically, still working under that name, to our Young Men's Christian Associations. Thousands of men have been led to enroll themselves as volunteers within the past fourteen years alone, and more than sixteen hundred of these volunteers have completed their preparation and have gone out to the mission fields under the regular missionary societies of the church, a larger number going in the past four years than in the preceding nine years.

Alongside of this movement among the young men has been developed the Student Young Women's Christian Association, which has wrought wonders among the women students of this country. I do not now pause to recount the exact facts of this organization, which now includes over three hundred and fifty colleges and schools with a membership of more than nineteen thousand college women. It may be stated, considering the difficulties, that they have had even more striking achievements than our Young Men's Christian Association.

GREAT BRITAIN.

I leave this continent and take you with me to the British Isles. The British College Christian Union began about seven years ago with seventeen Christian associations, or unions among students. There are now one hundred and thirty. That includes all of the great universities, and a large majority of the influential theological colleges and seminaries, and other institutions of higher learning. They do not yet address themselves as a movement to the secondary or preparatory schools. This organization of Britain, working in recent years in the midst of conditions which are certainly more difficult than those of a new country like Canada or the United States, has accomplished enough already to demonstrate convincingly that God is in their work. Take the matter of Bible study. I well remember, when I first attended one of their conferences, that some leading colleges had no Bible class. It would be difficult to mention a college of importance in the British Isles which does not now have one or more Bible circles as the result of the work of this movement. Last year they had two thousand students gathered in these classes, and their whole movement has in it now over four thousand members. This is a remarkable growth, considering that it has taken place within seven years. The Christward tendency among the British students is also increasing. Within the past few years they have had some remarkable spiritual awakenings in their great universities. If the Spirit of Almighty God can work as He has worked in these universities, it ought to encourage us to expect His marvels to be wrought in other parts of the student world. When the Volunteer Union was organized in Great Britain an investigation revealed the fact that only about three hundred British students expected to be foreign missionaries. They now have on their volunteer roll two thousand students, and of that number fully six hundred have already reached the mission field—a larger proportion than have gone out from the North American movement. The Archbishop of Canterbury has said that few things have inspired him with greater hope than the recent uprising of university men and women for the evangelization of the world. To my mind the largest result of the British movement has been the developing of the inter-collegiate or inter-university consciousness among the British universities and colleges. Before the movement had its rise, many of them were practically isolated. It is true that Oxford and Cambridge had annual conferences. But now they have had linked together in strong organization the many student centres. When we think of what Edinburgh University has wrought in the history of the world, or Oxford, what have we not a right to expect, and what does not our faith claim, now that the coming Christian leaders of church and state in Oxford and Cambridge, Edinburgh and Glasgow, St. Andrews and Aberdeen, Dublin and Belfast and other colleges are united in a common purpose and inspired by the same great objective? What may it not mean to the world-wide British Empire, and through that empire, to the unevangelized world itself?

GERMANY.

We go next to the great land of universities, Germany, one of the difficult fields of the western student world. The work there began in the gymnasia in the form of devotional Bible circles. Some said it would be an excellent thing if we could have a similar work in the universities. While people were expressing their doubts, and were discussing the matter, God was solving the problem. The gymnasia boys finished their education, entered the universities, formed their Bible circles, and the first thing we knew there was a student movement created in the German universities, created by Almighty God working in His own way. There are now Bible circles in seventeen of the twenty-one universities of Germany, and in many of the gymnasia. A striking thing about the German movement is, that every member of it belongs to a Bible circle. I wish we could say that of the theological section and the different college sections of this country. You ask me: "Are the students of Germany being led out of agnosticism and lives of sinfulness into the Bible faith in Jesus Christ?" Last year witnessed more men entering the Kingdom of God as the result of the work of the German movement than in any preceding year of its history. A German graduate said to me: "We had an eminent professor who attended some of our circle meetings, and as a result, came out into a clear faith in Christ," and he remarked: "He came like a little child." That is the way they will all come, whether they are the professors or the students in Germany or in other lands. It is only when they become as little children that they shall see the way, and shall have the spirit that will take them through the door.

The missionary spirit has also been developing in the German universities under the influence of the student movement. Now they have in their own Student Volunteer Movement nearly one hundred volunteers, and are planning to have a convention at Hallé next year, which will doubtless be the greatest student missionary convention ever held on the continent of Europe. It will be attended by evangelical students from all parts of that continent. I do not know how these facts concerning Germany impress you, but I have found few things in all my experience among students which have given me more hope. When we remember the influence that the German universities have had in the history of the church—that in them the great movements like the Reformation and the Pietist movement, and the missionary movement of modern times, in a very important sense, had their rise; when we remember that they hold a larger influence in the world of thought to-day than any other national group of universities (I include their theological faculties as well); when we recall their terrible moral and spiritual condition, as some of us have had an opportunity to see it and know it, are we not filled with gratitude to God, that He by His mighty Spirit has been pleased to move again in these universities, calling them into life and action even, on behalf of the world's evangelization?

SCANDINAVIA.

The Scandinavian movement is also of recent origin. It links together the Christian societies of university Christian men and women of Norway, Sweden, Denmark and Finland. They have their international conferences every two or three years. Three or four hundred students and professors assemble, and these are now among the most notable gatherings held in Europe. As the result of this movement, working out through the prayer life and the consistent living of the members of the local organizations, the religious life of the universities of Scandinavia has been greatly developed and quickened. Bible study is being promoted. Bible courses are being prepared. Work is being carried on to influence the boys in the gymnasia. The number of missionary candidates is increasing. I have found no students who impressed me as having greater strength than the Scandinavians. I admired their manliness, their thoroughness, their honesty of spirit and method. They are the most thorough students in the world. A man, after he has taken his arts course, has to study seven to ten years before he can graduate in medicine, four or five years before he can take a degree in theology, not less than five years before he takes it in law. These men go in training and stay in training, and come out thorough. They also have the missionary spirit. I expect not one of the largest, but one of the strongest contingents for the evangelization of the world from these universities of the Northlands.

SWITZERLAND—HOLLAND—FRANCE.

I shall not stop to relate the movement in the Swiss universities, more than to say that it has right of way in French-speaking Switzerland, and is just now beginning to develop in German-speaking Switzerland. It is very hopeful. It has recently secured the services of an able man as traveling secretary.

Nor shall I detain you to speak of the Dutch Student Christian Union, although it is one of the most interesting. They have a Christian organization in each of their universities, planted as the result of most prayerful effort, and in the face of difficulties they are doing great good. The missionary idea has been incorporated into their work within the last two years.

We shall not delay to consider the student movement of France—although there is much that might be said as a ground of encouragement—more than to say that in the most difficult field, the University of Paris, they now have an association numbering nearly two hundred men. The work has spread beyond Paris, until it is now established in five of the provincial universities of France. They have their missionary department, or section of the Student Volunteer Movement.

EGYPT.

On our way to the Far East let us stop in Egypt and go up the Nile valley, and look for a moment into Assiout, that wonderful college of the United Presbyterian Church. It seems to me that if foreign missions had done nothing else in Egypt than to plant that college, and to send out the results that have gone from it within these past fifteen or twenty years, they would have accomplished a great work. How it inspired me to meet with those students and professors and devoted missionaries who have planted their association! When I was there, I had the joy of leading some of those young men to devote their lives to Christian work. I think there were about twelve. They signed a little volunteer declaration of their own, and I cherish highly among my effects the little papers which they signed. The other day my friend Sallmon was induced, on his way back from Australia to this country, to touch that college, and he brings the word that the little band of ten or twelve has increased to eighty men, who had dedicated their whole lives to Christian work among their own people. It shows the germinating and dynamic power of this movement under the influence of the Spirit of God.

INDIA AND CEYLON.

We leave these inviting fields, and hasten on to India and Ceylon; India, that great country! Country? Let me change the word to continent. It is a continent with practically as many people as Europe, with many more lines of social cleavage than Europe has ever known, and certainly many more religions than Europe. It is a vast continent, and if we associate with it Ceylon and Burma, we find three hundred millions of people. Let me emphasize the fact that the student class holds the key to the situation in British India. There are about one hundred thousand young men in the universities, colleges, and other higher institutions, including the highest classes of the high schools of India, Ceylon and Burma. As go this hundred thousand and their successors, will go the three hundred millions of that great region and their successors. Some of us may be disposed to look down upon those Indian students. No man who has seen them, or worked with them, will do so. I have never been harder pressed in public argument or private interview than by those keen, subtle-minded Mohammedan students. If you are disposed to look down upon those men of our own blood, go with me to Oxford and Cambridge, and see how they are carrying off their share of the university honors.

It is a ripe field also. The student movement has become intrenched there. It began with a little group of societies. It now includes nearly forty, and its membership embraces the great university centres and the leading missionary schools of India and Ceylon. It has at its head several of the most experienced university workers whom we have been able to send out from the United States, Canada, Great Britain and Denmark. There are in all about ten university men who have dedicated their lives to molding, and guiding, and energizing, and spreading this movement on lines which have been wrought out in more favored countries. God is honoring their efforts. Their opportunities in the realm of Bible study are limited only by their time and strength. The way men will gather around them to learn the Word of God, and to study it and listen to lectures upon it, would stimulate some of us, if we knew the facts, to volunteer for foreign service in India. And men are being led to Christ. Henry Martyn maintained that he would about as soon expect to see a dead body rise as to see a Brahmin converted to Jesus Christ; and yet, believe me, dead bodies are rising in India as a result of this movement, as well as the result of educational missions and other agencies, so that not a year passes during these days in which strong Brahmins, Hindoos, and now and then Mohammedans, are not led out into a saving faith in Jesus Christ. Even the missionary spirit is beginning to show itself, although the conditions are very difficult. Take Ceylon, for example. Within the last year and a little over, the students in a college in the northern part of the island of Ceylon have started a missionary society, and have sent one of their own graduates to work among their own race in Southern India. They have caught the idea of Christ. Let us hope and pray that it may be planted and germinate in every one of these associations in India and Ceylon.

AUSTRALASIA.

We might, by way of variety, drop down into the Southern Hemisphere. It involved a journey of fourteen thousand miles for me to go down there and get back into the regular circuit that is usually taken around the world. I did not wonder at it, when I reached there, that God had taken me to that part of the world. I found in Australia and New Zealand and Tasmania a country as large as the United States and Canada, with a population nearly as large as that of Canada, a people combining the characteristics which mark

SIR WILFRID LAWSON.

off the Canadians and the Americans, and that is, by the way, a strong combination. I found universities there that stand much higher in their record and in their requirements than many of the universities in the two countries that we represent in this conference. These universities were given over largely to secularism. There were only five religious societies among them, and three of those did not bear the word "Christian." When they heard what the students were doing in Canada and Britain and the United States, their appreciation of the value of organization, that you find among Anglo-Saxons everywhere, responded to the suggestion, and they began to organize, and had some twenty-five societies organized as a result of their efforts before I left. That number has since increased to forty-five. Before I left they said: "We want a traveling secretary." Sallmon, the Yale secretary, was induced to go out there. He has returned after three years' labor, in which he has built up a movement which will compare with the best in the world. It includes all the universities, theological seminaries, and the other separate colleges. I did not find a Bible class among students in Australasia. I do not know one of those colleges which does not now have one or more Bible classes. I did not find a college in which I could discover that men had led students to Jesus Christ the year before. It would be difficult to find any prominent institution in which some men were not led to Jesus Christ last year by their fellow students. I found only nine men and women, I think, who were expecting to be foreign missionaries. They have now a volunteer roll of nearly one hundred, and of that number at least eleven have already reached the foreign field. They are looking out into the doorway of the three great mission fields of the world, Africa, India and China, not to mention the East Indies and the other islands of the Southern Seas. It is a great base for aggressive operations for the evangelization of the world. We hated to leave that country. We next went on that twenty-three days' journey through the Philippines until we came to China.

CHINA.

When I came to China, I came to the country which impressed me the most strongly of any I have ever visited. You ask me in what respect. Not so much because of the number of people; China has the numbers, there is no doubt about that—I was never out of sight of a living Chinaman, or the grave of a dead one; not so much on account of the difficulties, although China presents the greatest combination of difficulties of any mission field I have ever visited, not excepting the Mohammedan fields. You ask what, then, did impress me so much. The strength of the Chinese race. They combine the characteristics which have marked the greatest races of the world—industry, frugality, patience, tenacity, great physical vigor, great intellectual vigor as well, independence and conservatism. Some one pauses and says: "Is that the China that went down under the chariot wheels of Japan? Is that the China before which during these days are permitted to gather the fleets of Europe and America, and over which foreign powers are already beginning to extend their zones of influence?" No; that is an entirely different China. That China is composed of the officials. Who are the officials of China? They, to a man, belong to the literati. Who are the literati of China? They are the class which have passed through that old competitive examination system, which has in it, or has had in it, except in a very few cases, and that in recent years, no modern subjects of learning; no modern science, no political economy and sociology, no history of other countries, no geography of other countries no literature of other countries, no correct idea of their own country and its vast make-up and possibilities. Is it to be wondered at that men trained in that way have been the great obstacle in the way of its progress? You ask me: "What is the hope of China?" I found it in that fringe of modern colleges reaching from Canton on the south to Tientsin on the north, and back to Peking, and a very few in the interior. These colleges, planted by the missionaries, or at the suggestion of the missionaries, or as a result of the example of the colleges of the missionaries, are having trained in them natives, the leaders of the new China. What shall the leadership of the new China be? That is the burning question, and it is a far more important question than whether China is to be dismembered, or whether she is to preserve her integrity. One thing is certain, that within the very near future, scores of modern colleges will be planted in the provincial capitals of that country on the western model. In them will be trained many of the leaders of the new China. There is no more important question before the Church of Christ, and before us, therefore, as ministers of the church, than what shall this leadership be. Educational missionaries of all our denominations represented in China, and the student movement, unite in saying that that leadership must be made Christian, cost what it may. The missionaries have called the student movement. We did not go before their call. They united in a call, the like of which has come from few fields. To show the way they regard the matter, when I had the privilege of being there, we held the convention to form the national movement, and seventeen college professors left their work for from one to three weeks to come down to Shanghai and lay the foundation of this Student Young Men's Christian Association. When I reached China there were eight associations. Now we have forty-four; and five of our university men, whom we delight to honor—Lyon, Brockman, Gailey, Lewis and Southam—are in the leadership of this work, and are developing natives who will carry on these associations and make this organization indigenous to the soil. God is using this movement. They had the greatest revivals in the history of the colleges of China last year; a revival which, as some of us look at it now, was meant to nerve our fellow students there for the fearful ordeal before them. And down in the Fukien Province they had a revival only a few months ago, in which scores of students were led into the Christian life as the result of the work of their own fellow students.

Of the membership of the Chinese movement, over one-third are in Bible classes, and a more remarkable fact than that, five hundred and sixty of the number, that is, over a third, keep the morning watch; that is, they spend the first half hour of every day alone with God in Bible study and secret prayer. I wish we could say that all the members of our seminary associations and other sections of this movement begin the day with unhurried, recollected, purposeful communion with God, and with the application, day by day, of His truth to the life. What a different movement it would make! How it would cause these colleges and seminaries to pulsate with spiritual energy! It is not strange that we find in China, as a result of such honoring of the Word of God and such relation to Him in prayer, that the missionary spirit is developing. They have now about two hundred and sixty members, who are what we might call volunteers, who are turning from opportunities to give their lives to commercial pursuits, where they would receive two or three or more times as great salary, and are planning to devote themselves to preaching Christ to their own people. This is the secret of the evangelization of the world in the present generation.

We shall want leaders to go out from our home movements, but the rank and file of the workers must come from the ranks of the native students themselves.

JAPAN.

On to Japan, that most brilliant nation in the world; that country which has achieved greater progress in one generation than any other country has achieved in two, if not in three generations; that nation which has been going to school to the whole world, and which has learned her lessons with such remarkable facility. I found one hundred and fifty of those Japanese students in the German universities alone. These men have learned their lessons, and as soon as they learn them, they send back their foreign teachers. Japan has fifty thousand students. Of two hundred and fifty higher institutions of learning, about two hundred and fifteen are government institutions. In these two hundred and fifteen government institutions, I found that of three thousand three hundred professors and teachers, less than one in thirty-three was a Christian. That was three years ago. Less than one in thirty-three of the teachers of this progressive nation disciples of Jesus Christ! It does not require a prophet to predict what that means unless this proportion be changed, or unless some new factor be brought to bear. What can be done? The educational missionaries cannot work in these government schools and colleges. The government prohibits even Christian teachers propagating Christianity in connection with their work. What can be done? The government does allow Christian students to organize Young Men's Christian Associations and carry on volunteer work among their own fellow students. God, therefore, planned the idea. There were only eight of these societies three years ago. There are now about forty, including the great keystone of their educational arch, the Imperial University itself. A majority of the associations are in the government institutions.

FEDERATION OF STUDENTS.

Five years ago the leaders of the five national student movements then in existence came together in Sweden and formed the World's Student Christian Federation. Since then all these other national student movements which I have named have joined the Federation, so that now it includes over one thousand four hundred associations or unions, and a membership of sixty-five thousand students and professors, the largest student brotherhood in the world. What made it possible to bring together this combination? The Spirit of God suggested this basis: "The leading of the students of the world to become disciples of Christ, building them up in Christ, and sending them out into the world to work for Christ." It was found possible to sink denominational, national, and racial differences, and to link together people regardless of their jealousies and prejudices on this simple, yet secure platform. God has honored this combination of students in the name of Christ.

WHAT HAS BEEN ACCOMPLISHED?

It is more than an inspiring idea, although that would be sufficient to warrant calling it into being. It has organized six national or international Christian student movements. When we think what our own movement has meant to us in North America, we form some conception of what it means now that they have similar movements in all parts of the world. It has set these movements to acting and re-acting upon each other, making them acquainted with one another. As a result of that it has broadened the scope and improved the methods of every student movement of the world. This is what we should expect. The Spirit of God works in divers places as well as in divers manners. He has not revealed to the students of any one country the only way in which to accomplish His work in the world. I am coming to believe that the students of China and of India and of Japan have lessons to teach the student movements of the West, which will greatly enrich our lives and increase our efficiency in the service of building up the Kingdom of Christ in the world. This Federation also enables the strong movements to help the weak. And this is the will of God. If you could have been with me visiting the isolated colleges of China, Japan and India, and could have seen what an encouragement and inspiration it was to these groups of Christian students fighting against great odds to be linked up with these strong bodies of disciples of Christ in the West, you would cultivate this Federation bond with more assiduity and faithfulness than ever before. Moreover, the Federation enables the weak movements to help the strong. There is not a student nor an association in our movement that would not be moved by the heroism and the consecration and faithfulness of these struggling bands of students out on the battle line of the Kingdom of God. The Federation has broadened the horizon and enriched the sympathies of every intelligent member of the world-wide student brotherhood. It has set before us a grand and inspiring objective: Nothing less than the evangelization of the world and the complete establishment of Messiah's reign. It has helped to answer in a marked way the prayer of our Lord that they all may be one.

As I stood in the last conference of the Federation at Versailles the other day, when the officials and leaders of the student movements representing twenty-three countries had assembled in conference, and noticed the fellowship between the Spanish and American delegates, witnessed the mingling of the German and French delegates, and observed the British and Dutch delegates (understand, this was August, 1900) uniting in fellowship, and as I reminded myself that the Chinese and Japanese delegates had traveled for six weeks together to that conference as fellow passengers, and were discussing common plans for the evangelization of the Orient, I said to myself that this Federation is most impressively illustrating the reality of the truth that there is one fold and one Shepherd, and is revealing to Christians the world over their oneness in Christ our Lord.

SALVATION ARMY.

COMMANDER BOOTH TUCKER,
NEW YORK.

Hail, Prophet of the Poor! Discoverer
Of that sad, melancholy No Man's Land,
Where tears of widows, orphans, desolate,
Pour in one huge Niagara of woe,
And gather into lakes of sorrow, fathomless—
Immeasurable waste of human grief!
Hail, Noble Heart, that dares to seek to staunch
The source of heart-ache by the balm Divine
Of Calvary—who, passing boldly by
All earthly nostrums, steadfastly declares
That, come what may, thy lot with Christ is cast—
That for humanity's vast, gaping wounds
The wounds of Christ as solace sole exist!
Hail, Leader of our conquering hosts below,
Who, passing the church-cared professor by,
Has summoned every follower to thy side,
To dive to lowest depths of lost mankind,
And seek amid those water-caverns hid,
The priceless pearls for whom Christ's blood was shed!
Nor vain the quest! Millions of costly gems
Thy hand hath rescued from those realms of death,
To stud the jeweled crown of Christ thy Lord!
Amid the countless hosts who fight beneath
The Flag of Blood and Fire none love thee more,
Nor pledge more firmly to thy principles,
Than we, thy soldiers of America,
Who follow thee through life—to death—and rise
To hail thee in the Resurrection Morn!

* * *

IN THE fascinating records of the struggles and triumphs of the champions of the Cross who have fought and bled and died, through the ages, some of the most thrilling pages will ever be those on which are inscribed the wonderful history of the rise and progress of the Salvation Army.

The histories of all great religious organizations have in their earlier part been more or less the histories of the men from whose consecrated lives they have sprung. Thus the life of George Fox is the history of the Quakers of the seventeenth century; John Wesley's that of Methodism in the eighteenth; and the brilliant and tremendously active career of William Booth has impressed its stamp upon every development of the Salvation Army, the great religious crusade of the nineteenth.

William Booth started early that career of blood and fire which later was to fling a world-wide halo of love and veneration around his name. Although born and reared within the gates of the Church of England—he was baptized in a Derbyshire parish church in 1829—he began at the age of fifteen to attend the services held at a Wesleyan chapel. The clear and simple preaching of the Gospel produced a profound impression upon him. He was soundly converted, joined the church and soon became one of its most active members.

His father, who was an extremely able business man, had died some time previously, after meeting with reverses which left his widow with the remnants of a broken fortune, to struggle with adverse circumstances. From him William Booth inherited a keen business ability and a restless energy, while his mother, a rarely spiritual and pure and tender woman, must have endowed him with that intense spiritual enthusiasm which has ever been the predominating trait in his character.

This enthusiasm soon began to make itself felt. The ordinary methods of church work were not sufficiently aggressive to satisfy the young convert's thirst for the salvation of souls. When the long day's work in the store was over he would, after swallowing a hasty supper, hurry as fast as possible to the slumming purlieus of Nottingham, and, mounted on a chair or a soap-box, he would hold forth to the passing throng. Large crowds were nightly brought under the spell of the boy preacher's eloquence, and in the streets, or in some crowded cottage meeting, he would follow up the impression made, never happy unless he had the satisfaction of seeing some poor, ill-kempt sinner kneel and pour out his heart to God in prayer.

Thus the very foundations of the work of the coming Salvation Army were there unconsciously laid by the youthful evangelist. A number of young men gathered quickly around him to help carry on the warfare. His leadership was never questioned, even by those who were his superiors in age and social station. As later on in life, *he* went ahead, *others* followed. Singing, he would form his

GENERAL WM. BOOTH.

converts into a motley procession and march them down the streets—a prototype of the Salvation Army march that was to sweep the globe. Although the older members of the congregation eyed the uproar askance, yet he allowed nothing to dampen the ardor of his or his companions' enthusiasm.

Already then it was noticeable how a great, passionate love for the poor more and more filled his heart and consumed him with a flaming zeal. The horrible conditions of the slums among whose ragged denizens he labored burned its indelible seal upon every fibre of his soul. He who was to become the author of "Darkest England" here went through every grade of his apprenticeship. In the reeking atmosphere of drink and suffering and sickness and want was found the soul of him who later on was to be known in every clime as "The Apostle of the Poor."

It was at this period that a revival occurred in the Nottingham Circuit under the preaching of the Rev. James Caughey, an American revivalist. It was the first time that he had seen the wonderful effect of a sustained direct appeal to the moral sense of a semi-Christian community. The straightforward conversational method of teaching the truth of the Gospel, and the common-sense practice of pushing people up to the point of decision, made an immense impression upon his mind. It revealed to him the truth that in the spiritual as in the material world God works by law and not by caprice, and that if harvests are not reaped it is the husbandry that is at fault. He tells us: "I saw as clearly as if a revelation had been made to me from Heaven, that success in spiritual work, as in natural operations, was to be accounted for not in any abstract theory of Divine sovereignty, or favoritism, or accident, but in the employment of such methods as were dictated by common sense, the Holy Spirit, and the Word of God."

Twenty years later the Salvation Army sprang into existence, but its world-wide march of triumph is simply the result of the lesson then learned by the lad of sixteen. He stands now where he stood then, and all that was to come was simply development of the great truths he then grasped as they were flashed upon him with the force of a Spirit-born revelation.

The genius and enterprise that flashed forth in those early days were quickly recognized by his church. At the early age of seventeen William Booth was appointed to be a local preacher, and two years later his pastor urged him to enter the ministry. His health was delicate, and it is interesting to note that the doctor who examined him in order to report upon his physical qualifications, pronounced him utterly unfit for such a career, prophesying that it would land him in the grave within twelve months. For this reason he still remained in the ranks four years, until he finally, in London, on his twenty-third birthday, gave up his promising business career and entered the ministry of the Methodist Church.

We have dwelt so fully upon these early years because they supply the only clue to a full understanding of the marvelous history of the Salvation Army. It explains the secret of the remarkable influence its founder wields over his officers. People who wonder at the unquestioning obedience shown him by his followers never understood the impelling force of a great example. Already at twenty he wrote in a private letter to one of his friends: "Grasp still further the standard! Unfold still wider the battle flag! Press still closer on the ranks of the enemy, and mark your pathway still more distinctly with glorious trophies of Emmanuel's grace and with enduring monuments of Jesus' power! The trumpet has given the signal for the conflict! Your General assures you of success and a glorious reward! Your crown is already held out! Then why delay? Why doubt? Onward, onward, onward!" This letter is stamped with the spirit of leadership. The same glorious spirit has spoken from every action of his fifty years of Christian warfare even as it already then cast a beacon light across the monumental work he was destined to upbuild. It was in this spirit he commenced his labors in the Methodist churches as a credited evangelist.

In church after church the revival flame burst forth. Crowded audiences faced the young preacher, no matter whither he might turn his steps. Such was the number of the penitents that flocked to the altar for prayer that it became necessary, as a preliminary to each campaign, to construct a fence, which would keep back the crowd and enable the seekers to be properly dealt with by experienced persons. It was in the course of this work he first met the remarkable woman who was to play so important a part in his life and to impress so much of her nobility of soul and holiness of character upon the Salvation Army.

Catherine Mumford was born January 17, 1829, in Ashbourne, Derbyshire, England, and grew up in the almost Puritanical seclusion of her home. Her mother was a saintly woman, and through the physical sufferings of a very delicate childhood, her mother and her much-loved books were almost her sole companions. In this pure atmosphere her character was formed, and when later she attended the young evangelist's meetings, it was but natural that she should be drawn toward him. Between them sprang up an affection which later on found expression in one of the most beautiful courtships and blessed marriages ever known. The letters from the early days of their attachment are of a truly sublime character.

The wedding was quietly and unostentatiously celebrated on June 16, 1855, and from that moment not an onward step was taken in which Catherine Booth was not fully associated with her husband. It was not, however, till five years later, at Gateshead, that Mrs. Booth commenced the public ministry which was so remarkably blessed to thousands, and which was to open wide the door of opportunity for so many women who were encouraged by her example to follow in her footsteps.

Of Mrs. Booth and her remarkable life and labor volumes could be given without doing it justice. The title "The Army's Mother," under which she is affectionately known the world over, aptly describes her importance to the organization. She stood by her husband in the early days of persecution and hatred, she encouraged, advised, inspired and urged onward the ranks in every storm; she was the counsellor in every arising difficulty, and her sound common sense and judgment were invaluable in selecting the wisest path. Further than this, she unfolded an astonishing activity both in the pulpit and with her pen. Her gifts as a public speaker were of the highest order, and from her writings her fiery soul still speaks to millions. Well might Mr. Stead call her "A Maker of Modern England," and, speaking of her, say: "Among all those religious teachers who have left the impress of their thought and life upon England of to-day, Mrs. Booth is at once the most conspicuous, the most typical, and the most modern.

"Catherine Booth differed from all the others in almost every element of distinction. To begin with, she was a woman, and no woman before her exercised so direct an influence upon the religious life of her time. Her work was not the mere carrying on of an existing organization. She and her husband built up out of recruits gathered in the highways and by-ways of the land what is to all intents and purposes a vast, world-wide church. When she began to preach the Salvation Army had not yet been dreamed of.

"The Salvation Army is a miracle of our time. It is the latest revelation of the potency of the invisible over the visible, the concrete manifestation of the power of the spirit over matter.

"This vast organization, far greater than anything achieved by Fox or Wesley in their lifetime, is instinct in every fibre with the spirit breathed into it by Mrs. Booth. Though dead, she yet speaks from a thousand platforms. But this is merely one element of her influence. The action of the Salvation Army has stimulated the social and evangelistic activity of all other churches. The Church Army honestly avows its genesis without concealment. Other bodies which have sprung quite as directly into being from a desire to emulate the success of the Salvationists are less candid; but acts are more eloquent than words. Even where there is no organized effort to adopt Salvation Army methods, the community, from bishops to policemen, have publicly acknowledged the influence of the Booths. Another unique distinction of the Salvation Army is that it is the only religious organization of English birth which has produced any visible effect upon non-English-speaking peoples.

"George Fox preceded her in the theoretical proclamation of the truth; but despite some brilliant examples of Quaker women preachers, it was not until Mrs. Booth invented the Hallelujah lasses that there was anything approaching to a popular recognition of the capacity of women to teach, to organize, and to command."

It was with this woman at his side that William Booth approached the great crisis of his life, the turning point in his career. The successful evangelist was, in the midst of his spirit-crowned labors, yearning for that vast field, the churchless working classes, which had so stirred his youthful soul, and to which the seed he scattered within the church walls never seemed to reach. The traditions of the church rose like barriers on every hand to make the attainment of his life's great object impossible. He was pining for the street corners of his early career, for the God-forsaken audiences of the open air. He made many attempts to follow the call of the voice which constantly cried out in his soul, on behalf of the suffering multitudes, but in vain. At last he took the momentous step, and started out upon the deep alone. He says himself: "I couldn't rest; I wanted to get out into the wide sea of misery surging and sweltering around me. The Conference wouldn't let me do that special work, the only work for which I felt myself really fitted; and so, believing I was called to it by God, I went out and left every friend I had in the world."

"MOTHER BOOTH."

An old tent in a disused Quaker burial ground constituted the birthplace of the Salvation Army. It was amid the worse than heathen pandemonium of blasphemy and ribaldry for which the East End of London is so notorious, that the movement was born and cradled. After nine weeks of meetings the tent was blown down, and then the meetings were carried on, first in a low dancing saloon, and then in an old wool warehouse, and later on in music halls and theatres. But the open-air and indoor meetings were frequently upset by the rough audiences.

In fact, it was through tempestuous waters the frail Army bark at first had to battle its way. The persecutions with which it was met remind one of the early experiences of the Apostles. Throughout its later history instances of the most fearful and violent opposition abound. Every country it has invaded has furnished its thrilling chapters to this history of blood and martyrdom. But persecution never made either the General or his enthusiastic followers slacken their pace. It rather fanned the flame, which now began burning brightly in the hearts of the thousands that were reached. Drunkards, thieves and gamblers were won by the score, and William Booth provided plenty of opportunities for their new-kindled ardor. Passions, abilities, energies hitherto desecrated in the service of evil were enlisted in the warfare, and the lines of attack were constantly extended.

Thus the Salvation Army was not made, in the sense that it was originated by its founder, for the purpose it later on has served so wondrously. It simply grew, like a healthy plant, in the fertile soil of a great and crying need. Mr. Booth had at that day little idea of the momentous nature of the decision which formed the turning point of his life. His idea was merely to make converts for the churches. But he was reluctantly driven to the conviction that the converts were not welcomed by the churches, and that if they were not taken care of by him they would not be taken care of by any one else. So, gradually it dawned upon him that he would have to build up a whole religious society on permanent lines, the fundamental feature of which was the doctrine that no one can keep saved who does not try to save other people. Thus it was that the Salvation Army in fact, but not in name, was born. It was not invented; like Topsy, it "growed."

At first the movement was simply called "The Christian Mission." The decisive change which stamped the character of the organization occurred in 1878, when its present name was decided upon. It was chosen almost as if by chance, and Mr. Railton describes the historic occurrence in this fashion: "We were drawing up a brief description of the Mission, and, wishing to express what it was in one phrase, I wrote, 'The Christian Mission is a volunteer army of converted working people.' 'No,' said Mr. Booth, 'we are not volunteers, for we feel we must do what we do, and we are always on duty.' He crossed out the words and wrote 'Salvation.' The phrase immediately struck us all, and we very soon found it would be far more effective than the old name."

This was in 1878. Even before that date, however, there had been indications of development in a quasi-military direction. The evangelists of the Mission were called Captain, or Cap'n, by those who followed their lead, for with the common people Captain means leader. It is the more polite form of "Boss." The converts might have chosen the latter term. Had they done so, we might have had a great religious caucus with its bosses, instead of an Army with its officers. Gradually the other terms and designations incidental to a military organization were added. The rules and regulations of the British army served General Booth as a model. Again we quote Mr. Railton:

"When the Army name was definitely adopted, all this was made much plainer to the minds of all the people. What was inconsistent with the soldierhood for Christ was as rapidly as possible got rid of, and all that was useful in the teachings of earth's armies was carefully learned. Part No. 1 of Orders and Regulations for the Salvation Army was published in 1878, after long and careful study of the manuals of the British army."

In the question of uniform Mrs. Booth took a special interest. Herself careful to an extreme to dress with neatness and modesty, some of her most powerful anathemas had been directed from time to time against the fashions of the day.

Mrs. Booth set herself to work to devise for the women something which would be at once plain, distinctive and attractive. Shutting herself up in a room with her daughter and surrounded by a heap of bonnets of various sorts and sizes, she endeavored to discover what would be adapted to both. Some suited one, some suited the other, but the now famous "Hallelujah bonnet" was at length hit upon and pronounced equally suitable to all. Others who were consulted on the subject confirmed this opinion, and thus was settled the character of "the helmet of salvation" which was to be worn by the women warriors of the Salvation Army.

And then the wonderful onward march of the Salvation Army properly began. It soon spread over the borders of the United Kingdom, generally as the result of an urgent appeal from some emigrated Salvation soldier, who besieged the General with requests to send officers to commence the warfare in his domicile. Thus America was invaded in 1882, when Commissioner Railton and a party of officers were sent to open operations. France, Switzerland, Australia, New Zealand, Sweden, Holland, Africa and India followed rapidly. The onward swinging files have marched around the globe with the songs of a blood-bought liberty. To-day the cosmopolitan operations of the Salvation Army are carried on by 15,704 officers in 47 countries and colonies, and their literature is printed in 1,000,000 copies weekly in 21 languages.

SOCIAL SETTLEMENTS.*

Robert A. Woods,

BOSTON.

[The social settlement is an attempt to express the meaning of life in terms of life itself, in forms of activity. There is no doubt that the deed often reveals when the idea does not, just as art makes us understand and feel what might be incomprehensible and inexpressible in the form of an argument. A settlement brings to its aid all possible methods to reveal and make common its conceptions of life. All those arts and devices which express kindly relations from man to man, from charitable effort to the most specialized social intercourse, are tried. There are so-called art exhibits, concerts, dramatic representations, every possible device to make operative on the life around it the conception of life which the settlement group holds. The demonstration is made, not by reason, but by life itself.—Jane Addams, in "Hom. Rev.," August, 1901, page 177.—Ed.]

* * *

A group of young university men in Holland, some of whom had visited Toynbee Hall when they were in London, established a few years ago a society for "Toynbee work" in their own country. Last summer in Paris a distinguished French sociologist was found who showed no signs of recognition at the mention of social settlements in American cities; but when, for the sake of definiteness, Hull House was referred to, the savant responded eagerly that of course he had often heard of "the Hull Houses." These things suggest the shifting of interest from the idea and motive of a colony of young apostles of better things going to live amid the city's greatest need, to specific enterprises which have been able to show a degree of downright achievement.

So strong has the tendency become among settlement residents themselves to fix their gaze on results and to disallow tributes to their devotion that Canon Barnett, in the last report of Toynbee Hall, urges that "there is a distinct loss to a community when its members do not own up to their best qualities." It is this tendency in large part which led Dr. Fairbairn, in an address in the interest of Mansfield House, to say that much of the high enthusiasm for social reform which existed some years ago at Oxford has

---

*Appeared in "The Congregationalist," February 2, 1901.

ARNOLD TOYNBEE.

UNIVERSITY SETTLEMENT, NEW YORK.

to the Pacific. The term is used with such laxity that it is difficult to tell accurately how many genuine enterprises of this sort there are in the country, but it is safe to say that there are about 100, one-fourth of them being already sufficiently well established to give promise of permanent usefulness.

Dr. Coit called his undertaking a Neighborhood Guild, and though, as such, it came to no great success, the conception of the settlement set forth in his book, "Neighborhood Guilds," and since worked out to a degree by him at Leighton Hall in London, is to my mind the most satisfactory that has ever been set forth. After Dr. Coit's removal to London, the Neighborhood Guild was gathered up in the University Settlement, of which Mr. James B. Reynolds has been from the first the head worker. It now has on Eldridge street, a little east of the Bowery, the finest and best equipped building yet erected for settlement purposes. The settlement has a growing force of residents, and its work is constantly exceeding the capacity of the house and the strength of the staff. An important use of the large hall is that which is made of it by the Central Federated Union, the official body of delegates from the trade unions of New York, which formerly held its meetings amid very demoralizing surroundings. Mr. Reynolds has taken a leading part in the campaigns of the Citizens' Union, and is serving as a member of the Tenement House Commission appointed last summer by Governor Roosevelt.

Two years after the opening of the Neighborhood Guild, two settlements were established—so nearly at the same time that the matter of priority is an amiably mooted question—which have ever since stood as striking monuments to the public spirit, executive capacity and sound sense of the younger generation of American women—the College Settlement in New York, and Hull House in Chicago. The College Settlement in Rivington street has suffered somewhat through frequent changes in its leadership, but this may perhaps only have served to keep up the loyalty which college women have felt for it. Through this loyalty—in addition to the establishment of two other women's college settlements, one in Philadelphia, the other (Denison House) in Boston—it has come about that a large proportion of collegiate alumnæ are in spirit settlement women, and carry this motive into their home life and into their work. For the inculcation of this spirit the most influential personal force has been that exerted by Miss Vida Scudder, who has resided from time to time at each of these settlements, and has constantly been setting forth their motive with deep intensity and insight.

These three college settlements have each a force of from eight to twelve residents, a nucleus of the group remaining from year to year and gaining a deep influence in the home life and in the social affairs of the young people in their neighborhood. In all three cases the influence of the settlement is of a simple and personal nature, and the quiet, permeating influence of their work is certainly not the less valuable for being the less obvious and tangible.

Hull House stands easily first, both for achievement and significance, among American settlements. It is like Toynbee Hall in the originality and distinction which has characterized every part of its work, and in solid and abiding achievement, while there is determination and daring in its work such as is rather more characteristic of some of the other London settlements than of Toynbee Hall.

In its more obvious aspects Hull House represents a massing together of practically the whole variety of such appliances of charity, philanthropy and popular education as are demanded by the needs of a large and otherwise neglected immigrant neighborhood. The settlement has been compelled to build up the whole of this fabric, with the exception of a branch station of the public library and a small bathhouse, both of which are supported by the city. Among the specially interesting developments are a children's building, a co-operative home for working women, and a restaurant occupying beautiful and spacious quarters, with a theatre on the floor above. Manual training and handicraft are emphasized more and more, and it is proposed to have at the settlement a museum illustrating industrial processes.

The deeply impressive thing about Hull House, however, is that the finest quality of settlement spirit runs through all this complicated activity, holding it in solution, and leaving the remembrance, not of an institution, but of personality, in the mind of even the casual visitor. Hull House has come to exercise a profound influence upon the whole life of Chicago. As a rallying centre for all that in any way affects the uplifting and refinement of the great mass of the people of the city, it has a special pre-eminence, and no stranger who cares at all about the higher life of the Western metropolis neglects to see Hull House.

It is perhaps the fullest way to sum up what Miss Addams has accomplished to say that she was able at the beginning to draw into the service of Hull House a remarkable group of young women, several of whom still remain as the nucleus of what is without doubt the most resourceful settlement force to be found in either country.

Following soon after these first settlements came the South End House—originally the Andover House, and founded by President William J. Tucker, about whose work readers of "The Congregationalist" are perhaps sufficiently familiar; Whittier House in Jersey City, under the leadership of Miss Cornelia Bradford; Chicago Commons, the creation of Professor Graham Taylor; the Union Seminary Settlement in New York, which has had an encouraging growth; and the Nurses' Settlement, also in New York, which is under the direction of Miss Lillian Wald, has a peculiar quality of genuineness and inspiration about its work.

No settlement work in the country deserves more sincere respect than that which Professor Taylor, at great cost to himself in every way, is carrying on in Chicago. His district is to a large extent Protestant, and lends itself to such definite religious efforts as he is successfully carrying on. In these days, when it is the most anxious concern of the Protestant churches that they do not win the allegiance of nominally Protestant workingmen, it is a striking fact that a prominent teacher in the church should have sufficient political influence in his ward to turn the scales in favor of honest candidates, and should be nominated by the army of organized labor in Chicago as an arbiter in case of strike. Professor Taylor is now struggling with the problem of the adequate housing of Chicago Commons. Part of the new building, including rooms devoted to the services of a Congregational Church, is now complete, but $25,000 is needed for the remainder of the building. Considering all the facts, subscriptions for this purpose should not be limited to Chicago and its suburbs, but should come from different parts of the country, as recognition of Professor Taylor's great service to the whole denomination.

New York and Chicago both have a number of promising settlement undertakings beside those mentioned. Baltimore, Cleveland, Buffalo, Pittsburg, Louisville, Omaha, San Francisco and other cities all report progress with settlements that have developed chiefly within the past three or four years. Kingsley House in Pittsburg was established by Dean Hodges shortly before he left his parish in that city for the Episcopal Theological School in Cambridge. This settlement has just been presented with a fine old mansion, admirably situated and having three-quarters of an acre of ground around it. The Goodrich Settlement in Cleveland has a beautiful building, the gift of Mrs. Samuel Mather, and is a growing centre of influence in that city. Hiram House, also in Cleveland, is the result of a peculiar degree of devotion and purpose on the part of its head worker, who in a few years has built up an important enterprise. In Buffalo two churches have established settlements as centres for their work of social improvement in the districts assigned them under the successful "church district" plan.

It is the opinion of most sympathetic observers, as well as of settlement workers themselves, that, large as the total value of the work of all these settlements is in reviving the better life of neglected city neighborhoods, their still greater contribution is in the reflex influence which they exert upon the educated and prosperous classes in the community. The more sensitive social conscience, the removal of social barriers, the enlarged idea of life as a social service, the tendency toward a more thorough spirit of democracy as a vital element in Christian culture—these in many people were suggested, and in all have been re-enforced by the object lesson of the settlements.

It will in all probability be found, also, that the settlements have made a definite contribution toward practical Christian unity, by bringing together Christians of every name into enthusiastic joint action toward the bringing in of a more Christian city. In most cases, especially in this country, the settlement, if it became a mission, would at once alienate the majority of its neighbors, and thus defeat its specific end; but in every case settlement workers are encouraged to co-operate with local church work. The American settlement represents in most cases a friendly overture from Protestant Christians to Catholic Christians or to a Jewish population, which in many cases stands deeply in need of Christian helpfulness free from impossible conditions. Every consideration of national and social welfare demands that unity of feeling should be created between these separated and even hostile classes. The settlements are beyond all peradventure making headway with this task.

One of the incidental, yet highly important, outcomes of the growth of the settlement "movement" is the fact that at these centres men and women work together in a particularly normal way, with fairness and freedom, on the Christian basis of capacity for service as the basis for precedence, without regard to sex. The secret

FRANCIS E. CLARK, D.D.

of this is that the settlement is, in the first instance, simply an extension of the home in its finest conception, and offers a field, therefore, in which the trained and enlightened woman has an authority which no one would think of questioning. In all of the settlements men and women work together. Some have only men, or only women, actually in residence. At others there is a group of men residents and a group of women residents, living in different houses. At others still, especially where the tradition of co-education obtains, men and women residents live under the same roof.

Within the past few weeks two interesting documents have appeared which give impressive exhibits of the spread and substantial growth of settlement work. A fourth edition of the Bibliography of College, Social, University and Church Settlements has been prepared by Mrs. Caroline Williamson Montgomery, for the College Settlements Association. This is a pamphlet of sixty-eight pages and contains admirable résumés of the work of all known settlement houses throughout the world. Besides England and the United States, France, Holland, Germany, Japan and India are represented. Valuable lists of books and articles about settlement work are included, and there is a special list of books compiled from suggestions made by fifty experienced settlement workers as to the most useful reading for new recruits. The other document is in the shape of a preliminary report made in the Bulletin of the Bureau of Statistics of Labor of the State of New York as to the thirty-two settlement houses in that state. In addition to the accounts given by the various head workers, the report includes remarkably interesting statements from workingmen as to the value of settlement service.

CHRISTIAN ENDEAVOR.

Francis E. Clark, D.D.,
BOSTON.

[Nearly my entire ministry has been a blessed experience with Endeavorers. This experience has taught me how a pastor may help his society, and I name a few particulars.

First, be yourself an Endeavorer to the core. Know Endeavor from A to Z. Know its history, its evolution, its problems, its points of possible weakness, its towers of strength. Have its great ruling ideas like a fire in your bones. Be possessed with its rationale; believe in it like a prophet of God; catch every latest and best inspiration of it and ideal for it. Be, in short, its outward and bodily and inspiring presentment. From this, through the Lord Jesus, all the rest will flow.

Next, be on the active list. I do not mean the enrollment, though you should be on the roll; but I mean the real thing. Let no member of your society, or of any other, exceed you in society fidelity. The prayer meeting, the sociable, the business meeting, and the rest, be at, and be a power in; not by saying much, not by loading up with detail work. Be self-effacing. Be emptied of self. Be a presence, an atmosphere, a life. Be with the society as Jesus was with the twelve, they free, they speaking out without constraint their every thought, but Jesus, in His quiet, unobtrusive way, the life of all, the joy of all. But you will keep Jesus at the fore, not yourself.

Every minister has his aptitudes, his directions in which he can be specially helpful personally. With one it is the social side; with another, aptness to teach; with a third, singular winning capacity for the Lord Jesus, etc. Study yourself. Get in your best special work with a tact that never faileth. Your best, if it be too good anywhere else, is not a whit too good for your Endeavorers.

"And yet show I unto you a more excellent way." Love them. Love them as if they were each of your own body begotten. That will make you see their faults, but more their excellences and their vast possibilities; and the former love will gently extirpate, and the latter love will incite and unfold. Love them with a love like that of Jesus. Be a discoverer of all their glory and possibility and power, like Jesus, and, like Him, bring it out into actuality. Love is the fulfilling of the Christian Endeavor law.—David N. Beach, D. D.—Ed.]

* * *

The Society of Christian Endeavor was formed on the second day of February, 1881. It has now, in 1901, almost reached its majority. Its object was to increase the zeal of the young people of the

Williston Church, of Portland, Me., in which it was formed, to attach them more firmly to the church, to open their mouths in confession of Christ, to set them at work for Him in all appropriate and useful lines. The object of the Society to-day, though there are fifty thousand organizations, with nearly four millions of members, is the very same that it was twenty years ago. Including the Epworth League and the Baptist Young People's Union, which are branches of the same tree, Christian Endeavor numbers at least five millions.

During the last twelve years it has been my privilege to visit every state, province and territory in North America, almost every country in Europe and Asia, every colony but one in Australia, the Ottoman Empire, Egypt, and South Africa, Mexico, and some of the islands of the East and West Indies.

I would be a dull scholar indeed had I not learned some things from the book of experience concerning the essential and non-essential features of Christian Endeavor.

A thousand matters are left free and flexible in Christian Endeavor. Personal initiative, invention, resource; the constant leading of the Spirit of God, are possible. The Christian Endeavor constitution is no hard chrysalis which forever keeps the butterfly within from trying its wings. There is room even for experiments and failures, since we will always remember that the worst failure is to make no endeavor. Yet, while this is true, it is equally true that a universal movement must have universal principles that do not change with the seasons, do not melt at the tropics or congeal at the poles. A tree puts forth new leaves every year, but it does not change its roots. It simply lengthens and strengthens them. The roots of the Christian Endeavor tree, wherever it grows, are Confession of Christ, Service for Christ, Fellowship with Christ's People, and Loyalty to Christ's Church. The farther I travel, the more I see of societies in every land, the more I am convinced that these four principles are the essential and the only essential principles of the Christian Endeavor Society. Let me repeat them:

1. Confession of Christ. 2. Service for Christ. 3. Fellowship with Christ's People. 4. Loyalty to Christ's Church.

With these roots the Christian Endeavor tree will bear fruit in any soil. Cut away any of these roots in any clime and the tree dies. Believe me, I am not writing at random or without the most serious consideration.

The covenant pledge is simply a tried and proved device to secure frequent confession of Christ. It is essential to Christian Endeavor, but essential only because it secures, as nothing else has been known to do, the frequent and regular confession of Christ by the young Christian. It also secures familiarity with the Word of God, by promoting Bible reading and study in preparation for every meeting. There is sometimes an outcry against the pledge, as though we exalted a mere instrument to the place of a universal principle. This is not the case. We exalt the pledge as a builder exalts his plumbline and spirit-level. They are not his house, but he cannot build his house without them. We exalt the pledge as a painter exalts his brush, as a musician his violin, as a writer his pen. The brush is not the picture, the violin is not the music, the pen is not the poem; but the brush is necessary to the picture, the violin to the music, the pen to the poem, the pledge to the Christian Endeavor Society, because it insures regular and frequent confession of Christ. Then let no one speak lightly of our covenant pledge, or treat it lightly. In one aspect it is but a form of words, in another it is God's great agent used to raise His work among young people, to create a new agency of outspoken Christian activity.

Another universal principle of Christian Endeavor is *constant service*. If confession is the lungs of the movement, service is its hands and feet. In no part of the world have I ever found a good society whose members were not at work. Never have I found a true society that ignored its committees; for our committees make service possible and easy, systematic and efficient. The Society was not made for its committees, but the committees are for the Society, to make it a working organization. The most multifarious kinds of service have our societies undertaken, but all societies, the world around, that are worthy of the name are at work in some way. What are they doing? Ask the pastors and the Sunday-school superintendents in America and Great Britain and Australia. Ask the missionaries in the Punjab and among the Telugus, among the simple people of the Laos country, among the Armenians and the Zulus, the Karens and the Arabs, and they will all tell you the same story. "In the ideal society every member is responsible for some definite, particular task." This chorus of response is so universal and emphatic that it must have a significance that cannot be ignored. This feature of our Society is not a matter of indifference. It is not a late accretion. It is not a question of climate or race. From the first **day of the first society**, during all these nearly twenty years, this feature has characterized our movement, and, into whatever land it has spread, it has been known by this feature of systematic, organized, individual service.

Again, I have learned that a universal essential of the Society of Christian Endeavor is *fidelity* to its own church and the work of that church. It does not and cannot exist for itself. When it does it ceases to be a Society of Christian Endeavor. It may unworthily bear the name. It may be reckoned in the lists, just as an unworthy man may find his name on the church roll. But a true Society of Christian Endeavor must live for Christ and the church. Its confession of love is for Christ the head, its service is for the church His bride; its fellowship is possible only because its loyalty is unquestioned. This characteristic, too, I have found as universal as the Society. I have found no real exceptions. In city or country, in Christian land or mission field in Europe, Asia, Africa, or America, it is everywhere the same.

Because this is our ideal and our principle, and our earnest endeavor, let me urge older Christians, however, not to hold Christian Endeavorers responsible, as some are inclined to do, for every weakness among young Christians, which the Society is doing its best to remedy, but cannot wholly overcome. Because many young people do not go to church the Society is often blamed. Because some forget their vows the splendid fidelity of the rank and file is forgotten. Because the church pews are not filled or the Sunday-school enlarged, or the longed-for revival comes not, the Society is made the scapegoat by some unthinking Christians for these defects, for the very reason that its ideals on these matters are exalted.

Once more, *our fellowship* is an essential feature of Christian Endeavor. This, too, is not a matter of zones, or climates, or latitudes, or languages. Our fellowship is universal, God-given fundamental feature of Christian Endeavor. The movement to-day is more emphatically world-wide than ever before. In every land I have felt the heart-throbs of my fellow Endeavorers. Our Christian fellowship is expressed in different ways, but it is always the same fellowship. In Japan, I have prostrated myself on hands and knees with my fellow Endeavorers and have touched my forehead to the floor as they touched theirs. In China, over and over again, a thousand Endeavorers have stood up as I addressed them, and have shaken their own hands at me while I have shaken mine at them. In India they have hung scores of garlands about my neck, until I have blushed for my own unworthiness of such a flowery welcome. In Bohemia they have embraced me and kissed me on either cheek. In Mexico they have hugged me in a bear's embrace, and patted me lovingly on the back. Always I have felt that these greetings were far more than personal matters. They represent the fellowship of the cause. Always, whatever the form, the loving greeting of loving hearts is the same.

I confidently assert once more what the experience of twenty years in all lands has proved, that the fundamental, universal, enduring features of Christian Endeavor are confession, service, fellowship, fidelity. Hold to these fundamentals the world around, hold to these fundamentals, Christian Endeavorers; exemplify them in your societies and your own lives, and abundant as have been the blessings of God during the last twenty years, the next twenty will far surpass them. Hold to these principles, and you will understand more and more of Paul's superlatives, more and more of his "exceeding abundantly," when in the fulness of his life of confession, service, fellowship and fidelity he ascribed all to Christ, crying out: "Now unto Him that is able to do exceeding abundantly, above all that we can ask or think, according to the power that worketh in us, unto Him be the glory in the church and in Christ Jesus unto all generations for ever and ever."

* * * * * * * * *

[CHRISTIAN ENDEAVOR'S FIRST TWENTY YEARS.

In 1881, a single society. In 1901, societies to the number of 60,750.

In 1881, a membership of 57. In 1901, a membership of 3,500,000.

In 1881, a single denomination touched. In 1901, more than forty denominations permeated.

In 1881, an extreme corner of one country. In 1901, all countries on the face of the earth.

In 1881, the English language. In 1901, literature in Chinese, Japanese, Malagasy, Persian, Arabic, Turkish, Bulgarian, Armenian, Siamese, German, French, Italian, Greek, Spanish, Swedish, Dutch, Norwegian, Welsh, Austrian, Koptic, Mexican, Portuguese, Indian, the many tongues of India and Africa.

In 1881 no national organization dreamed of. In 1901, national Christian Endeavor organizations in the United States, Canada, England, Scotland, Ireland, Wales, Australia, France, Spain, Germany, South Africa, India, China, Mexico, Japan.

In 1881, no periodical thought of. In 1901, "The Christian Endeavor World," the English "Christian Endeavour," the Japanese "Endeavor," the Australian "Golden Link" and "Roll Call," the South African "Golden Chain," the Spanish "Esfuerzo Cristiano," the Mexican "Esforzador," the German "Jugend-Hilfe" and "Mitarbeiter," the India "Endeavourer," the Canadian "Banner," the Jamaican "Gem," the Irish "Endeavorer," the Welsh "Lamp," besides a throng of State, city, and denominational Christian Endeavor organs.

In 1881, only the Young People's Society. In 1901, the Juniors, Intermediates, Seniors, Floating societies, Mothers' societies, Prison societies, Travelers' societies, societies in factories, schools, colleges, almshouses, and asylums.

In 1881, a single newspaper article. In 1901, scores of books, hundreds of pamphlets, and Christian Endeavor articles by the thousand every week in the leading secular and religious journals of the world.

In 1881, no young people's religious convention even guessed at.

1. Portland, Me. 1882
2. Portland, Me. 1883
3. Lowell, Mass. 1884
4. Old Orchard, Me. 1885
5. Saratoga, N. Y. 1886
6. Saratoga, N. Y. 1887
7. Chicago, Ill. 1888
8. Philadelphia, Pa. 1889
9. St. Louis, Mo. 1890
10. Minneapolis, Minn. 1891
11. New York, N. Y. 1892
12. Montreal, P. Q. 1893
13. Cleveland, O. 1894
14. Boston, Mass. 1895
15. Washington, D. C. 1896
16. San Francisco, Cal. 1897
17. Nashville, Tenn. 1898
18. Detroit, Mich. 1899
19. London, England. 1900
20. Cincinnati, O. 1901

Its conventions now rank among the greatest in the world's history. Nothing short of circus tents will hold the throngs. More than fifty thousand came to the Boston convention in 1895. Fifteen thousand crossed the continent to San Francisco and met fifteen thousand more from the Pacific Slope. This convention is estimated to have involved an outlay of $9,000,000. The last convention, held in London, brought together about forty thousand persons.

In 1881, no Christian Endeavor unions. In 1901, important unions in practically all cities, counties, States, and Provinces of the English-speaking world and in many other lands, together with the denominational Christian Endeavor federations.

In 1881, three Christian Endeavor committees. In 1901, the lookout, prayer-meeting, social, missionary, temperance, flower, music, good-literature, Sunday-school, Christian-citizenship, information, executive, Junior, press, calling, relief, and—*whatsoever* committees, with all that they imply of out-reaching, practical effort.

In 1881, the young people neglected in church life. In 1901, the religious training of the young among the foremost purposes of every church.

In 1881, our young people had not been taught to give systematically for missions. In 1901, they had given, during the previous year, more than half a million dollars for this purpose alone.

The Detroit "News Tribune" of July, 1899, in viewing the convention, and in estimating the Christian Endeavor movement, is impressed by the rare spectacle of a vast concourse of modern men and women fascinated by a spirit of "other-worldliness," not by money-getting or other form of self-seeking:

"Every effect has its cause. The forces that have conspired to bring together 50,000 people from the four corners of the world must be real. All the other conventions that convene in this city of conventions are explicable. The purposes, objects and motives of them are known, and there is not the suggestion of mystery about them. Material well-being of some sort, usually of a pecuniary nature, is behind them all, and even the city that invites them to its hospitality is not without its selfish interest in receiving them. But here is the most stupendous concern of them all, from which these common motives are wholly absent. No pecuniary profit awaits these devoted members of the Christian Endeavor. No increase of knowledge in the modes and ways of getting on better in the pursuits that add to worldly and luxurious pleasures is to come to them out of the social conditions of the meeting; such gain would be loss, according to the ancient formularies of their faith. They come here wholly under the inspiration of an other-worldliness. They hold that the business of this life is not what the world calls gain, but to lay foundations for the life that has no end. The essential business of the meeting is to get increase of knowledge and fitness to bring this worldly world into the possession of the rich faith and hope they themselves enjoy. In other words, they come to give something and not to get something. It costs them time, money, and effort to do it, but they do it.

"This society has put to good use, in the church and for the church, the earnestness and religious enthusiasm of its young people. It has made this a mighty force, directing it, developing it, and pointing out to it the way to great results. It has formed the young people into a vast army, under one banner and under one Commander. Its work has been as wonderful as its growth. The society stands to-day the marvel of the religious world."—ED.]

BROTHERHOOD OF ANDREW AND PHILIP: REV. C. E. WYCKOFF.

THE Brotherhood of Andrew and Philip was organized in the Second Reformed Church of Reading, Pa., on the first Sunday in May, 1888. The Rev. Rufus W. Miller, who was at the time assistant pastor of the church, his father-in-law, the Rev. Dr. McCauley, being pastor, found his young men's Bible class did not feel the Young People's Society of Christian Endeavor exactly met their need. They requested him to organize something exclusively for young men, which he did. Major McCauley, U. S. A., a son of Dr. McCauley, was then living in Chicago, where he had heard of the Brotherhood of St. Andrew. He suggested that the new organization could profitably take the two rules and the ideas which bound that Brotherhood together. This suggestion was adopted and Philip was added to Andrew for the sake of distinction from the older Brotherhood.

The two rules and the aim of the Brotherhood are set forth as follows:

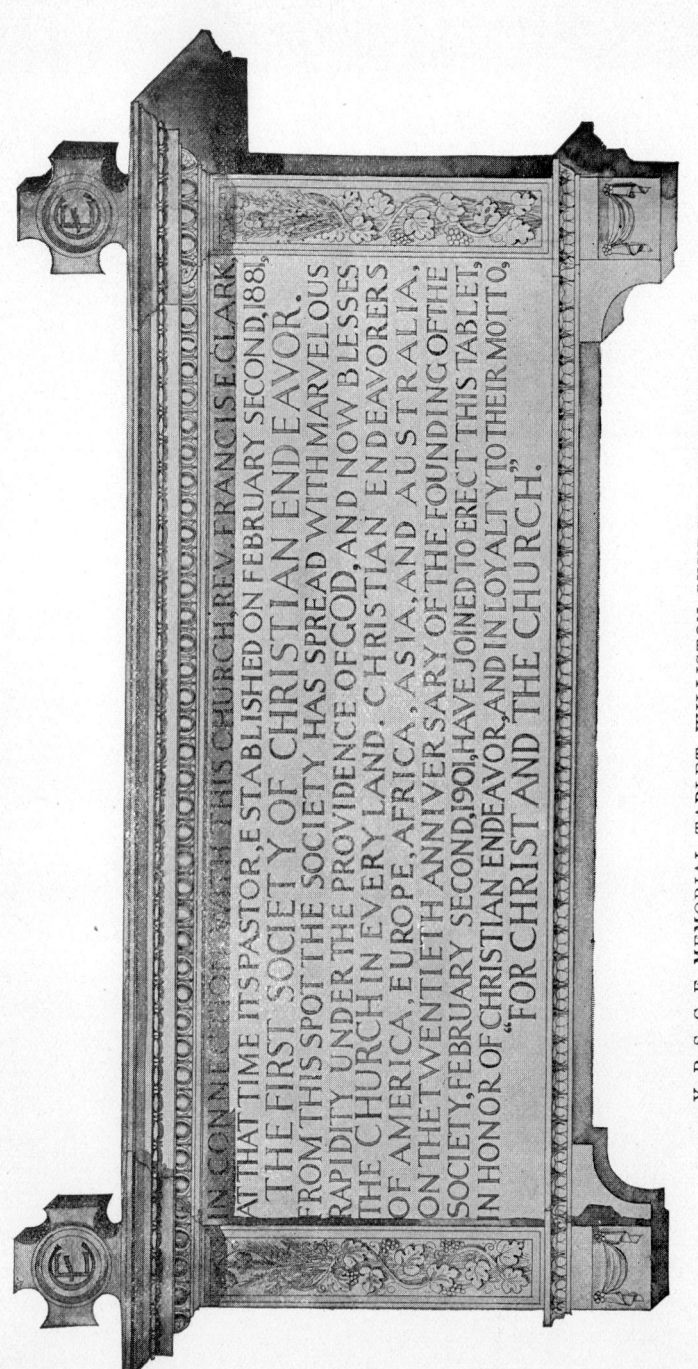

IN CONNECTION WITH THIS CHURCH, REV. FRANCIS E. CLARK, AT THAT TIME ITS PASTOR, ESTABLISHED ON FEBRUARY SECOND, 1881, THE FIRST SOCIETY OF CHRISTIAN ENDEAVOR. FROM THIS SPOT THE SOCIETY HAS SPREAD WITH MARVELOUS RAPIDITY UNDER THE PROVIDENCE OF GOD, AND NOW BLESSES THE CHURCH IN EVERY LAND. CHRISTIAN ENDEAVORERS OF AMERICA, EUROPE, AFRICA, ASIA, AND AUSTRALIA, ON THE TWENTIETH ANNIVERSARY OF THE FOUNDING OF THE SOCIETY, FEBRUARY SECOND, 1901, HAVE JOINED TO ERECT THIS TABLET, IN HONOR OF CHRISTIAN ENDEAVOR, AND IN LOYALTY TO THEIR MOTTO, "FOR CHRIST AND THE CHURCH."

Y. P. S. C. E. MEMORIAL TABLET, WILLISTON CHURCH, PORTLAND, ME.

SECTION 1.—The sole object of the Brotherhood of Andrew and Philip is the spread of Christ's Kingdom among the youth and older men.

SEC. 2.—The rules of the Brotherhood are two: The Rule of Prayer and the Rule of Service. The Rule of Prayer is to pray daily for the spread of Christ's Kingdom among men, and for God's blessing upon the labors of the Brotherhood. The Rule of Service is to make an earnest effort each week to bring at least one man or boy within hearing of the Gospel of Jesus Christ, as set forth in the services of the church, Young People's Prayer Meetings, and Young Men's Bible Classes.

SEC. 3.—The Brotherhood, believing in "the Holy Catholic Church, the communion of saints," and recognizing the special power of the young man's social nature, lays the personal obligation upon its members to utilize and manifest the spirit of comradeship and Christian fellowship in the church and in the varied walks of life.

It has been truly said: "The early church grew by cellular growth, one individual touching another. It was the contagion of Christian contact. One Philip found Nathanael at home, and another Philip found the Ethiopian in the desert. Each knew, and told what he knew, and through them these men became Christ's followers. Would you have spoken of Christ to these men, a neighbor, a stranger, if the opportunity had come to you? Would you have hesitated? Would you even have thought of it? The early church grew with such rapidity because Christians did think and did not hesitate. The Apostles could not possibly have won the world by preaching, any more than a battle could be won by generals. It was the rank and file who did the work. With what leaps and bounds would the church advance to-day if every one who knows Christ would think about some one who does not, would really care, would pray, would plan!"

Up to this time (Dec. 17, 1900), the organization has grown to 560 enrolled chapters, representing 23 denominations. These are found in almost all the states of the Union. Two have recently been organized in Canada and one in Japan. The number of members in the Brotherhood is estimated at 15,000. These statistics do not represent the growth of the movement. Many chapters or bands of young men have been organized under the Brotherhood name which have never been enrolled. In the course of years those who at first promoted the Brotherhood have become men in middle life, and the ambition of the Brotherhood is not only to enroll the young men, but also to gather together and develop the older men of the local church. To avoid confusion there are now recognized three Brotherhoods, graded according to age: the original Brotherhood, whose members are over twenty-one, up to any age the local chapter may decide upon; the Junior Brotherhood, enrolling young men from sixteen to twenty-one years, and the Boys' Brotherhood, which takes in those under sixteen years. All three branches of the Brotherhood are flourishing and have been copied more or less successfully under various names.

The chapters in any one denomination are organized as a denominational Brotherhood. These denominational organizations are pushed whenever they are thought to be strong enough to be self-sustaining. The Reformed, Presbyterian, Congregational, Methodist Episcopal and Baptist chapters have been so organized. Delegates from these denominational bodies are appointed every two years to sit in the Federal Council, which has charge of the whole work. Scattering chapters in denominations which are not so organized are under the direct care of the Federal Council. This council is unique as perhaps the first definite organized church federation modeled on the plan of our National Government. The president is the Rev. Rufus W. Miller, Reading, Pa., founder of the Brotherhood. The general secretary is the Rev. C. E. Wyckoff, Irvington, N. J. This Federal Council arranges for biennial conventions representing the whole Brotherhood. The denominational councils arrange for biennial conventions on the alternate years. The Federal Council publishes the only organ of the Brotherhood, called "The Brotherhood Star." It is published at the present time for the Council by the Rev. J. G. Hamner, Jr., 25 East Twenty-second street, New York City. The Council has supervision of all the departments of the publication, and acts as the Board of Editors.

---

*EPWORTH LEAGUE: REV. WM. D. GRANT, Ph.D.

A DOZEN years ago the Epworth League had no regularly organized chapter. To-day it has almost twenty-one thousand. Twelve years ago it had a total membership of twenty-seven. To-day it has a million and a half. Twelve years ago the Junior League had scarcely been dreamed of. To-day it is the most promising division

*Taken from "Year Book," 1901.

of the great Epworth army, having a membership of tens of thousands. Twelve years ago a suggestion to establish a newspaper organ was looked upon as a most doubtful experiment, and predictions of failure were freely made. To-day the organization has an official journal whose circulation exceeds that of any church weekly in the world, published at a financial profit greater than that of all other official papers of the Methodist Episcopal Church combined. Twelve years ago the Epworth wheel was just beginning to move in a slow and labored way. Its motions have been accelerated with each passing month, until now it is rolling with speed and triumph around the world. Young Methodism has been awakened to a vivid sense of its possibilities. The hosts of the League have been marshaled for systematic and aggressive Christian service. By the blessing of God we have been inspired by nobler ideals of intellectual and social life. But, best of all, we have been lifted to a higher plane of personal spiritual experience, and have consecrated ourselves to the great work of the world's redemption. "What hath God wrought!"

The Epworth League is the most extraordinary movement in Methodism for a hundred years. Its real significance was not appreciated at first. It is only partially apprehended now. We are yet too near to its beginnings. Twenty years from now the real meaning and bigness of the movement will be more manifest. The coming generations of Methodists will place Central Church, in the city of Cleveland, in the list of historic places whose names are mentioned with joy and pride, and will give May 15, 1889, a high place among the chief days in our denominational history.

*The Brotherhood of St. Andrew.

The Brotherhood of St. Andrew is an organization of laymen in the Anglican Communion. Its sole object, as stated in its constitution, is "the spread of Christ's Kingdom among young men." The words "young men" are understood to include all men of whatever age who need the friendship and influence of Christian men.

The Brotherhood began as a parochial guild in St. James's Church, Chicago. On St. Andrew's Day, 1883, twelve young men, with the approval of their rector, Rev. W. H. Vibbert, D.D., and under the leadership of Mr. James L. Houghteling, the teacher of

*Taken from "Year Book," 1901.

the parish Bible class, agreed to follow the example set by St. Andrew in bringing St. Peter into a personal acquaintance with the Messiah. To guide their efforts they adopted two rules: 1. That of prayer: "To pray daily for the spread of Christ's Kingdom among young men." 2. That of service: "To make an earnest effort each week to bring at least one young man within the hearing of the Gospel of Jesus Christ, as set forth in the services of the church and in young men's Bible classes."

Their efforts were successful beyond expectation. Information about the work spread from place to place and similar guilds were formed in several dioceses. In 1886 thirty-five of these scattered parochial guilds united in a general organization known as the Brotherhood of St. Andrew in the Protestant Episcopal Church in the United States. There are now in this country about twelve hundred parochial branches, or Chapters, with a total membership of about ten thousand men.

There are now National Brotherhoods in Canada, England, Scotland, Australia and the West Indies. There are in all branches of the Anglican Communion about fifteen hundred Chapters, with a total membership of about thirteen thousand men.

A convention is held each year, at which every chapter in good standing is entitled to be represented. The convention appoints a council, which is charged with the executive direction of the general organization. This council maintains an office in the Church Missions House, 281 Fourth avenue, New York, as headquarters for the Brotherhood and as a centre through which the different chapters are brought into communication with one another. It publishes the international Brotherhood monthly magazine, "St. Andrew's Cross," and other literature about Brotherhood work and methods.

The organization of the Brotherhood is marked by extreme simplicity. Complicated machinery has been avoided throughout. Everywhere emphasis has been laid upon individual responsibility for individual character, work and influence.

* * * * * * * * *

The Roman Catholics have just adopted, at Cincinnati, a constitution federating their societies, the membership of which is about 1,000,000.

The Baptist Young People's Union, closely allied to Christian Endeavor, and the Luther League may be learned of by applying for their "Year Books."

THE INTERNATIONAL ORDER OF THE KING'S DAUGHTERS AND SONS.*

REV. WILLIAM D. GRANT, Ph.D.,

NEW YORK.

THE Order of The King's Daughters and Sons began its existence in the union of ten women in New York City, each and all desirous of testing the question whether union and co-operation for their own greater advancement in true Christian living, and their usefulness in practical good works, could be promoted. They had no thought of a world-wide organization. They hoped each to become the centre of a better influence than had heretofore been exercised, and each the nucleus of some little group of friends that she might gather about herself, and infuse with her own spirit, each one of these becoming, in turn, a similar nucleus for ever-widening circles of usefulness.

They met for the first time at the residence of Mrs. Margaret Bottome, on the morning of January 13, 1886, and after consideration of the good to be gained and the good to be done, decided to organize themselves into an Order, or Sisterhood, of service.

Mrs. Bottome was chosen as president; Mrs. Mary Lowe Dickinson, Secretary; and Miss Hamersley, soon succeeded by Miss G. H. Libby, treasurer. The remaining members present were Mrs. Theodore Irving, Mrs. F. Payson, Mrs. C. de P. Field, Mrs. J. F. Ruggles, Miss S. B. Schenck, and Miss G. H. Libby.

Of the various names proposed for this Order, the one suggested by Mrs. Irving, "The King's Daughters," was most favorably received. Mrs. Irving, a well-known educator of New York City, had been in the habit of giving this name to young ladies as they went out into the world from her school, and this has given rise to the mistaken impression that the Order originated in these little groups of students.

The headquarters of the International Order are in New York

---

*In the preparation of this paper I have been greatly indebted to the secretary of the Order, Mrs. Mary Lowe Dickinson, for the courtesy of giving me access to her valuable manuscripts and leaflets.—ED.

City, at 158 West Twenty-third street, where also its authorized organ, the "Silver Cross," has its offices.

THE AIM OF THE ORDER.

There can be no doubt that the International Order of The King's Daughters and Sons is one of the most unique and remarkable of the great religious societies that have come into existence during the past quarter of a century. Its constitution states that its aims and purposes are "to develop spiritual life and to stimulate Christian activities," and that all who accept these "aims and purposes" and who "hold themselves responsible to the King, our Lord and Saviour, Jesus Christ," are welcomed to membership.

As the name indicates, the Order accepts and teaches the "Fatherhood of God and the brotherhood of man," and its first work is to strive to win the individual heart for Christ, so that the individual life may be governed and guided by His Spirit.

At the outset the Order accepted the disadvantages arising from the fact that it based its union upon an inward and spiritual tie, and left the question of outward organization to take care of itself. It knew the world's great need was character—the personal touch.

NO DIVIDING LINES.

The Order recognizes no dividing lines, whether of race, creed, or social conditions, among the children of God, but welcomes all alike to an earnest effort to love Christ and to serve Him. Referring to it on the platform, a public speaker recently said: "It is the only absolutely catholic organization known to me." The editor of a well-known religious paper wrote of it: "It is one of the two greatest human forces now at work in the world to bring about the unity of the church of God."

ITS PROGRESS.

Its founders desired as little publicity and as little organization as possible, but they have evidently been led by ways they did not choose, for the Order spread with amazing rapidity. Their badge, a small silver cross bearing the initials of their watch-word, "In His Name," is now worn all over the world, and the corresponding secretary is in official communication with nearly every nation. The organization was incorporated in 1889, and in 1891 the word "International" was legally added to its title, as long before that time its work had become world-wide.

The oldest member of the Order lives in Brooklyn, N. Y., and is one hundred and two years old; the youngest member was made such the day she was born. Within its ranks can be found not only the little child and the wayworn pilgrim, but some of the noblest men and women who, in the church, the state, the university and the business world, are to-day shaping the policy and guiding the affairs of the nation in this twentieth century of marvelous promise.

METHODS.

The Order works in groups called Circles. These vary in size, some having ten members, or even less, some numbering hundreds. There are state and county branches, chapters and city unions in America and Canada, and national branches in foreign lands. Its order of service is "the heart, the home, the church, and the world." While the organization is absolutely *inter*-denominational, perfect loyalty to that branch of the church to which its members belong is insisted upon, and all Circles at work in churches are under the teaching and guidance of their own pastor or rector.

WORK.

Just another of God's ways of blessing the world. How? By sending His Spirit to draw one heart and another and another into loving obedience to Christ. Every heart so drawn will love to find some little work, or large work, to do, such as Jesus would do if He were here. Anything, however simple, that brightens even an hour of another's life, that relieves pain, or poverty, or sickness, or distress, that makes the world a happier place to live in, that teaches others to know more and, especially, to love more—that is the Order's work.

The choice of work is left for each member to determine, but in the choice each should ask God to guide to that which will help most and that for which each is best fitted.

Individual members may work alone, but Circles may be formed wherever members love God and love each other enough to help each other to do better work than could be done alone.

What are they doing "for the love of Christ and in His name"? Everything that can help the souls and bodies of the children of God—building churches, paying mortgages on those already built, building and furnishing parsonages and rectories, educating young men and women for the ministry and for the foreign mission field, taking care of orphans and widows, of the old and the sick, building hospitals and infirmaries, maintaining day nurseries and kindergartens, sending trained nurses to the homes of the poor, and following the sailors out upon the lonely seas with evidences of loving care for their spiritual and bodily welfare.

GROWTH OF THE ORDER.

It was never the intention of the Council to keep strict records of work or of membership, and reports or registration are not insisted upon; but since the organization of the Order in January, 1886, with ten members, it has attained, in 1900, to a membership approximating 400,000.

At the present time it exists in greater or less numbers in North and South America, in Great Britain, Germany, France, Italy, Greece, Switzerland, Denmark, and Turkey, in Europe; in India, China, Japan, and Turkey, in Asia; in Australia, New Zealand, the Sandwich and Hawaiian Isles; in the Bermudas and Bahamas. There are individual members, and some Circles, in Palestine, effective bands in Smyrna, and several hundreds of members in mission fields abroad. In many of these places organization is well advanced, and there is not only a steady increase of membership, but, what is far better, there are evidences of consolidation, classification and adaptation to many practical lines of helpful work.

The Order has passed beyond such sentimentalism and sensationalism as was born, not of its principles, or its general management and conduct, but of its excessively rapid growth. This growth proved two things: first, that its projectors had been quite right in the supposition that there were multitudes of women eager and desirous of making their lives of value to themselves and of use to the world; and, second, that what they needed was not stimulation in order to make them willing to work, but education in the world's needs, and instruction as to the best methods of battling with its misery and sin.

But the transformation of this mass of womanhood into companies of well-trained soldiers, ready for an aggressive and successful movement against any one form of suffering or sin, has been a mighty work. The marvel is not that it should have been so imperfectly accomplished, but that such wonderful progress should already have been made. And how largely the movement was of God, and not of man nor of woman, is proven by the fact that even under the prolonged period of experiment the interest and enthusiasm have not died out, and the uplifting purpose is dominant in thousands of women's lives who have not yet found out the best way to make the most of themselves, or to do the most for the good of others.

The measure of this work is not in the number of large buildings erected, nor of new enterprises successfully carried on; its object has ever been the training of character until it should be a quiet, helpful force in good work already existing. Yet the Order can point to such an amount of new and aggressive work as would be a grand record if there were nothing else to be considered.

Hardly any class of people has been forgotten in its ministrations. Among the poor and the sick, in kindergartens, hospitals and jails, among the victims of flood, and fire and disease, the little cross has gone with its loving service. Missionaries in foreign lands, and the Indians on our own vast plains, have been helped. Special interest has always been shown in the care of the aged and of little children; and the distinctively educational work, in school and college extension by correspondence, among members of the Order, has no insignificant place among the varied activities of The King's Daughters and Sons.

The Order is urged to perform all these services silently, not to talk about them unless necessary in order to stimulate others to do likewise; to forget the good done as quickly as possible, and move forward to the next opportunity.

INDEX.

VOLUME II.

Abbott, Ezra, 159.
Abbot, George, Archbishop of Canterbury, 308.
Abeel, David, 310.
Ackerman, Jessie, 398.
"Acta Diurna," 172.
Adams, Wm., 315.
Addams, Jane, 432, 438.
"Age of Homespun, The," 126.
"Age of Reason," Paine's, 63.
Allen, James Grant, 18.
Allen, A. V. G., 116, 144.
Alliance of Reformed Churches, 319.
Alien population, 341.
Alexandrian School of Pantænus, 202.
Almy, Frederick, 84.
Almoners need to be instructed, 98.
Altruism before A. D., 72.
American Bible Society, 317.
"American Presbyterian Review," 314.
American paradise of labor, 48.
America for Rome, 223.
American ecclesiastical fraternity, 316.
Andrew, Elizabeth Wheeler, 398.
Andover House, 439.
Andreæ, Jacob, 295, 307.
Anglicanism and Greek Church, 309.
Anglican Orders and Roman Catholic Church, 319.
Angelo, Michael, life of, 102.
Animism stage in religion, 261.
Apostolic Church, the, 54.
Apostolic Succession, 214, 328.
Apostles' Creed, 252.
Appreciation of Martineau, 136-7.
Aquinas, Thos., and the Pope, 248.
Arian Controversy, 206.
Arminian bent in Greek Church, 308.
"**Army's** Mother, The," 427.

Arnold of Brescia, 219.
Arnold, Frederick, 108.
Art and Religious and Social Well-Being, 100.
Art in education, morality and worship, 101.
Art, absence of all, 102.
Art in Germany—Dürer, 102.
Art taught prior to Reformation, 102.
Art and Nature, 102, 112.
Art, aim of, 103.
Art and Puritan austerity, 105.
Art, influence of, 105.
Art in Architecture, 106, 107.
Art and the kitchen stove, 108.
Art and money values, 109.
Art Galleries always open, 109.
Art and the Bible, 104, 111.
"Association Men," 367.
Astruc, 167.
Athanasius, 205.
Atonement, Grotian theory, 125.
Attending church, 1.
Augsburg Confession, 306.

Bagehot, Walter, 97.
Bala, Chas., 63.
Bellamy, Ed., 44.
Baltimore, Moody in, 70.
Ballou, Adin, 51.
"Barbarism, first danger," 126.
Barrows, John Henry, 12.
Barker, Helen M., 400, 402.
Barnett, Canon, 432-4.
Barrett, Kate Waller, 376.
Barney, Mrs. J. K., 398.
Barton, Clara, 89.
Basil of Cæsarea, 205.
Baur, school of, 29.
Baxter, Richard, 252, 301.
Beach, David N., 442.
Beauchamp, Helen M., 402.

INDEX.

Beecher, Henry Ward, 171, 383.
Beecher, Lyman, 368, 388.
Beecher Ed., 65.
Belfast, Moody in, 69.
Believers, oneness of, 57.
Belgian, care of the poor, 82.
Bengel, 159.
Benevolence in United States, 1899, 78.
Benevolence imposed on, 97.
Berry, Chas. A., 323-4.
Bergen, Convent of, 295.
Bible, re-setting of, 6, 164.
Bible distributed, 12.
Bible better understood, 14.
Bible a new book, 30.
Bible, social wealth of, 53, 56.
Bible, Luther's translation, 104.
Bible illustrated, 111.
Bible Institute, 149.
Bible and D. L. Moody, 152.
Bible and Protestantism, 156.
Bible and Reformation, 156, 221.
Bible and research, 157.
Bible, first book printed, 172.
Bible and H. Heine, 222.
Bible kept from the people, 225.
Biblical Criticism warranted, 155.
Biblical Criticism, schools of, 158.
Bible study among students, 419.
Bismarck, 408.
Bliss, W. D. P., 54.
Blass of Halle, 160.
Black, Jas., 389.
Booth, Wm., 246, 223, 88.
Booth as a leader, 426.
Boards of Charities, 78.
Borgia, Cæsar, 217.
Borromeo, St. Chas., 289.
Bottome, Margaret, 453.
Brainerd, Cephas, 360-4.
Brewers' Association, 389.
Bridges, Cornelia, 370.
Bardford, Cornelia, 439.
Bradlaugh, Chas., 435.
Brooks, Phillips, 144.
Brooks, Phillips, biography of, 116.
Brooks, Phillips, a preacher, 144.
Browning, Robert, 332.
Brown, Mrs. M. M., 393.
Brooklyn, Moody in, 69.
Brotherhood of man, 4.
Brotherhood of Andrew and Philip, 448.
Brotherhood of Andrew and Philip, rules and aims, 449.
Brotherhood of Andrew and Philip, growth of, 449.
"Brotherhood Star," The, 450.
Brotherhood of St. Andrew, 451.

Buddhism, 73, 266.
Buell, Mrs., 396.
"Building of Character, The," 353.
Burt, Mary T., 392.
Burgon, Dean, 160.
Burns' "Cotter's Saturday Night," 8.
Burroughs, Jeremiah, 303.
Bushnell, Kate, 398.
Bushnell, Horace, 120.
Bushnell's literary activity, 123-6.

Cadbury, George, 330, 331, 336.
Calvinism, 308.
Calixtus, George, 299.
Cappadocians, the three, 205.
Capital and labor, 3.
Carlyle, and religious change, 10.
Carpenter, Lent, 127.
Carey, Wm., 237, 258.
Carpenter, Mrs. George, 391.
Cass, General Lewis, 388.
Caughey, James, 425.
Catechism of Free Church Council, 328.
Categorical Imperative, Kant's, 169.
Catholic and Protestant Socialism, 47.
Catholicism in 1800 and to-day, 189.
"Catholic World, The," 223.
Catholicism as a principle of progress, 227.
Catholic Unity League, 318.
Catholic Total Abstinence Society, 389.
Celsus, 202.
Cerularius, Patriarch, 201.
Chapman, J. Wilbur, 61.
Chalmers, Thos., 214, 368.
Charles V., Emperor, 293.
Channing and Martineau, 134.
Chamouni, Valley of, 112.
Charlemagne's Capitularies, 76.
Charity inspired by Christ, 76.
Charity organization societies, 95.
Charrington, F. N., 381.
Chateaubriand, 72.
Character related to teaching, 147.
Children's Country Holiday Society, 90.
Chinese Martyrs, 242.
Christianity, *Gains of*, 12, 23.
Christianity, aggressive, 13.
Christianity a vital force, 22.
Christianity in Modern Society, 1.
Christianity persecuted, 5.
Christianity a religion of service, 27.
Christianity a social force, 33, 34.
Christianity preëminent, 35.
Christianity a spirit, 55, 220.
Christianity and Philanthropy, 72.

INDEX. 461

Christianity in terms of life, 249.
Christianity self-renewing, 246.
Christianity, distinctive feature of, 250.
Christianity emasculated, 252.
Christianity, why the best religion? 256.
Christianity, unique, 264.
Christianity, universal and absolute, 270.
Christendom dominates, 276.
Christian Church, The, 12.
Christian fellowship, 14, 20.
Christian history in America, 20.
Christian coöperation, 20.
Christian sources attacked, 41.
Christian social movement, 42.
Christian Socialism, 43.
Christian Socialism in United States, 48.
Christian Socialism in Germany, 45.
Christian Socialism, works on, 52.
Christian Sociology, 52, 170.
Christian Social Union, The, 44.
"Christian Socialist, The," 43.
"Christian Nurture," 122.
Christian Apologists, the, 202.
Christian unity in mission field, 236.
Christian fundamentals and circumstantials, 247.
Christian progress and unification, 272.
Christian Church centre of unity, 275.
"Christian Union," 310.
"Christian Guardian, The," 315.
Christian Union and Church life in United States, 316.
Christian Commission, the, 361.
"Christian Mission, The," 430.
Christian Endeavor, 442.
Christian Endeavor, enthusiasm for, 442.
Christian Endeavor, principles and growth, 443.
Christian Endeavor, first twenty years, 446.
Christian coöperation and efficiency, 368.
Christian Endeavor Convention, 447.
Christian Endeavor Convention of 1899, 447.
"Christian Doctrine of Justification and Reconciliation, The," 140.
Christ's command to this age, 75.
"Christ in Theology," 124.
Christ is Christianity, 148.
Chicago, Moody in, 70.
Church, better known, 19.
Church's world-wide view, 22.

"Church Army," 44.
Church, labor and the poor, 50.
Church, social awakening of, 57
Church and social demands, 58.
Church according to Roman and Protestant, 220.
Church, dependent on, 230.
Church a fellowship of persons, 248.
Church discordant and powerless, 277.
Church, theory of, cause of failure, 278.
Church despotism and aggrandizement, 280.
Church Union in Scotland, 312.
Church of Scotland, 313.
Church Union Movements, 290.
Church Federation, 321.
Church Federation in the Old World, 322.
Church Congress, the, 322.
Churches of Asia Minor, 214.
Cicero and benevolence, 73.
City Mission and Tract Society, New York, 90.
Cities, religion and philanthropy of, 376.
Civilization and Roman Catholic Church, 181.
Clark, Lincoln, 314.
Clark, Francis E., 442, 317.
Clark, Myron H., 389.
Clement of Alexandria, 203.
Clergy, apathy of, 42.
Classes in America, 50.
Clifford, Dr., 335.
Cleveland, President, 398.
Cobbe, Frances Power, 131.
Coit, Stanton, 436.
Coleridge, 250.
College Settlement in New York, 437.
Columbian Congress of Religions, 19.
Commandment, the fourth, 8.
Communistic experiments, 51.
Communion in both kinds, 209.
"Communion of the Christian with God," 143.
Comparison of Christianity with other Religions, 255.
Concord, Formula of, 294.
Congress of Free Churches, a, 323.
Confession of Faith, 314.
Confession of a non-Catholic, 176.
Congregational Union, the, 44.
Congressional Library, 106.
Constantinople falls, 293.
Convalescents, care of, 90.
Controversy, theological, 14.
Coöperative parish work, 346.
Coöperative Calendars, 347.

INDEX.

Cox, Samuel, 368.
Corcoran Art Gallery, 106.
Crapsey, A. S., 272.
Creed, Ideal, 319.
Creeds in New York City, 343.
Crittenden, Chas. N., 380.
Critical Philosophy, the, 24.
"Critique of the Practical Reason," 25, 168.
"Critique of Pure Reason," 168.
Critical and Ethical Movements, 155.
Criticism of Bible needful, 155.
Critical Inquiry, purpose of, 155.
Critical Students of Bible—great names, 159.
Cromwell, Oliver, 328, 370, 385.
Crusius, Martin, 307.
Cummins, Miss, 398.
Cuyler Theodore L., 358.

d'Ailly, Peter, 219.
Dale, R. W., 155.
D'Aubigné, Merle, 368.
Day-Nurseries, 90.
Davis, Wm. F., 378.
"Debitum Legale," 76.
Defectives, care of, 91.
de Lavelaye, M., and Bible, 224.
Delitzsch, 158.
Dennison House, 437.
Denny, Prof., 143.
De Paul, Vincent, 289.
De Smet, Father, 193.
De Tocqueville, 17.
Dewart, E. H., 315.
Dickinson, Mary Lowe, 453.
Discontent, reasonable, 109.
"Dissertation on Language," 123.
Disappointment of Jesus Christ, 272.
"Disputes and Quarrels," 290.
Distilleries closed, 389.
Divine immanence, the, 26.
Divine transcendence, 25.
Divine unity, the, 135.
Disunion of Christendom, 272.
Dixon, A. C., 148.
Doctrinal Unity, 282.
Dodge, Wm. E., 338, 358.
Dodge, Hon. Wm. E., 372.
Doggett, L. L., 358.
Doré, Gustave, 111.
Dort, Council of, 252, 301.
Doyle, A. P., 176, 188.
Dow, General Neal, 389.
Drink traffic condemned, 385.
Drurie, John, 297, 298.
Drummond, Henry, 151.
Dunn, Dr., 386.
Dürer and religious art in Germany, 102, 104.

Dwight, Timothy, 106.

Early Christian Literature, 165.
"Ecce Homo," 73, 75.
Ecclesiastical Traditions, 176.
"Economic Review," the, 44.
Ecumenical Conference, 4.
Ecumenical Conference of Methodist Churches, 320.
Edinburgh, Moody in, 68.
Education and Art, 101.
Edwards, Jonathan, 120.
Edwards, Justin, 388.
Elizabeth's Statute, 77.
Eliot, George, 174.
"Elements of the Science of Religion, The," 261.
Emerson, R. Waldo, 289.
Emperor, William of Germany, 366.
Emperor, Julian's complaint, 74.
Employer and Employed, 96.
"Endeavors after the Christian Life," 132.
English social movements, 44.
English and American system of relief, 77.
English Presbyterians and Congregationalists, 302.
England, Moody in, 69.
England's system of poor relief, 79.
Engels, Friedrich, revelations of, 42.
Environment of Man, 109.
Epworth League, 450.
"Essays Theological and Philosophical," 132.
"Essays, Reviews and Addresses," 133.
"Essays and Addresses," Brooks, 144.
Essential Christianity, 245.
Ethical Problems, 170.
Evangelical Movement in England, 115.
Evangelical Alliance, 316, 337-40.
Evangelical Alliance, 368.
Evangelical Alliance, object of, 369.
Evangelical Alliance, branches of, 372.
Evangelical Alliance and Week of Prayer, 372.
Evangelical Alliance and Conferences, 373.
Evangelical Alliance and religious liberty, 373.
Evangelical Alliance and toleration, 375.
Evangelical Free Churches of Great Britain, 327.

Fabiola, a Roman lady, 74.
Fairbairn, Dr., 227, 228, 432.
"Faiths of the World, The," 255.

INDEX. 463

Faraday, Michael, 289.
Farrar, F. W., 386.
Farnsworth, Ezra, 378.
Fashioning the child nature, 353.
Fatherhood of God, 28.
Federation of Churches, 321.
Federation extension, 337.
Federation in the New World, 337.
Federation, political, 339.
Federation problem in America, 340.
Federation throughout the United States, 348.
Federation in New York City, 342.
Ferris, Frank A., 356.
Fermaud, M. Chas., 364.
Ferguson, Mr. and Mrs., 379.
Federation of Students, 409, 420.
Federation of Students and what has been accomplished, 421.
Fellowship with Christ ground of unification, 274.
Field, E. P., 373.
Fields, Addie Northam, 398.
Field, Mrs. C. de P., 453.
Fifty Years of Union Theological Seminary, 370.
Filioque Controversy, 207, 291.
"Five Views of Christian Faith," 129.
Finney, Chas. G., 21, 65.
Fisch, George, 368.
Fliedner, Pastor, 87.
Florence, Council of, 272.
Florence Mission, 380.
"Founders great in their unconsciousness," 126.
"Foundations of Belief," Balfour's, 134.
Founder of Christianity systematizes nothing, 247.
"Form, The," 107.
"Frankfort Journal," 172.
France's care of poor, 81.
Free thought interdicted, 296.
French Revolution, the, 38, 189.
Frederick, Wm. III. of Prussia, 305.
Frederick, Wm. II. of Prussia, 305.
Free Church Council Mission, 334.
Free Church Council Mission results, 335.
Free Church Council and South Africa, 332.
"Free Church Chronicle, The," 331.
Free Church Council, origin of, 323.
Free Church Council, objects of, 324.
Free Church of Scotland, 312.
"Freedom of the Christian Man," 229.
Froude, Mr., 224.

Fry, Susanna, M.D., 400, 402.
Fuller, Andrew, 63.

Gains of Christianity, 12.
Gale, George W., 65.
Garrison, Wm. Lloyd, 385.
Garvie, Alfred E., 139.
"Genius of Christ," the, 72.
Geneva, 308, 364.
Gerson, John, 219.
George, Henry, 44.
Germany's National Responsibility, 80.
Gifford Lectures, Prof. Tiele, 261.
Gladstone, W. E., 130, 217, 385.
Glespie, Rev., 312.
"God in Christ," 123.
Goodrich Settlement, Cleveland, 440
Goodman, Ed., 175.
Gordon, Anna A., 398, 400, 402.
Gospel and Greek Philosophy, 202.
Gospel of Beauty, the, 112.
Gospels alone sufficient, 249.
Gould, Helen Miller, 363.
Gough, Jno. B., 388.
Grant, Wm. D., 127, 212, 245, 368, 450, 453.
Gray, Wm. C., 171.
Grand Old Man of Maine, 389.
Greek Christianity, 200.
Greek Church replies to Pope Leo XIII., 200.
Greek Church includes, 201.
Greek Church oligarchical; Roman Catholic monarchical; Protestant, democratic, 207.
Greek and Protestant Churches friendly, 306.
Greek and Latin Churches divide, 290.
Greek Church surrenders to Rome, 292-3.
Greek Church, form of worship, 209.
Greek Church subordinate to State, Roman Catholic State subordinate to Church, 208.
Greeks scatter at fall of Constantinople, 293.
Green, Prof., 164.
Gregory of Nazianzus, 205.
Gregory of Nyssa, 205.
Gregory, 159, 160.
Grimm, Herman, 102.
Grotius, Hugo, 299.
"Growth of Law, The," 126.
Grundy, John, 128.
Guizot, M., and Bible, 224.
Gurley, Phineas D., 314.

Haldanes, the, 63.
Hall, Robert, 304.
Hamlin, Teunis S., 149.

Hamlin, A. D. F., 107.
Hammond, Burrell, 333.
Hamner, J. G., 450.
Hamersley, Miss, 453.
Häring, 141.
Harnack, 141, 165.
Harrison, Frederic, 130.
Hastings, Lord, 333.
Hatfield, Edwin F., 370.
Haupt, Prof., 162.
"Heart of a Continent, The," 196.
Heine, Heinrich and Bible, 222.
Hengstenberg, Prof., 164.
"Herbergen zur Hermath," 89.
Herrmann, 141.
Hiarm House, Cleveland, 440.
Higginson, Helen, 128.
Higher Criticism, 158, 162.
Higher Criticism Opposed, 163.
High Churchman and Dean Stanley, 15.
Hill, Rolland, 63.
Hill, Thos., 302.
Hillis, Newell Dwight, 115.
Historical Criticism, 29.
Historic Episcopate, 318.
"History of Pietism, The," 140.
"History of Dogma," 143.
"History of the German People," 216.
"History of the Popes," etc., 216.
Holland's care of the poor, 83.
Holy Trinity, Philadelphia, 144.
Holy Ghost, operations of, 179.
Holy Living and Roman Catholic Church, 183.
Holy Synod's Reply to Pope Leo XIII., 200.
Holy Scripture sufficient, 221.
Hodges, Dean, 350, 439.
Hodge, Charles, 311, 314.
Hoffman, Clara C., 400, 402.
Homer, 253.
"Homiletic Review," 386, 432.
"Home Prayers," 133.
Hopedale Community, the, 51.
Horton, 226, 336.
Horwill, H. W., 171.
"Hours of Thought on Sacred Things," 132.
House of Bishops, 317-18.
Housing the Poor, 92.
Houghteling, James L., 359, 451.
Hughes, Hugh Price, 327, 334.
Hull House, Chicago, 94, 432, 437.
Huntington, Wm. R., 338.
Hurst, Bishop, John F., 290.
Huss, 219.
Hutton, Mancius H., 1.
Hutton, R. H., 130, 213, 217.
Huxley, Prof., 130.

Ideal Creed, 319.
Imagery in Worship, danger of, 100.
Imperishable Greatness, 114.
Ingham, Mrs. M. A., 392.
Ingram, A. F. Winnington, 436.
Industrial Art, 105.
Infidelity, French, 63.
"Influence of Christ in Modern Life," the, 115.
"Influence of Jesus," 144
"Inner Mission," 46.
"Instruction in the Christian Religion," 140.
Institutions rejected, why? 214.
Institutional Churches, 58.
Intellectual Uniformity, 284.
Intolerance and State Church, 333.
"International Lesson System," 354.
International Y. M. C. A. Work, 360.
Introduction to the New Testament, 165.
Ireland, Archbishop, 223.
Irenic Movements since Reformation, 293.
Irving, Mrs. Theodore, 453.
Islam (universal religion), 269.
Israel's Downfall, 214.
Italy's care for the poor, 80.

Jackson, Samuel Macauley, 115, 117.
Jackson, A. W., 136, 228.
James, John Angell, 368, 371.
Jansen, J., 216.
Japan, regeneration of, 13.
Jay, Hon. John, 372.
Jerome, 219.
Jerningham's enumeration, 75.
Jesus Christ, Lives of, 14.
Jesus' method, 55.
Jesuits, 195, 309.
Jesus Christ the only Mediator, 228.
Jewish Canon, 161.
John of Damascus, 205, 206.
Johnson, Mary C., 392.
Justification by faith alone, 231.
Justification and Luther, 231.

Kant, movement led by, 24, 25, 101, 168.
"Kant, Lotze and Ritschl," 143.
Kaftan, 141.
Kaiserswerth, 89.
Keble, John, 289.
Keil, Prof., 164.
Kellogg, J. B., 379.
Ketteler, Bishop of Mayence, 47.
Kingdom of God, the, 56.
King of Catholic Italy, 366.
King of Portugal and Evangelical Alliance, 374.

INDEX.

Kingsley House, 439.
King's Daughters and Sons, 453.
King's Daughters, aim of the order, 454.
King's Daughters, methods and work, 455.
King's Daughters, growth, 456.
Kinnaird, Lord, 334, 374.
Kluge, Pastor, 366.
Knight, Wm., 137.
Knowles, 130.
Koran and care of sick and needy, 74.
Kritopulos, Metrophanes, 308.
Kuenen, school of, 29.

Labor Problems and Roman Catholic Church, 183.
Labor Colonies, 89.
Laidlaw, Walter, 321.
Lambeth Conference, 318.
Langdon, Wm. Chauncey, 360.
Lane, W. R., 331.
Latin and Greek Churches divide, 290.
Latin Church charged with heresy, 292.
Laurier, Sir Wilfrid, 398.
Lathrop, Mary T., 400, 403.
Leavitt, Mary Clement, 398.
Leckey, 74.
Leppington, C. H. d'E., 72.
Lewis, Dio, 390.
Libby, Miss G. H., 453.
Liberty, struggle for, 328.
Life, power of, 253.
Little Portland Street Unitarian Chapel, 129.
Livermore, Mary A., 400.
Liverpool, Moody in, 68.
Lollards, 219.
"London Spectator, The," 175.
"London Times, The," 174.
London Clergymen, group of, 45.
London Congregational Union, the, 44.
Lord's Prayer, 252.
Love of God, the, 27.
Love of Christ and Souls, Brooks' secret of success, 145.
Lowell, Josephine Shaw, 98.
Lower Criticism, 158.
"Lost Boy," poem, 405.
Loyal Temperance Legion, 403.
Lucar, Cyril, 308.
Luther's Bible translation, 104, 221.
Luther in Rome, 215.
Luther's Protest, 225, 245.
Luther and justification by faith, 231.

Lutheran and Reformed Union, 305.
Lyons, Council of, 272.

Maclauchlin, 226.
MacNeil, Esther, 390.
Maclaren, Ian, 328.
Mackennal, Dr., 331, 336.
Madison, James, 18.
"Maine Law, The," 389.
Mansfield House, 435.
Manchester College, 128.
Manning, Cardinal, 130, 218.
Marriages in London and New York, 344.
Mary, the Virgin, 186.
Martensen, Bishop, 225.
Marsten, Francis E., 100.
Martyn, Henry, 416.
Martineau, James, 127.
Martineau, Thomas, 127.
Martineau, James, in Dublin, Liverpool and London, 128.
Martineau appointed professor, 128.
Martineau in Germany, 129.
Martineau, estimate of, 130.
Martineau's literary labors, 132.
Martineau and Unitarianism, 134.
Martineau, honors to, 136-7.
Martineau, unique personality, 138.
Martineau's tribute to Roman Catholic Church, 188.
Marx, Carl, revelations of, 42, 43.
Massoretic School, 162.
Masses, condition of in Germany, 45.
Mather, Mrs. Samuel, 440.
Maurice, F. D., 130.
Medici, Giovanini, 217.
Meharry, J. B., 337.
Melanchthon, conciliatory, 294, 306.
Menzies, Allan, 255.
Metaphysical Society and Toleration, 130.
Methodism, Canadian union of, 315.
Methodism, Australian union of, 316.
"Methodist Times," 323.
Methodist Ecumenical Conference, 320.
Meyer, F. B., 334.
Middle Ages and the poor, 76.
Mill, John Stuart, 101.
Miller, Rufus W., 448.
Miller, J. R., 353.
Milton, John, 172, 242.
"Mind of the Master," the, 319.
Missions Problem, the, 4.
Missionary Heroes, 240.
Missionary Progress in Madagascar, Fiji, China, 241, 244.
Missions, Modern, beginning of, 237.
Missionary's message the same, 242.

INDEX.

Missions, foundations laid, 243.
Mission Organizations and their Work, 239.
Missionary statistics, 239.
Mohammed II. Recognizes Patriarch of Constantinople, 293.
Mohammedanism and Philanthropy, 74.
Monasteries Disendowed, 76
Moody, Dwight Lyman, 148, 21, 63, 358.
Moody's leadership, 148.
Moody described, 148-154.
Moody's message, 152.
Moody and Y. M. C. A., 360.
Moody's evangelistic campaigns, 68.
Montgomery, Caroline Williamson, 441.
Morgan, G. Campbell, 334, 336.
"Moral Uses of Dark Things," 126.
Moral Fallibility, 212.
Morality and Art, 101, 102.
Morley, John, 130.
Morrison, John, 224.
Moravians and Schleiermacher, 117.
Moravians and Missions, 238.
Morse, Richard C., 64, 358.
Mott, John R., 407, 358.
Mount Herman, 149.
Mozoomdar, 19.
Muir, Pearson McAdam, 313.
Munger, Theodore T., 120.
Mumford, Catherine, 426.
Mutual Aid by Christians, 74.
Mysius, Demetrius, 306.
Mystics, the, 219.
McAll Mission, France, 381.
McAuley, Jerry, 378.
McBurney, Robert R., 4, 358, 362.
McCormick, Cyrus H., 358.
McCauley, Dr., 448.
McCrie, Thos., 312.
McNeill, John, 335.

Nash, Henry S., 324.
National Religions, 365.
National Temperance Society, 386.
"National Philanthropist, The," 388.
"Nature and the Supernatural," 124.
Nature and Art, 102.
Necessarianism repudiated, 129.
Nestle, 159.
Neighborhood Guild, 437.
New Problems of Christianity, 1.
New York City, Moody in, 70.
New Gospel, the, 54.
Nettleton, Ashael, 64.
Newman, John Henry, 289.

"News Tribune," and Y. P. S. C. E. Convention, 447.
"Neuremburg Gazette," 172.
Nicæa, Council of, 74, 202.
Nightingale, Florence, 86, 89.
Nietsche, 170.
Nineteenth Century Marvelous, 71.
Northfield, Moody's home, 69, 149.
North End Mission, Boston, 377.
Nott, Eliphalet, 388.
Nottingham Revival, 425.
Nurses, training school for, 86.
Nurses' Settlement, New York, 439.

Oblate Fathers, 193.
"Obligations to the Dead, our," 127.
Oedipus and the Sphinx Riddle, 2.
Old Catholic Church, rise of, 140.
Old Testament, original text, 161.
Old and New School Presbyterians United, 315.
Organized and individual poor relief, 84.
Orr, Prof., 143.
Oriental Orthodoxy and Protestantism, 307.
"Our Country," 338.
"Outlook, The," on Protestantism, 226.
Overbeck, Johann F., 111.
Owen, John, 300.
Oxford House, 435.

Paganism in Worship of Greek Church, 209.
Page, Harlan, 370.
Painting is poetry without words, 104.
Palmer, Alice, 398.
Paleologus, Emperor Michael, 292.
Paleologus, Emperor John VII., 292.
Pantænus, of Alexandria, 203.
Parliament, Queen Elizabeth's last, 77.
Papal infallibility not impecability, 181.
Parkhurst, Chas. H., creed and orthodoxy, 250, 251, 1.
Parker, Joseph, 322, 333.
Parr, J. Tolefree, 331, 334.
Parrish, Clara, 398.
Parker, Theodore, 124.
Passmore Edward's House, 436.
Pastors unrestricted doctrinally, 252.
Pastor, Louis, 216.
Paton, John, 374.
Patton, Wm., 368-71.
Patton, Col. Robert, 370.
Patriarch, Jeremiah, 307.
Patriarch, Joseph II., 306.

INDEX.

Patriarch, Cyril Lucar, 307.
Patriarch, Michael Cerlularius, 201, 292.
Payson, Mrs. F., 453.
Payson, Ed., 172.
Persecution of Christianity, 5.
Person of Christ, power of, 147.
Pierson, Silas, Jr., 378.
Pierson, Arthur T., 377.
Pioneer work in missions, 243.
Pilate, Pontius, Holy Stairs, 216.
Phillips, Wendell, 21.
Philadelphia, Moody in, 69.
Philanthropy, 72.
Philanthropic Associations, 86.
"Philosophy of Art," Ruskin's, 101.
Physical Science, 31.
Plato and Art, 101, 203.
Polity of Greek Church, Oligarchical, 207.
Polity of Roman Catholic Church, Monarchical, 207.
Polity of Protestant Church, Democratic, 207.
Poor, Housing of the, 92.
Pope Leo III, 290.
Pope Nicholas I, letter of, 291.
Pope acknowledged successor of St. Peter, 292.
Pope Leo IX, 201.
Pope Clement VII, 293.
Pope Leo XIII, 319.
Pope Boniface, 213.
Pope Leo X, 215.
Popes Innocent—VIII, and Alexander VI, 217.
Population, urban and alien, 340-1.
Porphyry, 202.
Porteus, Bishop, 63.
Potter, Bishop, 21.
Prayer for the dead, 187.
Practical Christian Socialism, 51.
Preaching of the age transformed, 27.
Preaching of Martineau, 131.
Prentiss, George L., 370.
Prisoners' Aid Association, 92.
Prevention of Cruelty to Children, 93.
Presbyterian Church of England, 312.
Presbyterian Old and New Schools in U. S., 313.
Priest unknown in early church, 229.
Priesthood of all believers, 229.
Private Judgment, right of, 225.
"Princeton, Rev.," 310, 314.
Protest at Spire, 218.
Protestant defined, 219.

"Protestant Reformation in all Countries," 234.
Protestant Christianity, 212.
Protestantism and Bible, 156.
Protestant and Catholic and Socialism, 47.
Protestantism a failure, 232.
Propagation of the Faith, Society of, 196.
Protestantism in danger, 235.
Protestant Foreign Missions, 236.
Protestantism and Oriental Orthodoxy, 307.
Protestant Pat. of Constantinople, 309.
Protestant and Greek Churches friendly, 306.
Protestantism in Mexico, 319.
Protestant Episcopal Church and reunion, 317.
Protestant Episcopal and Presbyterian Churches, 318.
Providence, doctrine of, 26.
Pseudo-Isidorian Decretals, 293.
Pullman's model town, 109.
Purves, George T., 23.
Purgatory, 187.
Pusey, Dr., 289.

Raikes, Robert, 353.
"Rainbow" Bible, 162.
Rankin, Elizabeth, 127.
"Rationale of Religious Inquiry," 132.
Rechabites, order of, 388.
Red Cross Societies, 89.
Refining influences, 109.
"Reign of Law," 18.
Reformers and Bible, 156.
Reformation of 16th century, 215, 246.
Reformation of church attempted, 219.
Reformatory Councils, 219.
Reformation left something to be reformed, 246.
Reformation theory of unity, 281.
Reformation a reversion, 287.
Reformed and Lutheran Union, 305.
Religious Leaders, 114.
Religion, Speeches on, 118.
Religious liberty, 18.
Religious Thought, 23.
Religions, comparative study of, 35, 257.
Religious life changed, 41.
Religious Social Movements in U. S., 51.
Religion and Art, 101, 104.

"Religion Within the Limits of Pure Reason," 168.
Religious Press, The, 171.
"Religion in Hist. and Mod. Life," 227, 228.
Religion not a monopoly, 231, 248.
Religious systems depreciate, 245.
Religions Contrasted, 255.
Religions judged by value for human spirit, 260.
Religions morphologically compared, 260.
Religion, source of, 266.
Religion in our Lord's day, 273.
Renaissance of Learning, 102.
Rescue Work, 376.
Rescue Missions in N. Y. and other cities, 378.
Reunion of the church in God and in humanity, 288.
Reunion of the East and West attempted, 292.
Reunion of Protestantism and Prot. Episcop. Church, 317.
Revelation closes, 3.
Revolution brings people to front, 37.
Revelations of Marx and Engels, 42.
Revival Movements, 61.
Revivals still needed, 61.
Revival epochs, 63.
Revivals, group of, 63.
Revivals, fruits of, 63, 70.
Revivals in U. S., 63.
Revivals in Colleges, 64.
Reynolds, James B., 437.
Ritschl, Albrecht, 139.
Ritschl, school of, 29, 56, 141, 168.
Ritschl's publications, 140.
Ritschl, influenced by, 139.
Ritschlian theology, 142, 169.
"Ritschlian Theology, The," 143.
Robinson, John, 10.
Robertson, F. W., 108.
Robinson, Major, 175.
Robert, Charles, 96.
Robert Browning Settlement, 436.
Roberts, Brigham H., 403.
Rogers, Guiness, 322.
Rom. Cath. Christianity, 176.
Rom. Pontiff's infallibility, 176, 180.
Rom. Cath. Church developed, 177.
Rom. Cath. Church an organism, 178.
Rom. Cath. everywhere same, 180, 5.
Rom. Cath. power to remit sin, 185.
Rom. Cath. Missions, 188.
Rom. Cath. progress, 190-192.
Rom. Cath. foreign forces, 192.
Rom. Cath. Mission statistics, 197.
Rom. Cath. opposed by Greek Church, 201.
Rom. Cath. priority, 213.
Rom. Cath. Church of 16th century condemned, 217.
Rom. Cath. arrogance, 217, 218.
Romanism and Protestantism contrasted, 220.
Rome's denial of religious liberty, 227.
Rom. Cath. Church saves, 230.
Rom. Cath. Ch. and Prot. Reformation, 233.
Rom. Cath. Ch. dislikes Protestantism, 233.
Rom. Cath. Ch. and Anglican orders, 319.
Round-the-World, W. C. T. U., 398.
Rosenkranz, 321.
Royal Templars of Temp., 389.
Ruggles, Mrs. J. F., 453.
Rush, Benjamin, 387.
Russell, John, 389.
Russia and its poor, 81.
Ruskin, 21, 101.

Sabbath Observance, 7.
Sanderson, Mrs., 399.
Salvation Army, 423, 88.
Salvation Army's Mother, 427.
Scandinavia and its poor, 81.
Sacraments, Rom. Cath., 182.
Savonarola, 219, 289.
Sankey, Ira D., 68.
Schleiermacher, Friedrich, 117.
Schleiermacher's influence, 118.
Schleiermacher's discourses, 25, 230.
Schleiermacher a professor, 119.
Scheibel, Prof., 305.
Schürer, 141.
Schodde, George H., 155.
Schauffler, A. F., 353.
Schenck, Miss S. B., 453.
Scudder, Vida, 437.
Schell, M. Hermann, 227.
Schaff, Dr., 15, 158, 373.
Scrivener, 159.
"Seat of Authority in Religion," 133.
Seneca and benevolence, 73.
Septuagint or old Greek version, 161.
Seymour, Governor, 389.
Shaftsbury, Earl of, 42.
Shipton, Wm. E., 358.
Simeon, Charles, 115, 408.
Slack, Agnes, 398.
Social order and the Rom. Cath. Church, 183.
Sociological Bureau, 344.
Social Aspect of Christianity, 37.

Society an organism, 34.
Social Democracy, The, 38, 48.
Socialists and Sociology, 38.
Social conditions in America, 49.
Social system of New Test., 51.
Social conscience awakened, 53.
Social Settlements, 432, 58, 94.
Social settlements first in U. S., 436.
Social settlement work, 438.
Social settlements, character of, 440.
Social Settlement Bibliography, 441.
Social well-being and art, 104.
Société des Missions Etrangères, 197.
Somerset, Lady Henry, 398.
Sons of Temp. organized, 388.
Soul's immediate relation to God, 24.
Spinoza, 132.
Spring St. Presbyterian Church, N. Y., 370.
Smith, George Adam, 125, 151, 224.
Smith, Judson, 236.
Smith, Bishop B. B., 310.
Smith, Henry B., 314.
Smith, Gipsy, 331, 335.
Smith, Christopher, 365.
Stanley, Dean, 15.
"Standard, The," 175.
Stählin's "Kaut, Lotze and Ritschl," 143.
State Charities Aid Association, 86.
State Aid and individual relief for the poor, 84.
State Church and intolerance, 333.
Stead, W. T., 436.
Stead, F. Herbert, 436.
Stevens, Mrs. L. M. N., 393, 398, 400, 402.
Stevenson, Katharine Lente, 385.
Stewart, George H., 68.
Stewart, Mother, 400.
Stöcker, Pastor, 48.
Strauss, school of, 29, 41, 165.
Strong, Josiah, 338, 368.
Struggle for liberty, 328.
St. Simon, school of, 39.
St. Matthew's Guild, 44.
St. Basil the Great, 74.
St. Vincent de Paul, 87.
St. Francis of Assisi, 146.
St. Francis Xavier, 194.
St. Peter's primacy questioned, 200.
Stuart, Geo. H., 361.
Study of Scripture and sociology, 56.
Student Volunteer Movement, 13, 240, 410.
Stuckenberg, J. H. W., 37, 52.
"Studies of Christianity," 132.
"Study of Religion," 133.
"Studies in Theology," 143.

Student Missionary Movement, 363.
Students in Bible classes, 363, 419.
Student Movement, The World-Wide, 407.
Students and Religion, 407.
Students, Work for, 408.
Student Federation, 420; in America, 409; Great Britain, 411; Germany, 412; Scandinavia, 413; Switzerland, Holland, France, Egypt, 414; India and Ceylon, 415; Australasia, 416; China, 417; Japan, 420.
Sunday-School, 353.
"Sunday-School Times, The," 408.
S. S. teachers' helps and training, 354, 356.
S. S. Home Department, 354.
S. S. accommodation and equipment, 355.
Sunday-School leadership, 356.
Sunday papers discontinued, 330.
Swabian Concordia, 295.
Swing, Prof., 143.

Tacitus, 73.
Talmage, T. De Witt, 376.
Tammany Hall, 215.
Tauler, 219, 246.
Tayler, J. J., 129.
Taylor, N. W., 121.
Taylor, Graham, 439.
Teachers' helps and training, 354.
Tennyson, 130, 174.
Temp. Movement in America, History of, 386.
Templars of Hon. and Temp., 388.
Ten Commandments, 252.
Textual Criticism, 160.
Theodore of Tarsus, 76.
Thirty-Nine Articles, 252.
Thompson, Eliza J., 391.
Tischendorf, 159.
Tissot, James, 111.
Toleration and Liberty, 15; in Austria, Italy, Spain, France, Switzerland, Holland, Scandinavia, Brit. Empire, So. America, China, United States, 16.
Tolerance and D. L. Moody, 150.
"Toleration," lectures on, 144.
Tolstoi, 170.
Torgau Book, The, 295.
Tourjee, Eben, 378.
Toynbee Hall, 94, 432.
Tregelles, 159.
Trent, Council of, 218, 225.
Trinity Church, Boston, 144.
"True Wealth and Weal of Nations," 126.

INDEX.

Truth and Nature, 102.
Truth and Christian Union, 311.
Truth in terms of life, 432.
"Truth of the Christian Religion," 143.
Tucker, Booth, 423.
Tucker, Wm. J., 439.
Tübingen, school of, 164, 166.
Tyndall, 130.
"Types of Ethical Theory," 132.
Twining, Louisa, 86, 97.

Universities of England closed, 128.
Unity and the mission field, 236.
Universal religions, 266.
University Hall, 435.
University Settlement, 437.
Union Seminary Settlement, 439.
Union of Reformed and Lutheran, 296.
Union of churches in Scotland, 312.
United Presbyterian Church of Scotland, 312.
Union of Free and U. P. Churches, 313.
Union of Old and New School, 315.
Union of Canadian Methodism, 315.
Union of Australian Methodism, 316.
United Presby. Church, Assiout, 414.
"Union Signal, The," 403.
Upper and lower strata of society, 383.
Urban population in America, 340.
Usher, Bishop, 253.

Van Dyke's Irenicon, 310.
Varley, Henry, Brit. Evangelist, 68.
"Vicarious Sacrifice, The," 125.
Victoria, Queen, 398.
Vibbert, W. H., 451.
Vincent, Bishop John H., 392.
Vincent, Miss, 398.
Visitation, house to house, 93, 94.
Vest, Senator, 193.
Von Bodelschwingk, Pastor, 89.
Von Gebhardt, 159.
Von Hofmann, 168.

Wald, Littian, 439.
Wallace, Mother, 400.
Wanamaker, John, 69, 356, 358.
Ward, W. G., 130.
Ward, Mrs. Humphry, 436.
Warfield, 160.
Warnack, G., 170.
Warner, Lucien C., 364.
Warner, Amos G., 76, 78, 97, 98.
Washington and Am. Constitution, 20.
Washington, Booker T., 366.
Watson, John, Ideal Creed, 319.

W. C. T. U., 385.
W. C. T. U. named, 390.
W. C. T. U. organized, 392.
W. C. T. U. crusade, 390.
W. C. T. U. first officers, 392.
W. C. T. U. petition, 398.
W. C. T. U. first world's convention, 399.
W. C. T. U. "Do Everything Policy," 399.
W. C. T. U. honorable mention, 400.
W. C. T. U. early plans for work, 393.
W. C. T. U. extension, 400.
W. C. T. U. results, 401.
Weiss, Bernhard, 159, 161.
Week of Prayer, origin of, 372.
Wellhausen, school of, 29, 158, 164.
Westminster Confession, 252.
Weston, H. G., 149.
Wescott & Hort, 159.
Wesley, John, 245, 312, 424.
Westminster Assembly, 301.
West, Mary Allen, 400.
Wiclif, 219.
Wichern, John Henry, 45, 87.
Willard, Frances E., 392, 395, 402.
Willard, Frances E., Memorial Fund, 403.
Willard, Hon. Josiah F., 395.
Williams, Sir Monier, 19.
Williams, Sir George, 358, 365.
Willis, Nathaniel, 172.
Williams, Howard, 366.
Williston Church, Portland, Me., 443.
Whittier, 253-4.
Whittier House, Jersey City, 439.
Winthrop, John, 77.
Wiseman, Cardinal, 105.
Wittenberg, Congress in, 45, 306.
Wisbard, L. D., 363.
Wittenmeyer, Annie, 392.
Wolverhampton, Ch. Council, 326.
Woodbridge, Mary A., 400.
Woods, Robert A., 432, 44.
Worship and family religion, 8.
Worship, public, 9.
Worship and Art, 101, 103.
"Work and Play," 126.
World's Student Christian Federation, 363.
Wordsworth, Wm., 289.
"*World-Wide Student Movement, The,*" 407.
Wright, Carroll, 109.
Wyckoff, C. E., 448.

Xaxier, St. Francis, 289.

INDEX. 471

Y. M. C. A. Origin and Development, 358.
Y. M. C. A. Boston Jubilee, 366.
Y. M. C. A. R. R. department, 363.
Y. M. C. A. Navy department, 363.
Y. M. C. A. achievement, 358.
Y. M. C. A. international work, 360.
Y. M. C. A., origin of, 365.
Y. M. C. A., 13, 68, 93, 316, 410.
Y. W. C. A., 93, 363, 412.
Younghusband, Captain, tribute to R. C. missionaries, 195.
Younkin, L. D., 378.

Y. P. S. C. E., 442, 317.
Y. P. S. C. E., enthusiasm for, 442.
Y. P. S. C. E., first twenty years of, 446.
Y. P. S. C. E. principles and growth, 443.
Y. P. S. C. E. conventions, 447.
Y. P. S. C. E., convention of 1899, 447.

Zahn, Prof., 165.
Zenos, A. C., 200.
Zöckler, 161.

Date Due

9/20/41			

Library Bureau Cat. no. 1137